JOSEPH WRIGHT OF DERBY

Frontispiece *Self-portrait* c1767–8
(detail) Charles Rogers-Coltman
Cat 167

Joseph Wright of Derby

Painter of Light

Benedict Nicolson

Volume One
Text and Catalogue

STUDIES IN
BRITISH ART

The Paul Mellon Foundation for British Art 1968
London Routledge and Kegan Paul
New York Pantheon Books

First published in Great Britain 1968
by The Paul Mellon Foundation for British Art, 38 Bury Street,
London, S.W. 1 in association with Routledge & Kegan Paul Ltd.,
Broadway House, Carter Lane, London, E.C. 4

SBN 7100 6284 2
Library of Congress catalogue card no. 68–28393

Printed in the Netherlands by Joh. Enschedé en Zonen, Haarlem
Bound in the Netherlands by N.V. Boekbinderij P. M. Jansen
Designed by Paul Sharp in the offices of
The Paul Mellon Foundation for British Art

Contents
Volume one

Illustrations　Volume one

Dedicated to Charles E. Buckley
in memory of many fruitful
and pleasant excursions

Foreword

I suppose if one were to write a book about an artist like Turner, it would not be necessary to stray far beyond the bounderies of style. The heroic story is contained in the work. But Wright of Derby invites the biographer to speculate, as he himself speculated, on matters outside his artistic domain. He painted portraits of people in quite different walks of life; he studied scientific instruments and illustrations in treatises on anatomy, and volcanic eruptions and grottoes; and if one failed to enquire into the careers of these people, into the nature of these instruments and experiments, into these effects of rock structure and light, but was content to examine the art alone, that is to say the changes in style, technique and the use of light, and the successive influences on the work, one would have left one's task only half done. Wright was not an inward-looking man, but reacted to the world and to people around him, transforming himself, though never losing himself, in the process. And we have to get to know this world and these people in order to present him in the round.

I have therefore felt obliged to add one further section to those which a biographer of a painter is normally content with. There are the usual sections in the book dealing with the life (Part I) and the art (Part II), and at the end a *catalogue raisonné* (Part IV). But between the art and the catalogue is sandwiched a much longer section (Part III) entitled 'Wright and his Times', which approaches the artist from the other end of the tunnel; discusses who the sitters for the portraits were, who were the artist's friends, patrons and correspondents, what was the nature of scientific and industrial activity in his day and district. I am convinced that these marginal investigations shed light on the art of Wright itself. It might be argued that I would have done better to have woven this material, if I was to use it at all, into the section dealing with the artist's style. The advantages of so doing are obvious: a continuous narrative would have been the result. As it is, I fear that a picture like the *Orrery* is discussed in all four sections: in Part I, where I show that its exhibition in London contributed to the spread of the artist's fame; in Part II where it is treated as a moment in the development of style, and an object of aesthetic significance; in Part III in two separate chapters, as an object of interest to a scientifically-minded collector, and as an illustration of scientific activity in the Midlands; and finally in the catalogue I give all the facts about it that a catalogue is supposed to give. I decided that to incorporate a mass of material about eighteenth-century astronomy in a discussion of style, or *vice versa*, would only have had the effect of interrupting the narrative, and that their deliberate disjunction might even have the result of enriching the texture of the book as a whole. Just as when one comes on a much-loved stretch of country from an unfamiliar direction, it takes on a new, exciting aspect, so I am hoping that to approach a picture at different moments from different routes will be to give the book a liveliness that a more straightforward treatment would have lacked.

The decision to introduce Part III has led me, as it led the subject of my biography, into fields of study for which I am not professionally equipped. I have had to make do with my smattering of understanding of the behaviour of phosphorus, of the mechanics of the air pump and the iron forge, of the geology of Matlock High Tor, of mass production in cotton mills, of the tilt of Saturn's rings—of many subjects I never expected to have to contend with. I crave the indulgence of professional historians of science, medicine and industry, of geologists, astronomers and economists if any of them should chance to read this book, and ask them to remember that they would be equally at sea, were they told to translate into words the language of form.

Fortunately no biographer works in a vacuum, but is dependent on help from colleagues. I consider I have been particularly lucky in the advice and assistance I have received.

Private collectors and Museum and Gallery curators who have cooperated in supplying photographs, giving permission for their reproduction and helping in other ways such as checking dimensions and provenance, are not listed here among the acknowledgements, but owners appear alphabetically on p. 12. The list would have been even longer, had not a number of collectors preferred to preserve their anonymity in the catalogue. Thus the cryptic labels 'Private Collection, U.K.', 'Private Collection, U.S.A.' conceal further acts of kindness. I join with The Paul Mellon Foundation in hoping that one or two private owners with whom we have been unable to make contact will excuse the inclusion of their works among the illustrations. I must mention a few who have gone out of their way to be helpful. Among curators of public institutions I must single out Mr. David Piper, at the time of our correspondence about Wright Director of the National Portrait Gallery, who handed over to me his notes on an extra-illustrated copy of Bemrose (1885) once on loan to the Portrait Gallery; his successor as Director, Dr. Roy Strong who put all Wright material at the Portrait Gallery at my disposal, and gave permission for photostats to be made of the most important source of all, Wright's MS. Account Book; Mr. A. L. Thorpe, Director of the Derby Art Gallery, who never failed to answer questions with which I have been deluging him for years; and Mr. William A. Billington who took an enormous amount of trouble in supplying me with information and photostats relating to Wright in the Wedgwood archives at Barlaston (Stoke-on-Trent) and the University of Keele. Three private collectors have been especially cooperative and hospitable: Mrs. G. Anson of Catton Hall, near Burton-on-Trent; Sir Gilbert Inglefield, the Lord Mayor of London for 1967–8 and a Wright enthusiast, who gave me access to some unpublished letters from Wright to Hayley in his possession; and Colonel Peter Arkwright who gave me permission to quote from unpublished letters from Wright to Richard Arkwright junior. My enquiries from dealers on both sides of the Atlantic have invariably been met with courteous replies, but the two firms to which I am most indebted are Agnew's and the Sabin Galleries in Cork Street. I recall many pleasant afternoons in the company of Messrs. Kingzett, Joll and Drummond, having been summoned to their premises on the appearance of a new Wright.

It would be absurd to mention here everyone who has provided me with material, and once more I must pick and choose; but acknowledgements to individuals on specific points will be found continuously in the footnotes throughout this text volume. I offer my apologies in advance to anyone I have inadvertently overlooked. Mr. Brinsley Ford characteristically handed over to me the passages relating to Wright's way of life and reputation in Rome in 1774, in the correspondence of Father Thorpe with the eighth Lord Arundell of Wardour, when he should have kept these tit-bits for his own book on the Grand Tour. I am also much indebted to Mr. R. J. R. Arundell for permission to quote from these letters. Mr. John Jacob, formerly Deputy Director of the Walker Art Gallery, was most generous in letting me have references to obscure publications describing the activities of Liverpool slave-traders who had their portraits painted by Wright in the late '60's. Professor Ellis Waterhouse opened for my benefit his incomparable photographic files at the Barber Institute, as he had done once before when I was working on a study of Terbrugghen. I have also profited from the resources of the of the Witt and Frick Art Reference Libraries, from the Liverpool Public Library where I was able to consult the unpublished Daulby papers, and the Derby Public Library which is rich in Wrightiana. Professor A. W. Skempton gave me access to Michael Browne's Diploma thesis for the Imperial College of Science on Arkwright's development of the industrial site at Cromford. Brigadier R. G. Thurburn, Secretary of the Army Museums Ogilby Trust, saved me from committing many howlers over Wright's military portraits, by sending me succinct notes on uniforms. Professor Jules D. Prown of Yale University passed on to me his unwanted 'Copleys' which appear in my catalogue (Nos. 44, 91) as Wrights. Dr. Kenneth Garlick, Mr. David Carritt (who put me on the track of my catalogue No. 294) and Mr. Eric Robinson of the University of Manchester made useful contributions—and I could mention many others who went to the trouble of clearing up small points, though they had nothing to gain by doing so.

I am much indebted to two young friends who did some research for me, thus saving me many months of hard labour. Mrs. Ann Hills undertook without a murmur the God-forsaken task of working through thirty years of the *Derby Mercury*, noting references to public figures who were in one way or another associated with Wright. I only wish I could have used more of her references. But it transpired that these glib Derby journalists had little to recommend them beyond contemporaneity. She also checked several family trees; worked on manuscript and published material in the British Museum and at Derby; and obtained on my behalf some valuable information from local Record Offices, particularly at Lincoln. Mr. Christopher Charlton, Warden and Resident Tutor at Tawney House, Matlock, was well placed to put me right on the topography around Matlock and Cromford, in connection with Wright's activities as a landscape painter in these areas. I would not have been able to write the concluding paragraphs (pp. 164 ff.) on Arkwright's building operations unless he had exercised firm control over my pen.

I owe a considerable debt to the staff of The Paul Mellon Foundation for British Art for producing two such handsome and lavishly illustrated volumes. The credit for this must go chiefly to five people: first of all of course to Mr. Paul Mellon himself for initiating the project of 'Mellon Books' devoted to this unknown subject of British Art; to Mr. Basil Taylor who has shown enthusiastic interest in my work ever since he first suggested that I should undertake it, and has guided me at every stage of its production; to Mr. Douglas Smith who was in charge of the photography, and produced photographs of pictures which I knew to be hanging high up in obscure corners of country houses, but made them legible just as though he had them propped on an easel in his studio with arc-lamps trained on them; to Mrs. Patricia Barnden who has had the complex task of assembling the illustrations; and Mr. Paul Sharp who designed the book with scrupulous care, and understanding of the character of the subject-matter.

I have left to the last the greatest debt of all, which I can never repay: to the Director of the City Art Museum of St. Louis, to whom this book is dedicated. Charles Buckley and I drove cars from Lewes in Sussex to Carnforth in Lancashire, from Chester to Ipswich, from New Haven to Boston in pursuit of Wright, greeted at every door by screeching dogs. There was a time when it was assumed we would write the book together. But his move from New Hampshire to Missouri, though a tribute to his qualities as an administrator, proved a disaster for our joint enterprise. His duties at St. Louis grew too onerous, and it became clear that the book would have to appear under my name alone. Meanwhile on our many long drives and in our voluminous correspondence we had discussed every picture and drawing from every standpoint, so that I now no longer remember who said what first. I do not acknowledge to him in the course of the text (except when he has appeared in print), for to have done so would have meant mentioning him on almost every page. He must, however, take the credit for having contributed the passages in Part II on the early portraits up to 1773. If I have altered his wording, and added my own discovery of Thomas Frye and a few other pet theories, this was simply to bring the section into harmony with the remainder of the book.

The documentation is by way of being complete up to November 1967. Corrections made after that date are minimal.

B. N.

All illustrations in the text of Volume 1 are referred
to as Figures and those in Volume 2, as Plates. Unless
otherwise stated the works illustrated are by Wright and
are paintings in oil colours on canvas. The works by
Wright reproduced in Volume 1 occur again in their
chronological sequence in Volume 2. The caption to a
Figure also provides the work's Catalogue and Plate numbers.

I The Life of Wright

1 PRE-ITALIAN PERIOD 1734–73

A beautiful lucidity informs everything Wright did; whether he set himself the task of plotting the contours of the face as they curve from the bridge of the nose to the cheek, or describing a mere cork resting on a polished table. The spectator is never left in any doubt as to what is meant, or if he is, that is his fault for not probing deeply enough, or the restorer's fault for having falsified his intentions. This is because the facts of the physical world which were being passionately investigated in Wright's day in the Midlands demanded from the artist a clarity of vision no less rigorous than that to which Dutch artists a century earlier had been driven to submit in order to meet the assertions of science in their own day (and it is for this reason that Wright respected them above all others). The lucidity which shines forth from any task he undertook however menial is carried over into the actual events of his life: so that whatever remains unclear in the account of his life which follows must be put down to obtuseness on the writer's part, never to wayward 'genius' on the part of his subject. Wright is not one of the enigmas of history but an intelligible man, and there can be no excuse for writing off an ambiguity with a plea of interesting irrationality.

Joseph Wright, already known as 'Wright of Derby' in his lifetime in order to distinguish him from other artists of the same name, and because he elected to settle down in his native town more or less indefinitely, was born in Derby on 3rd September 1734, within a few months of an artist with whom he had some affinity, George Romney. He came of a well dug-in middle-class family which had emigrated from Staffordshire to Derbyshire in the late seventeenth century. Both his grandfather and father were attorneys, his father John (1697–1767) earning the nickname of 'Equity Wright'. His father had three sons and two daughters. The eldest son John (1729–96) adopted his father's and grandfather's profession. The second Richard (1730–1814) became a physician in his native town of Derby. The third is the subject of this book. Of Wright's two sisters, only the youngest child Anne Elizabeth or 'Nancy' who died unmarried in 1815 played any significant part in his life: his letters home from Italy are full of affectionate messages for her.[1] He was also close to his brother Richard, and in later years to one of Richard's daughters Hannah (1775–1867) who died as a spinster in her 93rd year and in the middle years of the nineteenth century composed a biography of her uncle Joseph, based on Wright's own papers, which remains the chief source of information about his life.[2]

Wright's birthplace, No. 28 Irongate, was pulled down in 1905[3] but old engravings of it show a snug house little larger than a cottage. The two elder sons were educated at Repton, to which the remainder of the family was temporarily evacuated when the army under Prince Charles Edward pushed South to Derby in December 1745. Joseph was sent to Derby Grammar School. Nothing is known of his scholastic attainments, but some anecdotes about his interest as a boy in mechanics were handed down to the nineteenth century, only

1 The Wright family tree was published by Bemrose, 1872–3, p. 176 and republished by him in 1885, opp. p. 4 (for full bibliographical references throughout these notes, see Bibliography).

2 MS. 2, Derby Public Library. It may be assumed that the factual material in this chapter comes from Bemrose, 1885, unless Hannah or another writer adds information he has missed, in which case the reference will be given.

3 According to N.P.G. extra-illustrated Bemrose.

1 Hudson and Roubiliac left London for a tour of Italy in July 1751, returning together in October. So Wright presumably went to him in the autumn of that year.

2 MS. 2, Derby Public Library. His niece Hannah tells us—this is perhaps an authentic tradition in the family—that he returned to Hudson 'not being satisfied with himself' and 'after lamenting he could not obtain better instruction, there being no one of eminence at that time in England.' Information about his apprenticeship with Hudson (1751–3; 1756–7) is passed on in a letter from Wright's brother Richard to William Tate, 18th September, 1797 (MS. Derby Public Library) just after the artist's death, but contemporary documents confirming these dates have not come to light. The information published by Richard is used by J. L. Philips, 1797.

3 The anonymous author of a 'Life of Mortimer, the painter', *Monthly Magazine*, 1796, p. 23 says Mortimer was with Wright at Hudson's. This writer tells us later *(Monthly Magazine*, 1817, Vol. 2, p. 27) that he was with Mortimer during his last days and after his death lived for years in his house in Norfolk Street. His evidence, therefore, carries some weight.

4 Gandon, 1846, pp. 21–2; Jones, 1951, p. 11. Gandon's son as editor of his father's *Life* says in a note that he often heard his father speak of 'the many pleasant hours he, early in life, experienced as a member of this society'. Born in 1742, James Gandon *père* is presumably recalling his experiences in the late '60's when he was in his twenties; Wright's membership of this Society certainly dates from before 1773 since Gandon goes on to tell us: 'Mr. Wright *afterwards* married...' (our italics).

5 MS. Account Book has the entry (? written at Retford): 'Came to Mr. Wades on Wensday 14 of Nov. [1759] went to Derby on the 24th January [1760] came to Retford on the 6th of March went to Lincoln on the 8. came to Retford again on the 9 of April'. We know the years are 1759–60 because this entry is immediately followed by 'The form of Drawing a Bill' dated 'Doncaster 20th 1760' [*sic*]; because a number of portraits in the Account

to be too avidly lapped up. Much of the information that has come down to us about his extreme youth bears a suspicious resemblance to stories told from Vasari onwards about innumerable other artists, and we are foolish to take them too literally. It would be surprising, all the same, if a young man who understood so perfectly the workings of the air pump and orrery, had not delighted as a child in mechanical contraptions of a similar nature.

His interest in drawing dates from about the time he was taken to Repton, but his earliest dated work is a chalk drawing of a certain John Rotherham done when he was sixteen [Plate 2]. He was never a precocious or rebellious youth, and when it dawned on him where his passion and talent lay, he knew they could prosper only under a regime of hard work. Accordingly he was placed in 1751[1] under Thomas Hudson in London, where he remained two years. Returning to Derby in 1753, he took to doing portraits of relations and friends, of himself, and of families in the neighbourhood. As far as we know the only illustrious family to employ him in the late '50's—no doubt out of kindness to young local talent—was that of Curzon of Kedleston, and two small portraits of Curzon children survive from these years [Plates 4, 5]. Not being satisfied by his progress he returned to Hudson in 1756 for a further fifteen months' training.[2] The choice of Hudson must have been dictated by the fact that Reynolds had been apprenticed to him in the early '40's (though their relationship had not been a happy one) and that at least his reputation as an instructor was established. Wright's fellow-pupil at Hudson's on his second visit was John Hamilton Mortimer (1740–79), and it is here that the seeds of a friendship with this boy six years his junior were sown.[3] Matthew William Peters, who also formed a close friendship with Mortimer, was at Hudson's as a boy in the late '50's, but we do not know what part if any he played in Wright's later life.

Wright was an accomplished musician and the story goes that as a young man he would attend weekly concerts at the house of a Mr. Denby, the organist of All Saints' Church. He records in his Account Book the purchase, about the early '60's, of a German flute, and we are told he used to play the flute, an object lovingly displayed in the Chase double portrait [Plate 50], at these parties, while his friend Peter Perez Burdett played the violoncello. We hear of others who played different instruments at these gatherings, but Denby and Burdett will be the ones to crop up most frequently in other connections in these pages. We are informed by the architect Gandon, a near-contemporary fellow-member, that Wright belonged (almost certainly in the late '60's), to a society called the Howdalian Society, designed to bring together 'ingenious men, principally eminent practitioners of the Fine Arts, embracing Music &c... on these occasions Mr. Wright was an efficient member, possessing an agreeable voice, and a perfect knowledge of music'. According to Thomas Jones, the Society was formed in memory of a certain Captain Howdall of the Artillery who had been posted in August 1766 to Minorca. It was a weekly club of young artists, 'instituted', writes Jones, 'at *Munday's* Coffeehouse Maiden Lane, of which my friend Mortimer was chosen President ... which for some years made a formidable party in the Society of Artists incorporated by charter'.[4]

He had sufficient confidence in himself by 1760 to embark in the early months of that year on a protracted tour of neighbouring Midland towns to the East, painting portraits of local middle-class families; he was at Retford and Lincoln in March, at Retford again in April, and also visited Newark and Boston, Thorne and Doncaster.[5] In all these places he was asked to paint several members of the same family. Thus at Doncaster he received the commission for portraits of the one-time Mayor, his daughter and son-in-law [Plates 21, 24, 23]; at Lincoln, the commission of portraits of two of Robert Cracroft's daughters [see Plate 25]. Of the portraits he painted on frequent visits to Retford, four have come to light, three of members of the Mason family, Cat Nos 104, 105 and 106, and *Kirke* [Plate 19]. After 1st February 1760 he painted members of the Carver family at Eckington in Derbyshire near the Yorkshire border [Plates 22, 26, 27, 28]. Most of these juvenile works have disappeared. On his return to Derby he was allowed to use the Town Hall as premises for exhibiting pictures. It is here that he showed his portraits of six members of the Derby Hunt, subsequently hung at Markeaton Hall [Plates 33, 34, 35, 36, 37, 38]. But the supreme achievement of these early years is the *Shuttleworth Group*, 1764 [Plate 51] which proves that before the middle '60's he had reached mastery in this branch of painting.

This is the crucial date in Wright's career when he came into his own; when he first discerned his power, his originality and a sense of direction, and set off, inspired, on a new course. At the very moment that he attained perfection as a portrait painter, within strictly self-imposed limits—since Wright was never one to experiment outside his area of experience—he embarked on a series of nightpieces, part portrait groups, part genre—a path, though trodden by others, never in his time with such competence. His talent blossomed suddenly in the two or three years before 1765; so when he decided the time had come to put his efforts to the test of the public in the middle '60's, he was ready to give of his best, and never again had anything better to offer. He first exhibited at the Society of Artists in 1765, appearing there continuously year after year until 1776, sometimes with one or two pictures only, once (1771) with as many as eight, generally mixing portraits with candlelights to prove he was equally adept at both.

The history of the formation, prosperity and dissolution of the various exhibiting societies in London in the late eighteenth century is no concern of ours, nor is there any point in telling once more the all too familiar story in anything but outline, as it affected Wright. The first public exhibition to be held in England (if we except the Foundling Hospital which had earlier opened its doors to the public) was in the premises of the Society of Arts in 1760 where all the best painters from Reynolds downwards had shown. Within a year the Society had gone downhill as an artistic enterprise and lost its best artists; those remaining under its patronage formally receiving the title of the Free Society of Artists, and continuing to exhibit as such until 1783. Wright showed twice with the Free Society, in 1778 (a portrait) and in the last year of its existence (a landscape and a genre piece)—a bare three pictures in all.

The best artists formed in 1761 a rival group called the Society of Artists of Great Britain and held a series of exhibitions throughout the '60's in premises in Spring Gardens.[1] This was the only place where an artist had the chance of attracting the public's attention, and so Wright was making no real choice between alternatives by exhibiting regularly with it. The Society received a Royal Charter, becoming the Incorporated Society of Artists, in the year Wright began showing there, and remained the chief exhibiting body until the foundation of the Royal Academy at the end of 1768. Then came the great split: most of the leading artists moved over to the Academy, whilst a small group of highly respectable painters, Wright among them, remained faithful to the old Incorporated Society.[2] The '70's saw the slow wheedling away of the diehards to the new Academy, until the fate of the Society of Artists was in its turn sealed.

It is significant that these 'diehards' were often Wright's personal friends or those for whom he would be expected to feel special sympathy. Thus in 1769 Stubbs appeared at the Incorporated Society in the company of Wright, although most of the other great names had departed. Mortimer remained a regular exhibitor until 1777. Stubbs, Romney, and Wright's friend from Derby, P. P. Burdett, were present with Wright from 1770 to 1772, and Stubbs and Burdett carried on for a year or so, but after 1772 Romney never showed again. In fact the early '70's marked the turning-point in the Society's fortunes. By 1776 it was heavily in debt and its handsome new premises in the Strand up for auction. Thereafter exhibitions were held in whatever galleries could be hired, until its last exhibitions of 1790–91. Wright continued to support this dying cause (the only artist of real distinction to do so except Mortimer) until 1776, and though he deserted it two years later by going over to the Academy, where he remained on and off for the following fifteen years, he was back at his old haunt in the last year of the Society's life (1791) with, among others, some Shakespearean scenes.[3]

His reputation in London had been high ever since he started exhibiting and, following on the wide dissemination in the late '60's and early '70's of engravings by leading print makers after most of his best subject pictures of the period,[4] his fame grew with the years. Thus, when Copley's enchanting *Boy with a Squirrel* was sent over from Boston to London in the autumn of 1765, it was brought to Reynolds's notice and exhibited at the Society of Artists in the following spring—the year of the appearance of the *Orrery*, and the one after that of the *Conversation Piece* which might so easily be the *Shuttleworth Group* with its striking though quite fortuitous echoes of Copley's early style. Benjamin West wrote to Copley

Book listed under these towns are repeated in another list headed 'Sitters for ffeb. 1st 1760'; and because Wright was at Retford shortly before 23rd February 1760—the date when William Kirke paid for his portrait by the artist.

1 It moved to new premises in the Strand, more handsome and better lit, and held its first exhibition there in 1772.

2 There is no truth in the statement made by S. Redgrave in his *Dictionary of Artists*, in Redgrave, ed. 1947, p. 106, in the introduction to the Derby 1934 catalogue, and elsewhere, that at the foundation of the Academy Wright enrolled as a student. The confusion has arisen because several 'J. Wrights' enrolled in the first years of the schools. One 'Joseph Wright' was admitted as a painting student in the Royal Academy Schools on 8th April 1775 (when Wright of Derby was in Rome). His age is given as seventeen '16th last July'. The author is indebted to Sidney Hutchison, the Librarian, Royal Academy, for checking the records.

3 Wright's pictures at the Society of Artists down to 1776, and again in 1791, are given in an Appendix A (pp. 273–5), as well as his submissions to the Free Society. It seems worth while publishing these once more, if for no better reason than that errors have crept into transcriptions, and that it provides an opportunity to add notes on purchasers and present locations, where known.

4 For an account of mezzotint engravings after Wright, see Buckley, 1957.

in Boston:

'Your picture first fell into Mr. Reynolds' hands to have it Put into the Exhibition as the Proformance of a Young American; he was greatly struck with the Piec, and it was first concluded to have been Painted by one Mr. Wright, a young man that has just made his appearance in the art in a sirprising Degree of Merritt...'[1]

Wright arrived in Rome in 1774 armed with letters from West whose admiration for the artist had by that time reached the ears of English residents in Rome. In a letter to Lord Arundell[2] Father Thorpe reports that West 'bestows very high encomiums upon his [Wright's] abilities' in candlelights. And years later West continued to maintain that Wright's 'forges and Blacksmith's shops were superior to anything of that kind which had been done in Italy...'.[3] In 1772 the young painter Northcote, a protégé of Sir Joshua, referred to Wright as 'the most famous painter now living for candlelights'.[4]

James Barry also had a high opinion of Wright as a painter, and must have been partly responsible for getting his name included among those artists thought suitable to decorate the Great Room of the new premises of the Society of Arts in the Adelphi. At the beginning of 1774 it was proposed that this room should be decorated with eight historical and two allegorical pictures, the former to be executed by Angelica Kauffmann, Reynolds, West, Cipriani, Dance, Mortimer, Barry and Wright, and the latter by Romney and Penny. The scheme fell through and Barry three years later offered to undertake the task single-handed.[5]

London was then as it is now the centre of artistic activity, but the foundation of the Royal Academy stimulated provincial centres to found cultural institutions of their own. Liverpool with its flourishing local culture took the lead. The Liverpool Society of Arts was founded in 1769, with Wright's friend P. P. Burdett, who had meanwhile moved from Derby to Liverpool, as first president, and 21 members including Richard Tate, a Liverpool merchant with whose family Wright soon became intimately associated; Peter Romney, a portrait painter and brother of the more famous George; and Dr. Matthew Turner, M.D., a physician friend of Josiah Wedgwood.[6] The Society was dissolved soon afterwards, and the great period of Liverpool's contribution to the arts had to wait another ten to twenty years. Nevertheless a sympathetic attitude towards the arts already existed there in the late '60's, and it was this knowledge, combined we can be sure with encouragement from Burdett, that induced Wright to try his luck there. He spent the better part of three years in Liverpool, from towards the end of 1768 to the autumn of 1771, boarding with Richard Tate.[7] Only occasional absences break the rhythm of his life there: a silence descends upon his movements in the summer of 1769, and we can imagine he would choose the warm season to visit his brothers and sisters in Derby. In the summer of 1770 he was painting portraits of Thomas Day and Erasmus Darwin in Lichfield. But Liverpool remained his base; and here in this busy city where art and industry advanced together, he was well supplied with commissions for portraits from leading local families, including the Heskeths [Plates 61, 62] and the Ashtons, a prosperous family of merchants [Plates 64, 65, 66, 67, 68]. He proved such a resounding success that he threatened to put rivals out of business. Peter Romney, for example, complained in a letter dated from Liverpool 5th November 1769:

'I have about a dozen pictures in hand here, but what further encouragement I shall meet with I cannot judge. Mr. Wright, a famous painter from Derby, is here, who swallows up all the business. He is indeed a true copier of nature: he is of a studious disposition, has a fine taste, and is, in short, qualified for a portrait-painter of the first class; but he seems to want a certain force of feeling and strength of conception necessary in history-painting'.[8]

It is not surprising, after the appearance of the *Gladiator*, the *Shuttleworth Group*, the *Orrery* and the *Air Pump*, the *Academy* and the splendid Liverpool portraits, to find Wright among the famous, though he was only thirty-five at the time.

Soon after his journey to Lichfield in 1770 Wright received the commission—his most important so far—to decorate an upstairs room in collaboration with his friend Mortimer at Radburne Hall, Kirk Langley, the residence of a Colonel Pole. There he painted a full-

1 For the whole story, see Whitley, 1928, I, pp. 215–17. The quotation from West's letter of 4th August 1766 is taken from Copley—Pelham, 1914, pp. 43–4.

2 Thorpe/Arundell MSS. letter of 12th February 1774.

3 According to Farington, Diary, p. 2889, entry for 8th January 1805.

4 Letter from James Northcote, London, 29th March 1772, see Whitley, 1928, II, p. 288. Describing the exhibition of the Society of Artists in its new premises in the Strand, Northcote mentions in another letter of June 1772 (quoted Whitley, 1928, II, p. 291): 'very fine candlelight pieces by Wright of Derby, who is in this way the greatest in the world'.

5 Barry, 1809. II, p. 388, pp. 409 ff. See also Derek Hudson and Kenneth W. Luckhurst, *The Royal Society of Arts 1754–1954*, London, 1954, pp. 22–3.

6 For further details, see Mayer, 1876, pp. 3 ff.

7 MS. 2, Dublin Public Library. Hannah writes: '...he appears to have passed a great part of his time from the latter end of 1768, to the autumn of 1771, at Liverpool & to have boarded with Mr. Rich.ᵈ Tate a Merchant there, at which time probably was formed a friendship with his son Mr. Tho.ˢ Moss Tate (then only a youth) which continued till his death...' There is in the Account Book a record of loans to, and expenses incurred by, Tate with the dates 14th December 1768; 16th April, 20th May, 3rd October, 18th December 1769; 11th and 25th April 1770; 14th April, 20th August, 3rd September 1771. More important, there are records of seven months' board paid to Tate on 18th May 1769; six months' board paid three times on 14th February 1770, 25th July 1770 and 25th January 1771; and seven months' and two weeks' board on 9th September 1771. This means he was at Liverpool at any rate most of the time from about October 1768 to September 1771. He paid 32½ months' board during these three years. The remaining 3½ months were spent in and around Derby as well as in Lichfield. The dates of the payments to Tate suggest an absence from Liverpool in the summer of 1769.

8 Romney, 1830. Appendix to the life of his father devoted to the life of his uncle Peter; p. 300.

length portrait of Mrs. Pole who, on her first husband's death in 1780, married Erasmus Darwin (whom she did not know when Wright was at Lichfield). If it is correct to infer that this picture, which formed part of the scheme of decoration, was at the Society of Artists in the spring of 1771, Wright must have been already at work at Radburne during the previous winter. He did not complete the decoration (which is still *in situ*) until 1772 when he painted the portrait of Colonel Pole and at least one of four candlelight overdoors for the room. This is the only occasion when Wright and Mortimer are known to have been together since their apprenticeship at Hudson's, except that we can guess that they were frequently in each other's company in the premises of the Howdalian Society in the late '60's, and we do not hear of them meeting again before Mortimer's untimely death in 1779. But then everything to do with Mortimer is shrouded in an intoxicating mist.

On 28th July 1773 Wright married a Miss Hannah or Anne Swift (1749–90) about whom nothing is recorded except for the occasional reference to her—never very revealing—in Wright's letters to his family from Italy. He was rather slipfaced about this marriage, concealing it from his brother Richard for fear of disapprobation, and only admitting to it when he was about to set sail for Italy in the following October. On this occasion he wrote to Richard:

'... I flatter myself *matrimony* has improved my Constitution and I am better able to bear the rude winds than heretofore. I have now now let slip a word, that from my own feelings ['makes one' crossed out] I pity yours; and the awkward situation I have always found myself in, upon a Declaration, make me on your account as well as my own, stifle it—now it is out give me leave to send the joint Love of me & my Dear Wife to you & Sister [Hannah]. And if I have done anything that wore the face of slight and Disaffection, say not, love was banished; but Fear stood foremost and prevented my actions. Last week my sister Nancy...'[1]

Wright's niece Hannah did not approve of the marriage, and her own views reflect those of the remainder of the family:

'... had he married differently, and been placed within the circle of those who could enter into his feelings & pursuits, he would probably have enjoyed it & been a different person in every respect. .'

And elsewhere she writes: '[He] married Ann Swift, a person in an inferior situation of life [so that] he did not mention this marriage at the time'.[2] Here we have the clue to the prim silence: poor Miss Swift was not classy enough for such a well-placed family. The backwaters of English provincial life are picturesque but smelly.

Wright had six children, three of whom died young. The eldest Anna Romana was born in Rome in 1774, and married a James Cade, a surgeon of Spondon. There are still members of the Cade family today, living on a beautiful promontory near Penzance, on the outskirts of Melbourne (Australia), and in Suffolk, still owning paintings by Wright, not only family portraits. His eldest son Joseph died as a baby, and the second who soon passes out of our ken, became a missionary in Bermuda. A third son died as a youth shortly after his father. Wright was invariably angelic to his children—a stern parent would say he spoilt them by over-indulgence. He had been too closely bound up with the Lichfield circle to escape Rousseau's influence. Whether he met or even read Rousseau is not known, but this much is certain: had *Emile* never been written, Wright's children would have been more firmly disciplined. Farington tells us:

'Among other singularities Dr. Darwin makes it a rule never to contradict his children, but to leave them entirely their own master—Wright silently imitates Darwin in this respect...'[3]

From all accounts, Wright remained a model family man, in spite of having retained the stubborn habits of a bachelor until middle-age.

1 MS. letter, Eardley Simpson extra-illustrated Bemrose. The passage is quoted in the niece's memoir. The remainder of the letter (on either side of the dots here shown) is quoted by Bemrose, 1885, pp. 27–8. Bemrose has a habit of cutting out the most interesting passages from Wright's letters, out of misplaced discretion.

2 These quotations are from MS. 2, Derby Public Library.

3 Farington Diary, pp. 805–07, letter of 20th October 1796.

Fig 1   Attributed to Richard Hurleston
Portrait of Joseph Wright with Vesuvius in background c 1774
$26\frac{1}{2}$ x $22\frac{1}{4}$ in / 67.3 x 56.5 cm
Mr and Mrs Paul Mellon

1 A fourth Nice drawing inscribed on the reverse 'Nice. 25ᵗʰ Decʳ 1773' was in a portfolio of drawings sold Sotheby's 20th July 1966 (209); see below, note 4.

2 The facts assembled in this paragraph are derived from a number of sources, mostly unpublished letters from Wright to his family in Derby in the Eardley Simpson extra-illustrated Bemrose, extracts from which are given by Bemrose, 1885, pp. 28ff., sometimes with wrong or no dates. Some passages are quoted in Hannah's memoir.

3 Humphry MSS. R.A., folio 2 (1774).

4 Thomas Jones (1951, p. 53) records meeting Hurleston in Rome in December 1776. A portrait of Wright in a turban with Vesuvius in the background, and therefore possibly done in Naples in the autumn of 1774, is in the Mellon Collection (an inferior version in the Arkwright Collection), exh. R. A. 1964–5 (233) as a Wright self-portrait (Fig 1). H. Graves lent to Derby, 1883 (99) a 50 by 40 in. half length purporting to be a portrait by Hurleston showing Wright with a palette, and Vesuvius in the distance. Such a strange attribution must have some basis in fact, and one wonders whether the Mellon picture (which is not by Wright though painted in a Wright-like, *Miravan*-like style) could not be Hurleston's only known oil painting. Four rather crude figure studies by him survive,

2 ITALY AND BATH 1773–77

Wright and his wife, who by this time was pregnant, kicked their heels a few days in Exeter —they were there on 23rd October 1773—and were again held up a week at a village called Shawcross in Devonshire, 'windbound'. They boarded the *Jupiter* on 31st October and sailed the following day. Wright made some 'slight sketches' as they were off Spain. After an appalling voyage in which they were both thoroughly seasick, they came into port at Nice on 5th December (the very day, by a freak of chronology, that Fragonard reached Rome from Provence), where they remained three weeks. Some drawings made by the artist at Nice survive (Eardley Simpson and Oppé Collections, and Derby Art Gallery), dated respectively 9th, 15th and 19th December.[1] George Romney had passed through Nice the previous May in the company of Ozias Humphry on their way to Rome, and Wright was to run into both of them further South. The Wrights left Nice on 28th December and arrived two days later at Genoa, where they remained another three weeks. They set sail from Genoa on 20th January 1774 and reached Leghorn 'well pleased... we had done with the sea. I sincerely hope I shall never have anything to do with the sea than just carry me from Calais to Dover', he writes, in one of his rare humorous moments. They arrived by the overland route at Rome on 3rd February.[2] Meanwhile a certain H. Spicer had written from London to Humphry at the English Coffee House in Rome (9th January): 'as to Wright of Derby I sopose by this time he is with you'.[3] He wasn't, but at least this meant there was a little warmth awaiting him on arrival in the form of a compatriot and fellow-artist who could show him the ropes.

On this ill-starred trip they were accompanied by a promising young artist named Richard Hurleston,[4] a pupil of Wright, whom he had known in London a few months before and whose address in Lincoln's Inn Fields he had given as his own in the catalogue of the Society of Artists' exhibition in 1773. Hurleston is said to have been killed by lightning while riding across Salisbury Plain. All Wright could find to say about this distressing episode, in a letter to his brother from Bath (9th March 1777), was: ''Tis a loss indeed to me, he was ever ready to serve me...' This callousness was not characteristic, but at times we all behave out of character. During the last stretch of the journey the Wrights were accompanied by James Paine, who had been brought up as an architect by his more famous architect father of the same name, but who also practised as a sculptor. 'Young Payne' as Father Thorpe calls him, was then in his late twenties. The even younger John Downman also accompanied them. Downman looked to Wright for encouragement and help: his watercolours and pen and wash drawings of Italian landscape (1774) are close to Wright's drawing style of this period.[5] Downman takes from Wright all he was capable of assimilating: he seizes on Wright's prettiness but ignores the underlying structure, and the results are dazzling.

6

Whom else of interest, one wonders, did he frequent in Rome besides Hurleston, Paine, Downman, Humphry and Romney?[1] Not Fragonard certainly—a more incongruous pair cannot be imagined. His long letters back home deal with topics we do not want to hear about, such as how the natives dressed, or what the weather was doing. He took it for granted his brother the Derby doctor and their young sisters would be bored or bewildered by accounts of intellectual life in the city. In any case Wright was too much taken up with the monuments of the past to pay attention to the prattle of the present. Elegant or clever talk had never been an accomplishment he aspired to, and in the company of Grand Tourists and Connoisseurs he would have felt *dépaysé*. This was his first trip abroad and he spoke no word of the language; even when in London he seized the first opportunity to rush back home. All the same he can hardly have avoided being drawn into the life of the English Coffee House, and running into Fuseli: 'Among the students in Painting', writes the sculptor Thomas Banks shortly before Wright's arrival, 'Fuseli cuts the greatest figure';[2] and it is to Fuseli in the Coffee House that Thomas Jones is at once introduced on reaching Rome three years later.[3] No doubt it was here that Wright cemented his friendship with the Scots artist, Jacob More, who settled in Rome, submitting his picturesque views of Nemi, Albano, Terni, Vesuvius, Etna—the lakes, cascades and volcanoes of Central Italy and Sicily—regularly to the Society of Artists throughout the '70's, and later to the Royal Academy, as Wright was to do.

We may be well documented about his journeys to and from Italy, but we learn little of significance about his way of life in Rome. All we are told is that he found a floor with six rooms on a hill, at the top of some steps, in a house where 'upwards of 40 English students' were also residing. This was unquestionably on the Trinità de' Monti (above the '*Ghetto degl'Inglesi*' which was the Piazza di Spagna), where English artists were in the habit of congregating. In the first spring and summer he worked hard copying the antique in the leading galleries open to students. He was at the Capitoline in the last fortnight of March and at the beginning of April, filling sketch books with beautiful outline drawings of famous statuary (Derby Art Gallery). This was the first public museum of antiquities in Europe, which had opened in 1734 under the Corsini Pope Clement XII, who had acquired part of the Albani Collection from Cardinal Albani and had added some well-known pieces to it, and which had been enriched by his successor Benedict XIV. From the middle of the third week in April he was copying the antique at the French Academy in Palazzo Mancini[4] and again in May. In June he was back at the Capitoline, and in the beginning of October in a *palazzo* in Trastevere. He also worked at the Vatican both this and the following year, and at Palazzo Barberini in March 1775. He was back at the French Academy in the spring of that year.[5] Throughout these months he was engaged on filling sketch books with figure and landscape studies.

The High Renaissance was another object, besides the antique and the scenery around him, of Wright's scrupulous investigation—the very objects, in fact, that Benjamin West advised Copley to study when he got to Rome, and no doubt recommended to Wright also. He occupied his time in 1774 in making large outline copies of the prophets, sibyls, and other figures in the lunettes and spandrels and on the ceiling of the Sistine Chapel. A volume of thirty-six sketches remained in the artist's possession until his death (later Collection William Bemrose). His associates Humphry and Romney also made drawings in the Chapel in the same year. Humphry wrote to Romney in Florence (13th January 1775): '...we may shortly see Rome surrounded by a Neapolitan army. This in the mean time, is likely to become such an impediment to my studies (the Capella [*sic*] Sistina, being shut) that I have thoughts of passing some months in Venice...'[6] Romney made sketches of the prophets and sibyls; possibly in Wright's company, though he preferred working on his own. There was a tradition in his family that Wright had injured his health by lying on his back on the cold floor of the Chapel and contracting a liver complaint. For this eccentric habit there is no first-hand evidence; and we might have felt inclined to dismiss the rumour as preposterous, were it not for the fact that Fuseli himself, who was more responsible than any artist—indeed any man—then residing in Rome for setting Michelangelo on a pedestal above all others, is on reasonably good authority also reported[7] to have lain, week after week, on his back with his eyes fixed on the ceiling. However this may be, we can safely

including a copy of the Raphaelesque *Jupiter embracing Cupid* in the Farnesina. Against two of them Wright has added colour notes, suggesting that they were executed on his instructions. These are contained in a portfolio of wash drawings and watercolours, sold Sotheby's, 20th July 1966 (209) and later on the London art market, inscribed on the cover in a contemporary hand: 'J. Wright's & Rich⁴ Hurleston's (his pupil) Drawings... when on Italian Travels...' Wright's drawings and watercolours are all of Italian landscape and belong to the same series as that in the Derby Art Gallery. Originally the portfolio contained many more drawings, with the leaves hinged in, but most have been torn out. One view of Vesuvius appears to be too bad for Wright and therefore to be by Hurleston: this could lend support to the view that the pupil accompanied the master to Naples and painted his portrait there.

5 Edwards, 1808, p. 253 says Wright accompanied Downman to other parts of Italy besides Rome, and implies that they returned together to London. No other authority has been found for this statement, but Mrs. Downman was in Parma with Wright in July 1775 (see Bemrose, 1885, p. 37), so the report may be accurate. The Downman drawings referred to are in the Oppé Collection. Father Thorpe is the only authority for the statement that Paine was with Wright on arrival in Rome (see Thorpe/Arundell MSS., letter of 12th February 1774). This was his second visit.

1 Romney, 1830, pp. 95, 99, tells us Wright first became acquainted with Romney in Rome. They later became good friends, largely through a third person, Hayley, who was more intimate with both of them than they were with each other.

2 Letter from Thomas Banks to Nathaniel Smith, dated from Rome 31st July 1773, quoted by J. T. Smith, *Nollekens and his Times*, ed. W. Whitten, 1920, II, p. 122.

3 Jones, 1951, p. 53, entry for 27th December 1776.

4 The French Academy was not transferred to Villa Medici until 1803.

5 The series is unpublished. The periods of his attendance at the various galleries can be deduced from dates and locations inscribed on some of the drawings themselves in Wright's own hand. A sketch book in the Department of Prints and Drawings, British Museum (No. 199–a 16), is inscribed with Wright's name and the date February 1774 both outside and inside the front cover, in his own hand. Some drawings are dated: the last date is the middle of May. It is from this source that we learn he was copying the antique at the Capitoline at the beginning of April.

6 Romney, 1830, p. 111.

7 A. Cunningham, *The Lives of the most eminent British Painters...*, II, London, 1830, p. 269.

7

take on trust Romney's lament (he, after all, was in an excellent position to know) to William Hayley the poet, that 'Wright the painter of Derby, had laid the foundation of those cruel nervous sufferings, which afflicted his latter years, by excess of application during his residence in Rome',[1] and Wright himself was to complain of this. Long hours in the cold Chapel and in the dank galleries of *palazzi* must have contributed to the deterioration of a frame which had never been robust.

However, as the summer wore on, we begin to detect a note of optimism in his letters home. On 22nd May he was able to write:

'[My health], thank God, is much better. This climate is certainly very Salutary, and would, I think, properly restore me, was not my attention and application continually engaged with the amazing and stupendous remains of antiquity, and so numerous are they, that one can scarce move a foot but the relics of some stupendous works present themselves. When I consider the immense size of the whole, and the beauty of the parts, I cannot help reflecting how trifling and insignificant are the present operations of mankind; we are no better than infants, and ought to wear daiding strings...'

And again on 10th August 1774: 'When I consider my time is entirely spent amongst antique statues and paintings'.

From the letters of Father Thorpe to Lord Arundell of Wardour we collect some curious gossip about this cautious, humourless, dedicated man from the English provinces, pitched in middle life into the incautious centre of the world. Father Thorpe recalls Wright's arrival in Rome laden with the *Alchemist* and the *Captive King* (two pictures he had failed to sell before leaving London and which he hoped to dispose of abroad): 'I have not seen either, but better judges who have say that he has merit in imitating the Flemish masters in such subjects' (12th February). By 26th February Father Thorpe had learnt that these pictures which Wright had brought with him from England were not being well received by the Italians, and that the artist, being 'unwilling to hear remarks on his night pieces that clash with his own opinion of them refuses to show them. Little more is here allowed to him than a mediocrity in imitating the Flemish masters of that stile'—a judgement we would regard as rather harsh, even were we to measure him by the highest Roman standards of the day. On 24th June his first daughter Anna Romana was born, and Father Thorpe notes (30th July): 'Mr. Wright of Derby... will not have his Child christened by any one hitherto. They [referring to other English artists as well] are a set of the most extravagant oddities imaginable...' And on 10th August the words 'peevish obstinacy' creep into Father Thorpe's correspondence—words that Wright can sometimes be accused of in dealings with his later patrons:

'... Mr. Wright of Derby is painting *the Captive* described in Sterne's *Sentimental Journey*. The Italians make no great account of this Artist whom they class among the modern mimicks of Flemish masters; he is here suspected to be a Jew, or Annabaptist, or something else that is not a Xian. He persists in not having his new born child baptised by any person or in any manner whatever. He shows a peevish obstinacy in this...'

His reasons for refusal to baptise Anna Romana are no doubt quite simply explained by his failure to find a suitable person to perform the ceremony (though it must be admitted we know nothing of his religious views): immediately on his return to Derby he had Anna Romana christened in St. Michael's Church, and showed no objection to the baptism of his first son two years later.

Writing to his brother on the very day[2] that Father Thorpe was writing to Lord Arundell, Wright had a different story to tell. 'My pictures are in great estimation here', he writes, 'I am shortly to be introduced to the Pope; it is thought he will honour me with his medal...' But the health of Clement XIV was already beginning to give way in June. He was unable to attend the exequies for Louis XV at the end of July. In August blood poisoning from a skin disease, which would not respond to treatment, was suspected. Only occasional audiences were granted, and then only to important Church dignitaries. Late in the evening

1 Hayley, 1809, p. 55.

2 10th August. Wrongly attached by Bemrose, 1885, p. 34 to a later letter. MS. Eardley Simpson extra-illustrated Bemrose. From Wright's many letters from Italy, published by Bemrose, we shall only quote the most significant extracts.

of 21st September he received Extreme Unction and died the following morning.[1] So Wright was done out of his audience and his medal. Evidently Father Thorpe did not know about the medal when he spoke ill of Wright in August, but when he next refers to the painter (3rd September) this weathercock is quite happy to report the opposite opinion (and maybe Wright's stocks were in fact going up that summer): '...Mr. Wright of Derby has finished the picture of Sterne's *Captive* with more success than his other pictures, & shows that he is improved by coming hither: he is very dear, gives nothing for less than a hundred guineas [the price he was asking for this second *Captive*] & indeed is thought to have more genius than any of the great number of English painters in town; but he has come late to this school...'

Earlier this year he had been fascinated by the carnivals and firework displays which for centuries had been such an exotic feature of the life of the City. 'The Romans seem to me all going mad', he had written in February at Carnival time;[2] no such insanity had ever possessed the stolid inhabitants of Irongate. Between then and the beginning of June he had witnessed a firework display from the Castel Sant'Angelo, known as the Girandola, on account of the radiating rockets and revolving wheels, causing a swirling movement of lights in the sky above the Castle.[3] As early as 4th June he made a study—not of the actual event since the monuments of Rome are rearranged to suit his pictorial pleasure—showing St. Peter's lit up by the fireworks cascading from the Castello in the foreground [Plate 154]. This proves that his interest in the subject preceded the festivities for the inauguration of the new Pope. But there is nothing surprising in this: these displays were organised, not only in honour of a new Pope (on these rather rare occasions they were on an even more lavish scale) but during the Festival of Holy Week and on the eve of the anniversary of Ss. Peter and Paul.[4] It must have been one of these that Wright witnessed. But he was still in Rome on the election of Braschi as the new Pope Pius VI (middle of February 1775), and so was present at the celebrations in his honour.[5]

From the time of Evelyn onwards, firework displays and illuminations of the great monuments had never ceased to thrill foreigners. Evelyn describes 'at least 20... fireworkes of vast charge and rare art for their invention before divers Ambass:[rs] Princes, and Cardinals palaces, especially that on the castle of St. Angelo, being a pyramid of lights, of great height, fastened to y[e] ropes and cables w[ch] support the standard-pole'.[6] At the end of June 1755, Robert Adam and the young Duke of Bridgewater watched the illuminations of St. Peter's when the great dome was lit up, and the Girandola from the Castello, which provoked Adam to write that it 'exceeded for beauty, invention and grandeur anything I had ever seen or indeed could conceive'.[7] Canova, a mere six years after Wright's visit, attended the spectacle of the Girandola from the Castel Sant'Angelo at which—and this fact is curiously relevant, as we shall see, to Wright's interest in the subject—a simulated eruption of Vesuvius opened and closed the proceedings.[8] Goethe a few years later witnessed the feast of St. Peter and St. Paul:

'yesterday we saw the illuminated dome and the fireworks of Castel Sant'Angelo. The illuminations are spectacular, like a scene from fairyland; one can hardly believe one's eyes... To see the Colonnade, the church and, above all, the dome, first outlined in fire and, after an hour, become one glowing mass, is a unique and glorious experience. When one thinks that, at this moment, the whole enormous building is a mere scaffolding for the lights, one realises that nothing like it could be seen anywhere else in the world. The sky was cloudless and the light of the risen moon softened the brightness of the lamps; but when the second lot of illuminations were set ablaze, the moonlight was eclipsed... The fireworks were beautiful because of their setting, but they did not compare with the illuminations of the Church. We are going to see them both a second time'[9]

The next visitor, an English lady, a few years later laid it on a little too thick—but allowances must be made for her since she had the misfortune to describe a romantic subject at the height of the Romantic Movement: 'The lighting of the *Lanternoni,* or large paper lanterns, each of which looks like a globe of ethereal fire [on St. Peters]... was nearly completed'. These lanterns were pale glimmers beside the illumination of St. Peter's that followed:

1 Pastor, *History of the Popes*, ed. London 1951, Vol. XXXVIII, pp. 522 ff.

2 Letter of 4th February 1774, wrongly dated 10th August by Bemrose, 1885, p. 33.

3 The first mention of such a display is in 1481; the last spectacle was in 1887 (for further details see Margaret R. Scherer, *Marvels of Ancient Rome*, London, 1955).

4 Charlotte A. Eaton, *Rome in the nineteenth century...*, London, 5th ed. 1852, II, pp. 127–8, says that in her day (*c.* 1817) the illuminations of St. Peter's and the Girandola were repeated on two successive evenings of the Festival of St. Peter.

5 Pastor, *op. cit.*, Vol. XXXIX, p. 20. Pius VI was crowned on 22nd February 1775.

6 Evelyn's Diary, ed. 1827, entry for 22nd November 1644.

7 See John Fleming, *Robert Adam and his Circle in Edinburgh and Rome*. London, 1962, p. 177.

8 Antonio Canova, *I Quaderni di Viaggio (1779–1780)*, ed. Elena Bassi, Venice—Rome, 1959, p. 111. Canova witnessed the spectacle on 27th March 1780.

9 Goethe, *Italian Journey 1768–1788*, translated by W. H. Auden and Elizabeth Mayer, 1962, p. 344, entry for 30th June 1787. Among Goethe's possessions are listed some famous engravings after Wright's subject pieces (see *Goethes Werke. Hrsg. im Auftrage d. Grossherzogin Sophie v. Sachsen*, XXXVIII, Weimar, 1897, pp. 377–8).

'As we passed the Ponte Sant'Angelo, the appearance of this immense magnificent church, glowing in its own brightness—the millions of lights reflected in the calm waters of the Tiber, and mingling with the last golden glow of evening, so as to make the whole building seem covered in burnished gold, had a most striking and magical effect... It seemed to be an enchanted palace hung in air... the exhibition of the Girandola, or great fireworks from the Castle of St. Angelo... commenced with a tremendous explosion, that resembled the raging eruption of a volcano. Red sheets of fire seemed to blaze upwards into the glowing heavens, and then to pour down their liquid streams upon the Earth...'[1]

1 C. A. Eaton, *op. cit.*

and so she goes on in the same vein, more evocative of John Martin than of Wright.

During the autumn of 1774, Wright made an excursion to 'the raging eruption of a volcano.' He left for Naples after 2nd October[2] and was back in Rome by 11th November. This visit he made: 'partly to satisfy my curiosity for seeing one of the most wonderful parts of the world, and partly to improve my health impaired by the intense heats and too close application to study'. As he climbed Mount Vesuvius he was reminded of his old Derby friend John Whitehurst who as a geologist would be less interested in the crust of the Earth than in what went on underneath:

2 One drawing in the Derby Art Gallery is inscribed in Wright's hand 'Lungara' with the date 2nd October. This means he was still at work in Trastevere then, no doubt at Palazzo Corsini or the Farnesina, both in the via della Lungara.

'I wished for his company when on Mount Vesuvius, his thoughts would have center'd in the bowels of the mountain, mine skimmed over the surface only; there was a very considerable eruption at the time, of which I am going to make a picture. 'Tis the most wonderful sight in nature...'[3]

3 Both quotations are from a letter to his brother, 11th November 1774, quoted Bemrose, 1885, pp. 34–5. The picture in question is probably the one now in the Derby Art Gallery [Plate 168].

Since Wright had never in his life set eyes on anything of the kind, it must have struck him as a singular phenomenon. But during his visit the volcano was not so spectacular as it had been eight years before, or was to be again five years later. Severe eruptions had taken place in 1766–7, but thereafter the mountain was content to pour out smoke, and now and then to throw up red-hot cinders and liquid lava, like the running of an open sore; it was not the infliction of the wound itself but its refusal to heal that Wright witnessed. No records survive of exceptional activity during the weeks Wright spent in Naples, and it was not until 1779 that eruptions broke out again on the same scale as before. However, if he witnessed lava pouring down the mountain side—as he must have done, to judge by his sketches made at the time—then he can be exonerated from sending home false reports: for Sir William Hamilton had laid it down that 'at Naples, when a lava appears, and not till then, is it styled an eruption'. Hamilton's account of the behaviour of the volcano in the '70's is the best indication of the kind of scene Wright witnessed:

'Since the Eruption of 1767... Vesuvius has never been free from smoke, nor ever many months without throwing up red hot SCORIÆ, which increasing to a certain degree was usually follow'd by a current of liquid Lava, and except in the Eruption of 1777, those Lava's broke out nearly from the same spot, and ran much in the same direction, as that of the famous Eruption of 1767. No less than nine such Eruptions are recorded here since the great one above mention'd, and some of them were considerable... I never fail'd visiting those Lava's, whilst they were in full force, and as constantly examined them, and the crater of the Volcano after the ceasing of each Eruption...'[4]

4 The two quotations are from Hamilton, 1772, p. 20, and Hamilton, 1779, p. 2 of Supplement, the latter a letter of 1st October 1779 to the President of the Royal Society.

5 The author is indebted to Mr. Noel Blakiston of the Public Record Office for this information.

6 See letter from Richard Cumberland to Romney, 14th August 1774 (Romney, 1830, p. 108) informing him that he is to be supplied with a letter to Hamilton 'to prepare him a reception when he arrives in Naples'.

7 An inscription on the fly-leaf of Hamilton's own copy of his *Campi Phlegraei*, which he presented to the British Museum, includes the name of Wright among collaborators in the

He does not say whether Wright accompanied him on any of these expeditions and it is not known for certain whether they met, but Hamilton was not in the habit of allowing an English traveller, especially an artist who had caught the bug of Vesuvius, to pass through Naples without seeking him out; and various letters from Hamilton[5] in November 1774 show him to have been continuously resident in Naples in that month. Romney is believed to have arrived in Naples that autumn armed with a letter to Hamilton,[6] and Romney had fewer claims on Hamilton's attention (before the entrance of Emma onto the scene) than Wright had. Moreover, it is possible that Wright contributed a sketch to Hamilton's splendid illustrated volumes on volcanoes, but the evidence is not conclusive.[7]

Wright kept a Journal (Ms., Derby Public Library) in which he noted down the places and objects which had struck him most forcibly on his trip to Naples. As often happens when someone does not express himself naturally in words, these impressions lose their vividness as they get translated from heart to paper, and one regrets he had no Fuseli or Barry at his elbow to lace them with a little zest. He notices the usual Titians, Raphaels and Correggios, but more revealing are comments on artists whom not everyone would have singled out for praise: such as Ribera at S. Martino, whose manner ('forcible and natural') would be expected to appeal to one who had spent his youth investigating dramatic lighting effects; and Salvator Rosa whose *Banditti* in the King of Naples's Palace 'are painted with great force and spirit'—like Mortimer's, he might have added.

He visited Pompeii and Herculaneum, and the Museum ('the most interesting place I have seen'), where he admired 'a satyr lying on a skin of wine, snaping [*sic*] his thumb & finger, the expression very good'.[1] Drawings by him of similar subjects from the antique survive. Like any tourist of the period, he would climb the hill above Naples to make sketches in Virgil's Tomb, and would make expeditions to grottoes in the Gulf of Salerno, just as from Rome he would pay his obligatory respects to Nemi and Albano, falling like everyone else into the usual tourist traps. All these themes and others developed on canvas into a regular stock-in-trade; and for the remainder of his life he would play variations on them, shifting the position of Castel Gandolfo from the left to the right, or introducing into Virgil's Tomb the mournful figure of Scilius Italicus, or into a grotto the figure of Julia, or leaving them desolate except for the moonlight streaming through them. Already when in central Italy he had embarked on this long series. Towards the end of 1774 he produced two cavern scenes inspired by two grottoes near Salerno [Plates 174, 175]—the first oil paintings of Italian landscape known from his hand, though not the first landscapes he had painted: one had been at the Society of Artists in 1772, and one (which could conceivably be identical with it) is at Radburne Hall [Plate 112]. He also did an *Eruption of Vesuvius* in the early months of 1775 which he hoped, but failed, to sell to the Empress of Russia.[2]

Wright delayed his departure from Rome till 10th June of that year ('I am like all other artists that come here', he wrote home in May, 'who much outstay their intended time'), but finally set off for Florence by way of Narni, Terni (which gave him the idea for a *Cascade* picture) and Perugia. In Florence he met a girl of about fifteen named Maria Hadfield, the daughter of a Manchester manufacturer who had opened a large hotel in the town before the middle of the century, and where no doubt Wright, like all English travellers, stayed. According to Northcote she was married in Florence to the miniature painter Cosway in January 1781.[3] When she was a very old woman she recalled in a letter from Lodi where she was then living:

'I had a number of Masters but painting had my preference... Mr. Zofani living in Florence my father aske'd him to give me some instructions. I went to study in the Gallery [Uffizi] & the Palazzo Pitti & copied many of the finest pictures; Wright of Darby passed only a few days at Florence & noticing my assiduity & turn for the art sprung me to the highest branch of it...'[4]

If any of the known facts were at fault, they would have cast suspicion on Maria Cosway's memory; but Zoffany was indeed in Florence at the time, polishing up his interminable *Tribuna*; and Wright indeed spent no longer than a fortnight in the city (19th June—4th July)—just long enough, though, to spring the young lady up to the top of the tree.

Wright was not willing to take much of a chunk out of his life in order to get to know Florence properly; a fortnight, even by the standards of the eighteenth century, was short. He found it disappointing: 'Titian's Venus, Florence, did not answer my expectation; when one has seen Rome, other places suffer by the comparison', he confided to his Journal. He was not prepared to give anywhere else in North Italy even as long as a fortnight. No doubt he decided slow travel was too complicated with a child a year old, and he was anxious to push home before the winter set in. Ozias Humphry who was in Florence to receive him wondered how he was going to fit everything in:

'Mr. and Mrs. Wright when they left Florence had no intention to continue in any part of Italy more than three weeks or a month [even this was an exaggeration]. They proposed to go from

volumes. This particular copy contains some original sketches by Fabris and others, bound in with the plates after these sketches. The inscription is not in Hamilton's hand and looks considerably later. No original drawing in the book is inscribed with Wright's name, and Hamilton makes no mention of him in his accompanying text. On the other hand one or two drawings do remind one of Wright and are too good for Fabris.

---

1 This is the famous bronze *Drunken Faun* [Fig 2] in the Museo Archeologico Nazionale, Naples. Wright's outline pen drawing of a reclining satyr, though similar, was done in Rome [Fig 3].

Fig 2 *Drunken Faun*
Museo Archeologico Nazionale, Naples

Fig 3 Drawing after a *Reclining Satyr*
c 1774–75
Pen $11\frac{1}{2}$ x $21\frac{1}{4}$ in / 29.2 x 53.9 cm
Derby Museum and Art Gallery

---

2 See letter to his sister, 4th May 1775, published Bemrose, 1885, p. 35. MS. Eardley Simpson extra illustrated Bemrose. The letter was finished on the 7th June. It may have been the same picture as that referred to by Father Thorpe (see p. 76).

3 Bell, 1938, pp. 23–4.

4 Williamson, 1897 pp. 10 ff. From a letter dated from Lodi, 24th May 1830.

1 Extract from letter to Mr. Stevens signed 'O. Humphry' and dated 'Florence July 18th 1775'. Humphry MSS. R. A. folio 31 (1775). This is the 'poor Mr. Stevens' mentioned in Wright's letter to Humphry from Parma, 24th July 1775, quoted by Bemrose, 1885, p. 37.

2 The quotations are from Wright's Journal, MS. 1, Derby Public Library. Most of the Journal is published by Bemrose, 1885, pp. 39–41, but he has made small errors in transcription which are here corrected, and omitted a long passage about Correggio, which should be inserted after 'Here is the famous picture of Correggio...' (p. 40). It is not worth quoting since he expresses himself in almost the same words in the letter to Humphry from Parma (see p. 12, note 1).

3 To single out the Northern pictures in the Palace of the King of Sardinia at Turin was not so eccentric as it might sound. Cochin in his *Voyage d'Italie*, Paris, ed. 1758, I, p. 11 also regards the Van Dycks, Rembrandts and Dous as outstanding, going out of his way to praise the Dou Wright mentions—evidently a famous picture in its day: '*un... représentant un médecin qui regarde une liqueur au travers d'une phiole; une femme malade, sa fille qui lui prend la main, et sa servante. Ce tableau est de l'exécution la plus prodigieuse...*' Cochin also refers to works by Teniers and Berchem in this collection.

4 See Hayley, 1809, pp. 60–1, and Romney, 1830, p. 127.

5 Letter from Wright to Humphry (see p. 12, notes 1 and 2). The Correggio in question was the *Madonna of St. Jerome*, in the Ducal Palace from 1765 onwards, before being transferred to Paris in 1796.
Cochin, *Voyage d'Italie...*, Paris, 1758, I, pp. 64–5, describes the Correggio, then in a room adjoining the Cathedral, and singles out the head of the Magdalen as '*le chef-d'oeuvre du Correggio, pour la couleur & le pinceau*'.

6 Copley had been in Rome for the winter of 1774–5 onwards, except for a month in Naples, and it is possible that the two artists first met then. He left Rome six days before Wright and reached Parma (via Florence and Bologna) soon

this City to Bologna and from thence to Venice where they expected to remain 10 or twelve days, barely time enough to see the principal things and to return again to Bologna and on to Parma immediately. Mr. Wright does not intend to copy the picture there [a Correggio] but to set forward with all expedition to England.'[1]

His itinerary was as follows: Bologna, Venice (a mere week in the middle of July), Padua, Vicenza, Verona, Mantua, Parma, Piacenza, Alessandria, Turin, which he left on 1st August to cross the Alps on muleback to Lyons. In none of these places except Venice did he remain more than three days, and only in Bologna and Parma as long as that.

In Venice he was disappointed in the vast Veronese in S. Giorgio, now in the Louvre: 'The large picture by Paul Ver. of the marriage in Canaan has an ill effect altogether, it is a confused multitude'. Of Titian's Frari *Assumption* he wrote: 'yᵉ colouring is become quite brown'; and of the *Martyrdom of St. Lawrence* in the Gesuiti—here, at last, one would think, was a picture after his own heart—he noted down: 'the figure of yᵉ Saint is very grand, the picture is become very dark, & I believe never had yᵉ effect of fire'. At 'Padua' [*sic*] he saw 'several Buildings by Palladio, in very good taste'. In the King's Palace at Turin he singled out the Northern pictures; he seems almost to be breathing a sigh of relief at reaching a city rich in transalpine associations: 'A man in armour on horse Back, as large as life, by Vandicke, very fine. The armour is a dark rich colour, full of beautiful reflections, & the lights most spiritedly touched'; other Van Dycks (including the *Three Children of Charles I*: 'such a sweet childish expression as I never before saw'); some supposed Rembrandts; some Teniers of Boors; landscapes by Both and Berchem, 'very fine'; and 'a great number of Gerard Dou, very fine, among which is a composition of four or five figures of the Doctor examining his patient's water'.[2] These satisfy him far more than the Carraccis and Domenichinos he had inspected in Bologna—and it will become clear in the course of this study that there is nothing mysterious about any of this.[3] It was only a pity that he failed to stop off at Brescia: here he would have found, in Savoldo and Romanino, two artists to his taste, who because they were also adventurous provincials, also made pictorial discoveries ahead of their time. But he tended to stick to what was accepted in the sights he visited, preferring to reserve his originality for his creative work.

Stories were circulating in Venice and Parma about Romney's adventures in these towns a few months earlier. He had left Rome in January 1775, and had proceeded north to Florence, Bologna and Venice. In a letter to Humphry he expressed more enthusiasm for the Titians in Venice, and remained much longer both there and in Parma, than Wright was to do. Romney spent a few weeks in Parma, 'where he was charmed with the works of Corregio, a painter whom he particularly admired...',[4] and returned to London at the end of June via Turin, Lyons and Paris. Wright on his arrival in Parma (24th July) reports to Humphry in Florence that Romney 'only painted the Magdalen's head [in a Correggio], the picture answered not his expectation'; and continues:

'Mr. Copeley [*sic*] has been hard at it five weeks, & says he will spend twice that time more over it but he will get it like the original. It is with infinite labour he produces what he does, but that is *entre nous*.[5]

Is there veiled hostility here to the young Copley, who had come over from Boston the previous year and was making his Grand Tour of Italian cities?[6] The words '*entre nous*' make one suspect it. In any case, one assumes from silence that the two artists (in theory well suited to one another) did not become friends. The reason may be that each resented the infringement by the other of his exclusive domain. There is an uncanny resemblance between portraits by the two artists in the late '60's, which may have disturbed both of them.

Wright got back to Derby on 26th September 1775. For some reason which has remained unexplained, he decided his best chance lay in filling the place left vacant in Bath since Gainsborough had left the town and settled in London (1774). He accordingly moved to Bath that autumn with his family, remaining there two years. It was an ill-advised step. He cannot have had any conception what he was letting himself in for. The toughest of his

Midland sitters were willing to accept without demur the dead-pan look he imposed upon their features as they sprawled in their chairs, because it was the reality of their success in achieving a solid social position, within a strict hierarchy, that they wished perpetuated, not some kind of lying glamour. But Bath was a different proposition. This was a tourists' centre, an off-shoot of London; the ladies parading around the Circus had the corrupting knowledge of how attractive they could be made to appear on canvas, with a little blurring of the edges and some expensive clothes; and Gainsborough with his canniness and his genius had known how to gratify them. Wright was quite unsuited to step into his shoes as a portrait painter; his candlelights of girls with far-away looks writing love letters, or kittens being dressed up, were more to the taste of this smart bunch. It is not surprising to find him writing from this pleasure resort to his sister on 15th January 1776:

'You'll scarce believe I have not had one Portrait bespoke, they one & all say it is a pity I should paint Portraits. Should they continue in that way of thinking, they will either pity me, or starve me to death. Notwithstanding my Candle light Pictures are so much admired here I have not sold one. I believe I am come to the wrong place...'[1]

Wright reached Bath on 4th November 1775.[2] He returned to his brother's house in Irongate, Derby for the summer of the following year[3] and it was then that his first son was born and baptised (14th July 1776), and that his intimacy with the poet Hayley first ripened. We hear of him in Hayley's company about the beginning of September, and it was more likely in Derbyshire than on his return to Bath that autumn that he painted (in September) the portraits of Erasmus Darwin's brother, sister-in-law and nephew [Plates 176, 177]. A further year had to be endured at Bath, Wright continuing to suffer from rheumatism. (It sounds as though this town was not living up to its reputation as a health resort.) On 13th June 1777 he came back with his family to Derby,[4] and during the course of that summer painted the portraits of Richard Cheslyn [Plate 190] and of an undergraduate of St. John's College, Cambridge, Thomas Gisborne, at the request of the headmaster of Harrow, Gisborne's old school [Plate 191]. On 6th October he went to lodge with a Mr. Eley opposite his brother's house[5] where he remained until the spring of 1779. The whole dismal Bath episode was over.

In the spring of 1779 Wright went to live at St. Helen's House on the outskirts of the town, a site now occupied by part of St. Helen's Street. His niece Hannah recalls that 'there was not any part of the house in which [the children] might not play, and they could even whip tops in the room where the pictures were arranged all round, and upon the floor'. This indulgent father and uncle who permitted top-whipping in his painting room, remained in occupation of this house for fourteen years. It was pulled down soon after he left it.

after the middle of June. 'I have begun my copy of the very fine Corregio', he writes to his mother on 25th of that month, 'for which I have a commission from an English Nobleman'. He had it almost finished by 22nd August (see Copley-Pelham, 1914, pp. 294–308, 328–33, 353.)

1 Additional passage, unpublished, from Wright's letter quoted by Bemrose, 1885, p. 44. From niece's memoir, MS. 2, Derby Public Library. The passage quoted by Bemrose is merely a postscript.

2 MS. 1, Derby Public Library has a note in Wright's own hand: 'Enter'd upon Mr. Sproules House 9th Nov. 1775. My horse went to Ward's Livery Stable. 29 Dec! 1775'. On the next page is: 'Had when I came to Bath 4th Nov! 1775 100 guineas...'

3 Niece's memoir.

4 Loc. cit.

5 MS. Account Books has note: 'Mem. My horse came to Mr. Eley's on Tuesday the 14th of Oct! 1777. Went to my Brother's Close 13th Dec! 77'. The information about the duration of his residence at Mr. Eley's comes from the niece's memoir.

3 THE LAST TWENTY YEARS 1778–97

1 Lists of exhibited pictures will be found in Appendix A, pp. 275–7.

Wright exhibited every year at the Royal Academy from 1778 to 1782.[1] This was good enough to qualify him for Associate Membership; and on being put up for election in November 1781, he received fourteen votes while none of his competitors received more than two. For some reason he failed to acknowledge receipt of the notification of his election from the Secretary until two months later. There may have been nothing in this so-called discourtesy but trouble was already brewing. A quarrel soon flared up but no-one has quite got to the bottom of the dispute. This much is clear: that in February 1783 he was defeated in the ballot for the Academicianship by the insignificant Garvey, but attained full membership the following year when a seat fell vacant on the death of Moser. When offered it, Wright declined the honour, and his name was erased from the list of Associates according to his desire. There is no need to pay any attention to the rest of the story, repeated though it is by Philips in his memoir of Wright on the strength of some preposterous gossip, that the Academy dispatched its Secretary Newton to Derby to make amends, but that Wright refused to relent.[2]

2 For the whole story and quotations from contemporary gossip, see Whitley, 1928, II, pp. 340–43. See also *St. James's Chronicle*, 3rd–6th May 1788 where the story about turning Newton out of doors is reported; Hodgson and Eaton, 1905, pp. 163–6; and Redgrave, 1866 (ed. 1947, pp. 106–07).

3 Quoted Bemrose, 1885, p. 63.

Wright's own explanation, coupled with that of his close friend John Leigh Philips, must be taken into account. On a second occasion in the early '90's when he quarrelled with the Academy—there is no getting away from the fact that he was a cantankerous man —Wright implied that he had 'been driven from their Exhibition before' because his pictures had been badly hung.[3] In a rather cryptic letter to Hayley of April 1784 he hints at further malpractices:

'I felt much satisfaction in reading your letter to Mr. Long respecting my rejecting or accepting being an Academician. If the ballance hung in equilibrium before, when I knew your sentiments up flew the Beam, & I refuse the honor, if it is one. I felt no inclination to become a member of a Society from whom I had repeatedly received the most humiliating treatment, the most flagrant abuse, & from w.ch being an Academician wou'd not have protected me, from "Envy, Hatred, & Malice &c...."'[4]

4 Inglefield MSS. The letter is dated 'April' from Derby but from internal evidence it is clear that 1784 is the year.

5 Philips, 1797.

6 Hayley, 1783; republished Hayley, 1788, pp. 141–47.

Philips also comes forward with the explanation about bad hanging, but adds that the successful candidature of Garvey contributed to Wright's disgust with the Academy.[5] Hayley's own observations, unfortunately, do not assist us, since he casts his defence of Wright in the form of an *Ode* to the artist, not the most convenient vehicle in which to conduct a line of argument.[6]

As evidence for the prosecution, it could be argued that many considerable artists have waited years before their election as A.R.A.'s and their attainment of full membership without kicking up a fuss; and Farington in 1794 lets the cat out of the bag by introducing the word 'pique' into his account of the episode.[1] His entry for 20th October 1796 is even more revealing:

'L. Philips mentions Garvey having been elected an Academician in preference to Wright. I told him it was in consequence of Sir Joshua Reynolds having represented to the members that there was not sufficient number able to act in performing the duties of the Royal Academy, and that they ought to elect persons who were resident in London—this, I said, with the interest which Gainsborough had made by canvassing for Garvey caused him to have a majority. Philips then said that Newton had been sent down to Derby to Wright afterwards with a Diploma, and that Wright had rejected it and turned Newton out of doors. This statement I did not think it now necessary to contradict, but it was as far as related to the Academy having sent Newton unfounded... Philips said He believed Romney & Hayley, both of whom are unfriendly to the Academy have, [sic] contributed to prejudice Wright against it'.[2]

So the truth seems to be that there were political reasons for electing Garvey; that Wright was upset by this election, but also by other alleged bad treatment from the Academy about which we are ill-informed; and that he desired that his name should be erased from the list of Associates (and indeed when he again exhibited with the Academy from 1788 onwards, his name is not printed in the catalogue as that of a member).

On breaking with the Academy, since he had to find some means of communicating with the public, he went in search of other platforms—as we have seen, he showed two pictures at the Free Society in 1783. His old haunt Liverpool had meanwhile been going from strength to strength as a cultural centre, and it was here that he turned his steps once more. The Art Society had been revived there in 1773; Dr. Turner had lectured on anatomy and P. P. Burdett on perspective, a subject on which he was an expert; and it held its first exhibition in 1774, to which Burdett had sent 'A print of Two Boys blowing a Bladder by Candlelight, from a painting by Mr. Joseph Wright (Wright of Derby)', and to which Daniel Daulby Jn., who was to become a friend and patron of Wright on the latter's return from Italy, had sent a landscape painting and two black chalk drawings which may or may not have been his own work. Richard Tate sent a copy of Wright's *Boys blowing a bladder by candlelight*, and William Tate, his brother, showed portraits. Burdett's financial crash and his disappearance to Germany were the principal reasons for the Society's collapse in the mid-'70's.

It was reformed in 1783 under the title 'The Society for Promoting the Arts in Liverpool' with Henry Blundell of Ince as President, Roscoe as Vice-President, and Daulby among the officers, and held an exhibition in September of the following year to which Reynolds, Paul Sandby, Fuseli and Wright sent contributions. Wright's pupil and young friend Thomas Moss Tate, the son of Richard and nephew of William, showed landscapes 'after Wright of Derby'. Wright himself sent seven pictures to this show. A second exhibition was held in 1787 under the presidency of a member of the Ashton family of Woolton Hall who had patronised Wright in Liverpool in the late '60's. Daniel Daulby and Roscoe were on the committee. On this occasion Wright showed five works.[3] Some of his Italian landscapes in both exhibitions (and his submissions consisted almost exclusively of these) entered Daulby's collection.[4]

After his break with the Academy Wright conceived the more or less unprecedented plan of holding a one-man exhibition of his works in London. Before the end of 1783 the idea was firmly lodged in his mind, and he was filled with apprehension at the prospect:

'O! that word [exhibition]', he writes to Hayley on 28th December, 'makes my heart ach, for shou'd I fail in my attempt I shall be thrown down forever, & I already see the invidious wth their pens diped in the blackest gall. Is it not vanity of the rankest sort for me to attempt to show alone? —You have most agreeably anticipated a request I have often wished to make to you, of publishing and connecting your charming Ode wth. my small insignificant catalogue...'[5]

In the autumn of the following year Wright fell ill again and the strain of the forthcoming exhibition grew more acute:

1 Farington Diary for 1794, p. 97: '...Wright of Derby, through pique at Garvey... being elected before him, declined the Diploma...'

2 *Loc. cit.* pp. 805–07. Walpole (1937, pp. 119 ff.) was of the same opinion: 'I have been told', he writes, 'that Wright is a splenetic man, and that the sole reason of his not being chosen was, that Wright residing in Derby and few of the directors attending, the society were obliged to elect one who would officiate'.

3 Lists of pictures exhibited by Wright in Liverpool in 1784 and 1787 will be found in Appendix A, p. 277.

4 For further particulars concerning the Liverpool Society of Arts, see Mayer, 1876, pp. 3 ff.

5 Wright to Hayley, N. P. G. extra-illustrated Bemrose. Hayley's *Ode* to Wright had been published that summer.

1 Wright to Hayley, Inglefield MSS.

2 Wright to Hayley, 17th February 1785, N. P. G. extra-illustrated Bemrose. The word 'Royalists' echoes a passage in Hayley's *Ode* in which he accuses the Academy of closing its doors against Wright:
  'Where Art, whom *Royalty* forebade to roam,
  Against thy Talents closed her self-dishonour'd Dome...'
Hayley's lines on Wright's picture of the *Attack of Gibraltar* appeared in the March 1785 issue of the *European Magazine*. Nothing further is known about the showing in Derby, nor about a proposed exhibition of his works in Derby, advertised in the *Derby Mercury*, 3rd October 1787 (see Bemrose, 1885, p. 24).

3 Lists of pictures exhibited at Robins's Rooms will be found in Appendix A, p. 278. It was announced in *The Morning Chronicle*, 18th April 1785 as: 'This & Every day will be exhibited...', and was visited on 4th May by Sylas Neville who noted 'Some pictures of great merit' (see *The Diary of Sylas Neville 1767–1788*, Oxford, 1950, p. 326).

4 *Public Advertiser*, 1st June 1785.

5 For further details about Carter's exhibition, see Edwards, 1808, pp. 234–38. Another case of a one-man show was that of Nathaniel Hone, who exhibited over one hundred works in St. Martin's Lane in 1775, following on an altercation with the Royal Academy. Copley also held private exhibitions of *The Death of Chatham* (1781) and *The Death of Peirson* (1784).

6 Hayley, 1823, p. 387, letter of 5th May 1789, quoted slightly differently by Bemrose, 1885, p. 81.

7 Wright to Philips, 15th April 1791, quoted by Bemrose, 1885, p. 64 from MS. Derby Public Library.

'...To be ill at any time is unfortunate, but at this period, 'tis most exceedingly unlucky,' he writes to Hayley on 22nd December 1784, 'My exhibition pictures have stood still these two months, & I feel not returning health enough to attack them wth spirit—but I must drag the pencil over the unfinished parts, or I shall be distanced. I am advised by some of my friends who live at some distance from the Town to make an Exhibition of my pictures here [in Derby] before I send them to Town; if there is no impropriety & I confess I see none, I shou'd like it very well, The pictures have only been seen by a few friends... and now my Dear Sir I must speak plain & beg the favor of you to compose the Catalogue for me as I have but few pictures it will be necessary to give some short historical or [word omitted] account of each...'[1]

By 17th February 1785 he had finished his enormous canvas, *A View of Gibraltar during the destruction of the Spanish Floating Batteries* and asked Hayley to produce a piece for the catalogue, explaining his intentions in this picture: 'together wth the rest of the Catalogue, wch I think with you shou'd be plain and simple...' He goes on to explain to Hayley that he proposes to open the exhibition in Derby 'in less than 3 weeks', and that he has 'secured Mr. Langfords Auction Room in Covent Garden' for the London showing. 'My exhibition in London will open some time about 16 April for I am advised to get the start of the Royalists'.[2] The exhibition opened at Mr. Robins's Rooms (late Langford's) 'No. 9 under the *Great Piazza, Covent Garden*' in the middle of April 1785, with contributions in the catalogue by Hayley. Twenty-five pictures by Wright were shown, only eleven of which were marked down in the catalogue for sale; the remainder being reserved by collectors.[3]

Three important pictures, *The Lady in Milton's Comus*, *The Maid of Corinth*, and *Penelope unravelling her Web* [Plates 246, 245, 242], were already earmarked for Wedgwood who before the mid-'80's had become one of Wright's most enthusiastic patrons, and took an active interest in the progress of his work. Others were Daniel Daulby of Liverpool who owned at least two pictures in this show; and John Milnes of Wakefield, the owner of Wright's largest and most audacious work, the *View of Gibraltar*, for which he charged more than for any other (£420) and of which all trace has been lost since the middle of the nineteenth century. It is odd that an object of this size should have been mislaid. The show does not appear, all the same, to have proved a success. One contemporary account[4] describes it as follows: 'Carter, as he justly deserves, and Wright of Derby as he very justly does *not* deserve, except for his caprice and spleen (for Wright is a very fine painter) both are losers on their experiments of separate exhibitions'. No doubt George Carter got wind of Wright's intentions, and determined to hold a one-man show of his own. He exhibited early in the same year, in a room in Pall Mall, one picture of the *Siege of Gibraltar*—a favourite subject at the time—, another entitled *Floating Batteries*, and views of the Fortress of Gibraltar which he had visited on his travels. His superior knowledge of the terrain was the only advantage he had over Wright, but this did not compensate for his lack of talent.[5]

No doubt partly on account of this disappointment, in 1788 Wright patched up his quarrel with the Academy and began exhibiting there again on three successive occasions. In 1788 and 1789 he was represented almost exclusively by Italian landscapes and a few genre subjects; the one exception being his famous *Dead Soldier* shown in 1789, engraved by Heath and thus widely disseminated, which moved his friend Hayley to tears:

'I shall beg you and Mrs. Beridge', writes Hayley to his wife in Derby, 'to call our friend Wright, and tell him from me, that I and all the lovers of painting with whom I have conversed, since my return to town, consider his pictures this year, as the very flower of the royal Exhibition. His dying soldier made me literally shed tears; his moon-light enchanted me.'[6]

In 1790 Wright showed two Shakespeare subjects—the Sarajevo of a new outburst of fury against the Academy. Wright claimed they were badly hung, and so he re-exhibited them the following year at the Society of Artists with a note in the catalogue to the effect that 'having been placed in an unfortunate position [at the Academy], owing (as Mr. Wright supposes) to their having arrived too late in London, and have since received alterations, he is desirous that they should again meet the public eye'. But as Wright explains[7] this soothing note was inserted simply because the Society of Artists wished to avoid altercation with the Academy. In private Wright expresses himself much more vehemently:

'I have lately sustained a real injury from the most *illiberal* behaviour of the Royal Academicians... 'Tis not the first instance of their base conduct... To put my pictures in places they could not be seen, and then to decry them is rank villany... I should have been very glad to have their behaviour publickly known, while it is recent, that if I should exhibit no more with them, the true reason may be known...'[1]

1 Wright to Philips, 11th June 1790, quoted by Bemrose, 1885, p. 63, from MS. Derby Public Library.

Wright did in fact exhibit once more with them, in 1794, the last time he showed publicly; and again on this occasion was represented by landscapes.

It need not be assumed that because he showed fewer portraits at this stage of his career, he had allowed this branch of his activity to take second place. Though now no longer such a prolific portrait painter as in his youth, throughout the '80's and early '90's he was producing some of his most famous likenesses, beginning with those of Brooke Boothby, 1781 [Plate 219] and the Rev. Henry Case and Mrs. Morewood, 1782 [Plates 223, 224]; continuing with his masterpieces of group portraiture, the members of the Coke family, *c.* 1781–3 [Plate 225] and the Gisbornes, 1786 [Plate 269]; and culminating in the portraits of the Arkwrights, headed by one of Sir Richard himself, who employed Wright to perpetuate his own features and those of his son, daughter-in-law and grandchildren [Plates 323, 325, 328, 329].[2] For these groups, Wright made the Arkwrights pay dearly, but being one of the richest families in the Kingdom, they could well afford it.

2 The author has deliberately excluded from this chapter a discussion of Wright's friends and patrons, who are only referred to here in passing.

It is a little difficult to draw general conclusions from the prices he charged, since he was quite capable of letting friends or cherished patrons have pictures cheap. However, prices for portraits were more or less standardised. A 30 by 25 inch canvas rose from six guineas in the '60's *(Bennett, Chases, Lygons)* to twelve or fifteen after the Italian journey *(Buckston, Foxes, Darwin, Mrs. Holland of Ford, Seward, Sacheverell Pole, Woods).*[3] A 'Kitcat' (Wright's description of a 36¼ by 28 inch canvas) remained more or less stationary between the late '60's *(Staniforth)* and the early '80's *(Whitehurst)* at fifteen to eighteen guineas. A 50 by 40 inch canvas began at twelve guineas *(Borrows, Pigots, Brooke, Carvers* and the Markeaton Hunt portraits) to end at twenty *(Day, Bakewell, Heskeths, Hurts)* unless practically the whole body was shown, in which case the price went up to £25–4 *(Pares, 'Stephen' Jones, Strutt, Holden, Whetham)*, or the whole body set in a landscape, for which Wright charged over £30 *(R. S. Bateman, Miss Duesbury, Col. Heathcote, 'Captain' Milnes, Case and Mrs. Morewood).* Group portraits were invariably the most expensive, except for the early *Chase* and *Shuttleworth* groups which he let go cheap; the *Coltmans, Mrs. Pole and her child* and the *Pickford Children* went up to £63 each, the *Coke* group and *Lady Wilmot and her child* to over £70, and the *Arkwright Children* to £94–10. The most expensive of all were the *Gisbornes* (£100–16) and *Richard Arkwright, his wife and child* (£126). More was charged (£105) for some subject or genre pictures dating from before the Italian journey, such as the *Academy*, the *Alchemist*, the *Hermit* and *Miravan*, than for corresponding pictures painted on his return, such as *Edwin, Maria, Comus* and *William and Margaret* (£84), though the latter were at least as large; but this can be explained by the fact that the earlier works contained more figures, and as we have seen from an analysis of the group portraits, two figures, even if one was a young child, were always more expensive than one. It is also understandable that he should have charged more for the *Air Pump*, the *Iron Forges* and *Blacksmith's Shops*, the *Orrery* and the Shakespeare scenes than for any portraits. Prices for landscapes between 1775 and 1795 varied according to size but not to period: they rose from a few guineas for a tiny lake or woodland scene to three hundred for a vast *Vesuvius* [Plate 214], but apart from the outsize landscapes purchased by Cockshutt and Catherine II of Russia, it was seldom that they fetched over £100. The Bishop of Derry was asked £105 for a *Vesuvius* [Plate 170] but Wright took objection to the Bishop's criticism of it and refused to part with it.

3 There was an intervening period in the early '70's when he charged ten guineas for portraits of this size *(Bathurst, French).*

Wright fussed more about health and his status as an artist than about money, but had there been the slightest justification for it, money would also have developed into an obsession, since he was born a prey to worry of every sort. He had the kind of middle-class frugality which would have made him mercenary, had he happened to be poor. It is true that he complained of the 'shabby price' Lord Hardwicke had paid for the *Earthstopper* [Plate 113], and that he was concerned about the low sum he was asking Benjamin Bates for the *Air Pump* [Plate 58]; that he was outraged by the behaviour of Alderman Boydell in offering him less for his scene for the Shakespeare Gallery [Plate 299] than he felt he ought to be getting; but all this was chiefly because he feared for his reputation if he allowed his prices to fall. He certainly kept a careful account book in which he noted down all expenses and earnings, but this is because he was by nature methodical. His correspondence is admittedly not free from haggling, but financial dealings play a smaller part in it than might have been expected. The explanation lies in the fact, not only that his pictures continued to sell well, but that he had inherited enough from his father not to have to rely entirely on his own resources; so that whenever he fell ill as he frequently did, he was at least spared the apprehension that he might no longer be able to support his family. For this we have the unimpeachable testimony of two close friends, Thomas Moss Tate and Philips, though at second or third hand. Farington reports: 'He [Wright] is in very good circumstances. Westall understood from Philips that Wright is worth £25000' (in 1796): and again three weeks later: '[Tate told me] Wright inherited from [his father] abt. £100 a year,... His eldest daughtr. is married to a young man who has abt. £200 a year near Derby.'[1] And in case we should feel inclined to dismiss Farington's observations as those of an inveterate gossip, here is Carey to back him up, who no doubt had his information direct from Philips with whom he was in touch: 'His [Wright's] circumstances were not only easy but affluent. He kept a handsome table, at which, without ostentation or profusion, he was happy to enjoy the company of his private friends; and at his decease, he left a property of from ten to twelve thousand pounds...'[2] Though necessarily Wright's financial transactions are noted down in his Account Book in a summary form, so that it is not always possible to extract the right information from them, they fully bear out what Farington and others report. To judge by numerous entries recording the receipt of interest on bonds, or of rent on property he owned, not only when in Italy but throughout his later years, he never had anything to worry about; and there are records of loans of large sums of money to associates.

So it seems that he was always rich enough to satisfy himself in his way of life. But what a paltry recompense this man's gift was, compared to God's gift of good health! The blight on Wright's life was not poverty or lack of recognition but constant illness. His body was already beginning to fail him in his early thirties: 'A series of ill-health for these sixteen years past (the core of my life) has subjected me to many idle days', he was writing in 1783[3]—which takes us back far past the cold floor of the Sistine Chapel, to 1767. 'I have laboured', he goes on, 'under an annual malady some years, four or five months at a time'. In 1783 itself he was prevented through ill-health from working literally throughout the summer.[4] In the late autumn of 1784, as we have seen, he was unable through illness to get ahead with his one-man exhibition, due to open the following spring. Towards the end of 1786 he is asked to contribute to the Shakespeare Gallery but wonders whether his health can stand up to it:

'If ever I felt mortifying circumstances from ill health, 'tis now—wch. will not suffer me to combat for the prize held out to me. Ever since I rec'd yours my mind has been strongly agitated wth. an ardent desire to contribute my mite to this noble work & a dread of not being able to compleat it, wch. in publick undertakings is a very serious business. Dec. 6th. The indifferent and very precarious state of my health, the dreadful size of the pictures & perhaps a limited time to compleat them in, had made me in my own mind give the matter up... Since I recover'd from a 4 months illness I have been employed in the puney works of an enfeebled frame, to go from half a yard of canvas to 12 feet is enough to over set me.'[5]

The next year showed no improvement: in the summer of 1787 he was laid low for almost four months without touching a pencil.[6] In 1791 he complains: 'I have had for some time past a nervous fever hanging about me, and am now much disturbed with an inflammation on my liver. Art stands still...',[7] and so the melancholy catalogue of woes continues, in

1 Farington Diary, entries for 4th October (p. 795) and 28th October 1796 (p. 813) respectively.

2 Carey, 1809, p. 20.

3 Wright to Hayley, 31st August 1783, quoted Bemrose, 1885, p. 61. The letter was with Maggs Ltd. in late 1920's and early 1930's.

4 Wright to Wedgwood, 23rd October 1783, Barlaston MSS. Wright was at Eturia in May and confesses he was unable to work between then and September.

5 Wright to Hayley, beginning 4th December 1786 and continuing two days later. N. P. G. extra-illustrated Bemrose.

6 Wright to Philips, 4th September 1787, quoted Bemrose, 1885, p. 88.

7 Wright to Philips, 24th June 1791, quoted Bemrose, 1885, pp. 89–90. Three days later he

letter after letter to patient friends. Much of all this was mere apprehension. But like many hypochondriacs, Wright was also a genuinely sick man; and so his friends had to be careful not automatically to dismiss his illnesses as illusory.

On 19th August 1790 his wife died of consumption, and the break up of his domestic life hastened his own end. About three years later he left St. Helen's House to go and live at 26 Queen Street, where he remained until his death.[1] His widowhood offered him the single consolation, that he now had more time for his friends, and in their company he discovered the solace of his lonely decline. The story of his last years is bound up with their names.

In a letter to John Leigh Philips of 30th May 1793, Wright announces: '...I shall shortly set my face towards Bootle Coffee House, I have worked very close since I left that place till lately & I begin to feel my painting spirits are near exhausted...'[2] We are fortunate enough in having an eye-witness account of that visit, and since it affords a rare glimpse into Wright's private life, it is worth quoting at length; and yet Wright's niece, the author of it, was so old when she committed her memories to paper, so conventional in her habits of thought, that even had she wished to, she could not have known how to bring her uncle to life for our benefit:

'In the summer of 1793, Mr. Wright, his two eldest daughters, his youngest son, his two sisters (who always lived with his Brother) & his Niece [the author of the account] went to Bootle, about 3 miles from Liverpool; here he enjoyed himself; there was not much company at the Hotel, [so] that the party dined at the public table, & spent the rest of the day in their private sitting room. Mr. Wright used to ride on the shore; the sea, with the different vessels that passed & other things were a constant amusement, likewise the shrimpfishers... His old and intimate Friend Mr. Tho.ˢ Moss Tate of Liverpool, came most evenings & staid till after breakfast... Mr. Blundel of Ince [living] about six miles from Bootle, having a collection of pictures which Mr. Wright was recommended to see, application was made for that purpose... Mr. Blundel was very much pleased & attentive, that the party was much pleased with the excursion. When Mr. Wright had been about 6 weeks at Bootle, he received a letter from Mr. Gisborne, who was then at the Lakes, in which he said, he hoped the date would bring a blush upon his face for not having visited that fine & interesting country & wished he would join him there; Mr. Wright & Mr. Tate set off, spent a week with Mr. Gisborne & returned highly delighted with all they had seen. After a sojourn of 2 months at Bootle the party returned home...'[3]

His niece Hannah tells us that he returned to Liverpool in July 1794, taking his eldest daughter, and went on from there with Tate to the Lakes. On his return from these two excursions to Westmorland and Cumberland, Wright did a series of Lake landscapes, among the last pictures he painted. Listed in his Account Book are some Welsh and Scottish landscapes, but one need not necessarily assume he visited these places also: they may have been adaptations of works by other artists.

Wright's friendship with Hayley had been intimate since the painter's temporary return from Bath in the summer of 1776 but they had not seen much of each other because Hayley could seldom be lured northwards from Sussex. But Hayley had placed his wife, who was mentally unstable, in the care of Dr. Beridge's widow in Derby in 1789, and Wright occasionally met her there. In October of 1793 Hayley's young son Thomas Alphonso, who had exhibited an early talent 'for the pencil', was sent to Hayley's wife (who was not the boy's mother) in Derby, and was placed with a Mr. Ward of Mickleover to study Latin and Greek. On 6th January 1794 he writes to his father: 'Your letter to Mr. Wright I delivered to his daughter, who happened to be with us when it arrived, and he has since been so good as to give me a few instructions in drawing.' On 22nd April he writes again in his usual priggish tone: 'I continue to draw, and, you will be glad to hear, with approbation of my great master' (Wright). It is clear that Wright went beyond what was required of him in kindness to an old friend by taking so much trouble over his pupil, who was only thirteen. But at the end of April that year the boy was suddenly called away by his father to help comfort Cowper who had fallen once again a prey to serious mental illness. Early the next year, Thomas Alphonso was bound to Flaxman as an apprentice. He died in terrible circumstances of slow paralysis of the limbs in 1800.[4]

complains to Richard Arkwright Junior that 'some disease of the liver enfeebles me & keeps me down & I fear till that is remov'd (if it ever will) I shall not be fit for business' (Wright to Arkwright, 27th June 1791, Arkwright MSS.).

***

1 Wright made regular payments for rent of a house amounting to £40 a year to Thomas Bainbrigge Jun. from 1st May 1793 to 27th May 1797, three months before his death. The receipts from Bainbrigge are recorded in the MS. Account Book. They are all in Wright's hand, including Bainbrigge's 'signatures', so they were evidently copied by Wright into his book. On 31st October 1796 the receipt reads: 'Settled with Mr. Wright for the Rent of his House due this Michaelmas last'. It seems reasonable to deduce that the property to which Wright moved in or before 1793 belonged to this man. (See also Bemrose, 1885, p. 102.)

2 MS. Derby Public Library.

3 Niece's memoir, MS. 2, Derby Public Library One ought not to pay too much attention to this visit to Ince, since by that time Wright was too much settled in his ways to profit from contact with, let us say, the Volaire *Eruption of Vesuvius*, or the four Wilsons (1763–67), representing though they did some of Wright's favourite subjects such as Tivoli. Perhaps he allowed his ill eyes to rest on them for a few minutes. 1793 was not necessarily Wright's first visit to the Lakes, as Gisborne thought it was: in a letter to Daulby of 7th February 1786 (see Bemrose, 1885, pp. 86–7) he announces his intention of visiting them that autumn. Of course he may have cancelled his plans, but there is a sunset view of Borrowdale recorded in the Account Book among pictures of *c*. 1786–8 which makes one think the journey was in fact undertaken.

4 Hayley, 1823, II, pp. 80, 87.

One of the great pleasures of Wright's declining years was the occasional visits he would pay his old friend Thomas Gisborne at Yoxall Lodge, his large, rambling house in the heart of Needwood Forest. He was there in 1793, the year the two men visited the Lakes together. He was at the Lodge again in the closing days of 1794, but this visit ended in disaster:

'The very severe winter we have had', he writes to Philips on 30th March 1795, 'has almost demolished me. Just after Xmas I paid a visit to my friend Gisborne. It was a young trick of me to sally forth at that time of the year, but he tempted me with sending his carriage; and wrapping myself up in Flannels, I thought myself invulnerable. Unfortunately for me it proved otherwise. I have been dreadfully ill ever since...'[1]

He never properly recovered from this journey, so wounded was he (as he put it) at so many points, but life dragged on a further two years. He was just in time to witness the marriage of his eldest daughter Anna Romana to James Cade in the spring of 1795 (which meant that the burden of looking after him in his last illness fell chiefly on his second, adolescent, daughter, Harriet [Fig 4]), and to set eyes on his first grand-daughter the following year. In 1796 one of the greatest poets of all time happened to pass through Derby, and in a letter to a friend, numbered Joseph Wright among the sights of the town: '...Derby is full of curiosities', writes Samuel Taylor Coleridge on 27th January 1796, 'the cotton, the silk mills, Wright, the painter, and Dr. Darwin, the everything, except the Christian...'[2]

Wright's health was fast failing. He sought the advice of Erasmus Darwin, who recommended 'a hot bath every night, from 94 to 96 degrees of heat, in which I stay half-an-hour'.[3] Two months later he reports: 'I have now been five months without exercising my pencil, and without a hope that I shall ever resume it'.[4] Not until October 1795 did he feel 'the dawn of inclination to resume it'[5]; but his optimism was shattered a few months later by severe fits of asthma, and suspected dropsy: 'I consulted Dr. Darwin in the last attack who has, I think with success, put me under a course of Foxglove for a dropsical habit, w[ch] he suspects is the cause of my difficulty in breathing...'[6] Philips reports to Westall in October 1796 that Wright has a liver complaint 'without a probability of recovery'. Darwin, says Philips (according to Farington):

'has regulated the life of Wright in whatever relates to Health for some years past, and has contributed to make Wright more valetudinary and unhappy, by encreasing his apprehension. Wright has lived in a state of terror of consequences which might arise from the most trifling deviations from rule. At present Darwin says Wrights liver is gone.'[7]

Next month we hear of failing eyesight: 'Wright of Derby, Philips says, is so shortsighted that he scarcely knows a person across a room'.[8] At this point his niece Hannah should be allowed to take over, since she was present at his deathbed:

'Mr. Wright had for sometime suffered from spasmodic asthma, he became dropsical, which with other painful complaints confined him to his bed in May 1797; during that time his nose bled to a great degree, which prevented him lying down, & from the feeble state he was in, he could not hold up his head long enough together, that a broad ribbon was fastened to each side of the head of the bed, upon which he rested his chin, which was a great relief to him...'[9]

He died on 29th August in his sixty-third year—but he seemed ten years older—in his house in Queen Street, and was buried nearby in St. Alkmund's Church.[10]

It must not be supposed from this description of his last painful years that he was never able to hold pencil or brush. He was still entering payments into his Account Book, albeit in a shaky hand, up to within three months of his death. One of his last pictures was a large *Head of Ullswater*. But when canvases of this size were beyond him; 'when', as Carey writes, 'the progress of his disorder, rendered him averse from the fatigue of working on large pictures', he took to small landscapes, 'which he generally finished in two days; that is, working at his ease, only a few hours, each day...'[11] When in October 1796 he began to

1 MS. Derby Public Library, quoted Bemrose, 1885, p. 95.

Fig 4 *Harriet Wright* (daughter of the artist) c 1790
Panel 10 x 8¾ in / 25.4 x 21.3 cm   Derby Museum and Art Gallery
Cat 175   Pl 322

2 *Collected Letters of Samuel Taylor Coleridge*, ed. Earl Leslie Griggs, I (1785–1800), Oxford, 1956, p. 99. Letter to Joseph Wade from Nottingham.

3 Wright to Philips, 30th March 1795; see note 1. above.

4 Wright to Philips, 29th May 1795, quoted Bemrose, 1885, p. 95.

5 Wright to Philips, 2nd October 1795, quoted Bemrose, loc. cit.

6 Wright to Philips, 11th April 1796, MS. Derby Public Library, passage not transcribed by Bemrose, 1885, pp. 96–7.

7 Farington Diary, entries for 4th October (p. 795) and 28th October (p. 813) 1796 respectively.

8 Farington Diary, entry for 19th November 1796, p. 830.

9 MS. 2, Derby Public Library.

10 His tombstone was discovered in July 1967 about three feet below the central aisle of St Alkmund's, in the course of work on the demolition of the church. There is no inscription apart from his name in capitals.

11 Carey, 1809, p. 19.

show signs of improvement, he succeeded in painting a little daily; yet 'he often requires the stimulus of some person to urge him to do what is necessary to finishing a picture, such as adding figures...'[1] Many of his last pictures remained unfinished at his death, and were impoverished by being rendered saleable by others.

The anonymous obituary in the *Gentleman's Magazine* (September 1797) is full of fine phrases signifying nothing, and only one merits our attention: 'His friends long urged him to reside in London, but his family attachments, and love of retirement were invincible...'[2] Wright was more content in his native town than he would have been in the Capital, finding himself not only well patronized there, but also at his ease in provincial middle-class society—like Joseph Priestley who deliberately turned his back on London to seek refuge in the Midlands, because in his case also, that was where his roots lay. And with Priestley, Wright would doubtless have agreed that there was more happiness, virtue and politeness to be found in the middle-class than in the upper.[3] Nevertheless, Wright was constantly in London, especially during the course of exhibitions at the Incorporated Society and the Royal Academy at which he was represented, giving various London addresses in successive exhibition catalogues; so that it may be presumed that he was well acquainted with the leading London artists and their productions.

Nothing is to be found in the obituary except empty words about his appearance and personality, and we are obliged to turn to the memoir published in the following month to find some of the deficiencies supplied—and yet, even here, how persistently words skirt around the truth! How amiably they pirouette! We must not kid ourselves into supposing that a pious memoir is a true picture of the man:

'In his person he was rather above the middle size, and, when young, was esteemed a very handsome man; his company was then much courted on account of his pleasing vivacity and convivial habits; his eyes were prominent and very expressive;... he was mild, unassuming, modest to an extreme, generous and full of sensibility, with the perfect carriage of a gentleman; honourable and punctual in all his transactions, he entertained the most utter contempt for every thing like meanness or illiberality; and his good heart felt but too poignantly for the misconduct of others'.[4]

From a series of self-portraits the accuracy (within its limits) of these statements can be tested: beginning with the youth in the Cade Collection [Fig 5] whose Baroque cloak and fancy Van Dyck collar and cuffs contrast with the stern oval of a face more noble than

1 Farington Diary, 28th October 1796 (p. 813), basing his information on a letter from Wright to William Tate.

2 Obituary, 1797. The same comments appeared in the *Derby Mercury*, 7th September 1797.

3 See the fascinating passage in the *Memoirs of Dr. Joseph Priestley written by Himself (to the Year 1795)...*, London, 1806, I, pp. 82–3.

4 Philips, 1797. Philips provided material for the obituary but his memoir is more detailed.

Fig 5 *Self-portrait* c 1758
30 x 25 in / 76.2 x 63.5 cm   Miss D. M. R. Cade   Cat 164   Pl 6

Fig 6 *Self-portrait* c 1767–70
30 x 25 in / 76.2 x 63.5 cm   Charles Rogers-Coltman   Cat 167   Frontispieces

Fig 7 *Self-portrait* c early '70's
c 28 x 24 in / 71.1 x 60.9 cm   Mrs Beryl E. Cade   Cat 169   Pl 120

Fig 8 John Holland of Ford (1800), after a lost
Wright of c 1779–82 *Self-portrait*
28 x 23½ in / 71.1 x 59.7 cm   Private
collection, U.K.   See Cat 170

Fig 9 Copy after Joseph Wright
Self-portrait 1793
30 x 25 in / 76.2 x 63.5 cm   Colonel Sir
John Crompton-Inglefield   See Cat 172

handsome; continuing with the tough candlelight painter in his mid-thirties who now sees himself as the Midlands Rembrandt [Frontispiece, and Fig 6]; then on to the contemplative portrait belonging to another branch of the Cade family [Fig 7] of a man bordering on middle age who is already ruffled by gusts of ill health, who has shed pugnacity in order to allow kindliness to come to the surface; passing on to a man in middle life wearing a floppy hat at a jaunty angle who appears temporarily—all too temporarily—at peace with the world [untraced: see Fig 8]; from there on to the haggard features of a man of 59 who has reached old age too soon, in the portrait Wright presented to his friend Gisborne on a visit to Yoxall in 1793 [untraced; see Fig 9]—all of them (and there are others in between, telling the same story) bringing out one side or another of this contradictory but in no respect unaccountable character: the vivacity and the mildness, the conviviality and the querulousness, the vigour and the frailty—many things short of duplicity and meanness.

The pictures which had remained in his painting room at Queen Street, except of course the family portraits, were dispersed at Christie's in 1801, and those that were bought in were resold at Derby nine years later.[1] A number in both sales returned to the family, but the remainder went to collectors rather than dealers and fetched good prices. For instance, in the first sale two views of the *Colosseum* and the *Indian Widow* [Plates 256, 247] were sold for considerably more than the value Wright himself had set upon them; as for the *Head of Ullswater Lake*, which had been described in his obituary as 'the finest of all his landscapes', it went for £315, a larger sum than he had obtained for any landscape in his lifetime. In the second sale the *Alchemist* fetched the enormous sum of £210—twice what Wright had asked for it.

For the next three quarters of a century, Wright's pictures remained locked up in country houses in the Midlands, except for the J. L. Philips (1814) and Hardman (1838) sales, and for the occasional exhibition at the British Institution or the Royal Academy to which, significantly, the same pictures (not always by Wright's hand) were loaned time and again; with the result that Wright is not honoured by a biography in Cunningham's lives of painters (early 1830's) though several half-forgotten artists are; and when the Redgraves came to compose their *Century of British Painters* in the 1860's, though they took the trouble to visit Derbyshire expressly to see some of his works,[2] they had insufficient evidence on which to base their adverse judgement of his contribution to the history of British art. And it was left to William Bemrose to do his hero justice, in a monograph (1885) which within its limits—it lays itself open to the charge of being more in the nature of a compila-

1 The catalogues of the 1801 and 1810 sales are reprinted by Bemrose, 1885, pp. 107–14.

2 Bemrose, 1885, p. 66 claims that they never saw his best pictures at all.

tion or anthology than a proper book—remains to this day the only reliable full-scale guide to the artist's life and work. Bemrose was able to draw on his experience, denied to the Redgraves, of the first representative exhibitions of Wright's works since 1785: those held in Derby in 1870 and 1883. And again at the Royal Academy in 1886 an important selection of his work was thrown open to a cultivated public. Two of his best pictures were in public collections by this time: the *Air Pump* which entered the National Gallery as early as 1863 and was therefore accessible to the Redgraves when they were engaged on their book, and the *Orrery* which was presented to the Derby Corporation Art Gallery in 1884. Since then the Derby Art Gallery has honoured its local painter by a succession of acquisitions, so that today Wright in all moods can be studied there better than anywhere else.

A loan exhibition of his works was held at Graves' Galleries in Pall Mall in 1910 which brought to light unknown pictures, many still in the possession of descendants of his patrons and friends. This was followed by a vast show at Derby in 1934 in commemoration of the bicentenary of his birth, comprising 156 items, some of which were copies or poor daubs.[1] Wright was too austere an artist to sail in on the new wind of taste which landed so many late eighteenth-century English portrait painters in mansions on Long Island, and partly for this reason serious Wright scholarship declined in the first decades of this century. The less said about a second monograph devoted to him in 1922, the better. And even as late as 1954 it was still permissible to omit a fine Wright double portrait [Plate 50] from the illustrations of a catalogue of the Courtauld Collection, where Matisse and Lautrec lithographs are given handsome treatment. It was not until after the second war that research began again in earnest, with the publication of Klingender's *Art and the Industrial Revolution* (1947), the first attempt ever made to relate him to his industrial background.[2] This was followed in 1953 by Waterhouse's Pelican History, providing a thoughtful but necessarily cursory survey of Wright's historical position. Since then some progress has been made. However, the stage has not yet been reached when all Wright's most significant works have been rediscovered, and it remains the art historian's duty to track them down. The author of this book is conscious that he has succeeded in unearthing a proportion only of what must exist among the factories of the Midlands and the North.

[1] It is symptomatic of the amateurishness of this show, that of the fourteen oil paintings (out of a choice of well over a hundred) illustrated in the catalogue, five were not by the artist.

[2] An intelligent effort to relate Wright's scientific pictures to science in his day in the Midlands was undertaken as early as 1923 by F. W. Shurlock (see bibliography).

Fig 10 Detail from *Francis Noel Clarke
Mundy of Markeaton* Cat 110 Pl 34

24

II The Art of Wright

1 EARLY PORTRAITURE

In this chapter we are concerned with the origins and early development as a portraitist of this subtle, changeable, yet invariably consistent artist. In exploring Wright's youth from this point of view we are fortunate in not being confronted with that succession of gaps in information that normally frustrates the art historian. Except later during the Bath period (1775–7) there is never any need to fall back on guess-work: for with the coming to light of so many forgotten portraits we can follow his progress more or less year by year from the age of twenty-two onwards. We can now account for the changes in the early portrait style and watch him move into independence when, with growing confidence, portraiture begins to alternate with artificial light subjects and finally with experiments in landscape. By 1764 he had broken entirely free from Hudson's apprenticeship and over the next ten years reached the peak of his career. While he was no less an artist on his return from Italy and continued to produce important work almost to the close of his life, he had made his deepest mark before leaving for abroad.

If we seek to uncover Wright's pre-history it is to the Derby Art Gallery that we must turn our steps. There in portfolios containing drawings of every period are some small studies in pencil and ink wash after indifferent engravings that must date from just before 1750, preceding by several years his first term of professional tuition under Hudson. Hard and clumsy though they are, these early efforts deserve at least a glance [see Plate 1]. Not only are they our first introduction to Wright, but by stretching our imagination we can perceive in them the glimmer of a dawn that broke in the early '60's. Already there is a concern with form, and in the primitive contrast between light and shade, the seed of experiments in artificial light effects is sown. Two drawings of a different character [Plates 2,3], chalk studies of an old man's head and a *Judith* expressed in a broader style, plot his conscientious progress from Kneller to Piazzetta. These are dated June and July 1751.[1] A few months later, soon after his seventeenth birthday, he left Derby to begin work with Hudson. As we have seen, there was a two-year stay in Hudson's workshop, followed by a return home to see what he could do on his own as a portrait painter. But with the first independence came the realisation of the need for further training, and another fifteen months with Hudson followed in 1756. In putting himself under Hudson, Wright had chosen an artist whose shop was at the centre of London's portrait trade. For well over a decade a stream of likenesses had flowed from the easels of this busy shop; there was still no lack of fashionable sitters anxious to be painted according to the conventions Hudson had long since perpetuated. But it was just this kind of romantic production that appealed to Wright at this stage, if for no other reason than it showed him the way towards achieving at least an acceptable standard of performance. Like his contemporaries in London whose skills were no less sought out, Hudson had long depended on shop assistants who could add

[1] The inscription below on the first: 'Joseph Wright fecit Old John Rotherhams Hand June 29th 1751. No. 2' and that on the second: 'Joseph Wright Fecit ... July 5th No. 6' (also obviously 1751) are in Wright's unformed handwriting. This means there were others of the same series. The second showing the head of Judith is copied from Piazzetta's *Judith and Holofernes*. The best known painted version is in the Accademia di San Luca, Rome (illus. R. Pallucchini, *Piazzetta*, Milan, 1956, pl. 60), but Wright clearly relied on a print. It is significant for his future development that Piazzetta's scene should take place by lamplight, and we are reminded of the hanging lamps in *Miravan*, *Penelope* and elsewhere. An unfinished black and white chalk drawing on blue paper of a *Counsellor Noel* is in fact recorded as having been done in his seventeenth year (Bemrose Collection, late nineteenth century) and no doubt belonged to the series.

Fig 11 Thomas Hudson
Mrs Matthew Michell and her Children,
Matthew and Anne c 1757–8   Leicester
Museum and Art Gallery

1 It is not possible to state categorically that
Wright collaborated on this picture, since its
date is not precisely known. However, the age
or ages of the children do not contradict the
required date of c. 1757–8. Mr. and Mrs. Michell
were married in 1749, and the children could be
about 7. The husband died in 1752.

2 An inscription in Wright's hand on this
portrait (now in a collection in Connecticut) has
a word following on his signature which might
be interpreted as reading 'Thorne'. In his
Account Book Wright records painting
portraits of two families at Thorne, the
Ellissons and the Fosters, but these were done in
1760, and he is not known to have travelled to
Thorne two years earlier. Still, there is no
reason why he should not have.

the needed drapery and backgrounds, thus helping him to meet the heavy demands on his time. Such a division of work had been an accepted part of shop organisation since the days of Van Dyck. An apprentice like Wright would have had no difficulty in such an environment in following the evolution of a portrait from the preparation of the canvas to the final touches. He would have been naturally eager to learn what he could of methods used by the shop to build up form, establish areas of drapery and bring them to a proper state of finish.

To judge from the portraits Wright produced in Derbyshire and Lincolnshire soon after his second stay with Hudson, his early style is stamped with all he had learnt as an apprentice. Form is solidly if sometimes too rigidly constructed, yet even in his stiffest portraits from these years there is a level of accomplishment that points back to the professionalism of his training. As a painter of drapery, especially, Wright seems from the beginning to have been more than just proficient. For even his first portraits reveal his identification with Hudson-esque formulae for painting lustrous materials and for picking out the patterns of lace. Perhaps in Hudson's shop Wright had been assigned to the speciality of drapery. There is no way of substantiating this. Yet when we examine a group portrait such as Hudson's full-length of *Mrs. Matthew Michell and her Children, Matthew and Anne* [Fig 11], parts of the drapery, and most of all the suit worn by the young boy, betray Wright's manner of treating folds and surfaces about 1760.[1]

In assimilating these shop methods, Wright could scarcely have avoided assimilating at the same time his master's by then well worn stock of compositions, as well as some of the mannerisms by which he dressed up a portrait. Although the latter are familiar enough once we have seen a number of Hudson's portraits, they go back to French sources, to Gravelot's engravings for example, and perhaps no less to Jean-Baptiste van Loo and Andrea Soldi, whose London vogue of a dozen years before had encouraged native-born painters to introduce Rococo elements into their work and to adopt a more fluid brush-work. In spite of his insistence on insularity, Hogarth himself was not above paying his respects to French taste and many of his portraits are embellished with Rococo flourishes. It mattered little if these once fashionable features had run their course by mid-century: they were still acceptable to Hudson's clients and Wright was to rely on them until well into the '60's.

Only two oil paintings survive from the period before Wright's second apprenticeship: two stiff waist-lengths within feigned ovals of the young *Nathaniel Curzon* and his sister *Caroline* [Plates 4, 5] which can be dated from the ages of the sitters about 1755–6. The request to paint these Curzon children must have been an exceptional stroke of good fortune for an artist still untried, indeed one who had not even completed his training: for next to the Cavendishes this aristocratic family was foremost in the county. Ironically enough, he never again painted anyone of such eminence (even *Richard Fitzwilliam* [Plate 49] was not quite in this class); drawing his sitters from then onwards from deeply rooted county families and the rising middle class where his brush was in steady demand. A portrait of an unknown boy evidently of much humbler extraction than the Curzons [Plate 8] is dated 1758,[2] and a series of portraits of six children of the Wilmot family [Plates 9, 10, 11, 12, 13, 15] follow within eighteen months to two years. They show an advance in subtlety on the three portraits of children of the late '50's. To a greater degree than before we find in the immediacy and freshness of the young Wilmots an expression of Wright's growing assurance in his ability to satisfy a patron. Even at this stage (1760) he was pushing beyond the limits of Hudson's instruction, to grope at naturalism. At intervals he painted his own portrait, and has left us records of his appearance from early youth to premature old age. The first likeness is a self-portrait in pencil in the Fitzwilliam Museum [Plate 7], a composition repeated exactly in his first self-portrait in oil [Plate 6]. Both can be dated about 1758. These two portraits show us the artist approaching his mid-twenties in an attitude that makes us realise how seriously he took himself from the word go. He looks out directly at the spectator (or rather, into his mirror) with large, questing eyes, and there is determination in the mouth. It is the face of a youth cut out for eminence.

Three portraits of about 1760 of members of the Lygon family still belong to descendants of the sitters [Plates 14, 17, 18]. In the female portraits, Wright has attenuated the figures, turning them into mannequins. *Mrs. Lygon* [Plate 18] wears a pale blue dress with slashed sleeves and a collar, fichu and cuffs of stiff lace; her daughter *Elizabeth* [Plate 14] has been given a plumed hat and a dress that matches her mother's in elegance. Here is the last stifled gasp of Rubens's *Chapeau de Paille*. In contrast to the finery of their dress, Lygon's [Plate 17] velvet coat is of plain cut, although the pale blue, and the brushwork that expresses its texture, are no less Rococo in spirit.[1] Several portraits survive from Wright's journey to counties east of Derbyshire in the early months of 1760. A forbidding portrait of a surgeon in Southwell (Notts.), *Nicholas Hutchinson* [Plate 20] shows Wright at his most prosaic. The portrait of William Kirke executed at Retford that winter is also no more than a routine performance [Plate 19]. The one time Mayor of Doncaster, *William Brooke* [Fig 12] brought out the best in the painter. Brooke is shown seated rock-like in his chair, much as we see *Richard Arkwright* [Fig 13] in the remarkable portrait Wright painted of him thirty years later, or many of the other male sitters whose practical grasp of affairs he so much admired. We are reminded of Hogarth's *Thomas Coram* whose pride in his station in life, in the solid position he had built up for himself, was no different from that of Brooke's or Arkwright's. Wright saw Brooke for what he was, a plain man who deserved a plain record. There is an element foreign to Hudson here; this may partly be put down to Hogarth, but also during his Lincolnshire tour Wright may have been struck by some early portraits painted in the county in the mid-'50's by

[1] A similar portrait, said to represent *Dorothy Anne, wife of Colonel Heathcote* [Plate 16] is obviously related in style to the Lygon portraits and must date from this period. Another portrait of an unknown young woman in a private collection (see Cat No 161) is also *c* 1760 but is too much damaged in the face to stand up to reproduction.

Fig 12 *William Brooke* 1760
50 x 40 in / 127 x 101.6 cm
R. D. Plant   Cat 25   Pl 21

Fig 13 *Sir Richard Arkwright* 1789–90
95 x 60 in / 241.3 x 152.4 cm
Colonel Peter Arkwright   Cat 1   Pl 323

Fig 14 George Stubbs *Sir John Nelthorpe as a Boy* Lt Col R. S. Nelthorpe

Stubbs, only one of which has so far come to light (but there were certainly others): *Sir John Nelthorpe* as a boy [Fig 14]—a family that still retains Wright's earliest genre piece [Plate 45].[2] Wright also painted Brooke's richly dressed daughter and her husband *William Pigot* [Fig 15, Plate 23] in attitudes scarcely less mannered than those he had employed for the Lygons. Brooke's genteel son-in-law rests an arm on an elaborately carved table of the type we find in some of Hudson's portraits, and he holds a decorated snuff box as though he were determined to establish his social superiority to his father-in-law. The entire organisation of his wife's portrait has been taken over from Hudson, since it follows closely the composition he used for *Elizabeth Cartwright* [Fig 16]. If Brooke comes to life again in Wright's portrait of Arkwright, we can say as much for the Pigots who stand in the same relation to the Doncaster Mayor as Arkwright's son and daughter-in-law [Plate 325] stand to the doughty old inventor.

[2] The connection between Stubbs and Wright at this early stage was pointed out by Basil Taylor in a lecture at Yale University in the spring of 1965. We hope it will be possible to be more specific when more early Stubbses turn up.

Fig 15 *Mrs William Pigot* 1760
50 x 40 in / 127 x 101.6 cm
R. D. Plant   Cat 121   Pl 24

Fig 17 *Mrs Ann Carver* 1760
50 x 40 in / 127 x 101.6 cm   Mr and Mrs
Ronald Tree   Cat 29   Pl 22

Fig 18 Mezzotint after Thomas Hudson
Duchess of Ancaster

1 Wright's use of Hudson's design was pointed out by John Steegmann, 'A drapery painter of the eighteenth century', *The Connoisseur*, June 1936, pp. 309 ff. Steegmann implies (though he does not actually state) that Wright employed a drapery man, but this is inconceivable. Wright was only just embarking on his career; moreover, the technique of *Mrs. Carver's* draperies is typical of his early style. He must, however, have relied on a drawing available in the Hudson workshop. Hudson's *Mary, Duchess of Ancester* is known from an engraving by James McArdell, but there also exists a three-quarter-length design by Hudson of

Fig 16 Thomas Hudson *Elizabeth Cartwright*
50 x 40 in / 127 x 101.6 cm   Mutual Households Association Ltd, London

Four members of the Carver family were painted at Eckington in 1760 on instructions from the father of the eldest: the widow *Mrs. Marmeduke Carver* [Fig 17] and her three children *Ann, Elizabeth* and *John* [Plates 26, 28, 27]. The Carver ladies outdo the Lygons in richness of dress, and it is on the diaphanous shawls that he concentrates his attention, hiding the faces behind masks. There is nothing perfunctory about these shawls as there is about the faces: they touched a deep chord in his nature, just as, in some male sitters, the passage from a cheek to a nose would cause him to explore every indentation. There were two sides to Wright's nature: a love of glinting surfaces, and a love of structure, and sometimes one is allowed to come to the fore, sometimes the other, and at his best the two converge. Mrs. Carver [Fig 17] supports her left elbow on a rock brought forward to suit her convenience, her fingers lightly brushing her cheek. For the design Wright has relied faithfully on Hudson's portrait of *Mary, Duchess of Ancester* [Fig 18]: the draperies are identical, and only the face is given a hasty make-up.[1] Her elder daughter [Plate 26] stands in profile before a landscape, her right hand extended in that aimless gesture that had stood for elegance since at least the days of Lely. She also is based exactly on a Hudson design: on his portrait of *Lady Northampton*, repeated in a half length of a member of the *Oxenden* family.[2] The younger daughter and the son [Plates 28, 27] are brought indoors and made to rest their arms on inadequate ledges. All four are shaped from the same mould as served to produce the Pigots and the Lygons. And there are others of the same type and period who are just as reticent about their personalities but are allowed a certain decorative charm: a member of the *Cracroft* family [Plate 25], as dazzling as any Carver; the unidentified ladies in St. Louis [Plate 31] and in a collection in Memphis, Tennessee [Plate 32], and a little girl at Temple Newsam [Plate 29]. The portraits of *Thomas Borrow* [Plate 39] and his wife[3] have developed further towards naturalism, and we are inclined to date them about 1762–3—dates in fact supported by their situation in the Account Book.

Between 1761 and 1764 Wright received a number of further portrait commissions. Six of these painted about 1762–3 as a series show strapping young men in the uniform of members of the Markeaton Hunt [Plates 33, 34, 35, 36, 37, 38]: navy blue coats, bright red waistcoats, yellow trousers. One, *Nicholas Heath* [Plate 37], wears his cap: one, *Becher Leacroft* [Plate 33] has parked his on a post; the four others carry theirs. These oddly contorted hats with their broad, crescent-moon peaks ask to be noticed, and Wright satisfies us by scrutinising them for the beauty of their shape alone. One of the sitters, *Francis Burdett* [Plate 38] echoes the *Rev. John C. Carver* [Plate 27] in reverse, and in the process turns him into a real man; another, *Becher Leacroft* [Plate 33] has a shot at *William Brooke* [Plate 21], but there are too many easy-going Leacrofts among his ancestors to make his act convincing: unlike Brooke, his status is too secure for him to have to insist on it. The relaxation of these six young men is new to Wright and in the forefront of British portraiture at that time. *Francis Noel Clarke Mundy* [Plate 34] stands before the rock face, his hound turning to sniff the severed brush of a fox. Here, as in Leacroft's left arm, hand and thigh, and in Peckham's handkerchief [Plate 35] are the first clear intimations in Wright's work of capabilities beyond those of a routine portrait painter. The detail of hound's head, brush, riding crop, gloves and plant in the *Mundy* [Fig 10] are conceived as a game still life in the Dutch fashion—leaving old Hudson far behind to plod along with his ordinary competence, pointing the way to immaculate still life details, beyond the young man taking notes in the *Orrery* [Plate 54] to the *Coke* and *Gisborne* groups of twenty years later and more [Plates 225, 269]. Leacroft's right hand is tinged with red from his waistcoat, and several dark blue coats blush under the waistcoats' impact. Wright was rushing ahead so far in advance of anything his smart sitters can have understood, that we are conscious that he was painting them for his own benefit as well as for theirs, building up an experience of form and colour in preparation for the subject pieces already in mind, and soon to follow on canvas. All of a sudden he has opened his eyes to light and grasped its value as an aid to defining form. The austerity of *Nicholas Hutchinson* and the Cade self-portrait [Plates 20, 6] has joined with the frivolity of the Carvers' veils to produce a synthesis, of form revealed by light. Up to that moment (for instance, on the backs of John Carver's and Bennett's [Plates 27, 30] hands), light had been used casually, as throw-away gestures. Now the humdrum lighting conventions of the Hudson studio—that habit of running a Neon streak down a shoulder—are used, as in *Nicholas Heath* [Plate 37], to give substance to the human body. Wright has swung into the highway of achievement, and the excitement mounts as we strive to keep pace with him. We become aware that *Mrs. Wilmot* [Fig 19], leaning forward on her fence in the most natural movement possible, has left the dolls of 1760 far behind her and taken on flesh and blood. She also is dressed in hunting costume, a whip in one hand, a plumed hat in the other, a tame fox in attendance. The new obsessions with light and still life—those feathers, those knuckles, that clenched glove—show that she belongs in spirit with the Markeaton huntsmen. She cannot be much more than a year earlier than Copley's *Mrs. Epes Sargent II* [Fig 20], also dressed for the hunt.[1] How strange that Wright and Copley should be racing in the same direction, yet unaware of each other's existence across those thousands of miles of sea!

Margaret, Lady Oxenden, repeating the composition. See also Alastair Smart, *The Life and Work of Allan Ramsay*, London, 1952, p. 41.

2 The full length of *Lady Northampton* was formerly on the London art market. A photograph of the half-length portrait of a member of the Oxenden family is in the Witt Library under Hudson.

3 The portrait of *Mrs. Borrow* has been so radically restored that it can no longer bear reproduction. The husband has also come in for some harsh treatment but has stood up better to the ordeal.

1 Jules D. Prown, *John Singleton Copley*, Cambridge (Mass.), 1966, I, plate 144. The Copley is signed and dated 1764.

Fig 19 *Mrs Wilmot* c 1762–63
50 x 40 in / 127 x 101.6 cm   Sir Robert
Wilmot, Bt.   Cat 148

Fig 20 John Singleton Copley *Mrs Epes Sargent II* 1764
49 x 39 in / 124.4 x 99 cm   Mr Oliver D. Knauth

Fig 21 '*Mrs Mundy*' c 1762–63
30 x 25 in / 76.2 x 63.5 cm   Sir Gilbert
Inglefield   Cat 112   Pl 44

Fig 22 *Mrs Francis Hurt* c 1780
50 x 40 in / 127 x 101.6 cm   Michael Hurt
Cat 93   Pl 203

1 Names of sitters in inverted commas indicate that the identification is not certain. The same goes for landscapes.

Two other male portraits of this period in private collections, one belonging to Gilbert Inglefield [Plates 43, 42], pursue the exploration of reality with the aid of light. Five female portraits bridge the gap between the Hudsonesque three-quarter lengths and the fully mature *Shuttleworth* group [Plate 51]: '*Mrs. Mundy*' [Fig 21],[1] *Mrs. Chase* [Plate 41], a lost and nameless young lady who is better ignored until she turns up [Plate 47], '*Mrs. Boyle*' [Plate 46] and *Miss Warren* [Plate 48]. This is also the moment of his first experiment in the conversation piece [Plate 50]. The most remarkable of the series is '*Mrs. Mundy*' [Fig 21], a dress rehearsal for *Mrs. Hurt* [Fig 22] of nearly twenty years later. She raises her right hand, perhaps a shade too artfully, to catch her pearls and veil. We saw realism taking shape in *William Brooke*, but the '*Mundy*' portrait has an intensification of character and unity of conception that take us beyond anything Wright had achieved so far. There is breadth in the handling of form; the contrast between the light raking the upper part of the body and the luminous shadow below is a quite new departure. Strong light plays its part as well in *Mrs. Chase* [Plate 41], falling with full force on her figure, and catching the edges of lace and the bows of the dress. Reflected lights add luminosity to the shadows which are painted with delicate pinks fusing into warm greys. Again Copley comes to mind but in the handling of colour and tone Wright is the more subtle: for he was steeped in the European tradition, able whenever he felt inclined to drench himself in the Old Masters in Midlands collections, particularly in the Dutch school where he was beginning to recognize his spiritual ancestry; whereas Copley had to rely on European engravings, causing him to realise his forms by abrupt transitions from yellowish lights to warm dark shadows, with the minimum of inner reflection.

In the portrait of '*Mrs. Boyle*' [Plate 46] the face has the same degree of delicate tonal variation that marks the other female portraits. But its most original feature is the treatment of the costume with its wide lace collar, and how this affects the way it fits over the shoulders. To describe it factually was important and he has done so in a highly realistic manner, but it was the intricate pattern of shadow cast on the bodice and sleeves by the 'islands' within the linear structure of the lace that captured his imagination. To paint what the mind knew, helped on by what the eye saw, instead of responding conventionally to drapery as he had done earlier, presented a problem every bit as challenging as the delineation of the lady's features. *Miss Warren* [Plate 48] kneels out-of-doors, her arm around the neck of a lamb which she draws close to her body. For the first time we note that a sitter is represented full-length (these are in fact the first feet in Wright's art); the landscape still smells of the studio but the setting was to develop by the end of the seventh decade into a major compositional scheme. He was probably already working on the large picture of *Mr. and Mrs. William Chase* [Plate 50] in 1762. As a work of art it cannot compare with the *Shuttleworth* group [Plate 51] of eighteen months later. Nevertheless, if we are prepared to overlook the clumsy relationship between the figures, it remains an ambitious effort. Wright appears to have sensed that for a work on this scale and involving sitters of some prominence, drapery alone was not enough and that the background demanded a more elaborate treatment: hence the country house grandeur with the Doric pillar, the heavy fold of curtain, the red lacquer desk, the Rococo scrollwork on the wall. William Chase dressed in dove grey handles an object of veneration to Wright, a flute, which he accordingly deals with venerably; while his wife wearing a rich dress of cold bluey-green coaxes her parrot to its perch. Wright has been at pains to describe minutely the construction, by the Pieter de Hooch window, of the parrot's domed wire cage (temporarily with its door open) which looks forward to the delicate scientific instruments which were soon to jingle from canvas to canvas. No matter if the demands of this composition proved too much for him: the *Chase* 'conversation' points unambiguously in the direction he was taking, and it was only a question of two years before his problems were resolved.

An attempt must be made to account for the speed of this progress from the mannequins of 1760 to the men and women of flesh and blood of 1762–3. Stubbs, as has been suggested, played perhaps a marginal role in this transformation. But Wright was more deeply indebted, soon after their appearance, to a series of some eighteen bust-length mezzotint portraits by Thomas Frye (1710–62),[1] first published in 1760 and 1761. Frye came to London from Dublin as a young man, set up in the '40's as a manufacturer of porcelain at Bow, painted some portraits and miniatures, and in the last year of his life issued this series, at least one of which crossed the Atlantic at once and was used by Copley as the pattern for the design of a pastel of *Mrs. Gawan Brown* (1763).[2] Wright could have been first attracted to Frye by seeing some oils, crayons, miniatures and engravings he exhibited at the Society of Artists in 1761, or he may have heard about him through his own later engraver William Pether who was Frye's pupil; in any case, if the mezzotints could reach Boston within two years, they could reach Derby more quickly, and there is little object in speculating about the channel of communication between the two men. We shall see in the next chapter what a vital part Frye's mezzotints played in the construction of heads and gestures in the famous subject pieces and genre scenes from 1765 onwards. For here at hand was the new realism, and a new way of using light and shadow that Wright sought—an attitude towards the human body that Hudson was of course unable or unwilling to supply. And it affected his portraiture also, to a lesser extent: a comparison between one of Frye's mezzotints of 1760 [Fig 23] and '*Mrs Mundy*' [Fig 21] will suffice to make the point. If Hudson had taught him the basis of procedure, it was Frye who opened his eyes to the real world. But not Frye alone. In the portrait of '*Mrs. Boyle*' [Fig 24] we are also riminded of Allan Ramsay of the turn of the sixth-seventh decade; of *Miss Woodford*,[3] for example [Fig 25] —though the differences between the two artists are no less revealing than their similarities. The two ladies wear the same type of shawl; but whereas Wright is anxious to tell us how his functions, Ramsay prefers to concentrate, in his, on what the casual eye observes. The comparison reveals that the realism of the one is based on knowledge, of the other on vision. Ramsay also lies behind *Richard Fitzwilliam* [Plate 49] and the *Shuttleworth* group [Plate 51], both of 1764. It was his softness of tone and luminosity that drew Wright to Ramsay, but he has also noted his way of composing a figure: *Mary Shuttleworth* is closely related to Ramsay's *Lady Susan Fox-Strangways* of 1761.[4] Frye and Ramsay, then, appealed to two seemingly irreconcilable sides of Wright's character: his austerity and his sweetness, and the two came together in his first masterpiece, the *Shuttleworth* group.

Not only are these figures painted with greater assurance and sensitivity than are the *Chases* but the articulation of the picture as a whole is more convincing. Shuttleworth stands in a natural pose, reminiscent of Batoni's full-lengths. His wife conducts us back to Helene Fourment *via* Reynolds and Ramsay. The little girl dangles a still life in the manner of Fyt. Having unified his figures in a physical sense he binds them all together more intimately by light which crawls thoughtfully over surfaces, bringing into sharp focus the smallest

Fig 23 Thomas Frye
Girl holding up pearls 1760
Mezzotint

1 The literature on Frye is meagre. The reader is referred to the *Ibernian Magazine*, January 1789, pp. 19–21; to the D. N. B; and for a summary of the evidence, to Hugh Tait, in an article on 'Bow' in *English Porcelain, 1745–1850*, ed. R. J. Charleston, London, 1965, pp. 42 ff. A letter from Wedgwood to Bentley, 25th June 1769 (quoted by Finer & Savage, 1965, p. 75) speaks of the daughter of 'that Fry [*sic*] who was famous for doing heads in mezzotinto, which you have seen…'

2 The source was discovered by Barbara Parker; see Prown, *op. cit*. I, p. 37 and plates 109, 110.

3 Exh. 'Realism and Romance in English Painting', Messrs. Agnew, November-December 1966 (10). The date is not known but it clearly belongs to the period *c*. 1759–62.

4 Illus. A. Smart, *op. cit*. plate XVIII (a). The figure of Mary Shuttleworth may also owe something to Reynolds's *Lady Caroline Keppel* of 1757–9 (Ellis K. Waterhouse, *Reynolds*, London, 1941, plate 47).

Fig 24 'Hon Mrs Boyle' c 1761–63
30 x 25 in / 76.2 x 63.5 cm   The Mackelvie
Collection, Auckland City Art Gallery,
New Zealand   Cat 23   Pl 46

Fig 25 Allan Ramsay *Miss Woodford*
30 x 25 in / 76.2 x 63.5 cm   Thomas Agnew
and Sons Ltd

details of costume and creating a lively play of cast shadow which reinforces the reality of
what we see. No less in his use of colour does Wright advance beyond anything he had
done before: for here we find colours harmonised and softened by the flood of light. From
the shadow cast by the column of the highly polished table on which Mary Shuttleworth
leans, to the high lights on the beaded choker around her neck, all is pure and unambiguous.
The stage is set for the *Gladiator* and the *Orrery*.

The next years were dedicated to subject pieces by artificial light, and accordingly he was
less active in portraiture, though not to the extent that he neglected this side of his art.
He still accepted sitters, particularly towards the end of the decade when he settled in
Liverpool, presumably for the sole purpose of seeking out new clients. Here he created
a stir, captured most of the local portrait trade, and soon had as much work as he could

Fig 26 *Mrs Gwillym of Atherton* 1766
50 x 40 in / 127 x 101.6 cm   City Art
Museum of Saint Louis, U.S.A.   Cat 69   Pl 55

Fig 27 Hendrick Terbrugghen *Penorcon Player*
Pen and white chalk on grey paper
$10\frac{1}{8}$ x $8\frac{1}{16}$ in / 25.7 x 20.4 cm   Kunsthalle,
Hamburg

handle. Only three portraits can be situated beyond question between the *Shuttleworth* group and the Liverpool series: the companion pictures of *Mr.* and *Mrs. Gwillym* [Plates 55, 56, Fig 26] dated 1766, and the *Bradshaw Children* [Plate 57] of about 1766–8. All three compare favourably with the Liverpool commissions. Robert Gwillym is painted from slightly below eye level, standing behind a balustrade drawn in exaggerated perspective—a trick Wright was to repeat effectively in *Mrs. John Ashton* [Plate 64], *Mrs. Bathurst* [Plate 84] and *Thomas Day* [Plate 80]. He rests his right arm on the stone coping as he surveys the scene before him with an air of satisfaction, the epitome of the landowner secure in his station in life. Wright felt no need to do more than present his subject as forthrightly as possible, even to the extent of recording the broken balustrade and metal stud which once held the upright member in place. What other English eighteenth-century artist would have made a virtue out of introducing such an incongruous note into a portrait? In the pendant Mrs. Gwillym wears a Van Dyck costume and stiff lace collar. In the devotion Wright lavishes on her lute, in her slashed sleeves, in the strong light which lends both magic and sense to form, in the treatment of the folds of the marvellous grey blue dress with its violet reflected lights, he seems to have relied on Terbrugghen, an artist of his favourite school, that of Utrecht. No painting by Terbrugghen is now known that corresponds with it, but a drawing in Hamburg [Fig 27] hints that such a one existed. The *Bradshaw Children* [Plate 57] are well up to Gwillym standards, but in their finery these children strike us as being out of place in a rustic setting. The effect of light is that of the painting room, as it was in the portraits of *Miss Warren and Mrs. Gwillym*. It was not until the *Coltman* group [Plate 91] that Wright learnt how to make people live at ease in the open air.

In his Account Book Wright lists twenty-eight names of sitters in Liverpool [Fig 28], but this could be extended because we know of several portraits not included in it. The

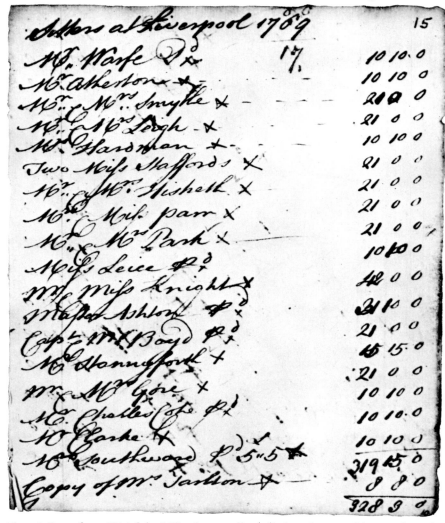

Fig 28 *Page from Wright's MS. Account Book listing sitters at Liverpool, 1769*
National Portrait Gallery, London

Fig 29 Mrs Katherine Thornhill
Mrs Sarah Clayton pastel
$24\frac{1}{8}$ x $17\frac{7}{8}$ in / 61.3 x 45.5 cm
Walker Art Gallery, Liverpool
See Cat 39

Fig 30 *Mrs Sarah Clayton* c 1769
50 x 40 in / 127 x 101.6 cm
Fitchburg Art Museum, Mass. U.S.A.
(gift of Miss Louise I. Doyle)
Cat 39 Pl 63

1 That Wright was interested in this portrait is
also suggested by the fact that its pendant of
Lord Fortescue (now also destroyed; see Ellis K.
Waterhouse, *Reynolds*, London, 1941, plates
34–5) appears to be the prototype for Wright's
Thomas Day [Plate 80].

2 A second portrait of *Mrs. Clayton* by
Katherine Thornhill [Fig 29] shows her as a
younger woman. For further details about this
pastel, see *catalogue raisonné* under 'Clayton'.

3 The use of the word 'spinster' to describe
'Mrs' Clayton will be explained in Part III,
chapter I, p. 99 where we outline Mrs. Clayton's
biography.

splendid likeness of *Mrs. Clayton* [Fig 30] is missing, and none of the five known *Ashton* portraits [Plates 64, 65, 66, 67, 68] is there except the one of the little boy [Plate 68]. The only other surviving Liverpool portraits that are listed are those of *Thomas Staniforth* [Plate 72] and *Mr. and Mrs. Hesketh* [Plates 61, 62]. The last three are of excellent quality. Staniforth turns to lean on the back of a chair—a pose, or rather the absence of pose, to which Wright returned more than once in the late '70's and '80's [Plates 190, 267, 268]. The head and hands are vigorously painted with short strokes of the brush setting down a broken pattern of brick reds and pale yellows. *Hesketh* is a development of the Markeaton Hunt series. He sits in the open air as though taking a rest after a shooting expedition. As so often in Wright's portraits we are made to feel that the sitter has momentarily laid down whatever he was doing at the painter's request and has held his pose in the same spirit as a busy man will drop his work to turn obediently to face the camera's lens. Wright's eye, ever attentive to revealing detail, has not missed the opportunity afforded by the hand-kerchief to develop, as he had done six years before in *Becher Leacroft* [Plate 33] a fascinating still life passage. With delight he pounces on the powder horn tucked into the pocket of the red coat, the metallic surface catching the light; he has been at pains to describe the ingenuity of the spout, persuaded that its proper functioning is as vital as that of the ratchets on an air pump. In the portrait of *Frances Hesketh* the subject is posed before the same distant landscape and stone balustrade (now repaired) as served for the portrait of *Gwillym*, a classical urn replacing the pineapple finial. She has less to do than her husband, so she plays with the end of her scarf like 'Mrs. Mundy' [Plate 44]—an excuse for the ghost of a hand printed on her dress.

Wright's friendship with the Ashtons brought him commissions for portraits of at least five members of the family, four ladies and a little boy. The boy *John Ashton* was destroyed in the second world war but has survived in Pether's mezzotint of 1770 and in a good copy of the early nineteenth century [Plate 68] where he is shown clasping, in the manner of *John Whetham of Kirklington* [Plate 195], his pet dog. The four ladies represent *Mrs. John Ashton* [Plate 64], her two daughters *Elizabeth* [Plate 66] and *Anna* [Plate 65], and her daughter-in-law *Mary* [Plate 67]. The finest of the group is the member of the older generation [Plate 64] who sits stiffly erect in her upholstered armchair, slightly above eye level as though on a dais, to suit her station as the wife of a prosperous slave-trader. We miserable spectators are left cringing at her feet, hardly daring to raise our eyes (invited though we are to do so by her sloping book and the diagonal of her arm resting on the arm of the chair) to that formidable face, for fear of a rebuke. *Anna Ashton* [Plate 65] is given the attributes of a shepherdess, though she is most elegantly attired in a low-cut dress with deep folds that trap the light. For the portrait of *Anna* and for the scarcely less successful portrait of her sister *Elizabeth* [Plate 66], Wright has selected more amiable surroundings than for the mother who in her struggle for a social position held graciousness of no account. All three are superior to the composition Wright settled on for *Mary Ashton* [Plate 67] who finds herself awkwardly seated in a landscape, a throw-back to *Elizabeth Pigot* [Plate 24]. In these Ashton portraits there is a strong hint of Reynolds: *Mary Ashton* can hardly have been painted independently of Reynolds's *Lady Fortescue* of 1756–7,[1] and *Mrs. Ashton* reminds us of *Anne Lennox* of about the same date.

The portraits of *Mrs. Ashton* and *Mrs. Clayton* [Plate 64, Fig 30][2] are among the finest in Wright's entire *œuvre*, for the simple reason that he responded with his deepest feelings to people whose youth had been spent rising in the world and had no time left for the *douceur de vivre*. He was stimulated by the contrast between them and his own smug middle class background which was embarrassingly solid and unshakeable, to give of his best in their presence. Mrs. Clayton sits at a polished table, a plan of her new house spread out before her, not like Mary Shuttleworth a dutiful wife, but a spinster[3] who has carved out a man's life for herself. A fold of dark drapery conceals what one takes to be artificial light; but whatever its source, the light is strong enough to throw parts of the figure into deep shadow while at the same time picking out the bows and pleats of her dress. We are again reminded of Copley whose native Boston provided him with sitters of the same up-and-coming middle class, who demanded a similar realistic treatment precisely at the moment Wright was at work in Liverpool.

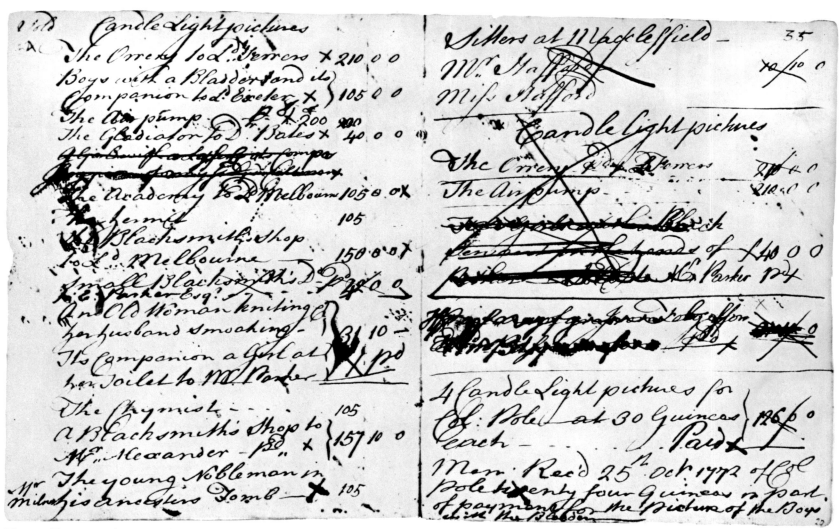

Fig 31 *Two pages from Wright's MS. Account Book, listing Candlelight Pictures*
National Portrait Gallery, London

Among Wright's list of candlelight pictures in his Account Book [Fig 31] is a heavily deleted entry: 'Two girls w[th] [?] their Black Servant...' Stylistically his *Conversation of Girls* at Charlbury [Plate 73] is datable in his Liverpool period, and was exhibited at the Society of Artists, along with a portrait of another child who was probably *John Ashton*, in 1770 during his residence in Liverpool. The presence of a young negress would not in itself be sufficient to establish its Liverpool origin, although most of Wright's clients there were trading with Africa and would have been better placed than anyone in Derbyshire to acquire a black servant; but the presence of the sea with a ship that can just be made out on the horizon, no doubt referring to the family's commercial interests, seems to clinch the matter. This completes the list of known Liverpool portraits. But there are others painted in Derbyshire and Lichfield at the same period which are no less realistic in approach: notably *Sarah Carver and her Daughter Sarah* [Plate 79] and *Erasmus Darwin* [Plate 78], where the brick reds and yellows of the Liverpool portraits have been carried over onto their faces and hands. Sarah Carver has grown more substantial than her Rococo relations of ten years before: Wright had invested too heavily in the new currency of realism to be able to abandon it where abandonment would have been diplomatic. The same goes for Darwin, though in his case realism was more appropriate. He is shown hunched forward to fill the canvas, his arms folded on the polished table. A more striking contrast between him and the portrait of *Thomas Day* [Plate 80], also painted in Lichfield in 1770, would be hard to imagine; but as we shall see in a later chapter, the differences in character and outlook of the two men account for differences in approach. Day is portrayed in a romantic attitude, with his arm resting lightly on the plinth of a column, before a dark and threatening sky, a 'toga' draped over his body. In this magnificent portrait, Wright's touch is as precise as ever, but Day's features come to life more through a subtle play of tone and colour than through modelling from darks to lights. This is the first indication we have of his willingness to modify realism in the direction of Romney's full-lengths which express the neoclassical taste of the late '60's.

Half-way between *Staniforth* and *Day*, is the melancholy young artist in a private collection [Plate 82]. We know he is an artist because he clasps a draughtsman's tool in his left hand; apparently his right arm rests on a grassy bank but the details are lost beneath the grime of two hundred years. We can guess from the nervous tension of cuffs and shirt ruffle (treated like a cabbage still life), and by the sympathy expended on the face, that he was a personal friend (in Derby? In Lichfield? In Liverpool? But Wright was moving about the whole time in 1769–70, so it could have been in any of these places). How we long for him to be Mortimer! But one of the few things we do know about Mortimer is his different, comical little marmoset face. It would be surprising if this young artist did not turn out to be someone who figures in these pages. This period (1769–71) marks the peak in Wright's career as portrait painter, and he never achieved anything comparable until the early '80's, with '*Christopher Heath*' and the *Coke* group [Plates 209, 225]. One portrait after another takes one's breath away. '*Mrs. Swindell*' [Plate 81] has the advantage over the young artist in being reasonably legible; preserving all the subtleties of tone that Wright has worked into her. Her greyish mauve dress (a favourite colour for these years) is set off by reddish lights in the folds, and the flesh tones are saturated with light.

A succession of military gentlemen sat for Wright in the early '70's.[1] The portrait of *Captain Bathurst* [Plate 83] has nothing specifically Wright-like about it except—inevitably—the light on the sword hilt; but that of his wife [Plate 84] has an originality that surpasses its pendant. There is nothing exceptional about the Cotes-like head; but the way she is shown just above eye level, her right arm bent to cradle the shepherdess' staff, its shadow defining the curve of her arm—nobody but Wright would have done this. Her straw hat seen in steep perspective proved irresistible, and we find ourselves transported back to the details of still life in the subject pieces of the late '60's. More sympathetic than *Bathurst* (for the very reason that he was a personal friend) is *Captain French* [Plate 85]. Again the sword hilt is a source of excitement, but the curve of the left hand holding the letter, and the shadow cast by the half-closed lapel of the uniform, add interest that *Bathurst* lacks. Similar portraits of *Sir George Cooke* [Plate 86] and an unidentified officer who used to be known as '*Admiral, Earl Howe*' [Plate 90] are in American public collections masquerading as Copleys. Wright has characteristically concentrated on the metallic gold braid on the lapels of Cooke's uniform and hat, and has imaginatively shown his sitter emerging from shadow into strong light. In the large portrait of '*Howe*' the sitter stands before a background of rocks, the light filtering through the upper part of the canvas. We are invited to contemplate the gloved hand, the other loose glove and the walking stick as shapes of interest for their own sake. The series of military portraits closes in 1772 with two small full-lengths of officers, *Colonel Heathcote* [Plate 115] and *Captain Milnes* [Plate 114]. The first [Plate 115] is only known from an old photograph but its composition is clearly as striking as that of the second. They are both closely related to the *Coltman* group [Plate 91], even to the extent, in *Captain Milnes*, of a repetition of the Stubbs-like motif of groom and horse in the background. The portraits of the *Coltmans*, of *Heathcote* and *Milnes*, in which sitters appear full-length under life-size, are among his most successful, and one wonders why he did not develop the series of these appealing 'conversations' which bring Devis alive and up-to-date. But whatever his reason, the type was abandoned, and on his return from abroad he reverted to life-size portraits.

The Coltman group of *c.* 1771–2[2] is another undoubted masterpiece, comparable to the *Shuttleworths, Mrs. Pole and her Child, Mrs. Clayton* and the *Cokes*. Though the triangular design of the figures and the diagonal of the tree are a development from the *Bradshaw Children*, here for the first time landscape comes into its own—the picture is in fact contemporary with Wright's first pure landscape [Plate 112]. For now people and animals actually inhabit their countryside instead of having to put up with token trees and houses dropped like stage scenery behind them. The Coltmans are about to set out on a ride. The charming young lady in her rich red riding habit is ready mounted, and her husband,

1 Much later, in the '80's, Wright painted at least two more military portraits; one of his nephew Richard [Plate 273], the other of a *Captain Salmon* which survives only in a copy [Plate 272].

2 It is just conceivable that this was the 'small Conversation' exhibited at the Society of Artists, 1771 (203). One would have expected a picture of this importance to have been shown [Fig. 33].

Fig 32 Detail from *Mr and Mrs Thomas Coltman* Cat 41 See Pl 91

Fig 33 George Stubbs Detail of John Milbanke from *The Melbourne and Milbanke Group* Private Collection, U.K.

dressed in a blue waistcoat and yellow breeches, waits beside her while his horse is brought up by a groom. He is not an intellectual but a rich landowner, at home with horses and dogs, happier in the open air than at his desk. He was a close friend of the artist and this is why Wright has exerted himself to do him full justice. It was clear to him that if he had to introduce horses (and there was probably no way out of it), one artist alone was in a position to help him, one who also reached the appearance of things through an analysis of their internal structure, one who also subjected realism to a certain classical poise and grandeur without losing sight of reality in the process: the animal specialist Stubbs. The young man in Stubbs's work who corresponds most closely to Coltman is John Milbanke [Fig 33] in the *Melbourne and Milbanke Family Group* of 1768–70. He was the brother of that remarkable Lady Melbourne (seated in a carriage in Stubbs's picture) who was probably instrumental in persuading her weak-minded husband to acquire Wright's *Academy by Lamplight* and *Blacksmith's Shop* [Plates 60, 100] during the very years in which the two portrait groups were painted[1].

Coltman was one of Wright's two most enthusiastic local patrons just before the Italian journey. The other was Colonel Edward Sacheverell Pole, who in about the winter of 1770–1 gave Wright the commission to paint four genre scenes [Plates 92, 93, 94, 95], as well as portraits of his wife and of himself [Plates 88, 87], for a room on the first floor of his house, Radburne Hall, Kirk Langley, not far from Derby. Wright was evidently not able to make much of the features of Colonel Pole [Plate 87] who according to Anna Seward was a disagreeable character (and more than with most painters, success or failure with Wright depended on how much sympathy he could muster for a sitter). With his wife and small son [Plate 88] it was a different matter. This astonishing full-length[2] holds its own among portraits by the most famous masters in the capital, surpassing the *Shuttleworth* group, and indeed all his earlier portraits, for sheer virtuosity. We have mentioned that *Thomas Day* owed something to Romney's influence. This artist again comes to mind with *Mrs. Pole*, but the white and violet draperies clinging to her figure, and the combination of the grand manner with the projection of a sitter in sharp relief, lie outside Romney's range. Somehow Wright manages to bring grandeur and simplicity together—the rich red drapery and the domestic preoccupations of Mrs. Pole—without making the one too pedantic, or the other too homely.

1 For the Melbournes as patrons of Wright, see below p. 106.

2 A gouache sketch on paper exists for this composition, in the Derby Art Gallery [Plate 89].

It should have become apparent, from the order of the illustrations if not from this text, that there is a marked change in style between 1768 and 1773. The late '60's saw Wright's moment of greatest vigour, where the opposite quality that contributed so richly to his success as a portrait painter, gracefulness, lay in abeyance. He was then the eager young bachelor in Liverpool, encouraged by the heady atmosphere of big business to transfer his sitters to canvas without any frills at all. Then in the early '70's the portraits recapture the charm of the *Shuttleworth* group. We shall see the same process at work in the candlelights: how they alter from the ferocious Coltman pendants [Plates 76, 77] of the late '60's to the almost Rococo grace of the Chandos-Pole quartet of two to three years later [Plates 92, 93, 94, 95]. By the early '70's, realism is modified, in the *Coltman* group, and in the full-lengths of *Mrs. Pole* and *Day*, and even some of the military gentlemen take on a certain amiability. A more demure approach to the human figure begins to creep in, which shall culminate, on his return from Italy, in outright Neo-Classicism. This change can also be observed in the self-portraits, though the dates of none of them before the Italian period are known for certain. The magnificent Rembrandtesque, almost Poussinesque, image of Wright in the Coltman Collection (Frontispiece) is painted on the reverse of a study for the *Air Pump*, suggesting a date in the later '60's. The vigorous style confirms it. Other charcoal self-portraits [Plates 69, 70, 71] look as though they were done about the same time,[1] though the one in the Ricau Collection [Plate 71] may show a slightly younger face. Quite different in conception is the fifth self-portrait belonging to a branch of the Wright family in Australia [Plate 120]. Whereas the first four are by the author of *Staniforth* and the *Air Pump*, the last is by the author of *Captain Bathurst* and '*Mrs. Swindell*'. A youth in the museum at Louisville, Kentucky [Plate 121] and two charcoals of the *Coltmans* [Plates 118, 119] in the Coltman family collection must be among the last he painted before leaving for abroad, and so close in style are they to his portraiture immediately on his return that we are deferring a discussion of them until he gets to Bath.

1 The charcoal self-portrait in the Mellon Collection [Plate 69] bears a date 1768 on the reverse. Whether this inscription is authentic or not, the portrait does seem to have been done about the same time as the other charcoal self-portraits, which for other reasons can be dated about then.

Fig 34 *Three Persons viewing the Gladiator by Candlelight* c 1764–65
40 x 48 in / 101.6 x 121.9 cm   Private Collection, U.K.   Cat 188   Pl 52

2 EARLY SUBJECT PIECES AND GENRE

It would not be correct to argue that Wright waited until he was entirely in command of his medium before encroaching on the dangerous territory of subject pieces and genre. The picture of a young woman reading a letter by candlelight, with a young man standing behind her gazing in our direction [Plate 45] is similar in style to the portraits of the early '60's, and (considering that it is in a collection in Brigg that was formed in the eighteenth century, and has been in Lincolnshire for at least one hundred years, long before Wrights began moving about), might even have been a direct outcome of his tour of Lincolnshire in 1760. Its style will become clearer when we consider it in relation to other letter-reading and letter-writing themes; that it is more clumsy than any of his other genre pieces is obvious. But it is of a modest nature. And we can be sure that nothing would have induced this prudent man to try out anything more ambitious along these lines before he had satisfied himself in the field of group portraiture, as he did in the *Chase* and *Shuttleworth* groups [Plates 50, 51]. It was the confidence these works must have inspired him with that encouraged him to go ahead with compositions outside portraiture of far greater complexity than the picture in Brigg. The astonishing years 1764–5 saw the production of two completely mature subject pieces, the *Gladiator* and the *Orrery* [Fig 34, Plate 54] and nothing he accomplished from then onwards was more masterly.

The *Gladiator* [Fig 34] shows three men seated around a table in a dark room of which nothing is visible except the door set at an angle to the picture plane, and a hanging lamp. They are viewing by candlelight a statuette of the Borghese *Gladiator* now in the Louvre, which had been famous in England since the early seventeenth century.[1] The statue is seen from one side, lunging forward, establishing with the thrust of the arm a strong diagonal into the void. An older man in spectacles on the left has the air of a connoisseur. One at least of the younger men is an artist, since he holds up his own drawing of the statuette and matches it against the object on the table, just as Daniel Parker Coke [Plate 225] matches a piece of paper against the landscape. The candle flame is masked by his shoulder, with the result that the light is not diffused but concentrated on these eager faces, and with its help we are made all the more acutely aware of undivided attention on the statuette. Later these friends may relax and enjoy one another's company over a bottle of wine, but for the time being they are not concerned about pleasure or human relations but about an idea. The nobility of the antique statue fills their minds, and justifies their earnestness. Its grace has lifted them above pettifogging everyday life, and from its contours their own features have borrowed refinement. There is nothing in the art of the time to compare with it. Wright had no predecessors in his own country who would have thought of doing such a thing. It is only in the art of the Low Countries of 130 years earlier that anything of the kind is to be found, but the discovery of a possible source in the Utrecht school does not detract

1 A bronze was made of it by Le Sueur for St. James's. This was at Hampton Court in Wright's time (see M. Whinney and O. Millar, *English Art 1625-1714*, Oxford, 1957, p. 120, note 4), but many reduced versions were in private collections.

Fig 35 C. H. Volmarijn *Christ at Emmaus*
Panel 35½ x 48 in / 90.1 x 121.9 cm
Ferens Art Gallery, Kingston-upon-Hull

from Wright's essential originality. Honthorst lies behind the *Gladiator*, but no known Honthorst evokes its spirit. We are forced to descend to a lower level, to the pale reflection of lost Honthorsts in the work of his Rotterdam imitator Crijn Hendricksz. Volmarijn before finding an apt parallel, and to try and imagine what a more elevated rendering of Volmarijn's theme would have looked like. In his *Christ at Emmaus* [Fig 35] the arm of the figure on the left masks the candle, and like that of the connoisseur in the *Gladiator*, his hand rests on the edge of the table; light throws weird shadows upwards, helping to bring out the spirituality of the faces; though in this case it is the miraculous Breaking of the Bread that is the object of the spectators' wrapt attention, not the miracle wrought by a Roman sculptor.

The distance between this and the *Philosopher giving a lecture on the Orrery* [Fig 36] meant a short step for its by now intrepid inventor to take. For in Wright's mind and in that of his Midlands contemporaries, modern science was no less of a miracle than the antique; the lecturer's equipment held the same beauty and purity of line and exacted the same devout contemplation. Taking the place of the statuette is an object known as an eidouranion or transparent orrery on the workings of which all attention converges. Far from taking liberties with its appearance, Wright has insisted on its remorseless logic, tracing with delight its elliptical metal bands as they encircle the air, catching the light as they twist around a corner just as an aeroplane will glint as it dips in the clear sky. Yet for him this logic is not a prosaic fact but magic, and it is magic and not common sense that he communicates by the light falling on surfaces, on those little moons and planets and on the

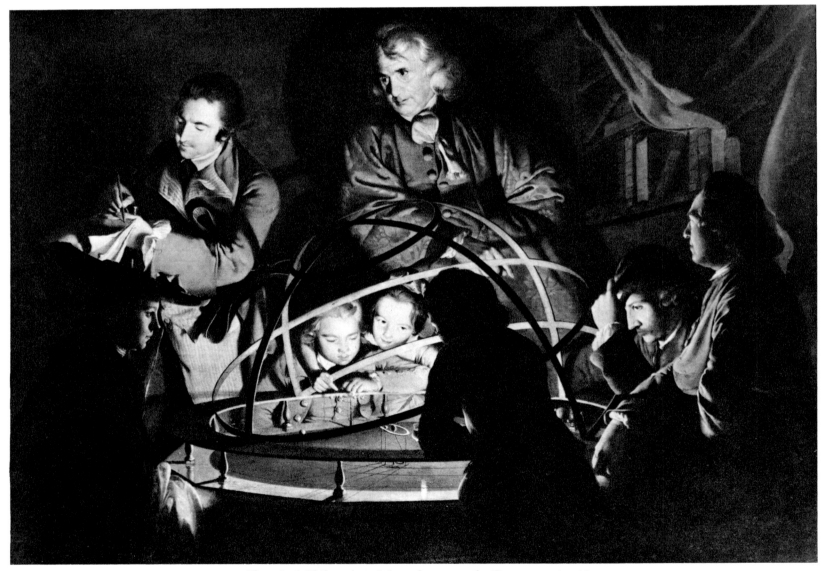

Fig 36 *A Philosopher giving a lecture on the Orrery* c 1764–66
58 x 60 in / 147.3 x 203.2 cm   Derby Museum and Art Gallery   Cat 190   Pl 54

delicate stands that hold them in place, on the buttons of a boy's coat or a young woman's necklace—each object facing the light in a circle around it like singers around a campfire, so that if we did not know where the source of light came from, we could plot its situation by the effect it had on its surroundings. It is in fact a lamp representing the sun in the centre of the solar system, hidden behind the boy in the foreground who in consequence is lost in shadow except for the pencils of light on his forehead, eye socket and coat. The demonstrator dominates his audience in the centre with his massive red sleeves and green gown, setting up a triangular design which was to remain Wright's favourite throughout life. The shadow of his back is thrown on to the wall behind him, and to his left are shelves holding his learned books on science. A young man stands to his right taking notes, another gazes at his equipment, and a third, corresponding to the artist in the *Gladiator*, follows his discourse. Two other children, their enraptured faces in full lamplight [Fig 37], crouch between the bands, and the shadow from one of the bands crawls across the little girl's cheek and chin, describing for our delectation their contours. Lugubrious shadows from bands meander over clothes and faces, fixing the space each shape occupies, as well as helping the controlled drama of the discourse along. A young woman sits brooding on the left. Her clean profile and poised hat nipped on the brim by light have the abstract quality of a Piero; the hat acting as a dish on which a still life of notebook, pencil, two hands, a cuff and the handle of a walking stick reposes [Fig 38]. Every slow movement is explained by the fall of light. Something of the abstract character of the instrument's ribs and planets has taken possession of the audience. The notetaker's hat tucked under his sleeve is as

Fig 37 Detail from *A Philosopher giving a lecture on the Orrery* See Fig 36

Fig 38 Detail from *A Philosopher giving a lecture on the Orrery* See Fig 36.

1 Compare Wright's painting of a Roman or Roman-inspired bust in lost profile [Fig 39].

heraldic as a medieval shield; the lost profile on the right has the impassivity and permanence of marble [Fig 40].[1] Yet real life is not lost in the gravity of the demonstration. The audience at the lecture is made up of individuals, each of whom is intended to be recognisable, and among them are Wright's friends and colleagues.

In the case of the *Gladiator*, the originality of the conception made it difficult to pin any ancestor on to it, and if we succeeded in finding a dim collateral, this did not endanger the explosive newness of Wright's picture. We shall be casting no aspersions on the uniqueness of the *Orrery*, either, in suggesting that Wright has turned for help once again to Thomas Frye's engravings. He appears to have made use of Frye's lady in profile [Fig 41] for his young lady seated on the left [Fig 38]; and it is tempting to argue that another figure [Fig 42] lies behind the slumped pose of the young man second from the right. Both of these

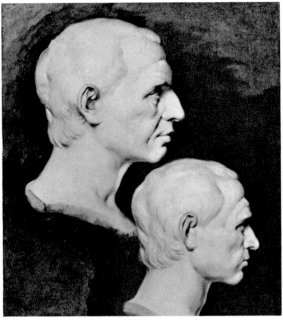

Fig 39 *Study after an antique bust, in two positions* c 1774–75
Oil on paper on canvas 20 x 16½ in / 50.8 x 41.9 cm   Charles Buckley
Cat 180   Pl 124

Fig 40 *Self-portrait*(?) Detail from *A Philosopher giving a lecture on the Orrery* See Fig 36

Fig 41 Thomas Frye *Portrait of a Lady* 1760–61   Mezzotint

Fig. 42 Thomas Frye *Portrait of a Young Man* 1760–61   Mezzotint

comparisons might have been dismissed as coincidences, were it not that into the next great subject piece of 1767–8, the *Air Pump* [Fig 43], Wright introduces a young boy with his head tilted back away from the picture plane [Fig 45] who is clearly inspired by Frye's figure of a man with his fingers to his lips [Fig 46]. This is a quotation unusually literal in an artist who preferred to conceal his sources, encouraging us to go on from there to identify as the origin of the demonstrator in the *Air Pump* [Fig 47] Frye's terror-struck youth clasping a candlestick [Fig 48].[1] He has stepped straight out of the pages of the *Castle of Otranto*; having evidently been interrupted by some creaking in the night, he probes with his flickering candle for the origin of the disturbance. If hair stood on end, his would. This is the figure in Frye's work best calculated to appeal to Wright, and we can understand that when given the chance to introduce into one of his own paintings a scien-

1 It is true that Fuseli (whom Frye's figure foreshadows) had already been in England before the *Air Pump* was painted—for about twenty months in 1764–5 and again from about October 1766 onwards—but there is no trace of any comparable figure in Fuseli's work of this period. The closest parallel to Frye is a pencil and chalk drawing, illus. F. Antal, *Fuseli Studies*, 1956, plate 17, but this is generally dated c 1780–2.

Fig 43 *An Experiment on a Bird in the Air Pump* c 1767–68
72 x 96 in / 182.9 x 243.8 cm   Tate Gallery, London   Cat 192   Pl 58

Fig 44 Detail of *An Academy by Lamplight* See Fig 50

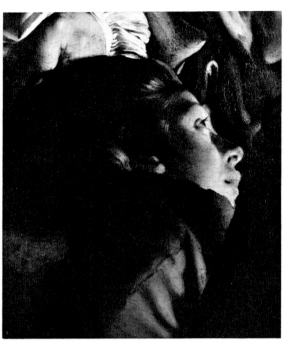

Fig 45 Detail from *An Experiment on a Bird in the Air Pump* See Fig 43

Fig 46 Thomas Frye *Portrait of a Young Man* 1760–1 Mezzotint

Fig 47 Detail from *An Experiment on a Bird in the Air Pump* See Fig 43

Fig 48 Thomas Frye *Figure with Candle* 1760 Mezzotint

tist at a moment of crisis betraying his fear by the flicker of light over his face, he would snatch at it. The *Air Pump* demonstrator has indeed reason to feel apprehensive—but before we go any further we must explain what is happening.

An experiment is conducted whereby air is pumped out of a glass bowl known as a receiver at the top of the picture, so that the bird inside is seen to be on the point of death. The demonstrator is about to reintroduce the air through a gadget to the right of the top of the receiver so that the bird may live, but the risk he takes in delaying the reintroduction of air until the last moment is stamped on his Frye-like features. This at any rate seems to be Wright's intention, if we may judge by the reassuring embrace bestowed on the young lady by the man standing on the right [Fig 49], and by the perkiness of the victim of the

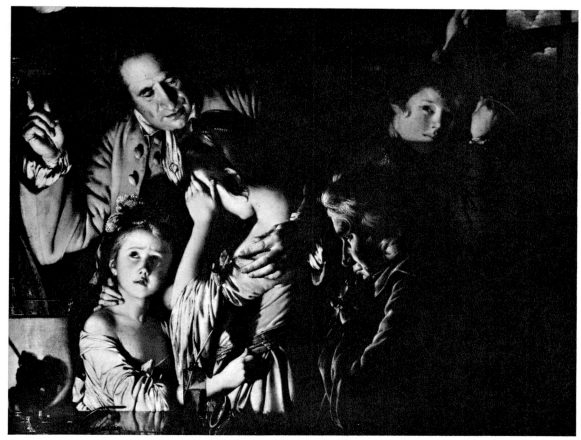

Fig 49 Detail from *An Experiment on a Bird in the Air Pump* See Fig 43

experiment. In a study for the *Air Pump* [Plate 59] on the reverse of a self-portrait, the demonstrator is more confident that the bird will live, and himself reassures the spectators—a far less dramatic idea than the one finally adopted.[1] If the bird is to recover, then the boy by the window is lowering the Gothic cage on a red cord so that the bird can re-enter it after its ordeal, not sadly slinging it up as though to tell us it will no longer be required;[2] and the young man with the watch in the left foreground is timing, not only the convulsions and the collapse, but also the revival. Wright in his title for the picture avoids the use of the word 'lecture', and indeed no lecture takes place, though one man explains what is going on to a young woman and her Reni-like sister [Fig 49], while other objects on the table not connected with this specific experiment but with the science of pneumatics in general lend the picture its didactic mood. The demonstration takes place by candlelight but we see nothing of the candle but its distortion in the fluid. Wright makes use of distortion to heighten the dramatic effect. Not only are faces bent out of shape by light, but the receiver gives an anxious twist to the demonstrator's arm, leaving us worried about his deftness and sense of timing. The picture is too dirty to yield much more information but if it were cleaned it would emerge as one of the triumphs of the eighteenth century. But then Wright is a 'minor provincial' who will have to wait his turn at the entrance to the restorer's studio at the Tate, before this verdict can be reversed.[3]

The *Academy by Lamplight* of about 1768–9 [Fig 50] shows a group of boys sketching a statue of the *Nymph with a Shell* [Fig 51] in the Louvre, formerly in Villa Borghese, an extensively restored antique that enjoyed wide popularity in Wright's time. Terracotta and marble versions of it were made in the late eighteenth century and it is possible that this was a marble copy and not a cast. In the background a copy of the *Gladiator* reappears, this time full scale. The location is a drawing academy for young students but all attempts to identify it have proved fruitless.[4] The statues are dotted about a vaulted gallery with slender, Ionic columns inspired by the Italian early Renaissance. The light issues from a hanging lamp concealed by a looped curtain, throwing the features of the boys and the statue they study into high relief. The boy with his back to us in the foreground is posed like the near-contemporary Liverpool portrait of *Fleetwood Hesketh* [Plate 61] and the one

1 The left hand side of this study is seriously damaged, the figure in the foreground being nothing but a comical ghost, but the demonstrator is reasonably well preserved, and his reassuring gesture can be trusted.

2 Todd, 1946, p. 11, however, assumes that the bird will die.

3 We reproduce [Fig 31] a page from Wright's Account Book in which the *Orrery*, the *Air Pump* and other candlelights are listed.

4 There is no justification for identifying it with the gallery of the Duke of Richmond in his house in Whitehall to which students had access from 1758 onwards and which was put under the control of the Incorporated Society of Artists about two years after the picture was painted (see Whitley, 1928, I, pp. 237–8). It may be presumed that Wright made use of this gallery's facilities since it became a favourite resort for those members of the Incorporated Society who held aloof from the Royal Academy, and since Wright's friend Mortimer was assiduous in his attendance there. But academies of this kind were not so rare in the late '60's as to enable us to identify the *Academy by lamplight* with any particular one.

Fig 50 *An Academy by Lamplight* c 1768–69
50 x 39⅞ in / 127 x 101.2 cm
Mr and Mrs Paul Mellon (on loan to the Tate
Gallery, London)   Cat 189   Pl 60

Fig 51 Detail from *An Academy by Lamplight*
See Fig 50

1 See. N. Pevsner, *Academies of Art Past and Present*, Cambridge, 1940, Figs 5 and 6.

on the left resting his arm on a plinth [Figs 44, 52] throws his head back like the boy in the *Air Pump* based on Frye's engraving. Once more Wright has hit on an original design, but the theme has a long and distinguished history, beginning with the engravings of Baccio Bandinelli's *Academy* in the Belvedere Court of the Vatican (1531) and in Florence (c. 1550) showing men and boys drawing by artificial light.[1] Wright would have been familiar with these early engravings but since his natural inclination was to look eastwards rather than southwards, his source is more likely to lie in Dutch or Flemish seventeenth-century studios where the subject was also popular; especially in view of the fact that he responded to that brand of intimacy and domesticity combined with gravity which was the Netherlanders' contribution. A precise source may never be found, but it is sensible to search for it among those Northerners who had had some experience of

Fig 52 Detail from *An Academy by Lamplight*
See Fig 50

Fig 53 Detail from *An Academy by Lamplight*
See Fig 50

the South: for as we shall often see it was the impact of the South on the North that most impressed him in others. We are reminded of the Wallerant Vaillant in the National Gallery, of a boy half turned away from us seated reading on a low chair in the presence of statuary, or of the boy formerly in the Cook Collection with his back to us, engaged in making a sketch of a picture of a bridge hung on the panelling in front of him, surrounded by studio props. The latter is generally but wrongly ascribed to Michael Sweerts, an artist after Wright's own heart—humble, humourless, moralistic, and drenched in the South; and the name of Sweerts at once conjures up the memory of that group in Haarlem of boys sketching from the male model [Fig 54]—not of course Wright's source, but there are analogies between it and the *Academy by Lamplight* that cannot be ignored.[1]

Wright transports this Netherlandish world of intimacy into his own day and place, and makes it his own. It is the world of bourgeois *sensibilité* to which Rotari, Jens Juel and Greuze also subscribed, and on a graver level, Chardin in his kitchen scenes where women and children are delicately converted into still life; revealing an attitude of mind that delighted in picking on the contrast between solemn adult activity and a child's incomprehension of it; that caused young children to gaze through the bands of an orrery and a girl to show anxiety as she watches the convulsions of a bird, and a little boy to stray by mistake into a drawing academy where he is too young to profit from instruction but, bored and distracted, to throw his arms around a friend's or elder brother's shoulders and to turn appealingly in our direction [Fig 53]. There are many such intimate details lurking in the recesses of the large subject pieces. And it is natural that Wright should wish to detach them from the solemn proceedings in which young children cannot be expected to play a worthy part, by letting them loose in genre scenes of their own. There exist several such scenes from the late '60's onwards on well-established themes like bubble and bladder-blowing that can be traced back to Netherlandish sources,[2] or could be if we were better informed about what was available at the time on the London market and in collections in the Midlands. But even if we can rarely lay our hands on precise models, there are many examples that can be cited that will not lead us too far astray.

The Utrecht school has left us a few such pictures and when we come to discuss Wright's genre scenes, it will be to Honthorst and Terbrugghen to whom we shall most often refer. We might have expected a candlelight painter of a later generation, Godfried Schalcken, also to have attracted his notice. A number of Schalcken's night pieces remained in England as a result of his visit to this country in 1692 and were accessible. For all we know Wright's late *Girl blowing on a charcoal Stick* formerly in the collection of Daniel Daulby but now lost, owed something to Schalcken's famous painting at Althorp showing a boy performing this act (though here again, it must be admitted that the theme was popular in Utrecht studios), and attempts have been made to identify copies of Lord Spencer's picture as Wright's original. But though Schalcken also specialised in half-lengths by candlelight, his style and handling of paint are quite different. There is only one demonstrable link between the two artists and this is confined to method. At about the time Wright was embarking on his night pieces, a description was published of the method Schalcken was supposed to have employed (whether he did so or not is irrelevant). This account explains how he sealed off a part of his studio from daylight, where he posed his models, and lit them by a lamp '*afin de s'assurer d'un point de lumière invariable*'. The account goes on:

'Par une ouverture faite en dehors de ce lieu, il examinoit l'effet que faisoit sur son modèle, cette lumière artificielle; ensuite il alloit mettre sur son tableau le même ton de couleur et les mêmes gradations, qu'il examinoit ensuite et étudioit à son aise: rien n'étoit abandonné à l'estimation arbitraire, la nature en décidoit'.[3]

Wright's own procedure for setting the scene for his night pieces (according to a generally reliable authority, his own niece) is so similar, though more complicated, that it is rash to write it off as sheer chance:

'The painting rooms at St Helen's House were not so convenient as those at his brother's, Dr. Wright's, in the Iron Gate, where one room opened into the other, so that by darkening the one

Fig 54 Michael Sweerts *Drawing Academy* $30\frac{1}{8}$ x $43\frac{1}{8}$ in / 76.5 x 109.5 cm Frans Halsmuseum, Haarlem

1 M. Waddingham (*Paragone*, 107, November 1958, p. 72 where the National Gallery Vaillant is illustrated, plate 28), has proposed Vaillant as the author of the 'Sweerts' formerly in the Cook Collection (See *Michael Sweerts en Tijdgenoten*, exhibition catalogue, Rotterdam, 1958, No. 39, illus). The Cook picture was sold at Christie's, 25th November 1966 (65).

2 A child with a bladder is represented in a *Meat Shop* by Willem van Mieris, signed and dated 1733 (on the London art market, 1966; see *Burlington Magazine* Supplement, December, 1966, plate XXI). This brings us close in time to the Wright.

3 M... [Dézallier d'Argenville], *Abrégé de la Vie des plus fameux Peintres...*, II, Paris, 1762, pp. 216–17. This was an enlarged edition of a book that had appeared in the '40's.

room he could introduce the proper light and subject he intended to paint, and view them to advantage from the other room. His mechanical genius, however, enabled him to construct an apparatus for painting candlelight pieces and effects of fire-light. It consisted of a framework of wood resembling a large folding screen, which reached to the top of the room, the two ends being placed against the wall, which formed two sides of the enclosure. Each fold was divided into compartments, forming a framework covered with black paper, and opening with hinges, so that when the object he was painting from was placed within the proper light, the artist could view it from various points from without'.[1]

The spirit of Honthorst, Terbrugghen and Schalcken was kept alive in England in the early eighteenth century by such artists as Mercier, who like Wright turned their backs on the low life elements and coarse humour of the Dutch but differed from Wright in converting the scenes into appealing but insipid Rococo. Wright had no use for them (except once at Radburne), but at least they ensured that the tradition was not lost, and its perpetuation accounts for the emergence, in the early work of Reynolds and Romney, of similar experiments. We hear of a painting in the collection of the younger Paine, who accompanied Wright on part of his journey to Italy, by 'Sir Joshua Reynolds. A Candlelight study made at the Academy in St. Martin's Lane', c. 1755;[2] and a decade later when Wright was beginning to paint candlelights, Romney also tried his hand at them, producing at least one work that provoked the comment:

'... with respect to the candlelight subjects, I can bear indirect testimony to their excellence; because there is in the family [of the artist] a portrait of his brother James, then a boy of sixteen, which was painted at this very time, and probably experimentally; he is holding a candle in one hand, and intercepting its lustre by the other, as if to screen it from the action of the air. The form of the hand is distinctly seen by the transmission of lights through its thinnest parts; but the chief effect is produced by the illumination of the face. Neither Schalcken nor Wright, could have surpassed this head; it is done in so clever a manner as to leave no doubt of his ability in this department of painting.'[3]

However, the only contemporary candlelight painter[4] who we can be sure influenced Wright's genre scenes was Thomas Frye; he alone, so far as we know, shared Wright's essentially serious and contemplative attitude to the human figure. In the examples that we shall cite, Frye will join the Utrecht School as the chief progenitor of the mode Wright made famous.

The picture of two girls dressing up a kitten [Plate 75] goes straight back to Honthorst; that is to say, the reddish-mauve sleeve of the girl on the left masking the candle, the dull dark red colouring of the faces, the saucy curl to the lips, the slanting shadow on the nose of the other girl, her eyes and eyelids, can all be paralleled in Honthorst's work even if the subject cannot. The cat theme appears in Netherlandish studios and again nearer Wright's time in Mercier[5] but Wright injects new life into it by pushing it further in the direction of Victorian sentimental genre than was then historically 'legitimate'. But we have to remember that the nineteenth century has a habit of cropping up in the eighteenth in the work of an artist so far outside the central artistic tradition that he is apt to make discoveries before they are due. The picture is an enchantment on account of a discarded doll, more human than *Caroline Curzon* [Plate 5], dressed in the height of fashion of the late '60's. Like the discarded hat in the portrait of *R. S. Bateman* [Plate 336] we are willing to excuse any amount of mawkishness when he offers us a throw-away line of beauty like this.

Three candlelights exist on the theme of letter-reading or letter-writing [Plates 45, 77, 92]. They all show a young woman seated at a table with her left hand to her cheek, reading a letter while a man behind her gazes over her shoulder. In each case the candle is concealed, twice by the letter itself which she holds up in front of her so that the light falls full on her face, once by a curtain beside her. In the case of the picture in the Nelthorpe collection [Plate 45] a young man looms out of the darkness to frown at us suspiciously as he pushes a curtain to one side and discovers us. In the Rogers-Coltman picture [Plate 77] he is replaced by an elderly man who reads the letter over her shoulder, with her acquiescence. In the Chandos-Pole candlelight [Plate 95] a youth raises a finger as though to warn us not to interrupt.[6] We shall not find the quest for meanings very rewarding: for

1 An account given in the niece's memoir, quoted Bemrose, 1885, pp. 51–2.

2 Whitley, 1928, I, p. 150.

3 Romney, 1830, p. 30.

4 The Danish painter Jens Juel deserves a glance here, although there is no indication that the two artists were aware of each other's preoccupations. Jens Juel painted a splendid self-portrait in about 1764 where the artificial light source is concealed behind his sketching block (Statens Museum for Kunst, Copenhagen; see Ellen Poulsen, *Jens Juel*, Copenhagen, 1961, plate 1). He also achieved a startling realism in the '80's, comparable to Wrights' *Brooke Boothby*.

5 See, for example, the Mercier in the National Gallery of Scotland, illus. R. Raines, 'Philip Mercier's Later Fancy Pictures,' *Apollo*, July, 1964, plate 8.

6 There is also a drawing on this theme in Wright's Account Book [Fig 55], closest to the Rogers-Coltman candlelight. It cannot be dated from Wright's notes superimposed on it, since they deal with cures for consumption that might have been jotted down at any time.

there is a deliberate reticence about these scenes which Wright intends us to respect. However, he lets a few dubious hints fall. In the Nelthorpe picture a book lies open at the title page with the words: 'The Guide or Art [of] Writing [a] Letter', and the letter she reads is addressed to 'Mrs. Eliza Jeltem'; evidently herself since she has broken open the seals. On the table lies a second letter she herself has started, with the words 'Dere Jack'. It sounds as though her intentions were no more romantic than to improve her literary style and spelling. The Rogers–Coltman picture offers no clues of this nature, but the one at Radburne [Plate 92] is more communicative. Here the lady reads over a letter, not addressed to her but written by her, beginning 'Dear Roger, The many hours and days that have elapsed since I was blest with thy composition…' This holds out the promise of love. But the absence in all three of any specific meaning indicates that we are not supposed to seek far for one, but must rest content with being charmed, as indeed we are, by the thought of a distant, male, correspondent reddening a girl's cheeks. The most vivacious of the three is the one in the Rogers–Coltman collection, datable in the late '60's; the Radburne candlelight is dated 1772. These dates prove that the genre scene in Brigg was done before 1765 [Fig 56]; it is also clearly at least two years earlier than the *Gladiator*. The light strays over the young man's face as it does over the face of Frye's near-contemporary *Young Man reading a book by candlelight* [Fig 57], and this is perhaps the source of its inspiration. If it is, then it cannot have been done on the Lincolnshire tour in the early months of 1760, because Frye's candlelight is dated that year. In the more mature Rogers–Coltman picture it is possible to detect the influence of Terbrugghen in the creases carved into the old man's face, in his large expressive hands, in his white scarf, in the way he peers at the letter through his spectacles. No such creases are to be found in Honthorst but this does not necessarily mean that Wright acknowledged Terbrugghen's separate identity: one of his works that had struck his fancy could easily have been masquerading under Honthorst's name, just as the supposed source for *Mrs. Gwillym* [Plate 55] he may have thought was a Honthorst. The source for the Radburne picture is not so obvious, but it has reminded one writer[2] of the Pietro Rotari genre scene in Munich.[3] The connection is not too close, but Rotari was giving shape to the same melancholy underground world in Venice that blossomed in Derby with the rise of a new bourgeois culture. A European revolution in ways of seeing was on the march, but in the great artistic centres it had not yet broken the polished surface.

Fig 55 *Page from Wright's MS. Account Book showing drawing of a Girl reading a Letter* National Portrait Gallery, London

2 Raines, *loc. cit.*, p. 32.

3 Carlo Donzelli, *I Pittori Veneti del Settecento*, Florence, 1957, illus. plate VIII in colour.

Fig 56 *A Girl reading a Letter by candlelight, with a Young Man looking over her shoulder* c 1762–63
35 x 27½ in / 88.9 x 69.8 cm   Cat 207   Pl 45
Lt Col R. S. Nelthorpe

Fig 57 Thomas Frye *Young Man reading by Candlelight* 1760   Mezzotint

The Rogers-Coltman candlelight has a companion of two boys fighting over a bladder [Plate 76], the most ferocious picture in Wright's *œuvre*. There is an intensity, no longer so reticent, about his work of the late '60's, from the *Air Pump* to the Liverpool portraits but surviving into the industrial scenes and the *Earthstopper*, conveyed by distorting lights, broken surfaces and harsh reds, that are not to be found at any other time, but in this picture alone he is lured further in the direction of expressionism—only to beat a hasty retreat from it by the time he gets to Radburne. In their struggle the candle has been overturned and threatens to set the whole picture alight. The boys twist each other's ears and their bodies are contorted in pain. The light is directed upwards to cast furious shadows on the face of the further boy, causing the structure of his throat and mouth to be lost, and the crouching, serpentine movement of the boy against the light makes it difficult to sort out whose arm is whose—but these uncharacteristic ambiguities enhance our awareness of the turbulence of the game that is rapidly degenerating from a game into a disaster. The other two bladder pictures are comparatively mild. One was probably done in Liverpool and survives only in copies [Plate 74]. The third [Plate 95] is one of the four candlelight overdoors done for Radburne Hall in about 1772. At one end of this beautiful room (which is still essentially unchanged since Wright's day) are two overdoors showing children at play: one a bladder-blowing, the other a bubble-blowing scene. There is a sweetness about them far removed from the spirit of the Rogers-Coltman companion pieces that recalls Mercier: though innumerable examples of bubble-blowing scenes could be cited from Netherlandish studios,[1] none is closer to Wright's picture [Plate 95] than the Mercier in Mrs. Christie's Collection,[2] although Mercier's version is cruder and unnecessarily rubs in the moral with the inscription: '*Sic transit gloria mundi*'. At the other end of the room are two groups of grown-ups where *gloria mundi* also seems to be evaporating. One is of the letter-writing scene [Plate 92] we have already discussed; the other [Plate 94] shows an elderly woman who reads over with disapproval a letter written by a young woman beside her who waits in trepidation for the verdict. The old woman's accusing little finger—poised as only an Utrecht painter like Terbrugghen would poise it—seems to be saying 'you must never speak to him again'; while the girl clasps her hands through which she has threaded her pen, like an Utrecht penitent Magdalen. No other English painter of the eighteenth century used fingers and hands for expressive purposes more subtly than Wright did, and it is only from Utrecht that he could have taken his cue.

About contemporary with the Radburne overdoors are the industrial scenes, the *Iron Forges* and *Blacksmith's Shops* (1772–3). Two of each survive: the *Iron Forge* seen from inside in the Mountbatten Collection [Plate 103] and from outside in the Hermitage [Plate 104]; and the *Blacksmith's Shop* seen in two versions from inside, respectively in the Mellon and a private collection [Plates 100, 101]. A fifth picture of a Farrier's Shop seen from outside is now known only from an engraving [Plate 102]. (We have lost a fine invention in that band across the boy's face.)[3] In these forge pictures, in spite of the differences in subject-matter, because science and industry were linked together in Wright's mind as part of a general pattern of change, the approach is the same as in the large scientific pictures: the concentration on the source of light in the centre, this time a white hot bar of metal, investing the figures surrounding it with a magical intensity that no normal illumination could hope to fabricate; the moon breaking through cloud in the night sky, competing unsuccessfully with the brighter light indoors; the rafters and beams [Fig 58] contributing to the gloomy atmosphere, yet never so persistent as to take the eye away from the centre of attention, the forging of an iron bar, any more than the darkened rooms in the scientific pictures distracted the eye from the experiments themselves; the contrast between hard work and the inquisitive tourists who have found their way into the forge, accompanied by their uncomprehending children turning in distress away from the light to find a refuge in their mothers' skirts—the thoughtful balance, in other words, between sense and sensibility, between the prosaic, necessary task efficiently performed which is going to benefit mankind, and the fear or amazement that its accomplishment inspires.

Though we hardly need his description, Wright has given us in his Account Book his ideas for 'Subject for Night Pieces'. '*A Blacksmith's Shop*', he writes:

1 The most relevant to the Wright are the *Soap Bubbles* by Frans van Mieris the Elder in the Mauritshuis (see Theodore Rousseau, Jr., 'A Boy blowing bubbles by Chardin', *The Metropolitan Museum of Art Bulletin*, April 1950, pp. 221 ff.) and a bubble-blowing scene attributed to Jacob van Oost the Elder, R. A. 'Flemish' exhibition, 1953–4 (468), and reproduced by A. P. de Mirimonde in *Koninklijk Museum voor Schone Kunsten*, Antwerp, 1965, p. 168, plate 41. The latter has the additional advantage of making use of light effects in a way that would have appealed to Wright.

2 See Raines, *loc. cit.* plate 5.

3 There also exist two drawings of glass-blowing factories [Plates 96, 97] and a study for the Mountbatten *Iron Forge* [Plate 99]. With these can be associated a beautiful, naturalistic drawing of a fireside [Plate 98].

Fig 58 Detail from *The Blacksmith's Shop* See Pl 100

'Two men forming a bar of iron into a horse shoe, from whence the light must proceed. An idle fellow may stand by the anvil in a time-killing posture, his hands in his bosom, or yawning with his hands stretched upwards, & a little twisting of the body. Horse shoes hanging upon ye walls, and other necessary things faintly seen, being remote from the light. Out of this room shall be seen another, in wch a farrier may be shoeing a horse by the light of a candle. The horse must be sadled, and a traveller standing by. The servant may appear with his horse in his hand, on wch may be a portmanteau. This will be an indication of an accident having happened, and show some reason for shoeing the horse by candlelight. The moon may appear, and illumine some part of the horses, if necessary.'

Fig 59 Detail from *The Blacksmith's Shop* See Pl 100

Fig 60 Attributed to Jan Molenaer
Iron Forge
Panel 26½ x 23½ in / 67.3 x 59.7 cm
Ponce Art Museum, Puerto Rico (The Louis A. Ferré Foundation)

It is gratifying to know that we see in the pictures what he saw; and also to have notes about the idle fellow in the time-killing posture [Fig 59], who is seated in the corner resting on his stick too old for work in the pictures illustrated in plates 100, 101, 103, 104. He has the dignified gaze of the philosopher. Wright's attitude towards him of sympathy and respect differs from the usual patronising tone taken up by the eighteenth-century middle-class townsman towards the picturesque villager. Similarly he invests the anonymous workmen with the heroic status of statuary in spite of their menial tasks. When he reached Rome he treated the urchins in the streets with the same gravity.

Attempts have been made[1] to trace the origin of Wright's industrial pictures to seventeenth-century representations of *Vulcan's Forge* in the Le Nain studios, and it is possible that he knew engravings of this character. But in our opinion they did no more than stimulate his imagination which was already ripe for attack on such themes. The boy seen against the light in the *Orrery* and the boy in the foreground of the Rogers-Coltman *Bladder* picture are the direct ancestors of the corresponding figures in the *Iron Forges* and *Blacksmith's Shops* and sufficiently account for them; and there is nothing in the forge pictures that had not been anticipated in embryo in the scientific scenes.[2] But if one had to find origins for these as well, it is in any case not sensible to argue that suddenly he should turn to French art for inspiration—even to French studios as Dutch in feeling as the Le Nains'. Here as always one would expect Holland to lie behind him. And in fact the closest known antecedent to Wright's *Forge* pictures is not a French *Vulcan's Forge* but a Dutch painting as pedestrian in subject as Wright's, by or attributed to Jan Miense Molenaer [Fig 60] where women and children play the part of amazed spectators.[3]

1 Notably by Klingender, 1947, pp. 50 ff.

2 Reference must be made at this point to the Swede Pehr Hilleström, the only other artist of the period of any consequence who painted industrial subjects. Although in any study of Hilleström's career, Wright would have to play a predominant part, in a study of Wright he is of no significance: for his industrial pictures begin when Wright's leave off (the last, the Hermitage picture, being dated 1773). He must have been familiar with engravings after Wright's pictures since his compositions are often strikingly similar. These essential points are not brought out in the standard work on the subject by Sixten Rönnow, *Pehr Hilleström och hans bruks-och bergverksmålningar*, Stockholm, 1929.

3 The supposed Molenaer is in the Museo de Arte de Ponce, Puerto Rico (catalogue by Julius S. Held, 1965, plate 77).

51

Fig 61 *The Alchemist in search of the Philosopher's Stone discovers Phosphorus* 1771–1795
50 x 40 in / 127 x 101.6 cm
Derby Museum and Art Gallery
Cat 195   Pl 106

Fig 62 Thomas Wyck *Alchemist*
50 x 40 in / 127 x 101.6 cm
Ham House, Richmond, Surrey

1 See *Ham House—A Guide*, 2nd ed. London, 1951, p. 18.

Wright completed his series of scientific pictures by the production in 1771 of his *Alchemist in search of the Philosopher's Stone, discovering Phosphorus* [Fig 61]. As in the *Air Pump*, the moment chosen is the culmination of the experiment, and again the demonstrator's face is transfigured by light as though he were one of Christ's disciples witnessing the Breaking of the Bread, and again his arm shoots out towards us, overcome with the prospect of success. This movement of the arm must have reached Wright from the Italian Baroque, but the whole character of the picture has its origin in Flanders. Like his many Flemish forbears he stresses the picturesqueness of the alchemist's profession but adds a new element to the old subject: the alchemist discovers, not gold, but phosphorus; showing that for all its romanticism his idea has a basis in serious scientific practice. The subject is to be found frequently enough in the work of Teniers, but the examples closest to Wright's picture are two by Thomas Wyck [see Fig 62], which were hanging at Ham House in his day[1] and therefore readily accessible on any of his frequent trips to London. The architectural setting of the Wycks, with their pillars and looped curtains, are more closely paralleled in Wright's *Academy by Lamplight* [Plate 60] than in his *Alchemist*; but that Wyck is the source for the latter is suggested, not only by the profusion of globes, papers, books and bowls on the tables, but by the light catching the face of the alchemist's assistant in the background.

The *Hermit Studying Anatomy* [Fig 63] is described in the catalogue of the 1801 Sale as a companion to the *Alchemist*. This may simply have been an idea of the organisers of the sale, but it was an intelligent one: for the figures (one main one in the foreground, two subsidiary ones behind) are on the same scale in both pictures in relation to their backgrounds; they are both night scenes; and they both show old men engaged on scientific research. The *Hermit* was painted in 1771–3 when Wright was in closest association with Mortimer. Mortimer with his *banditti* at once conjures up Salvator Rosa, and it would not be surprising if Wright passed through a brief Rosa-like phase just before leaving for Italy. He was well represented in English private collections, and Wright's first known pure landscape [Plate 112] dating from this time is the most Salvatorial in his entire work. We would be willing to leave it at that, did there not exist a Rosa on this theme, the *Democritus in meditation* in the Museum of Copenhagen [Fig 64], showing the philosopher seated in a romantic landscape surrounded by the bones of animals, with his right elbow resting on a

Fig 63 *Hermit studying anatomy* c 1771–73
50½ x 40½ in / 128.2 x 102.9 cm   Derby
Museum and Art Gallery   Cat 196   Pl 105

Fig 64 Salvator Rosa *Democritus in meditation*
135½ x 84¼ in / 344 x 214 cm
Royal Museum of Fine Arts, Copenhagen

classical relief and his hand to his brow. In Wright's day the picture hung with its companion *Diogenes* (also now in Copenhagen) at Foots Cray Place in Kent, a mere twelve miles from London, a fine Palladian villa belonging to Bouchier Cleeve. It is listed in guide books to the house of 1761 and 1766 as 'Democritus in the posture Hipocritus found him in near Abdera',[1] and we are informed in these guides that 'Admittance to see the house is by tickets from Mr. Cleeve, and the days are every Thursday during the summer season'. It need not be thought that visitors were restricted to the rich and distinguished. Artists were also welcome: for two years after the publication of the second guide, the collection was visited by William Gilpin who singled out Rosa's *Democritus* for special praise:

'Democritus by Salvator is a large and capital picture... The moral is good and the tale well told. The variety of objects about him which are subject to the decay of time; the contemplative figure of the philosopher; the dark and gloomy tint which prevails over the picture, in short the whole solemnity of the scene, and every part of it, contribute to strike that awe, which the painter intended.'[2]

The description alone is ready-made for Wright's pencil. Although it would have been simple for him to visit the house (where, incidentally, he would also have seen a 'Moon Light' by 'Vandeneer', 'a Smith's Shop' by 'Old Wyke', a 'Smith's Forge' by 'Brouwer' and 'Cat and Boys' by 'Old Mieris'), he was sure to have been familiar with Rosa's own etching after the picture, which Gilpin also refers to.

A fashion sprang up in the early '70's for macabre picturesqueness, and more than one artist took to playing lightly on the themes of death, decay and imprisonment. At the Royal Academy of 1773, Reynolds exhibited his *Count Ugolino and his Children* from Dante's *Inferno*, XXXIII,[3] but this was just one of many such signs of the times. In the following year J. Moore exhibited a *Count Ugolino* at the Free Society. We would expect Wright to plunge with enthusiasm into the new fashion. The *Hermit* combines all the elements best calculated to appeal to him: the romantic setting, the moral lesson, the interest in science, the magic of knowledge. In his *Miravan opening the Tomb of his Ancestors* [Fig 65] he has hit on an obscure and horrific moral theme from classical history. The young nobleman Miravan breaks open the tomb of his ancestors, which he is assured from an inscrip-

1 See Dodsley, *London and its Environs described...*, II, London, 1761, p. 316, and T. Martyn, *The English Connoisseur...*, I, London, 1766, p. 62. Cleeve's or Cleve's daughter married Sir George Yonge, who inherited the pictures and moved them to his house in London in 1772 when Foots Cray was sold (see J. P. Neale, *Seats, IV* (2nd series), 1828), so it is possible that Wright saw the Rosa in London.

2 *Southern Tour*, pp. 122–3. For Gilpin's visit to Foots Cray in 1768, see Barbier, 1963, p. 46.

3 R. A. 1773 (243). The author is indebted to Richard James for pointing out the relevance of the Reynolds and the Moore to Wright. The Moore is described in the Free Society catalogue (341) as 'Count Ugolino. A sketch. After Michael Angelo in the chapel of Sixtus the Vth [*sic*] in Rome...'

Fig. 65 *Miravan opening the Tomb of his Ancestors* 1772
50 x 40 in / 127 x 101.6 cm   Derby Museum and Art Gallery   Cat 222   Pl 107

Fig 66 School unknown, late 16th Century *Darius, son of Hispaspes, opening the tomb of Nicotris, Queen of Babylon*
Bronze plaque $5\frac{1}{8}$ x 7 in / 13 x 17.8 cm
Leonard Baskir

tion on it contains 'a greater treasure than Croesus ever possessed'. Wright copied his literary source, whatever it was, into his Account Book:

'... he was struck speechless with disappointment to behold nothing but a heap of Bones & Dust with this inscription over it. Here would have dwelt *eternal repose* a treasure that Croesus never possessed which thou hast driven hence being excited by an insatiable love of Gold, to disturb the sacred remains of thy progenitor. Had not thy reason been deluded by a false fancy she wou'd have told thee that the grave contains nothing but dust & ashes'.

The source has not been traced but Wright may have found the story in some contemporary collection of Persian fairy tales. Nobody now knows who Miravan was, but the same tale is told in Herodotus[1] of Darius, son of Hispaspes, opening the tomb of Nicotris, Queen of Babylon, who gave orders that her tomb should bear the inscription to the effect that incalculable treasures were to be found there, of which advantage should only be taken in case of dire necessity. The tomb remained untouched until Darius commanded it to be hacked open in his presence, only to find inside the Queen's decomposing corpse, with the inscription: 'If thou hadst not been insatiable for money and the victim of base cupidity, thou wouldst never have violated the repose of the dead'. Only two representations on this theme have come to our notice though there were certainly others: a bronze plaque of the late sixteenth century [Fig 66] where the perpetrator of the outrage covers his face in his hands as he retreats from the tomb, just as he does in Wright's picture;[2] and a painting by Le Sueur in the Hermitage.[3] This picture was engraved more than once in the eighteenth century (first by B. Picart in 1725) and one of these prints could have been the vehicle by which it was transmitted to Wright. It may have been quite famous in the late eighteenth century, if we are correct in thinking that an engraving of it hung on the walls of a common inn at Pontchartrain in 1764—but this is no more than a wild guess. In any case the existence there of the particular moral lesson to be drawn from Miravan's experience is evidence of the popularity of the legend at the time. The print is described by a certain Geneviève de Malboissière in a letter to a friend of 6th September 1764. She has just visited the inn and from Bourdonne writes:

'... une petite chambre charmante de l'auberge... Elle est ornée de petits tableaux au bas desquels sont de jolis vers, entre autres le *Soir*, le *Martin*, *Clothos*... et le *Soldat trompé* qui, croyant trouver un trésor, trouve un cadavre et fuit épouvanté. Vous voyés [sic] avec quelle exactitude je vous rends compte des moindres petites choses.'[4]

Though the style and composition of the Le Sueur are quite different from the Wright, the *idea* may have come to him from this source. It is significant that the Le Sueur was painted for a bourgeois client (Vedeau de Grammont) just as the Wright was (for Milnes), and that both clients would have interpreted their pictures as a use of 'antiquity as a means of pointing a moral which is intended can be applied to the problems of modern life'.[5]

Medieval histories were also popular in an age that saw West's *Death of Bayard*. Wright's contribution, the *Captive King*, painted in the winter of 1772–3, is lost, but three drawings for the composition are known [Plates 108, 109, 111] and a beautiful smallish sketch, as delicate as an Hubert Robert [Plate 110], almost monochrome but touched with pinks and light blues. This shows the captive reaching out from his grating, to fetch his bowl from the floor above; he is a special category prisoner and we see nothing of him but his hands—a typical neo-Gothic conceit. However, in the exhibited picture, the artist adopts the scheme outlined in the drawings.[6] One of the drawings [Plate 111] is a mere sketch of the architecture, noted down in the course of an explanatory letter. The two others [Plates 108, 109] show him reclining on straw above the grating, and one in the Derby Art Gallery [Plate 108] has a crucifix propped up against a pillar, which gives the clue to the subject.[7] Wright in his Account Book lists a painting of *Guy de Lusignan in Prison*, within a few entries of the *Captive King* and at the same price, so it must be the same picture. This young Frankish king had been defeated by the Saracens at the Horns of Hattin in 1187 and had been taken prisoner by Saladin. It was a decisive victory for the Muslim world: 'On the Horns of

1 We have consulted a pre-*Miravan* edition of Herodotus in English, that of 1737 in two volumes. The reference is Vol. I, p. 117.

2 The style of the plaque is not positive enough to enable us to pinpoint its geographical origin. It is known as School of Fontainebleau in a private collection in Northampton (Mass.).

3 See A. Somof, *Ermitage Impérial. Catalogue de la Galerie des Tableaux. Troisième Partie. Ecole Anglaise et Ecole Française*, St. Petersburg, 1903, No. 1450.

4 See *Une Jeune Fille au XVIIIè siècle: lettres de Geneviève de Malboissière à Adelaide Méliand, 1761–1766*, ed. Comte de Luppé, Paris, 1925, pp. 148–9. The author is indebted to Ronald Lightbown for this reference.

5 The quotation is from Anthony Blunt, 'The Hypnerotomachia Poliphili in 17th Century France', *Journal of the Warburg Institute*, 1937–38, p. 133. The Le Sueur is reproduced there on pl. 13C.

6 This is an argument in favour of the view that the small painting preceded the drawings. We know the exhibited picture showed the prisoner 'laying on the ground, a lantern hanging over him', as Horace Walpole says so (see A. Graves, *The Society of Artists of Great Britain 1760–91...*, London, 1907, p. 287).

7 Since Wright's *Captive King* is closely bound up with his relations with Peter Perez Burdett, we have postponed further discussion of the drawings and oil sketch for the lost picture until a later chapter (see below, Part III, p. 120).

Hattin', writes a recent historian of the Crusades, 'the greatest army that the kingdom had ever assembled was annihilated. The Holy Cross was lost',[1] and all that survives of it is the crude crucifix propped on the pillar. Guy was kept prisoner for some months, first at Nablus, later at Lattakieh, but was released the following year. If there was a colourful eighteenth-century description of the event which came to Wright's notice, we have not found it.

1 Stevan Runciman, *The History of the Crusades*, II, 1952, p. 460.

The last pictures he exhibited before leaving for abroad in 1773 were the *Captive King*, the Hermitage *Iron Forge*, and the *Earthstopper on the Banks of the Derwent* [Plate 113]; the following year during his absence saw the *Old Man and Death* [Plate 123] at the Society of Artists. In these last pre-Italian works as well as in the roughly contemporary *Hermit*, Wright makes his first experiments in landscape painting, although he had used landscape constantly as backgrounds for portraits, but in these cases (except in that of the *Coltman* group) the forms were generalised so as not to conflict with the sitters, and so hardly count. He also produced in about 1772 his first pure landscape [Plate 112], in the style of Rosa. In a later chapter[2] we shall discuss these few early ventures, noting the abrupt changes that took place in his style between them and the first views of *Vesuvius* and of the Roman Campagna. Meanwhile, since the *Earthstopper* and the *Old Man and Death* are also subject pieces, we must pay our respects to them here. The first shows a man who has ridden out with his dog by the light of the moon to fill up foxholes, so that on the following morning of the hunt, the foxes will be unable to take refuge in them. This is one of Wright's wildest landscapes, streakier, starker, more nervous even than the moonlights of the early '80's in the Cade and Booth Collections [Plates 236, 244] when for a glorious moment he manages to recover the breath of youth. Light collects from the lantern on the snapped tree trunk, coating it in glittering frost, and throws its beams upwards to pick out the earthstopper's ruddy face as he gets down to the job [Fig 67], just as 130 years earlier, unknown to Wright, Georges de La Tour had used a lantern to underline the concentration of the Holy Women on extracting arrows from St. Sebastian's side, and had turned their faces a deep red. Vegetation steals down the rock face in the night, disturbed in its descent by the unnatural light. An intelligent dog sniffs for foxes among the plants, and a white horse—too stupid to do anything else—just waits, displaying a patient rump that Stubbs need not have felt ashamed of.

2 See below, Part II, p. 75.

The landscape in the *Old Man and Death* [Plate 123] in broad daylight, is of a very different character, reminding us of Hobbema and Jan van der Heyden.[3] The figures in it oc-

3 Rosenblum, 1960, correctly points out that the crumbling Gothic ruin 'alludes to the melancholy transience of human life'. Another apparently autograph version of the *Old Man and Death*, showing only the area with the figures, is in the Walker Art Gallery, Liverpool [Fig 68].

Fig 67 Detail from *The Earthstopper* Cat 24 See pl 113

cupy a relatively inconspicuous place [Fig 68]. They repeat the fable of Aesop, in which an old woodchopper lays down his bundle of faggots and calls on death to release him from the burden of life; but when death arrives in the form of a skeleton and offers to help him up with his bundle, he wards death off, impotently clinging to life. It is a predicament many of us have faced at one time or another, in illness or in love. An English edition of Aesop's fables was published in Birmingham in 1761, and the illustration of this scene among the plates may have been known to Wright in near-by Derby where the skeleton carries the arrow of death instead of propping it on his shoulder, as in Wright's picture.[1] That Wright derived any visual satisfaction from this beastly little circular print is inconceivable. He must have searched further afield for a more edifying rendering; finding it perhaps in Marcus Gheerhaerts who engraved the subject for a series of plates in De Dene's *Set of Fables of Aesop* of 1567.[2] As for his skeleton, in spite of the gruesome subject, he would never have been content with it unless it stood up to the latest developments in anatomy (needless to say, the print of 1761 belongs to a pre-scientific age). Wright needed something like a skeleton or an orrery to tether him to facts whenever romance threatened to take charge. Like Stubbs with the anatomy of the horse, nothing short of accuracy was permissible. And it was to an up-to-date medical manual that he owed his instruction. The most reliable published in English before 1773 was the 1749 folio edition of Bernhard Siegfried Albinus's *Tables of the Skeleton and Muscles of the Human Body*, with beautiful whole-page plates by C. Grignion (1747). Three skeletons are shown: the human figure front and back, and a third Table showing the skeleton walking to the left with his left arm raised and his left leg trailing behind him [Fig 69]. Sharp shadows are cast from right to left; his ribs catch the light like the ribs of the *Orrery*; and as in Wright's picture, a lake with trees reflected in it completes the composition behind. For once we can do without that weak word 'probably' and can assert that this was the source for death in the Hartford and Liverpool pictures.[3] What is more, Mortimer owned a copy of this very edition.[4]

1 The comparison was made by Rosenblum, 1962, pp. 135–6 and plate 25c. By our implied criticism of the author we have no wish to deny the status of his article as the basic one on the iconography of the Hartford picture. Our own attempt of 1954 to explain the picture was a disaster. The illustration appears in *Select Fables of Esop and other Fabulists*, Birmingham, 1761, facing p. 29.

2 See F. W. H. Hollstein, *Dutch and Flemish Etchings Engravings and Woodcuts 1450–1700*, VII, p. 100. Although there are marked differences between Gheerhaert's and Wright's versions, this was a well-known book which had gone into four editions by 1617 and could easily have attracted his attention in some well-stocked library.

3 The author is indebted to Leonard Baskin for first suggesting Albinus as a source for the *Old Man and Death*. It was then merely a question of finding the most likely edition and engraved plate.

4 Mrs. Mortimer Sale, Christie's, 25th March 1808 (25).

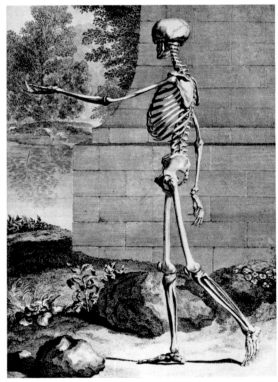

Fig 68 *The Old Man and Death* 1773
25 x 30 in / 63.5 x 76.2 cm
Walker Art Gallery, Liverpool   Cat 221

Fig 69 Berhard Siegfried Albinus   Anatomical Study from *Tables of the Skeleton and muscles of the Human Body* (ed. 1749)   Engraving

3 LATER SUBJECT PIECES, GENRE AND FIGURE STUDIES

On arrival in Rome, Wright set about documenting himself with his usual conscientious-ness on the antique and on Michelangelo. Just as a writer might transcribe into his notebook passages from the Roman poets which had struck his imagination, so Wright would treasure up notes in his sketchbooks, in the form of outline drawings of ancient statuary and the Sistine prophets, for possible later use in his own work. There they would remain, these *aides-mémoire*, ready to hand to be drawn on when the occasion demanded. Once many years later he instructed his friend Hayley to send on to Josiah Wedgwood a 'rude sketch' he had made of his proposed picture of the *Origin of Painting* which Wedgwood was contemplating buying. The sketch, he hastens to warn Wedgwood, has no light and shade in it, 'but it will shew you the actions'.[1] Similarly in his Roman copies, his aim is to rescue from oblivion the 'actions' for his own purposes.[2] The majestic, the pathetic, the imperious gesture—this is what he sought to retain at his beck and call, and this alone the art of ancient and Renaissance Rome could provide. The remainder could be filled in from his studies from real life.

A few copies survive, however, where he goes beyond the notation of movement to describe in more detail the interior forms. One is a noble copy after a Roman portrait bust [Plate 125]; but in this case one can understand that he would wish to elaborate the features with pen and wash. There could be no object in preserving just the outlines of a portrait; some characterisation also is necessary if it is to make any sense. The same goes for an even more splendid oil painting in monochrome of a Roman or Roman-inspired bust seen from two positions, one in sharp profile, the other (smaller) where the head is turned slightly away [Plate 122]. The concentration is on the modelling of the marble, not on its profile, meaningless in isolation. Though we know nothing of their origin, both presumably belong to his Italian period. Two copies appear to have been done in England, one before he left for Italy, the other on his return. The first is a careful study of the Borghese *Gladiator* [Fig 120], a statue famous in England in the '60's in innumerable casts and copies, large and small, and therefore readily accessible to him when he was engaged on his painting *The Gladiator* [Plate 52]—and indeed on general grounds one suspects the drawing was made in connection with this work, in spite of the fact that the statuette itself, and the image on the drawing held up by one of the participants, in this famous picture are shown from different angles. We can be sure there were other drawings of the *Gladiator*, with pen and wash to define the muscles, from other angles, since Wright had to learn the statuette by heart in all its twists and turns. The second is a pencil drawing of the Lysippean *Hermes* where quite uncharacteristically the artist is intent on defining with the aid of shading and white heightening the volume, not the contours, of the body seen (to judge by the chiaro-scuro) under artificial light. It stands quite apart from his Italian copies, and was very

1 See below, Part III, p. 145.

2 It must be borne in mind that Winckelmann's *Gedanken* (translated by Fuseli, 1765 and easily accessible to Wright) had put in an eloquent plea for the 'precision of contour'. Whinney, 1964, p. 155 also makes the point that young artists could not afford to buy expensive books of engravings and made tracings from them: 'such tracings would almost certainly have been in outline only, and would therefore have developed the habit of thinking in such terms'.

1 *Hermes putting on his Sandal*, Copenhagen. Formerly in the collection of 2nd Earl of Shelburne, Lansdowne House. By chance the illustration of the Lansdowne marble in Christie's catalogue, 5th March 1930, p. 151 is shown from the same angle (that, of course, from which the salient features can be studied). What makes one think that it was this version which Wright copied is that other versions (Louvre, Munich, Vatican), show both arms extended to the sandal. The statue was found by Gavin Hamilton in 1769 in Hadrian's Villa and sold by him to Lord Shelburne. It was delivered to Lord Shelburne before Wright left for Italy, but was probably not available for copying before his return (see A. Michaelis, *Ancient Marbles in Great Britain*, Cambridge, 1882, pp. 104, 464 ff.)

2 One outline pen drawing in the Derby Art Gallery, 20½ by 16½ in, is a copy of the prophet *Jonah* above the altar of the Sistine Chapel.

3 If there remains any doubt in the reader's mind that this is the head of the *Ganymede* and not that of the *Satyr*, it can be pointed out that the scribble on his left shoulder is the curve of the eagle's wing. The *Ganymede* remained at the French Academy until it was transferred in 1780 to Florence. It was one of Mengs's favourites.

likely done on his return to England on a visit to Shelburne (later Lansdowne) House where the original marble was preserved.[1] But these are the exceptions. The pages from sketchbooks now incorporated into two large portfolios in the Derby Art Gallery, and some pages with copies of ancient statuary in a sketchbook now in the British Museum, are almost exclusively made up of outlines, where nothing is indicated of the interior forms beyond what was essential to express the movement—mere anthologies, in other words, of pose and gesture. And the same was certainly true of the Michelangelo copies but these have almost all disappeared.[2]

We have been obliged to restrict our illustrations, out of well over fifty drawings after the antique, to the very best, but one day when Wright's name has become a household word the publication of the entire series will be justified. Not much of the unillustrated material, it has to be admitted, is up to the standard of the examples shown here. Some studies after antique sarcophagi are positively clumsy. But we have to remember that they were designed for his use alone; that polish was not what he was after; that there was no Wedgwood or Hayley to call him to order; that he was often working at speed in uncomfortable surroundings, remaining on his feet perhaps in draughty *palazzi*; that all he needed was to recall the pose. Some statues were too intricate to be expressed in a single frontal or profile view, and he found he had to move around them to catch and record their various facets, each facet presenting him with a new movement to contemplate and be amazed by. Thus the 'baroque' convolutions of the Barberini *Faun* (now in the Munich Glyptothek) inspired him to three of his most beautiful drawings [Plates 130, 131]; one a strange sideways view where the arm is thrown above the head at an angle sufficiently tortuous to satisfy Fuseli. He sketched the Capitoline Hellenistic *Venus* twice on the same sheet from two different points of view from the back, and a third time in profile five days later. One sheet carries two views of the *Satyr with a Panther* [Plate 132], to which he has added a head on the right of exquisite refinement—not the head of the satyr, but of the Hellenistic *Ganymede with an Eagle*, the subject of two separate and more detailed studies two days earlier [Plate 129].[3] The famous Hellenistic *Satyr*, in Florence since the early eighteenth century, was studied by Wright on three sheets from a version remaining in the French Academy [Plate 133]. The so-called *Dead Asiatic* from the Naples Pergamon group he sketched twice, from a version in Rome, on two successive days: on one occasion [Fig 86] selecting a most eccentric view where nothing is shown of the head but the hair. Again we are reminded that Fuseli was in Rome when Wright was at work on it. The *Drunken Old*

Fig 70 Drawing from a relief of a *Bacchic Procession* c 1774   Brown ink on white paper   21 x 14 in / 53.3 x 35.5 cm Derby Museum and Art Gallery

Fig 71 Relief of *Bacchic Procession* Museo Archeologico Nazionale, Naples

Woman in the Capitoline won his instant sympathy. He sketched her twice in pencil, once too hastily for competence [Plate 126] but the spirit of the tortured head and coarse hands has survived his speed.

Just as he would travel out into the Campagna to sketch the most famous sites, so he would settle on the statuary that was then most admired: on a *Satyr with a skin of wine* [Fig 3]; on the figure of Bacchus [Fig 70] from a *Bacchic Procession* from Stabia[1] [Fig 71]; on the Capitoline so-called *Dying Gaul*[2] [Plate 127]; on a copy of the Lysippic bronze (?) group of *Wrestlers* [Plate 135]; on a statue in the French Academy thought to derive from a bronze showing a figure connected with the chase [Plate 128]; on the Capitoline Hellenistic *Eros and Psyche*, the *Boy with a Goose*, and the *Youth playing the Lyre*; on the *Silenus with the Infant Dionysos* attributed to Lysippos; inevitably on the *Apollo Belvedere*—on all those visual tags that Mengs and Winckelmann had laid down should engage the attention of the visiting artist. Wright takes over whatever he is told deserves admiration, and finds it to his taste. But though the *idées* may be *reçues*, his interpretation of them is not. Out of the platitudes of the remote past he constructs works of art in their own right. What is so moving about these drawings is the extent to which he succeeds, in spite of an evident anxiety to remain faithful to the antique originals, in putting into them so much of his own personality. The seriousness he invariably displays, the skill with which he conveys the contour by a taut, uninterrupted penstroke, the choice of themes of death and dying, the emphasis on children and young people—all this is perhaps to be expected. More surprising is the occasional quirky angle of vision. The eagle is made to peck at Ganymede's cheek [Plate 129], and the heads of the Barberini *Faun* and the *Dead Asiatic* [Plate 130, Fig 86] are viewed from such odd angles that they are no longer conceived as heads but as dramatic, Fuseli-inspired shapes.

This is only a way of saying that he felt the intense vitality of the shapes he was copying, even though his models were in many cases themselves copies of distant prototypes. They were as alive to him as the people in the streets. It is a disturbing experience, for instance, to turn over the pages of the British Museum sketchbook of 1774 and not to be certain at a glance whether a given drawing is copied from a statue or from the living model, so intimately bound up together were ancient art and modern life in Wright's mind as he sauntered through the streets of Rome and encountered both at every turn. A statue will take on the immediacy of a human being, a beggar the timeless dignity of a statue. The young man gazing distractedly into the distance with his foot on a rock[3] [Plate 137] owes his stance to the ancients but he is studied from life. The boy asleep on the steps [Plate 141] is the modern counterpart of the *Dead Asiatic* [Fig 86]; the boy crouching in the corner of a doorway has dislocated his shoulder, so to speak, like the Barberini *Faun* [Plate 131]. What could be more classical than the youth asleep resting his head on a stone [Plate 134], with curls like Ganymede's? Far from being a hero of antiquity, he is a street urchin. Children have nothing better to do but lounge about, but unconsciously they take up classical poses [Plate 139]. This particular study proves that another, in one of the Derby portfolios [Plate 138], was also sketched in the streets of Rome at the same time. It encourages us to propose that several others in Derby belong to the same series of Roman life studies, though there is no indication on them that they were done there; such as the man studied twice in lost profile on the same sheet [Plate 136], and most dignified of all, that ragged, down-at-heel *contadino* seated on a rock [Plate 144], as sensitive and solid as a Giandomenico Tiepolo.

The British Museum sketchbook also deserves, one day, to be published in its entirety. There are two puzzling figures in it of disconsolate women [Fig 72], the purpose of which is not clear. Like so many of Romney's drawings which they vividly recall,[4] they may have been intended for some subject picture never carried out. There are studies of *écorché* figures [Plate 140], reminding us of Wright's scientific interests, done with the mastery we have learnt to expect from the author of the *Old Man and Death*. There are copies of statuary in the Capitoline and the French Academy, landscape sketches made in and around Rome, studies of children from life, of groups of passers-by—anything that happened to fall beneath his gaze as he took the air and turned to a fresh page.

Most of his daylight hours in Rome and Naples were thus given over to making visual

1 The most famous version is a relief of *Bacchus, Faun and Bacchante* from Stabia, now in the Archeological Museum in Naples [Fig 71], but this is not Wright's actual source. Nor did he use the similar figure on a large Gaeta vase signed Salpion in the Naples Museum. He must have used a third version, then in Rome. The author is indebted to Professor A. de Franciscis, Soprintendente alle Antichità, Naples, for his help over the identification of Wright's sources in antique art in Naples.

2 Wright's copy was done in the French Academy from another version. It probably represents a dying trumpeter.

3 A second drawing in the British Museum sketchbook shows the same figure in the same pose, more summarily treated in outline. This is also the case with the Romney-like disconsolate lady described below [Fig 72], and with the boy resting his head on a stone [Plate 134, Fig 80].

4 A remarkably similar drawing by Romney of a dejected lady is in the Yale University Art Gallery [Fig 73]. According to Patricia Milne-Henderson (see *The Drawings of George Romney*, exh. catalogue, Smith College Museum of Art, 1962, No. 9, plate XXV) it might represent *Andromeda* and have been executed *c.* 1777.

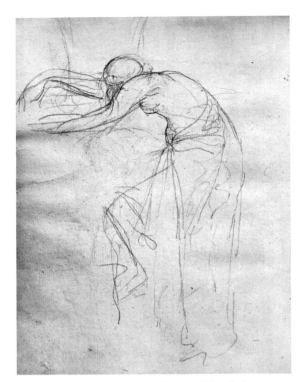

Fig 72 *Woman in distress* From Wright's 1774 Sketchbook   British Museum

Fig 73 George Romney *Captive or dejected woman; possibly Andromeda* c 1777
$20\frac{1}{4}$ x $12\frac{3}{4}$ in / 51.4 x 32.4 cm   Yale University and Art Gallery, U.S.A.   (Gift of Mr and Mrs J. Richardson Dilworth)

provision for the future, because he knew that time was limited and that he must scribble as much down on paper as possible while the going was good. Few canvases survive from this period, and few are recorded that have not come down to us. Only one subject piece, *The Captive* from Sterne's *Sentimental Journey*, is known to have been painted in Rome, and that in the late summer of 1774 after months of self-documentation in galleries open to artists. From Father Thorpe's letters we gather that he was engaged on this work in August and had completed it by the beginning of September.[1] Wright did two versions of the *Captive*, one turned to the left, known only from a poor copy [Fig 74], the other to the right [Plate 162], but we cannot deduce from Father Thorpe's letters or from any written source which was the picture in question. If it were not for a beautiful drawing in

1 See above, Part I, p. 8.

Fig 74   Copy of alost work by Joseph Wright *The Captive (from Sterne)*; original of 1774   40 x 50 in / 101.6 x 127 cm
Derby Museum and Art Gallery   Cat 217   Pl 162

Fig 75 *The Prisoner* 1774   Pen and wash with black ink
$9\frac{7}{8}$ x $13\frac{7}{8}$ in / 25 x 35.2 cm   Wadsworth Athenaeum, Hartford, Conn.

the Wadsworth Atheneum [Fig 75], resembling so closely Wright's Roman studies both of dejected beggars and of ruins in the Forum and elsewhere that it must have been done in Rome, we could never have guessed that the version turned to the left was the one described by Father Thorpe. This at any rate seems to be a reasonable deduction, considering that its composition follows faithfully that of the drawing manifestly executed in Rome at the same time. Whether the other version where the architecture is exactly repeated [Plate 162] but where the figure is quite different was also painted in Italy or soon after his return, must remain an open question, but judging by the tightness of the draughtsmanship it can hardly be later than 1777.

Before leaving for Italy Wright had no doubt already meditated on the theme of Sterne's *Captive* in the company of Mortimer. The latter exhibited a drawing of the *Captive from Sterne* at the Society of Artists in the Spring of 1774,[1] which is doubtless the one belonging to Richard Payne Knight, engraved as in his collection. A more summary Mortimer drawing (with wash) on the same theme but of uncertain date is now in the Oppé collection [Fig 76] and so close is it to Wright's figure that we are tempted to argue that it was executed before Wright's departure, by the autumn of 1773, and that Wright knew it as well. Wright possessed a drawing by Mortimer [Fig 77] which is also of obvious significance for his *Captive*.[2] The date is not known, but the very early '70's was the moment when Mortimer as well as Wright was preoccupied with themes of captivity, and so we are encouraged to identify it with a pen and ink study Mortimer had given him, and that Wright had lent his friend P. P. Burdett in Liverpool, and had never had back. Burdett had got into serious financial trouble early in 1774, and in August of that year, at the precise moment when Wright was engaged on his *Captive*, he became worried about the fate of his drawing, and wrote home asking one of the Tate brothers to retrieve it from Burdett 'w[ch] I would not lose on any account'.[3]

However, though Wright may have taken a hint from Mortimer, he owes little in his *Captive* to his own pre-Italian self. A visit to the fountainhead of art has meanwhile intervened and caused him to transform his style. It is instructive to contrast both his compositions of the *Captive from Sterne* with the *Captive King* [Fig 74, Plates 162, 110], dating from shortly before his Italian journey (though we are bound to admit the comparison is not quite fair, given that no canvas showing more of the figure of Guy de Lusignan than his hand exists). All the same it is not stretching the evidence too far to suggest that in the interval, Rome has lent Wright a certain monumentality, expressed in a new relationship between figures and their surroundings—a monumentality that only direct experience of the antique, of Michelangelo, of the inhabitants of Rome basking in the sun, could provide. We are not thinking merely of the obvious derivation, in the *Captive* turned to the right,

1 'The Captive, from Sterne's Sentimental Journey; a drawing in pen and ink', S. of A., 1774 (177).

2 The drawing is only known from the etching here illustrated, made by Thomas Hardy in 1805 (by which time its owner had been dead for eight years) and captioned in Hardy's plate: 'A Banditti [sic] made Prisoners. From an Original Drawing of Mr. Mortimer's, in the possession of Mr. Wright of Derby'.

3 Wright to his brother, 14th [sic] August, 1774, quoted by Bemrose, 1885, p. 33; from Eardley Simpson extra-illustrated Bemrose.

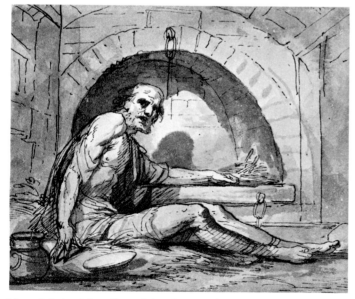

Fig 76 John Hamilton Mortimer *The Captive, from Sterne* Pen 4¼ x 5⅛ in / 10.8 x 13 cm D. L. T. Oppé

Fig 77 Thomas Hardy after J. H. Mortimer '*A Banditti made Prisoners*' Etching British Museum

1 Bemrose, 1885, pp. 69–70.

2 A second, slightly larger, picture of the same room from a different angle has recently come to light [Plate 285]. A fine drawing for the latter has survived [Plate 286]. The draughtsmanship is more pictorial than structural, which supports a late date for the paintings. It is in grey wash with brown ink, touches of pencil underdrawing, 13 by 17½ in. (H. C. Torbock Collection, Penrith).

3 Bemrose, loc. cit., tells us this Maria was studied from Mary, wife of a Richard Bassano, but the author has discovered no evidence to substantiate this statement, and Mrs. Bassano remains a shadow.

from the *Adam* on the Sistine Ceiling: even Bemrose, who did not go in for art history, spotted this.[1] But on a deeper level, Italian art and life are here shown to have made their full impact upon him for the first time; and from then onwards the link with Italy, though often tenuous, is never entirely severed. In a small prison scene, for instance, painted many years later, in the late '80's [Plate 284] perhaps in some cellar in Derby from where the spire of a church is half-glimpsed through the barred windows, where plaster peels from damp walls, where the vault is streaked with dark green spelling disease, where light picks up debris scattered over the unswept floor and catches the edge of a spindly trough, where a coatless and shivering captive snatches what sleep he can in a corner—Wright harks back to his *Captive*, recreating the spirit of the catacombs in his remote Midlands.[2]

On his return to England, once he had settled down in Derby again in 1777 after the abortive Bath interlude, Wright painted a companion to the *Captive* turned to the left, showing another episode from Sterne's novel, *Maria and her Dog Sylvio* [Plate 184]. The two distracted creatures, a man in prison and a girl imprisoned by love, sit facing one another but there can be no contact between them, so engrossed is each of them in his or her own misery. To compare *Maria* with another scene of despair in the countryside, the *Old Man and Death* [Plate 123] is to appreciate and be astonished by the distance he had travelled in a short period of four years. All the old dash has gone, to be replaced by a staid and pedantic classicism. The mood of the landscape is now quite different, reflecting the girl's own mood of melancholy resignation, and Maria is outlined against it as though superimposed on it in low relief. The landscape has changed, in fact, into an unobtrusive setting for a triangular plaque. It is not sensible to speak of her wearing clothes, she wears draperies which cling to her body as though chiselled out of a block of marble. Here we are being treated to the first fruits of his meditations in the presence of Hellenistic sculpture, tinged with the romanticism of Romney. Four years later he was to paint a second, much larger *Maria* in an upright format turned to the left [Plate 220], differing from the earlier one in being no longer a plaque in low relief but a statue in the round, in combining a delicate pale green with the white drapery, and in giving a little more individuality to the face;[3] otherwise the Romney atmosphere remains the same. Wright's sketchbook now in the British Museum surely lay open before him as he planned this picture: for in it are to be found studies from the antique and from nature of similar ladies resting their heads in their

Fig 78 *Edwin (from Dr. Beattie's Minstrel)*
1777–8   63 x 46 in / 160 x 116.8 cm
Lady Cynthia Colville   Cat 235   Pl 179

Fig 79 *Study of a Boy, here identified as Thomas Haden* c 1777   Pencil   7½ x 5½ in / 19 x 13.9 cm
Mrs J. Chandos-Pole

hands or wiping tears from their eyes.

Even more strikingly reminiscent of the studies in this Roman sketchbook is his figure of Edwin, inspired by James Beattie's poem *The Minstrel* [Fig 78], begun in the same year (1777) as the earlier of the two *Marias* [Plate 184] but used as a companion to the second *Maria* of 1781[1] [Plate 220]. We have already referred in another context to the youth asleep resting his head on a stone slab [Plate 134]. A second and more summary outline sketch of this boy [Fig 80], taken in conjunction with a study of a boy resting his foot on a low brick wall [Fig 81], is the unexpected source for *Edwin*: in spite of the fact that the head ('finely expressive of passion and enthusiasm' according to Horace Walpole)[2] is not that of a Roman urchin but of a middle-class Derbyshire boy of 16 or 17, a certain Thomas Haden who became an eminent Derby surgeon.[3] Wright did a pencil drawing of a boy of the same age who has every appearance of being the model for *Edwin* [Fig 79]. Perhaps he already had the picture in mind when the boy posed for him, and this would explain the retention of the poetical hand resting on the cheek. But in spite of his dreamy expression, young bourgeois Haden was still not poetical enough for an itinerant minstrel; and so was forced, for the final picture, to bare his breast, puff out his sleeves, smooth out the contours of his body, and at top speed grow ringlets over his shoulders. In the picture as finally executed, as in its companion, Wright treats the landscape as a backdrop, enlivening it with foliage and plants in the manner of Pieter Lastman simply in order to avoid monotony, but playing it down so that the two figures should not sink into their surroundings but stand out bold and triangular against them.

The fleeting but never quite eradicated impression that Italy left upon him can nowhere be better illustrated than in his heads of old men. These were designed as character studies of Apostles, or for possible use as philosophers in subject pieces, never as portraits. For portraiture in the accepted sense was not ordinarily[4] permissible in Wright's day on a lower social level than that of the middle-class; duchesses could appear as shepherdesses or housemaids but not *vice versa*. During the decade of the '70's he produced a series of these heads, similar in type but betraying marked variations in style. The first [Plate 122] is small, not only in dimensions but in conception. There is no trace of Italian influence here: the characteristic brown sleeves recall *Miravan*, and it is clearly to this moment, just before the Italian visit, that the little canvas must be assigned. Then suddenly we are confronted with

1 The R. A. catalogue of 1781 (100) notes that this second *Maria* was a 'companion to the picture of Edwin, exhibited three years ago' (that is, in 1778).

2 Quoted by Whitley, 1928, II, p. 397.

3 We only have Bemrose's word for this (1885, p. 69) but it can be accepted since he was in touch with Francis Seymour Haden who etched the picture of his ancestor, and who must have passed on this not too distant tradition in his family to Wright's biographer. Two of Thomas Haden's daughters sat to Wright as children at the end of the artist's life [Plate 343]. His son, Charles Thomas Haden (1786–1824), another surgeon, is a familiar name to Janeites, having professionally attended Jane Austen's father.

4 Reynolds's portrait of *Wang-y-tong* at Knole might be taken as an exception, but it is significant that the boy is posed in the genre tradition of Murillo.

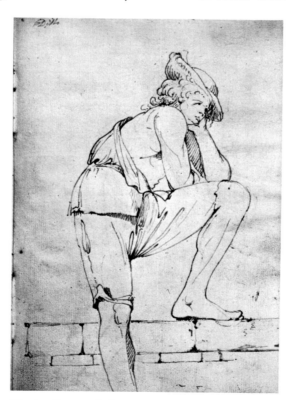

Fig 80 *Boy asleep* From Wright's 1774 Sketchbook   British Museum

Fig 81 *Boy with foot on wall* From Wright's 1774 Sketchbook   British Museum

1 Of the other two, in the Cade Collection at Porthcurno (Penzance), one shows him looking up to the right, the other down to the left, so the plan was to record as many positions of the head as possible.

2 The author has not seen this picture, which is in a private collection in Guelph (Ontario), and cannot therefore account for the poor drawing of the right hand. However, the painting comes from the Holland collection, and it is inconceivable that Holland would have owned anything but an original by his friend Wright, unless it were a copy after Wright by himself.

3 There is also a globe in the lower left foreground of the *Old Man's Head* [Plate 228] though it is scarcely visible in the reproduction.

four oil sketches on paper, fluent in handling, confident in design (two are here illustrated[1] [Plates 160, 161]). So Italianate are they in feeling that we can hardly believe they were done anywhere but in Italy—not necessarily in Rome, if we are correct in guessing that he has appealed for help to Piazzetta. In the last of the series[2] [Plate 228] dating from about 1780, when memories of Rome were fading and the art of the Netherlands was creeping back to take its place, we find ourselves once more in the world of Gerrit Dou, for whom Wright had had the impudence to express admiration when on sacred Italian soil; even though in the interval since his youth he may have gained, through contact with the South, a greater breadth of vision. The sitter, a certain John Stavely, was again used as a model for Wright's *Philosopher by Lamplight* [Plate 226], a subject piece of about the same date in the spirit of the *Alchemist* and the *Hermit*. This Dou-like figure, seated in a Gothic chair in sharp perspective with a globe behind him,[3] executing a pincer movement with forefinger and thumb, could never be mistaken for a Southerner. Yet the way he holds up his folio volume, that sleeve silhouetted against a white page on which the light falls from the lamp concealed behind the looped curtain—here we are reminded, just as much as we are of Dutch genre, of Ribera and Luca Giordano, and made to realise that the experience Wright had acquired in the South had not all been lost.

There is no object in entering at length at this stage into the question of Wright's subject pieces from 1783 onwards. His activity in this field for a decade or so (when it ceases altogether) is so closely bound up with his patronage by Wedgwood and Boydell, and with his dependence for choice and treatment of subject-matter on his sponsor Hayley, that it seems more sensible to postpone discussion of the whole topic to later chapters dealing with patronage and his preoccupation with literary themes. Meanwhile we shall confine our observations to a few isolated points of style.

It is understandable that his two paintings of 1783–4 on classical themes, the *Corinthian Maid* or the *Origin of Painting* [Fig 82] and its companion *Penelope unravelling her Web* [Plate 242] should be the most classical in style, though even here there are strong romantic elements: in the *Origin of Painting*, the Gothic arch framing a moonlit landscape, as anti-classical as the background to the *Alchemist* [Plate 106] or *William and Margaret* [Plate 241]; in the *Penelope*, the light issuing as usual from a hidden source so as to increase the dramatic

Fig 82 *The Corinthian Maid* 1783–84
42 x 50 in / 106.7 x 127 cm
Mr and Mrs Paul Mellon, U.S.A.
Cat 224   Pl 245

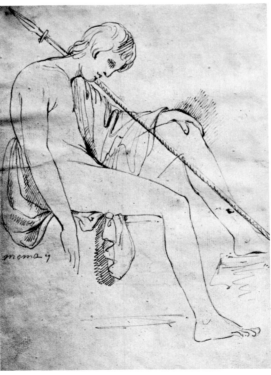

Fig 83 *Endymion* From Wright's 1774 Sketchbook   British Museum

Fig 84 David Allan *Origin of Painting: The Corinthian Maid* 1775
15 x 12 in / 38.1 x 30.5 cm   National Gallery of Scotland, Edinburgh

effect, and catching the profile and upraised arm and spear of the statue of Odysseus, Penelope's reddish-mauve draperies, the feverish limbs and unmade bed of the boy Telemachus, the gloomy recess and urn to the left. All the same Wright never produced another picture so uncompromisingly neo-classic as the *Origin of Painting*,[1] where two figures are flattened into a narrow plane in front of a bare wall, accompanied by Wedgwood jars as austere and undecorated as themselves. It is hard to see how the art of painting could be pushed further in the direction of relief sculpture than this. We are not surprised to learn that the figure of the sleeping youth is based directly on an antique relief, the *Endymion* in the Capitoline Museum, which Wright had sketched from memory in 1774 [Fig 83], had kept by him all these years, and now at last found an opportunity to re-use.[2] When we contrast his version with the other so-called Neo-Classic pictures on the same theme which preceded it, the Alexander Runciman at Penicuik House of 1771, and the David Allan in the National Gallery of Scotland of 1775 [Fig 84], both give the impression of being downright playful. No doubt Wright borrowed his general idea from David Allan.[3] But how decorous he is in comparison to Allan! How much barer his wall!

His two other pairs of subject pieces belonging to this period, the scene from *Comus* [Plate 246] and the *Indian Widow* [Plate 247] are literary in inspiration (though no precise literary source for the latter has been traced) and therefore remind us most vividly of earlier illustrations to literature where sad ladies play the principal role: the two versions of *Maria* of 1777 and 1781 [Plates 184, 220]. Like all his contemporaries Wright instinctively matched style to subject-matter; selecting classical forms for classical subjects, as in the *Origin of Painting*; Gothic forms for Gothic poems, as in *William and Margaret* [Plate 241]; classicism tempered by melancholy for ballads, Milton and the contemporary literature of sensibility, as in *Edwin*, *Maria* and *Comus*—all within the space of a few years. It was possible then—and of how many periods in the history of art can the same be said?—for an artist to practise without any sign of strain several different styles concurrently depending on his theme, since he was living in an age of artistic anarchy when anything from the most austere Neo-Classicism to the most outrageous Neo-Gothic was permissible. Yet even granting the fact that the intellectual climate was congenial, how are we to explain that a single human being should be capable both of the *Origin of Painting* and of *William and Margaret*, both of the *Dead Soldier* and the late views of Vesuvius, both of '*Christopher Heath*' and of *William Hayley?* We tend to label people as one thing or another, and expect them to stick to the rôle we allot to them, refusing to give them sufficient credit for flexibility, forgetting that so often the man in the office has a hidden streak of romanticism in his nature, and a man habitually living in the clouds will surprise us with his common sense. A business-executive will own an inaccessible island off Skye, and a poet a well-regulated washing machine. Wright was one of those not uncommon characters who will allow, now one, now another side of his personality to rise to the surface, and will not hesitate to give either its head, because to him there is no fear, no consciousness even, of self-contradiction. It is only in some such way that the romantic classicism of *Comus* and the *Indian Widow* can be suitably accounted for, following fast on the heels of strict classical themes. Two ladies sit deserted in the open air within sight of the sea. That old obsession, light, continues to haunt Wright's imagination and is used here to produce effects new to art. The young lady from *Comus* is startled by a sable cloud turning forth her silver lining to the night, and casting a gleam over the tufted grove. Behind the Indian Widow is a funeral pyre on the top of a hill, this time a man-made volcano in eruption; and through a break in the cloud, incongruous in the midst of the lightning, is a dazzling gap, for which no parallel can be found in British painting before the age of Turner.

In the process of defining Wright's vein of fantasy running through his depiction of fantastic events we had almost lost sight of the fact that when called upon he could also transform himself into a realist, and had indeed been engaged throughout these years on a series of realistic portraits far removed in spirit from the subject pieces; so that when inspired to paint an imaginary scene that might nevertheless occur in actuality, such as that provided for him by a vignette in Langhorne's *Country Justice*, he knew how to take realism also in his stride, or at any rate a sentimentalised brand of it.[4] His *Dead Soldier* from Langhorne [Fig 85], one of the pictures for which he was most famous in his day, shows a soldier

1 The author is quite legitimately quoted by David Irwin in *English Neoclassical Art...*, London, 1966, p. 79, note 5 as maintaining that the picture in the Mellon Collection is a copy of a lost work. Since then he has had the opportunity of restudying it at Yale and has concluded that it is probably the damaged original. It still does not make a satisfactory impression.

2 The source was traced by Miss Elaine Loeffler (see Rosenblum, 1957, p. 284 and Fig 7). Her identification is all the more convincing in view of the existence of the drawing in the British Museum sketchbook, which she evidently did not know.

3 If he did not know it in the original, he could have been familiar with Cunego's engraving of 1776. It is always assumed that David Allan received a prize for this picture in Rome in 1773. In fact he won the Gold Medal and first prize in the Concorsi Balestri in that year for his *Departure of Hector* (still in the collection of the Academy of St. Luke). The *Origin of Painting* dates from two years later. The author is indebted to Basil Skinner for clarifying this point. Wright must also have known an engraving of 1771 by Ravenet after Mortimer, or Mortimer's own drawing which shows the scene by lamplight. The lamp in Mortimer's composition is concealed by a looped curtain.

4 Only one representation of the scene before Wright has been traced: an aquatint by Henry Bunbury of 1783 (see Rosenblum, 1962, p. 25) but in this author's opinion Wright owes nothing to it.

Fig 85 *The Dead Soldier* 1789
40 x 50 in / 101.6 x 127 cm
James Ricau Cat 240 Pl 281

1 A close parallel is Smirke's illustration to *The Merry Wives of Windsor*, Act I, Scene I.

2 It is not being seriously suggested that Wright owed his figure of Romeo to the Michelangelo. The mention of the *Tityus* drawing is simply in order to indicate Wright's characteristic decision, when confronted with a grand Renaissance theme, to treat it in the Renaissance manner.

lying dead in the foreground beneath a tent hastily rigged up between branches of trees, while the battle continues to boom away in the distance, and his widow clutches his wrist and turns her head away in tears, and their baby aimlessly and unconcernedly wraps a fat fist around its father's fingers. Here was an episode belonging to real life that deserved to be treated realistically; and Wright does not disappoint us, with his soldier lying in steep perspective on the ground, taking up the pose of the *Dead Asiatic* from that eccentric angle he had once noted down in his sketchbook showing nothing of the head but the hair, his right arm twisted in agony behind his back [Fig 86]. It only goes to show that in Wright's mind there was nothing remote about Roman sculpture. It was just as much charged with emotion for him as a soldier of his own day dying on the field of battle. It would never have occurred to anyone to make such a remark in the eighteenth century, since it was then true of any decent painter. It is worth saying today because it is true of none.

But naturally enough in his illustrations to Shakespeare realism was not the appropriate idiom, and the element of fantasy is here reintroduced. In his scene from *The Tempest*, for example [Plate 299] Prospero, Ferdinand, Miranda and other minor characters perform their act in a cave such as Wright had once visited near Salerno and had used as a framework for several landscapes—that is to say, an actual cave but treated as though it were a setting for a dream; and the posturing figures are also dream-like, quite untypical of Wright, painted within a few months of his portrait of *Sir Richard Arkwright* [Plate 323], yet nobody relying on stylistic criteria alone could ever guess that the same hand was responsible for both. He has been careful to conform to what other contributors to the Boydell Gallery (for which the picture was destined) were doing, and this explains his unprecedented approximation to an artist like Robert Smirke.[1] In his scene from *The Winter's Tale* [Plate 304] he remains more recognisably himself, purveying his own speciality of the Derbyshire landscape in spite of the setting by the sea, introducing a snapped tree trunk in the foreground which we recall from the days of the *Earthstopper* [Plate 113]. And in the most impressive of the three, his illustration to *Juliet in the Tomb* [Plate 305] we are again on familiar ground, recognising the setting for *Miravan* [Plate 107] and the *Captive from Sterne* [Plate 162] and noting his preference for a triangular grouping of figures, but this time Wright has taken advantage of his large canvas to spread himself, to give Juliet the *Gladiator's* sweep of two arms, and Romeo a hero's death in the noblest traditions of Michelangelo's *Tityus*.[2]

Wright continued to produce a few genre scenes in later years in the spirit of his early series but they are not up to the same standard. The most famous is a *Boy blowing a Bladder* [Plate 320] which has undeniable charm but none of the old strength. To judge by innumerable copies in private houses in the Midlands, now beginning to find their way on to the international market, this represented the popular conception of Wright from the nineteenth century down to the second world war. A similar work of the period but probably not painted as a pair to it, showing a girl balancing a bladder on her hand [Plate 321] is also in the Arkwright Collection. If this book has gone any way towards demonstrating that Wright was capable of higher things than this sweet confectionery, it has not been written in vain.

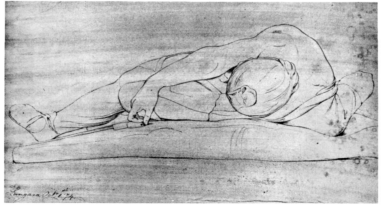

Fig 86 *Dead Asiatic* 1774 Pen on light mauve prepared paper
14¼ x 21⅜ in / 35.8 x 54.3 cm Derby Museum and Art Gallery

4 LATER PORTRAITURE

For obvious reasons, Wright gave up portraiture when he went to Rome, so there is a gap of two or three years before he took to it again; not a long time, but we might have imagined that the break would have precipitated an abrupt change in his style, especially since meanwhile he had the opportunity to observe at first hand what an artist like Batoni, with whom since the days of the *Shuttleworth* group he had some natural sympathy, was doing. But there is so little interruption that we are not always sure whether a portrait belongs to the immediate pre-, or post-Italian period. The charcoal heads of *Mr.* and *Mrs. Coltman* [Plates 119, 118] are on this borderline. We are inclined to place them about 1773 for a non-art-historical reason: Mrs Coltman's coiffure, where the hair as in Reynolds's portrait of *Mme Blanckart* at Althorp[1] is brushed high over the head, and the curls behind her ear do not break loose, as curls do later. The Reynolds is of 1771, and it is understandable that the simple Cheshire girl would catch up with the fashion within two years. This probably means that the handsome youth in Louisville, Kentucky [Plate 121] was also done just before the Italian journey: for the creases in his sleeve are defined by light as in the portrait of Coltman. The transition from these three to the portrait of *Mrs. Witts* [Fig 87] is gradual, compared to the decisive changes that were taking place in the subject pieces and landscapes of corresponding dates. We know Mrs. Witts was painted at Bath in 1776—she is the only certain Bath portrait remaining—and indeed her hair style has changed from the bunched to the straying curl, as in Reynolds's portrait of the *Countess of Harrington* at Harewood House (*c.* 1774–5).[2] She sits on a pinkish sofa dressed in light blue, propping up a book. Wright has felt ill at ease with her as he did with all his Bath sitters. His wretched and glorious insistence on honesty (which covered a very considerable range of styles, so that it was normally no handicap) did not suit a woman of her sophistication, and the result is an uncomfortable compromise between glamour and truth where glamour alone was desired by sitter and truth alone by painter. But she is saved from banality by a stiff veil sticking up of its own accord, by a kerchief over her head as decorative as that worn by the Kentucky youth, and by strings of pearls—all opportunities for those globules of light collecting on their surfaces which had delighted Wright ever since he sat the Carvers in front of him. In 1779 she was joined on the wall to her right by her husband, but since by this time Wright was back in Derby the Wittses were obliged to call in Romney, who did his best to accommodate himself to Wright's off-centre pose, and even paid his predecessor the compliment of switching Mr. Witts's buttons on like a torch [Fig 88].

Throughout this survey of later portraiture we shall often be conscious as we were before that success or failure depends above all on the amount of sympathy Wright was capable of extending to a sitter. If it is claimed that this is true of all portrait painters except the most obsequious or the most gifted, we can add that in his case more than in that of others,

1 Waterhouse, *Reynolds*, 1941, Plate 138.

2 Waterhouse, *op. cit.*, Plate 164.

Fig 89 'Elizabeth Kennion, Mrs Smyth'
c 1776–78
30 x 25 in / 76.2 x 63.5 cm
W. R. Kennion   Cat 131   Pl 188

Fig 90 George Romney *Miss Vernon as Hebe* 1777
38¾ x 40 in / 98.4 x 101.6 cm
G. & N. de Uthemann

1 To do Wright justice, it must be emphasised that the heads of both Kennion girls are suspect, especially that of *Mrs. Hall* who has suffered considerably.

2 Ward and Roberts, 1904, I, illus, opp. p. 45; II, p. 162. From the Collection of the Earl of Warwick; sold Sotheby's, 23rd November, 1966 (75).

sympathy meant deep understanding of what a sitter stood for in the world. If he held any ambiguity, Wright was not above making a hash of his features. So long as he was a friend, or so long as his social or intellectual situation within a known framework could be grasped, Wright knew how to turn his body into art without losing track of the body's substance in the process. Mrs. Witts represented an alien world of fashion and frivolity, who sat perhaps grudgingly, *de haut en bas*, to an anonymous provincial painter. With Erasmus Darwin's brother and sister-in-law [Plates 176, 177] he was on equal terms, of the same standing and culture, at ease with them in life and therefore in art. And though we do not know who he was, we suspect the young man in Kentucky [Plate 121] was either a friend or someone who commanded the painter's instant respect. If we knew nothing of his relations with the young *Thomas Gisborne* [Plate 191] we could guess that his sympathy for him extended further than that captivating embroidery on the sleeve of the scholar's gown, though this would have sufficed, as it sufficed for the young *Fitzwilliam* [Plate 49] to engage the interest of a specialist in light; in fact, Gisborne became one of his most intimate friends. This was also the case with Hayley and his wife, as we might have been able to tell in the presence of their marvellous portraits [Plates 182, 183]. His understanding of Hayley's background and status as a neo-classic poet has induced him to clamp his sitter down like a plaque on to his oval. He has taken the dangerous route beyond what the casual eye sees in order to express an idea, but at the same time never loses sight of the real man. He does the same for the poet's wife, but in her case it was not a question of finding a visual equivalent for the neo-classic couplet but of hinting at some strangeness in her make-up and background. Had rumour reached him of her mother's insanity, or was she herself already showing signs of mental derangement? The painter is the first outsider to spot it.

The portrait of *Mr. Witts* must have been the one occasion when Romney felt called upon to bow to Wright. Generally it was the other way round. As Wright drew closer to Hayley, he began to profit from the lesson of Hayley's friend Romney as well. The first trace of this is in *Mrs. Darwin and her Child* of 1776 [Plate 177] which appears to owe part of its inspiration to Romney's famous *Mrs. Carwardine and her Child* of the previous year, and part to recent contact with Italian High Renaissance *Madonnas*. In a series of female portraits of about 1777 Wright owes more to Romney than ever before or after. This was the year of the first of his two *Marias* [Plate 184] and the portraits begin to take on Maria-like, which is as much as to say Romney-like, characteristics. We hesitate to discuss *Mrs. Hodges* [Plate 189] who has bequeathed no more substantial a legacy than a poor photograph, but she looks the earliest of the group. The two girls of the *Kennion* family [Fig 89, Plate 187], one of whom married a *Mr. Hall* [Plate 186], and *Mrs. Beridge* [Plate 192], could convincingly have had Romney labels fixed to their frames, at a time when Romney was the more sought after of the two, but it would have been necessary to mask the light on the fingers and wrists of the Kennion girls in order to hide their Derbyshire origin from the trained eye, and to paint out the signature on *Mrs. Beridge*. Wright was not at home with the Kennion and Hall families,[1] though he has exerted himself to convey the toughness of Mr. Hall's personality. He may have leant too heavily on Romney to his own detriment. When we compare them to a relevant Romney, for example to the portrait of *Miss Vernon as Hebe* of 1777[2] [Fig 90], we can understand that this brand of sweetness did not become him. In *Mrs. Beridge*, on the other hand, he remains imperishably himself even when subjected to Romney's full pressure.

A series of portraits of distinguished middle-class citizens, mostly from Derbyshire (though Lynford Caryl [Plate 202] was Master of Jesus College, Cambridge, and the Rev. Thomas Seward [Plate 230] Canon Residentiary of Lichfield Cathedral) extends from about 1777 to the early '80's. The course of his style can be plotted with accuracy from *Flint* [Plate 196] to *Whitehurst* [Plate 227]; it charts an heroic journey of sensibility controlled by hard work. The portrait of *Flint* has survived in such immaculate condition that it can be read with no difficulty. The handling, as tight as in *Gisborne*, seems to place it earliest in the group, though *Pickering* [Plate 197] is a candidate for first place. These two were probably followed by *Henry Richmond* [Plate 198] and the unknown young man in the Gallery at Manchester [Plate 200] whose fingers take on the abstract quality of still life. Knuckles, like Mrs. Witts's, are studied for their own sake as shapes brought alive by light. Wright will seize on accessories or small details of apparel—on the tassels on Flint's coat or Pickering's cap, on the patterned buttons of Richmond's *sfumato* navy blue coat, on the leaves of a book or a polished table or the reflection of one in the other, on a stock or a cuff, and let the sun play over them so that light and shade can define their ins and outs as well as the material of which they are composed, and bring them to life. No background is without its glimmer of light. All shapes are explored with relish from end to end. Whereas Fragonard will swoop like a swallow over a face, Wright will crawl across it like a tortoise, registering every dent and bump. However, with him a face is but one element in a design; it is not the pivot on which all else hinges; he will crawl over a body also; Flint's tassels are as scrupulously studied as his eyes. Many portrait painters would have rested content, once they had captured Pickering's splendid ugliness, to leave the rest of him a suggestion of form to be filled in by the mind, but Wright goes on from his face to investigate with equal ardour the light on cap and scroll, and to make every inch of him solid as though he were a bust in the round, liberated from stone. He does not care to fall back on the portrait painter's shorthand—those seductive squiggles that serve for modelling—but must always insist on what is there.

Fig 91 Copy of a lost Wright *Maria Boothby* c 1780   30 x 25 in / 76.2 x 63.5 cm Sir Hugo Boothby, Bt   See p. 182

Fig 92 *Mrs Samuel Crompton* c 1780 30 x 25 in / 76.2 x 63.5 cm   Colonel Sir John Crompton-Inglefield   Cat 47   Pl 207

Three portraits belonging together take us down to about 1780: '*William Chase*', *Lynford Caryl* and *Samuel Crompton* [Plates 205, 202, 206]. Caryl in his bright red gown reflects no credit on the artist; he has tried to make up in light effects for his failure to establish a satisfying rhythm. The pose adopted by '*Chase*' takes a long journey back to Hudson and beyond. It served its purpose in 1760 for *Bennett* [Plate 30] and some of the *Wilmot Children* [Plates 9, 10, 13], but now is used with complete assurance to stand for dignity and calm. *Crompton* is one of the finest of all his half-lengths. Though we have been insisting on the abstract quality of this series—on Wright's habit of dealing with the human body as though it were a piece of machinery, every nut and bolt of which had to be scrutinised to make sure that it was in proper working order—the portraits of Crompton and his wife [Plate 206, Fig 92][1] as well as those of Pickering and Richmond, show how careful we have to be not to underrate his power to bring out character. *Thomas Seward* [Plate 230] can also hardly be described as characterless; and as for the paunchy '*Harrison*'[2] [Plate 199], how alive he comes with his shrewd eyes and sulky mouth! The last in the series, *John Whitehurst* [Plate 227] is looser in handling than any of the others, and perhaps slightly later, but there is no corresponding loosening of tension. The geologist Whitehurst is shown with a drawing of the strata of Matlock High Tor on his desk and a volcano in eruption in the back-

1 The reproduction here of a portrait of *Maria Boothby* [Fig 91] in conjunction with that of *Mrs. Crompton* [Fig 92] proves that the former is a copy of a fine lost work of this period, when Wright was also painting her brother [Plate 219]

2 *Pickering* and *Harrison* are placed, like other dubious sitters discussed in Chapter I, in inverted commas because we do not quite know who they were. It is therefore not possible to explain the significance of the geometrical figure at which Pickering points, though from our knowledge of similar 'props' in other portraits, we can be reasonably sure it was his own invention.

1 See below, Part III, p. 116.

2 Another half-length portrait in this series, that of *Samuel Ward* [Plate 229], though listed in the Account Book among pictures of 1781, seems to be looser in handling and may be slightly later. However, it cannot be far separated in date from the *Rev. Henry Case* of 1782 [Plate 223].

3 Waterhouse, *op. cit.*, Plate 130.

ground. The significance of these particular accessories will be explained in detail in due course.[1] We must emphasise at this stage that the links between objects and their owners is anything but tenuous, that their introduction is far from being a pretext for a display of skill in still life painting. The books people carry about with them may imply no more than that they are reasonably cultivated (though even to this rule *Brooke Boothby* [Plate 219] and '*Stephen Jones*' [Plate 268] are exceptions). But objects of a more specific character invariably hold a precise meaning, and if we fail to catch it, as in the case of *Pickering*, that is because the necessary information is lacking. Wright instinctively associates each sitter with his profession or class, and whatever he holds or displays before him are the symbols of his standing or attainments, as they were to the Dutch group portraitists on whom he modelled his style. The mathematician Pickering is inseparable from his diagram; the banker Crompton is committed to his scribbled note; Whitehurst's clever, brooding eyes would be inexplicable without the proud drawing under his hand.[2]

Intellectuals, scholars, heads of banking firms have their appropriate appendages, and so sometimes do industrialists. *Francis Hurt* [Plate 204], the founder of a prosperous mining business in Derbyshire, exhibits a lump of his own iron ore on the table. As usual when Wright is faced with power unaccompanied by social refinement, he allows the conventions of portrait painting to go by the board—a sacrifice that would be out of the question when undertaking commissions on behalf of public men in more sedentary, urban occupations; with the result that he achieves with men of coarser fibre a directness of vision almost without parallel in the art of his day. Though *Charles Roe*, the silk and copper manufacturer with other industrial enterprises to his credit, carries none of the symbols of his success, he could never be mistaken for the head of a Cambridge College [Plate 201]. If we did not happen to know who was the author of this portrait, we might have settled for an unknown *peintre de la réalité* (of the Macclesfield School, since this is where Roe lived) who had never bothered to acquire the tricks of the trade. For art as we have come to understand it from Wright's near-contemporary portraits of *Flint*, '*Harrison*' and *Crompton* [Plates 196, 199, 206] is gloriously banished in order to leave this hunk intact, seated too low on its canvas 'for art'; with those crafty button eyes, that graceless shoulder and that limp arm which make about as much attempt to seduce us as that seedy wig. A rude thing called a nose pokes out from a pudding face. Just as a writer like Sterne will throw literary artifice to the winds in order to call a spade a spade, so Wright when the appropriate moment presents itself, will defy the conventions of his own profession in order to paint a nose a nose.

A series of portraits of children dating from these years reveals a remarkable range of approach. The most informal are the boy and girl of the *Hope* family [Plates 180, 181]. Their parents were the artist's old friends, so he was free to paint them as they were. He was also a close friend of the father of the *Pickford Children* [Plate 185] and though he has preferred to pose these boys self-consciously mixed up with a dog to form a triangle, though the result is the opposite of a snapshot, their charm survives the ordeal. The beauty of the picture resides largely in the colouring of the children's clothes: the elder boy wears an exquisite lilac cloak over a pale yellowish-green dress and silver-white stockings; the younger, bright green with an ochre cloak. It is not possible to be so charitable towards the two sons of Francis Noel Clarke Mundy [Plate 222]. Wright could have made a success of them, had he been free to show two ordinary little boys playing at bows and arrows. But the elder one in particular, having a position to keep up as 'son of the house', is made to appear as a miniature grown-up practising the Noble Art of Toxophily, and try as he would, Wright could not bring off this kind of artifice. The admiration he felt for some Van Dyck children in Turin was for an achievement he must have known was beyond him. The idea for the Mundy children had perhaps come to him from Reynolds's *Viscount Sydney and Col. John Dyke Acland*,[3] but these were genuine adult archers who meant business, and to transfer their gestures to children without making allowances for childishness is to court disaster. The *Synnot Children* [Plate 221] deserve the same strictures but in their case, not on account of misplaced solemnity but sugariness. As with the *Pickford* group they are bunched together in the centre to form a triangle, surrounding not a dog but a wicker birdcage of ingenious construction, on which Wright has lavished his affection for the interplay of struts and perches in sunlight, as he once did in the *Chase* double portrait [Plate 50]. In front of the

Pickford group the eye seeks out the delicate *tempietto* drenched in light, peeping through the trees. In the presence of the *Synnots*, the eye is unable to settle for long on these simpering faces but must seek a resting-place in the lucidity and poetry of the cage.

Since we are on the subject of children, we may as well complete the survey down to the end of Wright's life. It is hard to account for the difference in approach between the group portraits of the *Leaper* and *Wood* children [Plates 243, 279]. To our eyes the first has breath-taking spontaneity and charm, the second is laboured and pedantic; though no doubt the kind of differentiation we make, even had it been apparent in the eighteenth century, would not have carried with it a value judgement. (It is not so much that one generation sees what another does not see, but that different points at different times seem to be worth raising.) We have too little information of the kind we need about Leaper and Wood *pères* but from our experience of other group portraits, it does not seem too daring to suggest that Wright was more at home with the Leapers than with the Woods. The *Thornhill Children* [Plate 278] stand half-way between the two. It is instructive to contrast these young cricketers (Gentlemen, not Players) with Copley's portrait of *Richard Heber* of about seven years earlier.[1] Accustomed as we are to Wright's realism, we think of the Thornhill boys as glamourised. But when we contrast them Copley's boy is the prince in the fairy tale: Wright's boys, the poor relations the prince befriends. Once again we find ourselves turning away from the younger boy's face to gaze in admiration at the bails he is about to fit on to the improvised stumps. For though Wright knows how to ape efficiently the picturesque portraiture then in vogue in the capital, it was not his *métier*, and so we cling with affection to these fragments of still life where he remains inimitably himself. The less said about *Miss Sally Duesbury* the better [Plate 337]. More rewarding is the portrait of *Richard Sacheverell Bateman* [Plate 336] though even here the stiffness and sentiment are disconcerting in an artist who ever since early youth had made the spontaneity of children his speciality. It has the same proto-Victorian touch as Banks's contemporary monument to Penelope Boothby in Ashbourne Church. The picture is saved by a discarded pale blue hat lying beside a child's book on the ground. No detail is more exquisite than this in the whole of Wright's late portraiture.

This survey of portraits of children (from which we have omitted the grandchildren of Sir Richard Arkwright [Plates 328, 329] who will be discussed later in connection with the mill owner himself) has carried us down, with *Miss Duesbury* and *R. S. Bateman*, almost to the close of Wright's life, and we can note in passing, what will probably have become apparent from the order in which the plates are arranged in this book, that as he adopts the current metropolitan conventions for sentimentalising children, so the forms become almost as generalised and summary as they do in the work of Hoppner. We must retrace our steps to the late '70's to discuss a series of greater interest and quite different character, the three-quarter-length and full-length portraits, single and in groups, which occupied his attention until about 1782 when he began to concentrate on subject pieces and landscapes in preparation for his one-man exhibition. This was a high point in Wright's career as a portrait painter (1776–81), as we have had reason to observe from a study of the busts and half-lengths ranging from the ovals of the *Hope* children and the *Hayleys* to *Whitehurst*, and as impressive a series in its own convention as the Liverpool portraits of the late '60's had been in theirs—provided we are prepared to overlook some partial failures such as the *Kennion* family, the *Mundy Children*, *Mrs. Witts* and *Lynford Caryl*.

There are no obvious failures among the three-quarter-lengths. The first is a fine portrait of *Richard Cheslyn* [Plate 190] of 1777. He is dressed in pale grey, lighter in tone even than the grey dress worn by his successor *Robert Holden* [Plate 193], and is seated on a dark green chair before a table laden with vellum-bound books. Wright was given the commission shortly afterwards to paint companion pieces of two friends, Robert Holden of Darley Abbey and John Whetham of Kirklington, while Romney who at this period (1777–9) has been intermittently flitting in and out of Wright's life, was asked to paint a third friend, Lord Middleton of Wollaton. The intention was that each of the three friends should receive versions of each portrait. It appears that Wright indeed painted three portraits of each of his two sitters, but only one of *Holden* has been traced: the prime original remaining in the family collection [Plate 193]. The original of *Whetham* in fancy dress[2]—he wears a bottle-

1 Jules D. Prown, *John Singleton Copley...*, Cambridge (Mass.), 1966, Vol II, Plate 424.

2 Christopher Hussey in *Country Life*, 5th May 1923 informs us that Whetham is represented in the fancy dress he wore at a ball at Clumber. Hussey may have had access to documents preserved at Nuthall Temple which are unknown to us. He and Lord Middleton married sisters, the Misses Chadwick of Kirklington.

1 For further details about portraits of Holden, Whetham and Middleton, see under HOLDEN in the *catalogue raisonné*.

2 It was Mr Brinsley Ford who suggested this portrait in his own collection as a possible source for the Wright.

3 Prown, *op. cit.* II, Plate 484.

4 The portrait of *Joseph Greenway* by Jens Juel in the National Gallery is a late example (1788) of the same tradition.

5 Waterhouse, 1953, p. 209.

Fig 93 Rev d'Ewes Coke, Detail from portrait group of *Coke Family*
Cat 40   See Pl 226

Fig 94 Daniel Parker Coke; Detail from portrait group of *Coke Family*
Cat 40   See Pl 226

green jacket and canary-yellow waistcoat and carries a spear—also survives in the Whetham family collection [Plate 195] as well as Wright's own copy in the Holden Collection [Plate 194].[1] In the first Whetham clasps a dog; in the second he rests his hand on a ledge. Perhaps Holden, when he came to discuss his version, found the dog objectionable and insisted on its removal. But there is nothing to choose in grandeur between the two. Another similar portrait (although preserving more of the Highmore tradition) is of *Robert Bakewell* [Plate 208], shown in black against a green shelf containing books (reminiscent of the background of the *Orrery*), and a reddish-brown curtain, contrasting with his ruddy complexion. But the most remarkable of all, to which nothing in Wright's entire œuvre as a portrait painter is superior, is the figure of an elderly man thought to be a certain *Christopher Heath* [Plate 209], though inevitably he has been called Doctor Johnson. All Wright's best qualities as a realist emerge here: his power to convey distinction without glossing over ungainliness; his conviction that so long as he stuck relentlessly to what he saw, art could be left to look after itself.

Brooke Boothby [Plate 219] is the only eighteenth-century English picture known showing a gentleman lying down like Venus in a wood. He has every right to be there. For he is a student of Rousseau and lovingly holds a volume of Rousseau under his gloved hand. An indoor setting for such a Child of Nature would have been an insult. The pose is not quite without precedent. A well-known tradition of portraiture stemming from Watteau and his early French imitators and transmitting itself in the middle years of the century to Gainsborough and Hayman, did not hesitate to show young men seated in informal poses under trees. This was taken up by Pompeo Batoni who probably in the early '60's showed *Sir Humphrey Morice* reclining in a landscape during a shooting party. Batoni's picture could be the prototype for *Boothby*[2] but the latter goes beyond it. Even Copley's portrait of *Thomas Lane and his sister Harriet*[3] of about 1783–8, for all its originality, does not attempt to rival Boothby in oddness. We find we have to wait till the late '80's for a true parallel: it was not until Tischbein posed Goethe in the Campagna, wearing a floppy hat similar to Boothby's and like Boothby surrounded by plants, indicating the recliners' interest in botany, that anything so eccentric was perpetrated again in portraiture.[4]

It is understandable that during this period of realism (1780–2) Wright should have wished to pose sitters in natural surroundings instead of against indeterminate dark walls, and three further portraits are of this kind. Two show the *Rev. Henry Case* and *Mrs. Morewood* [Plates 223, 224], he dressed in Van Dyck costume with something of the bearing of a Van Dyck sitter; she confronting him on a companion canvas, as *Maria* confronts *Edwin*. The third, the members of the *Coke* family [Plate 225], has been described as Wright's 'masterpiece of group portraiture';[5] showing the Rev. D'Ewes Coke in the middle with his arm around his wife's shoulder, and a distant cousin, Daniel Parker Coke, seated at the table and gazing out at the landscape. Wright has posed them in a triangular pattern around a plain garden table, like the *Synnot Children* around their birdcage, yet there is nothing artificial about the Cokes. All Wright's long training as a portrait painter is summed up in this large canvas: his interest in light, expressing itself in Mrs. Coke's green dress turning to yellow as the sun catches it, and in that transparent scarf which remained his signature for over thirty years; the very different personalities of the two men [Figs 93, 94], brought out by touches to eyelids, by the slope of a brow or a mouth; the naturalness of their movements; the still life with its sunshade and portfolio where every ring and tape has its logical place in the sun; the shadow of the stick curving around Daniel Parker Coke's leg and helping to define its roundness, just as the shadow of the stick behind the lantern in the *Earthstopper* [Plate 113] plots with its jagged smudge the slope of the bank behind it; the generalised landscape, held back from clear definition so that it should not interfere with its inhabitants.

Alone among the late group portraits, the one showing *Gisborne and his wife* [Plate 269] of 1786 is comparable to the *Cokes*. We do not wish to examine the Gisbornes too closely at this stage, since their significance can only emerge when we have learnt who they were and what part they played in Wright's life. We shall content ourselves for the moment with describing what is seen. Mr. and Mrs. Gisborne rest on a bank beside some fine old oaks. The ribs of a green sunshade, like the one resting on the Cokes' table but here shielding the Gisbornes from the sun, are geared to their taut canvas with the logic and delicacy of Gothic

Revival fan vaulting. Like Daniel Parker Coke's leg and walking-stick, the curve of the portfolio under Gisborne's arm is described by nothing more substantial than the slant of the tapes' shadows. The greyhound's sharp nose against his master's left hand is studied with the lucidity of a still life by Chardin. Judging by the brownish tints of the foliage, the season is Wright's favourite, autumn. Having feasted our eyes on the surrounding details, we turn to the young married couple. Gisborne is dressed from head to foot in black satin—a far cry from the embroidery on his scholar's sleeve [Plate 191]; his black, broad-brimmed hat is propped up against the bank beside him. Mrs. Gisborne wears an olive-green dress with yellow highlights, and a dark grey-green shawl. There is even more serenity in this master-piece than in the *Coke* group, and we become aware that between the two the shadow of Wedgwood has fallen. The intervening period saw the production of the *Origin of Painting* and *Penelope* [Plates 245, 242], and we can understand why, in this second portrait, Wright should have decided to dilute his realism with the demureness that his recent experience of neo-classicism had brought him, just as in the early '70's, he had diluted the realism of the Liverpool portraits under the impact of Romney. The period of his most intense realism (after Doncaster and Liverpool) had been the five years or so straddling 1780, from *Flint* to *Coke*. From then onwards, except when he was once again confronted with industrialists for whom no other style but realism was appropriate, new elements borrowed from neo-classicism or from the 'grand manner' current in London in the late '80's, left their mark on his style.

It might seem at first that these statements were contradicted by the existence of some splendid three-quarter-length portraits of 1785–8, where it cannot be denied that Wright is continuing the portrait style he had evolved for himself several years earlier. *Thomas Pares* [Plate 270], for example, cannot have been painted before the closure of the one-man exhibition, yet it retains the forcefulness of '*Christopher Heath*'. '*Stephen Jones*' of 1785 [Plate 268] and the *Rev. Basil Beridge* [Plate 267] of about the same date remind us, not only of the portraits of *Cheslyn* and *Holden* but of the relaxed pose adopted by *Thomas Staniforth* [Plate 72] in Liverpool as long ago as 1769. But when we come to look more closely we observe a breadth of handling, paralleled by that of the *Gisbornes*, that was not apparent before. We are tempted to invent a style called neo-classic realism in order to give it a convenient classification. Moreover, '*Stephen Jones*' and *Beridge* are not so realistic as they appear at first sight, to judge by the fact that they share the same body. Is it conceivable that *Staniforth* or '*Heath*' would have consented to borrow a body from someone else? This is the only case in Wright's surviving *œuvre* where he uses the same body in the same position, leaning on the same chair, for two different sitters,[1] even going so far as to repeat the precise folds from one dress to the other, though he has been obliged out of decency to give Beridge a more reverent costume, and to furnish Jones with a table on which to rest his account books and music sheet.

The same retreat from realism can be detected in the half-length portraits and busts from the late '80's onwards, though it is hardly necessary to insist on this point, since we have al-ready seen a parallel process at work in the group portraits of children over these years: how the comparative straightforwardness of the *Pickford* and *Leaper* children give way, by the end of the ninth decade, to the romanticism of the *Thornhill* cricketers. Close in date to '*Stephen Jones*' must be the disagreeable, supposed portrait of Wright's brother *Richard* [Plate 271], and possibly slightly later, because already more romanticised, the charming study of his nephew *Richard* in naval uniform [Plate 273], the son of Wright's other brother John, resting his arm on the barrel of a cannon. We have to be careful when speaking of Wright's 'development' not to deck it out with too neat a scaffolding, since as we have often had occasion to note, he will ring the changes on style to suit every new sitter. Thus, even at an advanced age, within a few years of his death, he will still be capable of such strik-ing character studies as *Sacheverell Pole* [Plate 342] and old *Mr. Buckston* [Plate 341]; and even the late portrait of Pole's step-father *Erasmus Darwin* [Plate 338] retains a certain asperity (though not as much as the subject deserved). But in general it is fair to claim that in late middle age Wright viewed his sitters through more benign spectacles than ever before. The *Woods* [Plates 276, 277] and the *Hollands* [Plates 274, 275] have a softness and sweetness that would have been anathema to *Crompton* or '*Chase*'; and as for *Mr. and Mrs. Fox* [Plates 340,

1 As we have seen (pp. 27–8), he did, however, in his very early years, take over costume patterns from Hudson.

1 An outline drawing after the antique in the Derby Art Gallery dated 12th March 1774 shows a young woman resting her elbow on a pillar, in a meditative pose. It is, however, not the specific source of *Dorothy Gell*.

2 Collection the Rev. Gregory Page-Turner; on loan to the City Art Gallery, Birmingham in the early 1960's.

3 See below, Part III, pp. 162 ff.

339] we can imagine them performing no more exacting a task than presiding over a tea table. This, unfortunately, was the direction Wright's art was taking, away from the heroic towards the cosy and the domestic, not only in portraiture. For even when faced with the majestic scenery of hills and lakes in Westmorland, he could make nothing of them but a tame mirage.

Two pictures of greater significance from the late '80's remain to be considered. *Dorothy Gell of Hopton* [Plate 266] is shown dressed like Mrs. Gisborne in olive-green, meditating beside a tomb on which are the words 'Sacred Friendship', separated from one another by a plant. She dates from the same year as the *Gisborne* group but her neo-classic origins are more thinly veiled. Though during his Italian journey Wright had sketched antique statuary on the theme of meditative women,[1] we do not have to look further than Romney's portrait of *Anna Seward* and other similar melancholy ladies of the '80's, to realise that Wright has taken over a popular fashion that suited his post-exhibition mood. The other is *Lady Wilmot and her Child* of 1788 [Plate 280] which is so much in need of cleaning that a description becomes necessary. A now almost obliterated column on the left descends to a plinth over which the curtain is draped. The curtain tassels fall to the ground at Lady Wilmot's feet. On the left is a cradle with a sophisticated classical ornament—in the same style as the stool on which Lady Wilmot sits—with above it a hood over which drapery is slung. The lady has just seized up her child, and the sheets and pillows are left in disarray. Light meanders over bedclothes and comes to settle on Lady Wilmot's blue draperies and on the edge of the stool. Wright himself described his picture as 'Lady Wilmot & her Child as a Madona', and no doubt he had in mind similar themes by or from the circle of Rembrandt where the Holy Family is enclosed in a domestic setting, and where soft light plays over cradle clothes. But he was also following a contemporary fashion: Cosway's portrait group of *Lady Francis Page-Turner and her son Gregory Osborne*[2] dated the previous year shows the mother lighting up the cradle to reveal the child; the cradle is similar; and she makes the Carracci gesture of silence as the child sleeps.

No account of Wright's late portraiture is complete without consideration of a group of portraits of industrialists painted around 1790. The best and most famous are of *Arkwright* and *Strutt* [Plates 323, 324]. There are two others, less successful, of the *Oldknow* brothers [Plates 334, 335]. But since the style of these pictures is so closely bound up with their subjects, it seems more sensible to postpone consideration of them until the problem of industrial progress in Derbyshire comes to be discussed.[3] The portraits of *Arkwright* and *Strutt* show that even at this late stage, he was capable of pulling himself together when the opportunity arose, and of producing two of the finest, most realistic portraits of his whole career; but by that time, nothing but industry could drag him back on to his true course.

5 ITALIAN LANDSCAPE

Though landscape occupies large areas of the *Earthstopper*, the *Hermit* and the *Old Man and Death* [Plates 113, 105, 123] Wright had had little experience of landscape painting before leaving for Italy. Only one pure landscape dating from before the Italian journey is known [Plate 112] and there can have been few others. From the examples that survive we are amazed by the audacity of these early experiments—how the pigment in the night scenes is slashed on, and how the surface is brought alive by dabs of frosty highlights on rock and tree trunk, and on pools and rivers craftily placed so as to catch the reflections of the moon, and how the trees shake like harridans their stark limbs at the night sky. In the one pure landscape, showing a waterfall among rocks in his native Midlands, uninhabited except for three tiny *banditti* armed with spears, no attempt is made to tidy up the barbarity of nature, but the vision is rushed down on to canvas in all its incoherence, and yet makes a coherent picture. Wright had noted similar effects in the landscapes of Salvator Rosa he had inspected in English private collections,[1] but the decorum of contemporary art is brushed aside in order to preserve the wildness intact. Nothing in his own work is quite comparable to this, and we recall few examples of the kind in British painting before the early nineteenth century. In this way Wright was sometimes able to steal a march on his fellow-artists: by shutting himself up in Derbyshire he defied the conventions and captured shapes that only enter the mainstream of English romantic painting at a later date.

Then all of a sudden the South is upon him in its warmth and serenity and his attitude to landscape alters. It is true that when he climbed to the summit of Vesuvius during an eruption the old exuberance came stealing back. But for the time being he is placid. Alexander Cozens[2] replaces Rosa in his heart. From the moment he lands at Nice he responds to the softness of the hill's contour [Plate 143]. As he proceeds southwards to the Campagna the majesty of stone pine and cypress guarding the classical villa over the garden wall takes hold of him, and he produces a classical drawing in the spirit of Breenbergh [Plate 142]. The branches of trees lose their fury, to assume the grace of the human beings now surrounding him [Plate 148].[3] Architecture becomes no less important to him than pure landscape. In one of his most beautiful watercolours [Plate 147] he explores, as Thomas Jones would explore, an ancient brick wall with a house built high on its summit. His eye is held by famous Roman ruins with picturesque shrubbery growing like tufts of unkempt hair out of their decaying arches [Plate 149]; often by the curve of the Colosseum itself [Plate 145].[4] Here he is candidly following in the footsteps of the Dutch Italianates of the early seventeenth century; nothing could be more natural than this, in an artist brought up in the Dutch Caravaggesque tradition. None of Wright's wash drawings are superior to a group of highly finished studies of views through arches: one [Plate 150] where we are invited to contemplate, not the arch alone but the gap it leaves, where the stone has been worn

1 The kind of Rosa in which he would have been most interested is the *Landscape with a Waterfall* in Glasgow (see L. Salerno, *Salvator Rosa*, 1963, pl. 81). Paradoxically enough, the most Rosa-like pictures, such as the *Hermit*, precede the Italian journey.

2 There are references in Wright's Account Book to copies he made of Cozens, once of a blot. The drawings after Cozens are listed among pictures of *c.* 1786–8—that is, as one would expect after the publication of *A New Method*... Wright's Italian drawings seem to prove that he was already interested in Cozens in the early '70's. A note in the Account Book under the date 4th December 1773 reads: 'Rec'd of Messrs. Denby & Greenwood for Cozens drawings... £2.2.0.' This was the day before he reached Nice when he was on the high seas, but he evidently copied the entry into his book on return to England from an account his brother had meanwhile been keeping for him in Derby during his absence.

3 This is the only pure tree study (with a crouching figure drawn the other way up) among several in the Derby Art Gallery that we can be certain was done in or around Rome in 1774, since it is on the reverse of a group of figures [Plate 138] known, for its connection with another in the British Museum sketch book [Plate 139], to be a Roman drawing of that date.

4 See *catalogue raisonné* for the reference to one in the Oppé Collection. One here reproduced [Plate 145] in the Huntington Library, San Marino, is from the portfolio of drawings sold at Sotheby's, July 1966, and therefore indisputable.

1 The same Temple is shown from the other side in a watercolour by John 'Warwick' Smith in the British Museum (1936 7.4.22), illus. Martin Hardie, *Water-colour Painting in Britain— I, The Eighteenth Century*, London, 1966, Plate 97.

2 There are, however, references to pictures he proposes to paint in Italy, such as a *View of Albano* for the Duc de Chabot (see *catalogue raisonné* under 'Albano, Nemi', p. 252).

3 For a full account of *Vesuvius* and *Girandola* subjects, see Appendix B, pp. 279 ff.

4 That is, if it was ever painted, but we are not even sure of this. The project might have been abandoned for all we know.

5 The annotations on the drawing show that he was uncertain about the limits of the composition: whether or not to include the Hermitage. This was the French Hermitage on the hill around which Thomas Jones made sketches on 15th June 1781 (see Jones, 1951, p. 105). A gouache by Hackaert in the Museo di S. Martino shows the lighthouse in the same position relative to the mountain as in Tate's drawing. The head of the Mole is not visible from the angle from which Wright and Hackaert sketched the lighthouse.

6 This at any rate is the author's impression after having motored from Naples to Posillipo, photographs in hand. However, it must be admitted that the coastline has been ruined by modern villas, and by a coast road, so that it is not always easy to distinguish between what Wright saw and what he invented.

7 Letters of 25th January and 11th February respectively (Thorpe/Arundell MSS.).

away by time and neglect; another [Plate 158] where he is intrigued by the contrast between the texture of smooth stone and dappled foliage; a third [Plate 149] which should be presented for inspection to anyone who doubted whether Wright was capable of answering a classical theme with a poised design. Even Breenbergh had nothing better to offer as a draughtsman than this. On one of his walks through Rome his attention was engaged by a farm built into the ruins of an Ionic temple. Here was a theme ready-made for the author of the *Blacksmith's Shop* where work is conducted in a medieval chapel, and he has left us a superb drawing [Plate 151] as a token of his admiration for the indivisibility of the ancient and modern world, first encountered in the North and then confirmed in the South.[1]

We have seen when considering his subject pieces how he would occupy his time in Rome in note-taking, in storing up impressions in sketchbooks to be drawn on at leisure. The same is true of his Italian landscapes. He rarely set up an easel in an Italian studio but preferred to document himself on famous sites, and then on his return home, time and again to play variations on the scenes he had witnessed, almost to the year of his death. Thus Nemi and Albano, Cosimato and the coast round Salerno, lighthouses in the Mediterranean, the Girandola and Vesuvius, pepper at irregular intervals his declining days. Only two surviving landscape paintings certainly belong to the Italian period,[2] two views of grottoes in the Gulf of Salerno [Plates 174, 175] done in the autumn or winter of 1774. A second pair showing the *Girandola* and *Vesuvius in eruption* [Plates 166, 167] are presumed to have been done about the same time. But these two are on a small scale, and belong with the many drawings that exist on the same themes as part of his documentation (though he would have felt free to dispose of the paintings later) and must be treated as such. He did paint at least one large *Vesuvius* in the winter of 1774–5 which is thought to be the canvas now in the Derby Art Gallery [Plate 168], but it is the only one on this scale of which we have any tangible evidence. Since the surviving material is richest in views of Vesuvius and the Girandola[3] it will be as well to begin with a discussion of these, and then to trace the course of the other themes separately one by one from the first flush to the last distant memory.

The sketches for *Vesuvius* divide themselves into two groups: studies of the mountain done for their own sake with no composition in mind, and studies for paintings. We can imagine him clambering up the mountainside with his portfolio under his arm, perhaps with Sir William Hamilton as guide to the more dramatic climbs, edging as close to the crater as he dared, jotting down the spectacle while the going was good. A beautiful gouache in the Derby Art Gallery [Plate 163] is too spontaneous and slapdash to have been done anywhere but on the spot. A conscientious pencil study in Derby [Plate 164] must have taken him much longer, as he has set out to register every crinkle in the smooth rock face, treating it scientifically as though it were a specimen of volcanic matter to be submitted to Whitehurst's analysis, but here he has selected a safer moment, if not a safer distance, and can wait. The same goes for another belonging to Sir Gilbert Inglefield [Plate 165], this time by moonlight with a view over the still sea, where he is not so much concerned with the texture of rock, as with its wavy sweep across the foreground. Only one composition drawing is known [Fig 95], and this for a painting for his friend Tate of which all trace has been lost.[4] It shows the Mole with the lighthouse looking out towards Portici, taken from the outskirts of Naples in the direction of Posillipo.[5] The same view is repeated, only further southwestwards towards Posillipo, in his small painting in the Sanderson collection [Plate 167], done as a pair to a *Girandola* now in Birmingham [Plate 166] and therefore probably not until his return to Rome. It is understandable that as soon as he attacks a canvas he should wish to rearrange the foreground to suit his pictorial requirements (and a certain licence he allows himself in the topography[6] cannot be taken as an argument in favour of a later date); whereas in the gouache and pencil studies he sticks faithfully to the facts.

During the winter of 1774–5 he painted a large picture of the top of Vesuvius. It is described by Father Thorpe in a letter of January 1775 to Lord Arundell: 'Mr. Wright's Vesuvius is not a landscape: it represents only the summit of the mountain...'; and three weeks later he returns to the subject '...his top of Vesuvius shows more abilities in the terrible way, but does not hurt Volaire...'[7] (the reference being to a French artist who was also engaged on painting eruptions). We would expect this to represent a fearsome eruption seen from the crater, and indeed there does exist a reddish picture of a theatrical kind in the Derby Art Gallery [Plate 168] which one would not think of describing as a landscape, and which fits Father Thorpe's description admirably, showing the lava pouring over the crater and collecting in pools around the cone. It appears to date from about this period. The picture in Aberystwyth [Plate 169], though we have no knowledge of its history, must fit into the series at this stage, either late on the Italian trip or soon after his return. It shows the mountain from approximately the same angle as that of the drawing for the lost picture [Fig 95] and as that for the Sanderson canvas [Plate 167], only this time the artist has crossed the Bay and moved up to Portici. He is determined to get as close, psychologically as well as physically, to what he calls 'the most wonderful sight in nature' as is consistent with picture-making, just as he had done with his waterfall in the Derbyshire hills. Again, as in the Sanderson picture, the wan moon is half-hidden by hills on the left in the direction of Naples, the rock is sprinkled with red-hot *scoriae*, and lava races to the valley. A halo of lurid light forms around the crater as it throws up its jet of liquid, causing the dark clouds to scamper like devils to either side of it. None of this looks like emotion recollected in much tranquillity, and it can only have been done while the fever of the mountain was still upon him. We can almost see him coming round to the view that immense natural forces are uncontrollable. Implicit in the assumption he had always made back in England, that man by intelligence can govern the operations of nature, that useful phosphorus will result from a dangerous experiment, that thanks to our ingenuity a bird will struggle for breath, but recover, in its glass bowl, is the danger that something may go wrong: the fear that nature may overwhelm us and upset our calculations. To judge by his early drawings and pictures of it, when first confronted with Vesuvius he must have had sensations of this kind; not horror at the prospect of the inhabitants being burnt alive—even he fails to anticipate the concept of compassion and there is never a suggestion of a personal tragedy in any of his renderings—but the more abstract idea that nature has to be reckoned with as a force superior to reason. Later, he retreated from this idea, ending by presenting the mountain only as a picturesque spectacle in a series of reflective canvases. This withdrawal is a proof of his disinclination to pursue the implications of disaster any further. Never again, after the picture in Wales, is there the same consciousness of a threat to our security, although the remaining views of Vesuvius of the '70's continue to hint at this aspect.

Probably the next in the series, dating from about 1775–8, is a large view by moonlight with a glimpse over the sea to the right [Plate 170], in the Cade Collection near Penzance.[1] It is more contrived; but then this can be accounted for by its large scale. Though Wright has retreated some distance, the volcano is still the centre of attention. Light collects in a nervous glitter on tree trunk and mountain slope, vegetation catches fire, and smoke rises from sizzling lava at the crater's edge. It has none of the measured pace of the picture in Moscow [Plate 214], painted in 1778 as a pair to a *Girandola* [Plate 213], from a viewpoint similar to that of the Inglefield drawing, which no doubt helped him with the design. By this time all sense of urgency, of involvement, has passed; though even here the branches of the tree to the right threaten to rustle in a sinister breeze that creeps up to it across the silent valley. This is the only surviving example in which he introduces the procession of St. Gennaro's head, moving with torches through a middleground of unnatural calm, in a futile attempt to placate the monster of death. The Saint's relic is carried under a red-roofed canopy on the shoulders of four men. Sir William Hamilton, reporting on these passive resistance marchers, allows the tip of his tongue to stray to his cheek: 'In the midst of these horrors', he writes, 'the mob, growing tumultuous and impatient, obliged the Cardinal to bring out the head of Saint Januarius, and go with it in procession to the Ponte Maddalena, at the extremity of Naples toward Vesuvius; and it is well attested here, that the eruption ceased the moment the Saint came in sight of the mountain...'[2] Wright, another scientist, was no doubt of the same persuasion, but since his job was to record, not to comment, there is no hint of its absurdity in his depiction of the dignified ritual.

His views of the volcano in the '80's continue this trend towards the contrived and the evocative. One of the most poetical[3] is an oval in a private collection [Plate 233] where the hill on the right is taken over from the hill in Mr. Sanderson's little picture [Plate 167] but where there is not the same hold on reality; in fact so far does he allow himself to go

1 Wright was specially fond of this work; having refused to part with it to the Bishop of Derry, he kept it in his possession till his death, and it is still the property of one of his descendants.

2 Hamilton, 1772, p. 35, describing the eruption of October 1767.

3 The date of this picture is not exactly known, but it was sold to Dr. Beridge at the same time as a *Lake of Nemi* [Plate 234] and its companion [Plate 235], and the companion bears the date 1782 on the reverse. Stylistically this date would make good sense.

1 The lost work engraved by William Byrne showing a similar view may be a few years earlier. The small copper panels belonging to Christopher Norris [Plates 288, 289] are also evidently late, though there is no external evidence for this. They are near monochromes, in brownish-red.

2 We must however, in all honesty, record that in 1794 he painted a near view of Vesuvius for John Leigh Philips (see Appendix B, No. 18), but in its absence we are safe in assuming it was a decorative, not an horrific, work.

3 Hamilton, 1772, p. 6, describing an eruption of March 1766.

4 This is neither signed nor dated, but exactly in the style of documented examples, such as the one in the Staatsgemäldesammlungen, Munich, illus. *Il Paesaggio Napolitano nella Pittura Straniera*, exhibition catalogue, Naples, 1962, Plate II. The author is indebted to Dr. Raffaello Causa to whom it belongs, for bringing it to his attention.

5 For further details about Volaire's career, see R. Causa, *Pitloo*, Naples, 1956, p. 50.

in the direction of abstraction that he fits a frayed collar on to the hill's neck in the form of two walls, to harmonise with his oval design. Still, this is realism in comparison to the lengths was prepared to go later. In the last of all, the two pictures in the Anson and Miller Mundy Collections of about 1788–9[1] [Plate 294, Fig 99] Wright has retreated almost as far as the Capo di Posillipo, so that Vesuvius is reduced to a low hillock in the distance, lost in a pink haze behind two phantom boats. All this time he has been moving further and further away from the source of the disturbance, in spirit as well as in actual mileage. Some of his first sketches were of the top of the mountain; his first large painting was of the crater itself; Tate's picture was taken from the Mole; the one in Wales was taken from nearer still, from the eastern side of the Bay of Naples. But in the end he allows distance to add enchantment to the view, and all that remains of the awfulness of the spectacle is an exquisite reverie of pink and green.[2]

By now it should be clear that there is little object in seeking for 'influences' on Wright's early *Vesuvius* views. Although the mountain had been popular in art since the middle of the century, although several *voyages pittoresques* had been undertaken by foreigners long before he set foot on it himself, he came to it fresh from the wild Derbyshire hills, and imposed his own wild vision upon it. He alone of all visitors to Naples had witnessed and recorded blast furnaces in operation, had watched scientific experiments conducted by the light of the moon. Sir William Hamilton observed that the lava resembled 'a river of red hot and liquid metal, such as we see in glass-houses',[3] and Wright's experience of glass-houses has stood him in excellent stead. All the same, here was a new subject, and like any sensible artist he looked around to see what others had made of it. Thomas Wyck, a possible source for the *Alchemist*, may have held more than academic interest for him. Several views of Vesuvius survive from his hand, in the late *bambocciante* manner of Lingelbach, and one in particular[4] shows an eruption in progress beyond the lighthouse on the Mole [Fig 96]—the very aspect Wright selected for his picture for Tate [Fig 95]. But from his contemporaries, the one artist from whom he had anything to learn at this early stage was Pierre-Jacques Volaire (1729– c. 1802)[5] who after a period in Rome (1764–9) had settled in Naples and by 1771 (three years before Wright arrived there) had established himself as a specialist in volcanic eruptions. He was the first artist to interpret Vesuvius in the new language of picturesque romanticism,

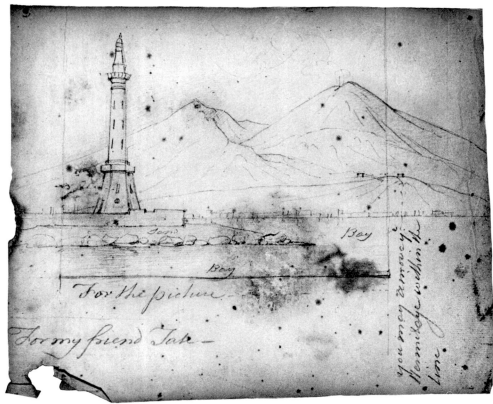

Fig 95 *Vesuvius from the Mole* 1774
Pencil $7\frac{5}{8}$ x 9 in / 19.3 x 22.8 cm   Derby Museum and Art Gallery

Fig 96 Thomas Wyck *Vesuvius in Eruption*
$23\frac{7}{8}$ x $19\frac{7}{8}$ in / 58 x 48 cm   R. Causa

Fig 97 Pierre-Jacques Volaire *Eruption of Vesuvius*
18 x 22 in / 45.7 x 55.9 cm Mrs Paulekas Rockefeller

Fig 98 *Vesuvius c* 1774–75 47½ x 67 in / 120.6 x 170.2 cm
Derby Museum and Art Gallery Cat 275 Pl 168

and a comparison of one of his close-up views [Fig 97][1] with Wright's first big canvas [Fig 98] demonstrates that, as far as we can speak of any source for Wright at all, this was it.[2] Volaire by his introduction of tourists stresses no aspect of the eruption but its sublimity—an aspect to which Wright in his turn responded; yet the very bleakness of Wright's vision goes beyond this to hint at its destructiveness and malevolent power—an attitude that did not become commonplace until the early nineteenth century. And when Father Thorpe claims that Wright does not 'hurt Volaire', to our way of thinking, with the advantage of hindsight, he does Wright an injustice. What stopped Wright on the brink of further dramatic probing is a more vexed question. The fact remains, in his later renderings of eruptions, he falls into line with the picturesque topographers. The two pictures in the Anson and Miller Mundy collections [Plate 294, Fig 99], though possibly the most lyrical, are not the most prophetic. Influences are therefore not so hard to detect at this late stage in his career. And it is obvious that he has taken his cue from Joseph Vernet who also enjoyed the spectacle of a ghost-ship silhouetted against the moonlit sky [Fig 100],[3] though Wright does not follow him in piling on the fantasy by adding to the moon and lava a picturesque campfire in the foreground.

1 The picture reproduced, belonging to Mrs. Rockefeller, is not signed or dated and may well be later, but the examples known from 1771 onwards betray a similar style.

2 Wright must also have been familiar with the drawings of volcanoes which Hamilton commissioned from Peter Fabris, an Englishman, soon after his (Hamilton's) return to Naples in January 1773, but Fabris's drawings are not very inspiring (see Hamilton, 1776, I, p. 5).

3 The picture reproduced, on the New York art market, is signed and dated 1780, but Vernet had introduced ghost ships earlier, such as in his moonlit landscape of 1767 (Dulwich College Picture Gallery) which Wright could have seen in the Desanfans Collection, and in another of 1769, sold Christie's, 29th November 1963 (68). Volaire introduces the same black

Fig 99 *Vesuvius from Posillipo* 178[?9]
40½ x 50½ in / 102.8 x 128.2 cm Major Peter Miller
Mundy Cat 267 Pl 291

Fig 100 Joseph Vernet *The Italian Coast, Vesuvius in the Distance* 1780
18¼ x 25¾ in / 46.3 x 65.4 cm M. Knoedler & Co, New York

rigging against the moon in his *Eruption of Vesuvius* of 1782 (Museo di Capodimonte; illus. *Il Paesaggio Napolitano...*, pl. VI). There are many other examples.

---

1 Hamilton, 1772, p. 8.

2 The reader is referred to the catalogue of the Exhibition *Settecento A Roma*, Rome, 1959 (1812) for not particularly relevant engravings of the 17th and 18th centuries showing the Girandola. One by Piranesi of this subject was also exhibited (No. 2217). The other engravings were re-used from time to time and redated because the character of the festivities changed so little.

3 Another pen and wash drawing shows a conflagration, perhaps caused by a stray rocket, in front of St. Peter's, of which nothing is visible behind the smoke except the Cross of the dome [Plate 159]. The date 4th June 1774 inscribed below to imitate an inscription on an engraving is a later addition, but there is every reason to suppose the drawing was done about the same time as the *Girandola* study.

4 We know this is the correct date because in a letter from Wright alongside the watercolour (see below) is a reference to his forthcoming Neapolitan trip.

5 Alongside the drawing is a mysterious letter from Wright to an unknown correspondent in Derby, explaining certain points about the design and asking for comments, from which we quote the only significant passage: '...before the Girandolo began the reflection of the Dome was seen on the water [*sic*] over the bridge the bridge being in shade but in the time of the Girandolo it was scarcely seen the water being so illuminated if you chuse to represent the Girandolo. At the finishing you may represent the Pesce which is thrown out at the same time [this is marked on his drawing issuing from the left side of the Castello]...'

'It is impossible', writes Sir William Hamilton of Vesuvius in eruption[1] 'to describe the beautiful appearance of these Girandolas of red hot stones, far surpassing the most astonishing artificial fire-work'. Yet Wright rated the Girandola from the Castel Sant'Angelo in Rome a comparable achievement, the best man could be expected to attain in tough competition with nature. He witnessed one of these festivities before midsummer 1774, and was so fascinated by it that for years he could not leave the theme alone. One would like to be better informed as to his sources for such an unusual undertaking.[2] Whereas in the case of Vesuvius, Dutchmen and Frenchmen had set their iconographic stamp on the mountain, in the case of the Girandola there was no firm pictorial tradition that went beyond mere pageantry. But there does exist an engraving with which he may have been familiar, and the fact that it was two hundred years old would not have deterred him from making use of it: this is an illustration by Ambrogio Brambilla in Lafreri's *Speculum* (1579) which shows how little the system of illumination had altered in the intervening years [Fig 101]. But of course he relied chiefly on his own notes made on the spot as he did with Vesuvius. He designed at least four distinct compositions, intending in all four cases to transform sketches into pictures. Only three paintings are now known although probably more than four were executed, and for two of these, drawings exist; for the third painting, no preliminary studies have come to light. The fourth view survives only in drawings. In order to bring some order into this confusion, it will be necessary to treat each scheme separately, even though in the process it will entail playing havoc with the chronology.

Perhaps the first is an imaginary view of the Castel Sant'Angelo in silhouette against St. Peter's, the latter lit up by the fireworks crackling away in front of it. On 4th June 1774 he made a wash drawing of this subject [Plate 154][3] but it must have been worked up in his studio from earlier studies done in the streets of Rome because he has juggled about with the topography of the city, adding the Pantheon on the left in a position from which it was never visible. Evidently it was his intention to produce a *capriccio* of Roman monuments, perhaps for the benefit of some patron who was ignorant of Rome or at any rate was indifferent to the visual impact it made, being more concerned that as many famous buildings as possible should be included. One of these early studies must have been the outline 'elevation' drawing showing a panoramic view of the Castello, St. Peter's and the Vatican from the same viewpoint [Plate 155] which although schematic, at least does not take liberties with architecture. Both drawings came to his aid when he was engaged on the painting in Liverpool [Plate 210], one by including the Pantheon, the other by showing the Cathedral from a much greater distance, from behind a hill. Nothing is known of the early history of the Liverpool picture and its dating is problematic. In style it reminds us of the Cade *Vesuvius* [Plate 170] of *c.* 1775–8; it has not reached the poise of the '80's; so a date soon after the mid-'70's seems reasonable. It is far from being one of his most inspiring works: the romance of the fireworks fails to harmonise with the niggardliness of the buildings, and one wishes that fewer windows had been given their correct architectural structure. But then Wright could never stand any ambiguity when it came to recording the works of man. We have seen how literal he could be in the presence of ancient ruins, and the same is true of his attitude to Renaissance architecture. It was only when confronted with untamed nature, and with boys fighting over a bladder, that he occasionally felt justified in letting himself go.

The next (conceived before October 1774[4]) is a view across the Tiber towards the Castel Sant'Angelo with St. Peter's in the distance on the left, where not only are the fireworks in full spate on the Castello, but the dome and façade of St. Peter's are studded with paper lanterns. A wonderful watercolour [Plate 152] is the first known sketch of this view, with another on the reverse of precisely the same view in outline in pencil [Plate 153]. He intended to work this up into a large drawing to be submitted to an unknown Derby collector, before finally transferring the composition to canvas.[5] And there may well have been a large picture of the subject for this collector which has disappeared. The canvas in Birmingham [Plate 166] based on this watercolour is unlikely also to have been intended for his Derby friend. For in the first place it is quite small, and in the second it was painted as a pair to the *Vesuvius* in the Sanderson collection [Plate 167], and therefore cannot have been in his mind till he left for Naples. Few of his small canvases are as sparkling as this, where in contrast to the picture in Liverpool, river, rockets and architecture are perfectly

Fig 101 Brambilla *Illustration of a Girandola in Lafreri's Speculum* 1579 (detail)   8 x 10 in / 20.3 x 25.4 cm
Metropolitan Museum of Art, New York, Dick Fund

Fig 102 *Girandola from the Castel Sant'Angelo* 1774–75
Pen $14\frac{5}{8}$ x $18\frac{7}{8}$ in / 37.1 x 47.9 cm   Derby Museum and Art Gallery

blended, where none of the vitality of the pre-Italian years has been sacrificed. With those reflections of fireworks in the Tiber, with that dead branch putting out feelers into the water, we are back with the *Earthstopper* [Plate 113]. The third group consists of an outline drawing [Fig 102] and a wash [Plate 156], of which no painted versions are known. Here St. Peter's is hidden behind the buildings on the left, and the artist faces the Castello, making it and the bridge the pivot of his design. Finally, for the fourth composition, we have only the large picture in Leningrad [Plate 213] dating from 1778–9 and painted some months after its pendant, the Moscow *Vesuvius* [Plate 214]. The latter had therefore to dictate what form the Girandola should take; the smoking Castello with its bright yellow halo had this time to be pushed into the distance in order to harmonize with the smoking crater; the tree had to fill the left foreground to balance its companion in Moscow on the right; the Tiber had to occupy an open space in the middle ground to match the Neapolitan valley; and the little boathouse with its delicate drawbridge proved as useful an interruption in the expanse of water as the procession of St. Gennaro's head had proved in an expanse of scrub. In the small pendants also [Plates 166, 167], Wright had carefully considered which features could be made to echo from one canvas to the other: the 'haloes' are again in the same relative positions, and a half moon in one is answered by the semi-circular dome of the cathedral in the other. In fact, in order to match its partner, the eruption in the Sanderson picture [Plate 167] has taken on the ornamental character of a firework display; the sparks shooting out of the crater with the regularity that man seeks but nature abhors.

During his trip to Naples, Wright made excursions to the Gulf of Salerno where he came on two outlandish grottoes,[1] one where the sea washed right into the cave, with a depth of water sufficient to serve as a garage for light craft, the other where sand and rock filled the entrance to the cave—a rendezvous, we can be sure, for much dubious trafficking. He made two drawings on the spot of the two interiors looking out to sea [Plates 171, 172][2] which in the early '80's he worked up into two once famous but now unknown moonlight and sunset views (formerly in the Hardman Collection; Cat Nos 279–80). The one at sunset showed a boat at anchor inside the cave. Some impression of what it must have looked like (whether an actual version or not) is conveyed by a copy of a lost Wright [Fig 103][3] where a forlorn boat waits for someone to unfurl its sails and steer it back into the open sea. Luckily two similar but unpopulated views of the same dimensions as the Hardman pictures exist, also worked up from the drawings, done before the end of 1774, one by morning, the other by evening light [Plates 175, 174]. Wright sought to avoid the mid-day sun, preferring the subtler light effects of the beginning and end of the day where pinks and blues glint on

1 They no longer exist—they are either blocked up or have crumbled—otherwise they would certainly be popular tourist resorts. There are still grottoes in this neighbourhood but as far as we have been able to ascertain, they are not the same shape.

2 The drawings are, as one would expect, more 'geological' than the paintings on which they are based, but only very slightly so: he introduced no essential changes into the later compositions, although the drawings are wider in relation to their height than the paintings are.

3 This was exhibited as an original at the Tate, 1958 (21), lent by Ralph Robotham.

Fig 103 Copy of a lost Wright
Cavern in the Gulf of Salerno
40 x 50 in / 101.6 x 127 cm
Mr and Mrs Paul Mellon

Fig 104 Sydney Parkinson *A perforated
rock in New Zealand (Tolago Bay)* 1769
Pen and wash 11¾ x 15 in /
29.8 x 38.1 cm   oval   British Museum

Fig 106 Peter Fabris *Fishing by
Torchlight in a Cavern near Naples* 1777
20½ x 25 in / 52 x 63.5 cm
Present whereabouts unknown

Fig 105 Detail from *A Grotto in the
Kingdom of Naples* Cat 277 See Pl 211

the rock surface; there are constant references in his Account Book to morning views with companions by moonlight or sunset, and several examples of such pairs besides the two cavern scenes survive. It is not easy to imagine two more Wright-like visions than these. The pelvis-shaped arch held all that was most precious to him, appealing both to his scientific and to his romantic temperament (and as we know there was no contradiction between the two): on the one hand, the logic of a firm structure of rock, geological in its fissures; on the other, the marvel of irridescent light. To his mind's content he established his solid design, and then proceeded to play about to his heart's content with colour. Just as in his early portraits he had felt free to experiment with fluttering veils and glinting pearls once he had tethered a body to a design, so here he felt free to explore the course of light as it glanced off the rock and bounded into the vault, once he had settled on his haunting shapes. What can he have had in mind? He was as familiar as we are with the grottoes that had mesmerised poetry since the days of Pope, and he must have turned over engravings extolling such preromantic habitations. He had seen pictures, no doubt, where St. George confronts the dragon at the entrance to a gaping cavern. But direct ancestors of his own grottoes were few, and what there were, were recent. It is possible that shortly before he left for Italy, an engraving came to his knowledge, published in 1773 after a wash drawing by Sydney Parkinson [Fig 104], showing a ship seen through the arch of a cavern in Tolaga Bay, New Zealand.[1] Joseph Banks when he saw it on Cook's first voyage to the Pacific in the *Endeavour* in 1768, was much struck by it:

'... we suddenly saw', he writes in his Journal, 'a most noble arch or cavern through the face of a rock leading directly to the sea, so that through it we had not only a view of the bay and hills on the other side, but an opportunity of imagining a ship or any other grand object opposite to it. It was certainly the most magnificent surprise I have ever met with; so much is pure nature superior to art in these cases...'[2]

Wright met with a similar surprise in the Gulf of Salerno, and understood the risk he was running in committing such a fantasy to the further fantasy of art.

He used the design of the dry cavern once more for his sunset view at Meynell Langley [Plate 211], painted on his return to England in the late '70's, but this time he has peopled the interior with a group of *banditti*, Mortimer's speciality. There are soldiers among them with spears, breastplates and preposterous plumed helmets, but they are not the brains of the group; they are there to carry out the orders of the civilian Mafia figure who sits brooding in the centre, half listening to the boy on the ground beside him who outlines some diabolical plan of banditry as he points out to sea [Fig 105]; while the setting sun streams into their lair, causing long spears of shadow to menace them from the pebbles, and bathing them in the soft, amber light of Adam Pijnacker. We saw how he turned to Breenbergh for help with classical ruins; now he puts on Pijnacker-tinted spectacles to gaze at caverns.

1 The engraving by J. Hawkesworth is included in *An Account of the Voyages undertaken by the Order of His Present Majesty for making Discoveries in the Southern Hemisphere*, London, 1773, 3 vols. II, pl. 17.

2 See Smith, 1960, p. 17. Wright naturally did not have access to Banks's account.

Wright never went further in romance than this. The bandits are not of this world at all but belong to the classical stage, plotting, we would say, not a routine robbery but the murder of Hector. We are reminded of a long European tradition of illustrations to classical drama, from Poussin to Gavin Hamilton, even though we may search in vain for any direct borrowing from it. It is always possible that some student of history painting will come forward with parallels to this astonishing group, but for the time being we are happy to put down our failure to trace them to Wright's originality rather than to our own ignorance. The only earlier picture known to us by another hand that bears the faintest resemblance to Wright's *Cavern with Banditti* is a scene of *Fishing by Torchlight in a Cavern*, signed by Peter Fabris, the artist who had been employed by Sir William Hamilton to make studies of Vesuvius, and dated 1777 [Fig 106]. It appears to represent the other cavern which the sea enters; but as we know from the picture at Smith College [Plate 174] Wright had fixed on his design for this three years earlier, and needed no additional instruction from Fabris.

In 1780 he used the watery cavern as a setting for his companion to the one with *banditti*, showing Julia, banished there by her grandfather Augustus [Plate 215]. Three years later the cavern reappears in another large picture on the same theme with the moon rising over the horizon (with the result that the interior became almost impenetrable), and Julia on a rock in the foreground, seated like Maria—her contemporary—bemoaning her fate. The picture is lost but in 1780 he did a small version which, if not precisely the same, must have foreshadowed this composition closely [Plate 216]. Two later landscapes of the same stretch of coast, one by moonlight, the other sunset [Plate 287], exist in the Bower and Inglefield Collections, and there are three views by moonlight of *Virgil's Tomb*,[1] two empty [Plate 231]—if one can call empty a tomb flooded with oppressive lunar light—and a third [Plate 232] with the figure of Scilius or Silius Italicus disclaiming Virgil. He was an eccentric poet living in the days of Nero and Trajan, who used to celebrate Virgil's birthday annually with ridiculous ceremony, and composed poor poems in the manner of his revered master. All three were done between the late '70's and early '80's, and so belong to a moment in Wright's career when he held a delicate balance between what actually was there, and what he liked to construct out of what was there. He may have lost his passionate involvement with stone and brickwork but there is no slackening of the inventiveness; the moon plays over the steps and lights up the tomb from inside as though it were being manipulated by some experienced stage designer. We have suggested that there is something stagy, also, about his vision of the crater of Vesuvius [Plate 158], that far from being a record of the thing seen, it could serve as a background for the witches in *Macbeth*. The *banditti* in the Meynell Langley *Cavern* are actors in a play.[2] Whether Wright had ever taken any interest in stage scenery is not known, but there are grounds for supposing that the painter William Hodges (1744–97) had designed scenery for the theatre in Derby when Wright was living there, and this might have been his introduction to it.[3] The best of all these pictures are those illustrated in Plates 231 and 287, but no doubt others were once up to this standard; only they have suffered in the course of time, one so badly (Cat No 278) that it is not even fit for reproduction. The same remarks apply to two views of the *Colosseum*, done at a high point in Wright's career from the early to the mid-'80's, with the breadth of vision of a Piranesi, and no doubt once as magnificent; but they have been so badly damaged, and so coarsely restored, that now one of them cannot be reproduced at all, while nothing but a photograph of the other before restoration, ghost though it is, can give any hint of its power [Plate 256]. This shows two figures (a tourist and his cicerone?) in the foreground admiring the sights, and its companion, a monk at his devotions before a shrine cut into the rock face, consisting of a shallow niche with inside it a crude statue of the Virgin lit up by candles. The significance for a specialist in candlelights of such a common Roman scene as this requires no emphasis.

Enough reasonably well-preserved examples remain of the romantic classicism of the early and mid-'80's to gain a clear insight into this confident phase in his career as a landscape painter. One of the finest is a *View of Tivoli* [Plate 260], the only painting of this district so far identified, although Wright has left us a beautiful watercolour of the cascade [Plate 251].[4] A view of Cosimato of 1786 [Plate 257] is followed several years later by two further exam-

1 A fourth view through an arch [Plate 296] in a collection in Milwaukee (Wisconsin) though similar in character, cannot be identified as a *Virgil's Tomb*. The style is of a later period, about 1790, and indeed the picture once bore this date which may have been genuine.

2 This encourages us to speculate as to whether Wright might have used theatre models in the manner of Gainsborough. One can imagine that an artist so much interested in light effects could only achieve his object by some device of this kind.

3 Hodges was apparently in Derby after studying with Wilson and before accompanying Cook on his second voyage to the South Seas—that is, perhaps, in the late '60's. He knew Whitehurst well and eventually married his niece. It is not impossible that Wright's portrait of a *Mrs. Hodges* [Plate 189] was the painter's first wife (see Smith, 1960, pp. 40, 74). A certain Hodges bought two Wright *Grottoes in the Gulf of Salerno* in the late '70's—just the kind of pictures one would expect William Hodges to admire—at about the time of Mrs. Hodges's portrait (see also Edwards, 1808, p. 242).

4 This does not look like a watercolour done on the spot, and belongs in style with the study [Plate 254] for an unidentified Midlands landscape dated 1786 in the collection of Mrs. George Anson. For one thing, it has no serial number in the top corner as most of the other Roman studies do; for another, it is more contrived than the watercolours of 1774. There also exists on the London market a lively sketch of a waterfall seen through an arch, with an illegible date in the '70's [Plate 173]. The figures resemble the Julia in the Meynell Langley picture [Plate 215]. It is not Tivoli and may turn out not even to be an Italian scene.

1 It shows the same view of the ruined villa as in an oval landscape dated 1782 [Plate 235].

2 Two drawings exist on either side of the same sheet [Plates 238, 240] for the picture shown in Plate 237 and for its companion in the Mellon Collection, a *Lake by Moonlight* [Plate 239]. It is instructive to observe how the latter retains the solidity of the early '80's, although a moon over a lake invites reverie. The situation would have been quite different a few years later. The drawing shows more clearly than the painting that the circular building is a *tempietto*. The small oval *Nemi* [Plate 234] has a companion of a *Lake by Moonlight* in the same collection, which we reproduce in colour [Plate 235]. It is the most enchanting of all his small Italian landscapes.

3 It is not always easy to distinguish the two lakes in art, as students of Wilson and the Cozenses know to their cost, and it is possible that we may be mistaken in one or two of our identifications. However, there are good reasons for these confident labellings, which will be found set out in the *catalogue raisonné*.

4 In the old days he had found a formula for waves, beginning in Derby before the Italian journey in an energetic squiggle but becoming more mechanical as time went on, though always adequate for his modest purposes. Here he has adopted a formula of a nervous, feathery touch to convey a general impression of light catching the crests of waves, which is most effective.

5 We are thinking in particular of the supposed Swanevelt in the Lugt Collection, reproduced in the catalogue *Artisti Olandesi e Fiamminghi in Italia*, Florence, 1966 (48), said to be a bridge near Tivoli, and of another attributed to H. Saftleven II in an exhibition at Houthakker, Amsterdam, 1964 (71). Many other similar examples are recorded. None of these bridges to our knowledge shows the one depicted by Wright, but the ramshackle character is the same in all of them.

6 For the sake of completeness, we must also record three pictures among our illustrations not mentioned in the text above: a *River in a Rocky Gorge* of 1787 in a private collection [Plate 263], picturesque but a little empty; a small late view probably of the Quirinal in the Dale Collection [Plate 348]; and a damaged *View of Florence* in the Chicago Art Institute [Plate 327], also late.

ples [Plates 282, 283] taken from approximately the same viewpoint. It seems possible to tell without reference to the dates which is the earliest: the picture at Kedleston [Plate 257] appears more solid, the other two more meditative, but perhaps it is simply that we know from clear cut cases that his art was taking a general direction towards meditativeness, and that we are reading into the *Cosimato* views a progression that is hardly perceptible there. However, the mauve hills of the Liverpool version [Plate 282], influenced by Dutch Romanists—again we are reminded of Pijnacker—are typical of the late phase. We saw how the difference between 1780–5 and 1790 could be illustrated by contrasting the three views of *Virgil's Tomb* [Plates 231, 232] with a fourth similar landscape [Plate 296] where form has almost dissolved in light. The same contrast can be drawn between the Wilson-like view of a bridge over a winding river at Leighton House [Plate 250] of 1785, and what we take to be a landscape close on 1790 showing a classical villa near the sea [Plate 295].[1] The latter is peculiarly satisfying in its dreamy evanescence. The composition is worked out in advance down to the last tree trunk, yet there is nothing stilted about it: for within the structure the light tries out its charm on the villa's walls, and the walls succumb.

To the early '80's also belongs Wright's direct adaptation from a Richard Wilson in Southampton: an enchanting sunset *Nemi* in a private collection [Plate 237] repeated in a small oval in the another collection [Plate 234].[2] The change in his style between the early and late '80's can nowhere be better shown than by contrasting the former picture with the last dream-like *Nemi* and *Albano* views. No landscapes in his entire work are more poetical than these final evocations of Claude. Two of the purest are the small companions in the Mellon Collection [Plates 316, 317], characteristically early morning and sunset, where full use is made of the low sun for lyrical effects. One of them, an *Albano*, and similar works at Radburne [Plate 314] and Cardiff [Plate 315] are probably taken from Wilson, and so reach Claude at one remove. The series is completed—but we can be sure more will come to light—by two versions of another view of *Nemi* in the Dale Collection and formerly on the London market [Plates 318, 319].[3] To the same period must be assigned two *Lighthouses in the Mediterranean*, one large [Plate 313], one small [Plate 312]; it should be clear by now, without the aid of the external evidence which indeed exists, that these non-revolutionary works can only belong to the final years (coinciding, incidentally, with the greatest revolution in history, but by now Wright had withdrawn too far into himself to be affected by the trend of events). We have traced two late views of Vesuvius to a source in Vernet. This is again obviously the inspiration of his picture in the Tate [Plate 313] where the same pink and green tints recur in the distant hills. The other showing a lighthouse on fire with a low moon and a boat tossing on a choppy sea [Plate 312] is altogether too precious for the explosive world that had just dawned.[4] Finally, we find nothing to surprise us in his *Bridge seen through a Cavern by moonlight* of 1791 [Plate 326], perhaps a view at Sorrento, a telling contrast to the *Lake by moonlight* in the Mellon Collection of ten years earlier [Plate 239]. All delight in the substance of things has vanished, and we are left with the dream of a sick and elderly man. The picture is quite personal, yet even at this late stage he still harps on his old love Holland. Similar spindly footbridges[5] which owe their picturesqueness to improvisation, were favourites with the Dutch Romanists, and Wright pays his respects to their memory for almost the last time.[6]

The trouble about pursuing themes in the work of a painter is that we tend to lose track of his development and we should at this point recapitulate, and define the changes in the style of the Italian landscapes between 1774 and 1791, now that we have all the available evidence before us. We began by drawing a contrast between the pre-Italian landscapes and the sketches in central Italy, and the differences are obvious to any sensitive eye. All the same, one is no more than a transposition of the other into a new key. Though the style may have become classical, there is the same grounding in reality behind the classicism as there had been behind the romanticism; with the result that Wright convinces us of the authenticity of his vision, whichever stylistic language he chooses to adopt. When in the presence of Vesuvius and the Girandola, romanticism comes once more to the surface (as it was bound to do, given the character of the subject-matter), his hold on real life is tight enough to persuade us that such improbable displays of pyrotechnics actually took place in his presence, that for all their hallucinatory quality those caverns at Salerno really existed. At first he is deeply concerned about their precise appearance: about the curve and fragmentation of rock, about lava sizzling at the water's edge, about the colour St. Peter's turns under a shower of sparks. But as time goes on the need to communicate the facts loses its urgency, and once the grip is relaxed, in the late '70's, we find him relapsing into generalisations. We see the first clear signs of this in the two large pictures in Russia. But whatever he may lose in vividness of direct observation, he gains in power of construction—that is, as far as it is possible for an artist primarily concerned with light effects. And it is understandable that he should turn at this stage to Richard Wilson, the only outstanding artist capable of giving him the sense of spaciousness he now desired. It is said that he and Wilson were close friends, and that Wright 'rarely failed to visit his great, but amicable Rival' when in London;[1] and a story is told which if not strictly true has the spirit of truth, that when it was a question of an exchange of paintings, Wilson said to Wright: 'with all my heart, Wright—I'll give you *air*, and you'll give me *fire*'.[2] He stole some air, then, from Wilson for his own use. The views of the early and mid-'80's, of Nemi, Virgil's Tomb, the Colosseum, Tivoli, Cosimato, have a new airiness that the first *Vesuvius* views and the *Girandola* lacked. He adopts a new Wilsonian romantic classicism, and we are suddenly reminded that this is the period of his closest collaboration with Hayley and Wedgwood, that the *Origin of Painting* [Plate 245] is roughly contemporary with the *Bridge* landscape at Leighton House. So for a time he achieves a nice balance between reality and the dream. But finally, in the last Nemi, Salerno, Sorrento and Vesuvius landscapes, in the lighthouse pictures, the dream takes over. What remains is the remembrance of things past, and all the melancholy such a phrase evokes.

1 Carey, 1809, p. 21. Though Carey is the only near-contemporary to refer to this friendship, he is probably repeating a sound tradition, since he knew Wright's great friend John Leigh Philips and could draw on his memory.

2 Carey, *loc. cit.*

Fig 107 *Matlock High Tor, moonlight* c 1777–79
24 x 29 in / 60.9 x 73.6 cm   Leicester Museum and Art Gallery   Cat 307   Pl 212

Fig 108 Alexander Cozens *High Tor, Matlock (on the River Derwent)* 1756
28 x 36¼ in / 71.1 x 92 cm   Private Collection, U.K.

6 ENGLISH LANDSCAPE

If it is thought that we have been insisting too much on the order in which things are done, that this approach to an activity essentially passionate and intuitive is too abstract, we reply that it is the only way of showing how a man's mind moves. The information is worth having if it can be extracted. But on turning to the English landscapes we find it not so easy to build up a chronology. We can seldom be sure that references in the Account Book to views of Matlock, Dovedale and Cromford correspond to known pictures, and so we are even denied the privilege of dating pictures from their proximity to works listed there whose dates are known. No English landscapes have come to light bearing dates before 1786, except as settings for subject pieces such as the two versions of *Maria* [Plates 184, 220], but the landscapes in these cases are of no real assistance as comparative material since they are modified, as are the backgrounds to portraits, to suit the status or mood of sitters. And yet it may be assumed that after the few pre-Italian essays in landscape, and the experience of Italy behind him, he would have felt disposed quite shortly after his return to try his hand at the hills and dales of Derbyshire. This means we may have to account for as many as ten blank years before the dates begin. We are forced to take refuge in comparisons with the style of datable Italian works. But this is not such a hazardous operation as it must sound to those unaccustomed to work along art-historical lines. For on general grounds it would make nonsense of this whole study, were it to be proved that Wright pursued a radically different course in his depiction of Derbyshire from the one he was pursuing concurrently in his depiction of the Campagna and the country around Naples. Moreover, the parallel between English and Italian scenes after 1786 when the internal evidence becomes clearer, is close enough for us to be able to infer that the same situation existed earlier. We encounter the same withdrawal into a dream world in the late English landscapes as in the contemporary views of Nemi and Vesuvius. This relieves us of the obligation to fall back on such a naive explanation as physical remoteness from the Italian scene, for the dream-like quality of the last Italian works.

One picture, of *Matlock High Tor* by moonlight, in the museum at Leicester [Fig 107] is in the style of the Aberystwyth and Cade views of Vesuvius [Plates 169, 170], and though the dates of these two may not be established beyond question, it is impossible to fit them anywhere into the sequence of Neapolitan views except towards the end of the Italian trip or within a few years of his return. All three have the same frosty highlights and the same sense of desolation, and hark back to the immediately pre-Italian years. Nothing of the kind is found in the landscapes of the mid-'80's where all scenery, however rugged, is tidied up and smoothed out; two views of *Nemi* and *Vesuvius* [Plates 237, 233] and the few other pictures we can safely place in the early '80's, are also more refined. The picture in Leicester may therefore have been painted about 1777–9 when the artist was doing his utmost to

1 Stars reappear in the Palmer-Morewood moonlight [Plate 292] of about ten years later, so it need not be assumed that these are later additions.

2 Wright to Long, Surgeon, Chancery Lane, 22nd April 1787 (Inglefield MSS.).

3 There exists such an excellent version in the Derby Art Gallery of the Miller Mundy *Vesuvius* [Plate 291], done by a genuine painter, that it is almost too good to be untrue, but one would be rash to claim it as autograph. Naturally there are many cases of autograph replicas of portraits, since different members of the same families required versions. Autograph replicas of subject pieces are also known.

4 Published by A. P. Oppé, *Burlington Magazine*, January 1954, p. 21. Oppé did not go so far as definitely to identify this as a Derbyshire landscape, but it was found by Messrs. Appleby at Derby, and the appearance of a second picture of *Matlock High Tor* confirms his suspicions that it could be this district. The pictures are now reunited in the collection of a descendant of Cozens living in Kent.

5 Pilkington, 1789, II, p. 124 lists among works of art at Kedleston 'Matlock High Tor, by Cozens. Vale near Matlock, by Cozens'. The context implies that these were paintings, not drawings; by Alexander, not John Robert. It is even conceivable that the very pictures here described were the ones once at Kedleston: in which case, Wright may have known them there, considering that he was painting portraits of two Curzon children at the time they were painted [see Plates 4, 5].

6 There are two figures in red in the picture in Leicester, close to the near bank, but they cannot be distinguished in the reproduction.

7 See above, Part II, p 75, note 2.

8 The identification of the subject was made by Buckley, 1955, p. 268.

recover from the too sophisticated atmosphere of Bath, by plunging back into his natural habitat of romance and solitude he had known as a youth. Unfortunately it is in poor condition, partly repainted, and superimposed on a portrait running in the opposite direction; the spectre of a face, the remains of eyes, nose and mouth, are disturbingly obvious on the original where the hills drop to the Derwent, like one of those puzzle pictures designed for children with the caption 'find the giant'. Nevertheless, though not every touch is to be trusted, enough survives to make us realise what a fine object it once was, with its tiny stars studding a turquoise sky,[1] its gashes of green and slate grey, its blue spots sprayed over the hill. Only two other pictures in the same category exist, in the Mellon Collection [Plate 218] and the Detroit Institute of Arts [Plate 217] of the same stretch of country, only showing this time what is known locally as Matlock Tor on the right, and the Derwent flowing in the direction of the spectator instead of away from him, as in Leicester. Wright is indifferent to the position of his moon; even in his own day he would not have qualified as a meteorologist. (He once made a startling admission: that 'Moon lights & fire lights are but a sort of guess work wth. me for I cant wth. impunity go out at night and study the former, & the latter I have seen *but once* [before 1787], at a time too, when I thought not of painting such effects'.)[2] Here in the Mellon and Detroit pictures he is facing in the opposite direction, yet the pale full moon is still there, casting its spell over the hill, and over the shabby white horse in the foreground, waiting for its rider to mount. The clouds again collect, like those scampering devils to either side of the crater of Vesuvius in the pictures in Wales and Cornwall [Plates 169, 170], delicately lined by the moon's light; and the water plunging over the stones has lost little of its impetus since the days of the *Earthstopper*. The Mellon and Detroit pictures— the only known case among the landscapes of a virtually exact replica[3]—begin to take on the grace of the mature landscape style, and may be as late as 1780. We have to remember that the small *Cavern with Julia* [Plate 216], which retains just as much of the romanticism of the '70's as these do, is dated that year.

We have suggested that Wright became interested in the drawings of Alexander Cozens when faced with Roman ruins in the Campagna, and it is understandable that he should be drawn to Cozens's oil paintings of the area around Matlock when he in turn came to transfer this spectacular countryside to canvas. Two oils by Cozens of Kit-cat size, both signed and dated 1756 and produced within a few miles of the town where the impressionable, budding artist of twenty-two was then living, are known of the neighbourhood; one of a not precisely identifiable scene under a sunset sky,[4] the other of *Matlock High Tor* [Fig 108].[5] By the standards of the '70's these panoramic views seen from a raised foreground are primitive, even quaint; they were experiments by an artist not used to working on a large scale in oils. Yet from no other source—not even from local topographical draughtsmen like 'Smith of Derby'—can Wright have derived his sense of sublimity. Predisposed though he was to do so already, it can only have been from Cozens that he gained confidence to subject the scenery to unusual light effects; and though the habit was widespread, it was perhaps from Cozens also that he borrowed the device of introducing into the immediate foreground figures so minute that their surroundings would appear all the more imposing in contrast.[6] From then onwards the pull of Cozens's oils slackened, and it is significant that the next time we hear of any spiritual contact between the two artists was after Cozens's death, when Wright made copies of his landscape drawings of a far softer, more picturesque character.[7] No trace survives of Cozens's influence in the daylight view of Matlock Tor [Plate 248] in the Fitzwilliam Museum, taken from precisely the same point on the Derwent as in the Mellon and Detroit pictures.[8] His interest in light effects—this time it is the sun breaking through cloud in an afternoon sky—has not of course diminished, but the whole mood has changed. Richard Wilson has now taught him to bring some geniality into the district. Now a tall tree, a picture-making tree, balances the Tor on the left, and its broken bough curtsies to the river. Wright had used this bough, which has a long history going back to Jacob Ruisdael, once before in his *Earthstopper* [Plate 113], but on that occasion for different, dramatic purposes. He was to use it again in his scene from *The Winter's Tale* for the Shakespeare Gallery [Plate 302]. In the Fitzwilliam picture the mood is no longer awe-inspiring but lyrical, with the sky passing from blue, to pink, to yellow as it descends. To take a midnight walk in the landscapes of the '70's would be to invite disaster, but anyone could entrust his limbs to the afternoon hills of the Fitzwilliam picture in safety. In the eyes of the guide-book writers of the late '80's Matlock has also lost its menace. Pilkington even goes so far as to describe Matlock Dale as 'this delightful place', where the Derwent 'flows in some parts with a noisy and rapid current, and in others with such a deep and gentle stream, that its unruffled surface' as in Cambridge 'clearly reflects the rocks and wood near its margin. Thus do rocks, trees, shrubs, and water conspire at once to fill the mind of the spectator with admiration and delight'.[1] The district has lost its Burke-like sublimity and acquired a Gilpin-like Picturesqueness.

1 Pilkington, 1789, I, p. 13.

Throughout the '80's and until about 1790, Wright painted a number of landscapes which appear to represent this district, but short of carrying out a detailed topographical survey, it is hard to identify the sites. One belonging to Sir John Crompton-Inglefield represents *Chee Tor* [Plate 265] in the neighbourhood of Buxton, described by the same guide-book writer about the time the picture was painted as 'a prodigious large rock, called Chee-Tor... In some parts it overhangs considerably, and is beautifully fringed with wood. There is great variety in the face of this rock... The rivulet, which flows at its foot, is likewise very beautiful. It is filled with large stones, and forms many natural cascades'.[2] This is a straight-forward sunlight view. Another in the same collection [Plate 290] shows a high central feature by moonlight with the moon reflected in the river. Two pictures with purple hills show the same rock formation on the skyline [Plates 308, 309]. They must date from about 1790, because the smaller of the two [Plate 308] belonged to his friend Holland, all of whose Wright landscapes were of this late phase. In any case, their style fits this period. They prove—though no proof is needed after the Fitzwilliam landscape—that though Wright would normally remain faithful to the general configuration of rock and winding water,[3] he would not hesitate to insert trees whenever the composition or a prospective client demanded it. One, a view of the boat-house near Matlock in the Mellon Collection [Plate 259], is so naturalistic that the tell-tale tree in the foreground on the right which is there to remind us that art and nature are not to be confused, comes as a shock. In these mature Derbyshire landscapes, Wright achieves a moment of calm, quite unlike anything in his work before. Sometimes as in *Chee Tor* [Plate 265] he will produce a naturalistic landscape with no trappings at all. But in company with most of his fellow landscapists he will generally find it necessary to combine the Real with the Ideal, by the introduction of foliage arranged to suit his convenience, to lend depth and balance. Nostalgia for a lost Rococo was in the air of the day. We have seen the same process at work in his views of the Campagna: how for example in the *Bridge* of 1785 at Leighton House [Plate 250], under the inspiration of Wilson he will adopt a framework of trees so contrived that we seem to have re-entered the world of the Rococo bookplate through which the romantic-classic valley is glimpsed. With the Romantic Movement coming between him and us, it requires an effort to reconcile such artifice with (in the case of the boat-house picture, for instance) such a keen grasp of the thing seen—more in his case than in that of others who have not his grounding in reality, from whom we do not demand real life, whose merits lie positively in shunning it. Similarly in the case of some late eighteenth-century poets whom we suspect of having something plain to say about the world—as it were, something about a primrose by the river's brim— we are disturbed by the too polished metre they adopt in which to say it.

2 *Loc. cit.*, p. 17.

3 An exception is the landscape in Sheffield [Plate 249].

Needless to say the most naturalistic landscapes of all are those done for his own use: those drawings and watercolours where there is no question of gratifying contemporary taste with amendments to nature. Here he was free to jot down whatever was there, unadorned. The best example is his watercolour of *Dovedale* [Plate 254]. This soft unemphatic valley of the Dove with its low wooded hills and pointed rocks would have required harsh treatment, had he investigated it in the '70's; harsher still in his early youth. No doubt this is why he then left it alone. He came to it in his docile, late middle age and found its melancholy congenial to his heart. A local topographer might be describing, not the country itself, but Wright's interpretation of it: 'These rocks, on both sides of the water, are of grey limestone, of every wild and grotesque variety of height and shape. Sometimes they stand single, like the fragments of a wall, or the tower of an old castle; sometimes they rise from a broad base in a kind of pyramid, at others slender like a pinnacle...'.[4] His *Dovedale* of 1786 at Kedleston [Plate 255], a pair to a *Cosimato* in the same collection [Plate 257], is

4 Bray, 1783, p. 141. Pilkington, 1789, I, pp. 25–6, in giving a similar account of Dovedale, speaks of Wright in connection with this district: 'Those, who have had an opportunity of seeing them', he writes of the Derbyshire hills, 'touched by the sweet and magic pencil of Mr. Wright of Derby, will easily conceive, how deserving they are of the attention that has been paid them'.

1 There are men in boats with fishing nets, not visible in the reproduction.

almost as free from cunning as the watercolour, except that small wild horses romp in the foreground, the usual device for making us appreciate the enormous distances covered by the surrounding hills. The swans in a landscape resembling *Dovedale* (though said not to of this district) at Catton Hall [Plate 252] dated the same year, perform the same function. We are not surprised to find that they are absent from the watercolour study in Derby [Plate 253] for this picture, just as the boating party[1] and the broken branch sloping across the river in the foreground are also absent; for in the privacy of his studio he had no need to parade any bag of tricks. In this picture as so often at this period (other examples are the Gisborne double portrait [Plate 269] and the landscape at Sheffield [Plate 249]) Wright selects the brown foliage of autumn, the season best attuned to his sick frame. We have reached at last the two pictures dated 1786 which are the flimsy scaffolding for a chronology of the English landscape style. We observe that the spongy appearance of the trees at Catton Hall [Plate 252] is repeated in both the Fitzwilliam and Mellon *Matlock* views [Plates 248, 259], encouraging us to accept a date for these two in the mid-'80's on more solid grounds than we have so far been able to establish. If the landscapes in Southampton and the Dale Collection [Plates 309, 308] are about 1790, then it seems permissible to date *Chee Tor* [Plate 265] in the intervening period. As for the moonlight belonging to Sir John Crompton-Inglefield [Plate 290], it still floats around unhappily in the late '80's, refusing to come to rest in any particular year. But to be dogmatic about a strict order would be foolish because no painter is logical. Two further *Dovedale* landscapes, one by daylight in the Crompton-Inglefield Collection [Plate 258], and what is believed to be its pair by moonlight in Oberlin [Plate 261] are close to the Kedleston *Dovedale* [Plate 255] and belong to this phase. They begin to take on the dreamy character of the circular landscape of 1787 [Plate 262] while retaining some hold on real life; but reality is combined in this case with an artful attempt on the part of the foliage to worm its way into position in front of the full moon, so that it can show off black against it.[2]

2 Another late landscape [Plate 264] belonging to Mr. H. R. Edwards is also believed to represent Dovedale.

The same pattern is repeated in the Cromford landscapes, though we do not propose to discuss them at this stage in detail, preferring to wait until we can turn to Arkwright's building operations in the area, from which they are inseparable. It is enough to say at present that a view of Arkwright's mills by moonlight [Plate 244] has the roughness and romance of the early '80's, belonging in technique (as far as we can judge from the damaged surface) and atmosphere, if not with the early picture in Leicester [Plate 212], with the *Matlock* landscapes in Detroit and the Mellon Collection [Plates 217, 218]. There are grounds, which will emerge in a later chapter,[3] for dating this crucial picture about 1783. A second view of

3 See below, Part III, pp. 164–5.

the mills [Plate 331] of some seven years later by daylight seen from approximately the same viewpoint, is of a relatively artificial character, a picturesque view with a high rock acting as a *repoussoir* on the extreme left, echoing another rock, equally unrealistic, in the right foreground of a companion to it, a view of *Willersley Castle* [Plate 330].[4] Even his pencil and watercolour drawing of Cromford, dated 1789 [Plate 297] has a similar con-

4 Willersley Castle was hardly in a fit state before 1790 to be painted. This enables us to date the daylight *Arkwright's Mills* quite accurately about 1790.

trivance in the right foreground, although, being a drawing for his own use, he studies the rock face with as much ease, as, fifteen years before, he had studied the area around the crater of Vesuvius. A small view of the *Cut through the Rock, Cromford* [Plate 333], also datable about 1790 for reasons which will become clear later, produces the same stagy effect. Now, when we turn back to the Matlock and Dovedale landscapes, with the Cromford views in mind, we can detect, what was not so clear before, a transition between 1780 and 1790 from romantic realism to a style which occasionally makes do with naturalism, but more often combines naturalism with picturesqueness. We are entitled to give the word Picturesque a capital 'P' at this stage, since this was the heyday of Gilpin, and though we do not know whether Wright and Gilpin ever came into personal contact, we can be sure he had absorbed Gilpin's ideas through their mutual friend Gisborne. The two views of Arkwright's mills are a perfect illustration of the change in his style; as we see it, a change for the worse. For had he continued after 1780 in the same general direction as before, perhaps diluting realism with naturalism but sacrificing none of the adventurousness of the preceding decades, he might have anticipated Girtin, the young Constable and Turner, and today be hailed, not as a precursor but as an initiator of the Romantic Movement, a kind of Midlands Pierre Henri de Valenciennes; whereas he allowed himself to

Fig 109 *Landscape with ruins, by moonlight* c 1780–82
25 x 30 in / 63.5 x 76.2 cm   Miss D. M. R. Cade
Cat 305   Pl 236

Fig 110 Pieter van Laer *Moonlight Landscape*
14 x 19½ in / 35.5 x 49.5 cm   Galleria Spada, Rome

be deflected into a convention of elegance which does not seem central to his nature, thus putting himself out of the running for such a title. Though not in years, he must have been too old already in mind to fulfil the promise of the *Air Pump*, and no longer sensed, or cared, along what paths the future lay.

Our frame work should by now be firm enough to justify the dating of the *Landscape with ruins, by moonlight* in the Cade Collection [Fig 109][1] early in the '80's, about the time of *Ark-wright's Mills by night* [Plate 244], the two moonlights in the Mellon Collection [Plates 218, 239], and the best version of *Virgil's Tomb* [Plate 231] where enough vigour survives from the preceding decade for the rough country still to be treated roughly with a loaded brush; later in the Oberlin and Crompton-Inglefield pictures, for instance [Plates 261, 258], the moonlights grow smooth and ethereal. No source in Wilson for the satisfying invention of the Cade *View of Ruins* has been discovered, and we hope we are safe in tracing its origin much further back to Wright's old favourites, the Dutch Romanists. There exists in the Spada Gallery in Rome[2] a Pieter van Laer at his most Elsheimerish, showing fishermen crouching by night over a campfire, with behind them a medieval castle and other old buildings [Fig 110]—a picture we might easily have overlooked as a source for Wright, had

1 A very fine pair to this, of a daylight landscape in the same collection, has not been photographed and therefore cannot be sensibly discussed here.

2 F. Zeri, *La Galleria Spada in Roma*, Florence, 1954, No. 302. Presumably one of the six octagonal paintings listed in a Spada inventory of 1759 as Cerquozzi, and therefore available to Wright when he was in Rome.

Fig 111 *Landscape with Dale Abbey* c 1786–8
28½ x 39 in / 72.4 x 99 cm   Sheffield City Art Galleries
Cat 331   Pl 249

91

not the sky been studded with stars as in Leicester, and were there not, as in the Cade moonlight, a pale moon suspended over a hill and casting its spooky reflection in the water. Wright used the same scene again in the daytime, in possibly the most beautiful of all his Wilson-like landscapes, the one in Sheffield [Fig 111], an autumn scene where pinks dance over hill and sky. It should be clear by now that it is later in the decade: about 1786–8, to judge by the similarity of touch to the unidentified river scene in the Anson Collection [Plate 252]. It could also be dangerously argued—but this brand of art history has long been discredited—that in the interval of a few years, bushes have sprouted on the far bank. So wayward is this argument that had we decided on other grounds that the moonlight was the later of the two, we would have merrily turned the argument upside down and gone on to maintain that Wright had either invented the foliage in the one or cleared it away from the other. That he was capable of manipulating nature like a pawn in his hand is proved in this unique instance by the elimination in the second version of the spur on the left with its medieval tower, as well as of the distant hill, in order to bring into prominence Dale Abbey on the distant bank—just what was wanted to give depth and air. There is in fact so much air in the Sheffield picture that until recently it was thought to be by Wilson himself. No doubt Wilson would also have been credited with Wright's circular landscape [Plate 262], had it not been signed on the reverse, and dated 1787, five years after Wilson's death. Like Wright's *Nemi* in a private collection [Plate 237], this *tondo* is based on a rectangular Wilson (a version was formerly in the collection of Lord Fairhaven), but as we would expect, the trees incline inwards to fit the new shape.

The facts of nature lose their excitement for Wright to such an extent that, by the late '80's, he is using landscape as a conventional backcloth for scenes of mild distress. Four pictures of *Cottages on Fire* have been traced [Plates 293, 303, 306, 307] where the same setting suffices: a moon, a ruined castle, a *repoussoir* bank, trees performing their customary minuet, changing shape slightly, but ever so slightly, from canvas to canvas. And on the bank is the cottage in varying stages of disintegration, and the inhabitants rescuing what they can of their pathetic belongings. Children are helped down the bank or cling to their parents in terror, as children cling to grown-ups in the *Blacksmith's Shop* [Plate 101]; picturesque Marias and Julias collapse outcast on the grass. One of them, in the Palmer-Morewood Collection [Plate 293] has a pair of a lake by moonlight [Plate 292]. In these two, instead of contrasting the times of the day, Wright contrasts red with green, a moon in a tree with a moon in a cloud, fragile people red from the light of the fire with fragile people green as though in a tank. This beautiful moonlight lake scene has the gently undulating vegetation of an aquarium. Like the late *Nemi* and *Albano* views, it has contracted out of this world and entered one of its own. It is the swan song of the *Air Pump* master, for which we may feel affection, but it does not clutch at the heart.[1] The last in the series is a small effect of a fire seen through a group of trees [Plate 332] in the Dale Collection in Ottawa, dated 1793. We noted how in his late *Bridge seen through a Cavern* [Plate 326] Wright was still paying his respects to his Dutch antecedents. Here again, within four years of his death, he leans heavily on Aert van der Neer or his circle—more heavily than, in the old days, he would have wished to lean on anyone.

The contrivance of some of these late works carries with it a new decorativeness, where flat areas of colour, harsh russet reds and greens, are spread over wide areas without modelling, freakishly prophetic of experiments conducted 100 years later by a group of audacious young men in the Breton village of Pont Aven; though naturally there is no suggestion in Wright's adoption of the device, of colour for emotive purposes. We have noticed something of the kind in his *Lighthouse* pictures [Plates 312, 313], and in the late pink and green *Vesuvius* views [Plates 291, 294] there is the same decorative tendency. The hills in what must be an imaginary scene, half-English, half-Italian, where Roman villas have incongruously come to settle on the Derbyshire hills [Plate 311] are subjected to the same treatment, and so no doubt is the lake scene with a little white house on the further bank reflected in the water [Plate 310], painted in the same year (1790) but in the foreground resembling the Dovedale landscapes of the mid-'80's. The picture has not been available for inspection, but we feel sure its mysteriously late date is accounted for by decorative colouring. The misty moonlight landscape dated 1792 belonging to Liverpool University

1 Waterhouse, 1953, p. 208 has pointed out that the organisation of this picture recalls the local topographical artist Thomas Smith, known as 'Smith of Derby' (d. late '60's). It is unlikely that Wright owed anything essential to Smith, to judge by the few surviving examples of his oil paintings, such as the *River Landscape* belonging to D.r Sheldon (exhibited Kenwood, 1967 (23)) which makes no advance on late Flemish Mannerism.

[Plate 344] is a further example of this tendency; and at least one landscape done about 1796 after the journey to the Lake District, an *Outlet of Wyburn Lake* [Plate 353] has the same character. In the *Landscape with a Rainbow* [Plate 347], on the other hand, of about 1794–5, the decorative element is not so pronounced. This is one of the most satisfying of his late English landscapes, where he recaptures the verve of former days. It may have been the thrill of the rainbow—like the lighthouse, a typical Wright feature that we were looking forward to all this time but had to wait till the end before finding—that jogged him back into his old form. How odd, now that we come to think of it, that he never painted an eclipse.

It is sad to have to round off a survey of Wright's entire career as an artist with the Lake District landscapes, but since they were painted last, they must come last. The subject is not conducive to a peroration. What more is to be said than that they evoke the charm of the period, the evanescence of the *fin de siècle*? That they hunt a pictorial tradition to its placid death? That others could do as well or better? How strange that the author of *Matlock High Tor* in Leicester, when faced perhaps for the first time with Wordsworth's paradise where possibilities for drama were at least as great as at Matlock, should have been content to sleep-walk and sleep-see through it! His Lake landscapes were much admired in their day by amateur artists of the same persuasion, but few have survived. There is the decorative *Outlet of Wyburn Lake* [Plate 353]; an unidentified lake scene that has also been floating around the market [Plate 346]; a view of *Ullswater* in a collection in Repton similar to a lost composition formerly in the Hardman Collection [Plate 355]; a *Derwent Water, with Skiddaw in the Distance* [Plate 354] in the Mellon Collection; and the famous *Rydal Waterfall* [Fig 112] in the Derby Museum. Two small lake scenes, not necessarily of this district, in the Dale Collection in Ottawa [Plates 349, 350] are among the best of the bunch; this is because in his old age, Wright retained the common touch when working on a small scale, and it is in the simplicity of his near-sketches that he gropes towards, and reaches, the younger generation. The one with the ruin on the hill [Plate 349] is built up of colour superimposed on a brown-stained canvas—producing an effect that would have delighted Cotman

Fig 112 *Rydal Waterfall* 1795
22½ x 30 in / 57.1 x 76.2 cm   Derby Museum and Art Gallery   Cat 324   Pl 352

Fig 113 Julius Caesar Ibbetson *Rydal Waterfall*
1798   36 x 26$\frac{5}{16}$ in / 91.4 x 66.8 cm
Walker Art Gallery, Liverpool

himself, had he ever seen it. But in his more finished works, can he be described as ever superior to other Lake District artists of the period whom we agree to call minor? He thought he was breaking fresh ground in his *Rydal Waterfall*: 'I was keen to produce,' he writes, 'an effect I have never seen in painting of showing the pebbles at the bottom of the water with the broken reflections on its surface...'[1] But is there much more originality here than in Julius Caesar Ibbetson's view of the same scenery [Fig 113][2] or in John White Abbott's?[3] And though his *Windermere with Langdale Pikes* survives only in the form of a copy [Fig 114], would the original have driven Ibbetson's version into the shade?[4] And did not Turner, after his flirtation with the Picturesque, cast them both into the shade for ever?[5]

1 Wright to Philips, 2nd October 1795, quoted Bemrose, 1885, p. 96. More quotations from this interesting letter are to be found in Tate, 1958, under No. 33. Evidently Wright was unaware that Leonardo had written *c.* 1508 (Libro A, 48): 'it [sculpture] cannot show [what painting can] small pebbles of various colours beneath the surface of transparent water'.

2 Walker Art Gallery, Liverpool. It bears a long inscription on the reverse: 'Correct view of the lower [*sic*] Rydal waterfall in S.! Michael le Fleming's Garden. Drawn from Nature October & finished December 1798 by Julius Ibbetson for Mr. T. Vernon of Liverpool...' R. A. 1799 (257). Vernon was one of Wright's patrons.

3 Exh. from Gilbert Davis Collection at Messrs. Spink, Duke Street, May 1952. Dated 11th July 1791.

4 Illus. Rotha Mary Clay, *Julius Caesar Ibbetson, 1759–1817*, London, 1948, plate 80.

5 We have mentioned or discussed all the illustrated material with the exception of a *Rocky Landscape with a Waterfall* [Plate 351] in a private collection in California, which the author has not seen since 1958, and then in a very grimy state. It is certainly late. The lost Arkwright *Ullswater* [Plate 345] will be discussed later (see Part III, pp. 168–9).

Fig 114 After Joseph Wright *Windermere with Langdale Pikes* c 1794–95
31 x 22½ in / 78.7 x 57.1 cm   Sir Gilbert Inglefield

III Wright and his Times

1 SITTERS TO THE FIRST PORTRAITS 1755–73

The reason why we should be surprised at the idea that artists in the eighteenth century could vary their approach to suit the character and status of their sitters is that this aspect of the history of portraiture has rarely been investigated. Artists only occasionally did so. Most of them rode roughshod over their sitters, bent on the pursuit of their own ideals of men and women, so that when we contemplate their portraits we are more conscious of an organic stylistic pattern than we are of style shifting back and forth to meet changing situations. Confronted with these, unless we happen to belong to the same family, we do not care too much about who is being shown. But there are others who will try to match their style to their subject. Wright of Derby was peculiarly eager to satisfy his clients in this respect, and was well qualified to do so, given his natural versatility; and on the few occasions when honesty came into conflict with what was required, as with *Mrs. Witts* [Plate 178], where he found sitters too alien to make his kind of sense out of them on canvas, he would still make an effort to accommodate himself to their wishes. If he failed to give satisfaction, this stemmed from some innate incapacity to produce what was required, not from a disinclination to do so on the grounds of integrity. Wright negotiated with his patrons on the same basis as his father might negotiate with transgressors of the Law or his brother with his patients: there were stylistic remedies for given physical types, just as there were legal or medical remedies for given disputes or diseases, and it was up to the professional to find them.

His portraiture can legitimately be approached, then, from two directions: his stylistic evolution under the impact of the art of other portrait painters, which we attempted to pin down in an earlier chapter; and the effect on him of his decision to convey the personality of his sitters by adopting different attitudes towards each, which we shall attempt to pin down in this, by studying who the people were who sat to him. Whereas in the first investigation a chronological survey was necessary in order to determine in which general direction he was moving, in this second we shall abandon the time sequence: for whereas meaning can be extracted from a development, however erratic, from Hudson to Ramsay or Stubbs, no lesson can be learnt from a perpetual oscillation, year by year, between the extremes of the icon and the real man, when style is not our main concern. We shall see that he can create a hieratic image like that of Reginald Lygon, and a human being like William Brooke, in the same year, both within the framework of the Hudson tradition, and will then develop his near-Rococo under the impact of Ramsay, to end up again in 1769–70 in Liverpool and Lichfield with a new modified realism in a quite different convention—a situation which if presented chronologically would make no sense. Instead we shall rearrange the portraits from the late '50's to about 1770 in a descending scale of sitters' social

1 The author has consulted the obvious published sources which are listed in the bibliography, consisting of tourists' accounts and memoirs, and histories of Derbyshire and Derbyshire families (Bray, Pilkington, Hulton, Davies, Lysons, Glover, Tilley and so forth). Detailed references to these are not given in these notes unless there is some special reason to do so. Unpublished sources, and less obvious printed ones, are given here. Much information comes from the files of the *Derby Mercury*. Further details about all sitters will be found in the *Catalogue raisonné*.

2 The author is indebted to Lord Scarsdale for filling in some gaps in the standard reference books.

eminence[1] and shall see that he tended to grow more boldly realistic, the lower he sank.

This is bound to involve us in an oversimplification of the issue. For in fact, the movement downwards from aristocrat to merchant is not invariably paralleled by a descending or ascending scale (however one likes to look at it) from icon to realism. There are times when Wright's own stylistic development appears to get the better of his determination to find an appropriate idiom for each sitter, as in the case of the heiress *Sarah Carver and her Daughter Sarah* [Plate 79] who 'ought' to be more idealised (unless there is some other explanation for the straightforwardness of his approach to them of which we know nothing), but the picture was painted at a moment (*c*. 1769–70) when the artist was evolving a highly original realistic style intended for other people which gets carries over willy-nilly to their features. The same remarks apply later in his career (in the early '80's) when he produced a startlingly unflattering image of Hannah Coke [Plate 225], another heiress, and wife of a respectable clergyman, whom we would have expected to be treated in a more considerate way. At other times an explanation is easier to find. For instance, the portrait of the cotton manufacturer Strutt [Plate 324] is not conspicuously more realistic than that of the land-owner Holden [Plate 193]. But then Strutt had a streak of idealism that Wright hoped to bring out by a hint of idealisation, and Holden a shrewd business sense that Wright could convey by sticking more faithfully to the facts than usual with men of his stamp; with the result that the two sitters were able to meet happily about half way. Moreover, it would be absurd to maintain that social distinctions were the only ones which conditioned different modes of representation: Wright was intrigued by personalities irrespective of their social origin, and strove to produce images in quite different styles of men with marked individuality, even though they might be socially indistinguishable. Thus, some middle-class intellectuals like Thomas Day [Plate 80] are idealised, while others like Darwin [Plate 78] are not. Other examples will occur to readers as we pass one sitter after another in review. However, so long as the occasional exception is borne in mind, the general rule can stand.

During the pre-Italian period Wright was associated with at least two aristocratic families and has left portraits of members of both of them. Among his earliest are two of Curzon children [Plates 4, 5] leading carefree lives in one of the most extravagant of Derbyshire houses, Kedleston.[2] (The grandest family of all, at Chatsworth, could not be bothered with a local painter, with the whole of London to pick from.) The little Nathaniel Curzon and his younger sister Caroline were brought up at Kedleston in security and style. The boy knew he would one day inherit the big house and was being groomed for his role: he was in the direct line of succession and nothing except death could take away his inheritance. His grandfather was then the owner but was to die shortly after the portrait was painted. His father was to rebuild the house on an even more lavish scale when he succeeded (1758). Wright has done his best to serve the aristocracy with the nonchalance of an aristocratic painter, but one senses that this effort went against the grain. He shows the boy in Van Dyck costume, giving the plume of his hat a necessary, quite uncharacteristic, Baroque flourish, but in the punctiliousness of the lace collar, and in the portrait of the prim little girl, he betrays his middle-class background as well as his extreme youth. He was more fortunate when faced with the undergraduate, the future *Viscount Fitzwilliam* [Plate 49]. Here he was spared the necessity for grandeur by the sympathy he would automatically have felt for a young scholar, and for his gorgeous gown, so much to his taste for the minute, the glittering and the intricate, however exalted the status of its wearer. All the same, Fitzwilliam is half way towards an effigy. And when it came to pinning down the features of a third family, the Lygons [Plates 14, 17, 18] which was heading for the aristocracy even if it had not yet got there, Wright showed himself painfully ill at ease. Here decorum in the Van Dyck tradition was called for; but all he could manage were stilted mannerisms —too long a neck, too stiff a skirt, too mean a ruff—, the very antithesis of his tastes and inclinations. Only in the dresses which gave him the excuse for some playful Rococo, was he able to follow his bent.

He was always at home with gay young heiresses since at least they encouraged his delight in rich dresses and finery, not caring to be shown portentous or sedate. No commissions he ever received for portraits came from a more elegant family than the Carvers

[Plates 26, 27, 28]; none at any period of his life earn the label of Rococo more deservedly than these Lely beauties transported into the idiom of a hundred years later, with their artificial gestures and semi-translucent veils caught by the sun and drifting in mid-air against all the laws of nature. The Carvers established themselves as landed gentry by a succession of diplomatic marriages. The elder of the two ladies in the Tree collection [Plate 22] was the daughter of the Rector of Eckington and Prebendary of Canterbury. Her son John [Plate 27] married the heiress to the fortune of the Middletons of Leam Hall; her daughter Elizabeth [Plate 28] married the vicar of Youlgreave who was steward to the Duke of Rutland. Later the Carvers were enriched by bequests of further Middleton estates.[1] Though not especially grand by origin, they had money on their side, and prize after prize dropped into their shimmering, satin laps. It is impossible to imagine them naked: they exist only in their rich clothes. How odd that an artist who was so thirsty for knowledge of the physical world, who did not balk at Sir Richard Arkwright's pot belly, should have known how to give these dragonflies the artifice they wanted! From the same social level comes James Shuttleworth (1714–73), also married (1742) to an heiress, the daughter of Robert Holden of Aston Hall,[2] rich enough to devote himself to leisurely country pursuits. Wright shows him with his wife and child back from a shooting expedition [Plate 51]; at any moment, one feels, he will journey to Rome and sit to Batoni. Like the Carvers he had his professional as well as his country gentleman side: member of Parliament for Preston (1741–54) and when Wright's portrait was painted (1764), for the county of Lancashire; sheriff of Yorkshire in 1760. One has to see the picture in the paint to realise how much Alan Ramsay overlays the realism; in human terms, how much elegance overlays a tough streak.

The same observations apply to the six portraits painted slightly earlier for Markeaton Hall, of Francis Noel Clarke Mundy and his five sportsmen friends [Plates 33–38]. The Mundys, who had been established at Markeaton for over two hundred years, were among the most prominent of Derbyshire families. Wrightson Mundy, one time M.P. for Leicester, had built Markeaton Hall in the middle years of the century. He came of a literary family, his father having been a friend and associate of Addison, Steele and Swift,[3] and these literary tastes were inherited by his son Francis (1739–1815) who preferred the life of poet and sportsman to that of public servant: we are hardly surprised to hear of him declining to stand for Parliament for the county in 1780. However, his wealth and sensibility were insufficient to induce him to acquire any paintings by Wright besides portraits, so far as we know. It was left to a member of a younger branch of the Mundys of Markeaton, a certain Edward Mundy of Shipley, to buy from Wright a *Cicero's Villa*, a *Vesuvius* and two *Dovedale* landscapes in the '80's [the last three Plates 291, 258, 261]—pictures one would have expected to appeal to the Mundys' Gothick taste. Like all Midlands intellectuals of his generation, Francis Mundy gravitated to the Lichfield circle, and we find him visiting Erasmus Darwin there in the early '70's.[4] Encouraged by Darwin and Miss Seward,[5] a volume of his poems, *Needwood Forest*, was published anonymously in Lichfield in 1776. It was no doubt from Mundy that Wright derived his limited experience of sport. In this poem occur the Gothick lines:

'...Whilst, as the silver moon-beams rise,
Imagin'd temples strike my eyes,
With tottering spire, and mouldering wall,
And high roof nodding to its fall.
His lantern gleaming down the glade,
One, like a sexton with his spade,
Comes from their caverns to exclude
The mid-night prowlers of the wood...'[6]

This very scene had appeared in Wright's *Earthstopper* [Plate 113] three years before, in which the sexton with his spade stops up the holes of midnight prowlers of the wood, as the silver moonbeams rise.

Two other members of the Markeaton Hunt painted by Wright later became Francis

1 Harleian Society, *Familiae Minorum Gentium* (Brit. Mus. 2099b), p. 839. The brother of the little girl in the double portrait of *Sarah Carver and her daughter Sarah* [Plate 79] inherited further riches from the estate of Jonathan Oxley of Leam, whose father had married a Middleton.

2 See R. Holden, *Nuthall Temple, Notts. Its History and Contents*, Nottingham, 1916. Wright's portrait of James Shuttleworth's sister (Cat No 130) is needless to say rendered in the same spirit.

3 Tilley, 1902, p. 130.

4 Seward, 1804, p. 59.

5 ' "Needwood Forest" is one of the most beautiful *local* poems that has been written...', writes the Swan of Lichfield (*op. cit.*). Mundy followed it up with a second poem, *The Fall of Needwood*.

6 *Needwood Forest*, Lichfield, 1776, p. 19. After the word 'sexton' is an asterisk referring the reader to a footnote: 'Earth-stopper'. A new version of this poem, again published anonymously, appeared in Derby, 1808. Here (p. 21) the 'sexton' is named Manuel, 'the Forest earth-stopper in the hunting days of the author'.

1 The obvious sources for the Burdett family have been checked and amplified from inscriptions on tombstones in Foremark Church.

2 Stevens, 1965, p. 20, entry for 13th May 1792.

3 The Burdetts of Sir Robert's generation had been closely connected with the Mundys. Portraits of the early '50's by Devis of Sir Robert Burdett and of his brother-in-law Sir Charles Sedley passed to the Mundy family (sold Christie's, 19th November 1965, Nos. 51 and 50) along with portraits of F. N. C. Mundy's father Wrightson, and two portraits of Mundy himself, his son and grandchildren by R. R. Reinagle, dated 1809. The portrait of Francis Mundy with his grandson by Reinagle (1809) has *The Fall of Needwood* and *Needwood Forest* on the table in front of him. The *Fall* bears the date 1808.

4 Hayley, 1823, ii, p. 339: 'This lady...has been long a favourite of the Hayleys...'

5 *Loc. cit.*, I, p. 418. Captain French owned Wright's *Chee Tor* [Plate 265] and was the artist's personal friend (see p. 155).

6 'The Economy of Vegetation', Canto III, line 308.

7 Information about Harry Peckham comes from the County Record Office, Chichester. A note in Wright's MS. Account Book reads: 'The letter in Mr. Mundys Picture to be dated from Amberley in Sussex [.] it may conclude with ["] Your friend Harry Peckham ["], not Henry [.] The Case upon the Latter's Table may be directed to Francis Mundy Esqr at Markeaton near Derby'. This still life may occur in another portrait of F. N. C. Mundy, now lost.

8 Wright painted a portrait of Sir Edward's daughter-in-law about the same time in a semi-realistic pose befitting her station [Plate 40]. A later generation of Wilmots of Chaddesden acquired the *Old Man and Death* [Plate 123].

9 See Roy Christian, 'Barton Blount Hall', *Derbyshire Countryside*, April–May 1964, pp. 28 ff. The Bradshaws acquired Barton Blount from the Cromptons in the early nineteenth century and the family died out at the beginning of this century.

Mundy's brothers-in-law: Francis Burdett, whose sister Elisabeth he married in 1770, and Nicholas Heath, who married his sister Mary two years earlier. Burdett (1745–94) also belonged to an ancient Derbyshire family,[1] and in Wright's portrayal of him [Plate 38] the image of accumulated eminence threatens to blot out the man. He himself achieved no special prominence apart from marrying a Wiltshire heiress, the daughter of the owner of beautiful Ramsbury; the only pen-portrait that survives of him conjuring up a peculiarly unattractive character: '...an over-grown Baby, the manly sensible seriousness of his son contrasts curiously with the flippant nonesense, the loud causeless Laugh, the hop-step-and-jump restless activity of the Father';[2] nor did his father Sir Robert,[3] who built Foremark in the Palladian style in the heyday of architectural enterprise, and was M.P. for Tamworth for thirty years—not at that time an occupation involving the expenditure of much energy or talent; however, his son Francis who succeeded his grandfather as 5th baronet, became the hero of Catholic Emancipation and the Reform Bill and is still studied by schoolchildren. Heath [Plate 37], who later changed his name to Nicholas, remains a shadowy figure, but his wife cut a tiny notch for herself in history by taking on the responsibility of looking after Hayley's wife in 1786 when she was suffering from a bout of acute nervous depression, and of trying to engineer an amicable separation between husband and wife.[4] Wright also painted Mundy's other sister Millicent (c. 1746–89), who married a Captain French. Millicent's portrait is lost and only her husband's remains [Plate 85]. Again it is the female side of the family which makes its mark: Hayley wrote after her death: '[Mrs. French] has an interesting tenderness of character, like the painting of Corregio';[5] and Erasmus Darwin just had time to squeeze a flattering obituary of her into his *Botanic Garden*.[6]

Of the other members of the Hunt painted by Wright, only one need detain us: Harry Peckham [Plate 35], the son of the vicar of Amberley in Sussex, today one of the *bijou* villages of England. He was Bencher of the Middle Temple and sometime Recorder of Chichester. He was extremely fond of hunting and died from a broken neck after an accident in the field.[7] We are presented, then, with a bevy of young sparks who have reached their social eminence through no effort of their own. Stark realism would therefore have been out of place when it came to perpetuating their features, and we must respect Wright for having lent them a touch of Reynolds's grand manner—a device which ensures that their superiority will appear genuinely effortless.

The Wilmot children [Plates 9, 10, 11, 12, 13, 15], on the other hand, are painted with greater sympathy, in a style equivalent to that of Liotard on the Continent. Their little faces are naive, questioning. They may not take so happily to their mock-military roles as the heir to Kedleston takes to his role of mock-grandeur, but being well brought up they dutifully adopt the poses their parents ask of them. There is no Van Dyck flourish here but a delicate realistic Rococo. If we did not know who these children were, we might guess they belonged to the landed gentry but on a lower social level than the Mundys and Burdetts, and this is exactly what we discover when we turn to the Wilmot genealogical tree. These were the children of a younger branch of the Wilmots of Chaddesden. Their father's elder brother was Edward Wilmot of Chaddesden, who had just been created baronet (1759), and was physician in ordinary to George II.[8] Their father Richard had married the only daughter of Sir Simon Degge of Derby and Staffs., and was rector of Morley, vicar of Mickleover and one time canon of Windsor. Those among the children depicted who survived into full adult life achieved distinction or wealth: Edward Sacheverell inherited a fortune from Elizabeth Sitwell of Renishaw on his elder brother Richard Staunton's death, adopted the surname of Sitwell, and married the daughter of a baronet; Robert followed his father in 1777 as rector of Morley—decent but not spectacular country gentlemen, in other words, for whom Wright finds the correct idiom. The Bradshaw children [Plate 57] are charmingly grouped in a park and do not need to tell us they are living secure country-house lives. They are the children of Joseph Baggaley of Holbrook, who became sheriff of the county in 1777 and a gentleman farmer. He acquired the name, arms and considerable fortune of the Bradshaws in 1767, at about the moment this picture was painted.[9] The fact that the children are *nouveaux riches* does not disturb them in the least.

Analyses of all the early portraits along these lines would make tedious reading, and in any case we know nothing of some of the sitters, such as the little girl at Temple Newsam [Plate 29], the lady in St. Louis [Plate 31], and the lady in a collection in Memphis (Tennessee) [Plate 32], though it would not be straining the evidence too far to assume that they also must have been born great or had greatness thrust upon them: they have settled down too comfortably to a Carver-like Rococo on Wright's canvases to have had to achieve greatness by their own efforts. The same cannot be said of the portraits Wright painted in Liverpool at the end of the seventh decade. So far in Derbyshire he had received commissions from descendants of ancient families, country gentlemen, sportsmen, public servants qualifying for their jobs by their position in society, farmers, the children of respectable clergymen, and had responded accordingly, giving them a Mannerist, Baroque, Rococo or 'grand manner' twist according to their circumstances. But here in Liverpool as the guest of a prominent merchant Richard Tate, he had encountered a hard-headed merchant class anxious to be commemorated in portraiture, and saw his chance of developing his bent for realism which had lurked at the heart of his earlier experiments but which out of propriety he had been obliged to play down. Suddenly he found himself precipitated into a progressive mercantile community ruled by a slave-trading and ship-owning oligarchy: 'throughout this large-built Town', writes a visitor only a few years before the abolition of the Slave Trade, 'every Brick is cemented to its fellow Brick by the blood and sweat of Negroes';[1] and in this atmosphere Wright's talents blossomed. The Carvers had been pretty puppets, the Lygons stiff puppets churned out like dolls on a conveyor belt, but now at last Wright had no inducement to drown the individual in the type.

Sarah Clayton survives in life as well as in art [Plate 63] as a dominant personality. If there were a phrase like 'blue-stocking' applicable to female industrialists, she would earn it. In 1745 she inherited Parr Hall, with its coal mine near St. Helens, and by 1757 when the Sankey navigation (projected by the husband of another of Wright's sitters, Mrs. Ashton) reached Parr, she had opened two new pits. She seems to have held with her nephews, the Case brothers (one of whom married Mrs. Ashton's daughter, whom Wright also painted) a leading position in the Liverpool coal market during the 'monopoly' period c. 1757–73. Unlike Liverpool merchants today who show no interest in artistic matters, she was also cultivated: advocating the use of John Wood as architect for the New Exchange (Town Hall) in Liverpool in 1749.[2] She laid down Clayton Square in the '50's[3] and took up residence there in 1767[4] just before Wright reached Liverpool. This was the largest house in the square, on the south corner site. We have entered into these details about her house because the architect's plan on the table in front of her in Wright's portrait agrees with the topography of the square. She became bankrupt in 1778 and her health was broken by this failure in the following year, but she has become part of the mythology of the place: it is much to her credit, for instance, that one of Liverpool's emergent Pop groups is called The Clayton Squares.[5]

Another local magnate who sat to Wright, *Fleetwood Hesketh* [Plate 61], was a member of a ship-owning family. He is posed just as informally as any of the Markeaton huntsmen but this time without a trace of the grand manner to help him along with his distinction. *Thomas Staniforth* [Plate 72] came to Liverpool from Yorkshire, marrying into a ship-owning family, the Goores, who were trading to Africa in the '50's. His father-in-law was interested in the Greenland Fisheries, and Staniforth carried on the business after his death in 1783. He was also a partner in a wine, rum and brandy firm, and in a firm of bankers in the '90's. He had shares in slaves, but he was a man of enlightened views, and interested in music. Wright shows this shrewd merchant in a startlingly natural pose, resting an arm on the back of a chair as though he were still discussing with the painter the best pose to take up—when the painter realised no pose was necessary.[6]

As for the Ashtons, they were slave traders on their way to becoming refined.[7] They belonged to an ancient Liverpool family but had only recently established themselves as leading merchants, and one can still see in the older generation represented by the formidable lady in the Fitzwilliam [Plate 64] the struggle for power carving its way into her features. Her husband John Ashton had made his money in the slave trade, had projected the Sankey Canal (the first, before the Duke of Bridgewater had come on to the scene),

1 Stevens, 1965, p. 436, entry for 20th August 1797.

2 Letter from Bath, 5th June 1749; published by S. A. Harris, *Trans. of the Hist. Society of Lancs. and Cheshire*, c, pp. 55–72.

3 Harris, *loc. cit.*, quoting a *Liverpool Town Book* entry dated 6th December 1752 referring 'to the field out of which she is laying out her intended square'.

4 She is not in Gore's Liverpool Directory of 1766 but her name is entered for the first time in the following year, with this address.

5 The author is extremely indebted to Mr. John Jacob for the information in this paragraph relating to Mrs. Clayton.

6 Information on Liverpool merchants in the eighteenth century has been obtained from the following publications. Gomer Williams, *History of the Liverpool Privateers... with an Account of the Liverpool Slave Trade*, London, 1897; John Hughes, *Liverpool Banks & Bankers 1760–1837*, London and Liverpool, 1906; Elizabeth Donnan, *Documents illustrative of the History of the Slave Trade to America*, Washington D.C., 1931, 2 vols.

7 For further details about the Ashton family, see Harris, 1951, pp. 161 ff.

and was an immensely prosperous salt manufacturer. Their son Nicholas worked as a young man in the salt works, and later made his fortune in the borough as a ship owner. It was in this generation that the Ashtons turned to the sweet things of life. Nicholas owned no less than four houses in Liverpool before 1772 when he acquired a country seat, Woolton Hall. He became a cultivated man; high sheriff of Lancashire in 1770, the friend of Roscoe, the patron of Robert Adam in the rebuilding of his country house, an amateur painter, and president in 1787 of the 'Society for Promoting the Arts in Liverpool'. As far as we know Wright did not paint him but we can deduce what the painter would have made of him from his portraits of the female members of the family. Wright confined his attention to Nicholas's mother [Plate 64], his two sisters Elizabeth [Plate 66] and Anna [Plate 65], to his wife Mary [Plate 67] and to their son John [Plate 68]. One sister was married to a slave trader, John Bostock; Thomas Case, the future husband of the one posed as a shepherdess, was a coal merchant and also probably a slave trader; but they are both well on their way to establishing themselves as country ladies. Wright does not flinch at bringing out the ugliness of Nicholas's wife, but she is moving as decorously as she can away from her father-in-law's exploitation of the negro by immersing herself in Thomson's *Seasons*— the page is inevitably open at 'Spring'. All three still have a long way to go before they assume the ease of the Derbyshire landed gentry. And as for the little boy [Plate 68], he still looks much more out of his element in this landscape than the countrified boy in the *Bradshaw* group [Plate 57].[1]

It is much to Wright's credit that he was able to move from this tough seafaring community to the placid cathedral city of Lichfield, the home of Dr. Johnson, without turning a hair, and with Erasmus Darwin to know how to cope with the same deftness as he had coped with Thomas Staniforth. We can imagine him finding his level without effort in the society of the Bishop's Palace, which was to remain the hub of intellectual life in the Midlands until Matthew Boulton collected a group of scientists around him in Birmingham. The Palace was presided over by the Rev. Thomas Seward, canon of Lichfield and Salisbury, who had gone to live in Lichfield in the middle of the century, and had taken up residence at the Palace shortly afterwards. In 1750 he published in collaboration with others an edition of Beaumont and Fletcher. 'He was a genteel well-bred dignified clergyman', writes Boswell when he and Dr. Johnson are invited to dine at the Palace one day in 1776. Boswell goes on to describe a conversation which would have made Wright prick up his ears: 'Mr. Seward mentioned to us the observations which he had made upon the strata of earth in volcanos, from which it appeared, that they were so very different in depth at different periods, that no calculation whatever could be made as to the time required for their formation...'.[2] Wright did not paint the dignified clergyman until the early '80's [Plate 230], but on that occasion it is significant that his daughter Anna, in some verses addressed to Wright, praises her father's portrait, not for the ennobling of his features, but for its life-like qualities—just the ones we would have expected to find there:

> 'Ingenious Wright! From thy creative hands,
> With outline bold, and massive colours warm,
> Rival of life, before the canvas stands
> My father's lov'd and venerable form!...'[3]

The portrait Wright painted at Lichfield in 1770 of Dr. Seward's friend Erasmus Darwin [Fig 115] was also recognised by Anna Seward as a good likeness: '... Dr. Darwin sat to Mr. Wright about the same period [1770]. *That* was a simple contemplative portrait, of the most perfect resemblance'.[4] Even had she not told us, and the portrait had vanished, we would have guessed that the doctor, passionately addicted to unravelling every secret hidden in man and nature, for ever inventing new devices, mechanical and medical, for making life more comfortable and more civilised, a rationalist, a philosopher, a poet, a wit, an eccentric, would not have wished to be fixed on canvas looking like anything but his own odd self; that is to say, 'never handsome, or personally graceful...; older much in appearance than in reality; lame and clumsy...'.[5] The rationalist like the merchant preferred

1 No other Liverpool portraits are known for certain, but it is significant that many other names in Wright's list of sitters there in 1769 (MS. Account Book; [Fig 28]) are familiar to us from the publications mentioned in note 6, p. 99. In a list published by Donnan, *op. cit.*, pp. 492–3 of the 'Company of Merchants trading to Africa... belonging to Liverpool, June 24th, 1752', besides the names of John Ashton and John Bostock, appear those of John Atherton, Pierce Lee, John Hardman, John and Edward Parr, Charles Goore, and John Tarleton. Wright does not give Christian names, so that we cannot be sure which of his sitters are the same person. 'Leigh' could be Pierce Lee; 'Gore' could be Staniforth's in-laws; and 'Tarlton' could be John Tarleton. The others, if not the actual slave traders mentioned, are likely to be members of the same family.

2 Boswell's *Life of Johnson*, II, ed. 1934, p. 467. Entry for 24th March 1776.

3 'Verses addressed to Mr. Wright of Derby, By Miss Seward. On his having painted her father's Picture', under the date 1783; see Seward, 1810, II, p. 140 and Walpole, 1937, pp. 119–22. The portrait is not known for certain, but one described as of Dr. Seward in a 1924 sale is most likely to be it [Plate 230].

4 Seward, 1804, p. 21.

5 In the words of Miss Seward, 1804, p. 154.

truth to grace in pictures as in everything else, and both were lucky enough to find a portrait painter at hand to satisfy them. Darwin weaves himself in and out of Wright's life from this time until the painter's death, both as a friend and as a medical consultant, but their period of closest intimacy belongs to a later chapter when Darwin became Wright's neighbour in Derby. It is sufficient at present to recall that Darwin came of an obscure middle-class family near Newark (Notts.) where he was born three years before Wright; that he was educated at Cambridge and Edinburgh, and moved from Newark to the more stimulating atmosphere of Lichfield in 1756, about the moment that Seward moved into the Bishop's Palace; that his wife died in 1770 and that Anna Seward is always said to have hoped to fill her place in his affections.

Around these two scholars and their soulful poetess, the brightest young stars from all over the Midlands hovered: Francis Mundy from Markeaton, and another well-born intellectual who became Wright's patron, Brooke Boothby from Ashbourne, attached themselves to the Lichfield circle in the '70's. The most eccentric of them all was a youth named Thomas Day (1748–89), chiefly remembered in history for a best-selling children's book, *Sandford and Merton*, who survives in the popular imagination, if he survives at all, as a prim Sunday School teacher.[1] He had been introduced to Darwin in 1768 in Staffordshire by his intimate friend Richard Lovell Edgeworth, and Darwin invited him to Lichfield. Day at this moment conceived the idea of educating two young girls in the approved Rousseau fashion, one as a possible future wife, and left for France with them in the autumn of 1769. Edgeworth tells us that he 'endeavoured to imbue them with a deep hatred for dress, and luxury, and fine people, and fashion, and titles...' On his return he parted with one of his pupils, finding her 'invincibly stupid'; he resolved to continue educating the other, but eventually cast her off as well—for ever—owing to some trifling misdemeanour. Like Anna Seward who had lapped up *La Nouvelle Héloise* as a child in her teens, Day was a passionate admirer of Rousseau. In a letter to Edgeworth from Avignon he writes: 'were all the books in the world to be destroyed, except scientific books (which I except, not to affront you) the second book I should wish to save, after the Bible, would be Rousseau's Emilius... every page is big with important truth...' Day was so much attracted to Darwin that he bought a house at Stowe Valley, near St. Chad's, with a splendid view of Lichfield Cathedral across the fields, on his return from abroad so as to be near him, and Edgeworth stayed with him there in the summer of 1770. The two young men were warmly received at the Bishop's Palace. Edgeworth became enamoured of Mr. Seward's

1 This is the implied view of him in *De Profundis*, ed. 1949, p. 63.

Fig 115 *Erasmus Darwin* 1770
30 x 25 in / 76.2 x 63.5 cm   G. P. Darwin;
on loan to Darwin College, Cambridge
Cat 50   Pl 78

Fig 116 *Thomas Day* 1770
50 x 40 in / 127 x 101.6 cm   The Lord Belper
Cat 58   Pl 80

1 For Edgeworth and Day at Lichfield, see Edgeworth, 1820, I, pp. 196 ff.; Gignilliat, 1932, pp. 67–70; Voisine, 1956, pp. 45 ff.

2 'Mr. Day's exterior was not at that time [c. 1767–8] prepossessing, he seldom combed his raven locks, though he was remarkably fond of washing in the stream' (Edgeworth, 1820, I, p. 180).

3 The catalogue of the Lunar Society exhibition, Birmingham, 1966 (55) states that the Belper version includes these inscriptions, but this is not correct.

4 Seward, 1804, pp. 20–1.

5 Keir, 1791, p. 86.

6 Edgeworth, 1820, I, pp. 180 ff.

ward Honora Sneyd whom he later married; Day turned his attentions, so as not to be left out of things, to the younger sister Elizabeth, but with less success. Day and Edgeworth left for France together shortly afterwards.[1] It was in the interval during their residence at Stowe Valley that Wright painted Day's portrait [Fig 116], which passed to Edgeworth after Day's death.

If we had not known who the sitter was, we might have supposed it represented an actor about to declaim, and in a sense this is true: Day in his shabby attire[2] seems to be on the point of haranguing a crowd on the iniquities of the slave trade. He had in fact just completed an anti-slavery poem-tract, *The Dying Negro*. It does not seem to have occurred to Wright that there was anything incongruous in hobnobbing with Liverpool slave-traders one month, and with a passionate abolitionist the next, but we have to remember the Ashtons were settling down as artists and patrons of the arts, that Wright had never known them in their savage days, and that in any case slave-trading was not then regarded as despicable—any more than we would call despicable a member of the New Party in the early 1930's. All the same, perhaps he had the decency to conceal the fact of his earlier associations from the wild young man in a state of nature who now took their place. The portrait was well thought of by Day's contemporaries. Miss Seward's description of it is quite inaccurate; it sounds as though she held an engraving in front of her as she composed it, since 'right' should read 'left' and *vice versa*, and she records inscriptions on the column and book which are not legible on either of the known versions.[3] However, she was at Lichfield when it was painted, and so some weight must be attached to her words. (Here again the likeness is said to be good, but this time fidelity to appearances is at once followed by a reference to the portrait's dignity—as though she felt, as we do, that unadulterated realism would have been out of place.)

'In the course of the year 1770, Mr. Day stood for a full-length picture to M.ʳ Wright of Derby. A strong likeness and a dignified portrait were the result... He stands leaning his left arm against a column inscribed to Hampden. M.ʳ Day looks upwards, as enthusiastically meditating on the contents of a book, held in his dropped right hand. The open leaf is the oration of that victorious patriot in the Senate, against the grant of ship-money, demanded by King Charles the first... The poetic fancy, and what were *then* [her italics] the politics of the original, appear in the choice of subject and attitude...'[4]

Two further quotations are necessary to interpret the portrait correctly: one from an anonymous memoir published after Day's death: 'In person Mr. Day was tall, strong, erect, and of a manly deportment. The expression of his countenance, though somewhat obscured by marks of the small pox, indicated the two leading features of his character, firmness and sensibility...';[5] the other, a tribute from his closest friend Edgeworth: 'It is but justice, and not the partiality of friendship, that induces me to assert, that Mr. Day was the most virtuous human being I have ever known...'.[6] We know that true friendship is not capable of justice but this does not make his words any the less affecting.

Wright's portrait of Day is no more a realistic image than Mundy's had been, or Booth-by's was to be. But we have found on other occasions and shall find again that he reserved realism for realistic people, and for the remainder preferred a more conceptual image—in Day's case, a theatrical pose expressive of his attractive other-worldliness. It would make an entertaining guessing-game, to imagine what convention he would have found for personalities he did not paint or whose portraits are lost to us: Miss Seward would have been immortalised as a neo-classic Juno or Hebe (but this task was left to Romney), whilst Wedgwood would have come in for the same down-to-earth treatment as was meted out to Darwin (but this task was left to Stubbs). This is where his talents as a portrait painter came into play: in his capacity to adapt his style to each new sitter. However, the contrast between his portrayal of Darwin, not as a 'philosopher' but as Darwin, and that of Day, not as Day but as a visionary, is more than a mere demonstration of his versatility. It takes us beyond the history of art into social history, by showing how attitudes of mind could alter in the space of a generation. In the first case, we are shown a middle-aged scientist, whose life is dedicated to reducing illusions to a minimum, who cannot conceive of reaching truth except by trial and error stage by stage up the slope of experiment; in the second, we are shown a melancholy young philanthropist carried away by *Emile*, who has decided on certain fixed rules for the conduct of life, and will put these rules so doggedly into practice that nothing, not even the prospect of causing misery to others, will deflect him from them. Yet the differences between them did not disturb the harmony of their relations. For in the first place Darwin was also attracted by Rousseau's theories of education, and most of all by his interest in botany, and had actually engineered a meeting with the French philosopher on a botanical excursion when Rousseau was staying not far from Lichfield at Wootton Hall three or four years before; in the second place, Darwin regarded Day's dogmatic Rousseauism with amused benevolence; while Day venerated the older man's omniscience. They met on some deep level of understanding where disastrous experiments in education could be written off as unfortunate miscalculations; where virtue and intelligence alone reigned.

We have only one further rung to descend down the social ladder; below that, Wright's portraits became character studies. This is the case of a self-made man painted by Wright in his youth (and there may have been others of whom we have no adequate record); who did not settle down like the Ashtons to a cultivated mode of life on making his pile, or lead a self-contained existence outside the community like the members of the Lichfield circle; who was represented on canvas, as we might have guessed, in the most realistic manner possible within the forbidding framework imposed by Hudson's tutelage; a man happy to expose his unsophisticated origin, proud of his business acumen and anxious that it should be written into his face: William Brooke, dealer in fabrics, Alderman and sometime Mayor of the provincial town of Doncaster into which not much gracious living had been permitted to penetrate [Plate 21]. We derive little impression of the appearance of Mr. and Mrs. Lygon, or of Miss Ann Carver, but we are left in no doubt as to what Brooke looked like, with his belly bursting out of his waistcoat and his bulk threatening to overpower his chair. One of his sons, far from becoming a Whig pamphleteer or amateur painter, took up the profession of merchant in Wakefield. His son-in-law Pigot, on the other hand, whom Wright also painted [Plate 23] has acquired a certain refinement from his upbringing in the vicarage of Doncaster, and has transferred some of it to his young wife the mayor's daughter [Plate 24] who will continue, during her five remaining years of life, to wear her expensive clothes as though she were as well established as the Lygons.[1]

Wright in his portrait of the mayor of a provincial town is permitted to display his qualities as a realistic portrait painter more openly than at any other time, until late in life when other self-made men, the Oldknows, the Hurts, Rowe, Strutt and Arkwright, would consent to sit to him, and also be shown as they really were. Though the *William Brooke* will strike the historian of form as a primitive work, most closely paralleled by the *Reginald Lygon*, the social historian will instinctively travel on thirty years to find its counterpart in the *Richard Arkwright*.

If we wish to find out where an artist's deepest preoccupations in the realm of portraiture lie, we must study what he made of his own body in the mirror. Two of Wright's early self-portraits [Plate 6, Frontispiece] show how he searched his body as though he intended to make a map of it. We must be grateful to Mrs. Nicholas Ashton, to Brooke and Staniforth, and to Erasmus Darwin, for encouraging him to search theirs as well.

1 For Brooke and Pigot, see Harleian Society, *Familiae Minorum Gentium*, pp. 763–7.

2 PURCHASERS OF THE FIRST SUBJECT PICTURES 1760–73

Until Wright began exhibiting in London in 1765 and so became known to the leading collectors, his clientele had necessarily been confined to Midlands families, chiefly Derbyshire but also neighbouring counties to the East. The family portrait was what was then wanted, which explains why he was more prolific in this genre in the early '60's than at any other period of his life. He is not known to have sold paintings other than portraits before the *Orrery* [Plate 54] and the *Gladiator* [Plate 52] but a *Girl reading a letter by candlelight* [Plate 45] does appear on stylistic grounds to be the earliest known of his candlelight subjects, and it is conceivable that he had disposed of it in Newark or Retford before any of the great collectors had a chance to get at it. As soon as he began exhibiting at the Incorporated Society, his subject pieces were in great demand, and he sold almost all the important ones. A few remained on his hands. The *Alchemist* [Plate 106] and the *Captive King* (lost) he took with him to Italy, thinking he might be able to dispose of them there; and the companion to the *Alchemist*, the *Hermit* [Plate 105], he left behind him in England, hoping to sell it to the Empress of Russia but she decided against it. These were the only important pictures, among those exhibited before he left England, that he was obliged to retain. The failure to dispose of the *Old Man and Death* [Plate 123] can be partly put down to his absence abroad during the period of its exhibition in 1774. As for a mysterious *Belshazzar's Feast* (Cat No 223), nothing has been heard of it since a casual mention of it in a letter from Wedgwood to Bentley of 1778.

The most sympathetic figure among his early patrons, the purchaser of the *Air Pump* [Plate 58], was Dr. Benjamin Bates, a half-forgotten hedonist who is worth resuscitating since he was the perfect embodiment of his age without having left any special mark on it; the kind of man who has all the clichés about the period loaded onto him, like a character out of Hogarth or *Tom Jones*; a dilettante of the best type, devoted to works of art but also making a fool of the puritan by sampling all the good things in life, over-indulging in them, and then instead of dying in agony at fifty, living to be nearly 100. He always kept his age quiet but he is said to have been born about 1736[1] in the North of England and to have studied medicine in Edinburgh.[2] About 1758 he settled as a physician in Aylesbury. He was married twice but only one child, a daughter Lydia (c. 1772–1850) who became an amateur painter, reached adult life. He became a member of the Hell Fire Club at Medmanham on the Thames near Henley, which has lived in history as the closest English equivalent to *Justine*. Long after its dissolution when Bates was its one surviving member, he would take pains to defend its memory by claiming that the scandalous stories circulated about the goings-on there were monstrously exaggerated—nobody knows with how much justification. In 1781 he was to have attended his friend and fellow-ex-member of the Hell Fire Club, Francis Lord Le Despencer, as personal physician on a tour of the Continent and

1 An inscription on a commemorative tablet to Bates, let into the floor of the church at Little Missenden adjoining his house, informs us that he died on 12th May 1828 aged 92 years. His age is not confirmed from any other known source, but if this turns out to be correct, then he was a year or two younger than Wright.

2 The author is, however, informed by Dr. V. E. Lloyd Hart that no Dr. Benjamin Bates graduated in medicine at Edinburgh University.

gave up his regular practice for this purpose, but his prospective patient inconveniently died, and Bates was deprived both of his patronage and of a huge annuity which was to have been settled on him for his services. He died at Little Missenden in 1828, in the same year as Bonington.[1]

Bates was passionately addicted to literature and art, and the few glimpses we catch of him as patron and art lover show him up in the most picturesque light. His friend Thomas Jones describes travelling down in August 1774 to the house Bates had acquired at Little Missenden: '...My principal business on this Occasion was pleasure, but my Ostensible business was to paint for the Doctor a view of the house at Chalfont St. Giles, whither, according to tradition, the Poet *Milton* retired during the Plague in London...' This was to be a small oval, with the addition of some figures by Mortimer describing a scene from *L'Allegro*; there was to be a companion piece with a scene from *Il Penseroso*. Jones goes on to describe how they drove over to a house near Amersham (that of a member of the Drake family whom Mortimer subsequently immortalised in a conversation piece for Shardeloes) a few days later to see some Vernets, and thence to Chalfont St. Giles, where they sat down to dinner in a room where they imagined Milton had often dined; and how Dr. Bates, 'over the second bottle', was heard '*spouting* with an elevated Voice, the *L'Allegro* and *Il Pensoroso* to an old woman who was spinning in One Corner of the Parlour...' A large room in the house at Little Missenden that Bates had designed purposely for the reception of his collection of paintings was then just finished, and he and Jones spent a day at the end of September 'arranging the pictures' in it. They must have got help with the *Air Pump*. Early the following year Jones again visited Bates at Little Missenden, to find Bates's closest friend John Hamilton Mortimer installed there, engaged on painting the figures in the two ovals.[2]

Bates later placed his former residence at Rickford's Hill, Aylesbury at Mortimer's disposal. Mortimer did not quite settle down there but commuted between Aylesbury and his house in Norfolk Street, London until his death (1779). Meanwhile Bates had assembled a collection of Mortimers, and before 1778 presented his *St. Paul preaching to the Britons* to the church at High Wycombe as an altarpiece.[3] Bates was also a close friend of Angelica Kauffmann; and after the death of Lord Le Despencer, bent on visiting Rome at all costs, he travelled there accompanied by his daughter Lydia, and by a new friend, the sculptor Flaxman. Just before leaving he wrote to Flaxman's wife (4th January 1787) telling her he had 'just now received a most beautiful specimen of a naked body from a Friend in the country, to all appearances wrought by the hand of Him who finished the Saviour of the Roman Capitol, & notwithstanding the extremities are mutilated, as all *true Antiques* ought to be, I have a few doubts concerning the period in wch this chef d'œuvre was produced which I have now the honour to present to you...' Relations did not remain so cordial. Flaxman had the misfortune to love Lydia; she paid insufficient attention to him, to judge by some cryptic letters he wrote home from Rome, and the friendship fizzled out in the early '90's.[4]

One can now understand why Bates, with his keen interest in antiques, should have wished to acquire Wright's first exhibited subject piece, the *Gladiator* [Plate 52], where figures are shown peering at a statuette of a naked body after the antique, and why he should also have possessed his greatest subject picture of all, the *Air Pump* [Plate 58],[5] where an experiment such as he might well have witnessed during his time as a medical student in Edinburgh, is conducted on a bird in a glass bowl. He must already have known Wright before 1765 through his Midlands connections: he was in Derby as a child, and lived there for a time before settling in Aylesbury;[6] and perhaps their mutual friend the mysterious Mortimer brought them closer together.

Considering the preoccupation with the subject-matter of art in the later eighteenth century, it would be surprising had the *Orrery* [Plate 54] not also been sold to someone with a special interest in the subject, in this case with astronomy. Wright simply tells us that 'Ld Ferrers' bought it. This was not of course the fourth Earl Laurence who had been tried by his peers in Westminster Hall for murder in 1760, and was hanged in May; nor his brother the sixth Earl Robert, from whom subsequent earls are descended, since he only became Earl Ferrers in 1778, a good thirteen or fourteen years after the picture was painted. In any case, it was put up for sale by the sixth Earl the year after he succeeded, and it is inconceivable

1 For information about Bates, apart from the obvious sources such as histories of Buckinghamshire, Wycombe, Aylesbury etc., see *The historical and the posthumous memoirs of Sir Nathaniel William Wraxall 1772–1784*, ed. Harry B. Wheatley, 1884, I, p. 209; and Robert Gibbs, *Buckinghamshire Local Occurrences*, 1880, entry for 12th May 1828.

2 See Jones, 1951, pp. 33–35.

3 See Gilbert Benthall, *John Hamilton Mortimer, A. R. A., Drawings and Engraved works*, n.d. (c. 1950–55), typescript, Victoria and Albert Museum Library, pp. 67–8. Benthall makes clear that financial problems were largely instrumental in persuading Mortimer to accept Bates's offer of the Aylesbury house, rather than (as used to be thought), ill health. The information about Bates's relations with Mortimer comes from an early source, an anonymous writer in the *Monthly Magazine*, 1796, p. 23, who sought Bates's advice when writing Mortimer's biography.

4 The letter from which a passage is quoted (Brit. Mus. Add. MSS. 39781, ff. 362–3) was kindly communicated to the author by David Irwin. The other letters referred to are Add. MSS. 39780 (ff. 42, 46–7, 51, 53–5).

5 Bemrose, 1885, p. 12 quotes a letter from Wright to Bates dated 12th September 1772 in which Wright asks £130 for an unnamed picture. Bemrose thinks this is the *Gladiator* but Wright's Account Book gives £40 for the price of this picture, which would be reasonable for his first exhibited work, not very much smaller than that asked for the *Earthstopper* of nearly ten years later (£52–10). Moreover the *Shuttleworth Family* (1764) only cost £42. The letter to Bates must therefore concern the *Air Pump*. In it he says the small sum 'might much injure me in the future sale of my pictures, and when I send you a receipt for the money I shall acknowledge a greater sum'. This would explain why the *Air Pump* is listed in the Account Book at £200 and £210—an understandable confusion about a phoney price.

6 See letter from John Holland of Ford to Wright's brother, 11th August 1801, quoted Bemrose, 1885, p. 111, asking him if he remembered Dr. Bates when he was living in Derby. In the letter quoted above, note 5, Wright describes himself to Bates as 'Your affectionate friend'.

1 The *Orrery* was then bought in, but was put up for sale again at Staunton Harold in 1787 and is said to have been acquired by a 'Bruce', but it may again have been bought in; if so, this would account for a mysterious phrase in a letter from the then Earl Ferrers to Copley of 5th June 1791 (quoted by A. Cunningham, *The Lives of the most eminent British Painters...*, V, pp. 181–2): 'However, if Mr. Copley would undertake to do a family piece for him [Ferrers] with about six figures, about the [evidently large] size of the picture he has of Mr. Wright's, with frame and all...' No other picture but the *Orrery* is known to have been acquired by the Ferrers family.

2 For further details about financial transactions involving Wright, Lord Ferrers and Burdett, see below pp. 117–8.

3 Pilkington, 1789, II, p. 83: 'The family... spent but little time here [at Melbourne]. When they are in the country, they principally reside at their elegant house, Brocketthall...' The evidence points to the same situation being the case eighteen years earlier.

4 See catalogue of the Francis Wheatley Exhibition, Aldeburgh and Leeds, 1965, under No. 92 for the most up-to-date information about the decoration of this ceiling.

5 Although the *Academy by Lamplight* was ready by 1769, it cannot have been acquired until 1770 at the earliest, the date when Peniston Lamb was created Lord Melbourne in the Irish peerage (the purchaser being described by his title in the entry in Wright's Account Book). Perhaps Lord Melbourne acquired it at the same time as the *Blacksmith's Shop* (dated 1771 and exhibited that year). Lord Melbourne was still employing Wright in the late '80's but only to repair pictures in the Collection (in his MS. Account Book Wright records the receipt of 3 guineas for this work, 27th April 1789).

6 D.N.B., *ad vocem*.

7 For fuller details, see Connell, 1957, pp. 19 ff.

that any patron until modern times would be so wayward as to buy a picture one year and try to dispose of it the next.[1] The intervening brother Washington Shirley, fifth Earl Ferrers from 1760 to 1778, the only respectable holder of the title among a poor bunch, was alone capable of being interested in such an original creation. He was made Fellow of the Royal Society in 1761 for his observations on the transit of Venus and for mathematical discoveries. Before 1763 he would hardly have been in a position to raise the two hundred guineas Wright was asking for the picture, but in that year he was regranted such estates as had been forfeited by the fourth Earl, and was financially secure enough by 11th July of that year to put his signature to a bond, undertaking jointly with P. P. Burdett to pay Wright £160 within a year. The association between Ferrers and Burdett is explained by the fact that the latter was also a keen mathematician, and was then residing at Staunton Harold where the Ferrers's chief property was.[2]

Whereas Lord Ferrers's astronomical calculations must have played a part in inducing him to acquire the *Orrery*, we need not seek for Warburgian motives for the choice by Lords Melbourne and Palmerston of the *Blacksmith's Shop* [Plate 100] and the *Iron Forge* [Plate 103] respectively beyond the appeal of picturesqueness. It may be thought surprising that prominent, prosperous peers with the whole of contemporary art at their beck and call should succumb to such bourgeois taste: that Lord Melbourne should also acquire the *Academy by Lamplight* [Plate 60] showing a group of anonymous boys sketching, with none of the distinction of connoisseurs examining the *Gladiator*, and—odder still—that Lord Palmerston should wish to possess Wright's most 'Victorian' picture, of two girls decorating a cat [Plate 75]. But when we examine the careers of these men, their craving for pictures of innocence and of unusual light effects begins to make sense. Peniston Lamb, first Lord Melbourne (1748–1829) had been brought up at Melbourne Hall, Derbyshire, his father Sir Matthew having married a Coke who on the death of her brother in 1751, had inherited the house. Sir Matthew had been legal adviser to the Cokes, and so was a *parvenu*, not an aristocrat. His son's taste for Wright's bourgeois art can therefore be put down partly to his humble origin, in the absence of evidence that he possessed any of that intellectual distinction which occasionally drives aristocrats to go slumming. It is also likely that rumours had reached him as a youth of the progress of the only respectable painter the county had yet produced. But not too much weight should be placed on local patriotism as a motive for his patronage of Wright; for in the first place, he spent most of his time in Hertfordshire, at his residence Brocket Hall,[3] when not in London; and in the second, as a very young man he employed Mortimer to paint the ceiling of the Saloon there (1771–2)[4] at precisely the same moment as he was buying Wrights,[5] which suggests he was keen on the latest English painting, rather than just a supporter of a Derbyshire man. During the same years he also purchased one of the early Stubbs enamels. If the truth be known, he was not up to much. We tend to assume that the father of one of our greatest Prime Ministers must also have been a Lamb of God. But the first Lord Melbourne was an insignificant Parliamentarian, a 'silent follower of Lord North',[6] who was under the thumb of his wife Elizabeth Milbanke, later the great friend of Byron. No doubt it was this remarkable woman who was the driving force behind his encouragement of these two young artists.

The origins of Henry Temple, second Viscount Palmerston (1739–1802), the father of another Prime Minister, were much more illustrious. He was a *bona fide* Whig aristocrat, but also an intellectual, and this explains how his eye came to roam so far afield as to light on a cat being dressed up—just as the noble families of Rome in the early Seicento would not confine their enthusiasm to Baroque ceiling decorations but would also collect cabinets of picturesque, realistic tavern scenes in the Campagna. Lord Palmerston was another failure as a politician; like Francis Mundy, he agreeably escaped from his obligations as a public servant in order to devote his life to the cultivation of friendship, to his collections, and to travel. He added hundreds of pictures to the ancestral collection at Broadlands. He stayed with Voltaire at Ferney.[7] He was in Naples in 1764 with Garrick, and with the ninth Earl of Exeter, who also acquired picturesque genre pieces from Wright, a scene of *Boys with a bladder* and its companion (both untraced). They both delighted in sentimental representations of children: Palmerston, on being given second choice in Sir Joshua Reynolds's will of any picture by him, chose the *Infant Academy*; and both he and Lord Exeter possessed versions of Nollekens's *Boy on a Dolphin*.[1] A taste for picturesque scenery is a short step forward from this. On a second Grand Tour in 1770 Palmerston was accompanied by William Pars whose job it was to sketch bas reliefs and lake views, and in the early '80's acquired from Wright a *Vesuvius* and a view of Etna.

Wright's other early patrons outside Derbyshire can be disposed of more rapidly. There was a certain E. Parker who acquired about 1770–2 a small *Blacksmith's Shop*, two candle-lights, and (unless the purchase was cancelled at the last moment) a 'conversation' of two girls with their negro servant (all unidentified except the last [Plate 73]); a well-known collector Robert Alexander of Edinburgh, patron of Alexander and John Runciman, who owned another *Blacksmith's Shop* [Plate 101] in the early '70's but got rid of it a few years later; a 'Mr. Milnes', the purchaser of *Miravan* [Plate 107] who may have been Wright's later patron, John Milnes of Wakefield;[2] and Philip, second Earl of Hardwicke (1720–96) who had been painted by Gainsborough as Lord Royston in 1763 and bought the *Earth-stopper* [Plate 113]. Wright's closest relations with Catherine II of Russia belong to a later chapter in his career, but she was already buying from him an *Iron Forge viewed from without* [Plate 104] as well as marine paintings by Richard Paton, with figures by Mortimer,[3] in the early '70's. It is astonishing to consider that the only ripple Wright ever stirred up on the European continent was in remote St Petersburg, before he was forty and before he had achieved comparable success in his own county town.

So far none of the people we have been considering were resident in Derbyshire, and none had such close connections with the county that, even though living outside it, their loyalty to it played a decisive part in their patronage of a local painter. Though some were attracted to Wright's work on account of its scientific content, none except perhaps Milnes had a stake in industry. There is no evidence that any Derbyshire industrialist or merchant bought his subject pictures before he left for Italy. His clientele for everything except portraits was more or less confined to the aristocracy or well-to-do middle classes centred on London. This is why he saw the necessity to appear regularly in public in the capital, knowing that he could not rely on local support. There are, however, two exceptions: Thomas Coltman and Colonel Edward Pole, both prosperous landowners in Derbyshire before Wright left for abroad, and both owners of genre pieces. But even they confined their acquisitions in one case to two candlelights (which may have been presents), and in the other to four overdoors (which are subordinated to their function as decoration), remaining impervious to the romance of the Industrial Revolution humming all around them, and to Wright's imaginative grasp of its possibilities as subject-matter for art, showing more concern for portraits of themselves and of members of their families than for the new world they must have seen encroaching on the old in their midst.

Thomas Coltman (1746–1826) was not even a Derbyshire man. The Coltmans had been landed gentry in Lincolnshire since they acquired their estate at Hagnaby Priory in 1715/16.[4] This is within a few miles of Boston and one wonders whether Wright had become acquainted with the family at Boston or Newark[5] in 1760 when Thomas was a boy. His life has come down to us in a most fragmentary form.[6] His father died at Bath in 1763, his elder brother in Marseilles in 1768, and he was left the head of the family;[7] but by the latter date he had already moved to Derby, where he lived in the parish of St. Werburgh's not far from Wright. He married Mary Barlow in her native town of Astbury in Cheshire in 1769.[8] She died in 1786 but by that time Coltman had moved back to Lincolnshire and had passed out of Wright's life: he was at Hagnaby again by 1780.[9] For many years thereafter he was Chairman of the quarter sessions of Lindsey, and from all accounts a conscientious magistrate. He corresponded regularly with Sir Joseph Banks from at least 1794 to 1797 on such subjects as the raising of militiamen in Lincolnshire. One phrase in a letter carries us back to Wright's double portrait of him and his wife [Plate 91]: 'I propose to go out with the Hounds in the Morning wch. I can do more easily than write a letter. No uncommon thing with a Sportsman.'[10] These are not the words of an intellectual. He does not look like one, either, in his beautiful portrait, and we must suppose that he patronised Wright for other than artistic reasons—chief among them family pride. He had himself and his wife painted separately in black and white [Plate 119, 118] as well as together about the same time and bought—or more likely was given—the

1 See Seymour Howard, 'Boy on a Dolphin: Nollekens and Cavaceppi', *The Art Bulletin*, June 1964, p. 178.

2 See below, Part III, p. 159.

3 These were four pictures showing the *Defeat of the Turkish Fleet at Chesme Bay in 1770*. Thomas Jones assisted Paton as well as Mortimer (see entry for end of August 1771 in Jones, 1951, p. 24). In the Hermitage is a landscape by Jones with figures of Dido and Aeneas by Mortimer, dated 1769, but this did not come to the Hermitage until near the end of the century. It is described by Jones, *op. cit.*, p. 19.

4 Most of the Coltman family deeds are now deposited with the Archive Committee at Lincoln, and Mrs. J. Varley, the archivist, has been most helpful in providing some relevant material. It appears from these documents that the Coltman fortune was made in London by Thomas's great-uncle Henry. It was he who purchased the Hagnaby property in February–March 1715/16. After the death of his only son he entailed all his Lincolnshire estates on his nephew John, subject to the life interest of his widow. Wright's patron was John's fifth child and second surviving son (christened 9th July 1746).

5 It does not appear from the family deeds that Thomas's father ever lived at Hagnaby, and his son John (Thomas's elder brother) is described as of Newark on attaining his majority in 1766.

6 See *History of the County of Lincoln*, London and Lincoln, 1834, p. 109; *Lincoln, Rutland and Stamford Mercury*, 27th October 1826.

7 This emerges from a letter from Coltman to an unknown correspondent dated from Hagnaby Priory, 30th August 1821, kindly communicated by the Records Office, Lincoln.

8 The marriage licence (kindly communicated by the Cheshire County Council) refers to 'Thomas Coltman of the parish of St. Wirburgh in the county town of Derby, and John Barlow in the parish of Astbury in Cheshire'.

9 Coltman does not appear in the land tax for Hagnaby prior to that date, but of course he may have left Derby earlier.

10 The correspondence with Banks is kindly communicated by the Records Office, Lincoln. The letters run from 12th May 1794 to the spring of 1797, generally written from Hagnaby. The quotation is from a letter of 10th November (? 1796).

artist's self-portrait (Frontispiece; *c.* 1767–8) and two candlelights [Plates 76, 77; late '60's]—the whole group (intact in the family collection) falling within the ten or so years that the two men were close friends. Whenever the artist mentions his patron in letters to his family, it is with unusually warm feelings. In a letter to his brother from Exeter just before sailing for Italy he writes:

'... My good friend Coltman has behaved wonderfully generous and genteel to me he wrote to Mr. Commersley the Banker to give me a Letter of Credit for £500. I refused taking any, but he insisted upon my taking one for three hundred...'[1]

When abroad Wright rented to him some property near his home, for which Coltman paid two years' rent.[2] We do not hear of the association continuing after Wright's return, but only three years were left between the time when Wright settled down again permanently in Derby, and Coltman's departure for Hagnaby, so no doubt the friendship was allowed to limp to a silent close.[3]

His relationship with the Poles of Radburne Hall, Kirk Langley was altogether more formal, as it had been with the Mundys. The Poles traced their pedigree back to the Middle Ages, claiming descent from the distinguished De La Pole family. Unlike the Carvers, the Bradshaws or the Ashtons who improved themselves by marriage or inheritance or speculation, they held firmly to a static position in society as prosperous landed gentry, below the aristocracy and above the professional middle class, carrying out their military or county duties but never deigning to get down to business.[4] The head of the family in the early eighteenth century, German Pole, had been friendly with the Mundys and the Burdetts; sheriff of the county in the '30's, and in company with the Burdetts of his generation, a supporter of the Stuart cause. Traces of his Stuart sympathies survive at Radburne. The magnificent, though not ostentatious room there on the first floor which Mortimer and Wright were employed to decorate in the early '70's, was in German Pole's time hung with two large maps.[5] 'If the ornaments are examined', writes his great-nephew Sacheverell Pole in 1803 when he himself was owner of the house, 'the principles of Mr. German Pole will be understood [.] over the picture on the chimneypiece [Wright's portrait of the author's father, Colonel Pole] is the bust of the Pretender [.] under it the prince of wales feathers [.] over the Hall door a Bust of Britannia... I have been told that this Mr. Pole was a well wisher to the Pretender...'[6] These relics of an innocuous underground movement have been dutifully preserved by his descendants, and Britannia still gazes on Bonny Prince Charlie across the room. Like some ancient French families who still support the Royalist cause, the Poles looked back to the more glamorous age of the Stuarts.

German's only son predeceased him and when he himself died in 1765 he settled all his estates including Radburne Hall on his nephew Edward Sacheverell (1718–80), then a man of nearly fifty with a distinguished military career behind him. He was Lieutenant-Colonel commanding the 23rd Foot, or Royal Welsh Fusiliers; he was present at the Battle of Fontenoy and in the next year saw the Young Pretender at Culloden. He also served in the Seven Years' War and was wounded at Minden. He became full Colonel on 19th February 1762,[7] and was out of the Army List after 1764. Within five years of his succession, he set about redecorating the Saloon on the first floor. The maps were removed but out of piety the Stuart emblems preserved. He employed Mortimer to paint two enormous history pictures to go either side of the door leading into the Hall: a *Belisarius*, and a *Caius Marius on the ruins of Carthage*.[8] Since the second was not exhibited at the Society of Artists until 1774, Wright did not have a chance of seeing the decoration completed until after his return from abroad. Mortimer was paid 100 guineas each for these, and fifty guineas 'for the little one over the hall door',[9] representing an allegory of the arts, also still *in situ*. At the same time Wright was commissioned to paint a three-quarter length of Colonel Pole in armour with his hand resting on the barrel of a cannon, in a landscape setting, to go over the mantelpiece [Plate 87], but since he was out of the army by then, he is not depicted in uniform;[10] a full-length of his wife to hang opposite [Plate 88]; and four candlelight overdoors [Plates 92, 93, 94, 95] to be set above the remaining four doors in the room (the smaller Mortimer occupying the fifth), showing four children at one end and four grown-

1 MS. 2, Derby Public Library.

2 See letter to his brother from Rome, 12th February 1774, quoted Bemrose, 1885, p. 29. Wright refers to the property as 'the Close'. In his Account Book under the date 20th July 1774 he notes: 'Recd. of Tho! Coltman Esq! one years Rent for the Close in St. Werb! parish [St. Werburgh's] & due Lady day 1774... £21-10-0'. The same sum is recorded the following year. In a letter of 22nd May 1774 of which Bemrose, *op. cit.*, p. 33 only gives an extract, he says a Mr. Brentnall is Coltman's subtenant.

3 Coltman family deeds, 1/8/16–18.

4 For the history of the Pole family, see Jeayes, 1896; Adam Wolley, *History of Derbyshire*, Brit. Mus. Add. MS. 6671.

5 A MS. inventory of the effects at Radburne, 1765 lists 'in the Salloon': '2 large Maps'. The author is indebted to Major J. W. Chandos-Pole for allowing him access to the family documents at Radburne.

6 From a MS. account of the house by Sacheverell Pole, 1803 preserved at Radburne. Sacheverell had not been born when German died but would certainly have heard about him from his father.

7 He was never Colonel of the Regiment, as stated in the catalogue entry to a half-length version of his portrait, sold Sotheby's, 3rd June 1959.

8 They are published for the first time by Waterhouse, 1965, Figs. 19–20. The *Belisarius* was criticised in *Candid Observations*, 1772 on the grounds that the legs of the young soldier were too large.

9 According to Sacheverell Pole, see note 6.

10 The author is informed by Brigadier Thurburn that the medal shown is likely to be a commemorative medal given by the Austrian Government, perhaps for Colonel Pole's services in the Seven Years' War.

ups at the other. The work occupied him intermittently from about the winter of 1770–1, till well on into 1772. Mortimer, who was still working for Lord Melbourne in the latter year, must have overlapped with Wright in the later stages.

Colonel Pole's wife, Elizabeth Collier, the illegitimate daughter of the second Earl of Portmore, had by him one son Sacheverell, the red-headed boy whom she carries in her arms in Wright's portrait, and two daughters. One of the daughters in the summer of 1777 fell ill and was attended by Erasmus Darwin. This quickly led to a romance between Darwin and Mrs. Pole. Fortunately Colonel Pole died in 1780 (it is not recorded whether Darwin attended him also, or if so, conscientiously), and Darwin was able to marry the widow early in the following year. The learned Doctor installed himself at Radburne for two years before finally settling in Derby, and reared a large family. This sudden twist in his fortunes caused some consternation in the Lichfield circle. Miss Seward in a deliciously bitchy mood, her pen sharpened, one imagines, by her situation as the rejected wife, wrote to a friend (1785):

'Almost five years have elapsed since Dr. Darwin left Lichfield. A handsome young widow, relict of Colonel Pole, by whom she had three children, drew from us... our celebrated physician, our poetic and witty friend. The Doctor was in love like a very *Celadon*, and a numerous young family are springing up in consequence of a union, which was certainly a little unaccountable; not that there was any wonder that a fine graceful, and affluent young woman should fascinate a grave philosopher; but that a sage of no elegant external, and sunk into the vale of years, should, by so gay a lady, be preferred to younger, richer, and handsomer suitors, was a marvel; especially since, though lively, benevolent, and by no means deficient in native wit, she was never suspected of a taste for science, or works of the imagination. Yet so it was; and she makes her ponderous spouse a very attached, and indeed devoted wife!...'[1]

In her memoirs of Dr. Darwin, intended for publication and therefore suitably more restrained, Miss Seward admits that 'Mrs. Pole was then [1778] in the full bloom of her youth and beauty. Agreeable features; the glow of health; a fascinating smile; a fine form, full and graceful...' and all the rest of it; instead, she now turns on the Colonel, throwing on his character a light which we do not obtain from any other source: 'Colonel Pole had numbered twice the years of his fair wife. His temper was said to be peevish and suspicious, yet not beneath these circumstances had her kind and cheerful attentions to him grown cold or remiss... He left her ... a son to inherit his estate, and two female children amply portioned...'[2]

One of the amply portioned female children married John Gisborne, the younger brother of Wright's great friend Thomas Gisborne. The son Sacheverell was painted again by Wright as a young man in about the early '90's [Plate 342], retaining in it that shock of red hair he had as a baby. He also led the life of a respectable country gentleman, married the daughter of a clergyman, became sheriff of the county in 1793, and to judge by the style of his account of Radburne preserved among the manuscripts in the house, like his mother could never have been suspected of a taste for works of the imagination. There is reason to suppose that he bought a view of *Albano* [Plate 314] at the sale of the contents of Wright's studio after his death, but from what we know of his character, he is unlikely to have done so without encouragement from his aged step-father. That Sacheverell remained on good terms with Erasmus Darwin is proved by the fact that he ordered from Wright a portrait of his step-father in 1792–3 [Plate 338].

The decoration of this room at Radburne is unique in the sense that it alone demonstrates how the taste of a Midlands landowner need not necessarily be confined to the heroic, but may descend, as Lord Palmerston's did, and as did the taste of the smart ladies in Bath, to the domestic. One can understand that Colonel Pole should wish to see himself represented as the soul of military virtue and his wife as an imperious Madonna, and that Mortimer should be asked to produce scenes from Roman history in tune with the heroic vision he had of himself; but why these should be combined with scenes of the most fetching domesticity is not so obvious. The key lies in the iconography of the Mortimers. Obligingly, he provides us with his sources in the catalogues of the Society of Artists: in 1772 for the

1 Anna Seward to Lady Marianne Carnegy, 21st March 1785 (see H. Pearson, *The Swan of Lichfield*..., London, 1936, p. 73). It is claimed that an old dog dancing to her tune in a portrait of Mrs. Pole in silhouette attributed to a certain Torond (exh. Birmingham, 1966 (63)), is Dr. Darwin himself. Attractive though this theory may be, the dog does not bear Darwin's features.

2 Seward, 1804, pp. 104, 150.

1 Waterhouse 1965, p. 77.

2 See the edition of 1787, published in Paris, where some *Lettres relatives à Bélisaire* to and from Marmontel and Catherine II are published (1767–8).

3 This 'skit' on *Romeo and Juliet* had a great vogue in the eighteenth century and would have been quite familiar to Mortimer with his interest in the theatre.

Belisarius, Marmontel, chapter 4, and in 1774 for the *Caius Marius*, Otway's play on this theme. A common denominator between these two must be traceable, and indeed it becomes clear that they are both 'histories in a Salvatorial version of the Grand Style... of the two examples in antiquity of the disavowal of military heroes'.[1] There is no evidence that any aspersions were ever cast on Colonel Pole's probity, and if Mortimer was trying to make a personal point (about virtue going unrewarded, for instance), it is lost on us. All we can say is that we are presented not with war but with the aftermath of war, and that in both cases the ex-soldier, as conceived by Marmontel in his *Bélisaire* (which so captivated Catherine the Great with its virtue that she insisted on translating one chapter into Russian[2]) and Otway in his play, *The History and Fall of Caius Marius*[3] has a distinguished military record behind him but is now out of the fray—the situation Colonel Pole found himself in at the time. His introduction of the Wright overdoors was his way of acknowledging that in this world of peace there was a place for the domestic virtues; and the result is a cosy view of life, where children gaze enraptured at balloons and bubbles, and young adults in love betray no more passion on their features than a vague apprehension or a dreamy longing for pleasures in store for them.

3 SCIENCE AND INDUSTRY IN DERBYSHIRE BEFORE 1774

Anyone reading this account so far would assume that nothing was stirring in Derbyshire, that it consisted of a series of country houses like Norfolk, set in parks, some grand, some modest, each inhabited by an ancient family keeping to its station in life, with affinities only with others of its kind, preserving a hierarchy as rigid as the strata of Matlock High Tor; shifting occasionally and then not dramatically when some son of the house married an heiress; that on a lower level existed the professional classes in the towns, the necessary doctor and the convenient advocate; that at a safe distance there were eccentrics reading *Emile* or tycoons making their fortunes in industry; and that below all this surged an anonymous rabble. There was also a local portrait painter who could be trusted to produce not too insulting a likeness, calculated to tone in pleasantly with portraits of ancestors lining the walls, who was reported also to be engaged on conversation pieces under peculiar conditions of light, but these were more suitable for the dilettanti of the capital. This is how it would have struck a contemporary, and his impressions would not be far off the mark. If we study Burdett's map of Derbyshire of the '60's, it consists largely of towns and villages interspersed with country mansions, with the names of the owners printed alongside the stateliest homes—a practice inconceivable nowadays even on the largest scale Ordnance Survey; and the tourists in their memoirs and the guide book writers tell us not only about the produce of the county, its geology, its antiquities, its mineral resources and its traditional trades but also about the bigwigs, their ancestry and relations; and if they mention the new ironworks or silk mills, they are oblivious of their destiny as the lords and masters of the future.

The reason for this is that a new spirit was spreading over the county so imperceptibly that no traveller could recognise it for the revolution it was. It took two forms, science and industry, and in both spheres of activity it was pushing its way upwards from underneath.[1] It had hardly pierced the surface; and even today we can travel to remote corners of Derbyshire and not be aware that the revolution has ever taken place, so traditional have habits of life remained. It was a middle-class revolution, set in motion in the towns by scholars and tradesmen, in the first case as the disinterested pursuit of truth, in the second as a means of amassing a quick fortune, sometimes a creative mixture of interest and self-interest, but calculated, whatever form the activity might take, to improve the lot of humanity.

Wright belonged to this class and was the first to exploit its artistic possibilities. He watched chemical experiments being conducted at night in darkened rooms. On the polished surface of the table would be set a lamp, and as the spectators crowded around to observe what was happening, shadows would play on their faces or hover menacingly on the wall behind them, shuddering as the flame flickered. A lost profile would survive as a pencil of light, an arm would loom gruesomely in silhouette against it. Someone would

[1] The account of science and industry in the Midlands that follows is of course confined to the significance of these subjects for the painter.

draw back the curtain and the moon breaking through a cloud would compete with the lamp on the table. Faces would grow tense as the experiment reached its climax; someone would cover his head in his hands, unable to bear the suspense any longer; and then the relief when the experiment was successfully concluded, and the moment of vision past. Or he would ride out at night under the light of a full moon to some ramshackle chapel with crumbling walls beside a swift stream where iron was being beaten into contrived shapes, and again the light would play fantastically over workmen's faces as they crouched and swayed over their anvil. And wherever he stood and gazed and sketched, in the lecture hall where the experiment was being conducted, in the forge where the iron glowed white, but also in the gallery of casts where students copied the antique and in the study where statuettes were displayed for the delight of connoisseurs, he was struck by the concentration on the matter in hand, by the indifference, for the time being, of the people to each other, and their absorption is a single inanimate object in their midst.

When we take a closer look at the audience witnessing the operation of air pump or orrery, we realise that some of them are not professionals at all, any more than are the well-dressed ladies touring the iron forge. There is the philosopher himself, alone in complete command of his subject, surrounded by a handful of eager students. But there are also women and young children who, though they may be watching entranced, can understand little more than that a bird may die unless something is done to save it, or that the planets revolve round the sun. The philosopher is lecturing to an uninstructed audience. He is not conducting an experiment for the benefit of fellow scientists which if successful will deserve a note in the *Philosophical Transactions*. There is nothing new to be extracted from his delicate machinery that is not known to experts already. These instruments were being constructed all over the country in the eighteenth century not because it was hoped that each new model would advance the cause of science, but because this was the age of the popularisation of science, when more and more instruments were required to satisfy an ever-growing curiosity in natural phenomena. Wright was not living in the greatest age of science; in his youth he witnessed no momentous discoveries to compare with those of Newton. It took a generation for even the best chemists to acknowledge that Lavoisier had truth on his side. It was, on the other hand, an age when the mystery of science was beginning to weave its thread into everyday life and play its part there as common sense, while still retaining, on its way to sense, the magic of the unknown. This precipitated a revolution of equal importance in its own way, and it is this shift in the attitude of mind of ordinary people that Wright sets out to communicate. In the *Air Pump*, for instance, it is not so much the discovery of something marvellous that arouses his interest, but the fact that the genius of the human mind is being brought down to earth and made accessible.

The air pump was invented in the mid-seventeenth century by Otto von Guerlicke of Magdeburg and was soon recognised as an ingenious device for demonstrating the effect of a near-vacuum on animate and inanimate objects. The basic principle is comprehensible to the layman: air is exhausted from the large glass bowl known as the receiver, and whatever has been placed inside the bowl ceases to function normally through lack of air. There were innumerable uses to which the pump could be put but the most spectacular was the imprisonment in the receiver of a bird or animal which, as the air was extracted, would be seized by convulsions; when the air was readmitted at a given signal, the creature would recover, though any miscalculation or planned delay would cause its death. The instrument was developed in England by Boyle and Hooke, Hawksbee and Smeaton, and became popular just after the middle of the eighteenth century. Joseph Priestley in his Memoirs[1] tells us that in Nantwich in Cheshire where he was living in the late '50's working as a schoolmaster, he purchased '...some philosophical instruments,... a small air-pump, an electrical machine &c. These I taught my scholars in the highest class to keep in order, and make use of, and by entertaining their parents and friends with experiments, in which the scholars were generally the operators, and sometimes the lecturers too, I considerably extended the reputation of my school...' Here we find the instrument used, as in Wright's picture, not only for the instruction of students but for the entertainment of their friends—Priestley's word 'entertaining' striking oddly on the ear, until we recall that the best

1 *Memoirs of Dr. Joseph Priestley written by Himself (to the year 1795)...*, London, ed. 1810, pp. 32–3.

scientists had passed on to something more complicated than this. Priestley goes on to tell us that when composing his *History... of Discoveries relating to Vision...* (it was more or less complete by the end of 1770, two years after Wright's picture was first exhibited), he enjoyed the companionship of John Smeaton, the engineer of the third Eddystone lighthouse, who was living nearby: 'he made me a present of his excellent air-pump, which I constantly use to this day [1787]. Having strongly recommended his construction of this instrument, it is now generally used, whereas before that, hardly any had been made during the twenty years which had elapsed after the account that he had given of it in the "Philosophical Transactions" '.[1]

The air pump also formed part of the equipment from the late '50's onwards of James Ferguson whom Boswell described as 'the self-taught philosopher'.[2] He had taught himself the principles of mechanics and had purchased an air pump from a London optician in 1756 'in order', writes his biographer, 'to add the subject of Pneumatics to his Course of Lectures'.[3] In his *Lectures on Select Subjects...* published in 1760 Ferguson describes the substance of eleven lectures he was in the habit of delivering, one of which has observations on the use of the air pump. To his explanation he appends a diagram of the air pump showing the various uses to which it can be put [Fig 117],[4] and we are not too surprised to find that it is quite different from Boyle's of eighty years earlier,[5] and basically similar to Wright's of eight years later. There is no need to explain the mechanism in detail. It is sufficient to record that Wright's instrument [Fig 118] is operated on the same principle as Ferguson's: that is, on the table is a machine consisting of two pistons encased in barrels and leathered together so tightly that they fit their barrels exactly. (Wright's barrels are the two ochre-olive-green ones, not the reddish ones which are purely ornamental columns.) When the handle is turned, it raises and depresses these pistons by means of ratchets, creating a vacuum in the barrels so that the air in the receiver is forced out through the pipe into the vacuum. (Wright shows his right-hand ratchet raised, demonstrating that a vacuum has been created in the right-hand barrel.) By a succession of turns of the handle, and the opening and shutting of valves in the barrels, all the air is extracted. At the end of the experiment the air can be readmitted by a simple mechanism at the top of the receiver.

1 *Op. cit.*, pp. 48–9.

2 *Life of Johnson*, entry for 26th October 1769.

3 Henderson, 1867, p. 216. Henderson had access to Ferguson's papers and any of his own comments are for this reason likely to be accurate.

4 Ferguson, 1760, plate XIV, opp. p. 185.

5 *Nova Experimenta Physico-Mechanica de vi aëris elastica*, Geneva, 1680, reproduced by Todd, 1946, p. 13.

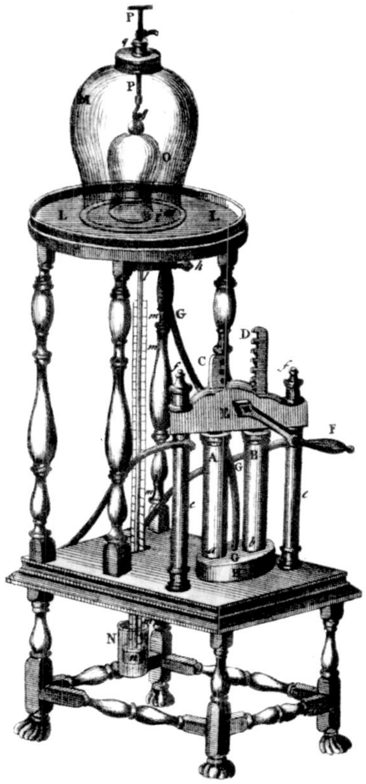

Fig 117 Engraving of an air pump, from Ferguson's *Lectures on Select Subjects...*, *1760*

Fig 118 Detail from *An Experiment on a Bird in the Air Pump*   See Fig 43

Having explained how his air pump worked, Ferguson then goes on to describe various experiments with it, one of which, the eighteenth, reads:

'If a fowl, a cat, rat, mouse or bird, be put under the receiver, and the air be exhausted, the animal is at first oppressed as with a great weight, then grows convulsed, and at last expires in all the agonies of a most bitter and cruel death. But as this Experiment is too shocking to every spectator who has the least degree of humanity, we substitute a machine called the *lungs-glass* in place of the animal; which, by a bladder within it, shews how the lungs of animals are contracted into a small compass when the air is taken out of them.'[1]

1 Ferguson, 1760, p. 200.

In Derbyshire, they were not so squeamish as to have to resort to that kids' stuff, the lungs glass, even in the presence of kids. Ferguson explains the use of the Magdeburg hemispheres, also the invention of Von Guerlicke, consisting of two cups which when fitted together and when the air was exhausted, could not be pulled apart by sixteen horses. The hemispheres are on Wright's table, awaiting their turn, now lying patiently and slackly apart; and there are other objects scattered about: some innocent, like a pair of spectacles in a case and a snuffer for the candle; others which one supposes will play their part in later experiments, like the liquid concoction which appears also in the study for the *Air Pump* [see Plate 59], a cork and a tap, the precise significance of which now eludes us.[2]

2 The cork is perhaps intended to help in sealing up the little bottle with its air inside, which will break outwards when the air around it is pumped out.

Ferguson also included the orrery in his course of lectures. This was a device for making the principles of astronomy palatable to the uninitiated, the eighteenth-century equivalent of the planetarium. In Wright's picture a lamp, masked behind the elder boy's sleeve, takes the place of the sun, and the earth, moon and planets are ranged around it at appropriate distances. The orrery is then turned, reproducing the motions of heavenly bodies at their correct relative speeds. The horizontal circle represents the plane of the elliptic in which the earth moves, and on it are inscribed the signs of the zodiac and the months of the year. The inclined circle is the Equator, and the great circles at right angles to it, forming a kind of armillary sphere, meet in the Pole.[3] The first orrery is said to have been constructed about 1709 by the clockmakers George Graham and Thomas Tompion which showed the motion of the earth and moon. But the instrument takes its name from a later invention of John Rowley who about 1712 made one for Charles Boyle, fourth Earl of Orrery; like the one in Wright's picture a lamp stands for the sun, and it has the plane of the elliptic in which the earth moves.[4] We hear of one in existence in Edinburgh in 1741[5] which like ours showed the motion of the earth, moon and planets, and was surmounted by an armillary sphere, but it was operated by wheelwork; whereas Wright's orrery shows no trace of mechanism, though as we shall see it may still be there. Ferguson's orreries, however, from the point of view of Wright's biographer, are the most instructive of all.

3 See Shurlock, 1923 for further interesting observations on Wright's orrery.

4 See Howard C. Rice Jn., *The Rittenhouse Orrery...*, 1954, commentary on an exhibition held at Princeton University Library; also F. Maddison, 'An Eighteenth-Century Orrery by Thomas Heath...', *The Connoisseur*, April 1958, pp. 163 ff.

5 Henderson, 1867, p. 42.

In 1743 he made a neat little orrery of which all the wheels were of ivory, and thereafter no less than six, all different: 'for', he says, 'I could never bear to copy one thing of that kind from another, because I still saw there was great room for improvements'. In 1748 he delivered lectures on the solar system, using an orrery he had made for demonstration.[6] This was a common practice and would have held no particular interest for us, had it not been that in 1762, about two years before Wright painted his picture, Ferguson made a tour through the Midlands, and in several towns there, gave his usual course of lectures on astronomy, mechanics, hydraulics and similar subjects. He gave his course in Derby itself; and 'during his sojourn', we are told by his generally reliable biographer, 'he frequently visited the ingenius Mr. Whitehurst, Clockmaker, from whom he received several curious papers and drawings of Escapements, Pendulums, and Hydraulic Engines'.[7] He also visited the great Silk Mill—one of the sights of the Midlands which must have been quite familiar to Wright from his childhood—built by George Sorocold for John and Thomas Lombe at Derby (1718–22)—the first large factory in England and still in the '60's a place of pilgrimage. We do not know precisely what Ferguson's equipment consisted of in his Derby course, nor on a second occasion in 1772 when he lectured to large audiences on astronomy and other subjects in the town, but in Bath in 1767 he lectured[8] on the orrery; and in his *Tables and Tracts* of 1762 he appends a catalogue of his apparatus, used in courses he is prepared to give within a hundred miles' radius of London, in which is included an air pump, an armil-

6 Henderson, *op. cit.* pp. 51–2; 123.

7 *Op. cit.*, p. 268. White, 1958 mentions the existence of a correspondence between Ferguson and Whitehurst, with coloured drawings by Whitehurst of clock parts and 'complicated astronomical movements and perpetual calendars', but unfortunately this precious material is untraced.

8 According to an advertisement announcing the course (see Henderson, 1867, pp. 338 ff.) on his Bath tour, Ferguson claims that his orrery was capable of describing 'all vicissitudes of Seasons and the Times, Causes, and Return of all the Eclipses of the Sun and Moon... together with the phenomenon of Saturn's rings...'

lary sphere, an orrery as well as a mass of other equipment.[1] There is no real reason to suppose that his luggage on the more distant Derbyshire tour was much less cumbersome.

It would be going too far to suggest that Wright shows Ferguson lecturing on the orrery. For one thing, he had a much leaner face.[2] For another, he had disappeared from Derbyshire probably before the picture was begun. In the third place, so far as we know, he did not construct an orrery of this type. In any case, no-one has ever suggested Ferguson as the sitter. It has sometimes been maintained on the flimsiest evidence[3] that the model was the organist of All Saints' Church, Mr. Denby, at whose house Wright used to attend concerts, but it is hard to see why a musician should be giving a lecture on astronomy. The same dubious source informs us that the Piero-like lady on the left [Fig 37] was a Mrs. Sale, and this is not impossible since she is known to have been a friend of Wright in his youth, and about the correct age. She was the daughter of Denby, and the confusion may have arisen on this account. It seems more likely that the philosopher was a philospher, and the only person who fits the role—that is, aged about fifty, living in Derby, a friend of the artist, a colleague of Ferguson, a man of immense distinction, famous throughout the Midlands—was John Whitehurst, clockmaker and geologist. Is it too fanciful to suggest, not only that he is represented, but that after Ferguson's departure he was inspired, as a clockmaker following in the footsteps of Graham and Tompion, to construct an orrery of his own? However this may be, James Gandon, the architect who had been interested in chemical experiments in his youth, who must have been constantly in touch with Wright at meetings of the Howdalian Society in London in the '60's, and was the designer of the Courthouse in nearby Nottingham, writes as follows, admittedly long after the event:

'… The lecturer introduced [into the *Orrery*] was the celebrated Mr. Whitehurst, an eminent watch-maker, of Derby, and well known for his knowledge of mechanics etc. The gentleman taking notes was a Mr. Burdett; the remainder of the audience were either relations or friends…'[4]

The problem is complicated by the fact that an engraved folding plate [Fig 119] [5] in John Warltire's *Analysis of a Course of Lectures in Experimental Philosophy*[6] shows an eidouranion or transparent orrery which is not only closer to Wright's in structure than any other

1 Henderson, 1867, pp. 343 ff.

2 See the engraved portrait of him in Henderson, 1867, frontispiece.

3 Bemrose, 1885, p. 76 mentions a print after the *Orrery* 'once belonging to the artist' with names written in the margin including that of Denby as the philosopher, and the date 1768. Nothing is known of this print, or of the author of the annotations.

4 Gandon, 1846, pp. 211–2.

5 We would like to thank Mr. A. H. Westwood, Assay Master, Birmingham Assay Office, for permission to have this pamphlet photographed, and to Dr. Kenneth Garlick for his kindness in arranging for the photography.

6 For Warltire, see Douglas McKie, 'Mr. Warltire, a good chymist', *Endeavour*, X, 1951, pp. 46 ff.

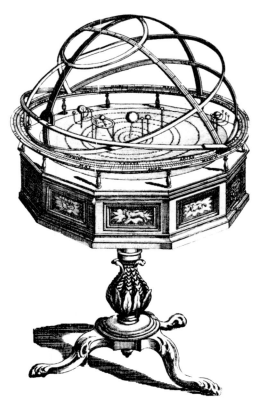

Fig 119 Engraving of orrery in John Warltire's *Analysis of a Course of Lectures in Experimental Philosophy* edition of 1767

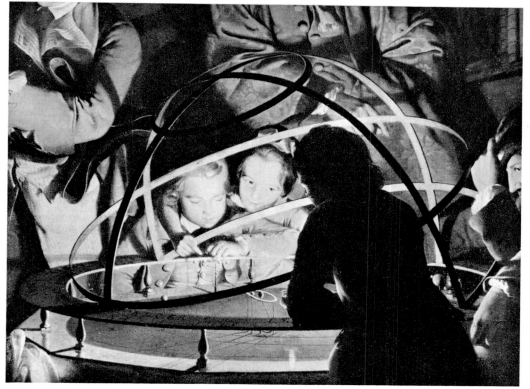

Fig 120 Detail from the study for an engraving of a *Philosopher giving a lecture on the Orrery* Cat 141 See pl 53

1 The details of the orrery are more legible in the study for the engraving [Fig 120] than in the reproduction of the picture in Derby [Plate 54].

2 Ed. 1767, pp. 24–5.

3 Darwin to Wedgwood, 8th November 1767 (quoted by Schofield, 1963, p. 76); 'He [James Keir] begs the favour of seeing your elegant manufactory, and hopes to meet our common friend, the philosopher, Mr. Whitehurst, at your house.'

4 See Whitehurst, 1792, pp. 6 ff; White, 1958, passim.

5 The third edition of 1792 is accompanied by this diagram along with others, as well as by an engraving after Wright's portrait.

Fig 121 *John Whitehurst F. R. S.*
c 1782–83
$36\frac{1}{4}$ x 28 in / 92.1 x 71.1 cm John Smith and Sons, Midland Clockworks Ltd, Derby Cat 141 Pl 227

recorded, but it will be obvious to anyone who examines it closely that all but one of the planets then known occur (among those visible) in Wright's picture in the same positions relative to the spectator as well as (more understandably) to each other.[1] What is more, the spectators' view of the axis of the hoops is also the same. In other words, one is copied from the other. It has not proved possible to discover the precise and crucial date of issue of this print, but it appears in the fifth edition of Warltire's book published in Exeter in 1767 (the edition we have used here), and is therefore about contemporary with Wright's picture. That Wright, who clearly in his scientific pictures relied on actual objects, copied Warltire is inconceivable, and the only remaining possibility is the other way round. We do not see Mercury or Venus in the picture since they are too close to the sun, and hidden behind the boy's body in front, but all the other planets accompanied by their moons are virtually duplicated, except Mars which has been shifted from a prominent place in the picture below the buttons of the coat of the boy facing the light, to another position, where it would have been obscured in the picture, at the same distance from the sun. The tilted Earth and our moon are the ones enclosed in a little circular frame nearer the sun in both representations. The complicated construction that absorbs the attention of the boy facing us is Jupiter with its four moons. Warltire's explanation in his *Analysis* of the function of these moons is too picturesque to miss: 'The use of these Moons or Satellites,' he writes of Jupiter, 'is the same as that of our Moon; to enlighten Jupiter's Nights, and to rise and agitate his Seas and Atmosphere'.[2] We can go on from there to observe that Wright devoted a lifetime to enlightening with our Moon the Thousand and one Nights of Earth. The planet on the extreme right in both print and picture, furthest from the sun, is Saturn with its five moons. Warltire's orrery also shows the signs of the zodiac and the months of the year around the outer rim, and a little handle for turning the instrument low down on the right. The existence of this handle makes us suspect that Wright's orrery was not necessarily hand-operated, but may conceal a handle behind the figures in the foreground.

All this might encourage us to argue that Warltire and not Whitehurst was the lecturer, but this is ruled out by Warltire's age: the date of his birth seems to be uncertain but he lived on to 1810, and the lecturer in the *Orrery* is certainly older than anyone could be who died forty-five years later. So we can rely confidently on Gandon's testimony, and stick to Whitehurst. This remarkable man was born at Congleton in Cheshire in 1713 and would therefore have been about fifty at the time of the *Orrery*. He came of a clock-and watch-making family in Cheshire and set up as a clock-maker at Irongate in Derby in 1736. He repaired the clock at the Town Hall in 1745. But he was much more versatile than this implies. He was in constant touch with all the leading Midlands intellectuals of the day, and a friend of Darwin and Wedgwood.[3] His political views can be deduced from the fact that he remained in correspondence with Franklin after the opening of the War of American Independence. On being appointed Stamper of the Money-Weights in 1775 created to regulate the standard of gold coinage, he moved to London, becoming a F.R.S. four years later. His Midlands friends feared he was lost to them for ever but thereafter he kept in contact with them by periodical visits to Derbyshire. His chief interests lay in geology and he more or less gave up clockmaking to devote himself to this science; in 1778 he published his *Inquiry into the Original State and Formation of the Earth* which he had been working on for years. He died in London in 1788.[4]

Wright painted a half-length portrait of him [Fig 121] after he had moved to London, no doubt on one of his Midlands visits—not accompanied with parts of the mechanism of a clock but with a section of the strata of Matlock High Tor before him; one of the diagrams in the *Inquiry* shows this very section designed by Whitehurst himself.[5] The volcano in eruption in the background is another reference to his interest in geology, and reminds us of Wright's wish when on Vesuvius to be accompanied by his old friend. Whitehurst was then close on seventy, but his appearance does not militate against the identification of him as the lecturer in the *Orrery*, allowing for the the fact that nearly twenty years separate the two pictures. As we would expect, his hair with age has lost its glossiness, and the contemplative gaze of a veteran has replaced the piercing eyes of a middle-aged intellectual. A description of his appearance in later life comments, oddly enough, on his expression as both penetrating and mild, the two aspects of the philosopher Wright contrives to bring out in his two portraits: 'As to his person', writes the author of a memoir after his death, 'he was somewhat above the middle stature, rather thin than otherwise, and of a countenance expressive at once of penetration and mildness. His fine grey locks, unpolluted by art, gave a venerable air to his whole appearance'.[1] Another account mentions that he was 'near six feet high, straight, thin, and wore his own dark-grey hair; was plain in his dress; and had much the appearance of a respectable farmer...'[2] This is based on a glimpse the author caught of him at Buxton three years before his death, and it fits Wright's half-length portrait to perfection. It also fits well enough the lecturer on the orrery, who indeed towers above his instrument, with a mop of hair unpolluted by art, though one does not feel so happy about his alleged emaciation: something must have happened to his metabolism as the years slid by.

We cannot do more than offer suggestions about other sitters in the subject pictures. That they are all portraits goes without saying, considering the very individual features Wright gives to each. A tradition in the Ferrers family maintained that the boy in the *Orrery*—presumably the one against the light who is the oldest [Fig 36]—was Laurence Rowland (1757–73), second son of the sixth Earl Ferrers and nephew of the purchaser.[3] At least he would have been the correct age. If he turns out to be the sitter, this would be an argument in favour of his uncle having purchased the picture before its completion. The suggestion has also been made that the man in lost profile on the extreme right [Fig 40] is a self-portrait, but he looks more than thirty. A slimmer and younger figure is seated in the same relative position in the *Gladiator*. Here is a more convincing candidate for Wright, since he holds up a drawing of the statuette, and there exists a study of this subject by the artist [Fig 122]. His known self-portraits do not, however, establish his identity here beyond question. We are quite at sea regarding the personalities in the *Air Pump*. One suggestion has been made that the demonstrator [Fig 47] is Warltire,[4] who in the middle '70's was invited by Darwin to help in experiments on the cooling produced in the receiver of an air pump on evacuation. He gave private tuition in chemistry to Darwin's and Wedgwood's sons in 1779, but no more is known of his residence in Derby at the time of Wright's *Air Pump* than at the time of the *Orrery*, and he could still hardly have been old enough for the part. Only about the young man in the *Orrery* taking notes [Fig 123] can we feel any real confidence. Gandon informs us categorically that this is Burdett, and there is every reason why he should be present at the ceremony. It is tempting to recognise his features as well in the central figure in the *Gladiator* but whether he is also the young man on the extreme left of the *Air Pump* must remain an open question.[5]

The birth date of Peter Perez (or Perey) Burdett is not recorded but to judge by his appearance in the *Orrery*, he was about Wright's age. In the '50's and '60's he lived partly at Derby and partly at Staunton Harold. It is not known what part he played in persuading the fifth Earl Ferrers to acquire the picture, but they were living close to one another at Staunton Harold in 1763 when on 11th July they were joint signatories to a bond, undertaking to repay the artist a loan of £160 within the year.[6] Burdett was by profession a cartographer[7] and during the mid-'60's (published 1767) produced a map of Derbyshire which in precision and elegance is matched by Wright's contemporary mapping of the faces of friends and neighbours. He also produced maps of Cheshire and Lancashire. By 1769 he was established at Liverpool, and so highly regarded there that in that year he was elected first President of the Liverpool Society of Arts. He exhibited at the Society of Artists in London from 1770 to 1773 some of the first aquatints to be produced in England. Though Paul Sandby is usually credited with the earliest aquatints, Burdett deserves to be reinstated as a pioneer in this field. The evidence is not perfectly clear, but it seems that on a tour of France in about 1771 he picked up and imported hints on early aquatint techniques which were further advanced there than they were in England, following on the researches of Saint-Non in collaboration with Delafosse, and later on those of Leprince (1768). In 1772 he was said to have discovered (but this was an exaggeration) 'A Mode of Etching, hitherto unknown in this country...'[8] and in that year exhibited at the Society of Artists 'An Etching, in imitation of a wash drawing', and another 'from a design of Mr. Mortimer's' which must have been among the first aquatints to be seen in England. In the following year he showed 'the effect of a stained drawing attempted, by printing from a plate wrought

1 Whitehurst, 1792, p. 18.

2 Hutton, 1791, p. 294.

3 *Stemma Shirleiana*, quoted by Bemrose, 1885, p. 76.

4 Robinson, 1958, p. 214.

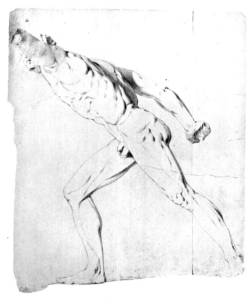

Fig 122 Study after a statuette of the *Gladiator* c 1764–65
Brown ink $20\frac{1}{4}$ x $17\frac{1}{8}$ in / 51.4 x 44.4 cm
(Part of drawing missing)
Derby Museum and Art Gallery

Fig 123 Portrait of P. P. Burdett from *A Philiosopher Giving a Lecture on the Orrery* See Fig 36

5 The marginal annotations on the print (see p. 115, note 3) also identify the young man taking notes as Burdett—for what this evidence is worth. Bemrose, 1885, p. 11 note, gives no source for his statement that the older man in the *Gladiator* is 'Old John Wilson, an inmate of the Devonshire almshouses'.

6 The bond is published by Bemrose, 1885, p. 77. Burdett's debt of his half of this sum is entered in the MS. Account Book: 'Burdett's Account. Lent July 1763... £80'. In the following two years, and again in 1771 Wright

made further payments to Burdett amounting in all (with interest) to £175–10–11 after a small deduction. Bemrose assumed that the 1763 bond was connected with the purchase of the *Orrery* but this is unlikely, since in the first place the *Orrery* was probably not begun so early, and in the second, it is hard to see why Burdett should be liable for half payment. When Wright saw no hope of being refunded at the time of Burdett's near-bankruptcy, he appealed to Lord Ferrers who had stood surety (see letter to his brother, 11th November 1774, wrongly dated by Bemrose, 1885, pp. 77–8; the passage there quoted should be inserted after 'unfit for study and application' in a letter of that date quoted *op. cit.*, p. 34). This Lord Ferrers agreed to do, according to a note of 1776 in Wright's hand on the reverse of the bond.

7 Dibdin, 1917–18, points out that he must have come from a good family since he is described in the document as a 'gentleman'.

8 *Candid Observations*, 1772, under 'Burdett'.

1 Only time and Mr. Eric Robinson will show what evidence exists for contemporary mechanical reproduction of Wright's paintings. No evidence that Boulton reproduced them by some such process has, so far as we know, been published, but is said to exist. Four paintings by Wright, two landscapes, a *Vesuvius* and a *Boy blowing a Bladder* (conceivably [Plate 320]) are reproduced by a 'Chemical & Mechanical Process' by the Polygraphic Society and exhibited along with the originals in 1792 by the Booth Society in London (see *Whitley Papers*, IX, p. 1177; the author is indebted to John Gage for this reference).

2 The copy of the aquatint in the Liverpool Public Library is inscribed in pen in a near-contemporary hand: 'First specimen of *Aquatinta* Invented in Liverpool by P. P. Burdett 1774 asisted [sic] by Mr. S. Chubbard'. (A Thomas Chubbard exhibited fifteen items at the 1774 Liverpool exhibition).

3 Wedgwood to Bentley, 23rd November 1771; see Finer & Savage, 1965, p. 116.

4 See letters quoted in Finer & Savage, 1965, pp. 117 ff.

5 Wright to his brother, 11th November 1774, see note 3, p. 61 above.

6 Whitley, 1928, ii, p. 30.

7 Letter of 21st February 1773; see Joseph Mayer, *History of the Art of Pottery in Liverpool*, Liverpool, 1855, p. 36.

8 Information about Burdett's later career comes from an interleaved Dibdin in the Liverpool Public Library, unpublished.

9 MS. Derby Public Library, passage in letter of 19th February 1794 not quoted by Bemrose, 1885, p. 93.

10 Dr. Turner is believed to have been a friend of Wright's also, if as seems likely it is to him that he refers in a letter to his sister of 13th April 1774, see Bemrose, 1885, p. 31. He could scarcely have spent so long in Liverpool without encountering him.

chemically, without the use of any instrument of sculpture',[1] and in 1774 produced two plates after Mortimer, and a beautiful aquatint after Wright's lost *Two boys blowing a Bladder* (for copy, see Plate 74).[2]

Burdett also conceived the notion of etching plates to be printed on pottery, and approached Wedgwood & Bentley in November 1771, claiming a new method: 'he is fully perswaded', writes Wedgwood, 'that he can, by his new method of ingraving, produce upon our ware, *Vases* and *Tablets*, the *full* and *complete* effect of painting *in one colour* ... his ingraving is done with a *Camel hair* pencil, by which he can produce every tone of Colour from the most tender and delicate wash to the deepest shade without a stroke of the graver.'[3] Relations between Burdett and the famous partnership continued amicably until February 1772 when he and Bentley met in London to try out experiments, but his process proved unsuitable for pottery and by the spring of that year the firm was discouraging him from continuing. Business dealings were terminated but there followed an acrimonious dispute over Burdett's fee, which was not resolved until March 1773.[4]

There must have been other reasons besides his failure to satisfy Wedgwood for the decline in Burdett's fortunes. Whatever they may have been—lack of skill and resourcefulness were not among them—he found himself heavily in debt in the early months of 1774 and obliged to leave Liverpool hurriedly. The news seeped through in Rome to Wright, who was worried about the repayment of a long-standing debt, and about a Mortimer drawing belonging to him in Burdett's possession [Fig 77]: '...he [Tate] tells me M.ʳ Burdett has sold up his goods and is off...'[5] Burdett must have sensed disaster on the way, for he was in correspondence with Benjamin Franklin in 1773, making tentative approaches. At first Franklin seemed to regard him as a great acquisition for the colonies, and writes: 'I should be glad to be informed where I can see some sample of your new Art of Printing in imitation of Paintings. It must be a most valuable discovery'.[6] But someone (Wedgwood?) must have warned him off. Burdett needless to say had more than one string to that bow, and was writing to the King of Prussia in February, months after his experiments with Wedgwood had proved a failure:

'I presume to acquaint Your Majesty that in making some chemical experiments I have now discovered a new, expeditious, and beautiful manner of engraving upon copper, so as to make impressions transferable to porcelain, and which, when vitrified, resemble and equal the most delicate paintings. The great fame of the Berlin fabric... strongly compels me to lay so important an article at Your Majesty's feet. Could I be encouraged to hope that abilities like mine deserve much honour.'[7]

He ended up by entering the service of Markgraf Karl Friedrich of Baden (the 'Prince of Baaden' to whom Wright hoped to sell his *Captive King)* in December 1774, entrusted with the task of preparing a topographical survey. Up to 1788 he lived at Rastatt and afterwards at Karlsruhe, until his death on 9th September 1793.[8] News of his death reached Wright eventually, for he writes to Philips five months later: 'I have thought much upon what you said about Burdett but I had in my own mind *so throughly given up the money* I lent him that I fear I rather wounded your feelings by my inadvertent inattention to it...'[9]

We have felt it necessary to enter into Burdett's career at length since with Mortimer and Stubbs, he was closest to Wright in spirit about 1770, and since it was above all from him (and from Whitehurst) that Wright acquired what knowledge he needed for his subject pictures—and we know from numerous later occasions that he always liked to get second opinions on such tricky problems. Friends like Denby were no help; and as for Darwin who would have been an obvious choice, he was too remote in Lichfield. It is significant that even after Wright had left Liverpool he was still seeking Burdett's advice on subject-matter. When asked about the theme of the *Alchemist* [Plate 106], Burdett modestly disclaimed knowledge of medicine, and turned the artist's enquiries over to a fellow-Liverpudlian, Dr. Matthew Turner, who lectured on anatomy at the Society of Arts at Liverpool in 1773 and was in a position to know.[10] All the same Burdett could not resist giving his opinion on, and sketching out, the composition [Figs 124–5], urging that 'the Chemist should be sitting on *this* side the Table turning his Head towards glass upon his assistants exclaiming upon the first appearance of the Phenomenon of the luminous exhalation from yᵉ Retort into yᵉ

Fig 124 P. P. Burdett   Drawing for the
Alchemist 1771   Derby Museum and Art
Gallery

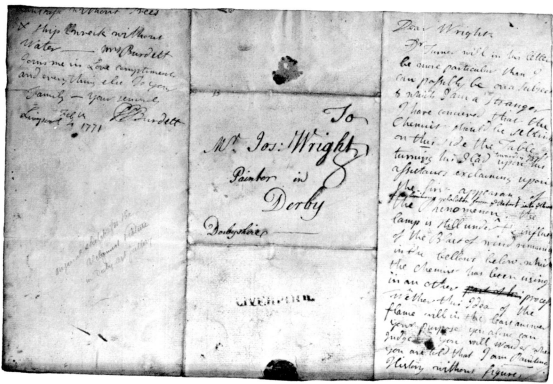

Fig 125 Letter from P. P. Burdett to Joseph Wright 4th February 1771
(on reverse of Fig 124)   Derby Museum and Art Gallery

Receiver... [Fig 125][1]—advice which Wright was quite willing to take. We do not know
what alternative scheme was proposed by Turner, but we can suggest a possible literary
source for the picture. That Wright should have consulted the literature on chemistry is
understandable, since he was always scrupulous about getting his facts right, and on a subject as remote from him as this, he would not have wished to rely solely on improvisation
and the advice of friends.

 The alchemist is also an astrologer, as we can guess from the globe. But like the philosopher in the *Air Pump*, he is not a relic of a pre-scientific age but a modern scientist who
discovers, not the phantom Philosopher's Stone, but phosphorus. This was first obtained
accidentally by Brandt of Hamburg about a hundred years earlier, and more than one
account of the process was published in England shortly before Wright painted his picture.
It is hard to say precisely which he consulted, but a translation from the French of M.
Macquer's *Elements of the Theory and Practice of Chymistry*[2] fits the picture admirably. But
first we must describe what Wright shows. The materials from which the phosphorus is
prepared are heated in a furnace and the phosphorus distilled over into a glass receiver. The
end of the retort protrudes from the furnace, and the receiver, known as a balloon, is luted
to the retort. The balloon is nearly half filled with water, and as the phosphorus distills over,
the upper part is filled with luminous vapour; while from a small hole in the top near the
neck of the balloon, the vapour rises in a luminous jet.[3]

 Macquer in his preface[4] describes the discredit into which the alchemist had fallen, and
points out that no sensible person any longer believed that you could produce gold by
chemical experiments. 'However', he goes on, 'as facts always promote the knowledge of
Nature, it happened that those experiments, though quite useless with regard to the end
for which they were originally made, proved the occasion of several curious discoveries',
among them phosphorus. The process of manufacturing phosphorus is described in great
detail, and we select the following passages which have the closest bearing on the picture:[5]

'Place your retort... in a reverberating furnace, so proportioned, that there may be an interval of
two inches all round between the sides of the furnace and the bowl of the retort, even where it
contracts to form the neck, which should stand inclined at an angle of sixty degrees... Fit on to the
retort a large glass balloon two thirds [*sic*] full of water, and lute them together ... In the hinder

1 The letter of 4th February 1771 is on the
reverse of a drawing showing the alchemist's
equipment, without figures [Figs 124, 125];
quoted inaccurately by Bemrose, 1885, pp. 83–4.
The drawing is always assumed to be by Wright,
and indeed it is competent. But the annotations
'Table', 'illuminated glass', 'carpet' etc. are in
Burdett's handwriting and are an integral part of
the drawing; what is more, the style, though
close to Wright's, is not convincing as his. The
letter on the reverse also supports the view that
the drawing is Burdett's.

2 2 vols. The author has consulted the 2nd
edition of 1764.

3 The author has relied heavily on Shurlock,
1923, who mentions a possible French literary
source without giving either author or title.

4 That Wright read Macquer in translation is
not pure guesswork. James Keir made a translation of Macquer's *Dictionary of Chemistry*
(published 1771) and when engaged on its
compilation about two years earlier became
intimate with Edgeworth. What more likely
than that Wright had listened to Edgeworth and
Darwin discussing the French writer in Lichfield
the year before the *Alchemist* was painted?

5 *Op. cit.*, pp. 261 ff.

part of this balloon, a little above the surface of the water, a small hole must be bored... The operation lasts four and twenty hours. [He goes on to describe the rising of the vapours in the balloon, the forerunners of the phosphorus. Then:] the first volatile Phosphorus... appears in about three hours after the white vapours first begin to rise ... there will issue out through the little hole of the balloon a stream of blueish light, which continues of a greater or shorter extent to the end of the operation... from time to time [it] darts out to the length of seven or eight inches, snapping and emitting sparks of fire....'

Wright's jet is shown at about its fullest extent. We could have trusted him to catch his alchemist at the most dramatic moment. What is more, his jet is *bluish*.

When engaged on his painting (now lost) of the *Captive King*, Wright again consulted Burdett in Liverpool, this time on the perspective scheme—a subject on which Burdett was due to lecture in Liverpool in a few months' time. Wright was touchingly dependent on his friend for help over a job of work which one would have imagined he was qualified to undertake single-handed. However, he seems on this occasion to have tried out a new perspective method recommended to him by Burdett since in one drawing [Plate 108] he has marked out a horizon line and vanishing point, and a scale, and in a letter with a drawing on it [Plate 109] he writes:

'I send you the above scratch for two reasons first that you may see & approve or disapprove of the disposition of the figure I intend for the Captive. I cou'd wish to have it just & striking as there will be but one in the picture and if this new method will permit I will finish it in the highest & most masterly manner I am capable of, to reward if possible my friend's pains...'[1]

Six weeks later he was going so far as to ask Burdett whether he might 'remove the window wch is in the left hand corner under the circular one... perhaps you'll think of something more consistent, but pray let me hear from you by return of the post as I cannot well go on without your assistance.'[2] Whether he was troubled, as well as by the 'new method', by the knowledge that Burdett had in mind a prospective customer such as the Margrave of Baden, and whether for some such reason he had to bow to his friend's demands, does not emerge from the surviving correspondence.

One crucial point becomes clear from the study of the literary sources of his scientific pictures whenever the facts can be ascertained: Wright took immense pains to get his equipment right, exactly as though it were going to be put to the test of an experiment. We can be sure the mechanism was accurate, down to those small details in which he invariably delighted, just as he would pounce delightedly on a well-wrought musical instrument or gun when there was an excuse for introducing them into his portraits. Even though there may be some difference of opinion about the level of the water (Wright following Burdett's instructions here, not Macquer's), the jet of vapour in the *Alchemist* is blue, and rises from the balloon precisely at the point where we are told by a chemist it should rise. The Magdeburg hemispheres make sense in the *Air Pump* just as they would in a diagram by an expert in pneumatics. The relative position of earth and moon is fixed in the *Orrery* as securely as it would be in the hands of an astronomer; the skeletons in *Miravan* and the *Old Man and Death*, the bones in the *Hermit*, would satisfy a professional anatomist. Only in the dramatic situation was fantasy allowed to play its part. It can be demonstrated that as far as machinery is concerned there was no question of artistic licence—and indeed no need for it: the existing gadgets were artistic enough. When we turn to industrial subjects we can be sure the equipment is once more faithfully recorded, even though the artist may manipulate his actors in order to produce the desired dramatic effect. This is certainly the case with Wright's iron forge which faithfully records the type of equipment which we know from documents and from existing examples was in operation in his day.

The purpose of the forge was to convert the cast or pig iron into malleable or wrought iron so that it could stand the force of the hammer. The iron was then sold to the smith for further working. The forge had the effect of diminishing impurities which the iron had acquired during the process of smelting. Generally the process was conducted in two separate hearths: in one the pig was melted down into malleable iron; in the other the iron

1 Dated 13th November (1772).

2 Collection Herman W. Liebert, New Haven (Conn.) [Plate 111]. Dated in postscript 'Friday morn. Xmas day'. Christmas fell on a Friday in 1772. On the address side of the drawing with the vanishing point is the beginning of a letter, presumably from Burdett to Wright since it seems to be in his handwriting, and the letter is stamped from Liverpool and addressed to the artist: 'Dear Joe, The sketch of the Barn is very incorrect in point of Perspective but if the subject pleases you I will send you a Projection exactly drawn [.] the same observation upon the inside of the ship [.] you was once thinking of reversing the View of the Ship. the main deck should be'—here the letter breaks off. The reference to the ship is mysterious: a drawing by Wright in the Derby Art Gallery [Plate 116] shows the plan and elevation of a ship, the latter fully manned, and another of a sea battle [Plate 117], but the purpose for which they were intended is not known. They might be drawings of *c.* 1772; on the other hand, there could be a connection between them and references to a 'sea engagement' which he proposes to paint in Derby in a letter to his brother from Bath, 15th and 30th April 1776 (transcribed by Bemrose, 1885, pp. 45–46).

was reheated for drawing out into bars. It appears that in Wright's forge only the second process was carried out, the earlier one of melting down the pig being conducted in another building. Such forges are recorded and they are of the most primitive type. Indeed the small building in which his forge has been erected is of a most rudimentary construction. Generally the early forges were of wood with a tiled roof, the foundation walls being of stone on account of the adjoining water conduits. In Wright's building the roof consists of beams and slats, surmounted by thatch, and there is brick as well as stone. His floor, however, is paved in tile, as was normal in the old forges. In the eighteenth century stone buildings became the rule because of the danger of fire, but of this innovation Wright takes no account.

He depicts a common type of helve or tilt hammer used in the oldest forges, the hammer head being of cast iron. The beam above and parallel to the hammer in its raised position is a spring board known as a 'rabbet'. The motion of the water wheel causes the axle-tree (just visible behind the arm-case in the Derby drawing) to revolve, and with it the arm-case, which is the barrel-shaped object seen behind the hammer. This causes the hammer to be jerked up against the rabbet. It then falls on the anvil with its own weight. In the Derby drawing [Plate 99], Wright shows the hammer resting on the anvil; in the final picture [Plate 103] the hammer has been raised to allow the iron bar to be inserted between it and the anvil.[1]

That Wright's is one of the earliest types of forges can be proved from descriptions of forges dating from the late sixteenth century, and from a few still in existence which were already old-fashioned in his time, such as the ancient helve hammer in the top forge at Wortley.[2] It goes without saying that he would not have used his imagination in such vital details as equipment—and we have the Derby drawing, clearly done on the spot, as proof of this. What is less obvious is that the building in which the forge has been introduced is also accurately transcribed. This is little more than an old barn with the remains of a brick archway, the kind of makeshift arrangement which was found adequate until mass production got under way—the only essential condition being that a dam and swift flowing river should be nearby to provide the power. To maintain that Wright transported his forges into imaginary settings is to misunderstand his whole approach to industry, which was a reverent acceptance of things as they were.[3] Similarly, his glass-houses (two drawings in the Derby Art Gallery [Plates 96, 97]) are no more than improvised barns where the plaster is peeling off the walls. This accommodation was found quite serviceable for the small scale production then carried on. These drawings were also made on the spot, and one, with the three 'eyes' [Plate 97], shows the furnace actually in operation. They were intended for a painting showing men at work, where Wright would also have respected the equipment and setting, but no trace of such a picture can be found.[4]

Equally there is no reason why the traditional trade of the blacksmith should not have been carried on in old buildings fit for no other use, and we need not feel too much surprised to find horseshoes being beaten into shape in some disused medieval chapel where angels clamber over arches [Fig 58], where stone walls crumble and are casually patched up, just sufficiently so that work should not be interrupted.[5] Admittedly between one version of the *Blacksmith's Shop* [Plate 100] and the next [Plate 101] he takes the liberty of removing a prominent beam; but one could no more argue from this that he failed to respect what he saw, than argue that he deliberately distorts reality in the *Iron Forge viewed from without* [Plate 104] because he has broken open an outside wall in order that the spectator should be allowed a glimpse inside: this was a pictorial convention understood by scientist and artist alike, just as in any treatise on hydraulics one might find engravings where for the purpose of elucidation, sections have been laid bare to reveal the hidden mechanism.

The magic had not gone out of industry, and for a man of Wright's class, upbringing and generation, it represented a hope for the future, not a betrayal of the past. Beckford, had he lived today, would have squeaked (his way of scowling) at every factory chimney in his path. But even he who had no faith in progress, recognised the sublimity of the ironworks in their still primitive state. On a visit to the north in 1779, before the mass production age had got to the point where the most profitable businesses were concentrated in the new factories, he noted:

1 The author has relied heavily in his account of iron forges on Schubert, 1957, pp. 272 ff. The diagram on p. 281 (Fig. 33) showing a hammer worked by water wheel is extremely close to the equipment depicted by Wright.

2 See Andrews, 1956, pp. 75–6.

3 For further observations on this point, see Robinson, 1958, p. 214.

4 The only record we have of such a work is a reference to 'The Glass-House, a Sketch: the Fire exceedingly well expressed', in the artist's posthumous sale at Christie's, 6th May 1801 (24).

5 This is not the opinion of Klingender, 1947, p. 50 who maintains that the setting must have been imaginary.

'... The hollow wind in the woods mixing with the rushing of waters, whilst the forges thundered in my ear. To the left, a black quaking bridge leading to other wilds. Within, a glowing furnace, machines hammering huge bars of red–hot iron, which at intervals cast a bright light and innumerable sparks through the gloom...'[1]

Here is the equivalent in words of Wright's early industrial pictures. Both artists are conscious of an overpowering romance. But each description adds an element that the other lacks. Beckford notes the intoxicating din; whilst Wright notes that a job is being properly done, and pays his tribute to efficiency by making sure that on his canvases also, the machines work.

[1] Quoted by B. Alexander, *England's Wealthiest Son*, 1962, pp. 73–4.

4 LANDED GENTRY 1775–97

The same general pattern in Wright's portraiture can be traced in the second half of his life, after his return from Italy, as in the first: that is to say, he continued to suppress his inclination towards realism when this would have been out of place, and only allowed it to break through when satisfied that this was what was wanted. Merchants and industrialists, and those among intellectuals and friends who preferrred to be shown as they were, continue to be treated realistically, and also a few others who had caught a breath of the new spirit of directness and are shown surprisingly life-like in spite of their exalted station. Wright himself thus began to impose his own taste and some submitted to it. But generally with his high-born sitters, he was still anxious to gloss over their features, giving them no longer a Rococo air—Rococo gaiety having long since evaporated—but a romantic or soulful Neo-classic one, sometimes wrapping them in the glamour of the 'English portrait style' of the last decades of the century—a style which we can all immediately recognise but which has never assumed the status of a concept owing to our suspicion of abstractions. Had Hoppner, Beechey and the mature Copley gone to work in Germany, we would have a name for 'it' as well as for them.

An essential difference between the patronage of the artist before 1775, and after, is that whereas in the earlier period his patrons in almost every case divided themselves into two groups, those who wanted their portraits painted, and those who wanted subject or genre works, in the later period it was a common practice for his sitters also to demand of him pictures of a less personal kind. This is partly because he more or less abandoned scientific and industrial scenes in order to concentrate on landscape and stories from literature, and these could be more easily assimilated by those who wanted their features perpetuated; partly because Wright on his return from abroad had established his reputation in the provinces as a leading painter whose excursions into landscape and literature it was now respectable to encourage. There is thus no longer any necessity to treat his portraits separately from his other works, since often the purchasers will be the same in both cases; and this new situation will enable us occasionally to throw light on a sitter's personality by examining what pictures of another kind he acquired.

One of the first representatives of the Derbyshire landed gentry both to have his portrait painted by Wright, and to become interested in the artist's landscapes, was Robert Holden (1722–1802) whose seat at Darley Abbey was 'situated in a very beautiful dale, upon the banks of the river Derwent, and at a distance of a mile from the town of Derby',[1] close to a medieval Augustinian Priory built in that, by now, fashionable twelfth century when Guy de Lusignan was taken prisoner by the Saracens. Holden has allowed himself to be represented [Plate 193] in a natural pose, resting his arm on the back of a chair, though in his situation as country gentleman he cannot quite be permitted the downright insolence of

1 Pilkington, 1789, ii, p. 197.

1 The two pictures are untraced. The Robert Holden listed in the Account Book as the purchaser must be the owner of Darley Abbey, not the later Robert Holden of Nuthall Temple, Notts., since the latter was only born in 1769 and the landscapes must have been painted before he reached his majority; they were not sold to him later, either, since the purchaser's name is added at the time the pictures are entered. (The fact that there is no trace of them at Nuthall before the destruction of the house in 1929 cannot be used as an argument that they belonged to the first Robert Holden, because his portrait and his own copy of the portrait of his friend Whetham [Plates 193, 194] passed from Darley Abbey to Nuthall). There is no evidence that the Nuthall pictures—the *Captive, from Sterne* [Plate 162] and a moonlight seascape [Cat No 285]—belonged to the first Robert Holden, so they are left out of this discussion. The two moonlights were not identical: the first Holden bought his for ten guineas, while the Nuthall picture was a 23½ by 30 in., a size for which Wright invariably charged more.

2 For further details see J. Nichols, *The History and Antiquities of the County of Leicester*, III, pp. 863–64.

3 Unless *Cromford Mills, by Day* [Plate 331] was painted for Arkwright but for this we have no evidence.

4 A. M. W. Stirling, *Coke of Norfolk and his Friends...*, London, ed. 1912, p. 74.

5 Letters of 4th February 1774, wrongly dated by Bemrose, 1885, p. 33 in August, by which time Coke had returned to England.

6 See letter of 12th February, quoted *op. cit.*, p. 30.

7 See Coke, 1880, pp. 89 ff. for further details.

Thomas Staniforth [Plate 72] who is also shown similarly relaxed. This casualness, combined with his decision to acquire from Wright at least two landscapes, shows that his taste was advanced for a man of his age—he was nearly sixty at the time (*c.* 1778–81). It is significant that he should have selected, not a conventional daylight *Dovedale*, but a view of *Nemi* by sunset, and a companion by moonlight.[1] A similar portrait, that of Richard Cheslyn (*c* 1717–87) [Plate 190], one would expect to represent someone in a similar social situation, and the little we know about him bears this out. A barrister of the Middle Temple he owned extensive property in Leicestershire, spending close on £5000 in about 1770 on plantations, gardens and pleasure grounds, and owing estates in Disworth and Castle Donnington[2] as well as the house he inherited, Langley Hall. However, neither Holden nor Cheslyn was as adventurous as a patron of the arts as was a member of the Coke family, Daniel Parker Coke, who has a unique place in history as both as a sitter to Wright [Fig 94] and as a purchaser of one of his industrial landscapes.[3]

Wright's association with the Cokes goes back to before his Italian journey, when he could not have failed to encounter the local M.P. for the town of Derby, Wenham Coke. He remained M.P. until 1774, by which time Wright had departed for Rome. His son Thomas William Coke, later the famous Earl of Leicester, was on the Grand Tour in the early '70's and was immortalised by Batoni in one of his most elegant portraits. He made a great impression with his good looks wherever he went. Lady Mary Coke records meeting him in Florence in the autumn of 1773: 'There are a great many English gentlemen here, among others, Mr. Coke... He is a very pretty man.'[4] He remained in Florence until early the following year but was in Rome again in February 1774 when Wright met him and was in his turn bowled over: 'The gentⁿ & ladies parade in their carriages up & down a long street whimsically dressed in masques, the most beautiful of wᶜʰ was young Mr. Coke, our Member's son'.[5] A week later young Mr. Coke honoured Wright with a visit,[6] and one can be sure there was no hint of condescension in his manner, as they gossiped of Derbyshire affairs. He left Rome shortly afterwards and Wright probably never saw him again, occupied as he was from then onwards with sheep farming in Norfolk. On his return from Italy, Wright became acquainted with a distant branch of the family which had settled in the Midlands, and this association bore fruit in the early '80's in possibly his masterpiece of group portraiture, *The Rev. D'Ewes Coke, his wife, and Daniel Parker Coke* [Plate 225].

The Rev. D'Ewes Coke (1747–1811), rector of Pinxton and South Normanton, was left an orphan at the age of eleven and was brought up by a guardian. He was educated at Repton and Cambridge. His guardian, a Mr. Lillyman, died when Coke was eighteen and on the death of the widow in 1780, he inherited Lillyman's house, Brookhill. The picture must date from soon after his occupation of the house. Through his marriage to Hannah, the daughter and heiress of George Heywood, he came into possession of Brimington Hall, as well as some property near Sheffield and Chesterfield. To judge by Wright's portraits of them they made an ill-assorted pair: he with his benevolent eyes [Fig 93], she with her sulky, hard mouth. Their biographer must have had access to papers testifying to the disagreeableness of her personality, for he writes that Mrs. Coke 'became her father's pet, which circumstance gave an unfortunate stamp to her future character'.[7] Mr. Coke was an etcher on copper and is said to have injured his eyesight by this occupation; Wright shows him dangling a pencil or engraver's tool in his left hand. His wife also must have been keen on drawing since on the table in front of her she props up a portfolio of drawings, one of which, showing a study of trees, peeps out from the rest. At the table is seated with them Daniel Parker Coke, who was so distant a cousin that he has no business there as a relation, but was no doubt just a friend. His parents had died in the late '70's and he remained a bachelor throughout life; this made him all the more dependent on the family life of others. He holds up a sheet of paper and seems to be matching it against the countryside. At the same time Mrs. Coke points at the paper and stares at the landscape. They are either planning some architectural scheme, or it is one of her own drawings that Daniel Parker Coke holds, representing the scene in front of them, and perhaps the rector is congratulating his wife on her success in catching the landscape's likeness, but she does not look as though she will allow herself to be seduced by his good nature. The most distinguished person present is D. P. Coke (1745–1825) [Fig 94]. He was admitted to All Souls, Oxford in 1762 and was afterwards called to the Bar. He was elected M.P. for Derby in 1776 and in 1780 was returned for the town of Nottingham, which he continued to represent for thirty-three years. The attention he paid to Wright seems to be confined to a short period in the early '80's, when he not only competed for and won a character study by the artist in a raffle but bought from him two views of Cromford, one showing Arkwright's newly erected cotton mills under the moon, during a night shift [Plate 244]. This indicated some innate romanticism in his nature; but his interest in recent developments in the factory system also contributed to his desire for its possession, understandable enough in someone who represented in Parliament a constituency like Nottingham in the very heart of the cotton-spinning area.

Distantly related to the Wilmots of Chaddesden who in 1810 acquired Wright's *Old Man and Death* [Plate 123] was the ancient family of the Wilmots of Osmaston-by-Derby, patrons like Daniel Parker Coke of Wright in his capacities both as portrait and landscape painter. Sir Robert Wilmot, second baronet with his seat at Osmaston, married in 1783 Juliana Elizabeth, a daughter of Admiral Byron, and Wright was commissioned five years later to paint her portrait with her young son, Robert, then aged about three, in her arms [Plate 280]. She died early in the year the picture was finished (1788) but their son survived to be third baronet, and on his marriage to Anne Beatrix Horton of Catton, took the name of Sir Robert Wilmot-Horton; his daughter inherited Catton Hall where the picture now hangs.[1] Sir Robert was the type of decent, easy-going baronet whom we have met frequently on earlier occasions, and consequently the Cosway-like, out-of-the-world portrait of his wife and child is as far removed from the realistic classicism of *Daniel Parker Coke* as Osmaston was from the cotton mills at Cromford. He served several times as sheriff of the county in the '90's and was married again to a Miss Howard in 1795—a circumstance that could have been left happily overlooked, had it not been that the minister officiating at the ceremony was his kinsman, that very Robert Wilmot, rector of Morley, whom Wright had painted as a little boy [Plate 15].[2] He had a younger brother Edward (d. 1795) who bought a *Vesuvius* from Wright, also in the late '80's. Whether Sir Robert acquired an Old Master collection himself it has not been possible to establish, but by 1811 a Cignaroli, a supposed Honthorst and a genre scene close to Manfredi were hanging at Osmaston[3] and one would like to think they were already there in 1786–88 when Wright was visiting the house: not that the beautiful Cignaroli would have meant anything to him, nor even the Terbrugghen, which was not the kind by which he was attracted; but his eye would surely have strolled in the direction of the supposed Manfredi, and most often of all towards a Moreelse of a shepherdess, who wears a hat similar to the one belonging to *Mrs. Bathurst* [Plate 84].[4]

Sir Robert Wilmot bought from Wright a *Vesuvius from Posillipo* on panel, in 1788 [Plate 294], a Derbyshire landscape painted in 1786 [Plate 252],[5] and a copy of a blot by Alexander Cozens done at about the same time. Wright also planned to paint for Sir Robert a picture on the theme of John Sargent's poetical drama *The Mine* (published in 1785), but we know nothing of its fate.[6] This more or less unreadable poem is based on a current story (which Sargent narrates in his preface in the form of a series of letters) concerning a Viennese nobleman, a Count Alberti, condemned to the quicksilver mines of Idria in Friuli for duelling with a General of the Austrian infantry against the Emperor's command. His wife insisted on sharing his fate, but Alberti was pardoned and they travelled in triumph to Vienna together. Sargent turns Alberti into a Hungarian nobleman named Count Maurice but retains the same macabre underground mine. Maurice's wife is called Juliana in the poem. A woman of improbable moral rectitude, she shares his fate but without revealing her identity for fear that he will refuse to allow her to remain in the mine if he discovers who she is—justifiably, for he also is in the habit of ruthlessly placing duty above happiness. Finally he is pardoned, and it is only then that Juliana is induced to throw aside her veil to reveal herself as his wife. They are released together, and all ends happily.

Hayley had been a school friend of Sargent and, sensing its possibilities as a theme for the painter, urged him to illustrate the poem. As usual Wright consults him as to the best way of turning words into shapes:

1 A MS. account preserved at Catton headed 'cleaning and varnishing' informs us that the picture was sent for restoration to Seguier in 1825. The charge for work done was £4–4.

2 *Derby Mercury*, 7th May 1795. Much of the information in this paragraph about the Wilmots of Osmaston comes from this source, but the author is also much indebted to the kindness of Mrs. George Anson, the present owner of Catton Hall, for allowing him to study family records in the house.

3 Recorded by Davies, 1811, pp. 277–9. The picture close to Manfredi is described by Davies as 'Soldiers playing with Dice in a Guard-Room; Ann. Caracci' and is published by B. Nicolson in *Studies in Renaissance and Baroque Art presented to Anthony Blunt*, London, 1967, pl. 8 and p. 112. The 'Honthorst' is either a damaged original or a good copy (see J. Richard Judson, *Gerrit van Honthorst*, The Hague, 1959, No. 133).

4 For the Terbrugghen *Beheading of St. John the Baptist*, now in Kansas City, see B. Nicolson, *Hendrick Terbrugghen*, London, 1958, No. A 12. The Moreelse *Shepherdess* is unpublished, but is of the same type as those illustrated in C. H. de Jonge, *Paulus Moreelse...*, 1938, Nos. 268–70.

5 Davies, *op. cit.*, 1811, mentions: '*View of Vesuvius and a morning scene;* Wright'. 'Two pictures by Wright', presumably these two, are in a MS. list at Catton, undated but about early nineteenth century, as having been removed from Osmaston Hall to 'M. J. Wilmot Horton Esq.ᵗ London'. They were sent for restoration to Seguier in 1825, and in the same year are destined for removal from Osmaston to Catton.

6 John Sargent, *The Mine. A Dramatic Poem*, London, 1785.

'... May I without interruption to your repose say a few words about my picture of the Mine, I mention'd to Lady Wilmot (who I think has fine taste & sound judgement) the point of time you thought I shou'd make use of, that is when the Lady throws back the veil & discovers herself to her Husband. She thinks that wou'd be striking & tells the story well, was there probability in it, but she says the whole circumstance of her attending her husband w.th only a thin veil so long undiscover'd, is highly unnatural & too much forced to be pleasing, indeed I think the Reviewers have made the like sort of criticism since. As the picture is for S.r R. Wilmot I am under the necessity of observing what they say... I have composed the scenery my friends say it is horribly grand...'[1]

Lady Wilmot's criticisms of the poem were justified, though we are not in fact told that the veil was thin; in any case, beneath it she wore, according to Count Maurice, 'dripping weeds and servile garb', and must have looked a scarecrow, not at all the dapper Budapest *maîtresse de maison* he remembered. We have no idea how Wright solved this problem, if he ever completed the picture. But though it may flit in and out of history like a bat through a lighted room, the brief glimpse we catch of it has its value as showing that Lady Wilmot had determined ideas about the kind of picture she wanted. Whereas Wright in other contemporary commissions selected scenes from literature calculated to translate themselves into the visual language of neo-classicism, Sargent's poem lent itself only to a picturesque interpretation—the dank cave; the illuminations from flints on revolving wheels; the blackened faces of condemned men hacking at the walls—and this is what appealed to Lady Wilmot, who also commissioned from the artist a highly romanticised portrait of herself as a Madonna, and owned three landscapes by him as far removed from the classical tradition as possible in the late 1780's.

Another of Wright's associates who sat—or rather lay—to him, and at the same time built up a collection of landscapes of the same romantic character as his portrait, was Brooke Boothby (1744–1824), a nobleman from Ashbourne who like Francis Noel Clarke Mundy was also an intellectual, very much in the swim of things. He belonged to a younger generation than Wright and Darwin, and was consequently more inclined to the theoretical than to the factual. He had a delicate constitution, which caused him to shun the brambles of the world instead of crushing them underfoot. His father Sir Brooke Boothby (1710–89) was the fifth in a line of baronets, and one feels that the boy Brooke cannot have looked forward with any relish to the prospect of shouldering the responsibilities incumbent on the sixth. When in the spring of 1766 Jean-Jacques Rousseau, fleeing from persecution in Switzerland, found asylum on the borders of Staffordshire and Derbyshire,[2] he was within a few miles of Ashbourne, and his presence hit Brooke Boothby as his vision outside Damascus hit St. Paul. He was not able to see much of Rousseau on this occasion, being part of the time away in Marseilles, so he wrote him a touching letter in his excellent French on his return to Ashbourne after Rousseau had gone. He seems quite proud of his imperfect subjunctives:

'Je sentis bien du chagrin de ne vous plus trouver à la compagne; je m'étois formé tant de petits projets de vous voir de tems en tems, surtout de vous amener dans des certains vallons où vous eussiez trouvé de quoi vous fournir biens des spéculations botaniques, et où vous eussiez vu tout ce que la simple nature à de plus beau... Je ne vous connois guère que dans vos écrits: c'est eux seuls parmi les modernes qui semblent fait pour inspirer l'amour de la vertu comme un sentiment, qui savent y intéresser à la fois le coeur et l'esprit. Je sens que je ne pourrois jamais fournir une amitié avec l'homme qui pourroit lire de tels écrits sans en aimer l'auteur... Il y a six mois que je me trouve chez mon régiment au Nord de l'Irelande. J'ai peur qu'une Vie militaire ne me conviendroit guère. J'ai le tempérament bien délicat, faute d'une mauvaise éducation, car j'ai les stamina vitæ bons. Je ne sais pas s'il me reste assez de force pour corriger un tel mal...'[3]

In the same letter he complains of the taxes which are crippling the poor and from which only the rich like himself do not suffer—a sentiment typical of his humanitarian generation, one which was well aimed at endearing him to the inhabitants of the Bishop's Palace at Lichfield, where inevitably he found his way in the '70's, hot on the heels of Thomas Day, and where he was received in the most friendly manner by Erasmus Darwin.

1 Wright to Hayley, 12th April 1786, N.P.G. extra-illustrated Bemrose, unpublished. This is the only mention of the picture in the entire literature. In his will of 1817 (MS. copy in the Fitzwilliam Museum), Hayley left a picture by Wright to John Sargent. The clause reads: 'A list of picture legacies to particular friends, June 25, 1817... To my friend and schoolfellow John Sargent Esq.r I give and bequeath my interesting picture called Tivoli or Horace (sic) Villa painted by my friend Wright of Derby...' (The author is indebted to J. W. Goodison for the transcription.) The only painting of *Tivoli* known cannot be traced back to Sargent, or to Hayley.

2 He was in Staffordshire from the second half of March 1766 until the beginning of May 1767. Richard Davenport placed his house Wootton Hall at Rousseau's disposal. Ramsay painted for Davenport a version of his famous portrait of Rousseau (see A. Smart, *The Life and Art of Allan Ramsay*, 1952, p. 136). The portrait of Rousseau in Indiana University, though firmly attributed to Wright, and given the illustrious provenance from Horace Walpole, is not by the artist, but a poor copy of Ramsay.

3 The letter can be taken as '*sic*' throughout, see *Correspondance Générale de J.-J. Rousseau...*, ed. T. Dufour, XVIII, 1932, pp. 136–8 (24th February 1768).

His letter to Rousseau had revealed his interest in botany '*dans des certains vallons*', and together with Darwin he founded the Lichfield Botanic Society. He even met with the approval of the waspish Anna Seward: 'Sir Brooke had not less poetic fancy than Mr. Day', she writes, 'and even more external elegance than Mr. Edgeworth possessed when he won Honora [Sneyd's] heart [1773]; elegance which time, its general foe, has to this hour [1804] but little tarnished in the frame of Sir Brooke Boothby…'[1]

On his return from a journey to Italy, Boothby passed through Paris and on 6th April 1776 visited Rousseau in the rue Plâtrière. Rousseau was then searching for someone to whom to entrust his manuscript of the *Dialogues*, then on the point of completion, and had in mind an Englishman, in the hopes that by this act he might repair some of the damage he had caused in his relations with a country he admired. Boothby's arrival was a gift from heaven. Rousseau writes:

…' Tandis que je vaquois à ce travail [the *Dialogues*], un jeune Anglois que j'avois eu pour voisin à Wootton passa par Paris revenant d'Italie, et me vint voir. Je fis comme tous les malheureux qui croient voir dans tout ce qui leur arrive une expresse direction du sort. Je me dis: Voilà le dépositaire que la Providence m'a choisi… Malheureusement, ma nouvelle copie n'étoit pas avancée, mais je me hâtai de lui remettre ce qui était fait, renvoyant à l'année prochaine à lui remettre le reste, si, comme je n'en doutois pas, l'amour de la vérité lui donnoit le zèle de revenir le chercher'.[2]

It does not seem as though Boothby went back the following year to fetch the remainder; perhaps he was discouraged from doing so, for Rousseau on having surrendered his manuscript, immediately had cold feet. At all events in 1780, two years after Rousseau's death, he published in Lichfield only the first dialogue,[3] Rousseau's first posthumous autobiographical essay to appear anywhere. It was accompanied by the following *Avertissement de l'Editeur*:

'Cet ouvrage me fut confié par son Auteur dans le mois d'Avril 1776, avec des conditions que je me crus fait un devoir sacré de remplir. J'ai cru un moment que ce seroit ici la place d'examiner l'effet que le traitement que l'Auteur reçut de son siècle devoit nécessairement produire sur une ame aussi sensible que la sienne: mais après avoir quelque progrès dans ce travail, une considération que je n'avois pas prévue, m'obligea à l'abandonner: forcé de citer des faits et d'entrer dans des détails, je voyois que je ne pouvois éviter d'y mettre un air d'apologie; et le role d'apologiste est trop au-dessous des sentimens de vénération que M. Rousseau m'a inspirés, pour que j'aye voulu paroitre m'en charger un seul instant. Au reste, l'ouvrage est assez fortement frappé pour pouvoir passer de Commentaire…'[3]

It is indeed '*fortement frappé*', and Boothby had no cause to lay it on any thicker. However, he does add that he expects virtuous, sensitive people to be disturbed by the anguish caused to this great and good man, reduced to the lamentable condition where he saw the whole world in league against him, and to be moved to avenge themselves on his persecutors.

Wright represents this virtuous and sensitive man [Plate 219], so far out of this world that even innocent Thomas Day is made to look like a tub-thumper in comparison, reclining in a '*certain vallon*' beside a stream surrounded by his botanical specimens, with a copy of *Rousseau Juge de Jean Jacques*, that had just come out in Lichfield, under his hand, in a Rousseau-like attitude more or less unique in the history of English painting up to that time.[4] How much better dishevelled Day would have played this part! Boothby with all his elegance has not caught the trick of living in nature. It is so much easier to imagine him at Chatsworth or at the courts of Rome than beside a stripling stream. All the same he had his romantic as well as his dandy side. He bought a number of other pictures from the artist, none of which can be identified, but we can tell from their description just why they should have appealed to him: landscapes needless to say, with a romantic twist, never those harsh neo-classic subject pieces which gratified the tougher-minded Josiah Wedgwood. Like Sir Robert Wilmot he was attracted to Alexander Cozens and bought two of Wright's copies after him; two views of bridges (sure to be crumbling to bits) in the neighbourhood of his beloved Rome, and no less than four views of Derbyshire, two of Matlock and two

1 Seward, 1804, pp. 57 ff. Anna Seward calls him 'Sir Brooke' because she is writing after he succeeded his father as sixth baronet (1789).

2 Jean-Jacques Rousseau, *Œuvres Complètes*, Bibliothèque de la Pleiade, I, 1959, p. 983. From the section '*Histoire du précédent écrit*'. See also pp. 1753–4; and Voisine, 1958, pp. 53–4.

3 Rousseau. *Juge de Jean Jacques—Dialogues… Premier Dialogue d'Après le Manuscrit de M. Rousseau laissé entre les mains de M. Brooke Boothby*, Lichfield, 1780. In the year that Wright finished his portrait, Boothby gave the MS. to the British Museum (Add. MS. 4925).

4 Strangely enough it was well received by the *Public Advertiser* of 2nd May 1781, which writes: '… he shews in the whole Length of the Gentleman lying down, the Powers of a *Portrait* painter in the *first* class…', but no doubt this criticism was rigged.

Fig 126 Sir Joshua Reynolds
Brooke Boothby 1784
73 x 62 in / 185.4 x 157.5 cm
Detroit Institute of Arts

1 Wright to Hayley, 22nd December 1784,
N.P.G. extra-illustrated Bemrose, unpublished.

2 The interesting accounts surviving of
Boothby's residence in Weimar would carry
us too far afield, but the reader is referred to
Goethes Gespräche. Gesamtausg. Neu hrsg.
v. Flodoard Frhr. v. Biedermann, Bd. 2 (1909),
pp. 508–9 and Bd. 5 (1911), p. 124 (visit to
Goethe by R. P. Gillies, 22nd June 1821),
published in Leipzig.

3 Sir Brooke Boothby to Lord Wellesley dated
from Dresden, 12th March 1806, from Brit.
Mus. MS. 37309, No. 102. See also letter from
George Sinclair to the Earl of Liverpool of
20th July 1822 (Brit. Mus. MS. 38575, No. 46),
pleading on Boothby's behalf for the award
in favour of the Boothby line of the Barony
of Burgh, then in abeyance.

of Dovedale. He also owned Wright's portrait of his patron and good friend Darwin, and one subject piece, a small romantic prison scene. He could not have been more like himself in his choice of Wrights. Though never intimate friends, the two men were on excellent terms. Boothby helped him with his one-man exhibition in 1785 by advising on advertisements, and by persuading his smart friends, over whom Wright himself had no influence, to take an interest. Boothby still moved in smart circles as he had in early youth. He was the opposite of Day in this respect: as immaculate in his manners and dress as Day was slovenly. Not only Wright's portrait but Reynolds's (in Detroit) bears witness to this [Fig 126]. Wright sees his chance of profiting from Boothby's social position and writes off to Hayley:

'Mr. Boothby was wth me the other day when we talked much of my Exhibition[.] he has most sanguine hopes of my Success, he is acquainted wth the Dutchess of Devonshire who you know heads the fashionable part of the female world, he will give her Grace such an opinion of it, as will he hopes make her patronize it, if so the business wou'd be half done.'[1]

Boothby's later career is clouded by a series of disasters. The first was to acquire a handle to his name in 1789 on his father's death. The next was two years later when his only daughter Penelope died at the age of five. Sir Brooke erected a monument to her, the most famous work of Thomas Banks, in the Boothby chapel in Ashbourne Church, which could claim a place of honour in the foyer of any Victorian exhibition, with inscriptions on it in various languages, one of which reads: '... The unfortunate Parents ventured their all on this frail Bark, And the wreck was total.' After the death of his daughter he separated from his wife. As a last straw, his financial affairs began to go to pieces, and he spent his declining years in self-imposed exile, a Settecento Oscar Wilde who had once seen Rousseau plain. It was through his good offices that the sixteenth-century stained glass windows from the Abbey of Herckenrode, near Hasselt in the South Netherlands were acquired in 1802 and installed in the Lady Chapel of Lichfield Cathedral. We find him in 1804 in Weimar in the company of Goethe.[2] He writes from Dresden in 1806 of 'pecuniary indiscretions' which 'I have more cause to lament than be ashamed of, and from indolence and penury and dejection with the prospect of public affairs, [I] have continued a solitary wanderer on the continent ever since.... I have in mind to return home but God knows when I shall find energy...'[3] He died, wifeless and childless, at Boulogne in 1824. Did the adolescent Sainte-Beuve, roaming the streets of his native town, ever think of jogging that handsome old head, stirring up memories of the great French philosopher in the woods of Staffordshire in the '60's, as Boothby lay on his death-bed at Boulogne-sur-Mer?

To move back from this captivating baronet to the humdrum existence of Derbyshire provincial life is something of a come-down, but we have one further family to consider, the Batemans, before turning to those more conservative Midlands families who demanded nothing more of Wright than the delineation of their own features. A certain Hugh Bateman of Hartington Hall (1758–1824) was J. P. for the county in 1777 and High Sheriff of Derbyshire in 1792. He was married in 1786 to Temperance, daughter of John Gisborne, and they had one son Richard Sacheverell (1788–94). Hugh was created Baronet in 1809. Wright is believed to have painted various members of the family in the early 1790's: Hugh and his wife; a 'Richard' who was possibly Hugh's brother; and Hugh's son as a child of about five [Plate 336] which like the Penelope monument in Ashbourne Church bears an inscription in Italian, put up in 1795 on instructions from Hugh Bateman to commemorate the boy's recent death. Wright probably painted him just before he died and the picture all too rapidly dwindled to a tomb effigy. It has a pious, sentimental air about it which fits the role it was destined to play. Some years earlier Hugh Bateman had purchased from Wright two Lake scenes, one by day, one by night [Plates 237, 239], and it is possible that he also owned other works by the artist.

It should have become clear that with a few notable exceptions Wright continued after his return from Italy to gratify his clients among the landed gentry by idealising their features. The point could be elaborated by considering some insipid portrait groups of children and examining their parents' backgrounds, but enough has been said. Sometimes we know so little about the people represented that it is tempting to speculate about their way of life on the basis of the painter's rendering of them, but this is full of pitfalls. Fortunately in the case of one of his most idealised portraits, that of *Dorothy Gell of Hopton* [Plate 266] we know something of her social situation, and this throws light on her appearance and mood in his picture. She was the daughter and co-heiress of William Milnes of Cromford, a possible alternative to John Milnes of Wakefield as purchaser of *Miravan* [Plate 107], a property speculator associated, not only with the gentry, but with the up-and-coming industrialists Arkwright, Strutt and Peter Nightingale of Lea.[1] In 1774 she married Philip Gell of Hopton, sheriff of the county in 1755 and a true gentleman of leisure. Writing to her father Jedediah, Elizabeth Strutt, who used to be a friend of 'Miss Dolly' as she called her, but who sensed in Dolly's marriage a gulf widening between them, observes:

'I had a letter from Miss Dolly during my dear Mother's illness whilst my mind was rack'd with a thousand hopes & fears. I could not answer it then—in a few days after she was married—& I have never answered it—I suppose it would be very improper to renew the correspondence now, having deferr'd wishing her happiness so long—if you think it would not, & can tell me how to address her in her elevated station it would be very agreeable to me, for there is something improving in her letters...'[2]

No doubt the Strutts who were great sticklers for etiquette on account of their social insecurity, would have intended by 'elevated station' nothing more sinister than Mrs. Gell's married state, but in Wright's portrait of her painted twelve years later, meditating beside a tomb, Miss Dolly has shed her property-speculating origins as well as her name, and is transformed into the embodiment of refined sensibility. The portrait is as far removed in spirit from that of *Mrs. Hurt* [Plate 203], the wife of the iron king and proud of it, as one could imagine it would be within the power of a single portrait painter to make it. Strangely enough Mrs. Hurt was born a Gell of Hopton and played Miss Milnes's role in reverse, by 'sinking' if one may so call it, from the life of the country gentlewoman to that of ironmistress; so it is she who ends up paradoxically the more down-to-earth of the two.

It would be instructive in one case, that of Samuel Crompton, to turn the argument upside down, and to consider first what we know about him, and then how he would be likely to be represented, before turning to the actual portrait which survives, thereby putting our theory to a hard test. Crompton came of a prosperous banking family, his father (d. 1757) being the first of the banking house and the founder of the family's wealth. They owned one of the finest buildings in Derby. The son whom Wright painted was High Sheriff of the county in 1768 and Mayor of the Borough in 1777 for the year ensuing. In 1775 Daniel Parker Coke had indicted Crompton for perjury at the Summer Assizes but even though Crompton was acquitted in the following year, he still felt he must clear his name, and two years later brought an action against Coke which was heard before Lord Mansfield at Westminster and a special jury, and a verdict was given for Crompton, the jury considering that there were not the least grounds for the indictment.[3] He died in 1782 and was succeeded in the business by his son Samuel who within a few months of his father's death was elected Mayor.[4] In other words, here was a family in business, which by offering its services to the community, was respected and respectable. Would we not expect a modified realism, something nearer to truth than to dignity? This is precisely what we obtain [Plate 206]. Between *Reginald Lygon* and *Staniforth* falls *Samuel Crompton*, banker and public servant. It would have been gratifying to go on from here to discuss '*Christopher Heath*' [Plate 209] and '*Stephen' Jones* [Plate 268], two of Wright's most magnificent portraits of the '80's which are near to the *Staniforth* end of the scale in directness of approach and naturalness of pose. But we are too vague about the sitters to be able to draw any deductions of a similar kind from them, and must suppress a temptation to speculate about their professional status.

1 He made a contract in 1776 with Richard Arkwright and in the same year sold his Cromford Estate to Nightingale; see Fitton and Wadsworth, 1958, p. 77.

2 5th September 1774; quoted *op. cit.* p. 149.

3 Kings Bench Judgement Roll, Crompton v. Coke. AB 122/413 membrane 5.30 (P.R.O.). This lengthy document, couched as it is in impenetrable legal language, reveals nothing of the true nature of the dispute.

4 Much information about the Cromptons can be extracted from the files of the *Derby Mercury*, but see also Pilkington, 1789, II, pp. 168, 179. Contrary to what is said in Tate, 1958 (18, 19), it was the younger Samuel who married the daughter of Samuel Fox, not the man painted by Wright.

5 PERSONAL FRIENDS 1775–97

Once Burdett, Whitehurst and Coltman had disappeared to, respectively, Germany, London and Lincolnshire, Wright was left in Derby with few friends of his own calibre. There were old family friends and their children of whom out of habit he was fond. But except for the two doctors Darwin and Beridge, we hear of no-one in the town who was both a friend and a stimulating companion during the last twenty years of his life. There were no artists to speak of, with whom to talk shop. When he travelled to the Lakes, it was in the company of friends and artists from outside. Perhaps there was something in what his snobbish little pipsqueak of a niece said, that his wife discouraged company at St. Helen's House. Perhaps he was driven by her lack of conviviality to satisfy a human need, friendship, in letters to people living at some distance: to the Tates in Liverpool, to Wedgwood at Etruria, to Hayley in Sussex, to Gisborne in Needwood Forest, to Daulby and Philips in Manchester. His loss is our gain: for his words which would have evaporated had he merely strolled up the street in order to deliver them, are preserved for us in the form of letters to these more distant kindred spirits. There remained in Derby a single consolation. Isolated and hypochondriacal as he was, it must hve been a relief to him when Darwin decided to join him there in 1783.

After having spent two years at Radburne (1781–3) Darwin moved with his new wife to Derby and remained there for the rest of his life (he died in 1802), except for a brief period at the end when he occupied Breadsall Priory, a Jacobean mansion outside the town, on the site of an Augustinian Priory.[1] He continued his practice as a physician but this was only one of his many activities. There was no department of intellectual life in which he did not seem to be playing a leading role. At Lichfield he had been constantly in touch with the young scientists, but at Radburne had missed their company. Whilst still living there, he had written to Boulton: 'I am here cut of [sic] from the milk of science, which flows in such redundant streams from your learned lunations; which, I can assure you is a very great regret to me'.[2] The move to Derby was designed so that he should be nearer the centre of things. (There was no question of returning to Lichfield: Anna Seward and the widow of Colonel Pole would have been scratching each other's eyes out.)

The reference in Darwin's letter to 'lunations' demands some explanation. For many years he had been closely in touch with a group of Midlands intellectuals who had formed themselves into a body which came to be known as the Lunar Society. At first it was a loose confederation of friends anxious to compare notes on the latest discoveries in the sciences, by occasional informal meetings and by correspondence. It traces its origin back to the '60's but it was not until the mid-'70's that the name 'Lunar' first appears, and when meetings are first recorded. Regular meetings did not take place before 1780. From that time onwards successive waves of Lunatics met regularly, generally at the house of Matthew Boul-

1 See Pevsner, 1953, p. 70.

2 Darwin to Boulton, 28th December 1782; quoted Schofield, 1963, p. 204.

130

ton in Birmingham.[1] Priestley recalls in his memoirs:

'I consider my settlement at Birmingham as the happiest event in my life, being highly favourable to every object I had in view, philosophical or theological... [I enjoyed] the society of persons eminent for their knowledge of chemistry, particularly Mr Watt, Mr Keir, and Dr Withering. These with Mr Boulton, and Dr Darwin [and others] and myself dined together every month, calling ourselves the *lunar society*, because the time of our meeting was near the full moon.'[2]

Whitehurst was another Lunatic, who would occasionally attend meetings on his visits to the Midlands from London. There were in all fourteen members over the years, many of whom were friends or acquaintances of Wright: besides those mentioned, Wedgwood (who did not often attend), Day and Edgeworth. But naturally enough Wright himself, being not in the remotest sense a professional philosopher or man of science, was never invited. As an artist he was content to keep the flag of the Lunar Society flying in his moonlit landscapes. Just as in these canvases the moon casts a romantic glow over Dove or Derwent, so it acts as a beacon for the philosophers as they ride home in the early hours from their sessions at Boulton's house.

Darwin founded a Philosophical Society in Derby soon after his arrival there, and wrote to Boulton inviting the members of the Lunar Society to join with the Derby philosophers in meeting at Darwin's house: 'We have established an infant philosophical Society at Derby, but do not presume to compare it to your well-grown gigantic Philosophers at Birmingham... our number at present [1783] amounts to seven, and we meet hebdomadally'.[3] Again Wright was not one of the elect, even in his home town, even though Wedgwood's daughter claimed that 'all the ingenious gentlemen in the town belong to it'.[4] Wright painted portraits or subject pieces for some of the other members of the Society: for Josiah Wedgwood (non-resident); Charles Stead Hope, whom he painted as a boy of about fourteen [Plate 180] and who had recently come of age; Brooke Boothby; possibly William Pickering [Plate 197]; and William Duesbury the famous porcelain manufacturer whose daughter Wright painted towards the end of his life [Plate 337]. Oddly enough we never hear of any connection between the painter and another member of the Society, Dr. Bage, a typical product of the period in that he was both a paper-mill owner and a disciple of Rousseau, later making his name as a novelist.[5]

Not content with being doctor, sanitary inspector, chemist, botanist, zoologist, mechanic, political theorist, Darwin had also to be a didactic poet. He had composed poetry as a young man, and again under the inspiration of Mrs. Pole. But it was not until the late '70's that he embarked on a lengthy poetical work, the *Botanic Garden*, on which he remained intermittently engaged for over ten years. He feared for his reputation as a doctor, were he to publish under his own name. Eventually the second part, 'Loves of the Plants' appeared anonymously in 1789 and was at once a best seller; so that he was encouraged to go ahead with the publication of the first. 'The Economy of Vegetation.' The story is well authenticated, how he would write round to all his Lunatic friends gathering information on every conceivable topic in which they happened to be experts, from steam engines to coining presses, all of which somehow or other wove their way into plant life. The immediate success of this long poem is not easy to explain since we are still suffering from 150 years of neglect of it. It was struck dead by the *Lyrical Ballads*, just as Wright's late landscapes were killed when romanticism became real life, in the hands of Turner, Girtin and Constable. But now we are beginning to drag our steps back to it. This is not a study of Darwin[6] and we have no wish to discuss any aspect of his work that has not a particular bearing on Wright. Even so, some of it is relevant to the painter, not merely the bouquet that Darwin hands out to him in the course of it:

'So Wright's bold pencil from Vesuvio's height
Hurls his red lavas to the troubled night;
From Calpè[7] starts the intolerable flash,
Skies burst in flames, and blazing oceans dash;

1 See Schofield, 1963, *passim*, and catalogue of the Exhibition 'Lunar Society of Birmingham', Museum and Art Gallery, Birmingham, 1966.

2 *Memoirs of Dr. Joseph Priestley Written by Himself (to the year 1795)*..., London, 1806, i, p. 97.

3 Darwin to Boulton, 4th March 1783; quoted Robinson, 1953.

4 Letter to her father, 13th March 1783; quoted Robinson, *loc. cit.*

5 An entertaining account of Dr. Bage is given in C. Kegan Paul, *William Godwin: his Friends and Contemporaries*, London, 1876, I, pp. 262 ff. Godwin describes Mrs. Darwin in the same letter (15th June 1797) as 'tolerably well bred'.

6 We are omitting the Darwin bibliography since recent biographies and critical studies cite all the books. His grandson's memoir is still the most readable study.

7 This is a reference to Wright's lost picture, *View of Gibraltar during the destruction of the Spanish Floating Batteries*.

1 *The Botanic Garden*, Part II, *Loves of the Plants*, Canto I, lines 175 ff. Some editions give 'birds' instead of 'bids' in line 5, but the latter makes more sense. The two parts of the poem are referred to below as E.V. and L.P.

Or bids in sweet repose his shades recede,
Winds the still vale, and slopes the velvet mead;
On the pale stream expiring zephyrs sink,
And moonlight sleeps upon its hoary brink.'[1]

It would be wrong to confine the parallels between poem and pictures to specific instances, because Darwin will swoop down from nymphs and dryads to the internal combustion engine or the future of aviation or the submarine and back again without turning a hair, and make us feel there is no difference in kind between one level of reality and the other; just as Wright will swoop down from Debutades's daughter to cotton mills operating a night shift, or will be occupied one day on an Æsop fable where a skeleton is made to saunter across a canvas, and the next on the forging of an iron bar. Galen and Whitehurst, Leander and 'Stephen' Jones, the head of San Gennaro and the valley of the Dove—they have equal strength as reality for him, so that there is no forced whimsicality in his use of the one, nor self-conscious defiance in his use of the other. To move from one canvas to the next is to be perpetually amazed, as we are when reading the *Botanic Garden*, by the way everyday life takes on the aspect of fantasy, whilst mythology and classical allusion are brought down to its level to join it. In the minds of both artists, the Wisdom of the Ages and the wisdom of the age meet half way on equal terms, and do not clash.

There are parallels in subject-matter, also, not merely in the taste that both men had for themes from Shakespeare and Milton. From the opening words of Darwin's 'Advertisement' to the complete work, we are put in mind of Wright's attitude to the world around him: 'The general design of the following sheets is to inlist Imagination under the banner of Science...', and from then on we are treated to eulogies of the iron forge, the pottery of Etruria, the orrery, the air pump, the cotton mills at Cromford, Hero and Leander[2]—all described with a sharp grasp of the visual, which makes us wonder why Darwin did not possess, so far as we know, a landscape or a subject piece by Wright. From many passages worthy of quotation we select one which reads so much like a Wright of the late '80's that we are tempted to deduce that Darwin had allowed his quill pen to be swayed, not only by nature herself, but by the many representations by the painter he must have seen of the neighbourhood of Dovedale and Matlock in the houses he was in the habit of frequenting:

2 The passages in question are respectively: E.V., II, lines 185 ff., 291 ff., 505 ff; IV, lines 135 ff.; L.P., II, lines 88 ff.; IV, lines 403 ff.

3 E.V., III, lines 19–24.

'Your lucid bands condense with fingers chill
The blue mist hovering round the gelic hill;
In clay-form'd beds the trickling streams collect,
Strain through white sands, through pebbly veins direct;
Or point in rifted rocks their dubious way,
And in each bubbling fountain rise to day.'[3]

Fig 127 *Erasmus Darwin* 1792–3
30 x 25 in / 76.2 x 63.5 cm   Major
J. W. Chandos-Pole   Cat 52   Pl 338

Wright painted a second portrait of Darwin in old age [Fig 127]. He has changed little since those philandering days at Lichfield but something tells us—it may be the poet's pen poised aloft, or a far-away look in the eye—that he has gained in spirituality with the passage of twenty years. Here is no longer the astute young scientist but the poet and the seer, who has conquered the material world around him and now looks into himself, who in a passage in his *Botanic Garden* on the abolition of slavery, can proclaim his contempt for human cruelty; the splendid old near-atheist who can join hands with Wordsworth in celebrating the rising of the French people: 'Do you not congratulate your grandchildren', he writes to James Watt soon after the outbreak of the Revolution, 'on the dawn of universal liberty? I feel myself becoming all french in chemistry & politics'.[4] Even to be old in that dawn was very heaven. His life-long friend, the chemist James Keir, shall have the last word: 'In benevolence, he thought that almost all virtue consisted. He despised the monkish abstinences and the hypocritical pretensions which so often impose on the world. The communication of happiness and the relief of misery were by him held as the only standard of moral merit...'.[5]

Such was Wright's constant companion and doctor during his last years. What, one wonders, was *his* opinion of religion and slavery, of the origin of species and democracy, of the dawn of the new order? How irritating it is that this painter, who was in constant contact with the most progressive minds of his day, should never have come clean about his own views! Perhaps he echoed to himself Copley's words: '... I am desireous of avoiding every imputation of party spir [it], Political contests being neighther pleasing to an artist or advantageous to the Art itself...',[1] extending this sentiment to embrace the entire social revolution in which he found himself, willy-nilly, involved. And yet, to think that he knew Arkwright, who was sinking a fortune in the factory system, now taken for granted as a basic economic principle but then a gamble for vast stakes; that he was the close friend of Wedgwood the Dissenter and Whig, who was writing to Darwin at the moment of the fall of the Bastille: 'I know you will rejoice with me in the glorious revolution which has taken place in France', and who manufactured a jasper-ware cameo with a slave in chains, with the motto: 'Am I not a man and a brother'; that he was on the best of terms with Brooke Boothby, courageous defender of the French Revolution against Burke and a saint of generosity and abnegation; the intimate of Gisborne, in his turn the intimate of Wilberforce! Was he of the same persuasion, as one might guess from some of the themes he hit on from English literature and the classics? If not to Day, then to Gisborne or Darwin, did he never confess to those unregenerate days in Liverpool, and did they pass his honesty off with a shrug? Or like Seurat was he happy to sit back in silence, as they planned the new society that was to transform the world? During those long winter evenings at Yoxall Lodge, did he and Gisborne do nothing but pore over drawings, or were there times when they put the portfolio aside and spoke with passion of the liberation of the slave?

We know little of the details of Wright's friendship with Gisborne[1] but enough to realise that it was one of the bright spots in a melancholy life. Their friendship dates from the summer of 1777 when Wright was given the commission to paint the portrait of this promising young Derby scholar. Thomas Gisborne (1758–1846) had been sent to Harrow in 1773 and had been admitted a Fellow Commoner at St. John's College, Cambridge three years later. In the year that Wright painted him [Fig 129] he won the gold medal for a Latin ode, a prize founded in 1774 for undergraduates under the will of Sir William Browne, President of the Royal College of Physicians. His academic attainments did not rest there: in 1780 he was sixth wrangler in the Mathematical Tripos, the only Honours Examination at that time, and won the First Chancellor's Classical gold medal. His old Harrow headmaster, Dr. Heath, was so proud of his progress that he arranged for Wright to paint him.

4 Darwin to Watt, 19th January 1790. The allusion is to Lavoisier.

5 Letter from James Keir to Robert Darwin, 12th May 1802, quoted Ernst Krause, *Erasmus Darwin*, London, ed. 1879, p. 35, in 'Preliminary notice' by Charles Darwin.

1 Copley to Benjamin West, 24th November 1770, quoted Jules D. Prown, *John Singleton Copley*, Cambridge, Mass., 1966, I, p. 78.

2 For further details about the relationship between the two, see Nicolson, 1965, *passim*. The passage that follows about Gisborne is reprinted from this article, with omissions and changes.

Fig 128 Detail from *The Rev and Mrs Thomas Gisborne* Cat 67 See Pl 269

Fig 129 *Thomas Gisborne* 1777
30 x 25 in / 76.2 x 63.5 cm Mr and Mrs Patrick Gibson Cat 66 Pl 191

This marked the beginning of a friendship which brushed aside the difference of twenty-four years in age between them, and lasted until Wright's death.

At this time he was plain Mr. Gisborne. It was only after graduation that he was ordained deacon (1781) and priest (1783). In the latter year he was presented to the perpetual curacy of Barton-under-Needwood, Staffs., and settled down at Yoxall Lodge, inherited by him on his father's death (1779), within three miles of his church. He became prebendary of Durham Cathedral. But he never aspired to high office in the priesthood: the country habit had him too firmly by the heart. A property in Derby was disposed of, and he remained contentedly at Yoxall for the remainder of his life. In 1784 he married Mary (1760–1848), daughter of a distinguished Leicestershire family of Babington, of Rothley Temple, and it is with her he is shown in a second portrait [Fig 128] painted two years after their marriage, seated under a tree in the once famous Needwood Forest near his home; no longer the proud undergraduate but the unworldly divine. The forest has now been stripped almost bare of its oaks, and Yoxall Lodge, a large, rambling house which used to nestle in the valley far from any tourist's gaze, was pulled down earlier this century. Nothing is left to remind us of its philanthropic owner except his tomb in the church nearby.

Wright was drawn to Gisborne, not only because he always enjoyed the company of the young, but because like Darwin he was attracted to this new generation of philanthropists —young men with deep religious convictions, so different from the rationalists of Wright's own generation, whose company he also sought, since they appealed to another, a scientific, side to his nature. Moreover he loved the peace of Yoxall. It is more than likely that his beautiful tree studies—those gnarled oaks in which the forest abounded—were done in the vicinity of the Lodge, on some of his frequent visits to it.[1] A common interest in art created a bond between them. We have it on good authority[2] that Gisborne, who had a natural taste and aptitude, used to draw with Wright in the mornings and play the flute with him in the evenings. Gisborne had a high regard for Wright's talent. In the very year of the double portrait, Wright painted two landscapes as companions, a *View of Dovedale* and a *Convent of Cosimato* [Plates 255, 257] as a reminder that the sublimity of nature was to be found equally in the English and Italian countryside, which remained at Yoxall until they passed to Kedleston; and two years later he noted in his Account Book the price of forty-two guineas for 'Gisborne's Eruption of Vesuvius' (now unidentified). Gisborne owned other pictures and drawings by him, mostly 'sublime' or picturesque subjects;[3] for of course the vogue for candlelight and scientific pictures had passed with the generation of rationalists, and even had Wright continued to paint them in the late '80's, their appeal would have been lost on the young country curate and amateur landscape draughtsman. A more personal token of their friendship is recorded in Wright's self-portrait at the age of 59,

1 Preserved in a portfolio in the Derby Art Gallery. They are all wash drawings, sometimes with single large trees, sometimes with groups of trees. One shows a hollow tree trunk. A selection is here illustrated [Figs 131, 132] along with a magnificent drawing of a boulder [Fig 130], which bears some resemblance to rocks in the vicinity of Needwood Forest, but it would be impossible ever to identify.

2 MS. 2, Derby Public Library; niece's memoir.

3 An exception is a copy by Wright of his portrait of Pickering (see Cat No 118). Gisborne would have been drawn to Pickering as a fellow-mathematician. There is a mysterious entry in Wright's Account Book: 'Mores account from Sep! 85 Rec'd of Mr. Gisborne for two large Drawings of Mores...£8'. This entry makes one think that Wright sold to Gisborne two drawings by Wright's friend Jacob More, on More's behalf. (That the word in the MS. should be read as 'Mores' and not 'Moses' as Bemrose, 1885, p. 124, first entry, believed, is confirmed by subsequent entries in this book where Wright records payments for lottery tickets, half of which are on More's behalf; Moses was no gambler). Jacob More is the type of landscape painter whom Gisborne would have been expected to admire; he had exhibited an *Eruption of Vesuvius* at the Academy in the previous year (1784), and was to exhibit an *Eruption of Etna* in 1788—the precise subject Gisborne chose for his description of a volcanic eruption in his poem *Walks in a Forest* (see below).

Fig 130 *Landscape with Boulders* late '80's
Pencil and wash 10⅛ x 14 in / 25.7 x 35.5 cm   Derby Museum
and Art Gallery

Fig 131 *Tree study* c 1786–90
Wash 9⅝ x 6½ in / 24.4 x 16.5 cm
Derby Museum and Art Gallery

Fig 132 *Tree study* c 1786–90
Wash 17¼ x 12⅝ in / 43.8 x 32 cm
Derby Museum and Art Gallery

painted on a visit to the Lodge in 1793 and presented to his friend with a touching Latin dedication on the reverse [Fig 9].

It was the habit in the last decade of the eighteenth century for clergymen to practise drawing from nature. Gisborne formed a close friendship in 1792 with a fellow-clergyman-sketcher William Gilpin, the apostle of the Picturesque, and it was no doubt through Gisborne that Wright became acquainted with Gilpin's ideas. Much light is thrown on Gisborne's character in Gilpin's letters. Soon after their first meeting, Gilpin is ecstatic about his new friend: '... I have seen, several times, also Mr. Gisborne, a Staffordshire gentleman', he writes, 'He is an ingenious man; & of so much simplicity of character, that he takes with me exceedingly. You can enter his mind without lock or key. He is a man of considerable fortune; but went into orders, not with any view of preferment, but merely, as it appears to me, to have a better pretence to be serious...'[1] And again a month later:

1 Gilpin to Mary Hartley, 17th September 1792; kindly communicated, along with the second quotation below, by Carl Paul Barbier.

'... I know not that I ever contracted so close an intimacy with any person in so short a time. He is a man exactly to my taste. You may imagine when I tell you, that I... am not *always* well-pleased, when people visit me, (for I am one of those odd folk, that like my own company better than the generality of company I meet with) but Mr. Gisborne, tho' he is continually stepping in, never comes amiss.—I am much pleased also with Mrs. Gisborne, who is a sensible unaffected, pleasant woman. Mr. Gisborne and I unite not only in our love of painting, (to which he is a pure devotee) but in all other subjects...'[2]

2 Gilpin to Mary Hartley, 11th October 1792.

The meeting with Gilpin, and the impact on Gisborne of the *Tour of the Lakes*, a new edition of which appeared in the year of the birth of their friendship, persuaded Gisborne to make up his mind to go on a sketching expedition to the Lakes in the following summer, and as we have seen, he suggested to Wright who was then staying at Bootle, near Liverpool, that he should join him there. Wright set off with Thomas Moss Tate and spent a week in Gisborne's company at the Lakes, returning to Bootle, according to Wright's niece, 'highly delighted with all they had seen.'[3] Gilpin followed up his encouragement of Gisborne with a letter which found Gisborne at Maryport in July 1793: 'Your situation near the paradise of England is enviable! Pray, when you see them next, give my respectful compliments to Skiddaw, Helvellin, Grasmire...'[4]

3 See above Part I, p. 19.

Practically nothing of Gisborne's work as an artist has been identified.[5] There exists among the Wright drawings at Derby a competent pencil and wash sketch of rocks and trees which we might have accepted as from Wright's own hand, had it not been for an inscription on the reverse; 'T.G. 1798', and then in pencil in a recent hand 'Sepia drawing after Wright (F.W.)'.[6] But it is too faithful a tribute to the memory of his friend to reveal

4 Gilpin to Gisborne, 1st July 1793, quoted by Barbier, 1963, p. 108, n. 2.

5 A water-colour of *Caerphilly Castle* belonging to Dr. Roderick Howell in Swansea is inscribed on the back 'August 1800', and on a label apparently of the early nineteenth century are the words: 'A picture by Rev⁴ T. Gisborne'. It seems inconceivable that this should not be an accurate attribution. A beautiful watercolour signed 'T. G.', in the manner of John 'Warwick' Smith, and evidently by Gisborne belonged in 1967 to the Sabin Galleries.

6 The initials are those of F. Williamson, Curator of the Derby Art Gallery in the 1930's.

Fig 133 Thomas Gisborne (?) *Warwick Castle* 1792
Sepia wash oval 6¾ x 10⅞ in / 17.1 x 27.6 cm   Derby Museum and Art Gallery

1 Wright to Philips, 17th January 1793, quoted Bemrose, 1885, p. 92. Moreland was a mutual friend of Wright and Philips.

2 29th December 1800; quoted by Barbier, 1963, p. 169, n. 4.

3 The author is indebted to Carl Paul Barbier for his opinion on the drawings. One is inscribed in Wright's hand 'No. 2 Dec.̲ 11ᵗʰ 1792'; another 'No. 3 Dec.̲ 22ⁿᵈ 1792'. We cannot be sure that Wright was at Yoxall at this precise moment but he was in the habit of visiting the Lodge in the winter months and may well have been given the drawings by Gisborne that December. One shows *Warwick Castle* [Fig 133] (Gilpin, 3rd ed. 1792, I, plate facing p. 39), a subject which Wright used for a moonlight canvas; another, a contracted valley (see I, plate facing p. 121); a third, rocky scenery at Matlock along the banks of the Derwent (see II, plate facing p. 217).

4 See below p. 156.

5 Robert Isaac Wilberforce and Samuel Wilberforce, *The Life of William Wilberforce*, I, London, 1838, pp. 10–11.

6 *Op. cit.*, p. 284.

7 He was at Buxton with Gisborne in mid-October 1789, and in November 1791 the two men visited Etruria together. Wilberforce was again at Yoxall in December 1791.

8 Quoted by John Campbell Colquhoun, *William Wilberforce, His Friends and his Times*, London, 1866, p. 200.

much of his personal handwriting. It is clear from the little evidence we have that Gisborne enjoyed experimenting in new techniques. These he had acquired from, among others, John 'Warwick' Smith, in whose confidence he was, if we are to judge from a postscript in a letter from Wright to John Leigh Philips: 'I am sorry I cannot fulfil my engagement with Mr. Moreland, Mr. Gisborne does not think himself at liberty to divulge Smith's mode of washing with water colours',[1] and there is a letter in existence from Gisborne to Gilpin in which he expresses his views on the use of body colour,[2] with some vehemence. It is possible that we have evidence of Gisborne's interest in the work of Gilpin in the form of four oval 'Picturesque' drawings [Fig 133] preserved in Wright's portfolio of drawings at Derby. These are rather poor copies of some aquatint illustrations in Gilpin's *Tour of the Lakes*. They are certainly not good enough for Wright but could be by Gisborne; especially since two of them bear dates in December 1792 in Wright's handwriting, which makes one think they were presented to Wright by Gisborne on a visit to Yoxall that winter.[3] This leads us on to consider what interest Wright himself took in the Picturesque movement. Since we do not know whether he was acquainted with Gilpin (all we know is that he was in correspondence with Gilpin's brother Sawrey before August 1790),[4] it is rash to speculate. That the ideas of the Picturesque were in the Midlands air in the '80's and that Wright absorbed them, there can be no question; but whether from Gilpin personally, or merely through his friendship with Gisborne, it is hard to say.

It is tantalising, also, that we should be so well informed about Gisborne's relationship with William Wilberforce, yet unaware whether he and Wright ever met. Gisborne and Wilberforce had been undergraduates together at St. John's, where according to Gisborne: 'My rooms and his were back to back, and often when I was raking out my fire at ten o'clock, I heard his melodious voice calling aloud to me to come and sit with him before I went to bed'.[5] Their acquaintance was interrupted when they left the University, but was later renewed by a letter of enquiry from Gisborne, when he first saw the name of Wilberforce connected with the cause of abolition. Thereafter Wilberforce frequently visited Yoxall where he enjoyed privacy, combined with the comforts provided by his friend's family. He also became friendly with Mrs. Gisborne's family, the Babingtons of Rothley Temple. He used Yoxall as a place in which to recuperate, though never to idle away his time; work continued there at high pressure, but free from the harrowing interruptions that made concentration so difficult at Westminster. He relished what he described as the 'innocent and edifying hilarity of the Lodge'.[6] Under his guidance Gisborne took an early stand against slavery. He was not the kind to venture as far as Westminster, but carried on propaganda in Derbyshire and Staffordshire in the early '90's in support of the cause his old friend had taken up. Wilberforce spent several weeks or months at Yoxall in early autumn, every year from 1790 to 1793[7]—precisely the period we know Wright was also frequenting the Lodge—but we cannot say more than that they shared a love of the autumn foliage of the Forest. Wilberforce never visited Yoxall in the spring till thirty years after Wright's death. In a letter of 1827 from the Lodge, he wrote:

'Well as I thought I knew this place, and much as I had admired it, I never saw its riches displayed in such overflowing profusion. I never was here before till late in the year, or saw the first foliage of the magnificent oak contrast with the dark holly, the flowering gorse, and the horse chestnut.'[8]

Gisborne was famous in his day, not as an abolitionist but as a man of letters. He was the author of numerous moral tracts which fortunately for us have no relevance to his friendship or artistic relations with Wright. He also composed a poem entitled *Walks in a Forest* (1794) which helps us to get back to the double portrait. It has a certain verve. It was written, as he tells us in his Preface—and this sets the tone for the whole book—'to inculcate, on every fit occasion, those moral truths, which contemplation of the works of God in the natural world suggests, and that reverence and love for the great Creator which it is adapted to inspire'. There is a stirring passage evoking the horrors of the slave trade; there is a description of moonlight in the forest which might have been inspired by a painting by Wright:

'Soon o'er the hill the yellow-tinctured moon
Rose through the twilight, and with slanting ray
Gilded the topmost boughs; while all the vale
And all its sloping boundaries lay wrapt
In shade unvaried...'[1]

1 *Walks in a Forest*, 7th ed., 1808, p. 44.

and there are excursions into the beauties of Dovedale, and into the sublimity of volcanic eruptions—reminding us that Gisborne had in front of him, on his walls at Yoxall, two paintings by his friend Wright of these very subjects. We hardly need to be told by Bishop Porteus or anyone else[2] that this book of poems was inspired by Gisborne's beloved Needwood Forest, but since the Bishop's description of a visit to Yoxall also gives us some information which rounds off the picture we have built up of life at the Lodge, a passage from his letter is worth quoting:

2 Francis Noel Clarke Mundy, for instance, who in his poem *Needwood Forest* (ed. 1808, p. 26) tells us: '...Here Gisborne penn'd his moral lay...'

'The former [Mr. Gisborne] has a very handsome and delightful habitation in the very heart of Needwood Forest, a large tract of ground belonging to the crown, and abounding with all those rude and picturesque scenes which produced his 'Walks in the Forest'. He lives in a style of plentiful hospitality, without luxury or parade...'[3]

3 W. Roberts, *Memoirs of the Life and Correspondence of Mrs. Hannah More*, II, 1834, p. 15; letter from Bishop Porteus to Hannah More, 31st August 1797.

This letter is dated 31st August 1797, two days after Wright's death. We can be sure that no hint had reached Gisborne from Derby of the painter's last painful illness. It is inconceivable that he would have entertained the Bishop so plentifully had he known his old friend was on his deathbed. When the news reached Gisborne of the artist's death, he sent a characteristically formal note of condolence from Matlock Old Bath to Wright's brother, holding back his grief out of a sense of propriety, in which he would commit himself no further than to say he felt 'sincere regret for a friend whom I had long known and valued highly.'[4]

4 Gisborne to Richard Wright, 3rd September 1797, Eardley Simpson extra-illustrated Bemrose; quoted Bemrose, 1885, p. 115.

We can now turn to the double portrait [Plate 269] with a fresh eye. We can appreciate how impeccably the painter has matched style to subject; how he has found in a restrained realistic classicism the form best adapted to convey the way of life of a decent middle-class couple, high-minded, dedicated to learning, the arts and the cause of freedom. We now realise that the portfolio under Gisborne's arm contains drawing paper; the picturesque landscape draughtsman is quite accustomed to making sketches in the open air of the forest scenery he knew and loved so well. Like the Rev. D'Ewes Coke's, his pencil is poised for the job. The decision to embark on a sketching expedition dressed in black satin need no longer mystify us. We are not surprised that a man should take the air so unsuitably dressed, or that he should succeed in conveying so much nobility with such utter simplicity. You feel you could enter his mind 'without lock or key'. The 'sensible unaffected, pleasant woman' who accompanies him rests against his shoulder and gazes into a secure future. She also is modestly dressed, as becomes a curate's wife; displaying no jewels; content to serve her husband 'without luxury or parade'; a woman of distinguished parentage who followed her husband into old age and died in the Year of Revolutions at the same age as he did of 88; endured a bare two years of widowhood; and was buried beside him in the church at Barton-under-Needwood within walking distance of the house where she had spent her whole 'innocent and edifying' adult life.

We are much less well informed about another painter and country gentleman who became Wright's close friend, John Holland of Ford Hall. He was similar to Gisborne in some respects: also rich, also coming from a well-established family, if we are correct in supposing that the Thomas Holland of Ford, sheriff of the county in 1763, was his father. He married in 1777 a Miss Borrows of Morton, 'an agreeable young Lady, with a very large Fortune',[5] and Wright's glamourised portrait of her [Plate 274] does not leave the impression that she was exactly impecunious. Since we hear nothing of Holland in connection with Wright until about 1780 when he came to the artist's studio to admire the *Synnot Children* [Plate 221], presumably their friendship did not ripen until then. Not only did he commission portraits of himself and his wife from the artist [Plates 275, 274], but also amassed a large collection of his landscapes: chiefly Italian lakes and sea-pieces [see Plate 318], a *Cottage on*

5 *Derby Mercury*, 16th–23rd May 1777.

Fire, a character study [Plate 228] (if this picture is really by Wright and not Holland's own copy from it), and many small sketches [Plates 308, 332, 333, 348, 349, 350] ranging in date from the '80's to the end of Wright's life. Only one letter from Wright to Holland has so far come to light, in which the subject of his health plays as usual a large part, but the rest of it is worth quoting since between the lines we sense the warm currents of affection that passed from one painter to the other:

'... The little bit of Rock Scenery wch you set by the Easel some time ago & wch you seemed to have a sort of an hankering after, I have twice attempted to pack up & send you; but not just meeting wth a case ready to my hand, I had not exertion enough left in my crazy frame to order one, but now having the opportunity of sending it in your chaise, a piece of brown paper will be a sufficient defence for it, I hope you will get it safe & give it a place in your Mansion wch will give pleasure, my dear Holland to your affectionate friend, Joseph Wright'.[1]

As an intimate friend of the artist he was one of his executors, and made himself responsible for bringing the facts about the sale of Wright's pictures at Christie's in 1801 to the notice of amateurs.[2] In a letter to Wright's brother at the conclusion of the sale[3] he draws a mock-modest picture of himself as a country bumpkin who has not set foot in London for thirty-three years; indeed he emerges from his correspondence, as well as from Wright's portrait, as an endearing, honest soul without a trace of pomposity. He showed his devotion to Wright by executing around the turn of the century a number of conscientious copies of some of his self-portraits and landscapes.[4] He had already been engaged in this occupation during Wright's life-time, as we discover from a letter to John Leigh Philips, asking for the loan of *Rydal Waterfall* [Plate 352] for this purpose:

'... I will tell you that Mr. Wright many times has entrusted many of his most choice pieces to me, & permitted me to take a copy & that they always were returned safe & unhurt.'[5]

Wright in his friendships ranged far further afield than Ford and Yoxall. His close relations with the Tate family date from his residence in Liverpool in the late '60's. He boarded with a merchant and patron of the arts there, Richard Tate, who had a brother William and a son (then only a youth) Thomas Moss.[6] Wright became friendly with all three. It is sometimes hard to decide to whom he is referring in his letters as he persists in describing at least two of them as 'Tate'. We shall attempt to define what each represented in his life.

Richard Tate (d. 1787) was a member of the first Society of Arts founded in Liverpool in 1769, and in 1774 exhibited a copy of Wright's *Boys blowing a Bladder*, and a shipwreck after Vernet, when the Society was reconstituted. This is precisely all we know about him. His brother William (d. 1806) was a portrait painter, friend and pupil of Wright. His master's style lies behind two portraits by him: one said to be a portrait of Wright himself [Fig 134], another of a woman and two children.[7] These date from the '80's, but he had been active as a portrait painter long before: he was a regular exhibitor at the Society of Artists from 1771 to 1775, showing again in the same year as Wright, in 1791. He describes himself in the early catalogues as a 'pupil of Mr. Wright of Derby', and in 1772 gives his residence as Manchester, though he was back in Liverpool two years later, exhibiting portraits there in that year. He also showed at the R.A. from 1776 onwards but like Wright he quarrelled with the Academy. Wright reports this in a letter of 1787 with ill-concealed satisfaction:

'My ingenious & very worthy friend Tate, whom you know, has not for several years past, owing to some ill treatment he met wth at the Academy exhibited any pictures, by wch omission he finds himself lost to the world & neglected. However he is now very advantagiously fix'd at Manchester where he is encouraged & respected equal to his wishes & as he intends exhibiting this year he wishes some friend woud say something handsome of his works wch will fix his reputation with his friends at Manchester, & the contrary might prove very injurious to him...'

Wright accordingly goes on to ask his correspondent to insert something in the papers

1 Collection Mr. William Dale, Ottawa. At the end is added in Holland's hand the date of the receipt of the landscape: 'Oct 10th 1795'.

2 A letter from John Holland to Joseph Banks, 29th March 1801, on this subject is preserved among the Banks MSS. at Kew.

3 Published by Bemrose, 1885, p. 111.

4 These are listed in the catalogue under Nos. 169, 170, 298. One of the self-portraits copied is illustrated in Fig 8.

5 Holland to Philips, 19th August 1799; MS. Derby Public Library.

6 The relationships are established from two sources: a letter from John Holland to J. L. Philips, 16th January 1798 (MS. Derby Public Library) mentioning 'Mr. W. Tate & his Nephew Mr. T. Tate'; and a letter from Richard Wright to William Tate, 18th September 1797 *(loc. cit.)* referring to William's 'nephew'.

7 The portrait which may well represent Wright, at Kedleston, is inscribed on the reverse: 'Wm. Tate pinx! 1782'. The portrait group of three figures, belonging to Mrs. Bell of Shepton Mallet and kindly brought to the author's attention by Dr. Kenneth Garlick, revealed the signature of William Tate on cleaning. The portrait of *Master Smyth* at Christie's, 7th July 1967 (123) as Wright is probably also by W. Tate.

about Tate.[1] It must also be to William that Wright refers in a letter to Philips in Manchester four years later:

'Your account of the base situation of my friend Tate's pictures in the R.A. hurts me much, tho' from repeated instances of this sort of behaviour both to myself and Pupil I am not much surprised...'[2]

Thereafter William Tate disappears from the scene, except for an occasional mention in Farington's diary,[3] and for one sinister reference in a letter from John Holland of Ford just after Wright's death: 'On Saturday I returned from Derby, where I left M.r Tate diligently & successfully employed in finishing some of our late Excellent Friends portraits...'[4] He owned at least one landscape by Wright, a *Convent of Cosimato* [Plate 282] and others destined in the Account Book 'for my friend Tate' may have belonged to him also.

Wright reserved his warmest feelings for Richard's son and William's nephew, Thomas Moss Tate. We do not know much about him either. He showed at the Liverpool exhibition of 1784 two heads in crayon and two landscapes, the latter both 'after Mr. Wright of Derby'. In 1787 he showed three landscapes, one of which was 'A view from nature, near Matlock'. He appears to have been almost exclusively a landscape painter and for this reason, as well as on account of Wright's affection for him, was considered a suitable person to make up the team of artists proposing to set out for the Lakes in 1786[5] and again in the early '90's. He took up watercolours in the mid-'90's[6] but of this occupation Wright did not quite approve: 'I am glad to hear my good friend [Tate] has laid hold of his brushes again. Paper and camel hair pencils are better adapted to the amusement of ladies than the pursuit of an artist'[7]—a sentiment which suddenly makes one realise how far out of touch Wright was with the preoccupations of the very young who were about to rewrite the history of British painting with the weapon of water-colour. The final reference in the literature to Tate comes from the most unexpected quarter: his name appears in the Company of Merchants trading to Africa in 1807.[8] Let us hasten to acquit him of any base dealings. The Company continued to exist for nearly fifteen years after the abolition of the Slave Trade, and Tate was merely one of those engaged in carrying the African investments through the transitional period during which other commodities were substituted for slaves. He was perhaps carrying on his father's own business. The name of Thomas Moss Tate appears a few entries after that of Thomas Staniforth's son, Samuel, commonly known as 'Sulky Sam'. He lived on until March 1825.

Though not the most important, Tate's collection of Wright's late landscapes, some of them presents from the artist, some purchases, was probably the largest in existence at the turn of the century. Not surprisingly he owned several Lake landscapes: a small *Borrowdale*, an *Outlet of Wyburne Lake* [Plate 353], one of the last works, and a view of *Windermere with Langdale Pikes* [See Fig 114]; a view in Wales; as well as a number of Italian and Derbyshire views which are entered in Wright's Account Book or were acquired at the posthumous sale simply as 'Tate', but one can assume that the nephew and not the aged uncle is intended.

It may have been through the Tates that Wright came to know Daniel Daulby of Liverpool, a man of considerable culture, who was married to Roscoe's sister, with a large library of books, prints and drawings, and a collection of Old Masters as well as of modern paintings. One does not require much imagination to realise how invaluable this collection must have proved to Wright with his passion for Dutch art. Daulby wrote a *Descriptive catalogue of the works of Rembrandt, and of his Scholars, Bol, Livens, and Van Vliet, compiled from the original etchings...*,[9] and many prints of the type he describes were in his own collection.[10] He had his portrait painted by William Tate, and owned a large collection of Wrights, consisting of landscapes and genre pieces of more than usual interest: a *Julia in the cavern*, a *Girl blowing on a charcoal stick*, a lake scene between Rome and Florence, a *Neptune's Grotto*, a *Girandola*, a moonlight *Vesuvius* and others. He was buying from Wright from the late '70's to the late '80's, and several of his pictures can be identified in the catalogues of the Royal Academy, the one-man show of 1785 and the Liverpool exhibitions; but the collection was dispersed and none of it can today be traced.

The collection of John Leigh Philips (1761–1814) was also dispersed, in 1814 after his

1 Wright to 'Mr. Long Surgeon' in Chancery Lane, 22nd April 1787; N.P.G. extra-illustrated Bemrose.

2 Wright to Philips, 20th May 1791; quoted Bemrose, 1885, p. 65 from MS. Derby Public Library.

3 Entries for 6th and 8th June 1802, pp. 2054–5. The second entry reads: 'Tate & his Uncle called & I went with them to Shees [Sir Martin Archer Shee] & to Hoppners'.

4 Holland to Philips, 16th January 1798; MS. Derby Public Library.

5 For the proposed visit to the Lakes in 1786, with Tate and Daulby, see Part I, p. 19, note 3.

6 See Bemrose, 1885, p. 26: '1795. I am glad to hear my friend, Tate, succeeded so well in water-colours'. This must be Thomas Moss and not William, since it is most unlikely that a portrait painter at a very late stage in his career should take up watercolours.

7 Bemrose, *loc. cit.*

8 See Elizabeth Donnan, *Documents Illustrative or the History of the Slave Trade to America*, Washington D.C., 1931, ii, pp. 655–6.

9 Liverpool, 1796.

10 His MS. notebooks recording his books, prints, pictures and drawings are preserved in the Liverpool Public Library. Since no dates occur in them after about the mid-'90's except for one or two obvious insertions, it may be presumed they were compiled about 1790–95. The author is indebted to the Librarian for permission to consult them.

death, but a few items in the sale have since come to light, such as *Rydal Waterfall* [Plate 352], a *Lighthouse in the Mediterranean* [Plate 312], two drawings of cavern scenes [Plates 171, 172], and a picture which probably once belonged to him, a *Bridge through a Cavern, moonlight* [Plate 326]. He also owned the large version of the *Dead Soldier* and numerous landscapes of *Vesuvius, Neptune's Grotto* and similar subjects. Carey sums up the character of the collection as follows:

'Mr. Philips, has, with some of his larger and capital landscapes, a few of the smaller class, painted in two days, and, then, priced at ten guineas. According to the gradual rise of Wright's reputation, since his death, they would now [*c.* 1809] probably sell for treble that sum...'[1]

Philips was, with Gisborne and Thomas Moss Tate, Wright's closest friend in his later years, and was entrusted with the task of writing his obituary. He was a successful silk and cotton manufacturer in Manchester, and owned a country house beyond Strangways, a mile from the town.[2] He was also a lieutenant-colonel of the first battalion of Manchester and Salford Volunteers. The character of his collection of Wrights was similar to Holland's and Tate's: picturesque landscapes of Central Italy and Central and Northern England, and the occasional subject piece; but never the suggestion of an industrial or scientific scene, in spite of the fact that his talents lay in mathematics and that he was a member of the Manchester Literary and Philosophical Society in 1781.[3] It is so easy to forget that when Wright ceased to paint the pictures for which he is today most famous, Philips was a boy of eleven, and it is not surprising that this side of the artist's achievement should have been crowded out, in the mind of his younger friend, by landscape and picturesque genre.

1 Carey, 1809, p. 20.

2 Farington Diary, 29th October 1796, pp. 813–4. There are further references to Philips in the Diary of no great consequence, but see the entry for 3rd June 1807 for a discussion of his *Villa Madama* by Wilson.

3 The author is indebted to the Local History Librarian, Manchester Public Libraries, for certain details about the career of John Leigh Philips.

Fig 134 William Tate *Joseph Wright* 1782
24 x 22 in / 60.9 x 55.9 cm
Viscount Scarsdale

6 THE POET AND THE POTTER: HAYLEY AND WEDGWOOD

Concerning the development of his friendship with two others, Hayley and Wedgwood, we are better informed. Though direct contacts between poet and potter occurred seldom,[1] they are as far as Wright's biographer is concerned inseparable, since the painter's relationship with the one was closely bound up with that of the other during the early '80's. Hayley took the place of P. P. Burdett in his life. The pictures earmarked for Wedgwood would be criticised by Hayley, and Wright would not only try to rectify the 'errors' in the light of Hayley's comments, but would pass them on to Wedgwood who in his turn would come forward with further criticisms. Poor Wright was the cat's paw at the mercy both of Etruria and Eartham; anxious to satisfy both, touchingly bowing to their judgement, yet at the same time the only one of the three a professional painter who had his own views about his own art which were not always shared by poet and potter. He knew both of them long before they came together in his letters, and so we shall trace the prologue of his friendship, first with one, then with the other, leading up to the moment when they can no longer be disentangled.

William Hayley (1745–1820) had been educated at Trinity College, Cambridge, where he struck up a friendship with John Beridge (c. 1745–1788), a fellow undergraduate. Beridge became a student of medicine in Edinburgh and in 1767 Hayley visited him there and they travelled about Scotland together. Beridge settled as a physician in Derby, and in the summer of 1772 Hayley paid him a visit, which is described in his *Memoirs*:

'He [Hayley] had promised to devote some months of the year 1772, to his highly-valued friend Beridge, who, having settled as a physician in Derby, and taken a very spacious house and extensive garden, bounded by the river Derwent, was kindly anxious to render his new pleasant abode, the summer residence of his early friend Hayley, and his two ladies. They visited their beloved physician in the beginning of July, and did not leave him till towards the end of September...'[2]

Both men married young: Beridge in 1766 to the daughter of George Buckston, a Derbyshire girl whose brother had been at Cambridge with him; Hayley in 1769 to a Miss Eliza Ball. The visit was repeated at the end of August 1776 when Hayley and his wife went to Derby to congratulate Beridge on his recent marriage. It was on this occasion that Hayley became intimate with Wright, though they may have met in Derby four years earlier. We quote again from the *Memoirs*:

'Towards the end of August [1776], the Hayleys were induced to take a very long journey, for the pleasure of congratulating their friend, Dr. Beridge, at Derby, on a most seasonable marriage, that restored him from a state of perilous discomfort to health and happiness... The visit to Derby

1 A letter from Hayley to his wife of 15th July 1792 (see Hayley, 1823, I, p. 439) informs us that Mrs. Hayley is about to visit Etruria, and recommends her to pay attention to Wright's *Penelope*.

2 Hayley, 1823, I, p. 122.

1 *Op. cit.*, p. 156.

2 It is not known who purchased some of the landscapes still in the same family collection but it may have been a later generation than George Buckston's, partly because they are mostly late, partly because there exists in the collection a copy of a Wright self-portrait by Holland, dated 1800. A *Nemi* and a *Lake by moonlight* of the early '80's [Plates 234, 235], and a *Vesuvius* [Plate 233], now in the collection, were, however, bought by Dr. Beridge.

3 Hayley, 1809, p. 68.

4 Hayley, 1823, I, p. 243; letter of 16th December 1781.

5 Wright to Hayley, undated (*c.* January 1783); Inglefield MSS.

6 Hayley, 1823, I, pp. 293–4; letter of 17th January 1783.

7 William Hayley, *Poems and Plays*, I, London, 1788, from 'An Essay on Painting in two Epistles to Mr. Romney'. These lines are from the second epistle (p. 37).

was productive of various delights. Hayley not only sympathized in the happiness of the restored physician [Beridge had suffered from gout and had tried a cure in Bath], but in the weeks that he passed under his friendly roof, he had the gratification of cultivating an intimacy with Wright, the admirable painter, of Derby, who, having injured his health by too assiduous an application to his art, had great comfort in the kind attention he received from the friendly physician, and took a pleasure in executing for Hayley two hasty little portraits in chiaro-scuro, of Mrs. Beridge and her husband, after painting for the Doctor the poet of Sussex and his Eliza.'[1]

The two hasty little portraits of Mr. and Mrs. Beridge have disappeared, but those of Hayley and his wife have remained in Mrs. Beridge's family ever since [Plates 182, 183], along with a portrait of Beridge's father-in-law, done in the old age of both artist and sitter [Plate 341].[2] The marvellous portraits of the Hayleys are quite unrealistic, but so, if it comes to that, were the Sussex poet and his painfully unstable Eliza. Once again Wright has suited style to temperament, and we are grateful to him for having gone so much further in imaginative invention than a mere record of what they looked like.

Until 1772 Hayley had practised drawing but in that year he suffered from inflammation of the eyes, and informs us that he does not recall ever having taken up the pencil again 'except once in Derbyshire, where I was tempted to copy two bold sketches in water-colours of the scenery about Matlock, that were kindly lent to me by my friend Wright, the excellent painter of Derby'.[3] This must have been later than 1776, and indeed Hayley was sometimes in Derby after that date though he was loath ever to move out of his country place at Eartham, near Chichester. For instance, in 1781 he writes to his wife from Derby: 'We are going to visit Wright and his pictures, and I must therefore bid you hastily fare-well'.[4] Two years later Wright presented him with a picture of *Virgil's Tomb* (Cat No 189):

'... I have at length obtained a desire, wch has long lived in me of presenting you wth a picture of his [Virgil's] Tomb—Accept it, as it is given, for the Esteem I bear you.—Your good friend Mr Beridge, who I suppose will deliver this to you, finished the picture by adding the Frame'.[5]

Hayley was delighted with the gift and writes to his wife: '...Romney [and others] have been lavish in their praise of this exquisite performance; and how it has delighted me, you, who are acquainted with my feelings, will be perfectly able to imagine'.[6] Their friendship was developing rapidly, and in the summer of 1783 Hayley printed and distributed his Ode to Wright from which we have quoted. He also wrote an epistle to Romney, who had become an intimate friend, in which the following lines occur:

'But see far off the modest Wright retire!
Alone he rules his Element of Fire;
Like Meteors darting through the gloom of Night,
His sparkles flash upon the dazzled sight;
Our eyes with momentary anguish smart,
And Nature trembles at the power of Art.
May thy bold colours, claiming endless praise,
For ages shine with undiminish'd blaze,
And when the fierce Vesuvio burns no more,
May his red deluge down thy canvas pour!'[7]

It is hard to decide which is more commonplace, the poetry or the art criticism.

Meanwhile, Mrs. Hayley was beginning to show signs of mental derangement (her mother had been insane), and she was taken in for a short time by the wife of one of Wright's sitters [Plate 37], Mary Heath, later Mrs. Nicholas, the sister of Francis Mundy. But Hayley was obliged to take her back. In 1786 Eliza began to go quite out of her mind and three years later a separation was arranged between husband and wife. Beridge died in the latter part of 1788, and Hayley placed his wife in the care of his widow a few months later. During the next eight years they corresponded continuously but Hayley thwarted all efforts on her part towards a reunion. It seems as though he treated her with some callousness but he claimed it was necessary for the sake of the peace of mind of both of them. His excuses have never carried conviction.

This takes Wright's relations to Hayley up to, and even beyond, the point where the poet and the potter jointly play a major role in the artist's life. He had known Josiah Wedgwood about the same length of time.[1] Their acquaintance dates from at latest 1773 when Wedgwood met Sir William Meredith 'at Mr. Wrights' in Derby.[2] It may have been on this occasion that he saw in Wright's studio his paintings of *Belshazzar's Feast* [Cat No 223] and the *Alchemist* [Plate 106], and contemplated buying something from the artist connected with the pottery industry he had established in the late '60's at Etruria, near Newcastle-under-Lyme. Evidently he had kept the idea in mind, since five years later he wrote to his partner Bentley:

'... I am glad to hear M.ʳ Wright is in the land of the living, & continues to shine so gloriously in his profession. I should like to have a piece of this Gentlemans Art, but think Debutades's daughter would be a more apropos subject for me than the Alchymist though one principal reason for my having this subject would be a sin against the Costume [.] I mean the introduction of our Vases into the piece for how could such fine things be supposed to exist in the earliest infancy of the Potters Art.—You know what I want, & when you see M.ʳ Wright again I wish you would consult with him upon the subject. M.ʳ Wright once began a piece in which our Vases might be introduced with the greatest propriety. I mean the hand writing upon the Wall in the Palace of Nebucadnazer.'[3]

In other words, he had no doubts as to what he wanted: something in tune with his own experiments as a potter, possibly a picture which could with propriety celebrate his vases; in any case executed in the new bourgeois-classicist taste for which he was at that moment successfully creating an international market. The *Alchemist* was not the answer. The subject of the *Corinthian Maid*, in spite of the fact that his vases cannot have been supposed to exist in the earliest infancy of the potter's art, was to bear fruit a few years later.

He had the chance to speak to Wright himself about the *Corinthian Maid* as a subject for a picture in the early autumn of 1778:

'... I was lucky enough to meet with M.ʳ Wright at Derby, & we had some little talk upon the subject of a picture for me, but my stay was too short to conclude upon anything, only that we are to meet again, & he has almost promis'd me a visit in the spring. He does not meet with the encouragement his superior talents ought to command, & would starve as a painter if the Empress of Russia had not more taste & sense than the english, to buy those pictures now, which we may wish the next century to purchase again at treble the price she now pays for them...'[4]

One may conclude from this letter that Wright had been exaggerating to Wedgwood his success with Catherine II, knowing that Wedgwood who was also being patronised by the Empress,[5] would be suitably impressed: in fact he had only sold one picture to Russia, the *Iron Forge* [Plate 104], by that date, though negotiations for the sale of a recent *Vesuvius* [Plate 214] may already have been opened. And if Wright claimed that his English patrons were being sluggish in their encouragement, this also was far from the truth: for he was rapidly disposing of nearly all six pictures he had exhibited at the Academy that spring to Cockshutt, Milnes and Daulby, and had been busy for over a year with portraits of the Hayleys, the Beridges, the Hope and Pickford children, Gisborne, the wife of the Rev. Basil Beridge, Richard Cheslyn and many others. This little episode places him, not Wedgwood, in an unpleasant light, but if the false impression he had succeeded in conveying was ever detected, it was not held against him.

Next year Wedgwood contemplated having his children painted in characteristic attitudes by Wright or Stubbs. It will be recalled that Priestley's assistant Warltire had been employed at Etruria in 1779 in instructing Wedgwood's children in chemistry,[6] and this accounts for Wedgwood's wish for those children old enough to benefit from it, to be shown conducting chemical experiments in one of the proposed pictures:

'The two family pieces... I mean to contain the children only, & grouped perhaps in some such

1 He probably knew Wedgwood's partner Bentley in Liverpool in the early part of 1769 where they had mutual friends in P. P. Burdett and Dr. M. Turner. Bentley who was four years older than Wright and had been brought up in Derbyshire, did not leave Liverpool permanently until August of that year (see R. B.[entley], *Thomas Bentley 1730–1780 of Liverpool, Etruria and London*, Guildford, 1927, pp. 14 ff.)

2 Wedgwood to Bentley, 27th March 1773; Wedgwood, 1903, p. 25. One could have argued that this was a different Wright, had it not been that Sir William Meredith paid rent to the artist for property leased to him during his stay in Italy. In letters home of 10th August 1774 (Eardley Simpson extra-illustrated Bemrose) and 11th November 1774 (see Bemrose, 1885, p. 34) from Rome, Wright expresses his doubts about the punctuality of Sir William's payments. In the Account Book he records receipts for payments between January 1775, and 1778.

3 Wedgwood to Bentley, 5th May 1778; Wedgwood, 1903, p. 315. Checked from Barlaston MS. 18834–25.

4 Wedgwood to Bentley, 10th September 1778; Wedgwood, 1903, pp. 336–7. Checked from Barlaston MS. 18850–25.

5 Catherine became interested in Wedgwood ware in the early 1770's, introduced to it by Lord Cathcart, with special emphasis on copies of antique art. She commissioned Baxter to open negotiations towards the end of 1773 for the manufacture of a 'vast cream-ware service... on which should be enamelled views of British scenery' (see Meteyard, *Life of Josiah Wedgwood*, II, pp. 272 ff.).

6 See above, part III, p. 117.

1 Stubbs exhibited a picture, showing labourers loading on to a cart, at the Academy of 1779, which convinced Wedgwood he would be competent to paint his children along the lines he suggests.

2 Wedgwood to Bentley, 30th May 1779; Wedgwood, 1903, pp. 380–1. Checked from Barlaston MS. 18894–26. Also published Finer & Savage, 1965, pp. 234–5.

3 Wright to Wedgwood, 15th July 1779; Keele MS. 669–1.

4 Wedgwood to Bentley, 21st July 1779; Wedgwood, 1903, pp. 388–9.

5 For further details see 'George Stubbs 1724–1806', exhibition catalogue, Whitechapel Art Gallery, 1957, especially under Nos. 9–11.

manner as this. Sukey playing upon her harpsichord, with Kitty singing to her which she often does, & Sally & Mary Ann upon the carpet in some employment suitable to their ages. This to be one picture. The pendant to be Jack standing at a table making fixable air with the glass apparatus &c.; & his two brothers accompanying him. Tom jumping up & clapping his hands in joy & surprise at seeing the stream of bubbles rise up just as Jack has put in a little chalk to the acid. Joss with the chemical dictionary before him in a thoughtfull mood; which actions will be exactly descriptive of their respective characters. My first thought was to put these two pictures into Mr Wrights hands; but other ideas took place, & remembering the labourers & cart in the exhibition,[1] with paying for tablets &c. I ultimately determined in favour of Mr Stubbs, & have mention'd a fire piece to Mr Wright in a letter I wrote him the last week to tell him I should be glad to see him here in a fortnight or 3 weeks. But what shall I do about having Mr S. & Mr W. here at the same time, will they draw kindly together think you.'[2]

By the time Wedgwood's letter reached Derby, Wright was away 'on a ramble for my health'. He had been ill since the spring:

'… Since the beginning of April I have not touched a pencil [this was in July]. When the weather is a little moderate, I intend paying you a visit to consult you about the subject of the Maid of Corinth, or any other & to make such sketches of your apparatus as may be necessary. As to painting the picture with you [that is, at Etruria] is impracticable. When I desired Mr Bentley woud ask you what you intend'd to have done, he mention'd some Portraits, wch made it necessary for me to enquire what, that I might be provided.'[3]

This provoked Wedgwood to tell Bentley that Wright 'will pay me a visit when the weather is moderate to consult about a subject for a picture & catch any help from our fires at Etruria.'[4]

When translating in imagination the description Wedgwood gives of the two proposed scenes with groups of children, into two-dimensional terms, we at once conjure up, not Stubbs at all, but Wright's candlelights at Radburne and elsewhere, and it is a little perplexing to find Stubbs considered as the right artist for the job. But we have to remember that Stubbs had been experimenting for nine years with enamel painting on copper plates, and unable to attain the size he required, had been driven to approach the firm of Wedgwood & Bentley which that very summer of 1779 was offering to supply him with china, instead of copper, tablets of a suitable size for his purposes, and he wished to do something for Wedgwood in return for his services. He was also a more forceful character than Wright, accustomed to getting his way, even with a man like Wedgwood as tough as himself. The plans for the conversation pieces were in fact abandoned but in the following year Stubbs spent several months at Etruria painting portraits of Wedgwood, his father and wife, and a group on a single canvas of the whole family, parents and children.[5] How Wedgwood broke the news to Wright that the commission for these portraits had been given to another artist is not recorded.

Wedgwood's letters on these topics as well as Stubbs's pictures bring home to us more vividly than any other sources the bond uniting classicism, realism and sentimental genre in the minds of artists and their patrons in the '70's; the way classicism, for example, could shade off into realism at the turn of the brush without loss of grandeur if the portrait of an astute business man was the matter in hand, or shy away from it if that is what the subject dictated. We no longer feel, when reading these affectionate screeds to Bentley, embarrassed at having to explain the conjunction on the walls of that upstairs room at Radburne, of children blowing bubbles, and heroic scenes from Roman history, because their juxtaposition was then quite normal; nor need we feel puzzled that within a few months of one another, Wright could achieve a portrait so startlingly lifelike as that of *Richard Cheslyn* [Plate 190], and a dreamy, sentimental minstrel like *Edwin* [Plate 179]. The shift from one mood to the next was in the air of the day, and Wedgwood's letters show that he took it for granted that a competent artist could accomplish the shift without strain.

The question of the *Corinthian Maid* [Plate 245] lay dormant for two years and a half but was reopened not by Wedgwood, but by Wright who had meanwhile become fascinated by the subject. The legend as told by Pliny, describes the daughter of a certain Dibutade, a

Corinthian potter, who drew her lover's outline so accurately from his shadow that her father cut away the plaster, took an impression from the wall with clay, and baked it with the rest of his pottery. It is not surprising that the subject should have grown suddenly popular in the dawn of the neo-classic age: it lent itself to a bas-relief design; it called for all the purity of outline that the taste of the time yearned for. Wright was not by any means the first in the field: the theme had been exploited in the early and mid-'70's by Runciman, Mortimer and David Allan; Mortimer's version had been popularized in an engraving as early as 1776.[1] It invaded poetry as well as the visual arts. Hayley introduced it into his essay on painting, and in a letter to him of 1784 Wright gives him the credit for having inspired his picture: 'Your elegant lines upon the Corinthian Maid,' he writes, '... I have painted my picture from your Idea'.[2] In this poem occurs the typical neo-classic couplet:

> 'Pleas'd she beheld the steady shadow fall
> By the clear lamp upon the even wall;'

steady, clear, even—the three adjectives also apply to Wright's picture, and set the slow pace for the period between the Rococo and the Romantic Movement.

Wright reopens the correspondence with Wedgwood early in 1782:

'...I have been employing myself in making a few historical designs, among wch is the maid of Corinth, which will certainly make the best Candlelight picture I have painted. Mr. Boothby and several of my friends have seen it, & approve of it much.

I take the liberty of mentioning it to you, as you sometime ago had thought of having that Subject painted.

If you still continue in that Intention I shoud wish to have your thoughts upon it. It seems to me the elegant simplicity of the subject shoud be disturbed as little as possible by other objects; an opening into another room, wth some elegant vases upon a shelf, others on the ground, much kept down, woud mark her fathers profession & enrich the picture without disturbing the effect, but I think I would not introduce a Furnace...'[3]

Flaxman himself could not have condemned these sentiments as too tempestuous.

Wright was soon thinking aloud to Hayley about the design. He sent him a 'rude sketch' of the work, and in a letter expressed his concern about the shadow:

'... She by retiring a Step or two shoud conveniently see it, & it must also be evident to the Spectator. As sleep is full of motion of the head at least, the Shadow is traced upon a dark wall wth a Sharp pointed instrument, wch leaves the tracing white while his head was more erect, and the present Shadow agreeable to the position of the head is much lower; I think it tells the Story better, than if they coincided as it is more conspicuous.

I once thought rapturous astonishment was the expression to be given to ye Maid, but I now think it too violent...her figure... shou'd fall into a loose & easy swing... her face—I leave you to tell me what it shou'd be—the uper part of her figure will be strongly illuminated falling by gentle gradations into half Shade... I wish to raise his left Leg. I have done it by a vessel lying down part of a Groupe I intend there; if you have no objection to it; but it seems to want Stability. Would it better if broken? Or what can be substituted that will not appear as put there for the purpose? I intend thro' an Arch showing another Room filled wth elegant Earthen vessels—The Lamp will be partly concealed by a Curtain, the flame intirely—

Be my *Friend* & tell me all my faults...'[4]

There can be few examples since the Renaissance where a painter has relied so heavily on a poet for so many details in a single picture—and there are further points that Wright raises in the same letter which we have omitted simply out of fear of growing tedious.

On 9th March he asks Hayley to send on the 'rude sketch' to Wedgwood accompanied by any criticisms he cares to make. The sketch, he explains to Wedgwood, has no light and shade in it, 'but it will shew you the actions'. He then proceeds to raise with Wedgwood the same points he had with Hayley: how love should possess the girl's soul and be the sole expression of her face; how, in order to be faithful to Hayley's line 'And, drawing, doated on the form she drew', he would have to withdraw her slightly from the action; how the tracing on the wall in a position before his head had sunk would have the effect of making

1 For a full discussion on the subject, see Rosenblum, 1957, *passim*; though he does not mention the Mortimer on this occasion.

2 Wright to Hayley, 22nd December 1784; Inglefield MSS. An undated letter from Wright to Hayley (before March 1782) among the Inglefield MSS. proves that Wright had already read the poem.

3 Wright to Wedgwood, 11th February 1782; Keele MS. 670–1.

4 Wright to Hayley, undated, about the end of February 1782; Inglefield MSS.

1 Wright to Wedgwood, 10th March 1782, the day after he asked Hayley to send on the sketch to Wedgwood. Barlaston MSS.

2 Wright to Wedgwood, undated but about March 1782; Keele MS. 671–1.

3 Wright to Hayley, undated but about January 1783; Inglefield MSS.

4 Hayley, 1809, p. 71 speaks of William Long (c. 1747–1818) as one 'to whom nature had given extraordinary talents for the pencil', but he took up surgery instead. Romney painted a portrait of Long for Hayley.

5 Wright to Wedgwood, 29th April 1783; Barlaston MSS.

6 He acknowledges receipt of the vases in a letter to Wedgwood, 29th May; Barlaston MSS.

7 Wright to Wedgwood, 23rd October 1783; Barlaston MSS.

8 Wright to Wedgwood, 20th April 1784. Barlaston MSS.

9 Wedgwood to Wright, 29th April 1784; quoted by Finer & Savage, 1965, pp. 276–7.

10 Wright to Wedgwood, 3rd May 1784; Keele MS. 673–1.

11 The passage in question is quoted at length in the catalogue of the 1785 exhibition; see Bemrose, 1885, p. 21.

it more conspicuous; how Boothby had suggested a tripod in place of the vase at the youth's feet, and how Darwin was not in favour of any vases being shown—all these ideas he throws out in order to have them knocked down by Wedgwood, in the hopes of getting his doubts resolved for him by a firm answer.[1] A further letter to Wedgwood raises the problem of lighting: he now thinks of lowering the concealed source of light so as to make the shadow 'more accurate'.[2] And then silence descends for nearly a whole year, or perhaps the discussion proceeds in a desultory fashion and the letters are not kept.

A solution is still hanging fire in the early months of 1783. Wright hesitated to go on with the picture because it was coming in for some sharp criticism. He felt himself bombarded with advice from all sides:

'...When I ask other peoples opinion, 'tis to profit by them [;] if they happen to coincide wth my own I am happy, if otherwise, they stagger my opinion, & leave me undetermined whether I shall go on wth the picture—I much approve Mr. Long's Idea of the female figure in the act of Drawing; the other hand up expressing a fear of waking the youth is good, & certainly tells the Story much better than mine, but I like not the thought of placing him on a Sopha, & his head raised wth an antique Bolster; here appears too much intention, when everything shou'd look like accident...'[3]

Everything is not like accident in the final version, but it is interesting to observe that Wright adopted some of Mr. Long's[4] ideas—if not the antique bolster, then the gestures of the Maid's hands.

He was sufficiently advanced with the picture by April of 1783 to be able to ride over to Etruria 'to have the accompaniments settled',[5] and Wedgwood sent him some vases to be introduced into the piece.[6] By October he had painted the adjoining room where the oven is, and asks Wedgwood for the 'forms of the long Irons w[ch] stand about the Oven'.[7] By the spring of the following year the picture was ready for Wedgwood's inspection, but he objected to the figure of the Maid on the grounds that 'the naked appears too much thro' the drapery'. Wright defended his brush by pointing out that 'the action she is in unfortunately makes the Drapery cling to the limbs but it is not on that account less Graecian [;] however', he adds with his customary humility, 'I will endeavour to alter it'.[8] Since this criticism was only passed on to Wright at second hand, through Darwin, Wedgwood felt under an obligation to explain more precisely what he meant, in a most friendly letter in which he expressed rapturous approval of every feature but the Maid's body:

'The objections [made at Wright's house by various ladies in Wedgwood's presence] were the division of the posteriors appearing too plain through the drapery and its Sticking so close, the truly Grecian, as you justly observe, gave that part a heavy hanging-like (if I may use a new term) appearance, as if it wanted a little shove up, which I only mention in illustration of the term hanging as used above... It is unfortunate in my opinion that the maid shows so much of her back, but I give it as my *opinion* only, with great diffidence, and entire submission to your better judgement...'[9]

Wright was aware that this was mere courtesy, and that he had better do something about the division of the posteriors. He reassured Wedgwood that he would 'cast a fuller drapery upon the Corinthian Maid w[ch] will conceal the Nudity, but her figure cannot be turned more in profile consistent with her employment...'[10] To judge by the final product, there is not a contour that the primmest lady in Derbyshire could raise an eyebrow at.

Meanwhile, in May 1783, Hayley had recommended Wright to paint one of two companions to the *Corinthian Maid: Penelope unravelling her Web* or the *Origin of Music*. Whilst the first (taken from the second book of the Odyssey, in Pope's translation[11]) would represent the 'ingenuity of Love in a Maiden', Penelope would 'display the same quality in a Wife'; the point being, that in her palace at Ithaca, persuaded that her husband Odysseus was still alive, Penelope would sit at her loom weaving a funeral robe for her father-in-law, expecting thereby to delay her choice of a suitor, and at night would secretly unravel the work of her daylight hours. Hayley assessed accurately the direction in which Wright's mind was moving; for it is hard to imagine a more typically Wright-like subject than that of a virtuous lady, secretly and by lamplight demonstrating her loyalty to a distant husband. It was not in Hayley's nature to leave it at that. He had to go on to dictate what should be represented: 'I think you may introduce a young Telemachus, a Boy about 10 or 11 sleeping of an antique Bed, you may venture to give him a sickly or feverish appearance & represent his mother... turning her head w.th a look of anxiety towards the Boy. The Chamber may be decorated w.th a statue of Ulysses...', and so Hayley goes on, outlining what the picture should look like. The alternative, the *Origin of Music*, would form a 'proper companion to the origin of her Sister art... I wou'd introduce Mercury sitting on a Rock w.th a few shells of Tortoise around him...', and again the whole scene is conjured up.[1] Wright had one of his usual bouts of illness from then until September and was unable to proceed with the work, but he managed to secure Wedgwood's approval of the idea of *Penelope* as a companion to the *Maid of Corinth*, and thereafter plans for an *Origin of Music* were dropped. He is worried about whether there exists any historical justification for the feverishness of the young Telemachus, and Hayley confesses it is his own idea: 'Let me only observe', he writes, 'that in such kind of historical or rather poetical subjects, you may take any liberties you please'.[2] It seems strange to us that a painter should be willing thus to be dictated to by a poet, but Wright relied pathetically on his friend, confessing to him that he felt 'a pleasing firmness when I rest upon your authority',[3] and goes on to raise endless points about the composition of *Penelope* [Plate 242] which one cannot help wishing he had resolved for himself in the secrecy of his studio. In a later letter to Hayley he points out that since the *Corinthian Maid* 'is much limited in its light & Shadow—I wish therefore to compose the picture of Penelope, in w.ch there is full latitude, with a strong effect of Candle light, I have therefore brought the Statue of Ulisses forward, & right before the Lamp for I always conceal the cause when I can do it naturally, that the affect [sic] may be brighter...'[4] But all this questioning, prevaricating, hanging on the words of others, only had the result of giving the two pictures the impression of being contrived.

Beridge now stepped in, by objecting to the nakedness of the statue of Odysseus, 'being unfit for the chaste eyes of our English Ladies,' with the result that Wright agreed to conceal 'the part w.ch may give offence' with a quiver 'w.ch might cross the bottom of the belly & render him perfectly decent to the chastest eye...'.[5] This little incident must have made him pine for those carefree months in Roman and Neapolitan palaces ten years before, when he could permit himself the luxury of copying antique statues in a state of nature since they were destined for the privacy of his portfolio. The quiver did not satisfy Hayley who maintained that this crafty substitute for a fig-leaf would only have the effect of making 'some saucy imaginations' exclaim 'Happy is the man that hath his Quiver full', and recommended a light drapery.[6] Again the poor artist complied, 'but cou'd scarce do little enough it so injured the outline of the figure'.

Not content with proposing the subjects (or at any rate the setting) for two of Wright's most ambitious subject pieces, Hayley suggested two more: scenes from the story of *Hero and Leander*, which might have struck him as appropriate from his reading of a translation of Musæus' *Loves of Hero and Leander* made by Dr. James Beattie in 1757. Wright took up the theme in the early months of 1783. Wedgwood's daughter visited him when he was in the process of painting them, and seemed to think they might be suitable for the collection at Etruria. Her letter to her father is worth quoting at length since the pictures have disappeared:

'We have this morning been paying a visit to M.r Wright... two pictures, The Story of Hero & Leander, which he is now painting upon... If you come to Derby you may perhaps get a sight of these two charming pictures one of them is the meeting of the two lovers, the moon shining extremely bright & a flaming torch at the top of the Castle where Hero had been watching for Leander & had left the torch there in her haste to meet her lover, who swims across a river every night to see her. He has one foot in the water & the other out to shew his impatience & the lovers are embracing—This is a beautiful picture but the other is quite sublime—The scene of the piece is the same but in this the moon is overcast & the lightening is flashing about particularly in one part which discovers Leander holding out his hand just expiring amongst the waves. Hero is running to the sea shore with the Torch extended in one hand behind her, which lights the Castle...'[7]

1 Wright to Wedgwood, 29th May 1783, quoting Hayley's letter; Barlaston MSS.

2 Wright to Wedgwood, 23rd October 1783, quoting Hayley's letter; Barlaston MSS.

3 Wright to Hayley, 5th November 1783; NPG extra-illustrated Bemrose.

4 Wright to Hayley, 3rd December 1783; Inglefield MSS.

5 *Loc. cit.*

6 Wright to Wedgwood, 31st December 1783, quoting Hayley's letter; Keele MS. 672–1.

7 Susannah to Josiah Wedgwood, 21st March 1783; Darwin MSS., Down House; kindly communicated by Mr. Eric Robinson.

1 Wright to Hayley, 5th November 1783; NPG extra-illustrated Bemrose.

2 At about the time of Wright's death, Heath tried to obtain them through Lord Lansdowne to be engraved; see letters from Heath to J. L. Philips, quoted Bemrose, 1885, p. 73.

3 Wright to Hayley, 28th December 1783; NPG extra-illustrated Bemrose.

4 Wright to Hayley, dated 'April' (1784); Inglefield MSS. The literary sources for *William and Margaret* and *Comus* are discussed in the next chapter (pp. 152–3).

5 According to Mrs. Marcia R. Pointon who is engaged in research on Milton as a source of inspiration in English painting at this period and later. There are engravings on the same theme after a design by E. F. Burney (1791) and after Westall (1795) which differ in composition from Wright's.

6 The author is indebted to Mr. Geoffrey Turner, Secretary of the University Museum, Oxford, for information concerning Indian technology. For further details, see Nicolson, 1962, *passim*.

7 A literary source was the diary of Peter Kalm, a Scandinavian naturalist who had travelled widely in North America; see *Travels in North America...*, 2 vols., London, 1772.

8 The picture (1789–90) is at Upton House. See 'English Pictures, 1730–1830, from National Trust Houses', Messrs. Agnew, 1965 (26), illus.

9 The portrait was also exhibited. Wright sent Wedgwood an account for all four pictures under cover of a letter to John Wedgwood, 26th June 1785; Barlaston MSS. The prices charged exactly tally with those given in the Account Book.

By the autumn of that year they were reserved for Lord Harington,[1] but passed to a member of the Lansdowne family.[2]

Again in 1783 Hayley proposed the subject of the *Indian Widow*[3] which the artist lost no time in attacking with relish, since the idea of a woman mourning for her dead husband fitted in like *Hero* and *Penelope* with his mood, and with the mood of the time. He even contemplated doing two pictures of this subject also, one before the storm, the other after. He wished to get ahead as fast as possible with a number of subject pictures, to be ready with his one-man show in the spring of 1785, and also worked concurrently at a *William and Margaret*, a scene from Percy's *Reliques of Ancient English Poetry* [Plate 241]. He reports progress to Hayley in April 1784:

'...I am ingaged wth. Margeret & Willm. for wch. I have done [sic], I hope it will prove a chilling picture [it is], I have arrived at an unpleasant sort of colouring, wch. will be well contrasted by the Corinthian Maid & penelope, between wch. I intend it to hang in my Exhibition [.] I have also nearly finished a Companion to the Indian Widow, the burst of light in wch. picture, suggested to M^{rs}. Beridge those lines from Comus: 'Was I deceived? or did a sable Cloud/Turn forth her Silver lining on the Night &c.' I never painted a picture so universally liked [as the *Comus*].—The Scenery, the Habiliments of War are finished in the Indians picture but the figure for want of knowing the Dress of a Mourner is only an outline [.] I wrote to you about it, but I suppose it escaped your notice—If you can give me any hints I shall be obliged to you also for your Idea of the figure.'[4]

The scene from *Comus* [Plate 246] comes straight out of Milton and can have presented no iconographical problems, in spite of the fact that no earlier representation of this episode in the poem is known.[5] But in order to produce a convincing widow of an American Indian Chief, seen mourning the death of her warrior husband in front of a blasted tree from which dangle his 'Habiliments of War' [Plate 247], he had to search further afield. If Hayley gave him any hints for his mourner, they cannot have been helpful. For Wright has fallen back on those well-worn neo-classic draperies which served for any distressed female this side of the Atlantic. On the other hand, the form of her head-band, the treatment of the feathers, the quilled cords and knife sheath, and the buffalo-robe painted on the skin side show know-ledge of Indian technology from at least as far West as the upper Great Lakes. This proves that Wright used authentic props—and we might have guessed he would have done so, remembering the passionate fidelity to detail he invariably displayed. The tomahawk was easy enough to come by since the type was manufactured in great quantities in the Mid-lands. And it may have been from the Shirleys at Ettington, near Stratford-on-Avon, who once owned his portrait of *Mrs. Bathurst* [Plate 84] and possessed equipment of this nature, that he derived the further documentation he needed.[6]

It is easy to understand how the concept of the Noble Savage reached England and found its way into art. Ever since Benjamin West had exclaimed in the presence of the *Apollo Belvedere*: 'How like a Mohawk Warrior!' or words to that effect, imagination had been stirred by accounts of the American Indian.[7] The heroic role allotted to the Indian in West's *Death of Wolfe* (1771) and *Penn's Treaty with the Indians* (1772) was a recent memory, and it grew fashionable to think of the Indian as a 'loyal' supporter of the British in the recent struggle against the 'rebel' Americans. Englishmen were beginning to turn out their T. E. Lawrences. William Augustus Bowles, for instance, took refuge among the Creek Indians, lived the life of an adventurer, and was depicted by Thomas Hardy dressed as an Indian Chief, only about five years after Wright's *Indian Widow* was painted;[8] and an engraving by J. R. Smith of a portrait by Hayley's and Wright's friend Romney of Joseph Brandt, Sachem of the Mohawks, appeared in the same year (1789) as Smith's engraving after Wright's picture.

When the exhibition opened in London in the spring of 1785, not only the *Corinthian Maid* and *Penelope*, but also the scene from *Comus* were reserved for Wedgwood. Wright also let Wedgwood have a *Self-portrait* (Cat No 171) which he had painted for his friend Jacob More in Rome but which Wedgwood had seen in his studio and had admired so much that he wished to possess it; and Wright agreed to do another for More.[9] It has always seemed puzzling that Wedgwood did not also acquire the *Indian Widow*, in order to make up two pairs of subject pictures; since like Hayley and Wright he liked to think of pictures *en série*. But there is no evidence that he hankered after the companion to *Comus* as well. One imagines that the contrast between the scene from Milton, 'much limited in its light & shadow' like the *Corinthian Maid*, and the *Indian Widow* where 'there is full latitude' as in *Penelope*, would have appealed to the potter's imagination. Here two women face one another, both done down by circumstances over which they have no control. They are resigned to loneliness, fixed into position by their stylised gestures, posed so artificially that they seem not to inhabit their landscapes but to have been clamped down there like figures in relief on Wedgwood plaques. No wonder the benighted porcelain lady gazing at the sable cloud took Wedgwood's fancy! It is only mysterious that he did not make off with her terracotta companion as well.

Having acquired three important subject pictures from Wright, along with a self portrait, for the immense sum of about £300, all within the space of a few months, Wedgwood had proved himself one of Wright's most ardent supporters. During all those tricky negotiations which could so easily have tipped over their friendship, they remained on the best of terms. Wright acknowledged his indebtedness to the potter by presenting him two years later with a landscape (Cat No 341), inscribed on the reverse: 'The gift of Joseph Wright to his friend Jos. Wedgwood Esq., the patron and encourager of living artists, 1787', and in 1789 Wedgwood presented Wright with a table service.[1] Wright also had cause to be grateful to the poet Hayley for supplying him with themes with which to attract the potter's attention, and as we have seen his relations with Hayley continued into the '90's to be more than cordial. In the second half of the '80's it was Hayley who proposed to him the subject of the *Mine* to be painted for Sir Robert Wilmot, and it was Hayley again who more than any other single friend was responsible for getting Wright's name included among the contributors to the Shakespeare Gallery. With his charming humility and good nature which never failed to come to the surface in his relations with true friends, banishing that petulance which seized hold of him when he suspected an enemy, Wright paid back what he owed to Hayley in constantly reiterated expressions of gratitude in letters, and in gifts of works of art; as well as in kindness to Thomas Alphonso, which he was careful to see exceeded what was required of him in civility, because he knew this son was loved.

1 An order from Wedgwood for the delivery of this service is preserved among the Keele MSS. (No. 677–1). It reads: 'table service green shell edge, for his [Wright's] own use, gratis, about 10 guineas value to be looked out very good'. Wright's receipt for the service dated 7th March 1789 is also noted. According to Bemrose, 1885, p. 81 Wedgwood also presented a dinner service of 150 pieces on the occasion of the marriage of Anna Romana to James Cade (April 1795).

7 WRIGHT AND LITERATURE

Wright was one of the first to turn to literature for themes for subject pieces but not the first: he had been anticipated by John Runciman's *King Lear in a Storm* (1767). For his *Old Man and Death* [Plate 123] he had used a fable from Aesop; for *Miravan* [Plate 107] some moral tale we cannot now lay our hands upon; for the *Captive King*, perhaps a near-contemporary account of the Crusades. As far as we know it was not until he left for the continent that he was drawn to that brand of contemporary literature which exploited the cult of sensibility. He was captivated by a book that was then on everybody's lips. Laurence Sterne had brought out his *Sentimental Journey* in 1768 and it was at once a best seller. A copy of it was a compulsory item in the luggage of any sentimental traveller to France or Italy in the '70's. We can imagine Wright reading it on his voyage to Genoa between bouts of seasickness, and being enthralled by its ironic tone, by the deviousness with which supposedly inartistic episodes are presented as art, by the substitution of men of flesh and blood for puppets (Wright himself had done the same in Liverpool, Lichfield and Doncaster), by the 'casual' style which by implication made a mockery of literary artifice. In the summer of 1774 he decided to paint a picture from one of these episodes, and it is characteristic of him to have selected, not Yorick's sentimental escapades with housemaids which were too Rococo for his taste, but a prison scene, similar to the one he had painted before leaving England of Guy de Lusignan incarcerated by the Saracens.

Sterne describes how Yorick had left England for Paris without his passport, which was obligatory as we were then at war with France. The Lieutenant de Police called on him at his hotel and he was threatened with imprisonment. There was never any real risk of his being locked up, but the idea of loss of liberty begins to prey on his mind and he imagines, more in fun than earnest, what prison life was going to be like. Since Sterne thought in visual images, he does not sit poor Yorick down in a dungeon to ruminate on his fate, but makes him watch a prisoner (himself) from outside:

'I took a single captive; and having first shut him up in his dungeon, I then look'd through the twilight of his grated door to take his picture. I beheld his body half wasted away with long expectation and confinement... in thirty years the western breeze had not once fanned his blood;—he had seen no sun, no moon, in all that time... He was sitting upon the ground, upon a little straw, in the furthest corner of his dungeon, which was alternately his chair and bed: a little calendar of small sticks were laid at the head, notched all over with the dismal days and nights he had passed there; he had one of these little sticks in his hand, and with a rusty nail he was etching another day of misery to add to the heap...'

Sterne makes Yorick 'take his picture'—an invitation to Wright to do the same. What

Yorick witnesses through the grated door belongs as much to the visual as to the literary arts. Wright's two versions of the *Captive* [Fig 73, Plate 162] are in this respect ready-made, a prefabrication by Sterne, even down to the calendar of notched sticks which dutifully he introduces into his pictures.

On continuing his journey southwards, Sterne/Yorick encounters on the road outside Moulins a distracted peasant girl named Maria 'sitting under a poplar.—She was sitting with her elbow in her lap and her head leaning on one side, within her hand:—a small brook ran at the foot of the tree... she was dressed in white... her hair hung loose'. Maria had appeared earlier in *Tristram Shandy* accompanied by a lover and a goat, both of whom had forsaken her. Now she has acquired a little dog called Sylvio 'which she kept tied by a string to her girdle'. Again with deceitful simplicity Sterne is asking for his words to be translated into shapes, and a neo-classic medallion leaps to the eye. On his return from a-broad Wright painted (1777) a companion to the *Captive* showing Maria seated facing him on an adjoining canvas, a fellow sufferer, reflecting his melancholy as in a mirror. She has every right to be there: for she also belongs to the world of the incarcerated, enslaved as she is by unrequited love. Though he does not follow Sterne's instructions regarding the poplar and the brook, Wright shows *Maria* [Plate 184] seated under his own kind of tree beside a sluggish river with her little dog Sylvio appealing to her from her feet. Her story demands a visual treatment on that borderline between neo-classicism and romanticism so close to the artist's heart; and we can sympathise with his decision to return to the theme four years later with a second and much larger *Maria* [Plate 220], this time as a companion to the contemplative young minstrel Edwin.[1] Here she has to turn her body round to the left to face Edwin, crossing her legs in emulation of his; holding a pipe distractedly in her hands as she was said to have been doing in *Tristram Shandy*, 'playing her vespers upon her pipe'; accompanying the young minstrel whose pipe also peeps out from his lap.

The literary source for Wright's *Edwin* [Plate 179] was a poem almost as immediately successful as Sterne's *Sentimental Journey* though it has not weathered the centuries so well. Dr. James Beattie, professor of moral philosophy at Marischal College, Aberdeen, published the first canto of *The Minstrel or the Progress of Genius* anonymously in 1771. The second canto was published with the first in a new edition (evidently the one Wright used) of 1774 under his name. In the preface he writes: 'The design was, to trace the progress of a Poetical Genius, born in a rude age, from the first dawning of fancy and reason, till that period at which he may be supposed capable of appearing in the World as A MINSTREL, that is, as an itinerant Poet and Musician...' Wright takes note of Edwin's dual accomplishments as writer and flautist, and of the description of the boy as he first appears on the scene (Book I, XI):

> 'There lived in Gothick days, as legends tell
> A shepherd-swain, a man of low degree...
> But he, I ween, was of a north countrie;
> A nation fam'd for song, and beauty's charms;
> Zealous, yet modest; innocent, though free...'

He does not borrow from Beattie, as he does from Sterne, any specific episode in the central character's career because Beattie, unlike Sterne, is more concerned with the idea than the visual image; but there is one stanza which comes close to the mood Wright settles on for his picture (Book II, ix) and he may have had this one in mind:

> 'One cultivated spot there was, that spread
> Its flowery bosom to the noonday beam,
> Where many a rose-bud rears its blushing head,
> And herbs for food with future plenty team.
> Sooth'd by the lulling sound of grove and stream,
> Romantic visions swarm on Edwin's soul:
> He minded not the sun's last trembling gleam,
> Nor heard from far the twilight curfew toll;
> When slowly on his ear these moving accents stole.'[2]

1 That the theme was popular in neo-classic circles is shown by its recurrence as a Wedgwood cameo mounted in cut steel by Matthew Boulton *c.* 1790 (Collection Josiah Wedgwood & Sons, Ltd; exh. Birmingham, 1966 (one of twelve under No. 99)).

2 The engraving after E. F. Burney reproduced as Frontispiece to Vol. I of the 1799 edition of *The Minstrel* illustrating Book I, liv, is clearly indebted to Wright's picture.

In accordance with his usual practice, he writes in January 1778 for Beattie's advice:

'I have read your Poem called the Minstrel or the Progress of Genius, which I much admire and have painted a picture from it... I have made him a beautiful youth of about 16 or 17 years of age, sitting under a rock or ellevated ground which cuts upon a Mountainous Distance. He holds a small pipe in his right hand and reclines his Cheek on his left, he looks contemplative and penetrating—his dress is plain and simple, something of the old English Dress with a loose Cloak...'

Wright proposes to engrave some verses on the rock 'supposing them to be *his* [Edwin's] *own compositions*, as poetry, as well as music was his study...', or alternatively some lines from *The Minstrel* itself; and contemplates placing a harp or lyre beside him. Beattie replies and Wright thanks him for his observations:

'I have now finished the young Minstrel', he writes a month later, 'I have made alterations agreeable to your remarks, have introduced a Gothick Spire, terminated the distance with the Sea and made a bright streaky light on the Horizon—but for the Harp the great characteristic of a Minstrel I cannot find room for [*sic*], indeed I have been hard set to bring in the scrolls of manuscripts without hurting the composition and effect of the picture...'[1]

It was no doubt on Beattie's instructions that the following three lines from Book II, XXIX were 'engraved' into the rock face behind Edwin, but since Beattie had never seen the picture, he cannot have been expected to recommend a more appropriate stanza:

'[Which, late,] exulting, view'd in Nature's frame,
Goodness untainted, wisdom unconfined,
Grace, grandeur, and ability combined'.

Throughout the '80's Wright continued to draw sustenance from poetry ancient and modern. This was the period of his closest intimacy with a poet of the sensibility cult, William Hayley, who was constantly supplying him with promising themes. It was no doubt Hayley who drew his attention to the story of *William and Margaret* and stimulated the production of one of Wright's least satisfactory works [Plate 241]. This was a ballad from Thomas Percy's *Reliques of Ancient English Poetry, consisting of Old Heroic Ballads, Songs, and of Pieces of our earlier Poets (Chiefly of the Lyric Kind)*, which appeared in 1765, long before the publication of *Edwin*—and in fact Beattie was merely being carried along on a wave of taste for ballads of the Dark and Middle Ages which had come in with mid-century Gothicism. Percy tells us in his preface that the greater part of these songs are extracted from an 'ancient folio manuscript, in the Editor's possession, which contains near 200 poems, songs, and metrical romances. This MS. was written about the middle of the last [seventeenth] century, but contains compositions of all times and dates, from the ages prior to Chaucer, to the conclusion of the reign of Charles I'. Among the more recent ballads is one entitled *Margaret's Ghost*,[2] telling the story of a Juliet-Comus-Maria-like maiden who had died of love for William because he had forsaken her and pledged himself to another. Her ghost appears in his bedroom and upbraids him for his inconstancy. Wright selects the following Wright-like moment:

'Twas at the silent solemn hour,
When night and morning meet;
In glided Margaret's grimly ghost,
And stood at William's feet'.

Next morning William visits her grave and dies as he bends his cheek to it. It is hard to treat this poem, and the picture Wright made out of it, more generously than as typical period pieces.

We have seen how the *Corinthian Maid* was painted from Hayley's idea; how *Penelope, The Indian Widow* and *Hero and Leander* would never have materialised but for his encour-

1 These two letters of 18th January and 16th February 1778 are published by Honour, 1956, p. 188 from the originals preserved among the Beattie MSS. in the University Library, Aberdeen, C300 and C302.

2 *Reliques...*, London, 1765, III, pp. 310 ff. The source is cited in the 1785 exhibition catalogue as 'Pierce's Reliques...' One wonders how many students have searched the general catalogue at the British Museum under 'Pierce' and drawn a blank.

agement; how it was he who came forward with the suggestion for the depiction of a tense episode in Sargent's poetical drama, *The Mine*. It could so easily have been Hayley—though in fact it was Mrs. Beridge—who proposed a subject from Milton where Comus, son of Circe and Bacchus, corrupts all travellers with his potion and transforms them into monsters. He is passing by night through a wood with his monstrous crew when he observes 'Some Virgin... Benighted in these woods', and decides to do his worst with her as well. So as not to affright her he appears before her in the guise of a harmless villager. She had been searching everywhere in vain for her brothers who had accompanied her as far as the wood; now she had nothing left to protect her except her chastity, but this gives her strength enough to carry her through. The passage Mrs. Beridge indicated as a proper subject for Wright's pencil gave him the fullest scope for those dramatic lighting effects he invariably demanded (and it is with relief that we are able, for a change, to quote some lines of genuine poetry):

> 'Was I deceiv'd, or did a sable cloud
> Turn forth her silver lining on the night?
> I did not err, there does a sable cloud
> Turn forth her silver lining on the night,
> And casts a gleam over this tufted grove...'[1]

1 *Comus*, lines 221–5.

To satisfy Wright, not only must the subject be steeped in macabre or doleful sentiment— a virtuous lady must be forsaken by husband, lover or brothers; a count must be condemned to quicksilver mines; an old man must waste away in a dungeon or, having called upon death to relieve him of his misery, must draw back from death when his wish is granted; a youth must retreat into the hills to play his pipe in solitude; a lover with every prospect of happiness must drown—not only must these conditions be fulfilled, but the weather and time of day must also be suitable: if there is no excuse for moonbeams slanting across tomb chambers or prisons, then at least there must be a storm brewing on the coast.

For his *Dead Soldier* [Plate 281], Wright selected a vignette from Langhorne; like the prison scene from the *Sentimental Journey* it represents an interruption in the main flow of the narrative, a set piece with little or no relevance to what comes before or what follows— the kind of self-contained word-picture that a painter would seize on in any work of literature. The vignette is from Langhorne's *Country Justice*, a poem in three parts bearing the date 1774 in the dedication, five years before the writer's death. The passage in question occurs in Part I entitled 'Apology for Vagrants':

> 'Perhaps on some inhospitable shore
> The houseless wretch a widow'd parent bore;
> Who, then, no more by golden prospects led,
> Of the poor Indian begg'd a leafy bed.
> Cold on Canadian hills, or Minden's plain,
> Perhaps that parent mourned her soldier slain;
> But o'er her babe, her eye dissolv'd in dew,
> The big drops mingling with the milk he drew,
> Gave the sad presage of his future years,
> The child of misery, baptiz'd in tears!'[2]

2 *The Country Justice*, Part I, 'Apology for Vagrants'. For further details, see Rosenblum, 1962, p. 136.

This touching scene which reduced Hayley to tears was engraved by Heath and hung up in every right-minded middle-class home.

Wright and Langhorne were almost exact contemporaries, and by sheer chance must have known one another in odd circumstances in their youth. Langhorne went to live in 1759 at Hackthorn near Lincoln, as preceptor to the sons of Robert Cracroft. He fell in love with one of the Cracroft daughters, who turned him down. Like any fictional character of the period, he took himself off, to lick his wounds in silence. This proud renunciation stood him in excellent stead: for the lady relented and they were married six years later. They

1 *The Poetical works of John Langhorne, D. D. ...*, London, 1804, contains (Vol. I) a memoir by his son who informs us of these facts (pp. 8 ff.) Langhorne remained at Hackthorn until the autumn of 1761.

2 See Shakespeare Gallery, 1790. Preface by John Boydell dated 1st May 1789. That the plan was put forward in 1786 as Hayley writes (1809, p. 109) and not 1787 as John Romney claims (1830, p. 151) is proved by the letters that passed between Wright, Hayley and Boydell in the earlier year (see below).

3 See Boase, 1947, pp. 95 ff. and Merchant, 1959, pp. 66ff. for further details.

4 Hayley, 1809, p. 112.

5 Walpole, 1937, p. 122, quoting a press cutting of 1786.

6 There is also a possibility that he was confusing Wright with Mortimer who did draw Bardolph's face.

7 4th and 6th December 1786, from which an extract is quoted; Part I, p. 18.

ought to have lived happily ever after but she died in childbirth a year after their marriage.[1] During the early part of 1760—precisely at the moment that Langhorne was living there—Wright was at Hackthorn, painting two of Mr. Cracroft's daughters, one of them Langhorne's future wife [Plate 25]. Can it ever be said that a biographer is better informed than the subject of his biography? Might this curious occurrence have slipped Wright's memory as he turned over the pages of the *Country Justice* close on thirty years later?

It was again in the late '80's that Wright received his most important commission for scenes from literature, and the prospect appalled him, though by that time he could not be said to lack experience. He was lucky in having his close friend Hayley in a position of power as adviser to the businessman financing the scheme, Alderman Boydell, and so could be sure of support in the highest places.

John Boydell made up for his lack of artistic talents by developing those of the *entrepreneur*. He set up in London as an engraver, employing other printmakers to work for him. His great *coup* was the dissemination of William Woollett's engraving after West's *Death of Wolfe*, out of which he made a fortune. This print was calculated to appeal to the not very sophisticated public Boydell saw could be reached. In 1782 he was made Alderman of the City of London, in 1785 Sheriff, and in 1790 Lord Mayor. It was in the autumn of 1786 that he embarked on his most ambitious programme: the publication by subscription of a series of prints illustrating Shakespeare, after pictures painted expressly for the work by English artists, and built a gallery in Pall Mall for their exhibition. The object was to pay for the gallery by the sale of prints abroad, and then to present it to the nation. This undertaking, writes Boydell three years later, 'originated in a private company, where Painting was the subject of conversation ... It is not now necessary to say, who first promulgated the plan—who has promoted it—or who has endeavoured to impede its success...'[2] To this day nobody quite knows who first came forward with the suggestion. It may have been that Romney proposed the Gallery, and George Nicol the publication of an edition of plates engraved after the paintings.[3]

Hayley who was present at the party thought of Wright as a suitable contributor, and wrote before the end of 1786 'a letter to engage my friend Wright of Derby to paint for the Gallery. My application to Wright was made at the earnest desire of the Alderman...'[4] Some journalist did not share this favourable opinion of the artist as an illustrator of Shakespeare, though he could have seen his one-man show eighteen months before, and have known not only that he was capable, after the *Siege of Gibraltar*, of a work on the scale required, but also that he had had wide experience of history painting: 'We are ready to allow', he writes, 'every merit to Mr. Wright of Derby: he was born to paint volcanos and founderies; but what has that to do with Shakespeare, unless indeed the artist confines himself to Bardolph's face?'[5] This observation about Bardolph throws a lurid light on the reaction of an arbiter of taste to Wright's realistic portraiture. Whose battered face can he have had in mind? That of *Whitehurst*, or of the artist himself, at the one-man show? The journalist shows himself blind to Wright's refinement, and evidently sees his portraits only as coarse character studies.[6]

Wright also—for different reasons—had doubts about his capacity to control 'the dreadful size of the pictures', and to meet what he feared was going to be a tight schedule. But it is easy to read between the lines of his reply to Hayley[7] the thrill he felt, mingled with the apprehension. At once he sets about discussing the subject Hayley has proposed, from *The Tempest*, Act IV, Scene I showing *Prospero in his cell with Ferdinand and Miranda* [Plate 299]; continuing as usual to think aloud to his friend about the composition; finding any excuse (this time, the magic powers exercised by Prospero) for taking liberties with the light in the cell—for he could never plan a composition before first deciding in what conditions of light it should be set:

'I wish it to be artificial, the view without of the sea shore illuminated faintly wth. the moon. This kind of effect will be better perhaps than day light at least make a variety in the picture. Caliban & Trinculo wth. his companion just coming ashore at a distance... prospero is to look angry & discomposed, and the happy engagement of the two Lovers shou'd be seen thro' their actions [.] They are thrown into [word omitted] by the emotion of prospero. But my dear friend if I paint this picture, or any other, let it be under your guidance. Tell me if you was to paint how you wou'd treat each figure how compose the whole. How shou'd they be drest?'

Thus before ever putting brush to canvas he has transformed a scene from Shakespeare into a Wright: that moon; that well-worn cave, now inhabited by Prospero instead of a phantom ship or the melancholy Julia; that familiar curve of the distant shore—all the elements in his repertory are present already. Yet strangely enough he still lacks confidence in himself; at the age of fifty-three he needs a poet to tell him what to do.

His friend Beridge, living conveniently nearby, also came to his rescue. He persuaded Wright to do a sketch of the scene which turned out to correspond roughly with what Hayley had in mind. In the sketch (as in the finished picture): 'The Dancers are risen above their heads [of the other figures] & agreeable to Shakespeare's Idea the furthest off has almost lost its form & vanished into thin air, while others are beginning to fade…'[1] By March of the following year Wright was seriously beginning to wonder whether he could undertake the work at all. He had only just acquired the canvas: '…I now find my frame,' he writes to his friend Mr. Long, the surgeon in Chancery Lane, 'much too feeble for 12 feet of canvass, the sight of it affrights me…'[2] By February 1789, after two years' silence, we find him in a more optimistic mood: '…I seized the favourable hours for the execution of my picture of prospero & have nearly finished yᵉ principal groupe…'[3] Details of the description he gives of the dresses to be worn by Ferdinand and Miranda, appropriate to their station, would be boring to repeat, especially since this scene from Shakespeare—largely owing to the worry Wright had over it, his incessant (and one cannot help feeling, unnecessary) recourse to Hayley and to Shakespeare's text, the oppressive size of the canvas which continued to nag at him with its emptiness—is not one of his successes; we may, however, be excused, in view of the fact that the picture is lost, for quoting one passage where he refers to colour: 'Prospero I have given a flowing gown of scarlet hue, wᶜʰ suits my purpose better than black, & keeps clear of the common stage conjurer'. Yet Prospero reminds us of nothing so much as a conjuror at a Christmas party, and Ferdinand and Miranda as stage-struck extras.[4] Romney had objected to the introduction of the figures on the seashore, but Wright retained them, knowing as no-one outside Derby could, that they are pushed sufficiently far into the background not to disturb the main groups. The care he took to get the drunken Stephano right, hanging on to Trinculo for support, his determination to catch Caliban in a 'cringing collected posture on tip toe', the consideration he gave to the costume of the distant Trinculo[5]—all these little details engaged his attention for months, and show how anxious he was to remain faithful to the play; too anxious in fact: for it was precisely his over-conscientious homework that contributed to the failure.

By March of 1789 the picture was ready[6] (though even then he could not leave it alone and had to go on tinkering with it), and later that year was dispatched to the Alderman. Wright had meanwhile been having words with Boydell over his status as a painter, and over the price, both of the *Tempest* scene and of another he planned for the Shakespeare Gallery, a scene of *Juliet* in the tomb. He was already proposing to do this second scene when the project for the Gallery was first mooted, in December 1786: 'Methinks I feel a desire to paint Juliet waking in the Tomb—if you write to Mr. Boydell pray mention it',[7] he tells Hayley. Evidently Hayley passed on the message and the Alderman gave his consent, for the question of the price cropped up a few days later:

'…I thought by my friend Hayley's letter', he writes to the Alderman, 'the pictures were to be of two sizes only the horizontal ones 12 feet by 8f 6i. [inches] & the uprights to be 8f 6i. [high] in order to range uniformly—the figures to be as large as the life, but by the size you propose for Juliet in the Tomb (viz) 5f 2 by 7f 2 long, the figures must be much less than the life, scarce 3 feet high, a size I had in my own mind given up painting. I also understood by him that you had classed the painters, & that the first, in wᶜʰ you had placed me, was to have 300 [guineas] a picture & more if the work met wᵗʰ encouragement to enable to do so, I find by my friend Mr. French, that in the papers I am promiscuously named sometimes in one class & sometimes in another wᶜʰ I think very wrong (if it is so, but I have not seen the papers) after what pass'd between me and Mr. Hayley…'[8]

1 Wright to Hayley, 23rd December 1786; Inglefield MSS.

2 Wright to Long, 28th March 1787; Inglefield MSS.

3 Wright to Hayley, 7th February 1789; Inglefield MSS.

4 Boase, 1947, p. 98 rightly criticises the figures: 'which are marred by excessive gesture and expression'. Merchant, on the other hand (1959, p. 73) speaks more highly of it.

5 All these points are raised in the same letter to Hayley, of 7th February.

6 Wright to Boydell, 12th March 1789; quoted Bemrose, 1885, p. 97.

7 Wright to Hayley, 4th and 6th December 1786; N.P.G. extra-illustrated Bemrose.

8 Wright to Boydell, 12th December 1786; MS Derby Public Library.

1 Wright to Hayley, 23rd December 1786, quoting Boydell; Inglefield MSS.

2 Reynolds and West were each offered 1000 guineas. Romney was paid 600 for his scene from the *Tempest* but felt slighted because the other two were offered more. 'He complained that the whole affair was being hurried through as a commercial matter, and that Boydell wished to include one or two expensive pictures by the leading names and then complete the gallery on the cheap by the works of younger, lesser men' (Boase, 1947, p. 98). Wright did not know at the time that Reynolds and West had been offered so much; had he done so, he would have been even more infuriated.

3 Wright to Boydell, 26th July 1789; MS. Derby Public Library. Since this important letter and Boydell's reply of 3rd August are available *in extenso* in Bemrose, 1885, pp. 98–100 they are not quoted in full here. Almost all the other quotations from letters in this chapter are unpublished.

4 According to a letter from Wright to Hayley, 12th September 1789, N.P.G. extra-illustrated Bemrose, what happened was that Wright consulted Hayley as to how to reply, and Hayley produced what must have been a tact-fully worded letter, which Wright transcribed *verbatim* and passed on to the Alderman. This had the effect of calming them both down. All the same the painter could not hold back a Parthian shot: 'I must further add, it is the poorest stipend I have recd for so much work, these many years'. Wright did not wish the Alderman to be left with the satisfaction of giving 'this extravagant price, in order to prove his own liberality', and so contemplated returning some of it.

5 Wright to Hayley, 12th September 1789, postscript, N.P.G. extra-illustrated Bemrose, shows that he still had work to do on the *Juliet* then: '∴ pray put down your ideas on the subject of Romeo & Juliet in Capulet's Tomb.'

6 See Shakespeare Gallery, 1790, Nos. I and XVII respectively, the latter as by Hodges. These are listed again in the 1802 catalogue (III and XXXII), this time with the correct attribution for the second. In the 1802 catalogue the engravings by Thew and Middiman after the two pictures are recorded.

7 The act of devouring takes place off-stage: it is reported by the clown to the shepherd. Wright paid close attention to this passage of description.

8 The reference to donkeys is to Wright's lost painting *An Old Man and his Ass, from Sterne* (Cat No 241); to parrots, his *Chase* double portrait [Plate 50]: the others are more obvious.

9 Sawrey Gilpin to Wright, undated, quoted by Bemrose, 1885, p. 98 from Hannah's memoir. In a passage Bemrose does not quote, Gilpin asks to be remembered to Mrs. Wright, so the letter is before August 1790 when she died.

10 Wright to J. L. Philips, 24th September 1792, MS. Derby Public Library, quoted by Bemrose, 1885, p. 90.

Boydell tried to maintain in reply that there was no question of classing the painters or the prices of their pictures, 'as it entirely depends upon the size of the picture & the number of figures, & the size of them...'[1] This proved not to be strictly true. The relations between painter and Alderman remained reasonably amicable, largely owing to Wright's ignorance of the true state of affairs at the time, but they soon deteriorated as he grew better informed, and as his suspicious nature was aroused. In this particular situation he had some right to be indignant, on discovering after the assurances that had been given, that Reynolds (with a much smaller picture) and West had been paid more handsomely for their contributions,[2] and demanded the same amount for his own. Unless he was paid at the same rate, he argued, he would 'not only lose the pecuniary advantage [with which, if the truth were known, Wright was not much concerned], but endanger my reputation, a point which I consider of far greater moment'.[3] Boydell fairly let fly in his reply, insulting Wright by saying: '...I am free to confess that had I ever presumed to have classed the historical painters of this country, perhaps Mr. Wright's name would not have stood exactly where he has been pleased to place it himself'. He goes on to criticise, with some justification, Wright's scene from *The Tempest*: 'however excellent the landscape part of it may be, the figures are very faulty, and so much out of drawing, that it will give no little trouble to correct it for the engraver'; and offers him 300 guineas and not a penny more. Rather lamely, Wright accepts the offer, but thinks of all kinds of ways of refusing part of it in order to preserve his dignity.[4] Both men made valid points, but both are to be blamed for putting their points so pettily. Taken all in all, the quarrel leaves a nasty taste in the mouth.

For some reason his picture of *Juliet* [Plate 305] in the tomb (Act V, Scene III) was not accepted for the Shakespeare Gallery, but was shown at the Academy in 1790 instead; its appearance there shows that it could have been ready for exhibition in Pall Mall had it been wanted.[5] There may have been another row hidden behind this rejection about which we know nothing, connected with the production by Northcote of a tomb scene for the Gallery. In its place Wright painted another picture for the Gallery for which he was willing to accept a more modest fee (£136) than for the *Tempest* scene, though admittedly it was much smaller: *the Storm in the Winter's Tale* [Plate 302].

This and the *Tempest* scene were shown together at the opening of the Shakespeare Gallery in 1789–90.[6] He did another version of the *Storm* concurrently [Plate 304], which was sold to the brother of his friend John Leigh Philips. They both showed an episode from Act III, Scene III where Antigonus is pursued by a bear—always a stumbling-block in any stage production where bears are hard to come by, but not in the art of painting where the artist is at liberty to select the act of pursuit or the moment of devouring,[7] depending on the nature of his obsessions. Needless to say Wright has taken pains to avoid a Rubensian scene of massacre and has settled for the pursuit; though his bear is so playful that one is at a loss to explain why Antigonus should be scared of it. He had to find out what a bear looked like. Horses, foxes, parrots, lambs, dogs, cats, donkeys[8]—he had had experience of all of them, but of bears none. So he applied to the animal painter Sawrey Gilpin for a sketch of one. Gilpin replies: 'I will go a Bear hunting to the Tower... and sketch one from nature, if possible [having sent him a rough sketch]...I think with you, that the pursuit is better than the horrid act of tearing'.[9]

The two versions are similar, the chief difference being that whereas in the one in the Boydell Gallery the ship has almost disappeared in the storm, in the Philips version (now at Kedleston) it is still well above the horizon, and a dead tree has been added, to balance the high rocks in the left foreground. These changes are mostly afterthoughts. Wright as well as his friends preferred the second:

'I have finished the "Storm"', he writes, after several attempts at retouching, 'except for the figure of Antigonus. Your brother Frank [Philips] seemed to like it much; indeed those who have seen it give it the preference to the other [for Boydell]. I have brought yᵉ ship nearer, which heightens the distress of the scene; and being much larger, the masts go above the horizon, and make a ballance to the other side of the picture'.[10]

It is no more surprising that he should settle on the tomb scene in *Romeo and Juliet* and on the storm in the *Winter's Tale*, than that he should wish to introduce a moonlit cave into the *Tempest*. Tombs had played their part in his world ever since he had depicted the young nobleman Miravan ill-advised enough to break open his ancestors' tomb, and the motif had passed into the Gothick vernacular of the day. As for Antigonus, any prospect of a storm on a coast could be relied on to quicken the artist's senses. A scene of this kind demanded a background in keeping with its romance; and Wright could find no landscape more appropriate than the rock formations around Matlock and Cromford over which, during these very years, he had been incessantly tramping. For his stage scenery he has transported Matlock to the coast, and created a phantom resort known as Matlock-on-Sea.

Wright exhibited the Philips version of the *Storm*, as well as his *Juliet*, at the Academy of 1790, but dissatisfied with both, he reworked them after the closing of the exhibition:

'The two pictures I exhibited last year [1790] in the R. Academy of "Romeo & Juliet" and Antigonus in the "Storm" were certainly painted too dark, sad emblems of my then gloomy mind. I have simplified the back ground of the former, enlarged the parts, and thrown more light into the Tomb, so that Julia is bright without being a spot ... I have a strange wish to see them well engraved as they are [that is, in February 1791, after retouching], though unworthy of adding to Boydell's collection...'[1]

It appears from his silence that Hayley did not think much of the *Romeo and Juliet* in the state in which it was first exhibited, but 'the Storm he speaks more mercifully of'.[2]

Meanwhile the Boydell pictures continued to be on show in Pall Mall. In 1789 there were thirty-four pictures; a year later this had risen to over sixty. In 1802 there were over 160, more than half of which were of large size. More than thirty painters contributed, and two sculptors. All the best artists (as well as many indifferent ones) were represented.[3] There had never been such stimulus exerted by a private speculator in the cause of contemporary British art. The stage ought to have been set for Boydell's apotheosis. But the wars of the French Revolution destroyed his chances of foreign trade, and by 1804 he had to apply to Parliament to dispose of his property by lottery. His dilemma can best be expressed in his own words:

'My receipts from abroad had been so large, and continued so regular, that I at all times found them fully adequate to support my undertakings at home. I could not calculate on the present crisis, which has totally annihilated them.'[4]

He lived to see every ticket in the lottery disposed of, but died (in December 1804) before the prizes were drawn.[5] It was a dismal end to an imaginative project. But one cannot suppress a suspicion that it was just as well that the Gallery was dispersed. The timing was at fault. The scheme was launched at a poverty-stricken moment in British painting; there was no longer sufficient genius to raise the execution up to the level of the idea.

1 Wright to Philips, 14th February 1791; MS. Derby Public Library, quoted by Bemrose, 1885, p. 101. They were re-exhibited at the Society of Artists in the spring of that year (see Part I, pp. 16–7).

2 Wright to Philips, 17th June 1790; MS. Derby Public Library.

3 Except Blake, and Stubbs, for whom nobody had the wit to propose the subject: 'A horse! A horse! My kingdom for a horse!'

4 Alderman Boydell to Sir John W. Anderson, 4th February 1804, and read by the latter in the House of Commons.

5 The Shakespeare Gallery fell to a Mr. Tassie, who sold it by auction at Christie's in May 1805. Wright's *Tempest* scene was bought by the Earl of Crawford and Balcarres and remained until recently at Haigh Hall. His *Antigonus* has not been seen since the sale.

8 THE INDUSTRIAL SCENE 1775–97

With the possible exception of Milnes, it was only on Wright's return from Italy that merchants and industrialists thought of adding art to wealth by acquiring from him subject pieces and landscapes, as well as getting him to paint their portraits. Before the Italian journey, even local landowners had hesitated to acquire from him anything more impersonal than their own features in two dimensions, and it was only because some well established men were also intellectuals like Boothby or progressives like Robert Holden, that he began as well to sell pictures of another kind locally on his return. The industrialists of the '80's repeated the pattern set by the gentry in the '60's: these laggards also preferred portraits and tended to look askance at landscape and genre. None of his patrons who had started from scratch and built up fortunes of their own seem to have demanded from him, at any rate until the '90's,[1] anything but portraits of themselves and of their families (that is to say, if we agree to leave on one side the unique case of Wedgwood, who was so much of an intellectual that we forget he made a fortune by the sweat of his brow alone); but that they should have sought out an artist of Wright's calibre when they might have been content with some hack journeyman no less close at hand, is remarkable enough, and without precedent in the history of British painting. Two industrialists who came from iron and cotton manufacturing families, Cockshutt and Milnes, did become interested in Wright's romantic landscapes, and not apparently in having their portraits painted. But it is significant that in both cases, so far as we can tell, these two had added to fortunes built up by their predecessors, and having achieved a certain position, had moved up into a different world.

About Josiah or Joshua Cockshutt we are forced to remain vague since only scattered, marginal facts have survived which do not add up to a consecutive story.[2] All we know is that he acquired from the artist before June 1780 three important South Italian landscapes datable 1777–80, all of which now hang at Meynell Langley (two are illustrated, Plate 215, Fig 105); that he was then living at Chaddesden, a village near Derby where a branch of the Wilmot family who had patronised Wright in the '60's (see *Mrs. Wilmot* [Plate 40]) had their seat; and that he belonged to a family of industrialists, the Cockshutts of Wortley, where there existed and still exists a helve hammer in the top forge very similar to the one depicted by Wright in his *Iron Forge*. But whether Wright's patron was an ironmaster himself is uncertain. By the late '70's the Cockshutts were well established in the district and had country house connections; this might explain the oddity of a member of an industrial family wishing to possess romantic Italian scenery. The dynasty was founded by a Matthew Wilson, who had built up the industry at Wortley, and on his death in 1739 the business appears to have passed to his nephew by marriage, John Cockshutt who, in spite of taking an active interest in the ironworks for the rest of his life (he died about 1765), was also a landowner. For the next eighty years until the early nineteenth century the forges

[1] There is no positive evidence that any of Wright's landscapes or genre pieces in the Strutt and Arkwright collections in the early nineteenth century was acquired by the first generation industrialists.

[2] The author is indebted to Mrs. Sandeman for permission to study documents preserved at Meynell Langley.

remained in the Cockshutt family.[1] But about Wright's patron, we have no specific information. The publication of this book may bring something to light about him. What a book leaves out can prove almost as useful as what it puts in, for this reason.

It is easier to understand why John Milnes of Wakefield in Yorkshire should have become interested in a Derby painter, since the Milneses claimed they were by origin small gentry from Derbyshire, moving to Wakefield in the reign of Charles II, and not only owned considerable property in Derbyshire but must still have had connections there, possibly with Milnes of Cromford, and with his daughter *Dorothy Gell of Hopton* [Plate 266].[2] John Milnes from whom Monckton Milnes, the friend of Swinburne and Florence Nightingale, was descended, was a rich Wakefield cotton manufacturer and had a monopoly of cloth in the district. He had intellectual pretensions, being a Dissenter and Whig, and was of ancient descent, not at all an upstart. We need not therefore be gravely disturbed to find him buying from Wright the same kind of romantic landscapes and subject pieces that took the fancy of men of quite a different stamp like Boothby or Sir Robert Wilmot.

Like Wedgwood he enjoyed possessing pictures *en série*, but not with the same intellectual content as Wedgwood's, where it was necessary to know what the stories were about in order to appreciate the relationship between one subject piece and the next. He preferred more straightforward landscapes where one canvas would form a contrast to its pendant by emphasising different lighting effects. Partly for this reason he bought at the Society of Artists of 1776 two large paintings of *Vesuvius* and the *Girandola*, 'the one', as Wright explains, 'the greatest effect of Nature the other of Art';[3] and acquired from the artist four large landscapes illustrating the four stages of the day: two views of the Alps in the morning and at noon, a sunset at Albano, and a moonlight on the coast of Tuscany. Farington's description of this quartet makes us realise how much we miss by its disappearance: 'He [Wright] painted 4 half length pictures [that is, about 40 by 50 inches] for M.ʳ Mills of Wakefield, Morning, noon (an Italian heated sky), evening and night. On these pictures He has said He shd. sooner choose to rest his reputation...'[4] Milnes also bought *Edwin* [Plate 179], the only one of his purchases to come down to us in the family, but in this case not its companion, *Maria* [Plate 220]. Perhaps he was not sufficiently drenched in literature to want both. This means that he was acquiring Wrights for at least fifteen years, beginning soon after the mid-'70's and continuing into the early '90's. It is possible that he began collecting Wrights even earlier. The Account Book notes that a 'Mr. Milnes' bought *Miravan* [Plate 107], a picture painted in 1772. That Wright was already associated with the Wakefield Milneses is proved by the appearance at the Society of Artists in that year of a portrait of John Milnes's son, Robert Shore, then an officer in the Royal Horse Guards [Plate 114]. In 1776 when in Bath Wright painted another small full length of another of John Milnes's sons (see Cat No 107). These portraits were probably not commissioned by the father. And as for *Miravan*, it is always possible that the entry in the Account Book refers to another purchaser, such as William Milnes, the father of Dorothy Gell. However this may be, John Milnes of Wakefield amassed one of the largest Wright collections, and acquired his most ambitious picture, the *Siege of Gibraltar*. By 1791 he had spent well over £1000 on the whole collection—more than any other single patron—which occupied more wall-space even than the Wright collections of Benjamin Bates and Arkwright.[5]

We know more about the genesis of the *View of Gibraltar during the destruction of the Spanish Floating Batteries* (Cat No 245) than about any other picture except the *Corinthian Maid* and his scene from *The Tempest*, but in its absence it would be depressing to enter into too many details. One is not grateful to, but curses, the guide who points at the blank walls of the Palais des Papes at Avignon and goes into raptures about frescoes that are no longer there. A few facts only need be recorded. On 13th September 1782 the British garrison at Gibraltar decisively defeated the Spanish floating batteries, thereby restoring some of that British prestige which had been shaken by the loss of the American colonies. The news had the same effect on public opinion in England as the Suez operation of 1956 would have had, if it had proved a triumph instead of a dismal failure. The subject was an obvious one for any history painter following in the footsteps of Benjamin West, and most of all for Wright whose speciality was fire, and who could visualise the contribution he alone could make to the events of that memorable day: the firing of red-hot missiles at the

1 For further details about the Cockshutt family, see Andrews, 1956, pp. 45 ff.

2 For the early history of the Milnes family, see T. Wemyss Reid, *The Life, Letters, and Friendships of Richard Monckton Milnes, first Lord Houghton*, London, 1890, I, pp. 1–7. A number of members of the family was painted by Romney (see Ward & Roberts, 1904, II, p. 106).

3 See Appendix B under 'A Pairs of "Vesuvius" and "Girandola"', p. 279.

4 Farington Diary, p. 813, entry for 28th October 1796. The pictures must date from about 1789–90, judging from their position in the Account Book. In a postscript to a letter from Wright to Philips, 15th April 1791 (MS. Derby Public Library; passage not quoted by Bemrose, 1885, p. 64) he writes: 'The two landscapes were gone to Wakefield before I got Tate's letter'. They were presumably two of these. To these four he soon afterwards added a *Needwood Forest* of the same size. This cannot have been one of the four: the only one we are not certain Milnes bought—the midday Alpine scene—must in fact have belonged to the set, and not the sunny cottage scene in Needwood Forest, because Farington specifically states that the midday picture was an Italian view.

5 See letter of Wright to Daulby, 11th January 1780 (MS. Derby Public Library) quoted in Appendix B, under No. 16 where Wright announces: 'Mr. Milnes has been a great friend to me, having laid out wᵗʰ me 7 or £800'. By 1780 it is not possible to account for more than £300 to £400 laid out by Milnes, but this is an argument in favour of the doubtful pictures having been acquired by him also.

1 Wright to Hayley, 9th January 1783; N.P.G. extra-illustrated Bemrose.

2 Wright to Hayley, 13th January 1783; Inglefield MSS. Copley received the commission for this subject from the Corporation of the City of London in the early months of 1783. George Carter applied to the corporation for the commission, but just too late, after Copley had signed his agreement. Carter claimed he had finished his picture by then (March 1783) but was probably exaggerating. He also claimed that he had obtained information from Sir Roger Curtis, and he no doubt was one of the people Wright had in mind when writing to Hayley (see Jules D. Prown, *John Singleton Copley*, Cambridge, Mass., 1966, II, p. 312, note 1). Copley and Dominic Serres had also obtained information from Curtis for their pictures of the Siege (Prown, *op. cit.* II, p. 324). George Carter's picture is reproduced in T. H. McGuffie, *The Siege of Gibraltar, 1779–1783*, London, 1965, p. 161. For Copley's beautiful sketch of 1788 in the Thomas Coram Foundation for Children, see exh. catalogue 'John Singleton Copley', Washington, New York, Boston, 1965–6, p. 111. His final vast picture in the Guildhall was only completed in 1791.

3 Wright to Hayley, 31st August 1783; quoted Bemrose, 1885, p. 61.

4 Wright to Hayley of that date, N.P.G. extra-illustrated Bemrose.

5 Wright to Hayley, 17th February 1785; N.P.G. extra-illustrated Bemrose.

6 Catalogue entry for No. XXIV, Robins's Rooms, 1785.

7 See letters of 14th November 1785 and 14th January 1786 to Daulby, quoted by Bemrose, 1885, p. 86.

8 Letter to Hayley, 12th April 1786; N.P.G. extra-illustrated Bemrose: 'I have disposed of my picture of Gibraltar for 420 gs to a private Gent^m. wch. will spare me many an awkward sensation excited by the Idea of having it raffled for ...'

Spanish ships; the ensuing conflagration in the harbour; the dramatic feature of the Mole; the proud garrison standing back to survey the blaze. Hayley and Beridge at once saw its possibilities for the painter and before the end of that year were urging him to get ahead with it. But Wright, whose direct knowledge of the topography was limited to a journey through the Straits nearly ten years before, realised he could only do so with the assistance of someone like Sir Roger Curtis who had played a heroic part in the defence of the Rock, and—more important for his purposes—had made drawings of the Engagement:

'...could I be *certain*', he writes, 'S^r. Roger Curtis, wou'd upon a personal application allow me the use of his drawings & give me those aids he has others, I shou'd be tempted to set forwards immediately in spite of wind & weather, but if I shou'd be denied such advantages I shou'd make a most uncomfortable return home'.[1]

He goes on to ask Hayley to find out whether Curtis would be willing to help, but urges him to make sharp: 'there is no time to be lost, as the Subject is by S^r. Roger's assistance already in the hands of several & will soon be a hackney'd one'.[2] It seems as though he never received the help he needed from Curtis, for we find him writing a few months later: 'Perhaps, had I... been furnished with proper materials for the action off Gibraltar, I should have begun my fire; but for want of such instructions, I soon sank into my wonted torpor again...'[3]

He worked hard on the picture during 1784, as far as failing health and torpor would permit, finishing it on 17th February of the following year.[4] He was worried about his ignorance of Naval affairs and wondered whether he would come in for criticism on that score:

'...I am unacquainted wth. naval business have therefore had many difficulties to combat wth. wch. if I could have foreseen, wou'd have deterred me from the prosecution of the work. After all I fear it is not the picture you expect to see, as the action is not principal & at too great a distance to discriminate particulars, even the men in the Gunboats that lie just off the New Mole (wch. makes a fine dark foreground to the picture) are not more than an inch high. however the floating Batteries in different degrees of burning make a fine blaze, & illuminate in a striking manner the noble Rock of Gib...'[5]

Wright had the idea of painting two pictures as companions: in the first (the only one executed) 'to represent an extensive view of the scenery combined with the action'; in the second 'to make the action his principal object'.[6] He also thought of raffling the picture,[7] but was relieved of this necessity by the appearance of Maecenas in the guise of John Milnes who carted the vast canvas off to Yorkshire,[8] paying him a more handsome sum for it than he had received for any other work.

It would not be correct to treat Cockshutt and Milnes as though they were self-made men. Behind them both lies a tradition of ease, of some inherited culture, and though both came from families of industrialists, there is no essential difference, as far as patronage of the arts is concerned, between them and some of the landed gentry whose careers we have already outlined. When we turn to Roe, the Hurts, the Oldknows, Strutt and Arkwright, we find ourselves up against quite a new type with no background except poverty and struggle. They had been too busy pushing their way up to find time for the enrichment of the spirit by art. But once they had sorted themselves out from others who had struggled with equal tenacity but through a combination of mismanagement and bad luck had come to grief, had reason to be proud of their achievement, and wished to see it immortalised, not by *banditti* plotting vengeance at the entrance to some sun-drenched cavern, nor by naval tactics in some distant bay, but in the shape of their own bodies, as an example to their descendants. Had Wright painted the portraits of Cockshutt and Milnes, he would doubtless have detected some traces of refinement which would have justified his turning a blind eye to what was actually there. With these new sitters, as with the merchants on Merseyside, there was no getting away from the facts.

Charles Roe (1715–81) is a copybook example of the self-made man [Plate 201], more familiar to us from biographies of nineteenth, than of eighteenth-century traders. Born in Derbyshire the son of the vicar of Castleton, he had settled in Macclesfield by 1742, and within a year to eighteen months had erected a mill there for the throwing of raw silk by water power. By the middle of the century he had entered into partnership with Samuel Lankford, a silk merchant (and member of a family whom Wright also painted), and on the latter's death in 1762, had joined with Lankford's son Harry and with others—for success then depended on being able to combine with rivals in the same line of business, just as on the intellectual plane the members of the Lunar Society could achieve nothing solid without propping each other up. Roe was also interested in copper smelting and was one of the chief promoters of this industry in Macclesfield. He was active as a propagandist for the building of a canal in the area to supply coal to the silk and copper factories at a cheaper rate, but unlike John Ashton ran up against strong opposition from the Duke of Bridgewater, and the scheme broke down.[1] As the son of a vicar he had preserved his piety through all the harsh competition of life, and in 1775 built Christ Church, Maccles-field, one of the most astonishing offshoots of the Industrial Revolution in the whole of the Midlands, which nobody except a student of the history of architecture would dream of dating before the early nineteenth century: dumped down as it is on a dreary, rain-swept slope, retaining no breath of the Rococo-Gothick spirit of its epoch but combining a heavy-handed Gothic with incipient Neo-Classicism; pointing into the future as men-acingly as Arkwright's cotton mills at Cromford, or Strutt's at Belper.[2]

On Roe's death in 1781, John Bacon was commissioned by his widow and children to erect a monument in this church (1784), than which it would be hard to imagine a more remarkable celebration in sculpture of the birth of the factory system. It shows the full-length figure of Genius clasping in one arm a medallion with the head of Roe, and holding in the other hand a broken cogwheel as though she were Britannia harnessed into the service of industry, mourning Roe whose achievements are honoured below in three bas-relief panels, representing his silk mill, the church itself, and his copper works. A quotation from the inscription on the monument will serve the dual purpose of providing more information about Roe's career than is given above, and of recreating the attitude of mind in the late eighteenth century towards a local benefactor whose greatness is put down to a nice blending of intuition, hard work, and moral decency:

'A Gentleman who with a slender Portion in his Entrance into Business carried on the Button and Twist Manufacture in this Town with the most active Industry, Ingenuity and Integrity and by a happy Versatility of Genius at different Periods of his life first established here and made instrumental to the Acquisition of an ample Fortune THE SILK AND COPPER MANUFACTORIES by which many thousands of Families have been since supported... By an intuitive kind of knowledge he acquired an intimate Acquaintance with the *Mineral Strata* of the Earth: and was esteemed by competent Judges greatly to excel in THE ART OF MINING... He dedicated to the Service of his MAKER, a Part of that Increase His Bounty had bestowed erecting and endowing at his Sole Ex-pence, the elegant [*sic*] Structure which encloses this Monument:—And which, it is remarkable, was built from the Surface of the Ground, and compleatly finished, both Inside and Out, in so short a space of Time as seven months...'

Shortly before Roe's death Wright was engaged to paint his portrait [Plate 201] which is preserved, unmolested by the knowing fingers of reliner or restorer, in the sacristy of Christ Church.[3] It is one of the most direct statements that he ever made, and that has ever been made by a professional painter.

The Hurts had established themselves at Alderwasley as the leading mining family in Wright's district by the middle of the century, and to judge by his portrait of the head of the family, *Francis Hurt* [Plate 204], shown at about the age of 58 with a lump of his own iron ore on the table beside him, he prefers like Roe to be remembered even in late middle age (by which time one might have expected the *douceur de vivre* to have softened his features), as the intractable materialist. The brittleness of the lump of ore—unique in the history of art?—indicates that it has reached the stage after the iron-stone has been smelted in the furnace and converted into metal, but before it has been given the malleability of iron in the

1 See Chaloner, 1950–53, *passim* for a detailed account of Roe's career, from which this summary is extracted.

2 The church was visited on 24th April 1776 by Thomas Buxton of Bradbourne, a close relation of Wright's patron George Buckston: 'y.ᵉ 24.ᵗʰ I dined with M.ʳ Rooe [at Macclesfield] and saw his new church... In y.ᵉ afternoon I went with M.ʳ Rooe to see his copper & Bras works, boath are very curious & valluable...' See MS. Buxton.

3 The portrait was discovered by W. H. Chaloner, who reproduces it in his essay on Roe, *loc. cit.*, opp. p. 133.

1 According to Pilkington, 1789, I, pp. 132 ff., who also mentions beds of iron-stone discovered at Wingerworth, Chesterfield and Stavely. One of the iron furnaces at Morley Park Farm is illustrated by Pevsner, 1953, p. 64.

2 For further details, see Farey, 1811, I, p. 403 and Lysons, 1817, p. CXCVII. We have no precise information about a comparable furnace at Alderwasley itself, but an iron forge is recorded there in 1807. The Morley Park furnace was in full operation in that year.

3 See W. H. Chaloner, 'John Wilkinson, Ironmaster', *History*, May 1951, p. 64.

4 *Derby Mercury*, 14th November 1777; 7th and 28th August 1778. The quotation is from the first issue cited.

5 See the family trees in Fitton and Wadsworth, 1958, pp. 325–6.

6 Records of the two portraits survive in old photographs pasted into the Eardley Simpson extra illustrated Bemrose, and a coloured stipple engraving by A. Delzers after the latter, published in 1911, exists [Plates 300, 301].

7 Unwin, 1924, p. 236. The author has relied heavily on this book for his account of Oldknow's career.

forge. This theory fits well with what we know of the Hurts. By the '80's one of the most valuable beds of iron-stone had been discovered at Morley Park, near Heage,[1] and a pyramidal furnace was erected there by a Francis Hurt for the purpose of obtaining the metal. Whether this Hurt was the father portrayed by Wright, or his son Francis, is uncertain, but it is clear that about the time of the elder Hurt's death in 1783 the family abandoned the small charcoal furnaces then in general use in Derbyshire and adopted at Morley Park a furnace of quite modern construction heated with coke.[2] The Hurts do not, however, deserve the credit for being pioneers in this field: for the process of smelting iron-ore with coke was invented by Abraham Darby I of Coalbrookdale as early as 1709 and was used by Wilkinson at Bradley soon after the middle of the century.[3]

The second generation of Hurts, though taking their business no less seriously than the first, blossomed out into public life, and into fun and games. Francis Hurt the Younger of Alderwasley became Sheriff of the County in 1777 when still in his twenties, and in the summer of the following year entertained a large gathering at the recently completed New Assembly Room in Derby 'at which the company were very numerous and brilliant; every Thing was well conducted, and in so generous a Style, that it bordered on Profusion'. A few days later he was married at Ashton-upon-Trent to Miss Shuttleworth, none other than the little girl in Wright's *Shuttleworth Group* [Plate 51] or her sister.[4] Like the second generation of Arkwrights and of the Milneses of Cromford, the Hurts were going up in the world. They continued to be bound by family ties to fellow-industrialists who were also reaping the benefits of their parents' drudgery. Thus Francis's younger brother Charles who had set up his own business nearby at Wirksworth, married the daughter of the first Richard Arkwright; Charles's daughter and Francis's son both married Arkwright's grandchildren; and one of Charles's sons married a Strutt girl.[5] Just as the later Arkwrights in Wright's portraits of them [Plates 325, 328, 329] have acquired a certain grace which the *pater familias* [Plate 323] lacks, so the second generation of Hurts, judging by reproductions of lost portraits by Wright of Charles Hurt of Wirksworth [Plate 300] and of his wife and child [Plate 301], are in a position to treat life more as it comes. Hurt is out walking with hat, cane and gloves; while his wife is seated on a rock under a tree, clasping her daughter, on whose right arm (stretched out to catch a butterfly) hangs a hat full of wild roses;[6] a far cry, in other words, from the chemical experiments Wedgwood imposed on his children, and from Mrs. Charles Hurt's austere parents-in-law.

The invention of Crompton's Mule (available to the public by 1780) gave great impetus to the manufacture of muslin, which demanded much more sensitive equipment than the usual calicoes. Samuel Oldknow, a member of a family of small traders, set up at Anderton as a muslin manufacturer in 1782 at the age of 26, and was the first to achieve real eminence in the business. From 1783 onwards he traded chiefly with London firms, but also with Manchester. It was in this year that he became primarily a maker of muslins, and within three years was recognised as the first in the Kingdom. He lacked capital, but was able to borrow large sums from Richard Arkwright which enabled him to start up his manufacture on a larger scale at Stockport. The new warehouse at Stockport was opened early in 1784. In 1786 he planned to enter into partnership with Richard Arkwright junior, who had his own spinning-mill at Bakewell, but negotiations broke down. In spite of this, during the next eighteen months Oldknow received large advances from the younger Arkwright. This encouraged him to take the decisive step towards the adoption of the factory system on a far more lavish scale by the extensive purchase of land and water power at Mellor (spring of 1787). He was overtaken by the disastrous trade depression (1787–8) but his trade recovered by the end of the decade. By this time, muslin accounted for nine-tenths of his sales. In 1790 he built a factory for spinning, worked by a Boulton and Watt steam engine, at Stockport, and laid the foundations of a larger mill (worked by water power) at Mellor: as Robert Owen put it, 'he desired to become a great cotton spinner, as well as the greatest muslin manufacturer'. But he appears to have set his sights too high, for from then onwards his fortunes began to decline. A recent biographer sums up his career as follows: 'he gained a fortune as a manufacturer and lost it as a spinner...Our records...seem to show that he owed his success more to creative aesthetic gifts than to mere business shrewdness'.[7]

From all accounts he was a genial, handsome man, endearing himself to his friends by his honesty, and by a certain incompetence in the conduct of his affairs which out of protectiveness they helped to set right. Some quality beyond mere cunning is brought out by Wright's full-length portrait of him [Plate 335], painted evidently before disaster overtook him. There is nobility as well as determination in those eyes. Wright pays lip service to the Grand Manner with his classical architecture and draped curtain, but the still life that rivets our attention is the strip of muslin slung over the parapet on which he proudly rests an arm, as Wright's nephew [Plate 273] rested his arm on a gun barrel to record his exploits as a sailor. Gun barrels no doubt belong to the history of portraiture, but muslin in its raw, unworn state decidedly does not. Conventional studio props are thus mocked at by this ungainly bundle, just as Hurt's circular table is mocked at by a lump of iron on its shiny surface. We are presented with Samuel Oldknow at the pinnacle of his fame. Nobody was to know that things were to go badly for him from then onwards. He lived on until 1828, moving out of Stockport and settling at Marple, but his brother Thomas whom Wright also painted in the last months of his life [Plate 334] died in his prime in 1791, before the family's downward lurch. Thomas was managing partner in the bleaching and printing works in his brother's business at Heaton Mersey from 1786 onwards, and died a rich man.[1]

There is no object in retelling the whole story of Jedediah Strutt, the hosier and cotton spinner (1726–97), since his achievement forms the backbone of a recent, well-documented study.[2] The son of a small farmer, he was born near Alfreton in Derbyshire, and was the inventor in the mid-'50's, in collaboration with his brother-in-law William Woollat, of a Derby rib machine which seems to have been an improvement on existing machinery. A partnership with Woollat and others was formed in 1758 and a patent granted in the following year. Strutt and Woollat got rid of their other partners in 1762 when they had served their purpose, and a more profitable association was started with a new backer, Samuel Need (1718–81), a Nottingham hosier, with whom Strutt maintained close business relations until Need's death. Strutt was also in business with Arkwright, but only until 1781, by which time both men were powerful enough to stand on their own feet, Arkwright remaining at Cromford, Strutt at Belper and Milford.

Wright in his marvellous portrait [Fig 135], for all the naturalness of the pose, does not show a man whose life has fallen comfortably into the pattern of that of others we have outlined—that is, an extrovert who with energy and common sense has slaved uphill for thirty years in order to bequeath a fortune to his descendants—but is at pains to bring out another, melancholy side to Strutt's nature. The portrait belongs to a late phase in the sitter's life when the struggle for power was over, but when long habits of discipline were too deeply engrained to allow the fruits of power to be plucked. It appears from letters to his wife and family that Strutt had a streak of melancholy even when the struggle was at its height; that he took an intellectual's delight in standing back and surveying from outside his own role in the struggle, intrigued (as men of action are supposed not to be) by evidence of weakness in himself, concerned with the moral implications in big business. Judging by the information that has been made public, he never quite admits to self-distrust, but the defiance with which on one occasion he extols money-making makes one think he has nervousness to cover up:

'I was this day thro' Cheapside', he writes to his wife in 1765, 'the Change &cc and cou'd not help imediately reflecting, that the sole cause of that vast concourse of people, of the Hurry & bustle they were in, & the eagerness that appeared in their countenances, was getting of Money, & whatever some Divines would teach to the contrary, this is true in fact that it is the main business of the life of Man & thou knowest not how solicitous I am while life, & youth, & opportunity lasts to acquire something that you & I, shoud we live so long, may not have the two great calamities of Human Life, poverty & Old Age, come upon us together...'

And the epitaph he composed for himself towards the end of his life reveals not only the pride of the successful businessman but also the self-consciousness of the intellectual and the scruples of the Dissenter:

1 The will of Thomas Oldknow is preserved in the Lancashire County Record Office, dated 2nd February 1791, from which it emerges that he left a widow and under-age children, and died with assets amounting to over £7500.

2 Fitton and Wadsworth, 1958, passim.

Fig 135 *Jedediah Strutt* c 1790 50 x 40 in / 127 x 101.6 cm   The Lord Belper   Cat 133   Pl 324

'Here rests in Peace J.S.—Who, without Fortune, Family or friends raisd to himself a fortune, family & Name in the World—Without having wit had a good share of plain Common Sense—Without much genius enjoyd the more Substantial blessing of a Sound understanding—With but little personal pride despisd a mean or base Action—With no Ostentation for Religious Tenets & Ceremonies he led a life of honesty & Virtue—& not Knowing what would befall him after death, he dyed resignd in full Confidence that if there be a future State of retribution it will be to reward the Virtuous & the Good

This I think is my true Character

J. Strutt'[1]

We are obliged to enter into the career of Richard Arkwright, or at any rate into the history of his building activities,[2] in greater detail because alone of all the industrialists he stimulated Wright, not only to record his features and those of his children and grand-children, but to bequeath to us a series of views of the area where he built up his industrial empire. Many such scenes survive from the hands of modest, topographical draughtsmen. But this is the only known case in the eighteenth century where an artist of Wright's calibre deigned to document the factory system in operation.

Richard Arkwright (1732–92) came of a poor family in Preston, and settled as a young man in Bolton as a barber, but later moved to Nottingham (1768), then the centre of the manufacture of cotton hosiery, a profession in which he saw better prospects of developing his gifts as an organiser. Here he was provided with sufficient funds by Jedediah Strutt and Samuel Need to improve existing machinery for the manufacture of cotton and to build a cotton factory run by horse power. Three years later he moved to the then unexploited district of Cromford near Matlock, where he built in partnership with Strutt and Need the nucleus of the Cromford Cotton Mills, to be run by water power. 'The decision to go to Cromford and apply water power to machinery still far from perfect was one of the turning-points in the history of the factory system'.[3] The site was selected partly because of the water supply from the Wirksworth lead mines, which was reputed never to have frozen, and possibly because Arkwright had social ambitions, and the proximity of Mat-lock Bath—then becoming popular as a spa town—gave him the opportunity of satisfying them.[4] He also had ambitions as an inventor, and during these early years at Cromford was engaged in perfecting a water spinning frame and in improving on traditional methods of carding cotton. He took out patents covering a series of inventions. Meanwhile, owing to these improvements in machinery and possibly to hostility on the part of Lancashire weavers, his Cromford mill was producing more yarn than he could use or sell, and so he and his partners decided to build a weaving workshop at Derby for the manufacture of calicoes to absorb the surplus yarn from Cromford (1773). Arkwright also began looking for further sites at Matlock, Bakewell and elsewhere, generally in collaboration with Strutt. Later, he extended his enterprises to the banks of the Clyde. He ventured into hosiery knit-ting as well. In 1781 he suffered a serious setback by the nullification of his carding patent, and four years later lost all his patents, but this did not prevent him from being honoured with a knighthood and becoming Sheriff of the County of Derby in the late '80's, and dying in 1792 one of the richest commoners in the Kingdom. He was an administrator of genius, but as an inventor, the evidence points to his powers having been restricted to the occasional improvement of other people's discoveries. He was a man of the utmost ruthless-ness, who never scrupled to appropriate the ideas of others for his own ends. Such is the nature of success in a rising capitalist society.[5]

The first news we have of Wright's association with Arkwright is in a letter of 1783 where he announces to Wedgwood: 'As soon as M^{rs}. Wright is brought to bed, wch she expects hourerly [sic]. I shall set off to Cromford by appointment to paint M^r. Arkwright and his daughter...'[6] Nothing further is heard of these portraits or this portrait-group: so far as we know he did not paint Arkwright till about seven years later, and the portrait of his daughter, Mrs. Charles Hurt, was also postponed. However, it must have been about this time (1783) that the artist conceived the idea of executing a view of Cromford Bridge and its companion of Arkwright's mills during a night shift, which were sold—not as one might expect to the owner of the mills who like other first-generation industrialists was

1 The two quotations are from *op. cit.*, pp. 108–10.

2 Throughout this account, we have been obliged to tread with the utmost cautiousness. For we have found during our investigation that sources conflict, later historians contradict one another, and that there is no general agreement on the basic facts. We have accordingly decided to take no statement on trust unless it is established beyond question.

3 The verdict of Fitton and Wadsworth, 1958,

4 The point is made by Chapman, 1965. Chapman elaborates the point in his excellent book, *The Early Factory Masters*, 1967, pp. 62 ff. In our opinion he exaggerates the part played by social ambition in Arkwright's move to Cromford, as we hope to demonstrate by implication in the remaining pages of this chapter.

5 This summary of Arkwright's career relies heavily on Fitton and Wadsworth, 1958, *passim*, and to a small extent on Browne MS. They supersede the biography of Arkwright in the D.N.B.

6 Wright to Wedgwood, 29th May 1783; Barlaston MSS. Wright's youngest daughter Maria was born a few days later (2nd June).

indifferent to landscape painting—but to the Fellow of All Souls and M.P. for Nottingham, Daniel Parker Coke. The view of the bridge has disappeared and only its pendant survives [Fig 137]. This date of about 1783 is suggested by the fact that the early '80's was the period when Coke is known to have been interested in the artist, and as we shall show, is not contradicted by the topography of the site.

That two mills had been built at Cromford by 1777 is known from documents. The first, upper mill,[1] was in operation before the end of 1771, the very year in which Arkwright moved from Nottingham to Cromford because the Nottingham mill had proved too unadventurous for his expanding business.[2] The second, lower mill was under construction in 1776–7, according to a contemporary eye-witness account; 'as large as the first,... new houses are rising round it, and everything wears the face of industry and cheerfulness.'[3] These two stone mills are shown on a map of 1777 [Fig 136] as of equal length and running more or less parallel to one another.[4]

Wright's picture [Fig 137] proves that this map, which is little more than a rough sketch, is inaccurate in at least two respects. He shows us a view of the mills towards the East-North-East; of this we can be certain, if for no better reason than that the two small contiguous brick buildings in front of the further mill are still in existence and unchanged. We can plot approximately the position Wright took up from the perspective in which they are shown. Two mills are visible. In front is a shortish one of five storeys (with an attic in the sloping roof), with at least nine windows to each floor. It is unlikely that more than one further window per floor is concealed behind the rock. This is the upper mill, constructed in 1771. Behind is a second which appears to be of double thickness with on one side a lean-to roof below the top storey. It is hard to say how many storeys it has but being further away from the spectator and apparently the taller of the two, in spite of being on a lower level, we can well believe the report that has come down to us, that it had seven storeys and was 120 feet long.[5] This is the second mill, constructed in 1776–7. To the left is the watercourse powering the two mills. The picture proves the map to be wrong; that not only were the mills at a sharper angle to one another, but that the later mill was the longer.[6]

1 Swindell, 1965, was the first to establish beyond question that the 1771 mill was the upper one.

2 This is known from an advertisement in the *Derby Mercury* of 10th December 1771, inviting applications for posts as clockmaker, wheelwright and for other trades at the 'Cotton Mill, Cromford'.

3 Bray, 1778, p. 119, writing of his own experience a few months before the end of 1777.

4 Plan of Cromford Moor Long Sough, dated 1777 (Bagshawe Collection, Department of Local History and Archives, Sheffield City Libraries). This map is too sketchy to be trusted, especially since it concentrates on another part of the district and shoves Cromford into a corner, but within its limits it confirms the evidence of the advertisement of 1771 and of Bray's statements.

5 For the evidence, see Fitton and Wadsworth, 1958, p. 99.

6 This is not clearly visible on the original which is damaged, but emerges more obviously from a copy in better condition (which has in other respects proved itself accurate) in the Oakes Collection; reprod. Klingender, 1947, pl. 16 and Michael Levey, *Rococo to Revolution...*, London, 1966, plate 101. What remains of the two mills today confirms their siting at an angle to one another.

Fig 136 Detail from *Plan of Cromford Moor Long Sough* 1777
Sheffield City Libraries (Bagshawe Collection)

Fig 137 *Arkwright's Cotton Mills, by night* c 1783
34 x 45 in / 86.3 x 114.3 cm I. M. Booth Cat 311 Pl 244

Fig 138 *Arkwright's Cotton Mills, by day* c 1790
23 x 30 in / 58.4 x 76.2 cm Formerly Colonel
M. H. Grant Collection Cat 312 Pl 331

No decent historian of the old school would accept this as evidence. But from our knowledge of the care he took to get things right, we can categorically state that Wright, though he may let his imagination rip when it comes to landscape, would not do so when it was a question of depicting industrial architecture.

About seven years later he painted a second view of the mills [Fig 138], this time by daylight, from roughly the same angle, again with Cromford Village to his rear, though on this occasion he has drawn closer to the mills, crossed the bridge and faced more or less due East, with the result that the upper mill is now squarely in front of him instead of at an angle, the two little brick buildings are hidden behind a tree, and the same watercourse flows from right to left instead of from left to right across his line of vision. Great changes have taken place in the interval dividing the two pictures. There are now at least fourteen windows per storey in the upper mill, which proves that between c. 1783 and c. 1790, this mill was extended in a northerly direction towards the Derwent (which lies in the valley on the other side of the hill feature on the left known as Scarthin Nick.) If this extension had not been made, it is possible that the corner of the lower mill would have become visible behind the upper. What is more, there is now a new watercourse running beside a newly constructed road, and carried over a wooden aqueduct to the upper mill. In 1783, this watercourse must have run into the old one above the bridge, 'off the picture', since there is no sign of it in the moonlit scene.[1]

Surrounding the mills, as can be seen in both of Wright's pictures, were a number of other, lesser buildings, chiefly warehouses,[2] and at a little distance, a model village of dwelling houses and shops, constructed to serve a whole community of workmen employed in the mills. By 1789 Cromford was absorbing several hundreds of workmen, with a terrifyingly high proportion of children. A Scottish spinner, Archibald Buchanan, who learnt his trade at Cromford in 1783, says the factory was kept going night and day: 'the spinning went on at night; the preparation [carding, roving etc.] was made in the day'.[3] In his first picture, Wright shows the night shift under the moon, with every window in the mills blazing with naked candles, concealing hundreds of inflammable spinners inside. Precautions against fire were not taken and conflagrations in factories were a common spectacle. Workmen and machinery burnt as merrily as they do nowadays in aeroplanes. It was left to a later generation—the humanitarian one—to introduce proper fire precautions by using metal in factory construction, thereby incidentally setting architecture off on a new course.

Nowhere in England was the future being plotted with such devastating accuracy. And like all revolutions it was deplored by traditionalists who saw the countryside going to

1 Astonishingly enough, this watercourse is included on the map of 1777 at Sheffield—but it is clear that the new stream was drawn in later.

2 Some of the smaller buildings are still in existence, such as the one in front of the upper mill, shown in the daylight scene, and the one on the extreme left of this mill in the same picture (not visible, as it should be, in the night scene, and therefore constructed in about the late '80's).

3 Quoted by Fitton and Wadsworth, 1958, p. 99.

rack and ruin under its scourge. The Hon. John Byng, later fifth Viscount Torrington, rightly saw in this beehive the destruction of the happy-go-lucky world he loved:

'Speaking as a tourist', he writes in 1790, 'these vales have lost all their beauties; the rural cot has given place to the lofty red mill, and the grand houses of overseers; the stream perverted from its course by sluices and aqueducts, will no longer ripple and cascade.—Every rural sound is sunk in the clamour of cotton works, and the simple peasant (for to be simple we must be sequester'd) is changed into the impudent mechanic... The bold rock opposite this house [the Black Dog at Cromford] is now disfigur'd by a row of new houses built upon it; and the vales are every way block'd up by mills. I saw the workers issue forth at 7 o'clock, a wonderful crowd of young people, made as familiar as an eternal intercourse can make them; a new set then goes in for the night, for the mills never leave off working... These cotton mills, seven stories high, and fill'd with inhabitants, remind me of a first rate man of war; and when they are lighted up, on a dark night, look most luminously beautiful...'[1]

Even Torrington had the grace to concede that Arkwright's sinister men-o'-war had unwittingly trailed beauty in their wake.

Wright's second picture resembles the present appearance of the site more faithfully than the night scene, because nineteenth-century additions to the Cromford site are here concealed behind the large upper mill in the middle distance which has altered little with the years,[2] and because nothing remains of the lower mill except its foundations. On this occasion the artist painted a companion piece to be hung to its left, showing the countryside continuing in a northerly direction to the Derwent Valley [Plate 330]. The two pictures do not quite form a continuous panorama, since the feature of Scarthin Nick is in actuality broader between the two. But this is as it should be, on the assumption that a gap would be left between the two landscapes as they hung on the wall, in such a way that the spectator could in imagination fill in the intervening space for himself, pursuing the course of the road as it disappears behind the rock outcrop.[3] The left-hand picture shows the Derwent winding through the valley toward Cromford Bridge in the distance, Arkwright's church, a fisherman's rest (now in ruins) beside the bridge, and on the top of the hill to the left, his new residence of Willersley Castle. Wright may have planned a third landscape to hang to the right of the daylight mills, to form a triptych: a much smaller picture showing a *Cut through the rock, Cromford* [Fig 139] continues the landscape in the direction of Cromford Market Place, but no work on the scale of the others is recorded. The creation of the A.6 has changed the topography to such an extent that the view is now barely recognisable, the high feature on the right, for example, having disappeared.

Hidden among the trees in the middle distance of the daylight mill scene below the lookout tower on the hill, is situated Arkwright's brick residence, Rock House, which is still in existence. He had selected this site so that he could survey his mills directly from above and make sure, day and night, that everything was running smoothly. By the early '80's the empire was sufficiently under control to enable him to switch his role from that of overseer to that of squire. He purchased most of the land around Cromford, and set about building a castle on the hill on the other side of the Derwent, from where the Cromford mills and his town planning were no longer visible, blocked from sight as they were by the high feature of Scarthin Nick. His new Masson Mills, built a little higher up in the early '80's, were also out of sight of the Castle. The siting as well as the architectural pretensions of this showy Estate is the most eloquent testimony to Arkwright's graduation from industrialist to country gentleman. But as it turned out the whole operation was conducted more for the benefit of his descendants than for himself.

He purchased the Estate in the late 1780's and employed a London architect, William Thomas, to build him a suitable residence in the medieval-Georgian taste. In June of 1789 Torrington visited it:

'[We] went to where Sr. R:A is building for himself a grand house (Wensley [*sic*] Castle) in the same castellated stile as one sees at Clapham; and *really* he has made a *happy* choice of ground, for by sticking it up on an unsafe bank, he contrives to overlook, not see, the beauties of the river, and the surrounding scenery...'[4]

Fig 139 *Cut through the Rock, Cromford*
c 1790
$18\frac{1}{8}$ x $22\frac{1}{8}$ in / 46 x 56.2 cm   Dr and Mrs William S. Dale
Cat 314   Pl 333

1 Torrington, 1935, II, pp. 194 ff., entry for 18th June 1790.

2 It lost two storeys in the 1920's. The wooden aqueduct to the right of this mill was replaced in 1821 by a stone and iron construction which is still there.

3 This road or track is still in existence in part but has been abandoned since the creation of the valley road.

4 Torrington, 1935, II, p. 40, entry for 14th June 1789.

1 *Op cit.*, II, p. 196, entry for 19th June 1790.

2 See Davies, 1811, pp. 484 ff.

3 This will is cited by Fitton and Wadsworth, 1958, p. 97.

4 J. P. Malcolm, *Gentleman's Magazine*, 1793, describes a visit to Matlock in August 1792 on the day of Sir Richard's funeral. From this account it transpires that Sir Richard is to lie in Matlock Church 'till a chapel now erecting and begun by him shall be finished'. Stevens, 1965, p. 47, entry for 29th October 1792 (after Sir Richard's death): 'Saw Sir Richard Arkwright's new church'. He explains that he had been riding through Matlock Dale, so this presumably is Cromford.

5 *Chartism*, Ch. VIII, *Miscellaneous Essays*, ed. Chapman & Hall, p. 166.

6 See Baines, *c.* 1835, pp. 163 ff.; Mantoux, ed. 1961, pp. 222–3.

7 Wright to Richard Arkwright junior, 12th December 1790; Arkwright MSS.

8 'Sir Rich.d was much pleased w.th the execution of his picture...' Wright to the younger Arkwright, 21st January 1790; Arkwright MSS.

9 Wright to Richard Arkwright junior, 16th January 1791; Arkwright MSS.

A year later Torrington pays it a second visit:

'... I took a short walk to look... at Sr Rd A's new house, (of which I spoke last year.) The inside is now finishing; and it is really, within, and without, an effort of inconvenient ill taste; ... the ceilings are of gew-gaw fret work...'[1]

It must have been about this time that Wright painted it. A year later it was damaged internally by fire[2] and it is hard to see how the old man ever had the chance of inhabiting it. It was still not ready at his death: for in his will he requested his son to complete it in the manner in which it had been begun.[3] In true Anglican spirit, a Castle had to be accompanied by a Church. Arkwright built his between the Derwent and the mills, and Wright dutifully records its presence near the bridge, looking forlorn but pretty. It was later gothicised.[4] Wright also shows the gatehouse by the entrance to Willersley and some buildings beyond it on the left, which are still standing.

At the same time (1790–91) the artist was employed to paint portraits of the family to be hung at Willersley [Plates 323, 325, 328, 329]. Sir Richard as the proto-*M. Bertin* had of course to occupy a canvas to himself, alone in his glory, in a style which would remind his descendants of his years of struggle, not of the squire he finally consented to become. Wright's vision of him is the same as that of Carlyle, who describes Arkwright as that 'plain, almost gross, bag-cheeked, pot-bellied Lancashire man, with an air of painful reflection, yet also of copious free digestion...'[5] Perhaps because aspersions had been cast on his qualifications as an inventor, he preferred to be shown accompanied, not by a plan of his industrial empire, the creation of his own undoubted genius, but by a model of the spinning frame he claimed to have invented, just as Hurt wished to be accompanied by a sample of his iron ore, and Oldknow by a bundle of muslin. This beautiful fragment of still life [Fig 140]—the one object Wright guarded in his studio from romping sons, daughters and nieces—is a faithful replica of the machine which revolutionised the cotton industry and remained the basic model for generations: consisting of a wheel which sets in motion the pairs of rollers of increasing rapidity of rotation, resulting in the production of a hard and firm thread calculated for warps, just as Hargreaves's spinning jenny was adapted for spinning weft, so that the two machines, in spite of occasionally coming into conflict, together transformed the economic structure of England.[6]

Before we number among Sir Richard's attainments that of patron of the arts, we should ask ourselves to what extent such an esoteric pastime ever engaged his mind. No evidence has come to light of his interest in this subject beyond a passing and enigmatical reference in one of Wright's letters: 'Sir Rich.d has sent the persons card where he saw the Groupe of Charity he sometime expressd a wish for me to paint, w.ch looks as if he continued his intention'.[7] This proves at least that he was not an utter Philistine. He also expressed his approval of his own portrait;[8] but narcissism and the dawn of the aesthetic sense are not the same thing. It is obvious that art to him was no more than a marginal preoccupation. Wright's letters to the son bear out what on *a priori* grounds we would have assumed to be the case: that the son and not the father was the artist's patron. The eight surviving letters on the subject of the portraits are all addressed to the son. What is more, the four large canvases—not only the portraits of the son's own family but the one of Sir Richard himself—as well as the *Boy blowing the Bladder* [Plate 320] were destined for the son's residence at Bakewell, not for the father's at Cromford; and it was only when the son succeeded to Willersley that the pictures were transferred there. The *Ullswater Lake* [Plate 345] was the son's, not the father's, purchase. It emerges from this correspondence that Wright painted the portraits of Sir Richard and of *Richard Arkwright, his wife and child* [Plates 323, 325] in his house at St Helen's in 1789–90; that they were hung side by side at Bakewell; that four portraits had already been commissioned by 1790 but that it was not until the following year that the series was completed with the two groups of children [Plates 328, 329] for the same room.[9] Instead of painting the children at Derby, Wright travelled to Bakewell in order to catch them against their own background. Evidently St Helen's was not regarded as a suitable setting for boys accompanied by a goat and an enormous kite.

In the room at Bakewell, later at Willersley, and today in a house near Stratford-on-Avon, what a contrast there was (and is) between this monument [Plate 323] to the triumph of ruthlessness (painted, we must remember, in the age of Hoppner and the young Lawrence), and the portraits Wright painted of the two succeeding generations [Plates 325, 328, 329]! That daughter-in-law, those grandchildren with their innocent goat and kite, that only son[1] who tricks us into supposing he is resting on his laurels but who, far from eating away his father's fortune, proved in his own way no less shrewd and died an even richer man—are now prepared to play their parts in the leisurely world just as though they were tracing their ancestry as far back as the Burdetts and the Poles. One may wonder whether Sir Richard would ever have settled down contentedly at Willersley. There can be no question that the second generation is at ease there. They even decided to cover the bare walls of the Castle with useless objects other than pious family portraits. At the sale of the contents of Wright's studio after his death, Richard Arkwright junior carted off to Willersley the large *Ullswater Lake* [Plate 345], one of the most famous of the artist's late landscapes; and this civilised gesture, symptomatic of the industrialist's new-found security, was noted with approval by a local historian ten years later: 'It [Willersley Castle] contains several excellent family portraits by Wright of Derby, particularly a whole length of Sir Richard Arkwright; and also some smaller pieces[2] by the same ingenious artist, as well as the sublime view of Ulls-water-lake…'[3] The moment was ripe for the absorption of a new breed of man into the mainstream of English social life.

1 Susannah Hurt was his half-sister, the daughter of Sir Richard's second wife whom he married (1761) shortly after the death of the first.

2 This historian (Davies) is presumably referring to a small *Grotto with Julia* [Plate 216] of 1780, and to two genre pieces showing a boy and a girl with bladders, one dated 1790 [Plates 320, 321]. It is not known when the first entered the collection. The bladder pictures were already at Willersley by 1793.

3 Davies, 1811, pp. 484–5.

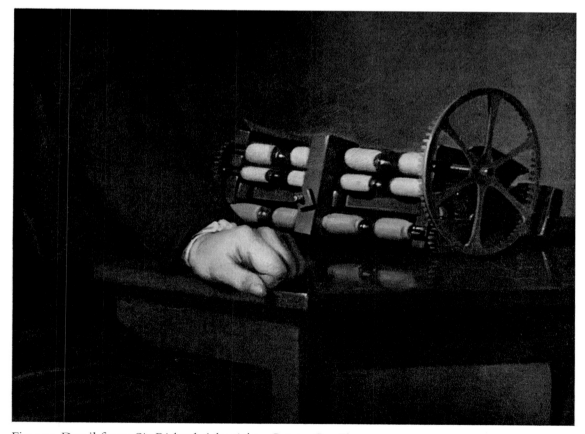

Fig 140 Detail from *Sir Richard Arkwright* Cat 1 See Fig 12

IV Catalogue Raisonné

The following catalogue embodies substantial quotations from Wright's Account Book and all such quotations are shown in Bold type. An attempt is made in the catalogue raisonné to record all paintings by the artist, although in practice the attempt must fail, since he did not record every picture in his Account Book and some that he omitted must have left no trace. All pictures entered in his Account Book are listed whether they can be identified or not. This system has the disadvantage that duplication is inevitable. Thus, an entry in the Account Book may not be sufficiently explicit to permit identification with a known picture (owing to the fact that a sitter has married since the picture was painted and has changed her name and so forth); the latter may, therefore, be listed elsewhere instead of in its proper place. The works have been divided into the following sections:—

1   PORTRAITS page 174

Throughout this section the material is arranged on a sequence of facing pages. On the left hand page are quoted all those entries from Wright's Account Book relating to Portraits and these are placed in alphabetical order of sitters' names. On the right hand page is the author's catalogue of extant portraits also in alphabetical order of sitters' names. In cases where a portrait mentioned in the Account Book is extant the catalogue entry for it will normally be found immediately adjacent on the facing page.

No differentiation is made between single and group portraits. Maiden and married names of female sitters are cross-referenced wherever necessary. In cases where the names of sitters of known portraits do not occur in the Account Book and where the title is given in inverted commas we cannot be sure that the traditional name is correct.

Biographies of and other information about the sitters are given here only in the cases where they are not discussed in detail in Part III.

Wright's Account Book has the following helpful note:

	f	I
The size of a Kit Cat frame is	3	$\frac{1}{4}$
by	2	4
A 3qrs is	2	6
by	2	I
An half length is	4	2
by	3	4

This means that wherever he refers to a Kit Cat portrait in cases where the original is lost, we know it was 36¼ by 28 in; a 3 quarters 30 × 25 in; and a half length 50 × 40 in. We must not be misled by the phrase '3 quarters' which has nothing to do with the extent of the body of the sitter shown, but only refers to the dimensions of the canvas—smaller in fact, than the normal half length. '3 qrs' is also used by Wright to describe the dimensions of some landscapes.

Sizes are given as 50 by 40 in, 30 by 25 in. etc. in spite of the fact that often a fraction of an inch has been lost in relining.

In Sections 2–6 the quotations from the Account Book are printed on the same page as the catalogue entries. In cases where the Account Book item is extant the catalogue entry follows immediately thereafter.

References are given to lost works only when it is reasonable to assume that these works were genuine: thus, portraits exhibited in the late nineteenth century by descendants of the sitters, or paintings of any subject which disappear at a certain stage, but when last heard of were in collections which can with reasonable certainty be traced back to the original purchasers, are given. Copies of lost works only are recorded, unless the copies of known works have some historical interest.

Drawings, water-colours, gouaches are not listed except in cases where works in these media are referred to because of a special significance (e.g. studies for known oil paintings, and some highly finished charcoal portraits).

Exhibitions are only cited in cases where information is given in the catalogue which does not appear here, such as earlier exhibitions.

It may be claimed by readers who have not gone into the matter deeply, that too much reliance is placed in the catalogue on dating on the basis of the location of an entry in the Account Book. But dated pictures (and those whose dates, arrived at on stylistic grounds, can hardly be disputed) have shown such a bewildering tendency to get listed *precisely* in the section of the Account Book where one would expect to find them, that dates suggested on this evidence alone for pictures in other categories are only positively rejected in cases where evidence is overwhelming to the contrary.

Only surviving pictures, or pictures about which some substantial record has survived, are numbered. The 340 odd pictures so numbered represent a mere fraction of his output.

BIBLIOGRAPHICAL REFERENCES
All sources referred to are listed in the Bibliography beginning on page 285. The abbreviations used are there explained and listed.

REFERENCES TO THE MAIN TEXT
Against each catalogue entry will be found not only references to Plates and Figures, but also page numbers corresponding to the pages in the text where the paintings in question are discussed or mentioned. Drawings are not indexed in this way since they are not separately catalogued; nor are incidental references to pictures in the catalogue and appendices where they occur under other headings. Numbers above the line refer to footnotes.

REFERENCES TO THE PLATES
The numbers in bold to the right of each catalogue entry refer to the plates in Volume II

OWNERS
For details of ownership reference should also be made to the list in Volume II.

Throughout this section the material is arranged on a sequence of facing pages. On the left hand page are quoted all those entries from Wright's Account Book relating to Portraits and these are placed in alphabetical order of sitters' names. On the right hand page is the author's catalogue of extant portraits also in alphabetical order of sitters' names. In cases where a portrait mentioned in the Account Book is extant the catalogue entry for it will normally be found immediately adjacent on the facing page.

ABNEY TO ARKWRIGHT

ABNEY

Half length of M.ʳ Abney, £25.4; D.º of M.ʳˢ Abney, £25.4; A Conversation picture of 3 of their Children (followed by an illegible word which resembles 'blond'), no price. Among pictures of late 1780s. *Portrait of W. E. Abney*, lent to Derby, 1866 (96) and 1870 (806) by Rev. E. H. Abney. Pilkington, 1789, II, p. 83 says that an Edward Abney was in occupation of Lord Melbourne's house at Kings-Newton at that date; he was the second son of an Abney of Mearsham.

ABSONOR

M.ʳ Absonor among sitters at Retford, undated. Winter 1759–60 or 1760.

ALDERSON

A 3 q.ʳˢ of M.ʳ Alderson, £12.12. This is followed by **D.º a copy of D.º**, also **£12.12**; among pictures which are chiefly late. A Mrs. Harriet Alderson was living at Wyaston Grove, near Ashbourne in the mid-nineteenth century.

ALLEN (see also **CARVER**)

Parson Allen, £6.6 among sitters at Derby, undated but among portraits of *c* 1760.

ARKWRIGHT

A full length of S.ʳ R.ᵈ Arkwright, £52.10. This is 1 opposite.

A 3 q.ʳˢ copy of S.ʳ R.ᵈ Arkwright, £12.12. This may be 2 opposite.

ABNEY TO ARKWRIGHT

1 SIR RICHARD ARKWRIGHT

Colonel Peter Arkwright

SIZE   95 × 60 in / 241.3 × 152.4 cm   pp 17, 27, 66, 74, 97, 103, 162, 168–9   **323**

PROVENANCE   Has remained in Arkwright family since it was painted.

ENGRAVED   Mezzotint by J. R. Smith dated 5th May 1802, which gives the date of the portrait as 1790.

EXHIBITIONS   Tate, 1958 (29) for further details.

Letter from Wright to R. Arkwright junior dated 21st January 1790 (Arkwright MSS) proves it was completed by then, and was therefore certainly started in the previous year. Destined for the younger Arkwright's residence at Bakewell and delivered there before 3rd March 1790 (as emerges from undated letter from Wright to Arkwright on which the latter or his deputy has added the note 'Paid by a bill 3^d March [£] 64–14', the additional items being frame, packing and transport).

2 SIR RICHARD ARKWRIGHT

Lord Belper

SIZE   30 × 25 in / 76.2 × 63.5 cm

PROVENANCE   Presumably the picture referred to in a letter from Richard Arkwright junior, 21st January 1790 (Arkwright MSS): 'As soon as I have finish'd a copy of Sr Richd Arkwrights picture for Mr Strutt wch will be in the course of this week if nothing prevents me…'

EXHIBITIONS   Derby, 1883 (73). Graves' Galleries, 1910 (24). Derby, 1934 (42).

The Belper version is the only one that has strong claims to be an original, but the one in the National Portrait Gallery is also excellent. Bemrose, 1885, p. 81 writes of a portrait of Arkwright painted for Wedgwood which was presented by Edward Buckley to the Manchester Royal Exchange. It is a copy.

Mrs Arkwright half Length, £26.5. This may have been a portrait of the daughter-in-law of Sir Richard, or of Richard Arkwright's wife before he became Sir Richard (1786). It is not quite certain that Wright has written 'Mrs' and not 'Mr'.

A Conversation of M^r and Mrs Arkwright & their little Girl full lengths, £126. This is 3 opposite.

A conversation picture of 3 of Mr Arkwright Children, £94.10; D^o of D^o, £94.10. These are 4 and 5 opposite.

ASHBY

A 3 q^{rs} picture of Mr Ashby, £12.12. Following on note of 1787.

ASHLEY, see **BATHURST**

3 **RICHARD ARKWRIGHT, HIS WIFE MARY and CHILD**

Colonel Peter Arkwright

SIZE $96 \times 62\frac{1}{2}$ in / 243.8 × 158.7 cm   pp 17, 27, 162, 168–9   **325**
Signed and dated on stone slab to Arkwright's right 'I Wright pinx! / 1790'.
PROVENANCE   Has remained in Arkwright family since it was painted.
EXHIBITIONS   Tate 1958 (30) for further details.
Letter from Wright to Richard Arkwright junior dated 1st December [1790] (Arkwright MSS.) proves it was completed by then. By 12th December it had been delivered and hung as pendant to that of Sir Richard (letter in same series of that date, and another of 18th December.) Paid for by 16th January 1791.

4 **THREE CHILDREN OF RICHARD ARKWRIGHT WITH A GOAT**
Colonel Peter Arkwright

SIZE 77×60 in / 195.6 × 152.4 cm   pp 17, 71, 162, 168–9   **328**
PROVENANCE   Has remained in Arkwright family since it was painted.
EXHIBITIONS   Tate, 1958 (31) for further details.

5 **THREE CHILDREN OF RICHARD ARKWRIGHT WITH A KITE**

Colonel Peter Arkwright

SIZE 77×60 in / 195.6 × 152.4 cm   pp 17, 71, 162, 168–9   **329**
PROVENANCE   Has remained in Arkwright family since it was painted.
EXHIBITIONS   Derby, 1883 (66). Graves' Galleries, 1910 (17). Derby, 1934 (144).
Letter from Wright to Richard Arkwright junior dated 1st December [1790] (Arkwright MSS.) proves that the two portraits had been commissioned by then. Letter in same series of 16th January 1791 shows that they had not been begun by then, but were to be very shortly. Letter of 27th June 1791 shows that they were then nearly completed.
The children in the kite picture are: left Robert (b. 1783); centre Richard (b. 1781); right Peter (b. 1784). Those in the goat picture are: left Elizabeth (b. *c* 1780); centre, on the goat, Charles (b. 1786) being supported by John (b. 1785). The little girl with her parents must be Anne.

6 **MRS JOHN ASHTON**

Fitzwilliam Museum, Cambridge (Reproduced by permission of the Syndics)

SIZE 50×40 in / 127 × 101.6 cm   pp 4, 33–4, 99–100   **64**
PROVENANCE   Given to Fitzwilliam anonymously in 1908.
c 1769. Elizabeth (1710–78), daughter of John Brooks of Liverpool.

7 **ELIZABETH ASHTON (MRS JOHN BOSTOCK)**

David Ashton-Bostock Esq

SIZE   *c* 50×40 in / 127 × 101.6 cm   pp 34, 99–100   **66**
c 1769
Elizabeth, daughter of John Ashton, married, first John Bostock; then (1777) Rev. John Yates. This might be the portrait referred to by Carey, 1809, p. 22: 'I lately saw in the possession of the Rev. Mr. Yate [*sic*] of Liverpool, the portrait of a lady, firmly drawn and painted by Wright...'

8 **ANNA ASHTON (MRS THOMAS CASE)**
Captain Everard Radcliffe M.C.

SIZE   *c* 50×40 in / 127 × 10.6 cm   pp 4, 34, 99–100   **65**
c 1769
Represented as shepherdess. Anna, daughter of John Ashton, married (1776) Thomas Case.

ASHTON

Master Ashton, £21.10; among sitters at Liverpool, 1769. This is 10 opposite.

ATHERTON (see also GWILLYM)

M.ʳ Atherton, £10.10; among sitters at Liverpool, 1769. This might be the Peter Atherton of Warrington who according to Baines, c 1835, p. 150 settled in Liverpool about this time. Richard Arkwright had sought financial help from him when Arkwright was a young man. On the other hand it might be a John Atherton, recorded as a slave trader in 1752 (see Part III, note 1, p. 100).

AYRE

Miss Ayre, among sitters at Boston, undated. 1760.

BAILEY

Cap.ᵗ Bailey, £6.6; among sitters at Derby, undated but among portraits of c 1760.

BAINBRIGGE

M.ʳ Bainbrigge, £12.12; M.ʳˢ Bainbrigge £12.12; among sitters from 1st February 1760. These are listed again: For 2 half lengths of M.ʳ & M.ʳˢ Bainbrigge, £25.4; and again a third time: M.ʳ Bainbrigge, £12.12; M.ʳˢ Bainbrigge £12.12; among sitters at Derby. Note in Account Book following immediately on a note dated 10th August 1761: To 2 ½ length frames C & G [carved and gilt] for M.ʳ Bainbrigge, £7.7. What must have been two further portraits are listed among sitters at Derby: M.ʳ Bainbrigge; M.ʳˢ Bainbrigge at £6.6. each. Also c 1760. Portraits of *Thomas Bainbrigge* and his wife lent to Derby, 1866 (100 and 101) by T. Bainbrigge. Thomas Bainbrigge of Derby; Sheriff of the County in 1760. J. P. 1760. Wright rented 26 Queen Street, Derby from 1793 onwards from Thomas Bainbrigge Jnr.

BAKER

M.ʳ Baker, £6.6; among sitters at Derby, undated, but listed with portraits of c 1760.

BAKEWELL

M.ʳ Bakewell, £21; among portraits of c 1777–80. This is 11 opposite.

BALGUY or BAULGY

A 3 q.ʳˢ w.ᵗʰ a hand of M.ʳ Balguy, £15.15; D.º of M.ʳˢ Balguy w.ᵗʰ D.º, £15.15. These entries come almost immediately after a date 1783. Two further pictures: M.ʳ Baulgy, M.ʳˢ Baulgy, £6.6. each are among sitters at Derby, undated, but listed with portraits of c 1760. They are therefore probably not the same people.

BARKER (see also CARVER)

A full Length of M.ʳ Barker of Bakewell, £52.10. Among pictures which are chiefly late.

BATEMAN

Miss Bateman, £3.3; among sitters at Derby, c 1760.
Hugh Bateman Esq.ʳ 3 q.ʳˢ w.ᵗʰ a hand, £16.16. This must be 12 opposite.

A 3 q.ʳˢ of M.ʳˢ Bateman, £17.17 (changed from 16 guineas). Listed in Account Book within a few entries of Hugh Bateman, and therefore presumably his wife Temperance, daughter of John Gisborne, whom he married in 1786.

M.ʳ Rich.ᵈ Bateman w.ᵗʰ a hand, £15.15; among pictures of c 1790. Possibly the Richard Bateman (d. 1821), son of Richard and grandson of the Hugh Bateman who died in 1777. He had a brother named Hugh who may be identical with the Hugh Bateman above.

9 **MRS NICHOLAS ASHTON**

David Ashton-Bostock Esq

SIZE   50 × 40 in / 127 × 101.6 cm   pp 4, 34, 99–100   **67**
PROVENANCE   Ashton family since it was painted; sale, Sotheby's, 7th July 1965 (143); acquired on London Art Market (1965–66) by another member of the Ashton family.
Mary Warburton Philpot (d. 1777, aged 37), married (1763) Nicholas, son of John Ashton. She was the heiress of the Warburtons of Hefferston Grange, Cheshire.

10 **JOHN ASHTON**

Formerly Ashton Collection

SIZE   50 × 40 in / 127 × 101.6 cm   pp. 4, 34–5, 99–100   **68**
ENGRAVED   Mezzotint by W. Pether 1770 (illus. *Connoisseur*, April 1923).
EXHIBITIONS   ? S. of A., 1770 (303).
1765–1815. Son of Nicholas and Mary Ashton. A copy by Williamson of *c* 1800 or later in Ashton-Bostock Collection [Plate 68]. The original was destroyed in the bombing of London, 1943.

11 **ROBERT BAKEWELL**

Richard Dyott Esq

SIZE   50 × 40 in / 127 × 101.6 cm   pp 17, 72   **208**
PROVENANCE   Robert Bakewell's daughter Frances died unmarried, leaving the portrait to a cousin named Dyott; in whose family it has remained.
EXHIBITIONS   Birmingham, 1833 (88), lent by General Dyott.
c late '70's.
Robert (later Sir Robert) Bakewell was made Deputy Lieutenant for the County of Derby on 2nd March 1762 when he was a very young man.

12 **HUGH BATEMAN**

Formerly Mrs. Sacheverell Bateman (1910)

SIZE   Unknown   p 128
EXHIBITIONS   Graves' Galleries, 1910 (44). Since the entry in the Account Book is on the same page as the portrait of the Bateman boy (see below), among pictures which are chiefly late, it is presumably a portrait of the Hugh Bateman (1756–1824) who was the boy's father. There was another Hugh Bateman who died in 1777 aged 87, who may have been this Hugh's grandfather.

A full-length of Master Bateman, £31 (? £51).10. This is 13 opposite.

BATHURST

BAULGY, see **BALGUY**

Cap. **Bathurst, £10.10;** listed among portraits of very early 1770's. This is 14 opposite.

BENNETT

M. **Bennet, £6.6;** listed among portraits of *c* 1762–65. All these entries are crossed out and the same picture is listed again among the same sitters: **A 3 q.** **of M.** **Tho.** **Bennet, £6.6.** This is 16 opposite.

BENTLEY

A Copy of M. **Bentley Kit Cat, £21;** listed among pictures just after 1780. This might conceivably have been a commemorative portrait of Wedgwood's partner Thomas Bentley who died in 1780. The portrait of Bentley at Leigh Hill Place is not by Wright, though ascribed to him.

A full Length of Miss Bentley, £31.10; among pictures which are chiefly late.

BERESFORD

M. **Beresford, £6.6;** listed among portraits of *c* 1762–65. All these entries crossed out and the same picture is listed again among the same sitters: **M.** **Beresford, £6.6.** His name occurs in the Account Book immediately after that of Boothby, so he is probably the Francis Beresford who had financial dealings with Wright and Boothby.

BERIDGE

Rev. **M.** **Beridge, £28.1** (changed from £25.4), among pictures of *c* 1782–85. This is 17 opposite.

D. [e.g. small head] **of D.** **Beridge, £8.8;** and **M.** **Beridge, small oval, £8.8.** Following

13 **RICHARD SACHEVERELL BATEMAN AS A BOY**

SIZE   50 × 40 in / 127 × 101.6 cm   pp 17, 48, 71, 128   **336**
PROVENANCE   Bateman family.
EXHIBITIONS   Graves' Galleries, 1910 (60). Derby, 1934 (1).
Richard Sacheverell Bateman (1788–94), son of Hugh and Temperance Bateman. A book lower left is entitled *L'Ami des Enfants*. This is followed by '*Par M.B....*', but the author's name is not legible. On right is a four-line verse in Italian:
'*Io sulla Tela solitaria e mesta*
Voi souvente [sic] in voi cerco, e trovo solo
Un silenzio, un orror, che d'alto duolo
M'empie, e gli occhi mi bagna, e'l piè m'arresta.'
('On the solitary, mournful canvas I often gaze at your image in search of you, but discover nothing but silence, terror, filling my heart with grief, bathing my eyes in tears, arresting my step.') The Italian is not good and may have been faultily transcribed.
Beneath is the name of Hugh Bateman and the date 1795, neatly printed and not necessarily in Hugh Bateman's own hand. The portrait must have been painted *c* 1794 or slightly earlier, just before the child's death.

Mrs. F. E. Fitz Herbert Wright

14 **CAPTAIN HENRY BATHURST**

SIZE   30 × 35 in / 76.2 × 63.5 cm   pp 17[3], 36, 38   **83**
Dressed as officer in the Blues. Son of Peter Bathurst who was the younger brother of 1st Earl Bathurst. Style of *c* 1770–71. He became Lieutenant in 1762, Capt./Lieutenant in 1767, and Captain in 1770. He was out of the Army List after 1787.

Lady Hervey-Bathurst

15 **MRS HENRY BATHURST**

SIZE   30 × 25 in / 76.2 × 63.5 cm   pp 33, 36, 125, 148   **84**
PROVENANCE   Shirley Collection, Ettington.
EXHIBITIONS   'Pictures from Hampshire Houses', Winchester/Southampton, 1955 (87), as artist unknown. Catalogue records attribution to Wright.
Companion to above. *c* 1770–71. Mrs. Henry Bathurst was the daughter of William Ashley of Derby and the wife of Captain Bathurst.

Lady Hervey-Bathurst

16 **THOMAS BENNETT**

SIZE   30 × 25 in / 76.2 × 63.5 cm   pp 17, 29, 69   **30**
PROVENANCE   Bennett family; Mrs. J. H. Powell (1934) by whom bequeathed to Derby.
EXHIBITIONS   Derby, 1866 (207) lent by Mrs. Bennett. Derby, 1934 (15).
A Derby attorney. On stylistic grounds one feels inclined to date this 1760, rather than slightly later as indicated by the Account Book.

Derby Museum & Art Gallery

17 **REV. BASIL BURY BERIDGE**

SIZE   50 × 40 in / 127 × 101.6 cm   pp 34, 73   **267**
PROVENANCE   Trustees of Rev. Basil Beridge Sale, Christie's, 8th April 1911 (29); John R. Vanderlip; Paris market; entered Museum 1912.
Catalogue of Kunsthistorisches Museum, 1938 (1721).
Beridge was ordained deacon, 1761; rector and Lord of the Manor of Algarkirk-cum-Fosdyke (Lincs.) from early 1780's to his death in 1808 aged 70 or 71.
Presumably painted *c* 1785 in view of the fact that his body is that of *Stephen Jones* (dated 1785; q.v.), though the portrait of his wife (see below) is dated 1777. The two pictures do not look like pendants.

Kunsthistorisches Museum, Vienna

on the latter entry is the note: **N.B. The D.ʳ paid for both the oval frames at the time he paid for his picture.** This proves his portrait was an oval also. They were therefore companion pieces. The pictures were painted in Derby soon after the marriage (1776) of John Beridge, M. D. to Miss Buckston. Hayley, 1823, I, p. 156 tells us they were done for Hayley in about September of that year, and were monochromes. Wright was on a visit to Derby from Bath that summer.

Two 3 q.ʳˢ Copies of D.ʳ Beridges Grandfather & Uncle, £25.4. Listed on page with a date 1782. It is reasonable to assume that the entry in the Account Book among pictures of *c* 1790: **A head of the late D.ʳ Lynn Beridge, £12.12,** is connected with one of these two, since the price is exactly right.

BINGHAM

M.ʳ Bingham, £6.6; listed among portraits of *c* 1762–65. All these entries are crossed out and the same picture is listed again among the same sitters: **A 3 q.ʳˢ of M.ʳ Tho.ˢ Bingham, £6.6.**

BISCOE

M.ʳˢ Biscoe 3 q.ʳˢ w.ᵗʰ hand, £17.17; among pictures which are chiefly late.

BLUNT

Cap.ᵗ Blunt, among sitters at Boston, undated. 1760.

BOLD OF BOLD, see **HESKETH**

BOOTHBY

A large picture of M.ʳ Boothby, £50.8. The Account Book also contains the entry; **Brooke Boothby Jun. Esq.ʳ D.ʳ to Jos.ʰ Wright. Sep.ᵗ 30.ᵗʰ 1780.** Then follows a number of items, among which is **A Full Length of himself, £50.8.** This was several months before the date on the picture, which is 20 opposite.

Copy of M.ʳ Boothby, £12.12; among portraits before 1777. **M.ʳ Boothby, £6.6.;** among portraits *c* 1762–65. Entry crossed out and the same picture listed again among the same sitters: **M.ʳ Boothby, £6.6.** This last entry has been corrected from £12.12., so there may be a connection between these three entries. They must refer to an earlier portrait or portraits of Boothby.

The bill of 30th September 1780 quoted above also has the item: **Altering Miss Boothby's picture...** What may be a copy of this lost work is *Maria Boothby,* collection Sir Hugo Boothby Bt., canvas 30 × 25 in. Maria (1758–1805) was the sister of Brooke Boothby. J. Steegman, *A Survey of Portraits in Welsh Houses,* Vol. 2, *South Wales,* 1962, No. 33, wrongly accepts as by Wright.

BORROW

M.ʳ Borrow, M.ʳˢ Borrow, £12.12. each; among portraits *c* 1762–65. All entries crossed out and the same pictures listed again among the same sitters: **M.ʳ & M.ʳˢ Borrow half L., £25.4.** On both occasions, Mr. Borrow is listed twice. This may mean there were two portraits of him. The two known portraits are 21 and 22 opposite.

18 **MRS BERIDGE**

SIZE 50 × 40 in / 127 × 101.6 cm   pp 68, 143   **192**
Signed and dated lower left: 'J. WRIGHT/PINX./1777'.
PROVENANCE   Same as above until Paris market. Christie sale No. 28.
EXHIBITIONS   Smith College, 1955 (3). New York, 1960 (19).
Wife of Rev. Basil Beridge (see above).
The same Christie's sale, also by order of the same trustees, had a portrait (30) described as
by Wright of Derby of the same male sitter; oval, 30 × 25 in, 'in black gown, with white
bands; powdered hair'. It is not known whether this Beridge was any relation of Dr.
Beridge of Derby.

Minneapolis Institute of Arts

19 **'HON. THOMAS BLIGH'**

SIZE 30 × 25 in / 76.2 × 63.5 cm   p 68   **200**
PROVENANCE   Purchased from Messrs. Agnew, 1901.
At Manchester as Anon. English School; formerly as Romney. No 'Bligh' appears in
Wright's Account Book and the name of the sitter has probably been lost.
c 1777–80.

Manchester City Art Galleries

20 **BROOKE BOOTHBY**

SIZE 58¼ × 81¼ / 148 × 206.4 cm   pp 17, 48⁴, 70, 72, 102, 127–8, 131   **219**
Signed on tree trunk right 'I. WRIGHT PINX!/1781.'
PROVENANCE   Sir William Boothby, Bt. Sale, Ashbourne Hall: paintings in supplemen-
tary catalogue 11th–12th November 1847 (5); bequeathed by Miss Agnes Ann Best to
National Gallery 1925 (N.G. No. 4132).
EXHIBITIONS   R.A. 1781 (245) as 'Portrait of a Gentleman'. Tate, 1958 (22). Tate, 1959
(380).

Tate Gallery, London

21 **THOMAS BORROW**
Derby Museum & Art Gallery

SIZE 50 × 40 in / 127 × 101.6 cm   pp 17, 28, 29³   **39**
See 22

22 **ANNE BORROW**

Derby Museum & Art Gallery

SIZE 50 × 40 in / 127 × 101.6 cm   pp 17, 28, 29³
PROVENANCE   Borrow or Borough family; Burton Borough Bequest to Derby, 1960.
Companion pieces in the style of the early 1760's.

BOSTOCK, see **ASHTON**

BOYD   Cap.! & M.ʳˢ Boyd, £21; among sitters at Liverpool, 1769.

BROAD   Miss F. Broad, £6.6; among sitters at Derby.

BROME   D.º [e.g. a 3 q.ʳˢ] of F. Brome Esq.ʳ, £12.12.

BROMHEAD   Miss Bromhead, among sitters at Lincoln. Undated. 1760. A portrait said to be of '*Mrs. Bromhead*', 26½ × 21½ in, at Christie's, 4th February 1927 (75).

BROOKE (see also **PIGOT**)   M.ʳ Brooks, among sitters at Doncaster. Undated. 1760. The same entry is repeated among sitters from 1st February 1760 onwards: **M.ʳ Brooks, £12.12**; and again, undated: **For a half Length of M.ʳ Brooks, £12.12.** In all cases the entries are preceded by others for portraits of Mr. and Mrs. Pigot. The portrait of '**Brooks**' is 25 opposite.

BROOKS, see **ASHTON**

BUCKSTON, see **BUXTON**

BURDETT   M.ʳ Burdet, £12.12; among portraits *c* 1762–65. All entries crossed through and the same picture listed again among the same sitters: **M.ʳ Burdet, £12.12.** This is 26 opposite.

BURNHAM   M.ʳ Burnham, M.ʳˢ Burnham, £12.12. each; among portraits of *c* 1790.

BUXTON   A head of M.ʳ Buxton, £12.12; among pictures of the mid-'90's. This is 27 opposite.

CALDWELL   A small picture of M.ʳˢ Caldwell, £8.8; among portraits of the late 1780's.

CARLEILL   A small Oval of M.ʳ Carleill, £8.8; frame & Case, 16/—. Bemrose, 1885, p. 52 recounts an anecdote which he dates October 1782 concerning the portrait 'of a young gentleman named Carleill'. This is very likely accurate, since five entries after the listing of the portrait in the Account Book, Wright adds the date December 1782.

CARVER   M.ʳˢ Carver, Miss Carver, Miss N. Carver, M.ʳ Carver; among sitters at Eckington, undated. 1760. These are listed again among sitters from 1st February 1760 onwards, at £12.12. each, except that the Christian name in 'Miss N. Carver' has been corrected to 'B.ʸ' (presumably Betty or Elizabeth). The same portraits appear a third time among portraits of 1760 as **For 4 half Lengths of M.ʳˢ Carver Miss &c for D.ʳ Griffith, £50.8.** These four are, in the order in which they appear above: 28, 29, 30 and 31 opposite.

23 **'HON. MRS BOYLE'**

Mackelvie Collection,
Auckland City Art Gallery,
New Zealand

SIZE   30 × 25 in / 76.2 × 63.5 cm   pp 30–31   **46**
PROVENANCE   'Hon. Mrs Boyle', Christie's, 27th July 1945 (120); with Messrs. Agnew.
c 1761–63.
The name of Boyle does not occur in Wright's Account Book and so the sitter's name may
be lost.

24 **BRADSHAW CHILDREN**

Peter Wilmot-Sitwell Esq

SIZE   63½ × 54 in / 161.3 × 137.2 cm   pp 33, 36, 98, 100   **57**
PROVENANCE   Bradshaw family, Barton Blount.
ENGRAVED   Mezzotint by Valentine Green, 1769.
EXHIBITIONS   Derby, 1883 (35).
The children are Francis, Annie (afterwards Mrs. Thomas Porter Bouch, of Duffield), and
Frances. The picture is datable c 1766–68. The daughter of Francis Bradshaw married a
Sitwell of Morley who was a son of one of the Wilmot children Wright painted (q.v.).

25 **WILLIAM BROOKE**

R. D. Plant Esq

SIZE   50 × 40 in / 127 × 101.6 cm   pp 17, 27, 95, 103   **21**
PROVENANCE   In Pigot family since it was painted.
William Brooke (1694–1763) was Mayor of Doncaster 1736, 1743, 1746 and 1751, and
Alderman from 1733 until his death. A man named John France was Mayor when Wright
was in Doncaster. Brooke's daughter married the son of the vicar of Doncaster, William
Pigot. Sale, Sotheby's, 23rd November 1967 (48).

26 **GEORGE BUCKSTON**

Private Collection, U.K.

SIZE   30 × 25 in / 76.2 × 63.5 cm   pp 17, 73, 141–2   **341**
EXHIBITIONS   Derby, 1934 (152).
The style confirms a very late date. Moreover, we know Beridge's father-in-law, George
Buckston of Bradbourne, did not die until 1810. Born in 1721, he looks here as though he
might be in his early seventies.

27 **FRANCIS BURDETT
OF FOREMARK**

Major Peter Miller Mundy

SIZE   50 × 40 in / 127 × 101.6 cm   pp 2, 17, 28–9, 97–8   **38**
PROVENANCE   Mundy family; Rev. Clark-Maxwell Sale, Christie's, 15th May 1936 (19).
EXHIBITIONS   Derby, 1934 (26).
One of six portraits of members of the Derby Hunt painted c 1762–63 and hung at Markea-
ton Hall, the home of Francis Noel Clarke Mundy, who later became Burdett's brother-in-
law. Mundy was included in the series. The other four are: Nicholas Heath, Edward Becher
Leacroft, Launcelot Rolliston and Harry Peckham.

28 **MRS ANN CARVER**
Mrs. and Mr. Ronald Tree

SIZE   50 × 40 in / 127 × 101.6 cm   pp 2, 17, 28, 96–8   **22**
See 31

29 **MISS ANN CARVER**
Mr. and Mrs. Ronald Tree

SIZE   50 × 40 in / 127 × 101.6 cm   pp 2, 17, 28, 96–8, 103   **26**
See 31

30 **MISS ELIZABETH
CARVER**
Formerly Athorpe Collection

SIZE   50 × 40 in / 127 × 101.6 cm   pp 2, 17, 28, 96–8   **28**
See 31

31 **REV. JOHN C. CARVER
OF MORTHEN**

SIZE   50 × 40 in / 127 × 101.6 cm   pp 2, 17, 28, 96–8   **27**
PROVENANCE   Painted for Rev. John Griffiths, D.D., Rector of Eckington (d. 1765). His
daughter Ann married Marmaduke Carver of Morthen, Yorks, who died in 1746 aged 34.
She was therefore a widow when Wright painted her, and this explains her presence at

Rev. John C. Carver's wife and daughter were painted by Wright *c* 1767–70. This is 32 opposite.

Wright's Account Book also has an entry for a much later picture, listed among works of the late '70's or early '80's: **Master Carver, £8.8.**

CASE, see **MOREWOOD**
(see also **ASHTON)**

CAVENDISH

A head of Ld Richd Cavendish, £12.12; listed among pictures of *c* 1787–88. This is repeated on another page.

CHADWICK, CHADWICKE

Miss Chadwick, among sitters at Lincoln, undated. 1760. **A half Length of Jo^s Chadwicke Esq, £25.4.** The entry is repeated: **A half Length of Mr Chadwick, £25.4.** Among late pictures. There is no reason to suppose there was any family relationship between these two.

CHALLENOR

Master Challenor, Miss Challenor, £8.8. each; among sitters at Derby, *c* 1760.

CHASE

Mr Chase, Mrs Chase, £6.6. each; among sitters from 1st February 1760 onwards. They are listed again among portraits of *c* 1760: **For a 3 q^{rs} P.** [picture or portrait] **of Mr Chase, For a 3 q^{rs} of Mrs Chase, £6.6. each.** The pair is listed a third time at these prices.

A second pair of portraits is as follows: **Mr Wm Chase, Mrs Chase, £12.12. each;** among sitters from 1st February 1760 onwards. They are listed again at these prices. Since the two portraits catalogued opposite are what Wright calls three-quarters (30 × 25 in) they can be considered as candidates for the six-guinea, but not the twelve-guinea, pair: 35 and 36 opposite.

Eckington. Her three children were: Ann; Elizabeth who married in 1781 Robert Barker (c 1736–1796), vicar of Youlgreave; and John (d. 1807) of Morthen. The latter's daughter-in-law was an Athorpe of Dinnington, Yorks, and the four pictures descended in the Carver family, a member of which in 1821 took the name of Athorpe. Athorpe Sale, Christie's, 27th April 1934 (93, 92, 94, 96).

The first two passed to the Collection of Ronald Tree by whom they were exhibited Derby, 1934 (126, 122) and New York, 1960 (3, 4). The second two were: Christie's 14th December 1945 (136, 135); Sotheby's 8th February 1950 (117, 116); Sotheby's, 12th July 1967 (109).

Formerly Athorpe Collection

32 SARAH CARVER AND HER DAUGHTER SARAH

SIZE   50 × 40 in / 127 × 101.6 cm   pp 35, 96   **79**
PROVENANCE   Same as above, until Athorpe Sale, lot No. 95; presented to Derby Art Gallery by Mrs. Rose-Innes, 1946.
EXHIBITIONS   Tate, 1958 (1) for further details.
John Carver's wife was the daughter of Thomas Allen of Eyam, and heiress to her mother Elizabeth Middleton of Leam Hall. Their daughter Sarah was still living unmarried in 1803.

Derby Museum & Art Gallery

33 LYNFORD CARYL

SIZE   30 × 25 in / 76.2 × 63.5 cm   pp 68–9, 71   **202**
A copy at Jesus was presented to the College in 1782 by Caryl's niece Miss Roberts, done from the original then in her possession. Quite recently, Jesus has acquired the original. Lynford Caryl was Master of Jesus from 1758 to his death in 1781. He had been Laurence Sterne's tutor at Jesus in the mid-'30's. The portrait was painted shortly before his death.

Jesus College, Cambridge

34 'MISS CATTON' or 'MISS COTTON'

SIZE   50 × 40 in / 127 × 101.6 cm   pp 28, 99   **31**
At St. Louis as Hudson but an authentic Wright of c 1760. A very similar portrait is at Temple Newsam of an unidentified girl (see Cat. 160).

City Art Museum of
St. Louis, Missouri

35 WILLIAM CHASE

SIZE   30 × 25 in / 76.2 × 63.5 cm   pp 69, 73   **205**
Inscribed lower left 'Mr. Willm. Chase/living 1745'.
See 36

36 MRS WILLIAM CHASE

SIZE   30 × 25 in / 76.2 × 63.5 cm   pp 17, 30   **41**
Inscribed lower left 'Mrs. Willm. Chase/living 1745'.
EXHIBITIONS   New York, 1960 (1 and 2). S. Brewin lent to Derby, 1883 (108 and 108A) two half-lengths of 'Mr.' and 'Mrs. Chase' which appeared at Christie's, 18th December 1911 (99) as 'William Chase, Esq., father of the above [referring to the William Chase in the double portrait catalogued below] … his wife … a pair'.
They were almost certainly the Yale portraits. It was Wright's custom, when he painted more than one member of a family, to differentiate in his Account Book by giving no Christian name to the eldest. From his lists of Chases alone one could deduce that the six-guinea pair represented an older married couple than the twelve-guinea pair, and that the 'M^r. W. & M^rs. Chase' catalogued below where they appear together were also the younger pair. Indeed this is borne out by the evidence: the two single portraits surviving are of an older generation than the double portrait, and it does seem reasonable to deduce (what was evidently a tradition in the family kept alive by the remarks in the sale catalogue) that Mr.

For a **Conversation picture of M.^r W & Mrs Chase, £25.4;** among pictures of the early 1760's.
This is 37 opposite.

The Parrot, £3.3; among pictures at Derby, *c* 1760. It sounds as though Wright did a separate picture of the parrot for the young William Chases.

CHESLYN

Rec.^d of Richd Cheslyn Esqr on account for his Picture, £21; under date 25th July 1777. The portrait must therefore have been painted that summer, since Wright only got back from Bath in the middle of June. This is 38 opposite.

For painting Mr Cheslyn's drapery, £12.12. This entry appears among pictures of the very end of his life, and may possibly refer to a touching-up of the picture of 1777.

CLARKE

Miss Clarke, £6.6; among sitters from 1st February 1760. This is repeated among the same sitters, *c* 1760: **For a 3 q.^{rs} Picture of Miss Clarke, £6.6.** It was therefore a 30 × 25 in. The entry is repeated a third time among sitters at Derby, *c* 1760: **Miss Clarke, £6.6.**

Mr Clarke, £10.10; among sitters at Liverpool, 1769.

COCKIN

Miss Cockin, £6.6; among sitters at Derby, undated but among portraits of *c* 1760.

COKE

A Conversation Picture of D. P. Coke Esqr, The Revd Mr Duse Coke & his Lady, £75.12; listed among pictures of the early 1780's. This is 40 opposite.

Mr Charles Coke, £10.10; among sitters at Liverpool, 1769.

Cap.ⁿ Coke of the Blues, £12.12. (Wright notes that he paid £15), among pictures of 1776–80.
See 'COOKE'. This is followed by the entry **Parker Coke Esqr,** to which no price is affixed, and the entry is deleted. This may imply that a portrait of D. P. Coke was projected but not executed. According to the *Derby Mercury* three troops of Horse Guards Blues arrived at Derby in October 1779.

COLTMAN

M.^r & Mrs Coltman a Conversation, £63, listed among pictures of 1770–71. Wright notes against the price **P.^d £100,** but the remaining £37 may be for other payments. This is 41 opposite.

and Mrs. William Chase the elder had a married son named William, and that we have portraits of all four. However, it is not as simple as that. In the first place, the elder Mrs. Chase's feigned oval turns into a Baroque scroll at the bottom, whereas her husband's does not. In the second place, the style proclaims that the two portraits do not date from the same period: Mrs. Chase being *c* 1761–63, he nearly 20 years later. (Cf. *Lynford Caryl* of *c* 1779–80). The answer may possibly turn out to be that the mother was painted first and her husband added later as a pendant. The older Mr. Chase is no doubt the 'eminent banker' recorded in the *Derby Mercury*, 20th May 1784 as having died in his 77th year.
For a full discussion, see Buckley, 1962, pp. 43 ff.

Yale University Art Gallery; gift of Junius S. and Henry S. Morgan

37 MR and MRS WILLIAM CHASE

Lord Butler
(at Gatcombe Park)

SIZE $54\frac{1}{2} \times 75$ in / 138.4 × 190.5 cm   pp 2, 17, 23, 30–1, 39, 70, 156[8]   **50**
Inscribed lower left in same hand as the Yale portraits: 'M.[r] & M.[rs] Will.[m] Chase/m.[d] [married] 1760'.
PROVENANCE   S. Brewin (1883); Sale, Christie's 16th December 1911 (98); Lord Lee of Fareham (by 1934); Samuel Courtauld; passed to the present owner by inheritance.
EXHIBITIONS   Derby, 1883 (97); 1934 (110). For fuller details, see *The Courtauld Collection* ..., London, 1954, No. 244.

38 RICHARD CHESLYN

Private collection, U.K.

SIZE   50 × 40 in / 127 × 101.6 cm   pp 13, 34, 71, 73, 124, 143–4   **190**
PROVENANCE   Barber family; Ethel Hallewell (1934).
EXHIBITIONS   Derby, 1866 (176); 1870 (306); 1883 (18); 1934 (98).
Cheslyn's house Langley Hall passed on his death to a nephew Richard Cheslyn (b. 1771) who married a Barber. He also inherited Wright's portrait.

39 MRS SARAH CLAYTON

Fitchburg Art Museum, Mass., gift of Miss Louise I. Doyle

SIZE   50 × 40 in / 127 × 101.6 cm   pp 34, 36, 99   **63**
PROVENANCE   T. A. Tatton Sale, Christie's, 28th February 1947 (102); Christie's, 18th April 1947 (74); Christie's, 25th June 1948 (135); New York Art Market, 1952.
EXHIBITIONS   Smith College, 1955 (5); New York, 1960 (7).
Sarah Clayton (1712–79) was unmarried and the 'Mrs' is a courtesy title. A pastel portrait of her as a younger woman (demonstrably the same sitter) was bequeathed to the Walker Art Gallery in 1906 by Rev. S. A. Yates. It can be identified as the portrait referred to in Sarah Clayton's will, 1778 (Picton, Tarleton MSS. 11 and 11a, Liverpool Public Library) as being 'The Crayon Picture painted by my late worthy friend M.[rs] Katherine Thornhill & w.[ch] hangs over y.[e] Glass in my dining room...'

40 REV. d'EWES COKE, HIS WIFE HANNAH and DANIEL PARKER COKE, M.P.
Derby Museum & Art Gallery

SIZE   60 × 70 in / 152.4 × 177.8 cm   pp 17, 29, 36, 39, 72–3, 96, 124–5, 137   **225**
PROVENANCE   Was in the Coke family since it was painted until acquired by Derby, 1964–65 (see N.A.C.F. *Report*, 1965, No. 2180).
EXHIBITIONS   Tate, 1958 (23) with further details.
Soon after 1780.

41 MR and MRS THOMAS COLTMAN

Charles Rogers-Coltman Esq

SIZE   50 × 40 in / 127 × 101.6 cm   pp 17, 33, 36–8, 55, 107   **91**
PROVENANCE   Has been in the Coltman family since it was painted.
EXHIBITIONS   British Council, Canada and U.S.A., 'British Painting in the eighteenth century', 1957–58 (81), illus. catalogue in colour. Tate, 1958 (9) for further details.

COPESTAKE

M.ʳ Copestake, Miss Copestake, at £6.6. each, among sitters at Derby. Undated. *c* 1760.

CRAYCROFT

Miss Craycroft, Miss Molly Craycroft; among sitters at Lincoln. Undated. 1760. These are the only two daughters who were still unmarried in 1760, of Robert Cracroft of Hackthorn Hall, near Lincoln by his first wife: Anne (1735–68) who married (1767) Rev. John Langhorne, and Mary (1737–1809) who married a Nelthorpe after 1762. In 1746 Robert Cracroft married *en secondes noces* Rebecca Waldegrave (b. after 1718–d. 1802). The daughters' portraits appear to be missing but one of 1760 said to represent their step-mother is still in the family collection. This is 45 opposite.

CREWE, see **SHUTTLEWORTH**

CROMPTON

M.ʳ Crompton, M.ʳˢ Crompton, £10.10. each, listed among portraits of *c* 1777–80. These are 46 and 47 opposite. What are presumably copies by Wright of these portraits (though the copies are more expensive) are: **Copy of M.ʳ Crompton 3 q.ʳˢ w.ᵗʰ a hand, £14.14,** and **Copy of M.ʳˢ Crompton, £12.12.** Immediately following on these entries are listed two more copies of *Mr.* and *Mrs. Crompton* at the same price.

3 q.ʳˢ of M.ʳ Jos. Crompton, no price entered, listed among pictures of *c* 1790. There were several Joshua Cromptons. This one could have been the son or brother of Samuel.

Miss Crompton, among sitters at Derby, undated. *c* 1760.

CURZON

Master Curzon, £3.3; among sitters at Derby, *c* 1760. Repeated as **Nathaniel Curzon, £3.3;** among sitters at Derby, *c* 1760. This is 48 opposite.

Miss Curzon, £3.3; among sitters at Derby, *c* 1760. This is 49 opposite.

42 THOMAS COLTMAN   See 43   pp 38, 67, 107   **119**
Charles Rogers-Coltman Esq

43 MRS COLTMAN   SIZE $21\frac{3}{8} \times 17\frac{1}{2}$ in / 54.3 $\times$ 43.8 cm each   pp 38, 67, 107   **118**
                              Pair of charcoal studies with white heightening on canvas.
                              Mrs. Coltman is signed and dated bottom right: 'J. WRIGHT/177..' The final digit of the
Charles Rogers-Coltman Esq   date is not legible.

44 SIR GEORGE COOKE,   SIZE   30 $\times$ 25 in / 76.2 $\times$ 63.5 cm   p 36   **86**
BART.   Nelson Gallery of Art as Copley.
                              Sir George Cooke was a cornet of the Royal Horse Guards (Blues). His commission is dated
                              10th April 1766. He became 7th Baronet in 1769 and served in the regiment until 1771. On
                              stylistic grounds the portrait is datable c 1770–71, and the uniform is that of the Royal Horse
                              Guards. It seems therefore as though the sitter's name has been correctly preserved, though
                              the artist's was lost. Wrights were liable to get changed into Copleys in American collec-
Nelson Gallery – Atkins Museum   tions. The picture is not, however, apparently listed in Wright's Account Book: it is con-
(Nelson Fund) Kansas City, Missouri   ceivably the portrait listed as 'Cap.ⁿ Coke of the Blues' among pictures of 1776–80 (see
                              above under 'COKE').

45 'REBECCA' CRACROFT   SIZE   50 $\times$ 40 in / 127 $\times$ 101.6 cm   pp 2, 28, 154   **25**
                              PROVENANCE   Has remained in the family since it was painted.
                              The sitter is identified by a later inscription on the canvas, but she seems to be a younger
                              woman than Rebecca was in 1760, and it is possible that one of the step-daughters is
Private Collection, U.K.   represented.

46 SAMUEL CROMPTON   See 47   pp 69–70, 73, 129   **206**

47 MRS SAMUEL   SIZE   Each 30 $\times$ 25 in / 76.2 $\times$ 63.5 cm   p 69   **207**
CROMPTON   PROVENANCE   Have been in the Crompton family since they were painted.
                              EXHIBITIONS   Derby, 1866 (210 and 212); 1870 (767 and 774); 1883 (14a and 15); Tate,
                              1958 (18 and 19), for further details.
Col. Sir John Crompton-Inglefield   Crompton died in January 1782, so the portraits were ready at latest by 1781.

48 NATHANIEL CURZON,   SIZE   19 $\times$ 15 in / 48.2 $\times$ 38.1 cm   pp 2, 26, 88⁵, 96, 98   **4**
SECOND BARON   The date 1762 on the frame must be false for reasons given below.
SCARSDALE   EXHIBITIONS   Derby, 1870 (772); 1883 (41); Graves' Galleries, 1910 (65).
                              Nathaniel Curzon (1751–1837) is shown as a boy of about five. A date c 1755–56 would be
                              stylistically reasonable; at latest, 1757. A copy is at Locko Park of the same size, also in
                              feigned oval, inscribed on reverse: 'Nathaniel 2nd Baron Scarsdale/Painted by Bethel/a
                              copy from Wright of Derby', according to Locko Park catalogue by Jean Paul Richter,
                              London and Derby, 1901, No. 13. See *Catalogue of the Pictures... at Kedleston*, Derby, 1861,
Viscount Scarsdale   p. 27.

49 LADY CAROLINE   SIZE   18 $\times$ 16$\frac{1}{8}$ in / 45.7 $\times$ 41.3 cm   pp 2, 26, 88⁵, 96, 98   **5**
CURZON   According to Locko Park Catalogue (see above), No. 16, it bears an inscription on reverse:
                              'The Honourable Caroline/Curzon painted by Wright of Derby'. However, the picture
                              has been recently relined and shows no trace of this.
                              EXHIBITIONS   'Works of Art from Midland Houses', Birmingham, 1953 (82). Matlock,
                              1964 (14). Caroline was Nathaniel's younger sister, and her portrait is a pair to the above.

Copy of Lady Curzon, £6.6; among sitters at Derby, *c* 1760.

2 of S.! Nat. Curzon, £12.12 (e.g. six guineas each), following on entry for *Lady Curzon*. These must have been painted between 1758 (when Sir Nathaniel Curzon, the husband of Mary Asheton, died) and 1761 (by which time the son of the above, the Sir Nathaniel Curzon who married Lady Caroline Colyear, had been created 1st Baron Scarsdale). Of course, it is conceivable that the portraits were painted even earlier, in which case they would represent the 1st Lord Scarsdale's father. There were evidently four portraits in all, two of him and two of her, for various members of the family, though one of Lady Curzon could have been by another artist, copied by Wright.

Master Penn Curzon; Master P. Curzon, £4.4. each, among sitters at Derby, *c* 1760. These were two portraits of the nephew of the 1st Baron Scarsdale, Penn-Asheton (1757–97), the son of Asheton Curzon.

M.! A. Curzon, £6.6; among sitters at Derby, *c* 1760. Asheton Curzon (b. 1729), younger brother of 1st Baron Scarsdale, and father of the Penn Curzon listed above.

DALBY

Miss Dalby, £6.6; among sitters at Derby, *c* 1760.

DARWIN

M.! Darwin, Miss Darwin, among sitters at Newark, undated. 1760. Erasmus Darwin left Newark in 1756, so these could easily have been relations.

A 3 q.rs of D.! Darwin w.th a hand, £15.15; among pictures of *c* 1790. This or another version is 52 opposite.

A Copy of D.! Darwin for M.! Strutt, £15.15; among pictures chiefly of the mid–1790's. This may be 54 opposite.

A copy of D.! Darwin for S.! B. Boothby, £15.15; among pictures chiefly of the mid–1790's.

49

Captain P. J. B. Drury-Lowe

A possible explanation of the presence at Locko Park of the original of her portrait, and a copy of the other, is that her niece, Caroline Esther (b. 1808) married a William Drury Holden of Nuthall Temple, Notts. who took the name and arms of Lowe (1849). The Caroline of the portrait was born in 1753 (she died unmarried in 1841), and so a date *c* 1755–56 would suit her as well as her brother.

50 **ERASMUS DARWIN**

G. P. Darwin Esq; on loan to Darwin College, Cambridge

SIZE   30 × 25 in / 76.2 × 63.5 cm   pp 4, 35, 96, 100–1   **78**

This is the version referred to by Bemrose, 1885, p. 80 note, as belonging to Reginald Darwin, D.D.; Exh. Derby, 1870 (782); Birmingham 1966 (56). The yellow and red flesh tints confirm the date 1770, when Wright was in Lichfield. Another original of this pattern is:

51 **ERASMUS DARWIN**

Mrs. C. R. H. Kindersley

SIZE   30 × 25 in / 76.2 × 63.5 cm   pp 4, 35, 96, 100–1

PROVENANCE   The picture has been in the Darwin family since it was painted; not in that of Erasmus but of his elder brother William Alvey, from whom the present owner is descended. On the stretcher is a near-contemporary label, in the same hand as the label on the stretchers of the portraits of *William Alvey Darwin* and his wife (q.v.): 'Erasmus Darwin, M.D. aged (40) ... A copy of the original both [*sic*] done by Mʳ Wright of Bath (formerly of Derby) 17(70)'. The figures in round brackets are added in a later hand. A version of the same size, not certainly an original, was acquired by the National Portrait Gallery in 1859. A portrait medallion in jasper, done after the *Darwin* of 1770 in Wedgwood's workshops in 1781, is at Leith Hill Place (illus. Finer & Savage, 1965, p. 6).

52 **ERASMUS DARWIN**

Major J. W. Chandos-Pole

SIZE   30 × 25 in / 76.2 × 63.5 cm   pp. 17, 73, 109, 132   **338**

Stevens, 1965, p. 65, entry for 2nd February 1793: 'Went with T. Sales and his wife to see Wright's Paintings—Darwin's portrait there taken for Poole—a strong but severe likeness. His Countenance is seldom without a smile playing around it...' This is the version at Radburne, and therefore datable 1792–93. Since Darwin was by now so famous it is not surprising that Wright had commissions for others of the same pattern.
Three are recorded:

53 **ERASMUS DARWIN**

Sir Robin Darwin

SIZE   30 × 25 in / 76.2 × 63.5 cm   pp 73, 132

PROVENANCE   Not traceable in the Darwin family before the nineteenth century. About early '90's.

54 **ERASMUS DARWIN**

The Lord Belper

SIZE   30 × 25 in / 76.2 × 63.5 cm   pp 17, 73, 132

EXHIBITIONS   Derby, 1883 (69); 1934 (25), with the reproduction of the mezzotint by J. R. Smith (which is different; dated May 1797).
The picture looks authentic. A copy by Rawlinson after Wright of the portrait of Darwin is recorded in Strutt catalogue, 1827, No. 38.

55 **WILLIAM ALVEY DARWIN**

Mrs. Richard Kindersley

SIZE   30 × 25 in / 76.2 × 63.5 cm   pp 13, 68   **176**

PROVENANCE   Has remained in the family of the elder brother of Erasmus Darwin, the sitter William Alvey, since it was painted.
William Alvey Darwin (1726–83). On stretcher is a near-contemporary label: 'William Alvey Darwin aged 50. 14th October 1776. Painted by Mr. Wright of Bath (formerly of Derby) in September 1776'. This is not strictly a pair to the following portrait group, since the latter alone has a feigned oval:

DAY

M! **Day 2 half lengths, £42** (e.g. 20 guineas each), among portraits of *c* 1770. It may be assumed that Wright prepared two of the same pattern. One is 57 opposite; the other could be 58.

DEGG

Mrs **Degg**; among sitters at Derby, undated, *c* 1760. The Degges of Derby were the family of the mother of the Wilmot children (q.v.).

DENBY

M! **Charles Denby, £12.12**; listed among works of the early '80's. Bemrose, 1885, p. 9 tells us that 'Mr. Charles Denby' played the second violin at concerts in the house of Mr. Denby (probably his father) when Wright was a young man. The information comes from Hannah's memoir. Postcript to letter to J. L. Philips, 31st December 1792 (MS. Derby Public Library): 'Tell him [Tate] our late honest & worthy friend C. Denby buried a fine boy about three weeks ago & in ten or twelve days after, gave up the ghost himself, sic transit etc.'

DIXON

M! **Dixon, £6.6**; among sitters from 1st February 1760 onwards. Following on this is: **M^{rs}. Dixon, £6.6.** These entries are repeated among pictures of *c* 1760: **For 2 3 q^{rs} of M! & M^{rs}. Dixon, £12.12,** and a third time among sitters at Derby of the same date and for the same prices. Wright has a note in his Account Book datable *c* 1760 which may refer to this family: **Dixon lives at Luton in Bedfordshire.** The entry is deleted.

DREURY or DREWRY

Master & Miss Dreury, £14.14; among portraits of *c* 1760. This double portrait is repeated among portraits of the same period: **For a Picture of Master & Miss Drewry, £14.14. Miss Drewry** and **Master Drewry** listed among sitters at Lincoln, undated. 1760. Though they are listed one after the other, they presumably also refer to the same double portrait.

DUESBURY

A full Length of Miss Sally Duesbury, £31.10; among pictures *c* 1790–95. This is 59 opposite.

56 **JANE DARWIN, and HER SON WILLIAM BROWN DARWIN**

SIZE   30 × 25 in / 76.2 × 63.5 cm   pp 13, 68   **177**

PROVENANCE Same as No 55.

Jane (1746–1835), daughter of Joseph Brown of Balderton. On stretcher is a near-contemporary label: 'Jane Darwin (wife of William Alvey Darwin) aged 30. 10ᵗʰ October 1776, and William Brown Darwin aged two years and an half. 12th August 1776. Painted by Mʳ. Wright of Bath (formerly of Derby) in September 1776'. The dates where the days of the month are given are the birthdays of the sitters, except in the case of the boy who was 2½ on 12th August.

Mrs. Richard Kindersley

57 **THOMAS DAY**

SIZE   50 × 40 in / 127 × 101.6 cm   pp 4, 17, 33, 34[1], 35–38, 96, 102, 127

PROVENANCE Richard Lovell Edgeworth; Mrs. Rose B. Montagu, one of his descendants (1930); sale Sotheby's, 10th December 1930 (115), sold with letter from Edgeworth dated 21st October 1789 offering the picture to Mrs. Day. This was the year of Day's death.

ENGRAVED Henry Mayer, 1820, reproduced Edgeworth, 1820, I, p. 350.

Edgeworth, Day's great friend, quotes the letter (now in the possession of the National Portrait Gallery) he wrote to Mrs. Day's nephew (1820, II, pp. 105–106): '...I have an excellent picture of Mʳ. Day by Wright; if Mrs. Day [his widow] should wish for it, it is at her service; she may be sure no other person shall have it, but one of my own children. Please to give her this message, with my best respects...'

National Portrait Gallery, London

EXHIBITIONS Birmingham, 1966 (55).

58 **THOMAS DAY**

SIZE   50 × 40 in / 127 × 101.6 cm   References, see 57   **80**

EXHIBITIONS Manchester Art Treasures Exh., 1857 (79); Derby, 1934 (30) and on other frequent occasions.

This excellent version also is original.

The Lord Belper

59 **MISS SALLY DUESBURY**

SIZE   50 × 40 in / 127 × 101.6 cm   pp 17, 71, 131   **337**

PROVENANCE George Dean (1883); Cade Bemrose (1910).

EXHIBITIONS Derby, 1883 (87); Graves' Galleries, 1910 (11).

Bemrose, 1885, p. 75, illus. when in collection of George Dean. Illus. *Apollo*, November 1956. Sally Duesbury, here shown at about the age of eight, was the daughter of the famous Mr. Duesbury of the Derby China Works.

Untraced in U.S.A.

ELLISSON

M.ʳ Ellisson, Mrs Ellisson, M.ʳ & Mrs Ellisson; among sitters at Thorne, undated. 1760. The entries are repeated among sitters from 1st February 1760: **M.ʳ Ellisson, Mrs Ellisson, £12.12 each; Master & Miss Ellisson, £6.6.** The third portrait showed two children, not grown-ups as is suggested by the first entry. The third time the three canvases are recorded, Wright is more specific (among sitters of c 1760): **For 2 half lengths of M.ʳ & Mrs Ellisson, £24.24 [sic]; For a small Picture of Master & Miss Ellisson, £6.6.** In the Account Book Wright records under the date 6th October 1760 the sum of 6 guineas he owed his frame-maker for **2 ½ length frames for M.ʳ Ellisson C & G** (carved and gilt).

FALLOWS

For a whole Length of Mas.ʳ Fallows, £16.16; among pictures of c 1760. This must be the grown-up Mr. Fallows to whom some seventeen years later Wright wishes to appeal to redress a wrong he has suffered at the hands of some 'rascally watermen' (see his letter to his brother from Bath, 9th March 1777, Bemrose, 1885, p. 47): 'Give my compliments to M.ʳ Fallows and tell him, as I spent a day over his picture, he will, I doubt not, do me this favour'.

FENTON

Miss Fenton, £6.6; among sitters from 1st February 1760. This is listed again among portraits of c 1760: **For a 3 q.ʳˢ of Miss Fenton, £6.6,** and a third time among sitters at Derby.

FISHER

M.ʳ Fisher, £6.6; among sitters at Derby.

FLETCHER

John Fletcher of Osmaston an old bald headed man, is a note in the Account Book which does not suggest a patron, but he might have sat for a character study (see page 233). Another Fletcher who was a *bona fide* patron is also listed:

M.ʳ Fletcher, £12.12; among pictures of c 1780; and on a third sheet: **M.ʳ Fletcher owes for Frame & Case £2.6.6,** among pictures of about the same date.

FORRESTER

Mrs Forrester, £10.10; among sitters c 1777–80. J. G. Crompton lent to Derby, 1883 (110) a '*Mrs. Forrester*' ($25\frac{1}{2} \times 28\frac{1}{2}$ in) and a '*Dr. Forrester*' ($25\frac{1}{2} \times 30\frac{1}{2}$ in).

FOSTER

M.ʳ Foster; Mrs Foster; among sitters at Thorne, undated. 1760. The entry is repeated among sitters from 1st February 1760 onwards, as at £6.6. each, and again a third time: **For a 3 q.ʳˢ of M.ʳ & Mrs Foster, £12.12.**

FOWLER

Mrs Fowler, £6.6; among sitters from 1st February 1760 onwards. This is repeated among portraits of c 1760: **For a 3 q.ʳˢ of Mrs Fowler, £6.6.** Mrs. Richard Hope lent to Derby, 1883 (33) a '*Mrs. Fowler*' of the correct size (26 × 30 in). Wright refers to a lady of this name in a letter to his sister from Rome, 4th May 1775 (quoted Bemrose, 1885, p. 36): 'Make comp.ᵗˢ to Mrs Fowler & to her most ingenious & agreeable daughter…'

FOX

Old M.ʳ Fox, £3.3; among sitters at Derby, c 1760. Mrs. D. Hamilton (née Fox) has a portrait called '*William Fox*', 30 × 25 in, which is certainly a copy after a lost Wright of c 1760. It probably reflects the original listed in the Account Book; however, William Fox is believed to have died in 1753 and it may be another member of the Fox family. The Mrs. Fox referred to in Wright's letters to his brother just before sailing for Italy, and soon after his arrival in Rome (see Bemrose, 1885, pp. 28, 30) must be related. In the second letter she is called 'our good friend Mrs Fox'.

To a later generation of Foxes belong the following: **Two 3 q.ʳˢ pictures of M.ʳ & Mrs Fox, £24.4** (an odd price, but perhaps a misprint for £25.4, making the portraits the normal twelve guineas each), among the very latest works (1793–97). These are 62 and 63 opposite.

60 **HON. RICHARD FITZWILLIAM, LATER 7th VISCOUNT FITZWILLIAM OF MERRION**

SIZE   30 × 25 in / 76.2 × 63.5 cm   pp 26, 31, 68, 96   **49**

PROVENANCE   According to the Register in the Fitzwilliam Museum labelled 'Fitzwilliam Museum Donation Book, 1817', p. 13, painted for Samuel Hallifax, P.D., 1764. Given by his son, Rev. Robert Fitzwilliam Hallifax, 1819.

EXHIBITIONS   'Treasures of Cambridge', Goldsmiths' Hall, 1959 (1).

See F. R. Earp, *A Descriptive Catalogue of the Pictures in the Fitzwilliam Museum...*, 1902, No. III, 1.

Lord Fitzwilliam (1745–1816), founder of the Fitzwilliam Museum, who succeeded his father to the title in 1776, was admitted a nobleman at Trinity Hall, November 1761, and took his degree from Trinity Hall in 1764. He is shown wearing the gown of an undergraduate nobleman fellow commoner, of a kind used on special occasions. It can therefore be assumed that he is represented before taking his degree in 1764. Samuel Hallifax, later Bishop of St. Asaph, was fellow and tutor of Trinity Hall and private tutor to Lord Fitzwilliam, and his son was the latter's godson.

Fitzwilliam Museum, Cambridge (Reproduced by permission of the Syndics)

61 **'HENRY FLINT'**

SIZE   30 × 25 in / 76.2 × 63.5 cm   pp 68–9, 73   **196**

PROVENANCE   Sale Sotheby's, 22nd May 1957 (150); Mrs. Arthur Barber (1958); Richard Roberts (1959); Maurice Quick (1963); Sale Christie's, 22nd November 1963 (70); Cyril P. Plant.

Datable on stylistic grounds *c* 1778–80. There is no certainty about the identity of the sitter. Henry Flint was Mayor of Derby in 1770 and 1786. In a letter from Rome of 12th February 1774 (quoted Bemrose, 1885, p. 30), Wright comments: 'M^rs. Flint's death alarmed me much, tho' I thought before I left Derby she declined fast'. This might possibly be the Flint for whom Wright painted a portrait of *Mr. Salmon* (q.v.), to judge by its situation in the Account Book in the late 1780's, when we know Flint was still alive.

D. R. Sherborn Esq, F.S.A.

62 **'FRANCIS FOX'**

See 63   pp 17, 73–4   **340**

63 **'DOROTHY HUNT, WIFE OF FRANCIS FOX'**

SIZE   Each, 30 × 25 in / 76.2 × 63.5 cm   pp 17, 73–4   **339**

PROVENANCE   Have remained in the Fox family since they were painted (as a pair).

EXHIBITIONS   Derby, 1866 (206, 209), lent by Rev. S. Fox who also lent (No. 208) the copy after Wright referred to opposite.

The identifications as Francis Fox (1724–89) and Dorothy Fox (1733–93) are from mid-nineteenth-century labels on the reverse. The same source gives William Fox as the sitter for the earlier portrait. These identifications must be wrong since the sitters in all three cases died before the pictures were painted. It is more likely that the two Wrights represent Mr. and Mrs. William Fox, from whom Wright recorded payments in the Account Book for 10th January 1784 onwards into the 1790's. Francis did have a younger brother called William, born after 1729, but the date of his death is not known. The Account Book also records: **Mem. Rec'd 27th April 1789 of M^rs. Fox three g^s for repairing three pictures for L^d. Melbourne.** This might be the same vixen.

Mrs. D. Hamilton

FRENCH   **Cap.ᵗ French, £10.10;** among pictures of *c* 1777–80. This is 64 opposite.

FYDELL   **M.ʳ Fydell; M.ʳˢ Fydell** listed among sitters at Boston, undated. 1760.

GELL   **A full Length of M.ʳˢ Gell, £5(?).10.** This is 65 opposite.

GISBORNE (see also **BATEMAN)**   **A 3 q.ʳˢ of M.ʳ Tho.ˢ Gisborne, £12.12,** following on the date 1777. This is 66 opposite.

M.ʳ & M.ʳˢ Gisborne, £21, listed among portraits of *c* 1777–80. Mr. and Mrs. Thomas Gisborne were not married until 1784, so this entry probably refers to Gisborne's father John (d. 1779) and mother. It may describe two small heads at ten guineas each, not a group portrait.

A Conversation picture of M.ʳ & M.ʳˢ Gisborne, £100.16. This is 67 opposite.

64 CAPTAIN RICHARD FRENCH

L. B. Sanderson Esq

SIZE   30 × 25 in / 76.2 × 63.5 cm   pp 17³, 36, 98   **85**

PROVENANCE   Passed from the Mundy family to a cousin; sold by his son, G. S. Clark-Maxwell, Christie's, 19th November 1965 (53) as '(Gilbert) Stuart'.

'Cap! French' is referred to as a 'good friend' in a letter from Wright to his sister from Rome, 13th April 1774 (Bemrose, 1885, p. 31). It is clearly the same person. Since the entry in the Account Book immediately precedes one for Miss Millicent Mundy (q.v.), this must be the Captain Richard French of the Royal Horse Guards whom Miss Mundy married. (Cornet R.H.G., October 1766; Lieutenant, April 1771; out of Army List after 1773; died 1801). Since Wright also charged ten guineas for the Mundy portrait, they were very likely pendants. One would have thought on stylistic grounds that this portrait was earlier than its position in the Account Book implies; the biographical and stylistic evidence points to c 1771–72. Moreover, Wright put up his prices for a 30 × 25 inch canvas to twelve guineas after his return from Italy (see, for example, *Gisborne*). The sitter is identified by a nineteenth-century label on the reverse: 'Richard French'.

65 DOROTHY GELL OF HOPTON

Lt. Col. John Chandos-Pole, O. B. E.

SIZE   93½ × 57 in / 236.8 × 144.8 cm   pp 74, 129, 159   **266**

Signed and dated: 'I. Wright pinx!/1786' on the central tree right.

PROVENANCE   Inherited by the Chandos-Poles from the Gells, who were no relations.

EXHIBITIONS   Derby, 1883 (23). No. 113 in this exhibition was also a *Mrs. Gell* lent by H. Chandos Pole-Gell and was no doubt the same picture, listed a second time in error. Graves' Galleries, 1910 (10).

Dorothy Gell (1758–1808), daughter and coheiress of William Milnes of Aldercar Park, Derbyshire and Cromford, married Philip Gell of Hopton Hall in 1774; his portrait by Reynolds is also in the Chandos-Pole Collection (recorded by Waterhouse, *Reynolds*, 1941, p. 90).

66 THOMAS GISBORNE

Mr. and Mrs. Patrick Gibson

SIZE   30 × 25 in / 76.2 × 63.5 cm   pp 13, 68, 133, 143   **191**

On the relining canvas is an inscription, perhaps taken from one on the original canvas which must have been near-contemporary though after 1780, which reads: 'Thomas Gisborne Esq! of Derby & Yoxall Lodge, Staffordshire/Before he was 20 he became a Fellow Commoner to S! John's Coll./Cambridge. M! Gisborne went to/ Cambridge October 1776, This picture was taken the next summer,/ He took Holy Orders when was of the proper age to do so./ in 1777—gained at Cambridge Brownes gold medal for the best Latin Ode/ 1780 took his degree—sixth wrangler and the Senior Chancellors Classical medal/ Painted by Wright of Derby in D[erby] 1777 [the last digit has been changed from a '6']/ D! Heath, the head Master of Harrow on/ the Hill, desired to have this picture taken of his/ Pupil M! Gisborne from the Doctor's high approbation of him'.

PROVENANCE   Sale, Christie's, 22nd December 1932 (46); Sotheby's, 15th February 1956 (118), bt. Agnew's. See Nicolson, 1965, p. 59.

67 REV. THOMAS AND MRS GISBORNE

Mr. and Mrs. Paul Mellon

SIZE   74 × 60 in / 188 × 152.4 cm   pp 17, 29, 72–3, 90, 134, 137   **269**

Signed and dated bottom right: 'I. WRIGHT Pinx! 1786'.

PROVENANCE   Mrs. Griffiths, Yoxall Lodge; Christie's, 26th March 1926 (127); Mrs. Florence H. Crane, Ipswich (Mass.).

EXHIBITIONS   Derby, 1883 (82). Richmond, Virginia, 1963 (256); R.A. 1964/65 (253). See Nicolson, 1965, pp. 58 ff.

GORDON, see **HOPE**

GORE M.ʳ & M.ʳˢ Gore, £21, among sitters at Liverpool, 1769. Conceivably related to Staniforth's (q.v.) wife's family, the Goores.

GOSPAL M.ʳˢ Gospal, among sitters at Newark, undated. 1760.

GREATORIX A Head of M.ʳ Greatorix, £12.12. A little lower down (and no doubt a pair to it, 30 × 25 in) is: M.ʳˢ Gretorix [sic] 3 q.ʳˢ, £12.12. These are among pictures of the early '90's.

GURNEY M.ʳ Gurney, £6.6, among portraits of c 1762–65. This entry is repeated among portraits of the same date.

GWIN A half Length of M.ʳ Gwin, £12.12, among portraits of c 1762–65.

HACKART A Copy of Col. Hackart, £12.12, among pictures of the early '90's. This entry is repeated elsewhere in the Account Book, with the additional item: **Frame for D.º, £2.12.6.**

HALL (see also **SMYTH**) M.ʳ Hall, M.ʳˢ Hall, Miss Hall, among sitters at Newark, undated. 1760. These Newark portraits are not identified but see 72 and 73 opposite.

HANCOCK M.ʳ Hancock 3 q.ʳˢ, £12.12, among pictures of the early '80's, or even slightly earlier.

HANMER (see also **LYGON**) Miss Hanmer, M.ʳˢ Hanmer, £6.6. each, among sitters at Derby, undated. c 1760. Also **Copy of M.ʳ Hanmer,** at the same price.

HANWAY M.ʳˢ Hanway, among sitters at Newark, undated. 1760.

HARDMAN M.ʳˢ Hardman, £10.10; among sitters at Liverpool, 1769.

HARPUR M.ʳˢ Harpur, among sitters at Derby, undated. c 1760. It is possible that this portrait is still at Calke Abbey, but the author has received no encouragement to investigate it, in spite of repeated efforts.

HARRISON D.ʳ Harrison, £12.12; among pictures of c 1781. This is probably 74 opposite.

68 **ROBERT VERNON ATHERTON GWILLYM**	SIZE 50 × 40 in / 127 × 101.6 cm Signed and dated bottom left: 'J. Wright Pinx!/1766.' See 69	PP 33-4	**56**

69 **MRS GWILLYM of ATHERTON**

SIZE   50 × 40 in / 127 × 101.6 cm   PP 33, 49   **55**
Signed and dated bottom left: 'J. Wright Pinx!/1766.'
Pair to above. In both cases the artist's name appears in block letters in the lower left corner, but has been painted out.
PROVENANCE   Both from Atherton family; acquired for St. Louis on London Art Market, 1965.
Robert Gwillym of Bewsey Hall, Warrington married Elizabeth, daughter and heiress of John Atherton of Atherton. Their son Robert Vernon Atherton Gwillym of Bewsey and Atherton (dead by 1787) assumed name and arms of Atherton in lieu of those of Gwillym; married (1763) Henrietta Maria (d. 1787) eldest daughter and heiress of Peter Legh (1706–92) of Lyme, Co. Chester. Wright's portraits must represent the second pair three years after their marriage. Sydney H. Pavière, *The Devis Family of Painters*, Leigh-on-Sea, 1950, plate 20, No. 64 shows a Devis signed and dated 1743 of *Robert Gwillym of Atherton*, who is the same sitter, in the company of William Farington. In the Mellon Collection (Catalogue No. 226) he appears again in the same pose, this time alone (see *St. Louis Bulletin*, 1965).

City Art Museum of
St. Louis, Missouri

70 **THE TWINS: SARAH and ANNE HADEN**

SIZE   21½ × 18½ in / 54.6 × 47 cm   p 63³   **343**
PROVENANCE   Has remained in the family since it was painted.
EXHIBITIONS   Derby, 1883 (67); Graves' Galleries, 1910 (12); Derby, 1934 (109).
Etching by F. Seymour Haden after this version, illus. Bemrose, 1885, p. 12.
Wright did a second version:

Private Collection, U.K.

71 **THE TWINS: SARAH and ANNE HADEN**

SIZE   c 21 × 18 in / 53.3 × 45.7 cm   p 63³
PROVENANCE   According to some family letters, this version was presented by the artist on 30th April 1796 to a friend, Mrs. Francis Boott, a direct ancestress of the present owner.
Daughters of Thomas Haden of Derby, surgeon: Sarah (1788–1860), married James Oakes of Riddings; Ann (1788–1869) married Kirk Boott and lived in America.
The portrait group must have been one of the last Wright painted.

David Richardson Esq

For Haden see also Edwin, under heading Scenes from Contemporary Literature.

72 **'H.B.' HALL**

SIZE   30 × 25 in / 76.2 × 63.5 cm   p 68   **186**
See 73

Hugh Wontner Esq, M.V.O., J.P.

73 **MRS HALL**

SIZE   30 × 25 in / 76.2 × 63.5 cm   p 68   **187**
These two were exhibited Derby, 1883 (89, 100) by Lorenzo K. Hall, along with a portrait of Elizabeth Kennion (101) who married a Rev. John Smyth. All three were sold at Sotheby's, 12th December 1956 (55, 56, 54). Mrs. Hall was formerly Martha Kennion, but her relationship to Elizabeth is not known (the family likeness and proximity in age suggest sisters). The portraits date from the late '70's: according to the 1883 catalogue, Mrs. Hall died in 1780.

Mrs. Nancie C. MacGilp

74 **'JOHN HARRISON'**

SIZE   30 × 25 in / 76.2 × 63.5 cm   pp 69-70   **199**
EXHIBITIONS   Derby, 1866 (98); 1870 (799); 1883 (91); 1934 (12).
Not only is the portrait listed in the Account Book among portraits of c 1781, it also belongs stylistically to this date or slightly earlier. The subject must therefore be wrongly identified as John Harrison, clock-maker and inventor of a marine chronometer who died in March

HEATH

Mr **Heath, £12.12;** among sitters of *c* 1762–65. All entries are crossed out and the same picture is listed again among the same sitters: **For a half Length of Mr Heath, £12.12.** This is 77 opposite.

Mrs **Heath, £9.9;** among sitters from 1st February 1760 onwards. This is repeated among sitters of the early 1760's: **For a Kitcat picture of Mrs Heath, £9.9.** The picture is listed a third time among sitters at Derby *c* 1760. Nicholas Heath did not marry F. N. C. Mundy's sister Mary until 1768, so this cannot be she.

Mr **John Heath, £21;** among portraits of *c* 1770. A picture described as by Wright of John. Heath, banker of Derby, 30 × 25 in, was sold Christie's, 25th June 1928 (44), but the photograph in the Frick Art Reference Library, New York shows a portrait (conceivably by Wright) which can hardly be later than 1760. In any case £21 is too high a price for a three quarters.

HEATHCOTE

Capt **Heathcote, £6.6;** among sitters at Derby, *c* 1760. This is very likely the Captain Heathcote whom Wright met in Rome (see his letter to his brother, 12th February 1774, Bemrose, 1885, p. 30 where he asks to be remembered to Colonel Heathcote, see opposite). He might also conceivably be the 'Mr Heathcote' who had a friend at Pisa (see Wright's letter of 4th February 1774, Bemrose, 1885, p. 29).

Col.^l **Heathcote small full Length, £31. 10;** listed among portraits of very early '70's. This is 79 opposite.

1776 before Wright got back from Bath. Wright calls him a doctor, so he is probably the 'surgeon in the Wardwick', Mr. John Harrison, in whose house the daughter of Edward Wilmot of Duffield died (see *Derby Mercury*, 24th September 1786). He is described in *Derby Mercury*, 11th October 1787 as having died: 'surgeon aged 64...' The portrait could show a man of *c* 56.

Private Collection, U.K.

75 **WILLIAM HAYLEY**   See 76   pp 65, 68, 71, 142–3   **182**

76 **MRS WILLIAM HAYLEY**   SIZE   Each $13\frac{1}{4} \times 11\frac{1}{2}$ in / 34.3 × 29.2 cm   pp 68, 71, 142–3   **183**
Grisaille bust ovals on canvas.
The pictures were painted in Derby soon after the marriage (1776) of John Beridge to Miss Buckston. Hayley, 1823, I, p. 156 tells us they were done for Beridge in about September of that year. Wright was on a visit to Derby from Bath that summer.

Private Collection, U.K.

77 **NICHOLAS HEATH**   SIZE   50 × 40 in / 127 × 101.6 cm   pp 2, 17, 28–9, 97–8, 142   **37**
PROVENANCE   Mundy family; Rev. Clark-Maxwell Sale, Christie's, 15th May 1936 (22).
EXHIBITIONS   Derby, 1934 (19).
One of six portraits of members of The Derby Hunt painted *c* 1762–63 and hung at Markeaton Hall, the home of F. N. C. Mundy.
For the other five, see BURDETT.

Major Peter Miller Mundy   Nicholas Heath changed his name to Nicholas Nicholas.

78 **'CHRISTOPHER**   SIZE   50 × 40 in / 127 × 101.6 cm   pp 36, 65, 72–3, 129   **209**
HEATH'   A portrait said to be of Christopher Heath (banker and proprietor of the Cockpit Hill Pot and China Works; Mayor of Derby 1774; died August 1815) by Wright was exhibited Derby, 1866 (187) lent by J. Hudson; 1870 (811), lent by Mrs. Hudson; 1883 (2), lent by H. Barber. It is not known whether this passed to its present owner's family, but the evidence is overwhelmingly in favour of its identity with the so-called '*Samuel Johnson*' in that Collection. The arguments in favour are: first, the portrait is not of Johnson, yet according to the reviewer of the 1883 exhibition in the *Derbyshire Advertiser*, 22nd March: 'The subject of the portrait [of 'Heath'], in wig and brown coat, ponderous and sedate, reminds one greatly of the well-known portrait of Dr. Johnson'; he is shown writing a letter on which the word 'Derby' can be read, though the picture is now too dirty for other letters or figures to be clearly deciphered; the description of '*Christopher Heath*' in the 1883 catalogue runs: 'Seated looking to right; [this was the convention adopted in this catalogue: 'right' meant from the point of view of the sitter, as we can prove from its description of Mrs. Hall and Miss Kennion (see HALL) who are said there to be 'to right'] writing letter dated "Derby, May, 1781". Handkerchief in left hand. Canvas 50 × $39\frac{1}{2}$'; and the date of the portrait of 'Heath' could be *c* 1781. This portrait was exhibited Derby, 1934 (102) when a date '?1778' was read.

Private Collection, U.K.

79 **COLONEL CHARLES**   SIZE   50 × 40 in / 127 × 101.6 cm   pp 17, 36   **115**
HEATHCOTE   EXHIBITIONS   S. of A., 1772 (369 or 370). This is only known from a photograph in the National Portrait Gallery, extra-illustrated Bemrose. The only Heathcote in the Army List of the period (and out of it after 1773) was Lt. Colonel Charles Heathcote, 35th Foot (today the Royal Sussex Regiment) who commanded it from 1769 to 1772.
A similar picture is of a *Captain Milnes* (q.v.). The extra-illustrated Bemrose also contains a photograph of an unknown picture described there as:

(Untraced)

80 **'DOROTHY ANNE,**   SIZE   ? 30 × 25 in / 76.2 × 63.5 cm   p 27[1]   **16**
WIFE OF COLONEL   Judging by the style, this dates from *c* 1760.
CHARLES HEATHCOTE'
(Untraced)

HESKETH

M.^r & Mrs Hisketh, £21 (that is to say, most likely ten guineas per portrait); among sitters at Liverpool, 1769. These are 81 and 82 opposite.

HODGES

A 3 q^{rs} of Mrs Hodges, £12.12; among portraits of *c* 1780. This is 83 opposite.

HOLDEN

A Half Length of Robt Holding Esqr., £25. 4; among pictures of the very early 1780's. This must be the portrait of Holden catalogued opposite (84), since on the same sheet of the Account Book is listed a half length of Whetham at the same price, and the pictures were painted as pairs.

81 **FLEETWOOD HESKETH**
82 **FRANCES HESKETH**

See 82   pp 4, 17, 34, 99   **61**
SIZE   Each 50 × 40 in / 127 × 101.6 cm   pp 4, 17, 34, 99   **62**
EXHIBITIONS   Festival of Britain Exhibition of local Art Treasures, Atkinson Art Gallery, Southport, 1951 (153 and 149), both illus. catalogue.
Fleetwood Hesketh of Rossall and North Meols married Frances, daughter of Peter Bold of Bold. He was the son of Roger Hesketh and Margaret Fleetwood of Rossall, and was painted as a child with his parents and sister by Devis *c* 1742 (see Sydney H. Pavière, *The Devis Family of Painters*, Leigh-on-Sea, 1950, No. 66). He died in 1769, so that we can be sure the pictures were painted by then.

Trustees of the Hesketh Settled Estate

83 **MRS HODGES**

SIZE   30 × 25 in / 76.2 × 63.5 cm   pp 68, 83³   **189**
PROVENANCE   Sale, Christie's, 22nd May 1908 (194) as Gainsborough; bt. Agnew's.
The author's only knowledge of this picture is a photograph in the Frick Art Reference Library, New York, which shows a half-length figure in a feigned oval. It belongs in style with the *Beridge* portrait in Minneapolis (1777).

Formerly
Humphrey Roberts Collection

84 **ROBERT HOLDEN**

SIZE   50 × 40 in / 127 × 101.6 cm   pp 17, 71, 73, 96, 123–4   **193**
EXHIBITIONS   Derby, 1883 (31). 'Pictures from Shropshire Houses', Shrewsbury, 1951 (47).
Three portraits of three friends: *Robert Holden* (1722–1808) and *John Whetham of Kirklington* (1731–81) by Wright, and *Lord Middleton of Wollaton* (1728–81) by Romney, were painted as companion pieces. There is a tradition in the Holden family (see R. Holden, *Nuthall Temple, Notts. Its History and Contents*, Northampton, 1916, p. 16) that 'each [sitter] had a copy of these three portraits'. This may be literally true, since we do know that Wright painted three versions of the *Whetham*: a near full-length; a copy of it (which is probably the version hanging as a pendant to the *Holden)*; and an oval bust (see WHET-HAM). Romney did at least two versions of the *Middleton*. In a MS. list of his portraits and accounts (Victoria and Albert Museum Library), under 1781 is: 'Lady Middleton/Her Ladyship's portrait W.L. [whole length] £73.10/ Lord Middleton Dº—Dº £73.10'. Then a note against December 1781: 'Recᵈ. on account £105.0.0'. The balance of £42 is recorded as being paid later. Then a note under 1782: 'Receiv'd of Lady Middleton for Lord Middleton['s] Portrait sent into Derbyshire/ a copy—£73.10/ Frame my own— £16...' The former is evidently the version for Wollaton; the latter for the Holden family. Portraits of all three sitters are likely to have been ready by 1781 since Whetham and Middleton died that year; Middleton sat to Romney in the spring of 1779 (see Ward and Roberts, 1904, II, p. 103), and stylistically the *Holden* is nearer to the late '70's than the very early '80's (cf. for example, the *Cheslyn* of 1777).
A branch of the Holden family was later in occupation of Nuthall Temple, Notts. where the Holden version of the three pictures remained until the 1920's (see C. Hussey, *Country Life*, 5th May 1923, where they are shown hanging on the walls).

Major H. R. Holden

85 **JOHN HOLLAND of FORD**

SIZE   30 × 25 in / 76.2 × 63.5 cm   pp 73, 137   **275**
Signed and dated behind Holland's back: 'J. Wright/pinxᵗ/1787'. Inscription on relining canvas (obviously transferred from a genuine inscription): 'John Holland, painted by his friend, Joseph Wright, 1787. "However odd the phyz portrayed/ What artist has a better made"'.
EXHIBITIONS   Derby, 1934 (28).
A water-colour study of this portrait is in the Derby Art Gallery: oval, 7⅝ × 5½ in, from the Cheney Bemrose Bequest, 1954. It is hard to say whether it is by Wright or Holland.

Gladwyn Turbutt Esq

HOLLAND   Mrs Holland, £12.12; among portraits of *c* 1790. This is 86 opposite.

HOPE   Mr C. Hope, £6.6; among sitters from 1st February 1760 onwards. This is repeated among sitters at Derby, *c* 1760: **For a 3 q^{rs} of Hope, £6.6.** It was therefore a 30 × 25 in. A portrait of **Mr C. Hope** is listed again among sitters at Derby *c* 1760 but priced at £9.9. It sounds therefore as though two portraits were ordered, one of which was a pair to the Kit Cat of *Mrs. Hope*. The '3 q^{rs}' is probably 87 opposite

Mrs C. Hope, £9.9; among sitters from 1st February 1760 onwards. This is repeated among sitters at Derby *c* 1760: **For a Kitcat picture of Mrs Hope, £9.9.** It is listed a third time at this price, and was therefore a 36¼ × 28 in. This is 88 opposite.

Master Charles Hope Sm (i.e. small), £8.8; among portraits of *c* 1776–78. This is 89 opposite.

Miss Harriot (sic) **Hope D^{o}** (i.e. small following an entry for the young Charles Hope who can only have been her brother). This is 90 opposite.

HURST   **Miss Hurst,** among sitters at Boston, undated. 1760.

HURT   M^{r} & Mrs **Hurt,** £42 (that is to say, twenty guineas each); among sitters of *c* 1770–80. These are 92 and 93 opposite.

86 MRS HOLLAND OF FORD

Gladwyn Turbutt Esq

SIZE   30 × 25 in / 76.2 × 63.5 cm   pp 17, 73, 137   **274**
EXHIBITIONS   Derby, 1934 (29).
Mrs. Holland is shown in a feigned oval, whereas her husband is not. Her position in the Account Book also suggests that her portrait was not conceived as a pendant at the time.

87 REV. CHARLES HOPE

(Untraced)
Formerly Hope Collection

SIZE   ? 30 × 25 in / 76.2 × 63.5 cm
EXHIBITIONS   Derby, 1870 (753); Graves' Galleries, 1910 (50); on both occasions lent by members of the Hope family.
Rev. Charles Hope (1732–98), vicar of St. Werburgh's, Derby. It was no doubt he who played the harpsichord at concerts in the '50's at which his contemporary Wright was present (see Bemrose, 1885, p. 9).

88 SUSANNAH HOPE

(Untraced)
Formerly Hope Collection

SIZE $36\frac{1}{4}$ × 28 in / 92.1 × 71.1 cm
Susannah Hope (1744–1807), daughter of Benjamin Stead, married very young (1760) the Rev. Charles Hope, and their portraits were painted soon after their marriage. No trace has been found of the portrait of Mrs. Hope. One said to represent her in the Fitzwilliam Museum of about the correct date, and to be by Wright, is the wrong size to be the picture listed. It is an oval, $27\frac{1}{4}$ × $21\frac{3}{4}$ in (painted surface $29\frac{3}{8}$ × $24\frac{3}{4}$ in). This was bequeathed to the Fitzwilliam by Lady St John Hope on her death in 1952. In the author's opinion, it is not by Wright.

89 CHARLES STEAD HOPE AS A BOY

Private collection, U.K.

SIZE $13\frac{1}{2}$ × $11\frac{1}{2}$ in / 34.3 × 29.2 cm (oval)   pp 70–1, 131, 143   **180**
EXHIBITIONS   Derby, 1870 (792) when still in the Hope family; 1883 (86), lent by N. C. Curzon.
Rev. Charles Stead Hope, M.A. (1762–1841), son of Charles and Susannah Hope, shown as a boy of about fourteen. The style confirms a date c 1776–77. He became Mayor of the Borough in 1797. The *Derby Mercury* for 11th April 1793 announces his marriage to a Miss Mellor, an ancestress of a recent owner of the following:

90 MISS HARRIET HOPE

H. R. Edwards Esq

SIZE   14 × 12 in / 35.5 × 30.5 cm (oval)   pp 70–1, 143   **181**
EXHIBITIONS   Graves' Galleries, 1910 (22), lent by Vernon Mellor; Derby-Leicester, 1947 (10). Born in c 1768, she married a man named Gordon. An old inscription on the stretcher gives her Christian name as 'Susannah', but Susannah must have been the sister who married in 1786 the nephew of the Duke of Somerset, Edward Seymour Biscoe.

91 'RICHARD, EARL HOWE'

National Gallery of Art, Washington, D.C.

SIZE   50 × 40 in / 127 × 101.6 cm   p 36   **90**
PROVENANCE   From Curzon family, Lockington Hall, Derbyshire. Mellon Collection, 1940, as Copley. A typical Wright of the early '70's. The identification of the sitter is quite uncertain, but Lord Howe the Admiral (1726–99) did have political connections with Nottingham, though he sat at the time of this portrait as a member for Dartmouth (see Fitton and Wadsworth, 1958, pp. 70–72). He is not wearing naval uniform, which had white facings, and he may not be in uniform at all.

92 FRANCIS HURT of ALDERWASLEY

See 93   pp 17, 70, 161–2   **204**

93 MRS FRANCIS HURT
Michael Hurt Esq

SIZE   Each 50 × 40 in / 127 × 101.6 cm   pp 17, 30, 129   **203**
The portraits were painted before 1783 when Francis Hurt died.

A full Length of M.ʳ C. Hurt,£52.10; listed among pictures of *c* 1790. This is 94 opposite.

A full Length of Mʳˢ C. Hurt & her Child,£81.18; listed among pictures of *c* 1787–90. This is 95 opposite.

INGE

M.ʳ Inge,£12.12; among pictures of the very early '80's.

INWOOD

Miss Inwood, among sitters at Retford, undated. 1760. This is repeated among sitters from 1st February 1760 onwards: **Miss Inwood,£6.6.**

ISHMAY

M.ʳ Ishmay, among sitters at Boston, undated. 1760.

JOHNSON, see HEATH

JONES

A half Length of M.ʳ Jones,£25.4; among pictures of *c* 1782–85. This is 97 opposite.

JUDSON

M.ʳ Judson, among sitters at Retford, undated. 1760. The entry is repeated among sitters of 1st February 1760 onwards: **M.ʳ Judson,£6.6;** and a third time: **For a 3 q.ʳˢ of M.ʳ Judson, £6.6.**

KENNION, see HALL and SMYTH

KIRK

Cap.ᵗ Kirk, among sitters at Retford, undated. 1759–60 or 1760. This is 98 opposite.

KNIGHT

M.ʳ & Miss Knight, £42 (i.e. twenty guineas each); among sitters at Liverpool, 1769.

LANDER

Mʳˢ Lander,£12.12.

LANKFORD

M.ʳ Sam. Lankford, Mʳˢ Lankford,£10.10 each; among portraits of *c* 1777–80. These are immediately followed by an entry for Roe, so he must be a successor to the silk merchant, Samuel Lankford, who entered into partnership with Roe in or before 1750 (see Chaloner, 1950–53, I, p. 137). It cannot be Roe's partner, who died before 1762.

LATUFFIERE

M.ʳ Latuffiere, £12.12; (he paid ten guineas); among pictures of *c* 1776. Fitton and Wadsworth, 1958, p. 162 quote a letter from Elizabeth Strutt to her father Jedediah, 30th August 1775: '…M.ʳ Arkwright brought his Sister [? Susannah, later Mrs. Charles Hurt] to Derby last Tuesday but one to go to School at M.ʳ Latuffieres,…' This must be the same schoolmaster. Maria Edgeworth, the daughter of Wright's acquaintance Richard Lovell Edgeworth, was also educated at this establishment in the late '70's.

LEACROFT

M.ʳ Leacroft,£12.12; among portraits *c* 1762–65. All entries crossed through and the same picture listed among the same sitters: **A half Length of M.ʳ Leacroft, £12.12.** This is 99 opposite.

94 CHARLES HURT
of WIRKSWORTH

Formerly
Hurt Collection

SIZE $90\frac{1}{2} \times 54\frac{1}{2}$ in / 229.9 × 138.5 cm   p 162   **300**
EXHIBITIONS   Derby, 1866 (172); 1883 (47), lent by members of the Hurt family; Graves'
Galleries, 1910 (4), lent by F. Woolley-Dod.
Charles Hurt was the second son of Francis and Mary Hurt of Alderwasley. The only
record of the picture known to the author is an old photograph pasted into the Eardley
Simpson extra-illustrated Bemrose.

95 SUSANNAH, WIFE OF
CHARLES HURT AND
DAUGHTER OF
SIR R. ARKWRIGHT

Formerly
Hurt Collection

SIZE $90\frac{1}{2} \times 54\frac{1}{2}$ in / 229.9 × 138.5 cm   pp 162, 164   **301**
EXHIBITIONS   Derby, 1866 (189); 1883 (53), lent by members of the Hurt family; Graves'
Galleries, 1910 (8) lent by F. Woolley-Dod. 1911.
Being the same size, a pair to the above, though more expensive because there were two
figures.
Mrs. Charles Hurt, m. 1780. Her daughter Mary Ann, m. 1805 Peter, son of Richard
Arkwright II.

96 NICHOLAS
HUTCHINSON

Jeremy Hutchinson Esq, Q.C.

SIZE   30 × 25 in / 76.2 × 63.5 cm   pp 27, 29   **20**
PROVENANCE   Has remained in the Hutchinson family since it was painted.
Nicholas Hutchinson (c 1733–98) came from Newark and was very likely painted there in
the early weeks of 1760. The style confirms this date. He became a surgeon in Southwell,
Notts.

97 'STEPHEN' JONES

Sir Gilbert Inglefield

SIZE   50 × 40 in / 127 × 101.6 cm   pp 17, 34, 70, 73, 129   **268**
Signed and dated bottom right 'I. Wright Pinx!/ 1785'. A book on the table is labelled
'Rental' and a music sheet has the word 'Andante'.
EXHIBITIONS   Derby, 1934 (40); Tate, 1958 (26), for further details.
Evidently this Jones was an estate agent fond of music. Lord Vernon's agent Stephen Jones
is said to have been an amateur musician and it may well be he. The body is the same as
that of *Rev. Basil Beridge* (q.v.) whose portrait (originally at the same price) is listed on the
same page of the Account Book.

98 WILLIAM KIRKE

Rear Admiral
David Kirke C.B.E.

SIZE   30 × 25 in / 76.2 × 63.5 cm   pp 2, 27   **19**
William (1715–73) and his brother Edmund Kirke were close friends of the Masons of
Retford whom Wright also painted (q.v.), Edmund leaving all his property to their daughter.
The Kirkes lived at Mirfield Hall, East Markham. In William Kirke's accounts he states:
'Jan 23 1760 By Picture to Mr. Wright £6. 6.0.
Aug 26 1760 By Picture Frame   £1.14.1'
(Information kindly supplied by Mrs L. C. E. Currie).

99 EDWARD BECHER
LEACROFT of
WIRKSWORTH

Major Peter Miller Mundy

SIZE   50 × 40 in / 127 × 101.6 cm   pp 2, 17, 28–9, 34, 97   **33**
PROVENANCE   Mundy family; Rev. Clark-Maxwell Sale, Christie's, 15th May 1936 (20).
Sale Christie's 16th June 1950 (105).
EXHIBITIONS   Derby, 1934 (83).
One of six portraits of members of The Derby Hunt painted c 1762–63 and hung at Markea-
ton Hall, the home of Francis N. C. Mundy. For a list of the six sitters, see BURDETT.

M.ʳ Leacroft, £6.6; among sitters at Derby *c* 1760. This is a separate portrait of Leacroft who lived at Markeaton. The two preceding entries are of Mundy children.

LEAPER

A Conversation picture of three of M.ʳ Leaper's Children, £84 (changed from £72.15), immediately followed by the portrait of *Jones* of 1785. This is 100 opposite.

LEICE

Miss Leice, £10.10; among sitters at Liverpool, 1769.

LEIGH

M.ʳ & M.ʳˢ Leigh, £21 (e.g. ten guineas each); among sitters at Liverpool, 1769. Possibly members of the prominent Lee family. A Pierce Lee is recorded as a Liverpool slave trader in 1752.

LINDIGTON or LINDEGTEN or LIGDINTON

M.ʳˢ Lindigton, £6.6; among sitters from 1st February 1760 onwards. This is repeated among sitters of the early '60's: **For a 3 q.ʳˢ of M.ʳˢ Lindegten, £6.6**; and a third time among sitters at Derby *c* 1760, this time as **M.ʳˢ Ligdinton.**

LINTON or LYNTON

M.ʳ Lynton, among sitters at Boston, undated. 1760. John Linton lent to Graves' Galleries, 1910 (37) a portrait of *Rev. John Linton.*

LOW

M.ʳ Low, £3.3; among sitters at Derby, *c* 1760. An early note of *c* 1760 in the Account Book is headed **Money given to my father.** There are various items, including five guineas which his father had given him back **to pay M.ʳ Lowe's Bill.**

LUMB

For a small 3 q.ʳˢ of M.ʳˢ Lumb, £2.2; among sitters of *c* 1760.

Copy of M.ʳˢ Lumb, £2.2; among sitters from 1st February 1760 onwards. The entry is repeated among sitters at Derby, *c* 1760.

LUSHINGTON

Cap.ᵗ Lushington, £12.12; among sitters from 1st February 1760 onwards. This is repeated among sitters of *c* 1760: **For a half length of Cap.ᵗ Lushington, £12.12.** The entry is repeated a third time among sitters at Derby.

LYGON

M.ʳ Lyggon, M.ʳˢ Lyggon, Master Lyggon, Miss Lyggon, at £6.6. each, among sitters at Derby *c* 1760. The portrait of the Lygon boy is not traced. The other three are 101, 102 and 103 opposite.

MACAULEY or MACAULAY

Wright to his brother from Bath, 15th April 1776 (quoted Bemrose, 1885, p. 45): 'I am now painting a half-length of D.ʳ Wilson [q.v.] & his adopted daughter, Miss Macauley...'

100 **THE LEAPER CHILDREN**

SIZE 68 × 54 in / 172.7 × 137.2 cm   pp 71, 73 **243**

EXHIBITIONS Robins's Rooms, 1785 (22); Derby, 1883 (24), lent by C. E. Newton; Graves' Galleries, 1910 (7); Derby, 1934 (38).

John Leaper Newton (1754–1819) of Mickleover; town clerk of Derby 1777–91; succeeded to the estates of his cousin Robert Newton of Mickleover in 1789 (about four years after the picture of his children was painted) and assumed the name of Newton; sheriff of Derbyshire 1798. The girl in the centre, Sarah, married Francis Mundy of Markeaton.

Private Collection, U.K.

101 **REGINALD LYGON**

See 103   pp 17, 26–8, 96, 99, 103, 129 **17**

102 **MRS SUSANNAH LYGON**

See 103   pp 17, 26–8, 96, 99, 103 **18**

103 **MISS ELIZABETH LYGON**

SIZE Each 30 × 25 in / 76.2 × 63.5 cm   p 17, 26–8, 96, 99 **14**

PROVENANCE Have remained in the Lygon family collection since they were painted.

Reginald Pinder (c 1714–88), eldest son of Reginald Pinder and Margaret Lygon, assumed the name and arms of Lygon; married Susannah, daughter of William Hanmer. (Wright also painted members of a Hanmer family). His daughter Elizabeth married Hon. John Yorke, son of Lord Chancellor Hardwicke. Another portrait in the collection of John Yorke, is attributed to Wright but is not by him. Mr. and Mrs. Yorke had an only daughter Jemima, who married Rt. Hon. Reginald Pole Carew. A portrait of her as a young girl in the collection is attributed to Wright, also wrongly: it dates from about 1770 when Wright's style was quite different. The 'Master Lyggon' in Wright's lists is William (b. 1747), only son and heir of Reginald and Susannah Lygon; later (1806) Lord Beauchamp.

Private Collection, U.K.

MASON

M.ʳ Mason, M.ʳˢ Mason, M.ʳˢ G. Mason; among sitters at Retford, undated. 1759–60 or 1760. These are 104, 105, 106 opposite.

MEAD, see **WILMOT**

MELLAND

M.ʳˢ Melland, £6.6; among sitters at Derby, c 1760.

?MILLERS

Copy of M.ʳ Millers (?), £2.2; among sitters from 1st February 1760 onwards.

MILNES

Cap.ᵗ Milnes Ditto (i.e. small full Length), £31.10; among portraits of very early '70's. This is followed by entry: **Paid at the same time for frame etc.** (?). This is 101 opposite.

MONK

M.ʳ Monk, M.ʳˢ Monk, Miss Monk; among sitters at Lincoln, undated. 1760. The portrait of Mrs. Monk is again listed twice, at £12.12 among sitters from 1st February 1760, and among sitters of c 1760, where it is described as a half length.

MORE

M.ʳˢ More, £12.12; among pictures of the early 1780's. The entry is deleted, and so the portrait may never have been painted.

MOREWOOD

Small full Length of M.ʳˢ Morewood, £36.15, and **D.º** (e.g. small full length) of **M.ʳ Case, £36.15.** The same sheet of the Account Book has the entry: **A 3 q.ʳˢ of M.ʳˢ Morewood w.ᵗʰ a hand, £15.15,** but it is crossed through and so the portrait was probably never painted. On another sheet, just above the date **Dec.ʳ 1782** is the entry: **A small copy of M.ʳˢ Morewood, £15.10.** The whole lengths are 108 and 109 opposite.

MORTIMER

A head of M.ʳˢ Mortimer, £10.10; among pictures of c 1781.

MUNDY

M.ʳ Mundy, £12.12; among sitters from 1st February 1760 onwards. This is listed again as: **For a half length of M.ʳ Mundy, £12.12;** among sitters of the early 1760's, and a third time among sitters at Derby of the same period. This is 110 opposite.

M.ʳ Mundy, £6.6; listed among Markeaton Hunt pictures and therefore of the same period, only smaller. Conceivably the picture here catalogued as 113.

Miss Mill. Mundy, £10.10; among portraits of c 1777–80. Millicent Mundy (1746–89) married Captain Richard French whom Wright also painted (q.v.), no doubt as a pendant to this picture. She was a sister of F. N. C. Mundy.

104 **MR MASON**   See 106   p 2

105 **MRS MASON**   See 106   p 2

106 **MRS G. MASON**   All three (30 by 25 in) still or until recently in the Mason family at Mirton Hall, near East
Sir Paul and Lady Mason   Retford (Notts.).
                                                                                                       p 2

107 **'CAPTAIN' ROBERT**   SIZE   50 × 40 in / 127 × 101.6 cm   pp 17, 36, 159   **114**
SHORE MILNES   EXHIBITIONS   S. of A., 1772 (369 or 370), along with full length of *Col. Heathcote* (q.v.);
                                 New York, 1960 (9).
                                 This must be the Captain Milnes referred to in a letter from Wright to his brother from Bath,
                                 8th May 1776 (quoted Bemrose, 1885, p. 45): 'Have in hand a small full-length of Mr.
                                 Miles, brother to Capt. Miles I painted at Derby some time ago' (that is to say, about five
                                 years earlier). The portrait of the non-military brother is untraced.
                                 The Thaw portrait was certainly painted *c* 1771–72, and in view of the proximity of the
                                 entry in the Account Book to that of *Colonel Heathcote*, and of its description there, must
                                 represent Milnes. He is dressed as an officer in the Royal Horse Guards. There is no Milnes in
                                 the Army List at the correct date except Robert Shore Milnes who did not become a Capt./
                                 Lieutenant until 1776 and was a Lieutenant in 1772. Unless there is some other explanation
                                 that has not occurred to us, Wright must have been mistaken in his rank. Robert Shore
                                 Milnes (1747–1837) was the son of Wright's patron, John Milnes of Wakefield. It is not
                                 impossible that a young man of 25 is represented. Rev. Percy Sumner, *Journal for Army
                                 Historical Research*, XXII, p. 63 claimed him to be General Conway on the grounds of an
                                 alleged resemblance to Gainsborough's *Conway* at Inverary Castle, but Conway was then
                                 over 50. The problem is complicated by the fact that the portrait of Milnes by Romney
Mrs. Lawrence Copley Thaw   (Ward and Roberts, 1904, II, p. 106) is difficult to reconcile with Milnes's appearance in the
                                 Wright.

108 **REV. HENRY CASE**   SIZE   50 × 40 in / 127 × 101.6 cm   pp 17, 70², 72   **223**
(afterwards   Signed and dated bottom right: 'I.W.P. 82'.
CASE-MOREWOOD)   See 109

109 **HELEN MOREWOOD**   SIZE   50 × 40 in / 127 × 101.6 cm   pp 17, 72   **224**
                                 Signed and dated bottom left: 'I.W.P. 82'.
                                 EXHIBITIONS   Derby, 1934 (95 and 105).
                                 Henry Case, rector of Ladbroke, Co. Warw., married Helen Goodwin, widow of George
                                 Morewood, in 1793 when he assumed the name of Morewood. This pair was painted
                                 eleven years before their marriage. Helen Morewood's first husband George (sheriff of the
                                 County, 1761) died in 1792 and bequeathed Alfreton Hall to his widow. On the death of her
Palmer-Morewood Collection: on   second husband Henry Case, Mrs. Morewood willed the house and contents to her sister's
loan to Brighton Art Gallery   children, the Palmers who were no relation of the Morewoods.

110 **FRANCIS NOEL CLARKE**   SIZE   50 × 40 in / 127 × 101.6 cm   pp 2, 17, 28–9, 97, 102   **34**
MUNDY OF   PROVENANCE   In Mundy Collection since it was painted; Rev. Clark-Maxwell Sale,
MARKEATON   Christie's, 15th May 1936 (21).
                                 EXHIBITIONS   Derby, 1934 (147).
                                 One of six portraits of members of the Derby Hunt hung at Markeaton Hall, Mundy's
                                 home. For the five other sitters, see BURDETT. F. N. C. Mundy succeeded to Markeaton
Major Peter Miller Mundy   in 1762, and the series must have been completed soon afterwards.

Master Mundy, Miss Mundy, £6.6. each; among sitters at Derby, *c* 1760. He cannot be either of the two boys who appear in the following picture, painted about twenty years later.

Two Master Mundys full Lengths, £73.10; among pictures of the early '80's. This is 111 opposite.

NEVIL

M⁏ˢ Nevil, Miss Nevil, among sitters at Lincoln, undated. 1760.

NEWTON, see **LEAPER**

NICHOLAS, see **HEATH**

NOWEL

M⁏ & M⁏ˢ Nowel, £12.12 (that is, six guineas each); among sitters from 1st February 1760 onwards. These two are listed again among sitters of *c* 1760: **For a 3 q⁏ˢ Picture of M⁏ Nowel, D⁰ of M⁏ˢ Nowel, £6.6 each;** and a third time among sitters at Derby. These were 30 × 25 in. Wright also did:

M⁏ Nowel, £12.12 among sitters from 1st February 1760 onwards; also listed a second time among sitters at Derby. This was a 50 × 40 in, as emerges from a repetition of its listing: **For Nowell's ½ length Picture, £12.12,** among sitters of this date. In a framemaker's account is the item: **June 25th 1761 a ½ length frame C. & G.** [carved and gilt] **for Nowel, £3.13.6.**

OLDKNOW

A full length of the late M⁏ Oldknow, £52.10; among pictures of the early '90's. This is 114 opposite. This entry is followed by:

D⁰ (a full length) **of M⁏ Sam. Oldknow, £52.10.** A cross against this entry refers to a note at the top of the sheet of the Account Book: **Mem. on the 3ʳᵈ June 94 rec'd £10 on account.** This is 115 opposite.

PARES

Half Length of M⁏ Pares, £25.4; among pictures of the late 1780's. This is 116 opposite.

A half length copy of M⁏ Pares, £25.4; among pictures of the early 1790's. This is listed again among sitters of the same period. **D⁰** (half length) **Copy of M⁏ˢ Pares, £25.4** is deleted as though it was not carried out.

PARK

M⁏ & M⁏ˢ Park, £21 (i.e. ten guineas each); among sitters at Liverpool, 1769.

PARKER

A copy of the Late M⁏ Parker half Length, £25.4; a half Length of Miss Parker, £25.4; both among portraits of *c* 1781.

PARR

M⁏ˢ & Miss Parr, £21 (e.g. ten guineas each); among sitters at Liverpool, 1769.

PEACHALL

M⁏ Peachall; among sitters at Eckington, undated. 1760. This is repeated among sitters from 1st February 1760 onwards, and again a third time: **For a 3 q⁏ˢ of M⁏ Peachall, £6.6.**

PEART

Miss Peart; among sitters at Lincoln, undated. 1760. Also what one takes to be her three younger sisters: **Miss Molly Peart; Miss Nancy Peart; Miss Nelly Peart.** A Mr. Peart was a Lincoln attorney and political agent for the Monsons, but the family is not traceable in the Lincoln area.

111 **TWO YOUNG GENTLEMEN IN THE CHARACTER OF ARCHERS**

Oscar and Peter Johnson Ltd., Lowndes Lodge Gallery, London

SIZE $71\frac{1}{2} \times 54$ in / 181.6 × 137.2 cm   pp 70–1   **222**

PROVENANCE   Mundy Collection; sold by the son of a cousin of the Mundys, G. S. Clark-Maxwell, Christie's, 19th November 1965 (54).

EXHIBITIONS   R.A., 1782 (165); Graves' Galleries, 1910 (5), lent by Mrs. Mundy.

Francis and Charles, sons of Francis Noel Clarke Mundy, according to later inscription on the picture itself. The elder boy is shown at about the age of eleven. Since F. N. C. Mundy married Elizabeth Burdett in 1770, it would make sense to date the picture 1781–82 just before it was exhibited. This is confirmed by the style. The elder boy Francis married Sarah Leaper whom Wright also painted (q.v.).

Two portraits are thought to represent members of the Mundy family but this has not been confirmed:

112 **'MRS MUNDY'**

Sir Gilbert Inglefield

SIZE   30 × 25 in / 76.2 × 63.5 cm   pp 30–1, 34   **44**

EXHIBITIONS   Matlock, 1964 (10) as 'Mrs. Miller Mundy'.

A portrait of a middle-aged woman of c 1762–63.

113 **'MR MUNDY'**

Sir Gilbert Inglefield

SIZE   30 × 25 in / 76.2 × 63.5 cm   p 30   **43**

A portrait of a young man, bearing a strong resemblance to the Markeaton Hunt pictures and specially to Mundy himself, and done at this period.

114 **THOMAS OLDKNOW**

D. R. Sherborn Esq F.S.A.

SIZE $86 \times 56\frac{1}{2}$ in / 218.4 × 143.5 cm   pp 74, 163   **334**

PROVENANCE   Lent by Mrs. C. J. Pooley to the Leeds Art Gallery Committee, 1897. Sale, Christie's, 5th July 1929 (70), as Robert Oldknow. (No 'Robert' is recorded). Sale, Motcomb Galleries, 24th March, 1965, as Raeburn, when bought by the present owner. Thomas Oldknow became managing partner of the bleaching and printing works in his brother Samuel's business. He died in 1791. The picture was therefore painted c 1790–91.

115 **SAMUEL OLDKNOW**
Leeds City Art Gallery
and Temple Newsam House

SIZE   c 85 × 55 in / 215.9 × 139.5 cm   pp 74, 163   **335**

PROVENANCE   Lent by Mrs. C. J. Pooley to the Leeds Art Gallery Committee, 1900. Given to the Gallery, 1950.

116 **THOMAS PARES**

Major J. Pares

SIZE   50 × 40 in / 127 × 101.6 cm   pp 17, 73   **270**

PROVENANCE   Has been in the Pares family since it was painted.

EXHIBITIONS   Derby, 1934 (119).

Could be as late as c 1785–88.

Thomas Pares of Hopwell Hall, Derby (1716–1805).

PECKHAM

Ditto (half length) **of M.ʳ Peckham, £12.12**; among portraits of *c* 1762–65. This is listed again among the same sitters. It is 117 opposite.

PHILPOT, see **ASHTON**

PICKERING

M.ʳ Pickering, £6.6; among sitters from 1st February 1760 onwards. This is repeated among sitters of the same period: **For a 3 q.ʳˢ picture of M.ʳ Pickering, £6.6.**; and again among sitters at Derby.

A portrait of nearly twenty years later (*c* 1777–80), not necessarily of the same Pickering, is 118 opposite.

PICKFORD

A Conversation piece of two of M.ʳ Pickford's Children, £63; among portraits of *c* 1776–77. This is 119 opposite.

PIGOT (see also **BROOKE**)

M.ʳ Pigott; M.ʳˢ Piggott; among sitters at Doncaster, undated. 1760. The entries are repeated among sitters from 1st February 1760 onwards: **M.ʳ Pigott; M.ʳˢ Pigott**, at £12.12 each; again a third time: **For a half Length of M.ʳ Pigott; For a half Length of M.ʳˢ Pigott, £12.12** each. A note in the Account Book (preceding an entry of 17th July 1762) reads: **M.ʳ Edward Miller has given To Piggot 2 Guineas for his frame to be returned to Dubourg** (the frame-maker). These are 120 and 121 opposite.

POCKLETON

Miss Pockleton; among sitters at Newark, undated. 1760. Also: **M.ʳ R. Pockleton; M.ʳ J. Pockleton.**

POLE

Col.ˡ Pool, £21; listed among pictures of 1771–72. This is 122 opposite.

His wife Elizabeth Collier was painted by Wright at the same period: **M.ʳˢ Pool & Child, £63.** A note in the Account Book reads: **Mem. The Size of the pannel that M.ʳˢ Poles picture is to be is in Length 7 ft. 8½ by 5 ft. 8½. ⅛** [? thickness]. This is 123 opposite.

117 **HARRY PECKHAM**

SIZE   50 × 40 in / 127 × 101.6 cm.   pp 2, 17, 28–9, 97–8   **35**
PROVENANCE   Mundy family; Rev. Clark-Maxwell Sale, Christie's, 15th May 1936 (23).
EXHIBITIONS   Derby, 1934 (154).
One of six portraits of members of The Derby Hunt painted c 1762–65 and hung at Markea-
ton Hall, the home of Francis Noel Clarke Mundy. For the others in the series, see
BURDETT.

Major Peter Miller Mundy

118 **REV. WILLIAM (?)
PICKERING**

SIZE   30 × 25 in / 76.2 × 63.5 cm   pp 68–70, 131, 134³   **197**
EXHIBITIONS   Derby, 1866 (99), lent by C. Sanders as 'Rev. G. Pickering'; Derby, 1934
(149); Tate, 1958 (27) for further details.
A John Pickering was vicar of Mackworth 1731–90. What makes it possible that he is
represented is that Wright lists a copy he made of the portrait at a time when he can be assumed to have died, and Wright records his death: **A copy of the late M.ʳ Pickering w.ᵗʰ a
hand. for M.ʳ Th.º Gisborne, £15.15;** among pictures chiefly of the '90's. On the other
hand, a Rev. William Pickering was a member of the Derbyshire Philosophical Society in
the mid-'80's, and the geometrical diagram suggests someone who would be elected to this
body.

Sir Gilbert Inglefield

119 **PICKFORD CHILDREN**

SIZE   58 × 48 in / 147.3 × 121.9 cm   pp 17, 70–1, 73, 143   **185**
EXHIBITIONS   ? R.A., 1779 (361); Derby, 1866 (180); 1870 (310); 1883 (61); 1934 (130).
One of the boys (1773–1836) became Rev. Joseph Pickford and was a Fellow of Oriel, 1794.
Bemrose, 1885, pp. 55–56 quotes a passage from Mozley's *Reminiscences*, p. 65, in which he
tells us the father of these boys was an architect and builder 'and the intimate friend of
Wright', and of Whitehurst. He had built in the Friargate a 'house of some architectural
pretensions' and the sons had divided it. Mozley is inclined to date the picture c 1785 (not
1775 as Bemrose quotes him as saying). It is in fact datable in the late '70's.

Private Collection, U.K.

120 **WILLIAM PIGOT**

See 121   pp 2, 17, 27–8, 103   **23**

121 **MRS WILLIAM PIGOT**

SIZE   each 50 × 40 in / 127 × 101.6 cm   pp 2, 17, 27–8, 34, 103   **24**
William Pigot (d. 1782 aged 53) was the son of Hollis Pigot the vicar (1728–62) of Doncaster.
He married (1756) Elizabeth (1727–65), daughter of William Brooke, mayor of Doncaster.
Sale, Sotheby's, 22nd November 1967 (46) and (47).

R. D. Plant Esq

122 **COL. EDWARD
SACHEVERELL POLE**

SIZE   c 36 × 30 in / 91.4 × 76.2 cm   pp 5, 37, 103   **87**
Signed and dated on cannon: 'Jos. Wright/1772'.
PROVENANCE   Painted for the room at Radburne Hall where it still hangs.

Major J. W. Chandos-Pole

123 **ELIZABETH, WIFE OF
EDWARD
SACHEVERELL POLE,
and HER SON
SACHEVERELL**

SIZE   91¾ × 68¼ in / 233 × 173.3 cm   pp 4–5, 17, 36–8, 108–9   **88**
Signed and dated on plinth: 'Io. Wright Pinx. 1771'.
PROVENANCE   Painted for the room at Radburne Hall where it still hangs.
EXHIBITIONS   ? S. of A., 1771 (200); Tate, 1958 (7) for further details.
A gouache sketch on paper with some brown wash, 18¼ × 11¾ in, for this composition is
in the Derby Art Gallery; from a branch of the family of Darwin into which Elizabeth Pole
married on the death of her first husband. It has colour notes on the plinth: 'Purple and
Straw'; and a label on the reverse: 'E. G. Wheler from E. S. Galton'.

Major J. W. Chandos-Pole

A full length of Mrs Poole Wth her Child; no price listed, among pictures of *c* 1794. It is hard to explain its position in the Account Book, but it can hardly refer to any other picture but the above, unless it was an otherwise unrecorded portrait of Mrs. Pole's daughter-in-law.

The Poles' son Sacheverell (b. 1769) was again painted by Wright as a young man: **Sach! Poole Esq! D?** (i.e. **3 q^{rs} with a hand)**, no price, among pictures of *c* 1794. One imagines that the following entry must relate to the same portrait, in spite of being listed among pictures of *c* 1787–89:
A 3 q^{rs} Picture of M! Pole, £12.12 followed by **Frame for D? £2.2.** This is 124 opposite.
Mrs Poole 3 q^{rs} with hand, no price. This immediately precedes an entry for the portrait of Sacheverell and was presumably intended as a pendant, but the entry is heavily deleted as though the portrait were never executed. A portrait of Sacheverell's wife, Mary Ware, (whom he married *c* 1791) by Beechey hangs as a pendant to the one of himself at Radburne.

RASDALE and/or **RASTALL**

Mrs Rasdale; M! Rasdale; M! W. Rasdale; Mrs W. Rasdale; Old Mrs Rasdale; among sitters at Newark, undated. 1760. **2 Masters Rastall** are listed at eight guineas each among sitters of *c* 1760, and a **M! Rastall** (corrected from 'Rasdale') at fifteen guineas among sitters of the mid-'80's.

ROE

M! Rowe, £10.10; among sitters of *c* 1777–80. This is 126 opposite.

ROLLESTON

M! Rolleston half Length, £12.12; among portraits of *c* 1762–65. This is 127 opposite.

ROUSSEAU

A copy of Rousseau, £12.12 among pictures of *c* 1790. It is conceivable that the portrait of Rousseau given to Wright but by an unknown artist, in Indiana University, Bloomington, reflects this lost composition.

SALES

E. Sales, £2.2; among sitters at Derby, *c* 1760. **A Head of Master C. Sales; D? of M! R^d** [Richard] **Sales,** at ten guineas each, listed among pictures of *c* 1787–88.

SALMON see also **FLINT**

D? (3 q^{rs}) of M! Salmon for M! Flint, £12.12 followed shortly afterwards by an entry: **A 3 q^{rs} of M! Salmon for B. Boothby, £12.12;** among pictures of *c* 1787–88. They must have been done before 1789 when Boothby became 6th Baronet, because Wright always referred to him as 'Sir Brooke' after that date.

A portrait (30 × 25 in) traditionally and no doubt correctly described as that of a Captain Salmon, exists in an English private collection. It is a copy of an unknown painting by Wright of the late '80's. Exhibited: Graves' Galleries, 1910 (62). Plate 272.

SCARSDALE, see **CURZON**

SEWARD

M! Seward, £12.12; among pictures of the very early 1780's. This is 128 opposite.

Miss Seward, £15.15 follows on the entry for her father but it is deleted, and one can assume that it was not painted: otherwise Anna Seward would surely have recorded the fact.

124 **SACHEVERELL POLE**

Major J. W. Chandos-Pole

SIZE   30 × 25 in / 76.2 × 63.5 cm
EXHIBITIONS   Derby, 1934 (155).
Datable in the early '90's.

pp 17, 73, 109   **342**

125 **HENRY RICHMOND**

Professor Oliffe Richmond

SIZE   30 × 25 in / 76.3 × 63.5 cm
PROVENANCE   Has remained in the Richmond family since it was painted.
Henry Richmond, born *c* 1751; son of the Rector of Stockport. The picture dates from *c* 1777–80.

pp 68–9   **198**

126 **CHARLES ROE**

Parish of Christ Church,
Macclesfield

SIZE   30 × 25 in / 76.3 × 63.5 cm
The picture was painted in the late '70's, after the building of the church in 1775, and not long before Roe's death in 1781. See Chaloner, 1950–53, *passim*, especially II, p. 81.

pp 70, 160–1   **201**

127 **LAUNCELOT ROLLISTON**

Major Peter Miller Mundy

SIZE   50 × 40 in / 127 × 101.6 cm
PROVENANCE   Mundy family; Rev. Clark-Maxwell Sale, Christie's, 15th May 1936 (34).
EXHIBITIONS   Derby, 1934 (90).
One of the six portraits of members of The Derby Hunt painted *c* 1762–63 and hung at Markeaton Hall, the home of F. N. C. Mundy. For the other five, see BURDETT.

pp 2, 17, 28, 97   **36**

128 **REV. THOMAS SEWARD**

(Untraced)

SIZE   30 × 25 in / 76.2 × 63.5 cm
PROVENANCE   White-Thomson Sale, Christie's, 1st February 1924 (158) illus. catalogue.
The picture looks excellent from the catalogue illustration.
Rev. Thomas Seward (d. 1790 aged 81), Canon Residentiary of Lichfield Cathedral.
ENGRAVING   dated March 1811 reproduced as frontispiece to Vol. II of Anna Seward's *Letters* (Edinburgh, 1811).
The author is indebted to Canon D. A. Hodges, Precentor of Lichfield Cathedral, for informing him that the portrait is untraced in Lichfield, in spite of widespread enquiries.

pp 17, 68–9, 100   **230**

SHERRING Cap.! **Sherring, £6.6;** among sitters at Derby, *c* 1760.

SHUTTLEWORTH M.! **Shuttleworth; M.ʳˢ D.º; Miss D.º;** at twelve guineas each among sitters at Derby, undated, *c* 1760. These must have represented James Shuttleworth of Gawthorpe and Aston-on-Trent, his wife, Mary, and one of his daughters (Mary or Elizabeth). They were shown again on a single canvas:

Family Picture of M.! Shuttleworth, £42. The entry is deleted along with others on the same sheet, and the picture is listed again: **For a Conversation piece of M.! M.ʳˢ & Miss Shuttleworth, £42.** This is 129 opposite.
M.! Holding Shuttleworth, £10.10; among sitters of *c* 1777–80.
James Shuttleworth was dead by this time, so this presumably refers to one of his sons (? Robert) whose grandfather on his mother's side was Robert Holden of Aston Hall. She was an only daughter and inherited the Holden property. Wright also described the other Robert Holden of Darley Abbey (q.v.) as 'Holding', so this must have been an alternative form of the name.

SIKES M.! **Sikes;** among sitters at Newark, undated. 1760. In the early nineteenth century the Chauntry House, Newark contained portraits by Wright of *Mr. and Mrs. Joseph Sikes*, according to Bousfield, 1832, p. 8, who tells an amusing anecdote about a terrier licking his master's image on the canvas.

SIMPSON **Lynne Simpson Esq.ʳ; M.ʳˢ Simpson; Miss Simpson;** among sitters at Retford, undated. Winter 1759–60 or 1760.

SMYTHE M.! **& M.ʳˢ Smythe, £21** (i.e. at ten guineas each); among sitters at Liverpool, 1769.

M.ʳˢ **Smythe** is not the same as 131 opposite.

SOUTHWARD M.ʳˢ **Southward, £10.10** (a note to say she had paid five guineas); among sitters at Liverpool, 1769.

STAFFORD **Two Miss Staffords, £21** (i.e. at ten guineas each); among sitters at Liverpool, 1769.

M.! **Stafford, £10.10** and **Miss Stafford,** no price named; among sitters at Macclesfield. It is hard to date this entry from its position in the Account Book, but a **M.! Stafford** is listed again at the same price among pictures of *c* 1777–80, along with 'Rowe' whose portrait still hangs in a church at Macclesfield. So he is presumably the same. He is accompanied in this second entry by **M.! Will.ᵐ Stafford, £10.10.**

STAMFORD **Miss Stamford; Miss L. Stamford** at £ 8.8 each; among pictures of *c* 1784.
STANIFORTH M.! **Stannyforth, £15.15;** among sitters at Liverpool, 1769. This is 132 opposite.

STAVELY (see **CHARACTER STUDIES** and **SCIENCE, PHILOSOPHY,** under *A Philosopher by Lamplight*)

STEAD, see HOPE

STENTEN or STENTON M.! **Stenten; M.ʳˢ Stenten,** at £6.6 each; among sitters from 1st February 1760 onwards. These are repeated among sitters of the same period: **For 2 3 q.ʳˢ of M.! & M.ʳˢ Stenton, £12.12.**

129 **JAMES SHUTTLEWORTH, HIS WIFE AND DAUGHTER**

Lord Shuttleworth

SIZE   56 × 72 in / 142.2 × 182.9 cm   pp 2–4, 17, 30–2, 34, 36–9, 67, 105[5], 162   **51**
Signed and dated on plinth left: 'J [?—partly hidden by frame] Wright Pinx!/1764'.
EXHIBITIONS   ? S. of A., 1765 (164); Derby, 1934 (13), illus. plate II.

130 **ELIZABETH SHUTTLEWORTH, MRS JOHN CREWE**

Lady Cynthia Colville

SIZE   30 × 25 in / 76.2 × 63.5 cm   p 97[2]
A portrait of her as a much younger woman is at Leck Hall (Lord Shuttleworth), signed by Vanderbank and dated 1732. Born c 1711, she married John Crewe of Crewe Hall, Cheshire. Her son John became 1st Baron Crewe of Crewe. Wright's portrait dates from about the mid 1760's at the time of their son's marriage. She was the sister of James Shuttleworth represented in 129.

131 **'ELIZABETH KENNION, MRS SMYTH'**

W. R. Kennion Esq

SIZE   30 × 25 in / 76.2 × 63.5 cm   pp 68, 71   **188**
PROVENANCE   Sale Sotheby's, 12th December 1956 (54), sold with portraits of Mr. and Mrs. Hall (q.v.).
EXHIBITIONS   Derby, 1883 (101), lent by Lorenzo K. Hall.
It is uncertain whether the sitter is correctly identified. Elizabeth Kennion married a Rev. John Smyth. The portrait is of the late 1770's, *en suite* with the Hall portraits.

132 **THOMAS STANIFORTH**

Tate Gallery, London

SIZE   36¼ × 30 in / 92.1 × 76.2 cm   pp 17, 34, 36, 73, 99, 124, 129   **72**
PROVENANCE   Sale, Christie's, 2nd April 1965 (150); purchased by Tate, 1965.
Thomas Staniforth (1735–1803), from Darnall, Co. Yorks; married Elizabeth Goore (1760), daughter of Charles Goore (d. 1783; q.v. GORE). A portrait of his wife by Henry Pickering, signed and dated 1761, was in the same Christie sale (No. 82).
15 gns. is the expected price for a picture of this size (a Kit cat).
For further details, see *Tate Gallery Report 1965–66*, H.M.S.O., 1967, pp. 21–22. The Reports quotes from an old label on the stretcher giving biographical details.

STORER	**Miss Storer**; among sitters at Derby, undated, *c* 1760.
STOW	**M.ʳ Stow; Mʳˢ Stow; M.ʳ S.ᵗ** (? Stephen) **Stow**; among sitters at Newark, undated. 1760.
STRUTT	**An half length of M.ʳ Strutt, £25.4;** among pictures of *c* 1790. This is repeated among portraits of the late 1780's. It is 133 opposite.
	A copy of M.ʳ Strutt wᵗʰ a hand, £15.15. This must have been the upper half of the Belper near full-length.
SUTTON	**P. Rob.ᵗ** (Robert) **Sutton;** among sitters at Newark, undated. 1760.
	M.ʳ Sutton and **Mʳˢ Sutton;** among sitters at Retford, undated. 1760. **M.ʳ Sutton** is given twice more: among sitters from 1st February 1760, *£7.7;* and among sitters of the same period: **For a Kitt Cat of M.ʳ Sutton, £7.7.**
SWAN	**Miss Swan, £6.6;** among sitters from 1st February 1760 onwards. This must be the same lady as listed among sitters of *c* 1760: **For a 3 qʳˢ of Mʳˢ** (altered from 'Miss') **Swan, £6.6.** She is recorded a third time among sitters at Derby as 'Miss Swan'.
SYNNOT	**M.ʳ Sennit's 3 Children, £73.10.** This is 135 opposite.
TARLTON	**Copy of Mʳˢ Tarlton, £8.8;** among sitters at Liverpool, 1769. Perhaps a member of a slave-trading family in Liverpool, the Tarletons.
TATTON	**Mʳˢ T. Tatton, £10.10;** among portraits of *c* 1780.
TAYLOR	**Miss Taylor; Miss K. Taylor,** at *£6.6* each; among sitters at Derby, undated, *c* 1760.
TEAD	**For a Kitcat of Mʳˢ Tead, £9.9;** among portraits of the early 1760's. The entry is repeated among sitters at Derby of the same period, and again among entries from 1st February 1760 onwards.
THOMPSON	**Governor Thompson,** among sitters at Lincoln, undated. 1760. Other Thompsons are listed among sitters at Boston of the same date: **M.ʳ Thompson; Mʳˢ Thompson.**
THORNHILL	**Two full lengths in one picture of Master Thornhill's, £73.10;** among pictures of *c* 1789–90. This is 136 opposite.
TIPSON	**M.ʳ Tipson; Mʳˢ Tipson,** at *£6.6* each; among sitters at Derby, from 1st February 1760 onwards. This is repeated as **For 2 3 qʳˢ of M.ʳ & Mʳˢ Tipson, £12.12.**
TRAVELL see **WITTS**	
WARD	**M.ʳ Ward, £12.12;** among pictures of 1781. This is 137 opposite.
WARFE	**M.ʳ Warfe, £10.10;** among sitters at Liverpool, 1769.

133 **JEDEDIAH STRUTT**

The Lord Belper

SIZE   50 × 40 in / 127 × 101.6 cm   pp 17, 74, 96, 163–4   **324**
EXHIBITIONS   Manchester Art Treasures, 1857 (84); National Portrait Exhibition, 1867 (861); Derby, 1870 (821); Nottingham, 1878 (50); Derby, 1883 (62); 1934 (135) illus. catalogue plate VIII—and on other occasions.

134 **'MRS CATHERINE SWINDELL'**

Leicester Museum and Art Gallery

SIZE   28 × 22 in / 71.1 × 55.9 cm   pp 36, 38   **81**
EXHIBITIONS   Derby, 1934 (11), lent by Messrs. Agnew. See catalogue of the Leicester Museum, 1958 (176), illus.
The name of the sitter is uncertain, but there can be no doubt about the artist.
c 1769–72.

135 **SYNNOT CHILDREN**

Mrs. Michael Hawker

SIZE   60 × 49½ in / 152.4 × 125,8 cm   pp 70–2, 137   **221**
Signed and dated bottom right: 'I. Wright [Pinx!?] 1781'.
PROVENANCE   Hart-Synnot Trustees Sale, Christie's, 5th July 1918 (61).
ENGRAVED   By J. R. Smith, London, published 25th April 1782.
EXHIBITIONS   R.A. 1781 (181).
Sold by Lord Beaverbrook to Mrs. Patricia Hawker of Medindie, S. Australia; left Beaverbrook Gallery February 1961.
Bemrose, 1885, p. 52 describes the visit of Mrs. Morewood (q.v.) and Mr. Holland (q.v.) to see the picture at Wright's house. The children are Marcus, Walter and Maria Eliza. Their father, Sir Walter Synnot, came from Co. Armagh.
An undated press cutting (V. & A. Library, Vol. I, p. 204, indexed under 'Press Cuttings') describes the picture, thereby definitely identifying it as R.A. 1781 (181).

136 **THORNHILL CHILDREN**

Private collection, U.K.

SIZE   57 × 48½ in / 144.8 × 123.2 cm   pp 71, 73   **278**
PROVENANCE   Has remained in the family since it was painted.
EXHIBITIONS   Derby, 1870 (256); 1883 (78); 1934 (124).
The two boys were the sons of Bache Thornhill (1747–1830) of Stanton-in-Peak; Sheriff of the County, 1776. The older boy, Henry Bache, was born in 1780 and is indeed shown at about the age of 10. The younger boy William was born in the following year. They died in 1822 and 1851 respectively. Haddon Hall is shown in the background. This house is visible from Stanton Hall, the seat of the Thornhills.

137 **SAMUEL WARD**

Derby Museum & Art Gallery

SIZE   30 × 25 in / 76.2 × 63.5 cm   p 70² **229**
PROVENANCE   Bequeathed to Derby 1947 by Mrs. Samuel Ward, the wife of a descendant of the sitter.
Clearly this does not refer to the same person as Wright mentions in a letter from Bath, 9th March 1777 (quoted Bemrose, 1885, pp. 47–48): 'Since M! Ward is dead, we are happy Miss Ward did not regard our importuning her to stay here...' The picture can hardly be before the early '80's and may even be a little later, and a nineteenth-century label on the reverse gives his dates as 1732–1820 'of Derby and later of Richmond'.

WARREN

Miss Warren, small, £10.10; among pictures of 1776–79. Another portrait of a Miss Warren is listed twice: **A whole length of Miss Warren, £16.16**; among portraits of the early '60's; and among sitters from 1st February 1760 onwards at the same price: **Miss Warren.** This is 138 opposite.

WHETHAM (see also **HOLDEN)**

Half length copy of Mᵣ Whetham, £25.4; among portraits of *c* 1780–82. This entry is followed by: **a small Oval Dᵒ of Dᵒ** at eight guineas. The oval destined for Lord Middleton has not come to light. The prime original (which Wright does not list) is 139 opposite. The **Half length copy** is 140 opposite.

WHITEHURST

Mᵣ Whithurst Kit Cat, £18.18 (note added by Wright that nine guineas had been paid); among portraits of the early 1780's. This is 141 opposite.

WILDE

Mᵣ Wilde; Mᵣˢ Wilde, £6.6 each; among sitters from 1st February 1760 onwards. These entries are repeated among sitters of the same period: **For 2 3 qᵣˢ of Mᵣ & Mᵣˢ Wilde, £12.12**; and again among sitters at Derby, *c* 1760. This could be the Anthony Wilde who paid Wright rent during his absence in Italy: the Account Book has a note under the date 5th April 1774: **Recᵈ of Anthony Wilde one Years Rent for the Close e** (etc.) **due Lady Day (O.S. (Old Style) 1774); £8.**

WILLBY

Mᵣ Willby; among sitters at Boston, undated. 1760.

WILLS

Mᵣ Wills; among sitters at Lincoln, undated. 1760.

WILMOT

Master Simon & Harvey Wilmot, £6.6; among sitters from 1st February 1760 onwards. Other entries make clear that there were two portraits: **For a 3 qᵣˢ Picture of Master S. Wilmot; Dᵒ of Master Harvey Wilmot, £3.3** each; among sitters at Derby of *c* 1760. Another sheet of the Account Book has among sitters at Derby: **Master Wilmot; Miss Wilmot; Master C. Wilmot; Master R. Wilmot; Master S. Wilmot; Master Harvey W.**, at £3.3 each. This makes 6 Wilmot children, if **Master Wilmot** is taken as the eldest and thus too grand to have a Christian name: five boys and one girl. They are 142–147 opposite.

138 FRANCES WARREN

Mrs. Gerard Sweetman

SIZE   50 × 40 in / 127 × 101.6 cm   pp 30, 33   **48**

On the stretcher is an inscription (? nineteenth century) in a semi-educated hand: 'Frances Warren dau of/The Hon John Pollard Warren/by Wright/of Derby'.

139 JOHN WHETHAM OF KIRKLINGTON

Mrs. Daphne M. Smith

SIZE   50 × 40 in / 127 × 101.6 cm   pp 17, 34, 71–2   **195**

PROVENANCE   The present owner is a direct descendant of the sitter. She acquired the portrait from her father, Major S. A. Boddam-Whetham, D.S.O., M.C.

EXHIBITIONS   Graves' Galleries, 1910 (52) lent by J. W. Boddam-Whetham.

140 JOHN WHETHAM OF KIRKLINGTON

Major H. R. Holden

SIZE   50 × 40 in / 127 × 101.6 cm   pp 72, 124[1]   **194**

EXHIBITIONS   Derby, 1883 (39) as 'Mr. Cheetham', lent by John Holden.

Whetham died in 1781. The prime original at any rate must have been done by this date.

141 JOHN WHITEHURST, F.R.S.

John Smith & Sons, Midland Clock Works Derby Ltd.

SIZE   36¼ × 28 in / 92.1 × 71.1 cm   pp 17, 68, 70–1, 116, 154   **227**

PROVENANCE   Nephew of sitter (see Davies, 1811, p. 220); Bemrose Collection.

EXHIBITIONS   Robin's Rooms, 1785 (25); National Portrait Exhibition, 1867 (714); Derby, 1870 (803); 1883 (9); 1934 (21); Birmingham, 1966 (57) and often elsewhere.

ENGRAVED   Frontispiece in Whitehurst, 1792 as half-length, by J. Hall, published 2nd January 1786. Again as tondo by A. Smith published 10th October 1788 (*Universal Magazine*, November 1788).

Wright's niece Hannah (MS. Derby Public Library) quotes a description of *c* 1785 (source untraced) of the portrait as 'not mentioned in the catalogue' of the Robin's Rooms exhibition, showing an 'ingenious gentleman well known in the learned world'. Hannah adds Whitehurst's name in a note. No. 25 in the 1785 exhibition catalogue as a 'portrait of a gentleman' must have been the one.

142 RICHARD STAUNTON WILMOT

See 147   pp 26, 69, 98   **9**

143 DOROTHY WILMOT

See 147   pp 26, 98   **11**

144 EDWARD SACHEVERELL WILMOT

See 147   pp 26, 98   **12**

145 ROBERT WILMOT

See 147   pp 26, 98, 125   **15**

146 SIMON WILMOT

See 147   pp 26, 69, 98   **13**

147 HARVEY WILMOT

Peter Wilmot-Sitwell Esq

SIZE   each 20 × 16 in / 50.8 × 40.6 cm   pp 26, 69, 98   **10**

The six Wilmot children were all born between 1747 and 1753 and are therefore shown at ages ranging from 13 to 7. They are the children of Richard Wilmot (d. 1771 aged 89) and Dorothy Degge. They were married in 1746 and the children are: Richard Staunton (1747–72); Dorothy (1748–79); Edward Sacheverell (1749–1836); Robert (1750–1803); Simon (1752–81); and Harvey (1753–74). The only puzzle in Wright's list of the sitters is 'C' Wilmot who is not recorded, but perhaps one of them had a nickname beginning with that letter (? Edward Sacheverell).

Mrs **Wilmot, £12.12**; among sitters of *c* 1760. The entry is repeated: **A half Length of Mrs Wilmot, £12.12**; among sitters of the same period. This is 148 opposite.

A full Length of Lady Wilmot & her Child, £73.10. On the reverse of a letter dated August 1788 is an account made out to **Sir R^t Wilmot** including among other items: **Lady Wilmot & her Child as a Madona**, at the same price. This is 149 opposite.

WILSON

Master Wilson; Miss Wilson; among sitters at Lincoln, undated. 1760. Letter from Wright to his brother from Bath, 15th April 1776 (see Bemrose, 1885, p. 45): 'I am now painting a half length of Dr Wilson & his adopted daughter, Miss Macauley' (q.v.)... 'The Doctor is a very popular man and is fighting in my cause stoutly, for he thinks me ill-treated...'
Dr. Thomas Wilson (1703–84), prebendary of Westminster and rector of St. Stephen's Walbrook; son of the Bishop of Sodor and Man. He was in Derby in 1773 and settled soon afterwards in Bath (see *The Life of... Thomas Wilson, D.D., Lord Bishop of Sodor and Man*, Oxford, 1863, I, pp. xi ff. See also the disobliging remarks about him in Stevens, 1965, p. 50, entry for 12th October 1792).

WINN

Mr **Winn, £12.12**; among sitters of *c* 1760.

WOLLOT

Miss Wollot, £6.6; among sitters at Derby, *c* 1760.

WOOD

A conversation of 3 of Mr Woods Children, £84. This is 151 opposite.

3 q^{rs} of Mr Wood; D^o of Mrs Wood, £12.12 each. The entries follow on those for the children. They are 152 and 153 opposite.

?WOODVILLE

Bemrose, 1885, p. 55 records a portrait of Mrs. Woodville supposedly painted by Wright. In his day it had been cut down from a full length (90 × 54 in) to a 'Kit-cat'. He also lists (p. 124) a full length of Mr. Woodville.

YATES, see **ASHTON**
YORKE, see **LYGON**

End of sequences of entries from Wright's Account Book devoted to identified sitters. On the subsequent pages quotations from the Account Book will be found incorporated in the catalogue entries and set in bold type.

148 **MRS WILMOT**

Sir Robert Wilmot, Bt.

SIZE   50 × 40 in / 127 × 101.6 cm   pp 29, 98⁸, 158   **40**

EXHIBITIONS   Manchester Art Treasures, 1857 (82); Derby, 1866 (173); 1870 (779); 1883 (79); Graves' Galleries, 1910 (67); and on other occasions.

She was Mary Woollet or Woollett, wife of Robert Mead Wilmot who became 2nd baronet on the death of his father, Sir Edward Wilmot of Chaddesden, in 1786. The portrait was painted shortly after her marriage in 1759. It is sometimes incorrectly described as of Sir Edward's wife, Sarah Marsh Mead.

149 **LADY WILMOT AND HER CHILD**

Mrs. George Anson

SIZE   c 79 × 66 in / 200 × 167.7 cm   pp 17, 74, 125   **280**

PROVENANCE   From Osmaston Hall; Sir Robert Wilmot's son Robert married a Horton of Catton, which explains the picture's presence at Catton.

EXHIBITIONS   Derby, 1883 (29); R.A., 1886 (5).

She married in 1783 Sir Robert Wilmot, Bart. of Osmaston-by-Derby. The child in the picture is Robert John, b. 1784, succeeding his father as 3rd Baronet. Lady Wilmot died in March 1788, so the picture was started at the latest early that year.

150 **MRS EDWARD WITTS**

Major General F. V. B. Witts

SIZE   30 × 25 in / 76.2 × 63.5 cm   pp 67–8, 71, 95   **178**

Inscribed bottom right: 'WRIGHT/pinx!/1776' in another hand but probably still eighteenth century.

She was Agnes Travell, b. 1748, m. 1775 Edward Witts of Upper Slaughter in whose family the portrait remains. He was High Sheriff for Oxfordshire, 1779. His portrait by Romney, inscribed 'ROMNEY pinx!/1779' in the same hand as on the Wright portrait, hangs as a pendant, and may well have been painted three years later as such. It is catalogued in Ward and Roberts, II, 1904, p. 173. Romney's sitter book records sittings in April and May 1779, which gives one confidence in accepting the date 1776 for the Wright. If this is correct (and the style confirms this dating), it is the only known Bath portrait unless, as is conceivable, the portraits of *William Alvey Darwin* and his wife (q.v.) were painted there. Its absence from the Account Book is understandable since other Bath portraits are missing from it as well.

151 **WOOD CHILDREN**

Derby Museum & Art Gallery

SIZE   66 × 53 in / 167.7 × 134.7 cm   p 71   **279**

Signed and dated below Robert Wood's foot: 'I.W.P/1789'.

PROVENANCE   Remained in the Wood family until 1934; sale, Christie's, 1st June 1934 (62), illus. catalogue, withdrawn by consent of owner, R. H. Wood who sold it to N.A.C.F. (see Report for this year, p. 36).

EXHIBITIONS   Derby, 1934 (34); Tate, 1958 (28) for further details.

The children are: left, Robert; centre, John; right, Mary. Their parents were Hugh and Sarah Wood of Swanwick, Derbyshire (see below).

152 **HUGH WOOD**

See 153   pp 17, 73   **277**

153 **SARAH WOOD**

Private Collection, U.K.

SIZE   Each 30 × 25 in / 76.2 × 63.5 cm   pp 17, 73   **276**

PROVENANCE   Wood Collection until 1934; R. H. Wood Sale, Christie's, 1st June 1934 (64, 63); Christie's, 1st June 1954 (53, 54), bought back by a member of the Wood family. The style confirms a date c 1789.

End of catalogue of portraits of identified sitters.

154 'INDIAN CAPTAIN'

(Untraced)

'Indian Captain'
EXHIBITIONS   S. of A., 1767 (188) as 'Portrait of a Gentleman, whole length'.
Described in *Le Pour et Le Contre*, 1767 as:
    '...His Indian Captain makes the Critics stare,
    And awes their envy with his martial air...'
This was most likely an officer in the East India Company.

155 **YOUNG MAN IN FUR CAP**
J. B. Speed Museum,
Louisville, Kentucky

SIZE   *c* 16 × 12 in / 40.6 × 30.5 cm Charcoal   pp 38, 67–8 **121**

156 **YOUNG ARTIST**
Private Collection, U.K.

SIZE   *c* 50 × 40 in / 127 × 101.6 cm   p 36 **82**
c 1770

157 **YOUNG MAN**

Private Collection, U.K.

SIZE   *c* 30 × 25 in / 76.2 × 63.5 cm   p 30 **42**
Feigned oval, ruddy complexion, dressed in dark olive green, seated resting his arm on a table.
c 1762–64

158 **PORTRAIT OF A BOY**

Mr. and Mrs. Karl F. Milde

SIZE   22 × 18 in / 55.9 × 45.7 cm   p 26 **8**
Signed and dated bottom left: 'J Wright / [illegible word resembling 'Thorne'] pinx!/1758'.
PROVENANCE   Acquired by the present owners at the Plaza Auction Galleries, New York, 1939, appearing in the sale catalogue as by 'T. Wright'. The signature and dates are recorded there, though the picture had been repainted.

159 **FEMALE PORTRAIT**

Dr. and Mrs. Merlin L. Trumbull

SIZE   30 × 25 in / 76.2 × 63.5 cm   pp 28, 99 **32**
PROVENANCE   Christie's, 25th February 1949 (112); New York Art Market, 1952, where purchased by the present owners.
c 1760. Similar to the portraits at Temple Newsam (see below) and St. Louis (see 'CATTON').

160 **YOUNG GIRL**
Leeds City Art Gallery and
Temple Newsam House

SIZE   16 × 13 in / 40.6 × 33 cm   pp 28, 99 **29**
c 1760
At Temple Newsam as Allan Ramsay.

161 **FEMALE PORTRAIT**
Private Collection, U.K.

SIZE   30 × 25 in / 76.2 × 63.5 cm   p 27[1]
c 1760

162 **FEMALE PORTRAIT**
(Untraced)

Old photograph pasted into extra-illustrated Bemrose (National Portrait Gallery), un-captioned, *c* 1761–63.   p 30 **47**

A 3 q^{rs} of a Girl with Doves, £ 15.15; among pictures of early '80's. The entry is deleted but not in such a vicious way as to make one think the order was cancelled.

163 **TWO GIRLS AND A NEGRO SERVANT**

Heirs of Oliver Vernon Watney

Two Girls wth [?] their Black Servant in the hands of Pether Sold to Mr. Parker, £40. The whole entry except the name of the purchaser and the price is deleted. The entry is not datable within a narrower bracket than the late 1760's to early 1770's.
SIZE   50 × 40 in / 127 × 101.6 cm   pp. 35, 107 **73**
PROVENANCE   At Charlbury since before 1895.
EXHIBITIONS   S. of A., 1770 (155) as a 'Conversation of Girls'; R. A. 'British Portraits', 1956–57 (336).
c 1769–70, on stylistic grounds.
Pether had it, presumably, to engrave, but no engraving by him is known to the author.

164 **SELF PORTRAIT**

SIZE   30 × 25 in / 76.2 × 63.5 cm   pp 21, 26, 103   **6**
In Van Dyck costume; c 1758.
PROVENANCE   In Wright family (through his daughter Anna Romana) since it was painted.
EXHIBITIONS   ? Derby, 1870 (793); 1947 (18).
An approximately contemporary, similar self-portrait drawing, head and shoulders, though
not in Van Dyck costume, is in the Fitzwilliam Museum (No. 895) from Collection of Sir
Francis Seymour Haden; pencil (oval), $4\frac{3}{8} \times 3\frac{3}{4}$ in. On reverse of mount is an old inscrip-

Miss D. M. R. Cade

tion: 'Jos. Wright Esq!' / for Eliza Haden / from Miss Wright.' Illus. Morris, 1932, p. 35.

165 **SELF PORTRAIT**

SIZE $16\frac{3}{4} \times 11\frac{5}{8}$ in / 42.5 × 29.5 cm   p 38   **71**
Charcoal on bluish paper with white heightening.

James Ricau, U.S.A.

In fur cap and kerchief around it; c 1765–68.

166 **SELF PORTRAIT**

SIZE   17 × $11\frac{5}{8}$ in / 43.2 × 29.5 cm Charcoal.   p 38[1]   **69**
In turban. Faintly inscribed and dated on wooden backing '1768', though not in a

Mr. and Mrs. Paul Mellon

contemporary hand. This is in fact about the correct date.

167 **SELF PORTRAIT**

SIZE   30 × 25 in / 76.2 × 63.5 cm   pp 21, 38, 45, 103, 108   **Frontispieces**
In fur cap and kerchief around it; c 1767–68.
EXHIBITIONS   Graves' Galleries, 1910 (27).
On the reverse is a study for the *Air Pump*, which indicates (though it does not establish)

Charles Rogers-Coltman Esq

a date not later than 1768. Though he looks older, Wright was then still in his mid-thirties.

168 **SELF PORTRAIT**

SIZE   21 × $14\frac{1}{2}$ in / 53.3 × 36.8 cm Charcoal.   p 38   **70**
In fur cap; c 1767–70.
EXHIBITIONS   Derby, 1883 (43), lent by W. Bemrose; Norwich, 1959.
Similar to the *Self-portrait* in the Rogers-Coltman Collection (see 167), but with a fur

Derby Museum & Art Gallery

collar.

169 **SELF PORTRAIT**

SIZE   c 28 × 24 in / 71.1 × 60.9 cm   pp 22, 38, 138[4]   **120**
Right hand to chin. c early '70's.
PROVENANCE   In Wright family (through his daughter Anna Romana) since it was
painted.
EXHIBITIONS   ? Derby, 1870 (798).
Copy by John Holland of Ford (Turbutt Collection) exhibited Derby, 1934 (79). The copy
bears inscription on reverse: 'M! Wright from an original of his painting by J. Holland'.

Since Holland's copy of Wright's self-portrait in a broad-brimmed hat (see 170) is dated 1800, it is possible that a label pasted into p. 104 of the National Portrait Gallery's extra-illustrated Bemrose refers to this picture: 'Joseph Wright/ from the original, by himself/ This copy is dedicated to/Thomas Borrow Esq.' who's good nature will excuse/what his judgement may condemn/in the more feeble pencil/of his obedient/Servant/J. Holland/ Ford/Oct.' 18/1802'.

Mrs. Beryl E. Cade

170 SELF PORTRAIT

SIZE 28 × 23½ in / 71.1 × 59.7 cm   pp 22, 138[4], 142[2] **Fig 8**
In broad-brimmed hat. ? c 1779–82.
ENGRAVED By James Ward, February 1807, as in James Cade Collection.
Many versions are known, but probably the best is: Derby, 1883 (46) and 1934 (76), lent from the Cade Collection. Version in Derby Art Gallery, not autograph, exhibited Tate, 1958 (34). A copy, dated 1800 with a semi-illiterate inscription on the reverse (due to it having been faultily transcribed) by John Holland of Ford, in a private collection, U.K. In a letter from Holland to J. L. Philips, 31st December 1800 (MS., Derby Public Library), he says he made two copies from Wright's portrait 'with the hat on'.

Formerly Cade Collection

171 SELF PORTRAIT

Before April 1784   pp 148, 154
EXHIBITIONS Robins's Rooms, 1785 (20) as 'Portrait of an Artist'.
Letter from Wright in Derby to Wedgwood in London, 20th April 1784 (Barlaston MSS): '...D.' Darwin also mentioned how much you admired my portrait and advised me by all means to let you have it and paint another for my friend More of Rome... [postscript] If you should have my portrait I hope you'll indulge me with it, to put in my Exhibition' (at Robins's Rooms the following spring).
Letter from Wedgwood in London to Wright, 29th April 1784 (Finer & Savage, 1965, p. 277): 'you will oblige me very much in letting me have the portrait I was so much struck with in your room. To say nothing of the enthusiasm with which I admire the author I shall place his portrait Considered as a painting only as the gem of my little collection...'
Letter from Wright to Hayley, 26th September 1784 (National Portrait Gallery's extra-illustrated Bemrose): 'I have now in my possession a finished portrait of myself w.ch I painted for my friend More at Rome but M.' Wedgwood being much pleased w.th it, wished to be the possessor of it; ... I have let him have it...'
It is not known whether Wright painted the duplicate for Jacob More, but Wedgwood had his picture, as we know from its listing in an account presented by Wright to John Wedgwood, 26th June 1785 (Barlaston MSS.): **...my portrait, £16.16.**

(Untraced)

172 SELF PORTRAIT

Aged 59, no hat; 1793.   pp 22, 134–5 **Fig 9**
PROVENANCE Rev. Thomas Gisborne; Mrs. Griffiths.
EXHIBITIONS Derby, 1883 (52), lent by Mrs. Griffiths.
Bemrose, 1885 uses this portrait as his frontispiece. It is not the same as the one now belonging to Col. Sir John Crompton-Inglefield (exhibited Derby, 1934 (78)), which is not good enough to be an original. The latter bears an inscription on a relining canvas (incorrectly transcribed) no doubt from the inscription on the original canvas: 'JOSEPHUS WRIGHT/Anno Dom. 1793/Ætat 59/Manu propriâ/Tabulam hanc/Amico suo T. Gisborne/Dono dedit/Pictor.'

Formerly
Collection Mrs. Griffiths

JOHN WRIGHT (Father)

What may have been an original of 30 × 25 in was lent by Miss Cade to Derby, 1870 (768); 1883 (71). An early portrait, probably done in the '50's.

HANNAH WRIGHT (Mother)

What may have been an original of 30 × 25 in was lent by Miss Cade to Derby, 1870 (773); 1883 (51). This also was a juvenile work.

173 'DR RICHARD WRIGHT' (Brother)

Mr. and Mrs. Paul Mellon

SIZE 30 × 25 in / 76.3 × 63.5 cm

p 73 **271**

PROVENANCE Mrs. Lemann; Sale, Christie's, 2nd November 1963 (63).

EXHIBITIONS R.A., 1964–65 (235).

Said to be a portrait of his brother, though described in the sale catalogue as 'Rev. Dr. Richard Wright'. Whether the brother or not, it is an autograph work.

174 HANNAH WRIGHT (Sister)

(Untraced)

SIZE 30 × 25 in / 76.3 × 63.5 cm

A half-length in a feigned oval, three-quarter-face to right with left arm resting on left cheek and brow, c 1760, existed. It may have been the one lent by Miss Cade to Derby, 1870 (781).

A copy is known from an old photograph pasted into the National Portrait Gallery's extra-illustrated Bemrose, which used to be in a caravan on the Cam and is now in Spain.

ANN WRIGHT (Sister)
(Untraced)

What may have been an original was lent by Miss Cade to Derby, 1870 (791).

175 ANNA ROMANA WRIGHT (Daughter, as child)

Miss D. M. R. Cade

SIZE 30 × 25 in / 76.3 × 63.5 cm

EXHIBITIONS Derby, 1934 (84).

Anna Romana is shown at the age of about three or four which gives us the date c 1777–78. The portrait is unfinished.

A pencil drawing in the Derby Art Gallery, 14 × 9 in, shows the child in the same pose but unaccompanied by the dog.

176 ANNA ROMANA WRIGHT (Daughter, nearly grown up)
Miss D. M. R. Cade

Early to mid 1790's.

177 TWO OF WRIGHT'S CHILDREN (? Joseph and Harriet)
Formerly Cade Collection

Early 1780's. Illus. Bemrose, 1885, opp. p. 56, as in Cade Collection.

EXHIBITIONS Derby, 1883 (75) as 'John and Maria'.

178 HARRIET WRIGHT (Daughter)

Derby Museum and Art Gallery

Panel. 10 × 8⅜ in / 25.4 × 21.3 cm

p 20 **322**

PROVENANCE T. A. G. Pocock, by whom sold to Derby Art Gallery, 1967.

This sketch in brownish monochrome has a label on the reverse in a hand of about the mid-nineteenth century; there is no reason whatever to doubt its accuracy: 'Portrait of Harriet Wright daughter of Jo Wright of Derby by her Father. given by him to his favorite friend Mary Tunnaley & by her to her daughter named Harriet after Miss Harriet Wright./Harriet B. Lores [?]' followed by an illegible word which may be a house or town.

Wright's second daughter Harriet (1778–1860) is shown aged about eleven. The style of the picture also suggests a date c 1790. She is so much older than the little girl in the double portrait (see 177) that it is not possible to say whether it is the same daughter.

179 RICHARD WRIGHT (Nephew)

Private Collection, U.K.

A 3 qrs. of my Nephew Rd Wright; among pictures of 1786–88.

SIZE 30 × 25 in / 76.2 × 63.5 cm

pp 36[1], 73, 163 **273**

EXHIBITIONS Graves' Galleries, 1910 (61), lent by C. J. Cade. (The present owners are members of the Cade family and descended direct from the artist.)

Richard (1757–89) was son of the artist's brother John. He is shown at about the age of thirty, in naval uniform. According to M. S. Robinson of the National Maritime Museum (to whom the author is indebted) there were no commanders named Richard Wright at the period, so he may have been a warrant officer.

1

Mr Wright; Mrs Wright; among sitters at Derby, undated *c* 1760.
For these he charged six guineas each, which he would be unlikely to do if they had been family portraits. The only family portrait entered in the Account Book, and there unpriced, is that of the most remote, the nephew (see 179).

COPIES AFTER OLD MASTERS

Copy of Lady Rubens, £12.12; among pictures of the '70's. This was presumably a copy of a Rubens female portrait.
Wright is also alleged to have done a copy (14 × 10 in; Derby Art Gallery) after a contemporary portrait of the secretary of Charles I, *Sir John Coke*, but the evidence of his authorship is inconclusive.

180 **STUDY AFTER AN ANTIQUE BUST IN TWO POSITIONS**
Charles E. Buckley

SIZE   20 × 16½ in / 50.8 × 41.9 cm
Oil on paper, laid down on canvas.
PROVENANCE   William Bemrose, acquired by the present owner on the London Art Market, 1964.

pp 42¹, 57   **124**

CHARACTER STUDIES

An entry in the Account Book **John Fletcher of Osmaston an old bald-headed man** does not imply that Wright painted him, but he might have sat for a character study.

A large head of Jᵒ. Stavely, £18.18; among pictures c 1780. This is repeated among pictures of the same period: **A Kitcat of old John Stavely for Mʳ Holland, £18.18.** (Wright notes that Holland paid half of this sum).
This is probably:

181 **HEAD OF OLD MAN**

Mrs. Edward Maclean Stewart,

SIZE   36⅛ × 27⅞ in / 91.7 × 70.8 cm   pp 63–4, 138   **228**
PROVENANCE   From Holland Collection; Sale of estate of Flora C. Hall, 25th September 1946.
c 1778–81. Illus. Morris, 1932.
A half torn label on the reverse reads: 'Josʰ Wright/ ... the character of an...' The missing words can be supplied from the title of a Wright at R.A., 1782 (231), which might easily be this picture: 'Old Man's Head, in the character of an Apostle'. Another label on the reverse reads: 'Dining Room/Nᵒ 14/a Portrait of an Old Man -/C.A./J.G.' Both inscriptions go back at least to the early nineteenth century. Stavely also sat for the *Philosopher by lamplight* (see SCIENCE, PHILOSOPHY).

A Small head of Old Stavely, £12.12; among pictures of the same period.

182 **OLD JOHN, HEAD WAITER AT THE KING'S HEAD INN**

The Lord Belper

Old John at the Kings Head Raffled for & paid, £12.12; among pictures of c 1780.
SIZE   30 × 25 in / 76.2 × 63.5 cm   p 125
PROVENANCE   According to Bemrose, 1885, p. 10, exhibited at the Town Hall, Derby, raffled for ten guineas and won by Daniel Parker Coke; passed to Strutt family (listed in Strutt, 1835, No. 66). It has remained with the Strutts ever since.
EXHIBITIONS   Derby, 1870 (800); 1934 (91).
c 1779–80.

183 **HEAD OF OLD MAN**

Four studies   pp 63–4   **160–61**
SIZE   (Three) each c 19 × 14 in / 48.2 × 35.5 cm
         (One)   c 19 × 12 in / 48.2 × 30.5 cm

184 **HEAD OF OLD MAN**

185 **HEAD OF OLD MAN**

186 **HEAD OF OLD MAN**

Private Collection, U.K. (2);
Miss D. M. R. Cade (2)

Oil on paper pasted on board.
EXHIBITIONS   Derby, 1883 (20, 22, 26, 28) lent by members of the Cade family; 1934 (51, 52, 61, 62) all lent by Miss D. M. R. Cade.
Two of these (1934 Exh., Nos. 52, 62) are still in Miss Cade's collection at Porthcurno, Penzance; the others (here illustrated) passed to another branch of the family in Suffolk. Probably Italian period.

187 **HEAD OF OLD MAN**
Sir Gilbert Inglefield

SIZE   10⅜ × 8⅝ in / 26.3 × 21.9 cm   p 63   **122**
Pre-Italian journey, c 1770–73.

I STUDENTS AND CONNOISSEURS

**188 THREE PERSONS
VIEWING THE
GLADIATOR BY
CANDLELIGHT**

Private Collection, U.K.

The Gladiator to D.ʳ Bates, £40

SIZE   40 × 48 in /   101.6 × 121.9 cm   pp 4, 32, 39–42, 57, 104–6, 117   **52**
Signed on base of statue 'I. Wright. Pinx.'
PROVENANCE   Dr. Benjamin Bates; Lansdowne Collection, Bowood.
ENGRAVED   Mezzotint by William Pether published 10th July 1769.
EXHIBITIONS   S. of A., 1765 (163). Tate, 1958 (3) for further details.
It is wrongly stated in the Tate Exhibition catalogue that Bates paid more than £40 for the
picture. The correspondence between Wright and Bates on the subject of an unnamed
picture refers to the *Air Pump*. £40 is a reasonable price to charge for the *Gladiator* before
the mid 1760's though not later. The picture dates from shortly before its exhibition,
c 1764–65.

A drawing by Wright of the statue of the Borghese *Gladiator*, showing the left arm half
masking the face, is in the Derby Art Gallery (brown ink, $20\frac{1}{4} \times 17\frac{1}{8}$ in / 51.4 × 43.4 cm).
Part of the pedestal below has been cut off.

**189 AN ACADEMY BY
LAMPLIGHT**

Mr. and Mrs. Paul Mellon;
on loan to Tate Gallery

The Academy to L.ᵈ Melbourne, £105

SIZE   50 × $39\frac{7}{8}$ in / 127 × 101.2 cm   pp 4, 17, 37, 45–7, 52, 106   **60**
PROVENANCE   1st Lord Melbourne; remained in the Melbourne Collection until acquired
by Sir G. Buckston Browne, who presented Down House, Downe (Kent) with its con-
tents, as a memorial to Charles Darwin and his picture collection to the British Association
for the Advancement of Science, 1929; purchased for the Mellon Collection from the
Royal College of Surgeons, 1964.
ENGRAVED   Mezzotint by William Pether, 1772.
EXHIBITIONS   S. of A., 1769 (197); Tate, 1958 (6) for further details.
The picture belongs stylistically to the year or so before its exhibition (*c* 1768–69).

190 **A PHILOSOPHER GIVING A LECTURE ON THE ORRERY**

Derby Museum & Art Gallery

The Orrery to L.d Ferrers, £210. It is listed twice.
SIZE 58 × 80 in / 147.3 × 203.2 cm
pp 3–4, 17, 23, 29, 32, 39–42, 51, 56, 72, 104–6, 114–7, 120   **54**
PROVENANCE Washington Shirley, 5th Earl Ferrers; Ferrers Sale, Christie & Ansell, 3rd June 1779 (113), bt. in at £84; resold Ferrers Sale, Staunton Harold, 25th June and following days 1787, 5th day (54), bt. 'Bruce' (possibly bt. in), 95 gns.; Francis Wright of Osmaston (who took the name of Osmaston); purchased after the dispersal of John Osmaston's Collection in 1884 by Derby Corporation Art Gallery.
ENGRAVED Mezzotint by William Pether, published by Boydell 20th May 1768 when it was already in the Ferrers Collection.
EXHIBITIONS S. of A., 1766 (195). Tate, 1958 (2) for further details.

191 **A PHILOSOPHER GIVING A LECTURE ON THE ORRERY**
Mr. and Mrs. Paul Mellon

SIZE 17¾ × 23 in / 45 × 58.4 cm   p 116[1]   **53**
PROVENANCE Acquired for the Mellon Collection on the London Art Market, 1966.
A monochrome study for the *Orrery* by the artist himself. It is clearly a study for the engraving.

192 **AN EXPERIMENT ON A BIRD IN THE AIR PUMP**

Tate Gallery, London

The Air pump, £200. Against this entry was written later **P.d £200,** but the name of the purchaser is not given. On another sheet of the Account Book the price is given as £210, but neither of these two prices neeb be the correct one (see note 5, page 105). On a further sheet is the entry: **Mem. Rec.d of D.r Bates thirty pounds in part payment for the Picture of the Air pump.**
SIZE 72 × 96 in / 182.9 × 243.8 cm
pp 4, 17–8, 23, 43–6, 50, 52, 104–5, 112–4, 117, 119–20   **58**
PROVENANCE Dr. Benjamin Bates; Walter Tyrrell; presented by Edward Tyrrell to the National Gallery, 1863. Transferred to Tate Gallery, 1929.
ENGRAVED Mezzotint by Valentine Green, published by Boydell 24th June 1769. This is inscribed 'Jos Wright Pinxit 1768 Val Green fecit... 1769'.
EXHIBITIONS S. of A., 1768 (193); Re-exhibited in London to the King of Denmark in September of that year, under the auspices of the Society of Artists (No. 131 in the printed catalogue). Davies, 1811, p. 204 tells us the King of Denmark 'arrived at the George' in Derby in this year; Tate, 1958 (5) for further details.
The caption to this Green engraving may well record a signature on the picture which is now not visible in its dirty state. In any case, *c* 1767–68 is the correct date.
Robinson, 1958, note 9 quotes a passage from the Journal of the Austrian traveller Karl, Graf von Zinzendorf (entry for 29th April 1768): '*Puis à Spring Garden où la Société des Artistes étale ses tableaux et sculptures, il y a là un tableau d'une Expérience avec la machine pneumatique, qui se fait de nuit, qui est très beau...*'
A study for the *Air Pump* is on the reverse of a self-portrait (see Cat 167).

193 **STUDY FOR THE AIR PUMP (verso of 167)**

Charles Rogers-Coltman Esq

SIZE 24½ × 30 in / 62.2 × 76.2 cm   pp 38, 45, 114   **59**
EXHIBITIONS Graves' Galleries, 1910 (27).
The self-portrait is of course an upright, but the canvas has been turned on its side to accommodate the *Air Pump* study.

194 **A PHILOSOPHER BY LAMPLIGHT**

Private Collection, U.K.

SIZE 50 × 40 in / 127 × 101.6 cm   p 64   **226**
PROVENANCE Remained on the artist's hands: Sale, Christie's, 6th May 1801 (56), bt. in at £19.19; resold Derby, 11th October 1810 (3) to 'Mr. Tate, Liverpool' for £43.1.
EXHIBITIONS R.A., 1781 (23).
Stavely served as model (see *Head of an Old Man* under CHARACTER STUDIES No. 181). The picture dates from *c* 1778–81. It cannot therefore be identical with 'A Philosopher by lamp light' at S. of A., 1769 (196).
(See Appendix A, note 11).

195 **THE ALCHEMIST IN SEARCH OF THE PHILOSOPHER'S STONE, DISCOVERS PHOSPHORUS**

The Chymist, £105

SIZE   50 × 40 in / 127 × 101.6 cm   pp 8, 17, 22, 52, 64, 104, 118–120, 143   **106**

Signed and dated on extreme right: 'J. W. Pinx! 1795'; (for explanation of the late date, see below).

PROVENANCE   Remained in the artist's possession; taken by him to Italy in 1773 (see Bemrose, 1885, p. 27) but back in England by 1775; sale, Christie's, 6th May 1801 (62) for £80.17, bt. in; resold Derby 11th October 1810 (8), bt. Col. Wilson of Wooton Lodge; anon. sale, Christie's, 5th February 1881 (665), bt. McLean; purchased by subscription in 1883 for Derby Art Gallery.

ENGRAVED   Mezzotint by William Pether, 1775.

EXHIBITIONS   S. of A., 1771 (209); B.I., 1817 (118), lent by Thomas Wilson; Tate, 1958 (10) for further details.

It has been maintained there were two versions of this picture, one painted in 1771, the other in 1795, on the grounds that Pether's mezzotint of 1775 of the 'first' version differs in small particulars from the picture in Derby dated 1795. It seems more likely that there was only one picture, which was altered and dated at the time of the alterations, because the style of the picture in Derby is that of the early 1770's. But this cannot be proved.

Drawing by P. P. Burdett suggesting the composition for the *Alchemist*, without figures (sepia on paper, $15\frac{1}{2} \times 11\frac{1}{2}$ in / 39.4 × 29.2 cm) is in the Derby Art Gallery. On the reverse is a letter from Burdett to Wright dated from Liverpool, 4th February 1771. Wright had invited criticisms. The picture was therefore painted early this year, before its exhibition in the Spring. Thomas Bentley tried to induce Wedgwood to buy it but Wedgwood rejected it (see Wedgwood, 1903, I, p. 315, letter of 5th May 1778).

Derby Museum & Art Gallery

196 **HERMIT STUDYING ANATOMY**

The 1801 sale catalogue describes the following as a companion to the *Alchemist*:

The hermit, £105   pp 17, 52–3, 55, 64, 75, 104, 120   **105**

SIZE $50\frac{1}{2} \times 40\frac{1}{2}$ in / 128.2 × 102.9 cm

Signed bottom left: 'I. Wright Pinx!'

PROVENANCE   Remained on the artist's hands; sale, Christie's, 6th May 1801 (63) for £70.17, bt. Borrow; remained in the Borrow or Borough Collection until acquired by the Derby Art Gallery by bequest, 1960.

ENGRAVED   Mezzotint by William Pether, 1786.

EXHIBITIONS   Tate, 1958 (11).

This picture was painted just before Wright left for Italy, c 1771–73. In a letter from Rome to his brother dated 12th February 1774 (Bemrose, 1885, p. 30) he writes: 'Nancy tells me she has heard the Empress of Russia has taken ye picture of the Iron Forge, but does not like the Hermit'. The picture may have been sent to St. Petersburg for the Empress's inspection, since on 13th April 1774 Wright adds in a letter to his sister (Bemrose, 1885 p. 31): '...I must desire you to tell him [Tate] I shall be glad if he would look after the picture of the Hermit, see whether any accident has happened to it, and deliver it safe to Sotheby to keep till I return to England'.

Derby Museum & Art Gallery

The head of the *Hermit* in the University of Kansas Museum of Art, canvas, $11\frac{3}{4} \times 10\frac{3}{4}$ in (29.8 × 27.3 cm), exhibited New York, 1960 (8) does not appear from the photograph to be an original.

Galen for Ditto (Dr. Bates); among pictures of the early '60's. Wright notes in the Account Book that Dr. Bates has paid for this, but nothing is known of its fate.

197 AN IRON FORGE

Admiral of the Fleet the
Earl Mountbatten of Burma

The picture of the Iron Forge to L.ᵈ Palmerston, £210

SIZE   48 × 52 in / 121.9 × 132.1 cm   pp 17, 50–1, 106, 121   **103**

Signed and dated on stone slab bottom right: 'Jo. Wright/Pinx.!/1772'.

PROVENANCE   MS. Catalogue of 2nd Lord Palmerston's collection (Broadlands) has: 'An Iron Forge, bought direct from the artist 1772 for £200. 47 × 52 in'. A notebook kept by 2nd Lord Palmerston (Broadlands) has under general heading 'Pictures bought at home': 'An Iron Forge Wright 200–0–0'. It has remained in this family ever since.

ENGRAVED   Mezzotint by Richard Earlom, 1st January 1773, for Boydell.

EXHIBITIONS   S. of A., 1772 (373); Tate, 1958 (13) for further details. Here, wrong dimensions are given.

A preliminary study for the *Iron Forge* without figures is in Derby Art Gallery (pen and wash heightened with white, 12⅝ × 20½ in / 32 × 52 cm), inscribed in Wright's hand: 'Original Study for the Iron Forge/J. Wright 1772'. (Pl 99).

A reduced copy was made of the picture in the year after it was painted, by H. Faber, signed and dated 'H. Faber ['H' and 'F' in monogram] Pinx 1773', on a stone bottom right (with John Mitchell, Ltd., London, 1963).

According to Robinson, 1958, the *Iron Forge* was reproduced by Matthew Boulton by his mechanical process for reproducing oil paintings.

Candid Observations, 1772: 'If ever a Picture could be called perfect, certainly this may; nothing in colours can exceed this wonderful Production...'

198 AN IRON FORGE VIEWED FROM WITHOUT

Hermitage Museum, Leningrad

Picture of an Iron Forge viewed from without, to the Empress of Russia, £136.10

SIZE   41 × 55 in / 104.1 × 139.7 cm   pp 17, 50, 55, 107, 121, 143   **104**

Signed and dated on chest in the right foreground: 'J. Wright Pinx.!/1773'.

PROVENANCE   In a letter to his brother from Rome, 12th February 1774 (Bemrose, 1885, p. 30), Wright says: 'Nancy tells me she has heard the Empress of Russia has taken ye picture of the Iron Forge...'

EXHIBITIONS   S. of A., 1773 (371).

Hermitage catalogue, 1958 (359), illus.   A. Kroll, *English Painting of the XVIth–XIXth centuries at the Hermitage Museum*, Leningrad, 1961, plates 31–33.

199 THE BLACKSMITH'S SHOP

Mr. and Mrs. Paul Mellon

The Blacksmith's Shop to L.ᵈ Melbourne, £150

SIZE   50½ × 41 in / 128.2 × 104.1 cm   pp 17, 37, 50–1, 106, 121   **100**

Signed and dated bottom right: 'Jo.ˢ Wright/Pinx.!/1771'.

PROVENANCE   1st Lord Melbourne; remained in the Melbourne collection until acquired by Sir G. Buckstone Browne, who presented Down House, Downe (Kent) with its contents, as a memorial to Charles Darwin, and his picture collection to the British Institution for the Advancement of Science, 1929; purchased for the Mellon Collection from the Royal College of Surgeons, 1964.

ENGRAVED   Mezzotint by Richard Earlom for Boydell, published 25th August 1771.

EXHIBITIONS   S. of A., 1771 (201); Tate, 1958 (8) for further details.

A painting on glass after this composition is at Burghley House, signed and dated bottom left: 'Eglington. Marg.ᵗ Pearson, 1789'. A similar glass painting after this composition is in the Derby Art Gallery.

Small Blacksmith's D.º (i.e. Shop) to E. Parker Esq.ʳ, £42   p 107   **102**

EXHIBITIONS   S. of A., 1771 (202) as 'A Small Ditto [i.e. Blacksmith's Shop] viewed from without'.

ENGRAVED   By W. Pether as 'Farrier's Shop', published 2nd December 1771.

'A Smith's Forge' which might have been an original considering it was sold in Wright's lifetime, was sent by R. Price Jones to Christie's 26th February 1791 (91). It was conceivably the following:

200 **THE BLACKSMITH'S SHOP**

A Blacksmith's Shop to M.ʳ Alexander, £157.10
SIZE 49½ × 39 in / 125.7 × 99 cm pp 17, 50–1, 92, 107, 121 **101**
Signed on tool box bottom left: 'Jos. Wright Pinx.ᵗ/1771'.
PROVENANCE Robert Alexander of Edinburgh; his sale Christie's, 31st March to 1st April 1775, where it fetched £68.5; ? R. Price Jones (see above); Robert Hyde Greg before 1875.
EXHIBITIONS S. of A., 1772 (372); on loan to City Art Gallery, Manchester for a period until 1961.

Its presence at the Society of Artists in 1772 can be deduced from the description in *Candid Observations*, 1772: 'The Picture though somewhat like the one of the same Artist's last year [i.e. Lord Melbourne's] is yet very different; the introduction of the little Girls is a happy change; but the back Ground is not improved by the alteration'. Wright in a letter to his sister Nancy of *c* 1771 (Bemrose, 1885, p. 48; we know this must be the date since Wright refers in the letter to his painting *Miravan* which is dated 1772) writes: '...have worked very hard, have finished my Smith's Shop—'tis as good or better than the last' (i.e. the one for Lord Melbourne).

Private Collection, U.K.

See *Manchester City Art Galleries, Annual Report*, 1958, illus. pl. VI.
Wright exhibited at S. of A., 1775 (223): 'A Smith's Forge, altered from his first design'. It is hard to say whether the Alexander picture was re-exhibited at the time of its sale. All one can be sure about is that this picture dated from before the Italian journey, since Wright was still in Rome that spring and not in a mood to paint forges there.

V BUBBLE BLOWING, LETTER READING, BLADDERS

4 Candlelight pictures for Col. Pole at 30 Guineas each; £126. This is followed by: **Mem. Rec'd 25ᵗʰ Oct.ʳ 1772 of Col. Pole twenty four Guineas in part payment for the Picture of the Boys with the Bladder** (which is one of the four)
The overdoor of the *Girl Reading the letter* is signed and dated on the pages of the book under her left elbow: 'Jo.ˢ Wright pinx.ᵗ 1772'. It may be assumed the other candlelights belong to this or the previous year.

201–4 **CANDLELIGHT OVERDOORS**

Major J. W. Chandos-Pole

PROVENANCE Painted for the room at Radbourne Hall where they still hang.
pp 5, 37–8, 48–50, 108–10 **92-95**
The themes of letter-reading and bladder-blowing (which are two of the four overdoors) are repeated in the following pictures:

A deleted entry reads: **A Girl with a Letter its companion for my friend Coltman,** no price stated. They may have been gifts. These are:

205 **A GIRL READING A LETTER WITH AN OLD MAN READING OVER HER SHOULDER**

See 206 pp 38, 48–50, 108 **77**

206 **TWO BOYS FIGHTING OVER A BLADDER**

SIZE Each 36 × 28 in / 91.4 × 71.1 cm pp 38, 50–1, 80, 108 **76**
PROVENANCE Have remained in the Coltman Collection since they were painted.
EXHIBITIONS Graves' Galleries, 1910 (43, 46); *Boys fighting over a Bladder*, Tate, 1958 (4) for further details.
Late 1760's.

Wright showed a small candlelight and its companion at S. of A., 1767 (189, 190) and two candlelights the following year. The Coltman pictures may have been two of these; the other two may have been Lord Exeter's (see below). *Critical Examination*, 1767, p. 21 proves that No. 189 in the first year had more than one figure ('...The disposition of the figures...'); that the two candlelights shown in 1768 were companion pieces we know from the catalogue of the exhibition in September of that year to the King of Denmark (Nos. 132–133) where they are so described.

Charles Rogers-Coltman Esq

207 A GIRL READING A LETTER BY CANDLELIGHT, WITH A YOUNG MAN LOOKING OVER HER SHOULDER

A Girl reading a Letter by Candlelight, £12.12. Since only one picture is known of this description besides the Pole and Coltman candlelights (which appear elsewhere in the Account Book) this could be:

SIZE   35 × 27½ in / 88.9 × 69.8 cm   pp 27, 39, 48–9, 104   **45**

PROVENANCE   A label on the reverse reads: 'Exhibited by [?] Sutton Esq.', probably not earlier than the mid-nineteenth century. The Suttons were related to the Nelthorpes. Wright painted Suttons in Newark and Retford in 1760, and one of these Suttons might have acquired the picture; alternatively, the picture might have entered the Nelthorpe Collection through Mary Cracroft whom Wright painted and who afterwards married a Nelthorpe (see 45).

EXHIBITIONS   R.A., 1934 (303).

Lt. Col. R. S. Nelthorpe

Redgrave, ed. 1947, plate 38. The picture is Wright's first known candlelight (c 1760–63).

The following bladder pictures besides the ones so far listed are recorded. They are catalogued here as far as possible in the order of execution.

Boys with a Bladder and its Companion to Lᵈ Exeter, £105. These are listed in the Account Book among candlelights of the '60's, and may therefore be S. of A., 1768 (194). The ones shown at the Society of Artists in the previous year are described in the catalogue as small, and Lord Exeter would never have paid so much for small pictures.

SIZE   ? c 36 × 28 in / 91.4 × 71.1 cm   pp 15, 50, 118, 138

208 TWO BOYS WITH A BLADDER

Numerous copies of a lost early original exist, the best (though not the original) in the Huntington Library, S. Marino (Calif.). The original is unlikely to have been Lord Exeter's since the surviving copies are too small; besides, there are no known copies of the companion. The composition is used by P. P. Burdett for an aquatint (1774), and this is probably the composition copied by Richard Tate about the same time. This suggests that the original was in Liverpool about 1770. See Plate 74

(Untraced)

A Boy blowing a Bladder, £4.4

It is impossible to date this entry in the Account Book but it follows immediately on a **Boy with a Candle** at the same price. They were therefore probably companion pieces, both very small, to judge by the price.

A Boy blowing a Bladder fetched 8 guineas at Christie's, 23rd–24th January 1771, sold by 'a nobleman', bt. Lord Warwick; the *Girls decorating a Kitten* (212) was in the same sale.

A 'Boy blowing a Bladder' was at the Free Society of Artists, 1783 (89) which is unidentified.

209 BOY AND GIRL WITH BLADDER

Boy and Girl wᵗʰ a Bladder; among pictures of the late 1780's. This must be the same as the following entry, also among pictures of the late 1780's.

A Boy & Girl wᵗʰ a Bladder. Sold to Mʳ Hardman Manchester, £52.10

EXHIBITIONS   R.A., 1789 (87); Manchester Institution, 1831 (131).

Wright in a letter to J. L. Philips, 5th May 1789, (Bemrose, 1885, p. 88) fixes the price of 50 guineas on the picture. Letter from Wright to Philips, 4th December 1789 (MS. Derby Art Gallery), postscript: '...Pray give my compᵗˢ to Mʳ Hardman who I hope still enjoys the bladder wᶜʰ robbed all my other pictures [in the exhibition] of commendation'.

Formerly Thomas Hardman (1831)

A Boy blowing a Bladder, £31.10; followed by **A Girl looking thro' a bladder,** at the same price. These are listed among pictures of *c* 1790 and immediately precede an entry for an Arkwright conversation piece. They are therefore:

210 **BOY BLOWING BLADDER**	See 211	pp 66, 118[1], 168, 169[2]	**320**

211 **GIRL LOOKING THROUGH BLADDER**

SIZE Each 30 × 25 in / 76.2 × 63.5 cm   pp 66, 169[2] **321**

The *Boy* is signed and dated outside the feigned oval: 'I. Wright pinx!/1790'.

Letter from Wright to Richard Arkwright junior, 6th December 1790 (Arkwright MSS) proves that the *Boy* was completed by then. It was delivered to Arkwright at Bakewell soon after the 18th (letter in same series of that date).

A second version of the *Boy* from the Holland Collection (now belonging to William Dale, Ottawa) bears an inscription on the stretcher: 'The Gift of Richd Arkwright Esq/Mr J. Holland 1793'. The Holland-Dale picture is not an original.

EXHIBITIONS International Exhibition, 1862 (55, 54); Derby, 1883 (76,68); Graves' Galleries, 1910 (41, 38); Derby, 1934 (97, 121).

The picture of the girl must be about contemporary with the other. They do not look, however, as though they had been painted as pairs: neither the ovals, nor the design, correspond.

Col. Peter Arkwright

'A Boy and Girl with a Blown Bladder: the countenances full of lively expression, and the whole delicately and lightly finished,' bt. in by Jo. Wright at £40.19. at Christie's, 8th May 1801 (40).

Various versions of a picture of this description (different from the Hardman picture) exist but no original is known for certain. One decent copy belonging to Mrs. Fenwick-Owen is 25 × 30 in (76.2 × 63.5 cm); a picture of this description belonging to Mrs. Wheler is not known to the author except from the illustration in Smith and Bemrose, 1922, opp. p. 134. It is probably the best surviving.

VI CANDLELIGHTS, GENRE

These are listed approximately in order of execution.

A candlelight piece for Bates, among pictures of the early '60's. No price stated. This is conceivably the *Gladiator*.

212 **TWO GIRLS DECORATING A KITTEN BY CANDLELIGHT**

SIZE 35¾ × 28½ in / 90.8 × 72.4 cm   pp 48, 106 **75**

PROVENANCE Sale, Christie's, 23rd–24th January 1771 as 'Two girls decorating a cat by candlelight', sold with a *Boy Blowing a Bladder* (q.v.) by a 'nobleman', bt. Lord Palmerston, £7.7; 2nd Lord Palmerston; MS. Catalogue of pictures (Broadlands) has: 'Girl playing with a cat by candlelight', with the annotation 'sold 20th century'; with Messrs. Leger, then Agnew, 1946; Miss Craze.

EXHIBITIONS Winchester, 1938 (50), lent by Lord Mount Temple.

ENGRAVED By Thomas Watson, as 'Miss Kitty dressing', by 'R. Wright', published 20th February 1781.

Mrs. C. Margaret Riley

An Old Woman Knitting & her husband smoking. Its companion a Girl at her Toilet to Mr Parker, £31.10 for the pair. These were S. of A., 1771 (206, 205), the girl being described in the catalogue as undressing.

A Boy with a candle, £4.4. Presumably a pair to a *Boy blowing a Bladder*, listed next to it in the Account Book at the same price (p 239). The date cannot be ascertained.

Two girls w.ᵗʰ a Charcoal Stick; among pictures of the late 1780's.

213 **GIRL BLOWING A CHARCOAL STICK**

A girl blowing a charcoal stick. Sold to M.ʳ Daulby, £42; among pictures of *c* 1789.
EXHIBITIONS   R. A. 1789 (153).   p 47
Letter from Wright to J. L. Philips, 5th May 1789 (Bemrose, 1885, p. 88) fixes the price of the picture at 40 guineas. Letter from Wright to Daulby, 15th July 1789 (MS. formerly with Maggs, 1914 and Peter Murray Hill Ltd., London): 'I never produced a truer effect...' (than this picture). According to this letter, he received payment that morning from Daulby. It is entered in Daulby's MS. notebooks (Liverpool Public Library) of *c* 1790–95, but deleted—which means that it was sold about this time.

Formerly Daniel Daulby, Jnr.

VII PRISON SCENES

picture of a Captive King (the word 'King' inserted later, perhaps in order to distinguish the entry from a later one, *Captive from Sterne*) **to the Prince of Baaden, £52.10;** among pictures of 1772–73. Against the entry is the note: **'Mem: not sent'.** Since a crucifix appears in one of the drawings for it, it must have represented *Guy de Lusignan in Prison* and is presumably identical with an almost contemporary entry at the same price **Lusignan in prison.** This is:

214 **THE CAPTIVE KING**

SIZE   (small, to judge from the price)   pp 8, 54–5, 104, 118, 120, 150
PROVENANCE   Remained on Wright's hands and taken by him to Italy (see Bemrose, 1885, p. 27).
EXHIBITIONS   S. of A., 1773 (370).
That the picture showed a lamp is proved by a letter from Father Thorpe to Lord Arundell of 12th February 1774 (Thorpe/Arundell MSS., folio 24 *verso*): '...One of the pictures [which the artist brought to Italy with him] represents... a prison with a lamp on it'. Wright sent at least three drawings for this composition to P. P. Burdett in Liverpool for his criticism during the autumn and winter of 1772–73. It was therefore painted between then and its exhibition in the Spring of 1773.
There is an oil study for it:

(Untraced)

215 **THE CAPTIVE KING**
Basil Taylor Esq

SIZE   12 × 14¼ in / 30.4 × 36.2 cm   pp 54, 61, 150   **110**
PROVENANCE   William Bemrose; London Art Market (1965).

A 'Lusignan in prison' appeared at Robins's Rooms, 1785 (21). This was no doubt a second version. One or other was in Wright's sale, Christie's, 6th May 1801 (59) as 'Lusignan in prison—The interior finely illuminated, capital', bt. in at £60.18 and resold Derby, 11th October 1810 (4), kept by Wright's son-in-law Chappell of Arnold. The measurements are given as 40 × 50 in (101.6 × 127 cm).

216 **THE CAPTIVE, FROM STERNE**

SIZE   40 × 50 in / 101.6 × 127 cm   pp 8–9, 60–1, 66, 150–1
PROVENANCE   Begun before 10th August 1774 and completed by 3rd September, in Rome (according to Thorpe/Arundell MSS., letters of these two dates); sale, Christie's, 1780 by a 'nobleman', along with a *Maria*, from Sterne (No. 236) and other pictures fetching £51.9; by 1790 in collection of Edward Pickering along with the *Maria* (see Shakespeare Gallery, 1790 (31) where a drawing by Josiah Boydell is catalogued as after the 'Captive (from Sterne)': 'in the possession of Edw. Pickering Esq.'); remained with a branch of the

Pickering family in Shrewsbury along with the *Maria* till earlier this century but now untraced.

The Christie 1780 catalogue describes the picture as a 'Captive King', but this must be an error, since a typescript inventory of June 1913 of property belonging to I. E. Pickering (which remains with a member of the Pickering family in Colwyn Bay) describes a picture exactly corresponding with the *Captive, from Sterne* turned to the left, as we know it in the following copy (reduced or cut):

Derby Art Gallery, formerly Vickers Collection; 35 × 45 in (88.9 × 114.3 cm).

Moreover, it is unlikely that a *Lusignan* should be accompanied by a scene from Sterne, and very reasonable that two scenes from the *Sentimental Journey* should remain together. *The Captive* is in any case correctly described in the Shakespeare Gallery Catalogue of 1790.

ENGRAVED   By Ryder, published for Boydell, 1786.

That this is the picture described by Father Thorpe, and not the other version (see below) is more or less proved by the existence of a pen and wash study with black ink, $9\frac{7}{8} \times 13\frac{7}{8}$ in (25 × 35.2 cm) in the Wadsworth Atheneum, Hartford (Conn.), purchased in London, 1955. It bears inscription lower centre: 'Cavedone'—someone's bright attribution. The drawing belongs in spirit with others done in Italy. *The Universal Magazine*, June 1795, describes trouble with the Customs on the picture's return to England.

Formerly Pickering Collection

217 THE CAPTIVE, FROM STERNE

Sterns Captive, £105; among pictures of *c* 1775–77, probably refers to the second version. Wright did not keep careful accounts in Italy and this may have been done after his return.
SIZE   40 × 50 in / 101.6 × 127 cm   pp 60–1, 66, 124¹, 150–1   **162**
PROVENANCE   Holden Collection, Nuthall Temple, Notts. (where it is shown hanging on the wall in an illustration in *Country Life*, 5th May 1923); Nuthall Temple Sale, 27th–28th March 1928 (471), sold for £6; Mrs. Lousada gift to Derby, 1953.
ENGRAVED   Mezzotint by J. R. Smith, 1779, reprod. Morris, Engravings, 1932.
EXHIBITIONS   Derby, 1883 (38), lent by J. Holden.

Derby Museum & Art Gallery

One or other of the last two was R.A., 1778 (360), and one or other was sold Christie's, 14th–15th March 1783 by Charles Hamilton for £25.4.

A small prison Scene sold to M.ʳ Boothby, £12.12; entry just before a memorandum of July 1787.   p 128
Wright exhibited at R.A. 1789 (67) 'The Prison of the Capitol', which is unidentified.

A small prison, £16.16; among pictures of *c* 1787–90.

An internal View of a prison, £23.2; among pictures of the same date. This is probably: Exhibited Liverpool, 1787 (121): 'An internal View of a Prison'.

The last two are not known to have been sold, so they may be the ones in his sale at Christie's 6th May 1801 (60): 'A small Prison Scene, with a single Figure, £31.10 to Smith for Wakefield, and (61) 'A Ditto, £17.17' to Borrow.

218 SMALL PRISON SCENE

Two of them may have been:
SIZE $15\frac{1}{2} \times 18\frac{1}{2}$ in / 39.4 × 47 cm   p 62   **284**
Signed bottom right 'I W'.
PROVENANCE   Purchased on the London Art Market, 1965.
A date in the late '80's seems established, considering that no other similar pictures are recorded at any other period. The other (apparently of the same date) is:

Mr. and Mrs. Paul Mellon

219 SMALL PRISON SCENE
SIZE   19 × 27 in / 48.2 × 68.5 cm   p 62¹   **285**
PROVENANCE   Christie's, 31st March 1967 (36) as 'Wright of Derby' *tout court*.
A drawing for 219 is known (Collection H. Cornish Torbock).

Private Collection, U.K.

220 **THE OLD MAN AND
DEATH**

Wadsworth Atheneum,
Hartford (Conn.)

The Old Man & Death, £63

SIZE   40 × 50 in / 101.6 × 127 cm   pp 55–6, 59, 62, 75, 104, 120, 125, 150   **123**

PROVENANCE   Remained on the artist's hands; sale, Christie's, 6th May 1801 (58), bt. in at £51.9; resold, Derby, 11th October 1810 (5), bt. Sir R. Wilmot of Chaddesden for £84; remained in the Wilmot family till 1952; purchased by Hartford, 1953.

EXHIBITIONS   S. of A., 1774 (321); Derby, 1866 (177); 1870 (267); 1883 (30); R.A., 1886 (6) and on numerous other occasions.

Letter from Wright to his sister, 13th April 1774 (quoted by Bemrose, 1885, p. 32 in part): 'Tell Tate to take notice whether my picture [the only one he showed that year] is hung advantageously in the Exhibition... I have set 80 guineas upon it, but I would take 70 rather than not sell it. Tate can enquire of Miles if anybody has bid money for it, if it is necessary to mention the abatement to him, it must be done cautiously'. As it turned out, he was willing to take less than 70.

221 **THE OLD MAN AND
DEATH**

Walker Art Gallery, Liverpool

See Buckley, 1953 and Rosenblum, 1960 and 1962. A smaller version, showing the central portion is:

SIZE   25 × 30 in / 63.5 × 76.2 cm   pp 55³, 150   **Fig 68**

PROVENANCE   Rev. John Yates, the second husband of Mrs. John Bostock (7 under Portraits); bequeathed by Rev. Samuel Yates to Allan Bright; to his daughter Mrs. Lloyd; by whom presented to Liverpool.

EXHIBITIONS   Derby, 1934 (86).

The highly impressive provenance dispels whatever doubts one might have had about the authenticity.

222 **MIRAVAN OPENING
THE TOMB OF HIS
ANCESTORS**

Derby Museum & Art Gallery

The young Nobleman in his ancesters Tomb, Mr. Milnes, £105

SIZE   50 × 40 in / 127 × 101.6 cm   pp 17, 53–4, 66, 107, 129, 150, 157, 159   **107**

Signed and dated bottom right: 'I. WRIGHT, pinx!/1772'.

PROVENANCE   Presented to the Derby Art Gallery through the N.A.C.F. by Mr. and Mrs. A. L. Nicholson, 1937 (see N.A.C.F. *Report*, 1938, p. 41).

ENGRAVED   Mezzotint by Valentine Green published for Boydell, 18th December 1772.

EXHIBITIONS   S. of A., 1772 (417); Tate, 1958 (12), for further details.

Undated letter from Wright to his sister c 1772 (quoted Bemrose, 1885, p. 48 but wrongly dated from Bath, c 1775–76): 'Have upon the Stocks the young Nobleman, whose avarice caused him to break open the Tomb of his ancestors, in hopes of finding vast treasures, from an inscription there was upon it: "In this tomb is a greater treasure than Croesus possessed". This, I think, will be a favourite picture'. Wright was fascinated by the moral implications in the story, to judge by a long quotation transcribed in his Account Book, and by diagrams of the worn inscription (deliberately semi-legible) on the tomb, which he tried out in the Account Book. The inscription is repeated in a drawing in the Derby Museum of two girls leaning over railings.

223 **BELSHAZZAR'S FEAST**
(Untraced)

Picture of Belshazzer at the Feast when the Hand appeared writing on yᵉ wall; among pictures of 1771–73.   pp 104, 143

224 **THE CORINTHIAN
MAID**

The Corinthian Maid, £105

SIZE   42 × 50 in / 106.7 × 127 cm   pp 16, 64–5, 73, 85, 143–9, 152, 159   **245**

PROVENANCE   Purchased by Wedgwood from the artist, 1784–85. A picture of this subject was lent by John Greaves to the Manchester Institution, 1831 (130), and the subject as by Wright is recorded in the following sales: Charles Meigh, Christie's, 20th June 1850, bt. in at £84; Christie's, 1859, for £40, bt. Bentley which reappeared in John Bentley sale, 15th May 1886 (72) as a 41½ × 51 in, bt. McLean. The Mellon picture was acquired from Ralph Robotham.

EXHIBITIONS   Robin's Rooms, 1785 (13); Tate, 1958 (25) for further details; R.A., 1964–65 (234).

Painted as a companion to *Penelope unravelling her web* (225) during the two years or so leading up to its exhibition in 1785. The scheme to paint a picture of this subject was already afoot in July 1779 (letter of Wright to Wedgwood, 15th July 1779; Keele MS.), and had been mooted in the previous year. For fuller details, see Rosenblum, 1957, *passim*, especially p. 284 for a discussion of the iconography; and Nicolson, 1962, p. 114.

Mr. and Mrs. Paul Mellon

225 PENELOPE UNRAVELLING HER WEB

penelope unravelling her web. Candlelight. for M.ʳ Wedgwood, £105

SIZE   40 × 50 in / 101.6 × 127 cm   pp 16, 64–5, 73, 146–9, 152   **242**

PROVENANCE   Purchased by Wedgwood from the artist, 1784–85. Has remained in a branch of the Wedgwood family since it was painted.

EXHIBITIONS   Robins's Rooms, 1785 (14); Smith College, 1955 (13); New York, 1960 (20).

Mr. and Mrs.
Hensleigh Wedgwood

Painted as companion to the *Corinthian Maid* (224). Begun shortly before 3rd December 1783.

Margaret & William—framed, £63; Margaret & Wᵐ., £84. It sounds as though Wright did two versions since they are listed at different prices. One is:

226 WILLIAM AND MARGARET

SIZE   48 × 56 in / 121.9 × 142.2 cm   pp 17, 64–5, 148, 152   **241**

PROVENANCE   One of them remained on the artist's hands; sale, Christie's, 16th May 1801 (53), bt. in at £39.18; resold, Derby, 11th October 1810 (6), to Miss Wright of Spondon for £105; in a branch of the family until: Miss E. E. Cade sale, Spondon, July 1922 (317), sold for £86.

ENGRAVED   J. R. Smith, published 12th April 1785.

Col. Sir John Crompton-Inglefield; on loan to Judges' Lodgings, Derby

EXHIBITIONS   Robin's Rooms, 1785 (3), or the other version; Derby, 1866 (197); 1934 (143).

227 THE SPINSTER WITH COLIN SINGING A BALLAD

The Spinster wᵗʰ Collin singing a ballad; among late pictures.

SIZE   *c* 76 × 63 in / 193 × 160 cm

EXHIBITIONS   Derby, 1934 (23).

A picture of this subject of about this size was at Derby, 1883 (98) lent by George Wheeldon. The catalogue claims it was left unfinished at Wright's death. The picture here catalogued indeed owes a lot to a later hand.

Col. Sir John Crompton-Inglefield; on loan to Judges' Lodgings, Derby

A large picture of Hero & Leander. The entry is deleted, as well as the price which is not legible. The picture is listed again with a companion: **Hero & Leander Storm, £105; Its Companion Moon Light, £105;** both sold to 'the Hon. Tho.ˢ Fitzmaurice'. These are:

228 HERO AND LEANDER —STORM

See 229   pp 147–8, 152

229 HERO AND LEANDER —MOONLIGHT
(Untraced)

EXHIBITIONS   Robins's Rooms, 1785 (9 and 8).   pp 147–8, 152

Wright was working on these pictures in March 1783. Hon. Thomas Fitzmaurice (1742–93), younger son of the first Earl of Shelborne.

230 ANTIGONUS IN THE STORM, FROM THE WINTER'S TALE

The Storm in the Winters Tale, £136 (altered from £147).

SIZE   *c* 70 × 95 in / 177.8 × 241.3 cm   pp 66, 88, 156–7   **302**

PROVENANCE   Purchased by Boydell for the Shakespeare Gallery, 1789–90; Boydell Galleries Sale, Christie's, 20th May 1805 (17), bt. for £82.

ENGRAVED   By S. Middiman, published 4th June 1794 by John and Josiah Boydell at the Shakespeare Gallery.

EXHIBITIONS   Shakespeare Gallery, 1790 onwards, at first as by Hodges.

Formerly Boydell Collection

---

231 ANTIGONUS IN THE STORM, FROM THE WINTER'S TALE

A Storm wth Antigonus pursued by a Bear for Mr Henry Philips, £105

SIZE   61 × 85 in / 154.9 × 215.9 cm   pp 16–7, 66, 156–7   **304**

Signed and dated bottom in the middle: 'I. W. Pinx^t/1790'. The picture was in fact reworked after its dating (see below).

PROVENANCE   Henry Philips; at Kedleston by 1870.

EXHIBITIONS   R.A., 1790 (221); reworked 1790–92 and re-exhibited S. of A., 1791 (219), for sale; Derby, 1870 (271); 1883 (1).

Wright to Philips, 24th June 1791 (quoted Bemrose, 1885, p. 89 from MS. Derby Public Library) reveals that J. L. Philips's brother Henry is after the picture, and he quotes the price of 100 guineas.

Viscount Scarsdale

---

232 ROMEO AND JULIET

Romeo & Juliet

SIZE   70 × 95 in / 177.8 × 241.3 cm   pp 16–7, 66, 155–7   **305**

PROVENANCE   Rejected by Boydell; remained on the artist's hands; sale, Christie's, 6th May 1801 (51), bt. in at £47.5 and resold Derby, 11th October 1810 (7), again unsold; purchased from Wright's executors by the uncle of Henry Moseley who subsequently owned it; bought from him in 1857 by Mrs. Thomas Hope; in Oakes Collection before 1883.

EXHIBITIONS   R.A., 1790 (1); reworked by the artist, 1790–91 and re-exhibited S. of A., 1791 (220). Derby, 1883 (93).

A drawing (7¼ × 8¾ in / 18.4 × 22.2 cm) in the Derby Art Gallery shows the setting. Where the figures appear in the final composition are the words in pencil: 'The seat of ye figures'. Below in pen in Wright's hand: 'perhaps the Niech wch contains the Sarcophagus w^d be better removed a little more to the right, wch w^d give a greater breadth of illuminated wall'. This was done.

J. M. Oakes Esq

---

233 FERDINAND AND MIRANDA IN PROSPERO'S CELL

A large picture of Prospero in his Cell, shewing a visionary Spectacle to Ferdinand & Miranda—12 f. by 8 f.6, £315

SIZE   102 × 144 in / 259 × 365.8 cm   pp 17–8, 66, 154–7, 159   **299**

PROVENANCE   Purchased by Boydell for the Shakespeare Gallery, September 1789; Boydell Galleries Sale, Christie's, 20th May 1805 (55), bt. Earl of Balcarres for £69.6; remained in the Crawford Collection until sold in November 1946 from Haigh.

ENGRAVED   Robert Thew, published 4th June 1800 by John and Josiah Boydell at the Shakespeare Gallery.

Formerly Earl of Crawford and Balcarres

---

234 THE LADY IN MILTON'S 'COMUS'

A moonlight from Comus, £84

SIZE   40½ × 50¾ in / 102.8 × 128.9 cm   pp 16–7, 65, 148, 153   **246**

PROVENANCE   Purchased by Wedgwood before June 1785; presented by the widow of William Rathbone (in whose collection it was by 1881) to Liverpool in 1902.

ENGRAVED   Mezzotint by J. R. Smith, 1789.

EXHIBITIONS   Robins's Rooms, 1785 (1); Liverpool Art Club, 1811 (24); R.A., 1962 (299) for further details.

Companion to the *Indian Widow* (243).

Walker Art Gallery, Liverpool

Nearly complete by April 1784. See Nicolson, 1962, *passim*.

X SCENES FROM CONTEMPORARY LITERATURE
(see also PRISON SCENES)

235 EDWIN, FROM DR. BEATTIE'S MINSTREL

The Minstrel sold to Mr Milnes, £84

SIZE   63 × 46 in / 160 × 116.8 cm   pp 17, 63, 65, 72, 144, 151–2, 159   **179**

PROVENANCE   John Milnes of Wakefield; has remained in the Milnes family ever since it was painted.

ENGRAVED   Mezzotint by J. R. Smith published 30th December 1778 from this version.

EXHIBITIONS   R.A., 1778 (359); Derby, 1883 (58); R.A., 1886 (9); Derby, 1934 (10) and on other occasions.

Companion to *Maria* (237). See Honour, 1956, who shows that Wright began one version of this picture in 1777. It was completed by February 1778. In a letter of that date to Dr. Beattie, Wright announces: 'In all probability I may paint the subject again ere long...' Whether he ever did so is uncertain. Other versions are known for which authenticity has been claimed. One belongs to Major H. E. Morritt, Rokeby Hall. Another (which is not autograph) passed from the Montagu collection to the United States. It was in Captain F. J. O. Montagu Sale, Christie's, 26th July 1957 (168), and is reproduced by Honour.

A drawing for the head of *Edwin* showing the young Thomas Haden sketched from life belongs to Mrs. John Chandos-Pole, the wife of the owner of *Mrs. Gell* (No. 65).

Lady Cynthia Colville

---

236 MARIA, FROM STERNE

SIZE   32½ × 49½ in / 82.5 × 125.7 cm   pp 62–3, 65, 68, 87, 151   **184**

Signed and dated on tree trunk left: 'I. Wright pinxt/1777'.

PROVENANCE   Sale, Christie's 1780 by a 'nobleman' along with a *Captive, from Sterne* (No. 216) and other pictures, fetching £30.9; by 1790 in collection of Edward Pickering along with the *Captive* (see Shakespeare Gallery, 1790 (27) where a drawing by Josiah Boydell is catalogued as after this *Maria*: 'in the possession of Edw. Pickering Esq.'); remained in a branch of the Pickering family in Shresbury till earlier this century; sale, Sotheby's 13th July 1949 (93).

Private Collection, U.K.

EXHIBITIONS   Lichfield, 1953 (24).

---

237 MARIA, FROM STERNE

A full length of Maria, £84

SIZE   63 × 45½ in / 160 × 115.6 cm   pp 17, 62–3, 65, 72, 87, 151, 159   **220**

Signed and dated bottom right: 'I. W. Pinxt/1781'.

PROVENANCE   Remained on the artist's hands; sale, Christie's, 6th May 1801 (49), bt. in at £38.17; Bemrose collection; on London and New York art markets after first world war; purchased by Derby, 1925.

ENGRAVED   Mezzotint by J. R. Smith.

EXHIBITIONS   R.A., 1781 (100); Derby, 1870 (319); 1883 (64); 1934 (16) and on other occasions.

Derby Museum & Art Gallery

Companion to *Edwin* (No. 235).

---

238 THE DEAD SOLDIER

A large picture of the dead Soldier, £105   pp 16, 65–6, 140, 153

PROVENANCE   Bemrose, 1885, p. 70 claims as having been bought from the easel by Heath who sold it to Philips but this must be a confusion with a smaller version (see below). J. L. Philips Sale, Manchester, 31st October 1814 (33), bt. 'Gould', £315.

ENGRAVED   By Heath as in J. L. Philips Collection, published 4th May 1797. (Another inferior print by W. Dickinson published June 1804.)

(Untraced)

EXHIBITIONS   R.A., 1789 (236).

The following has a strong claim to be an original:

---

239 THE DEAD SOLDIER

SIZE   40 × 50 in / 101.6 × 127 cm   pp 65–6, 153

PROVENANCE   Artist's sale, 6th May 1801 (21), bt. Heath for £5; described as unfinished in catalogue. This must be the version in Miss Heath-Stubbs's sale, Sotheby's, 17th December 1947 (105), since she was a descendant of the engraver; London Art Market, 1951.

Formerly Miss Heath-Stubbs

Waterhouse, 1953, pp. 209, 214 (note), plate 171B, is inclined to accept as an original.

246

240 THE DEAD SOLDIER

James Ricau

The following is an original:
SIZE   40 × 50 in / 101.6 × 127 cm
Signed and dated 'I.W.P/1789'.   pp 65–6, 153   **281**
EXHIBITIONS   New York, 1960 (24).
This version may have been completed by another hand. See Rosenblum, 1960 and 1962, illus. on both occasions. The owner has no knowledge of its provenance and it may turn out to be identical with the Heath picture.

241 AN OLD MAN AND HIS ASS, FROM STERNE

(Untraced)

PROVENANCE   J. L. Philips Sale, Manchester, 31st October 1814 (19) sold for £34.13
EXHIBITIONS   Manchester Institution, 1831 (134), lent by Hirkman.   p 156[8]
The picture was left unfinished at Wright's death. See correspondence between Heath and Philips of 1797 and 1805 (quoted Bemrose, 1885, pp. 73–74), proving the landscape was added by Corbould. A study for the figure of the peasant was also in Philips's sale among the drawings, No. 42, sold to Hardman.

XI SCENES FROM CONTEMPORARY LIFE

242 THE EARTHSTOPPER ON THE BANKS OF THE DERWENT

Derby Museum & Art Gallery

Picture of an Earth Stopper to Lord..., £52.10
SIZE   38 × 47½ in / 96.5 × 120.6 cm pp 18, 50, 55, 66, 72, 75, 81, 88, 97, 105[5], 107   **113**
Signed and dated bottom left: 'J. WRIGHT PINXT/1773'.
PROVENANCE   Philip, 2nd Earl of Hardwicke; anon. sale, Christie's, 17th March 1950 (123); Benedict Nicolson; acquired from him by Derby Art Gallery, 1955 (see N.A.C.F. *Report*, 1956, p. 39).
EXHIBITIONS   S. of A., 1773 (372); Tate, 1958 (14) for further details.
Whitley, 1928, I, p. 247 quotes a letter from Wright to the Secretary of the Society of Artists, c 1773–74 complaining of the 'shabby price' Lord Hardwicke is to pay for the picture.

243 THE INDIAN WIDOW

Derby Museum & Art Gallery

an Indian Chiefs Widdow, £63
SIZE   40 × 50 in / 101.6 × 127 cm   pp 22, 65, 148–9, 152   **247**
Signed and dated bottom left: 'I.W. 1785'.
PROVENANCE   Remained on the artist's hands; sale Christie's, 6th May 1801 (64), bt. Borrow for £73.10; remained in this collection until acquired by Derby with the Borough Bequest, 1960.
ENGRAVED   J. R. Smith, published 29th January 1789.
EXHIBITIONS   Robins's Rooms, 1785 (2), for sale; R.A., 1962 (301) for further details.
See Nicolson, 1962, *passim*. Companion to *Lady in Milton's 'Comus'* (234). The setting was ready by April 1784 having been started at the end of the previous year, but the figure and implements of war were finished between then and the following spring.

244 THE INDIAN WIDOW

Formerly McNiven Collection

Wright painted a second version:
PROVENANCE   Remained in the Manchester family of McNiven between 1792 and earlier this century when it was burnt by a McNiven.   pp 65, 148–9, 152
EXHIBITIONS   B.I., 1844 (146) lent by C. McNiven.
Letter to J. L. Philips, 29th November 1792, quoted Bemrose, 1885, p. 91: 'I thank you for your friendly advice about the "Indian Widow", and tell our friend Tate, who I suppose will communicate it to Mr. McNiven, that in consideration of a little of his assistance to lay out my property to advantage, I will deduct 10 g[s] I sent it off by Shawcross last Monday, and hope it will be safe in Manchester ere this gets to hand...'

245 **THE SIEGE OF
GIBRALTAR**

(untraced, ? destroyed)

The Siege of Gibraltar Sold to M! John Milnes, £420. Milnes still owed him 200 guineas for it on 15th September 1787, having bought it before 12th April 1786.

PROVENANCE   John Milnes of Wakefield; Milnes Sale, Egremont House, Piccadilly, 12th June 1806 (60), bt. Vernon, a Liverpool merchant (according to Farington, Diary, entry for 26th June 1806, p. 3337) for £71.18; Lord Overstone (1857).
EXHIBITIONS   Robins' Rooms, 1785 (24); Manchester Art Treasures, 1857 (81).
Wright already had the idea of doing the picture by the beginning of 1783 but it was not completed until 17th February 1785.   pp 16, 131[7], 154, 159–60

LANDSCAPES

I ROME

i Colosseum

246 THE COLOSSEUM, DAYLIGHT

247 THE COLOSSEUM, MOONLIGHT

Derby Museum & Art Gallery

parts of the Colleseum sunshine; D.º its Companion moonlight, at £52.10 each, among pictures of the early to mid 1780's. These are:

SIZE   41 × 51 in / 104 × 129 cm   pp 22, 83   **256**
See 247

SIZE   40 × 50 in / 101.6 × 127 cm   pp 22, 83

Since restoration the pictures bear inscriptions 'I.W. 1789', but these may be faulty reconstructions of semi-obliterated signatures. The style suggests a date earlier in the '80's.
PROVENANCE   Unsold; Sale, Christie's, 6th May 1801 (54 and 55), bt. Borrow for £74.11 and £85.1 respectively; Borough Bequest to Derby, 1960.

A bit of the Ruins of the Coleseo sun shine sold to Mr. Machlin, £16.16; and A bit of the Ruins of the Colleseo, sun shine, £21, among pictures of the late '80's.
Since the dates fit perfectly, these must be: R.A. 1789 (74 and 107). The latter is described as 'with banditti'—and there are no banditti in the Borough pictures. This is claimed as the picture:
Ruins—with banditti round a fire, exhibited Derby, 1883 (13) lent by W. Bemrose.

A 'Part of the Collosseum' was at S. of A., 1791 (222), which might conceivably have been one of these.

A drawing *The Colosseum,* pen and brown wash, $14\frac{7}{8} \times 19\frac{5}{8}$ in (37.7 × 49.8 cm) in the Oppé Collection (see 'The Paul Oppé Collection', R.A., 1958 (1)). Other similar drawings are known.

ii Quirinal

248 QUIRINAL (?) BY MOONLIGHT
Dr. and Mrs. William S. Dale

SIZE $10\frac{1}{2} \times 15\frac{1}{2}$ in / 26.7 × 39.4 cm   pp 84[6], 138   **348**
Oil on paper
PROVENANCE   Holland Collection

iii Girandola. Full details will be found in Appendix B.
The known pictures are as follows:

249 **FIREWORK DISPLAY AT THE CASTEL SANT'ANGELO**
Birmingham Art Gallery

SIZE $16\frac{3}{4} \times 28$ in / 42.5×71.1 cm
See Appendix B, No. 5.

pp 76, 80–1   **166**

250 **FIREWORK DISPLAY AT THE CASTEL SANT'ANGELO**
Walker Art Gallery, Liverpool

SIZE $55\frac{1}{4} \times 68\frac{1}{8}$ in / 140.3×173 cm
See Appendix B, No. 8.

p 80   **210**

251 **FIREWORK DISPLAY AT THE CASTEL SANT'ANGELO**
Hermitage Museum, Leningrad

SIZE $63\frac{3}{4} \times 84$ in / 161.9×213.3 cm
See Appendix B, No. 4.

pp 77, 80, 85   **213**

II CENTRAL ITALY

i Albano, Nemi

The following known pictures can be identified with ones mentioned in early sources:

The Lake of Nemi Sun Set 3 q^{rs} Its Companion moon Light, £63; Frames for D^o at 2 G^s & $\frac{1}{2}$ p^r frame, £5.5. Then a note: **Mem. sold to Hugh Bateman.** Among pictures of very early '80's. These are:

252 **LAKE OF NEMI, SUNSET**
Private Collection, U.K.

SIZE $24\frac{1}{4} \times 29\frac{3}{4}$ in / 61.6×75.5 cm
Signed bottom right: 'I.W.'

pp 84, 87, 92, 128   **237**

253 **LAKE BY MOONLIGHT**

Mr. and Mrs. Paul Mellon

SIZE $24\frac{1}{4} \times 29\frac{3}{4}$ in / 61.6×75.5 cm
PROVENANCE   Mrs. Sacheverell Bateman (1910); Comm. and Mrs. Lister-Kaye (1934); Sale, Sotheby's, 4th December 1957 (161, 162).
EXHIBITIONS   Graves' Galleries, 1910 (77, 78); Derby, 1934 (120, 123).
The composition of *Lake of Nemi, Sunset* is taken from Richard Wilson which exists in several versions, the best known being that in the Southampton Art Gallery (called by Constable, plate 101b, a *River View*). Another version was in the Holland Collection (see Constable, p. 125), which Wright could well have known; a third (small) belongs to Sir Gilbert Inglefield, a beautiful original. Wright did another copy of the Wilson (see 254 below). Constable, plate 91a called *Lake Nemi* (1760) shows a similar stretch of the lake. A drawing in the Derby Art Gallery, black chalk with white heightening and wash on light green paper, $7\frac{1}{4} \times 9$ in (18.4×22.8 cm) shows a lake scene similar to the picture here catalogued (especially in the formation of the branches of the tall tree right); and on the reverse, a study in pen and wash with white heightening, for the Mellon moonlight.

pp 84, 91, 128   **239**

A small oval of the Lake of Nemi & its companion wth frames. Sold to Dr Beridge, £23.2, among pictures of very early '80's.
These are:

254 **LAKE OF NEMI**

See 255

pp 77^3, 84, 142^2 **234**

255 **CLASSICAL VILLA BY SEA SHORE**

SIZE   Each 12×14 in / 30.5×33.5 cm. Oval
PROVENANCE   Passed from Beridge to his wife's family, Buckston.

pp 77^3, 84^1, 84^2, 142^2 **235**

EXHIBITIONS Derby, 1870 (327, 576); 1934 (73, 72).

Lake of Nemi is a small version of the Southampton (ex-Lockinge) Wilson. The moonlight scene bears an inscription on the reverse on the relining canvas (presumably copied from the original canvas): 'Jos. Wright/1782'. It shows the same view as 294.

Private Collection, U.K.

256 NEMI

SIZE 17 × 24 in / 43.2 × 60.9 cm   p 84   **318**

PROVENANCE From Holland Collection.

Probably late evening, since the fading light is in West. The building on the hill on the right is apparently Gensano (cf. the Wilson in the Metropolitan Museum, New York; Constable, pl. 95a).

Dr. and Mrs. William S. Dale

Two sketches of yᵉ Lake of Albano & Nemi sold to Mᶜ:Nevin, £21 the pair; among pictures of the early '90's. These are:

257 ALBANO

See 258   p 84   **316**

258 NEMI

SIZE Each 14¼ × 21½ in / 36.2 × 54.6 cm   p 84   **317**

PROVENANCE Mrs. Burrows, from whom Mr. and Mrs. Mellon bought the pictures (1965) is a direct descendant of the McNiven to whom they were sold by the artist.

Early morning (with tall tree left; *Albano*) and sunset (with tall tree right; *Nemi*), violently contrasted. The same view of Albano is shown in the Pole picture (No 259).

Mr. and Mrs. Paul Mellon

259 ALBANO

SIZE 17½ × 25 in / 44.4 × 63.5 cm   pp 84, 109   **314**

PROVENANCE Sale, Christie's, 6th May 1801 (48) had a pair of views of Albano and Nemi, sold for £63 to 'Poole and Tate'. It seems sensible to infer that the one that went to 'Poole' is the *Albano* now at Radburne.

Major J. W. Chandos-Pole

260 ALBANO

SIZE 39¼ × 48 in / 99.7 × 121.9 cm   p 84   **315**

PROVENANCE F. J. Nettlefold (Grundy and Roe, *Catalogue... Nettlefold*, IV, p. 160, reprod. in colour). Presented to Cardiff by Nettlefold, 1946. Constable, 1953, p. 237 and plate 144b as *Nemi*, attributed to Wilson. Constable thinks the buildings on the right are Gensano, but the Cardiff picture has also been called Albano and the resemblance to Gensano is not close. He does not regard the picture as by Wilson and thinks that both it and the Wright at Radburne go back to a painting or drawing by Wilson. However this may be, the Cardiff picture is just as obviously by Wright as Major Chandos-Pole's.

National Museum of Wales, Cardiff

One further surviving picture of these subjects exists about which no early history can be traced:

261 NEMI

SIZE 17¾ × 25½ in / 45 × 64.7 cm   p 84   **319**

EXHIBITIONS 'Realism and Romance in English Painting', Agnew's, 1966 (28), illus.

On the stretcher in a very early hand (? early nineteenth century) is in ink: 'Lake of Nemi/ J. Wright of Derby pinxt'. It is very similar to the Dale picture (No 256), and has the same clear light effects. Probably also late evening.

Private Collection, U.K.

The following mentioned in the sources are not identified:

A small one (sketch) **on pannel of yᵉ Lake of Albano sold to L. Philips, £10.10;** among pictures of the early '90's.

Wright to Philips, 24th September 1792 (quoted Bemrose, 1885, p. 90): 'The finished one is on pannel'. From this letter we learn it was a sunset. In a letter of 29th November that year (Bemrose, *op. cit.*, p. 91) he writes to Philips: 'The little picture on pannel is too square...' In a letter to Philips of 31st December 1792 (Bemrose, *op. cit.*, pp. 91–92) he speaks of a 'Morning Effect on the Lake of Albano', as a companion to Wilson's 'Evening Effect' for Tate. It is not quite clear whether Philips acquired this, but one of these two was in the Philips Sale, Manchester, 31st October 1814 (18), sold to H. Wright for £18.18.

A 3 q^{rs} of the Lake of Albano with the Monte Jove seen thro' the arch of a Aquaduct, among pictures of the mid 1780's. A picture tallying with this description was sent to Philips at Manchester and is referred to by Wright in a letter to him 15th April 1791 (MS. Derby Public Library): 'Shall I exhibit the moonlight wth the dark arch, wch I sent to Manchester 'tis 3 q^{rs} consequently a frame may be easily procured...' It was at S. of A., 1791 (223).

A pen and watercolour sketch of the *Girandola* in the Derby Art Gallery has a letter of before October 1774, unsigned but in Wright's hand, along the margin. It contains the phrase: '...when I go to Naples, as I must go some time hence to make a view of the Lake of Avernus as a Companion to the Lake of Albano for the Duke of Chabaud...' This is the Duc de Chabot, of whom Mrs. Hervey, the wife of the Bishop of Derry, writes from Rome, 1st December 1778: 'They [the Duc and Duchesse] are much liked. They seem well bred and unaffected...' (Childe-Pemberton, 1925, I, p. 225).

The Lake of Albano Sun Set ½ length for Mr Milnes, £63; among pictures of *c* 1790. One of a series of four painted for John Milnes of Wakefield. The other three are two morning and noon scenes in the Alps, and a moonlight on the Coast of Tuscany. At least two were despatched to Wakefield in the spring of 1791.

Sale, Christie's, 6th May 1801 (50): 'A Landscape, View of the Lake of Albano, a beautiful warm scene', sold for £53.11 to Borrow.

D^o (a small picture) **of the Lake of Albana, Sunset, £26.5;** among pictures of the late '80's.

A Sun Set of the Lake of Nemi, £52.10.

A small picture of the Lake of Nemi sun set, and its Companion Moon light. Sold to Robt Holden Esq., £21.

Lake of Nemi Sun rising, £26.5; among pictures of the mid-'80's.

Lake of Nemi on pannel; among very late pictures (*c* 1794).

One of these might be: 'A view of the Lake of Nemi, a warm Evening Scene', Christie's, 6th May 1801 (22), sold to H. Wright for £12.12.

ii Cosimato (See also Unidentified Italian landscape Cosimato)

A view in Dove Dale & its Comp. of Cosmato for Mr Gisborne at 50 Gs., £52.10.

The companion is:

SIZE   18 × 25 in / 45.7 × 63.5 cm   pp 83–4, 89, 134   **257**

PROVENANCE   Mrs. Griffiths, Yoxall Lodge; Marquess Curzon (before 1922).

EXHIBITIONS   Derby, 1883 (27).

The companion to it of *Dovedale* (Cat 315) also at Kedleston is dated 1786, so this is of the same date.

A View of St Cosimato on pannel sold to Honble A. Thomson, £42

SIZE   24 × 32 in / 60.9 × 81.3 cm Panel   pp 83–4 · **283**

Signed and dated bottom right: 'I.W. P.1789'.

EXHIBITIONS   Presumably the 'View in Italy' lent by 'Chief Baron Thompson' to B.I., 1817 (76) and a picture under the same title lent by Thomas Pares to B.I., 1824 (168); Derby, 1883 (83) lent by E. H. Pares.

That Wright should have asked 15 guineas more for this than for Gisborne's picture is understandable since it is the larger.

262 **CONVENT OF S. COSIMATO**

Viscount Scarsdale

263 **CONVENT OF S. COSIMATO**

J. T. Blundell-Turner Esq on loan to Derby Museum & Art Gallery

264 **CONVENT OF**
S. COSIMATO

Walker Art Gallery, Liverpool

A small picture of Cosmato given to my friend W. Tate; among pictures of the late
'80's.

SIZE $19\frac{7}{8} \times 25$ in / 50.5 × 63,5 cm   pp 83–4, 139   **282**

PROVENANCE   Tate family; William Claxton; bequeathed by E. I. Claxton to Liverpool,
1958.

In pencil on the stretcher is written: 'Convent of Cosimato/Bought by Wᵐ Claxton
of South Hill Grove Liverpool in April 1849 having formerly belonged to his friend Jno
Moss Tate Esq/ by Wright of Derby Pᵗ 1794 gift to Jno Moss Tate Esq.' Unless as seems
unlikely Wright painted another *Cosimato* which is otherwise unrecorded, these statements
are erroneous: the picture was presented to William Tate and was painted six or seven
years earlier than Claxton says.

John Moss Tate is unknown. He was presumably a son of either Richard or William Tate.
Bemrose refers to a man of this name (1885, p. 5) but this may be a confusion with Thomas
Moss Tate.

The Convent of Sᵗ Cosimato, £26.5. This is followed by an entry: **Dᵒ for Mʳˢ Hayley
mem. not paid,** with the same price repeated but since the 'Ditto' and the second price
are deleted, one can assume she acquired the first, and only, version. Among pictures of *c*
1794. This might be the one referred to in a letter of Wright to Philips, 29th June 1794
(MS. Derby Public Library; a short passage from it quoted Bemrose, 1885, p. 93): '...I
shall not be sorry if Mʳ Wakefield buys the picture of Sᵗ Cosimato, it will pay part of my
expenses in visiting the Lakes...'

The only ones which qualify for R.A., 1788 (98) are Gisborne's and Tate's.

iii Neptune's Grotto

Neptunes Grotto sold to Mʳ Milnes, £31.10; among pictures of the late 1770's.
Letter from Wright to Daulby, 11th January 1780, quoted Appendix B, under No. 16,
R.A., 1779 (360). It was about the same size as Milnes's small *Vesuvius* (29 × 34 in / 73.6
× 86.3 cm).

A 3 qʳˢ of Neptunes Grotto wᵗʰ the Sibyls Temple &C. given to My friend Tate;
among pictures of *c* 1783.

Daulby's MS. *c* 1790 lists a *Neptune's Grotto at Tivoli* in Daulby's Collection, 15 × 19 in
(38.1 × 48.2 cm). R.A., 1778 (411). Probably the one that reappeared Liverpool, 1784 (119).

A small picture of Neptunes Grotto, to Leigh Philips, £14.14; among pictures of the
late '80's. Letter from Wright to Philips, 28th February 1791 (MS. Derby Public Library):
'...I shᵗ be glad to have [*Neptune's Grotto*] as soon as you please that I may get it enlarged,
and attack it when the humour takes me...' The humour had taken him by 23rd April 1791
(see letter to Philips quoted Bemrose, 1885, p. 65), on which occasion he improved the
picture. Philips Sale, Manchester, 31st October 1814 (5), sold to E. Flack for £24.3.

iv Terni

The Cascade at Terni 3 qᵗ given to my friend Tate, £31.10. 'Given to my friend' is
added after the picture had been priced.

A Large Dᵒ (picture) of the Cascade of Terni, £63.10; (changed from a sum over £70)
among pictures of *c* 1782. Probably the same as: **The Cascade of Terni framed, £63,**
among other pictures of that date. Since this appears next to a *William and Margaret*, it is
likely to be the one at Robins's Rooms, 1785 (4). And since no purchaser is recorded, it is
perhaps: Sale, Christie's, 6th May 1801 (47), bt. Borrow, for £40.19.

v Other Tivoli Subjects

The inside of a Stable near Tivoli sold to Jⁿ⁰ Henderson Esqʳ., £21; among pictures of the early '80's.

Its Companion (of a view of the 'Ponte Saloria') **sun set of Tivoli, £36.15;** among pictures of the mid 1780's.

265 VIEW OF TIVOLI

Derby Museum & Art Gallery

SIZE   30 × 38 in / 76.2 × 96.5 cm   pp 83, 126[1]   **260**
PROVENANCE   Borough Bequest to Derby, 1960.
Here identified as a view of Tivoli overlooking the Campagna (Cf., for example, Constable, 1953, plate 115a).

vi Maecenas's Villa

Mecena's Villa on Dᵒ (panel), **£42;** followed by entry: **Cicero's Villa on Dᵒ., £42.** They were evidently pairs of *c* 1788; they follow an entry for Sir Robert Wilmot's *Vesuvius* of about that date. This makes one think they were R.A., 1788 (81, 83). A letter from Thomas Kerrich to his aunt, dated Rome 16th April 1774 (when Wright was there) describes a visit to 'ye country seats of Maecenas' at Tivoli (see A. M. W. Stirling, *Coke of Norfolk and his Friends...*, London, ed 1912, p. 77).

vii Ponte Molle

A view of the ponte Mola sold to Sʳ Broke Boothby, £21.10. After 1789 when Brooke Boothby took this title.
Two miles beyond the Porta del Popolo.

viii Ponte Salario

A view of the ponte Salario half length, £52.10; among pictures of *c* 1790.

A morning view of the ponte Saloria, For Dᵒ., (i.e. Boothby) **£36.15;** among pictures of *c* 1786–88. It had a companion of the same price of *Tivoli* (q.v.). The first of the last two entries may be referred to in a letter to Philips, 24th September 1792 (quoted Bemrose, 1885, p. 90) as unfinished.
The Ponte Salario, over the *Anio*, about two miles outside the Porta Salaria.

ix Capua

A sepulchral Monument at Old Capua Moon light; among pictures of the late '80's.

III VESUVIUS

Full details will be found in Appendix B. The known pictures are as follows:

266 VESUVIUS IN ERUPTION
Miss D. M. R. Cade

SIZE   49 × 71 in / 124.4 × 180.3 cm   pp 17, 77, 80, 87–8   **170**
See Appendix B, No. 29.

267 VESUVIUS FROM POSILLIPO
Major Peter Miller Mundy

SIZE   40½ × 50½ in / 102.8 × 128.2 cm   pp 78–9, 84, 88[3], 92, 97   **291**
See Appendix B, No. 30.

268 **VESUVIUS WITH THE PROCESSION OF ST. JANUERIUS' HEAD**
Pushkin Museum, Moscow

SIZE $63\frac{3}{4} \times 84$ in / 161.9 $\times$ 213.3 cm
See Appendix B, No. 3.

pp 17, 77, 81, 85, 143   **214**

269 **VESUVIUS FROM POSILLIPO**
Mrs. George Anson

SIZE 25×33 in / 63.5 $\times$ 83.8 cm Panel
See Appendix B, No. 31.

pp 78–9, 84, 92, 125   **294**

270 **VESUVIUS**
Private Collection, U.K.

SIZE 12×14 in / 30.5 $\times$ 33.5 cm Oval
See Appendix B, No. 28.

pp 77, 87, 142[2]   **233**

271 **VESUVIUS FROM POSILLIPO**
Christopher Norris Esq

SIZE $7\frac{1}{2} \times 9$ in / 19 $\times$ 22.8 cm Oval on copper
See Appendix B, No. 33.

p 78[1]   **288**

272 **VESUVIUS IN ERUPTION**
Christopher Norris Esq

SIZE $7\frac{1}{2} \times 9$ in / 19 $\times$ 22.8 cm Oval on copper
See Appendix B, No. 34.

p 78[1]   **289**

273 **VESUVIUS**
L. B. Sanderson Esq

SIZE $16\frac{3}{4} \times 28$ in / 42.5 $\times$ 71.1 cm
See Appendix B, No. 6.

pp 76–7, 80–1   **167**

274 **VESUVIUS IN ERUPTION**
University College of Wales, Aberystwyth

SIZE 40×50 in / 101.6 $\times$ 127 cm
See Appendix B, No. 32.

pp 77–8, 87–8   **169**

275 **VESUVIUS**
Derby Museum & Art Gallery

SIZE $47\frac{1}{2} \times 67$ in / 120.6 $\times$ 170.2 cm
See Appendix B, No. 35.

pp 10[3], 11[2], 76[7], 77, 83   **168**

IV AROUND NAPLES AND SALERNO

i Amalfi, Capri, Sorrento

A small view at Almalfa, £14.14. What may well be the same entry is repeated on another sheet of the Account Book, where the word **sunset** is added. *c* 1783.

Two small pictures of the Island of Caprea; among pictures of 1783–84.

A Bridge seen thro' a Cavern on the coast of Sorente moonlight, To L. Philips, £31.10
This might well be:

276 **BRIDGE THROUGH A CAVERN, MOONLIGHT**

SIZE 25×32 in / 63.5 $\times$ 81.2 cm   pp 84, 92, 140   **326**
Signed and dated bottom left 'I.W.P. 1791'.
PROVENANCE   Philips Sale, Manchester, 31st October 1814 (30), bt. by H. & A. W[right] for £42; Rev. E. L. Simpson (1883); presented to Derby, 1939.
EXHIBITIONS   Derby, 1883 (32); Graves' Galleries, 1910 (81).
In a letter of 23rd April 1791 (quoted Bemrose, 1885, p. 63) Wright refers to a *Moonlight* for Philips at 30 guineas, which is presumably this.

Derby Museum & Art Gallery

A drawing of this bridge, without the cavern framing it in, is in the Derby Art Gallery. It is inscribed top left 'Sorente'. It is not by the artist but by an unknown imitator. It does at least help to identify the Philips picture with that in Derby.

ii Cicero's Villa

Ciceros Villa in the Bay of Naples sold to M.ʳ Smith. Rec'd on account £20; £36.15.
Also listed on the reverse of a letter of August 1788 in the Account Book. The first entry
is followed by:

A large one of D.º sun seting after a shower sold to Edward Mundy Esq., £81 (?£84).
This is the only large *Cicero's Villa* listed, so presumably it is the companion to the Moonlight on the *Coast of Tuscany* sold to Milnes (q.v.) Both were ? exhibited R.A., 1789 (26,9).

Cicero's Villa on D.º (panel), £42. This and a *Maecenas's Villa* (q.v.) were evidently pairs
of *c* 1788, which makes one think they were R.A., 1788 (81, 83).

iii Grottoes at Salerno (see also UNIDENTIFIED ITALIAN LANDSCAPES, *Caverns,
grottoes*)

277 A GROTTO IN THE KINGDOM OF NAPLES, WITH BANDITTI: A SUNSET

G. Meynell Esq, M.B.E.

A Grotto with a Banditti sold to M.ʳ Cockshut, £157.10
SIZE 48 × 68 in / 121.9 × 172.7 cm   pp 17, 82–3, 158 **211**
Described in 19th century notebook at Meynell Langley as signed and dated lower left,
close to the figures: 'J. Wright 1779'. No inscription is now visible. Since it is hard to get
away from the fact that this was the work shown at the R.A. the previous year, the date
must have been misread. We know a date on the *Virgil's Tomb* at Meynell Langley (286)
was misread by the same annotator, so a second error would not be surprising.
PROVENANCE Passed from Cockshutt to C. Heathcote, a descendant of his son-in-law
Bache Heathcote. Letter at Meynell Langley from C. Heathcote to Godfrey Meynell,
dated 20th March 1840, offering to Meynell this, its companion with the figure of Julia
(278), and a *Virgil's Tomb*, saying they 'had never been restored in any way'. This letter is
followed by a declaration signed by Godfrey Meynell, dated 28th March saying he had
taken the three Wrights. They have remained in the Meynell family since then.
EXHIBITIONS R.A., 1778 (358); Tate, 1958 (16) for further details.
Letter from Wright at Meynell Langley addressed to 'Jos.ʰ Cockshutt Esq.ʳ Chaddesden'
dated 29th August 1780: 'Sir, Within I have sent you a Bill of the two Pictures, the dis-
charging of w.ᶜʰ I beg you will consider [at] your own convenience'. The two *Cavern*
pictures are listed by Wright on the back of the letter, but in the Receipt dated June 1780
(quoted Tate, 1958, p. 23) *Virgil's Tomb* is added to the other two.

278 GROTTO WITH THE FIGURE OF JULIA

G. Meynell Esq, M.B.E.

A Grotto in the Gulf of Salernum with the figure of Julia. Companion to that w.ᵗʰ Banditti sold to Mr. Cockshutt, £105
SIZE Unknown   pp 83, 158 **215**
Described in 19th Century notebook at Meynell Langley as signed and dated on the rock
right 'J. Wright Pinxt 1780'. No inscription can now be read.
PROVENANCE Same as 277.
EXHIBITIONS R.A., 1780 (203).
London Courant, 5th May 1780, reviewing the Academy Exhibition, complains that 'the
inside of the cave seems to want some degree of tone; it is mere colourless light and shadow'.

A large Grotto in the Gulf of Salernum Moon rising sold to M.ʳ Daulby, £84;
among pictures of the early '80's.
Letter from Wright to Hayley, 28th December 1783 (National Portrait Gallery's extra-
illustrated Bemrose): 'I was just putting the last stroke to one of my exhibition pictures
[Robins's Rooms], when your letter arrived w.ᶜʰ put me into such good humour... that I
view'd my picture... w.ᵗʰ uncommon pleasure... The picture is a dark Cavern, faintly
illuminated w.ᵗʰ a large glowing colour'd Moon, almost clear of the Horizon, the figure of

Julia given up to despair, sits on a part of the Rock in the foreground, w.th her head down to her knees…' It was shown at Robins's Rooms, 1785 (7) but was still on the artist's hands on 14th November 1785 (see letter of that date to Daulby, quoted Bemrose, 1885, p. 86). In letter to the same, 14th January 1786 (*loc. cit.*, pp. 86–87) we learn it is offered to Daulby on approval. Letter of 7th February (*loc. cit.*, pp. 86–87) proves the picture is on the way. It reached Daulby on 16th February, according to a note in Daulby's hand at the end of Wright's letter to him 25th March (MS. Derby Public Library): 'I know the situation of my friend Tate's room, it has not light enough to shew it to advantage, moonlight pictures require a good light and not a glaring one…' A note in the Account Book informs us that Daulby is to pay 'lawful interest' on the picture until the 80 guineas are fully paid.

EXHIBITIONS   Liverpool, 1787 (117); Liverpool R.I., 1823 (111), lent by John Moss.

Grotto in the Gulf of Salernum moon light ½ length, D.° its Companion Sun Set sold to Mr Hardman, Manchester, £84; among pictures of the early '80's. These are:

279 GROTTO IN GULF OF SALERNO, MOONLIGHT

See 280   p 81

280 GROTTO IN GULF OF SALERNO, SUNSET

SIZE   Each 40 × 50 in / 101.6 × 127 cm   p 81

PROVENANCE   William Hardman; Thomas Hardman Sale, Manchester, 19th October 1838 (5) was *sunset* cavern.

EXHIBITIONS   R.A., 1781 (61, 112); *Sunset* Cavern, Manchester Institution, 1831 (127). Letter to Daulby, 14th November 1785 (quoted Bemrose, 1885, p. 86) saying the pictures are dispatched on that day. Letter to Daulby, 14th January 1786 (*loc. cit.*, p. 86) again expresses hope that Hardman will not reveal the low price he paid for the *Caverns*. Letter to Daulby of 7th February 1786 (MS. Derby Public Library) says the cavern scenes are now paid for.

The Hardman Sale catalogue of 1838 reveals that the *Sunset* showed a boat at anchor in the cavern; the size of a '½ length' is here confirmed (40 × 50 in). Two drawings in the Philips Sale, Manchester, 31st October 1814 (50) are said in the catalogue to be 'the originals from which the two celebrated pictures in the collection of the late Wm. Hardman Esq. were painted'. This statement is certainly true. They were bought by a Hardman; Hardman Sale, 1838, bt. by a member of the Wayne family; now in a private collection in England. Both black chalk on paper, 11¼ × 18½ in (28.5 × 46.9 cm). **171, 172**

Formerly Hardman Collection

Two Grotto's by the sea side in the Gulf of Salerno for Mr Hodges, £105 (increased from another sum); among pictures of 1777–80.

Conceivably purchased by the painter William Hodges. Wright did a portrait of a *Mrs. Hodges* (q.v.) who may be connected.

281 A CAVERN, MORNING

SIZE   40 × 50 in / 101.6 × 127 cm   pp 11, 76, 81–3   **175**

Signed and dated: 'J. Wright 1774'.

EXHIBITIONS   New York, 1960 (12) for further details. See Buckley, 1955, p. 266.

Mr. and Mrs. R. Kirk Askew Jr.

Pendant to the following:

282 A CAVERN, EVENING

SIZE   40 × 50 in / 101.6 × 127 cm   pp 11, 76, 81–3   **174**

Signed and dated: 'J. Wright/1774'.

EXHIBITIONS   New York, 1960 (13) for further details; Indianapolis, 1965 (19).

See Buckley, 1952, p. 165.

Wright did not go to Naples till the autumn of 1774, so they were painted between then and the end of the year.

Smith College Museum of Art

283 **GROTTO WITH THE FIGURE OF JULIA**

R. D. Plant Esq

SIZE $15\frac{1}{2} \times 20$ in / 39.4 × 50.8 cm   pp 83, 88, 169² **216**
Signed and dated bottom right: 'I.W. 1780'.
PROVENANCE   Arkwright Collection; Cyril Plant.
EXHIBITIONS   Derby, 1883 (85), lent by F. C. Arkwright.

iv Naples and Salerno Coast Scenes

A small Moonlight on the coast of Naples, with note: **The picture is paid for.** 1783.

The Companion (to Bacon's *Vesuvius*) **Sun Set in the Bay of Salerno sold to my friend Holland, £18.18** (changed from £21.10). A note on the same sheet of the Account Book reads: **Mem. Rec'd in two payments of my friend Holland 14 Guineas for the picture of yᵉ Gulf of Salerno Jan 7th.** The date at the top of this sheet is 1783, so he may have been paid for the picture in January of that year. For further details, see Appendix B, under No. 10.

284 **SUNSET ON THE COAST NEAR NAPLES**

Sir Gilbert Inglefield

SIZE $25 \times 29\frac{7}{8}$ in / 63.5 × 75.9 cm   p 83 **287**
PROVENANCE   Ralph Robotham (1934).
EXHIBITIONS   Derby, 1934 (104).
The picture is wrongly described in the 1934 catalogue as a 'Grotto in the Gulf of Salernum —Sunset'. The scene, which does seem to be Neapolitan, is unidentified.

285 **MOONLIGHT ON THE COAST NEAR NAPLES**

Alban Bower Esq

SIZE   23 × 30 in / 58.4 × 76.2 cm   pp 83, 124¹
PROVENANCE   Holden Collection, Nuthall Temple.
EXHIBITIONS   Derby, 1883 (17).
Similar in composition to the picture above. It bears the 1883 exhibition label (as lent by Holden) on the reverse of the frame. A Nuthall Temple provenance is not to be sniffed at. However, as it stands the picture is not up to Wright's standard and one can only suppose that it was an original but has been tampered with by another hand.
A copy lent by Major Griggs to Derby, 1934 (106) was sold Christie's, 17th June 1966 (1).

v Virgil's Tomb (see also Ruins)

286 **VIRGIL'S TOMB**

G. Meynell Esq, M.B.E.

Virgil's Tomb for Cockshutt Esq., £63   pp 83–4, 158
SIZE   39 × 50 in / 99 × 127 cm
Described in 19th Century notebook at Meynell Langley as signed and dated 1787 or 1781 on the right. This is certainly a misreading since Wright notes the sale of the picture to Cockshutt in June 1780 (for further details, see Tate, 1958 under No. 16).
PROVENANCE   Same as for *A Grotto in the Kingdom of Naples with Banditti: A Sunset* (277). Datable *c* 1779.

287 **VIRGIL'S TOMB**

Col. Sir John Crompton-Inglefield

Virgil's Tomb, £63 (a later price is £42); among pictures of 1778–79. This might well be:
SIZE   40 × 50 in / 101.6 × 127 cm   pp 83–4 **232**
Signed and dated bottom right: 'I.W. 1779'.
PROVENANCE   Mrs. C. E. Arkwright (1934).
EXHIBITIONS   The only certain *Virgil's Tomb* where the figure of Scilius Italicus appears is this one. It is therefore likely to have been R.A., 1779 (359)—the date on the picture. The poet also appears in the *Virgil's Tomb* at Liverpool, 1784 (115) but this may have been a smaller picture. Tate, 1958 (17) for further details.

A picture of *Virgil's Tomb* with Scilius Italicus is in the Derby Art Gallery, but it is hard to say in its present condition whether it is an original.

288 VIRGIL'S TOMB
Private Collection, U.K.
(Barton Blount Estates Company)

A large picture of Virgil's Tomb, £63 followed shortly afterwards by the date December 1782.
This might well be:
SIZE   40 × 50 in / 101.6 × 127 cm   pp 83–4, 91   **231**
Signed low in the centre 'I. Wright Pinx./1782'.
PROVENANCE   According to the present owner this came from the Gisborne Collection.

289 VIRGIL'S TOMB

Virgil's Tomb by Moonlight, £63; date uncertain from the position in the Account Book. It is not known whether the following was a 40 × 50 inch or a smaller picture but the entry might be:
SIZE   Unknown   p 142
PROVENANCE   Presented by the artist to William Hayley, 1783, and by the latter to Amelia Opie, 1817; bequeathed by Mrs. Opie to Thomas Brightwall 1853.
EXHIBITIONS   ? Robins's Rooms, 1785 (5).
See Cecilia Lucy Brightwall, *Memorials of the Life of Amelia Opie*, Norwich/London, 1854, pp. 179 ff., for the subsequent history of the picture.

Formerly Thomas Brightwall

Virgil's Tomb sun breaking thro' a cloud small picture, £31.10; among pictures of *c* 1790. Though the date as recorded does not quite coincide with what one might expect, this might be the one that passed to the Strutt Collection. Strutt, 1827 (68); 22 × 26 in / 55.9 × 66 cm.
EXHIBITIONS   Nottingham, 1878 (83); Derby, 1883 (11), described as 'sun breaking through a cloud' and signed 'I.W.P. 1785'.

A small picture of Virgil's Tomb, £21. *c* 1782. This could be the one in the sale, Christie's, 6th May 1801 (37), bt. Rawlinson for £17.6.6.

V FLORENCE AND NORTH ITALY

i Tuscany (See also *Lighthouses*)

290 DISTANT VIEW OF FLORENCE

A view of the City of Florence sun rising, £52.10. This entry is inserted among late pictures in the Account Book but it may even be before 1790 (see below). The following seems too small for a picture at this price and must be a second version:
SIZE   22½ × 29½ in / 57.1 × 74.9 cm   p 84⁶   **327**
PROVENANCE   ? N. Philips; ? Thomas Borrow; William Bemrose; by whom presented to his daughter Mrs. R. G. Wheler (1908); her sale, Sotheby's, 10th December 1958 (114); Chicago and London art markets; presented to the Art Institute in the mid-1960's.
EXHIBITIONS   New York, 1960 (23).
A label on the reverse is said to read: 'this painting by Mr. Wright of Derby was presented to me by my nephew Nat Philipps Wed. Aug. 28 1794. Thos. Borrow J. P. Original picture left as a gift to Mrs. R. G. Wheler by her father Wᵐ Bemrose 19/8/08'. It is clearly a modern inscription, which casts a little doubt on whether it is in fact the Philips/Borrow picture. That N. Philips did own this or the larger version is proved by a letter from Wright to J. L. Philips, 27th December 1794 (quoted Bemrose, 1885, p. 94) informing us that N. Philips bought the *View of Florence* 'some time ago'. The picture is in poor condition and for this reason the author cannot vouch for its authenticity.
A version, which could be the existing one, was in the Thomas Hardman Sale, Manchester, 1838 (40), 22 × 30 in (55.9 × 76.2 cm): '...the River Arno running through a finely wooded country...' A drawing, 11⅞ × 13⅞ (30.1 × 35.2 cm) in the Derby Art Gallery translates this composition into an oval, as though intended to serve for a work in another

Art Institute of Chicago

medium (? pottery). Pencil strengthened with pen. It is not certainly by Wright, and may have been done by someone extremely competent under his guidance.

Moonlight on the coast of Tuscany in the Mediterranean Com(panion) **to the larger picture of Cicero Villa for M.ʳ Milnes, £63.10;** among pictures of the late '80's. A large *Cicero's Villa, sunset* is entered a few items before this; it was sold to Edward Mundy (q.v.) Its companion was one of the four 'stages of the day' for Milnes; for the other three, see under the Milnes *Albano*. Possibly identical with the *Lighthouse by moonlight* at R.A., 1789 (9), see *Lighthouses*.

ii North Italy

A view in the Alps in the Dutchy of Milan. half length. Noon. £63. This is followed by:

The Companion D.º Morning. For Jn.º Milnes Esq., £63; among pictures of *c* 1790.

These are two of the 'stages of the day' for Milnes; see under the Milnes *Albano*.

A picture of the Alps on the side next Italy, in the Dutchy of Milan sold to Poploe (? Peploe) **Birch Esq., £36.15;** among pictures of the late '80's. ? R.A. 1788 (234).

A view on the Lake of Como in Italy warm Sun set. On pannel; among pictures of *c* 1790.

VI UNIDENTIFIED ITALIAN LANDSCAPES
(see also XIV)

i Bridges, River Scenes

291 **BRIDGE WITH TURRET OVER WINDING RIVER**

Leighton House (Royal Borough of Kensington and Chelsea Public Libraries)

A small picture of a Bridge in Italy Sun Set on pannel, £31.10; among pictures of *c* 1789.

SIZE   30 × 38 in / 76.2 × 96.5 cm   pp 84–5, 89   **250**
Signed and dated on rock right: 'I.W.P./1785'. Presented to Leighton House by executors of Sir Claude Phillips.

ii 'Cosimato'

292 **ITALIAN LANDSCAPE**

Mr. and Mrs. Paul Mellon

SIZE   40½ × 51 in / 102.8 × 129.5 cm   p 92   **311**
Signed and dated bottom left on rock: 'I Wright/Pinx/1790'.
PROVENANCE   Bentley Collection (before 1831): John Bentley Sale, 15th May 1886 (71), bt. 'F.B.' Described in sale catalogue as formerly belonging to 'Mr. Mills, Yorkshire'. However, it cannot be identified with any of John Milnes's known pictures. B. Nicolson; London and New York art markets.
EXHIBITIONS   Manchester Institution, 1831 (145); Richmond (Virginia), 1963 (39).
The picture has been known since at least the early 19th century as a view of *Cosimato* but it does not resemble closely enough the landscapes of this district. Wright may even have introduced elements from Northern landscape, and at any rate used his imagination freely.

iii Miscellaneous

293 GROTTO WITH WATERFALL
Ian Appleby Esq

SIZE $15\frac{1}{4} \times 19\frac{1}{2}$ in / 38.7 × 49.5 cm
Signed and dated bottom near centre 'IW 177 [?]'

p 83[4]   **173**

294 CLASSICAL VILLA BY SEA SHORE

Mrs. V. Martin

SIZE 21 × 36 in / 53.3 × 91.4 cm
A 19th century MS. list in the owner's possession states that the picture comes from the W. Hardman Collection. It would be surprising if it did not turn out to be the picture in the Thomas Hardman Sale, Manchester, 19th October 1838 (22): 'An Italian Scene, of great picturesque beauty, enriched with Classical Italian Buildings, and coloured with all the freshness of nature, under the warmth of an Italian Sky'. The description certainly corresponds to the known picture but the measurements are given as 23 × 30 in (58.4 × 76.2 cm). The same view is shown in 255.
A view in Italy warm Sun Set, £10.10; among very late pictures.

p 84   **295**

iv Lakes (see also 253; under Nemi)

A small moon Light of a lake sold to Mr. Daulby, £14.14 (changed from £16.16); among pictures of the early '80's.
This was 'A Lake between Rome & Florence Moonlight' $16\frac{1}{2} \times 21$ in (41.9 × 53.3 cm) which according to Daulby MS. *c* 1790 was shown at Liverpool, 1784 (120).

A 3 q^{rs} picture of a Lake in Italy Moonlight, £31.10, followed by **A small D^{o}. of D^{o}. by D^{o}., £21.10.** The second entry has (deleted): **Sold to Mr. Holland Mem. 5 pages on.** We turn 5 pages on, to find that Holland pays twenty guineas for the small moonlight between 1784 and 1787. They are both listed, needless to say, among pictures of *c* 1783.

v Lighthouses

A Light House in the Mediterranean, to L. Philips, £10.10; among pictures of the early '90's. The next entry in the Account Book includes the words: **both sketches,** meaning that the Lighthouse was also a sketch. An entry in the Account Book, crossed through, among pictures of the same period, reads: **Sketch of a Lighthouse on y^{e} Mediterranean, £10.10,** and is no doubt the same picture. This is:

295 LIGHTHOUSE IN THE MEDITERRANEAN

K. J. Blunt Esq; on loan to Derby Museum & Art Gallery

SIZE $14\frac{1}{4} \times 20$ in / 36.2 × 50.8 cm
PROVENANCE   L. Philips; sale, Manchester, 31st October 1814 (27), sold to Pares for £36.15; Commander and Mrs. Lister-Kaye (1934). Has been on loan from Mr. Blunt to Derby Art Gallery for some time in the early 1960's.
EXHIBITIONS   Derby, 1883 (80), lent by E. H. Pares; 1934 (49), lent by Commander and Mrs. Lister-Kaye. The lighthouse is shown by moonlight. In Philips's sale catalogue, his sunny evening *Vesuvius* (see Appendix B, No. 25) is described as a companion. A label on the stretcher reads: 'This Picture by Wright is the property of Thos. Pares Esqr Hopwell...'

pp 84, 92, 140   **312**

296 LIGHTHOUSE ON THE COAST OF TUSCANY

SIZE $40 \times 50\frac{1}{2}$ in / 101.6 × 128.2 cm
PROVENANCE   Fitzherbert Wright; purchased on London Art Market, 1949.
EXHIBITIONS   ? R.A., 1789 (9); Derby, 1883 (25); 1934 (39); R.A., 1951–52 (11).
According to note in Algernon Graves, *The Royal Academy of Arts*, 1906, Vol. VIII under Wright, the 'moonlight' at R.A. 1789 (9) was 'with a lighthouse'. This is the only recorded picture which is a plausible candidate (Mr. Blunt's being too small). Letter from Hayley to his wife, 5th May 1789 (quoted Bemrose, 1885, p. 81) says R.A. 1789 (9) had 'enchanted'

pp 84, 92   **313**

Tate Gallery London

him. This may be identical with 'Moonlight on the coast of Tuscany in the Mediterranean' for John Milnes of Wakefield (q.v.).

vi Ruins

297 RUINED ARCHWAY

SIZE $24\frac{1}{2} \times 17\frac{1}{2}$ in / 62.2 × 44.4 cm   pp 83[1], 84 **296**

Not a view in Virgil's Tomb because the brickwork is different. When the picture was on the London Art Market in the early 1950's, there were two figures seated on the steps. These disappeared when the picture was cleaned, as well as the inscription bottom right 'IWP/1790'. The figures appear from old photographs to be quite characteristic of the artist and it is possible that they, as well as the inscription, were done by his own hand.

Private Collection, U.S.A.

VII ELSEWHERE ON EUROPEAN CONTINENT

According to letter from Wright to Daulby, 11th January 1780, Milnes bought from the artist a view of Mount Etna, as a companion to a *Vesuvius*. He is never known to have visited Sicily but this was not necessary. The picture may have passed to Lord Palmerston (for fuller details, see Appendix B under No. 16).

Its (a small *Vesuvius*) **Companion by the Lake of Geneva moonlight For Col. Grevill, £21.** See Appendix B, under No 27.

VIII IN AND AROUND DERBYSHIRE, General

picture of a bridge wth. the effect of a rainbow sold to M^r. N. Philips, £52.10; among pictures of *c* 1794–95. From letters from Wright to J. L. Philips of 27th December 1794, 2nd October and 18th December 1795 (quoted Bemrose, 1885, pp. 94–96) it is clear that at the end of 1794 N. Philips ordered the picture which he intended sending to America; that it was ready at the beginning of October 1795; and that it was sent off to Nottingham before the end of that year.

298 LANDSCAPE WITH A RAINBOW—'VIEW NEAR CHESTERFIELD'

picture of a bridge wth. the effect of a rainbow, following on the last entry. This is:

SIZE   32 × 42 in / 81.2 × 106.7 cm   pp 93, 138[4] **347**

PROVENANCE   Sale, Christie's, 6th May 1801 (46), bt. in by Tate at £59.17; Cade Collection; acquired by Derby, 1913.

EXHIBITIONS   Tate, 1958 (32) for further details. A copy by John Holland of Ford, signed on stretcher and dated 1799, belongs to Sir John Crompton-Inglefield. There is no rainbow. As early as 30th May 1793, Wright informs Philips (MS. Derby Public Library): 'I am trying my hand at a rainbow effect'. There is no evidence that the bridge was anywhere near Chesterfield.

Derby Museum & Art Gallery

299 LANDSCAPE WITH FIGURES AND WAGGON
Southampton Art Gallery

SIZE   40 × 50 in / 101.6 × 127 cm   pp 89–90 **309**

The river valley has not been identified, and it may not even be Derbyshire. The only point about the topography that is obvious is that the same view is shown in the following:

300 RIVER VALLEY (? DERBYSHIRE)
Dr. and Mrs. William S. Dale

SIZE $11\frac{3}{4} \times 17\frac{3}{4}$ in / 29.8 × 45 cm   pp 89–90, 138 **308**

PROVENANCE   Holland Collection

301 LAKE SCENE
Mr. and Mrs. Michael D. Coe,
U.S.A.

SIZE $21\frac{1}{2} \times 30$ in / 54.6×76.2 cm   p 92 **310**
Signed and dated extreme right 'I.W. Pinx/1790'. Formation of the rocks right suggests Derbyshire scenery but the district has not been identified.

A half length Landscape of a Cottage Scene in Needwood Forrest for M.ʳ Milnes, £63. c 1791. Letter from Wright to Philips, 25th April 1791, postscript (MS. Derby Public Library): 'Milnes likes his pictures so well [the four 'stages of the day'], he has given me a commission to paint him a Cottage Scene the size of his other pictures'. Penultimate paragraph of the letter to Philips, 20th May 1791 (quoted Bemrose, 1885, pp. 65–66) should read (MS. Derby Public Library): 'I have just finish'd for M.ʳ Milnes another picture of the size of the last, with w.ᶜʰ he is much pleased, of a Cottage Scene in Needwood Forrest, the effect of sunshine, in w.ᶜʰ according to the opinion of my friends particularly M.ʳ T. Tate I have succeeded. 'tis a pleasant picture'.

Another picture of this subject appeared at Christie's 6th May 1801 (52), bt. Tate for £63.

IX BUXTON, MATLOCK

A small picture of Chee Tor. About late '80's. This might well be:

302 CHEE TOR

SIZE 17×23 in / 43.1×58.4 cm   pp 89–90, 98⁵ **265**
PROVENANCE R. French (according to label on reverse); Mrs. C. E. Arkwright.
EXHIBITIONS Derby, 1934 (138).
A near-replica ($17\frac{1}{2} \times 23\frac{1}{2}$ in / 44.8×59 cm) was lent to Derby, 1934 (141) by Miss Oakes. The author has not seen this version but to judge from a good photograph, it may turn out to be an original.

Col. Sir John Crompton-Inglefield

A 3 q.ʳˢ picture of Matlock high Tor by moonlight sold to M.ʳ Boothby, £26.5 (the price of £31.10. is also given). Among pictures of c 1780. This is listed again in the Account Book among pictures purchased by Boothby, at £31.10, dated 30th September 1780. **Another Matlock Tor by moon light. Sold to M.ʳ Brooke Boothby** occurs a few items further on, with the same prices. This also is listed in the account of 30th September 1780. Both pictures are referred to obliquely by Anna Seward in her poem on Wright of 1783 (see Walpole, 1937). Wright lists elsewhere (among pictures of c 1780) **Two Views of Matlock, £63,** an entry which could be a repetition of the Boothby pictures. The price is just right. However, the entry could equally well relate to the following:

Two Views of Matlock for M.ʳ Emes, £63. c 1777–80.

A distant View of the high Tor at Matlock. Date uncertain. The description could fit the picture in Leicester (see No 307).

A view at the boathouse near Matlock Town for M.ʳ Denby, £21. c 1790.

View of the Boathouse, Matlock. About the same period as above and perhaps identical with it. The following could well be one or other or both:

303 VIEW OF THE BOATHOUSE NEAR MATLOCK
Mr. and Mrs. Paul Mellon

SIZE 23×30 in / 58.5×76 cm   pp 89–90 **259**
PROVENANCE Acquired for the Mellon Collection from the London Art Market, 1966.

It is difficult to say which of these were Robins's Rooms, 1785 (12), or which were the Views in the neighbourhood of Matlock at Christie's, 5th May 1801 (28, 38) both of which passed back to the family. However, 'A mountainous and woody Landscape, a View in the Neighbourhood of Matlock', in the 1801 Sale (38), 'Mr. Cade, in', may be:

304 'VIEW NEAR MATLOCK'

Miss D. M. R. Cade

SIZE   25 × 31 in / 63.5 × 78.7 cm   p 91[1]

EXHIBITIONS   ? Derby, 1866 (179), lent by T. C. Cade but described only as 'landscape'.

A pair to this is:

305 LANDSCAPE WITH RUINS, BY MOONLIGHT

Miss D. M. R. Cade

SIZE   25 × 30 in / 63.5 × 76.2 cm   pp 55, 91–2   **236**

Possibly 'A pleasing view of a lake by moonlight' in the 1801 Sale (32), 'Mr. Cade, in'.

EXHIBITIONS   ? Derby, 1866 (174), a 'Moonlight' lent by T. C. Cade.

Elements in this landscape have been re-used for the Sheffield landscape (see No. 331). If the entry in the 1801 sale refers to this, it is wrong in thinking the water constitutes a lake.

306 VIEW NEAR MATLOCK BY MOONLIGHT

Col. Sir John Crompton-Inglefield; on loan to Judges' Lodgings, Derby

SIZE   15 × 23⅛ in / 38.1 × 58.7 cm   pp 89–90   **290**

307 MATLOCK HIGH TOR, MOONLIGHT

Leicester Museum and Art Gallery

SIZE   24 × 29 in / 60.9 × 73.6 cm   pp 87–8, 90, 93   **212**

PROVENANCE   Arkwright Collection; purchased by Leicester from London Art Market, 1946.

EXHIBITIONS   R.A., 1886 (8 or 12).

High Tor on left bank; looking southwards.

308 MATLOCK TOR, MOONLIGHT

Mr. and Mrs. Paul Mellon

SIZE   25 × 30 in / 63.5 × 76.2 cm   pp 88, 90–1   **217**

PROVENANCE   Bought during 2nd World War by Edward Wolfe in an antique shop in Bristol.

EXHIBITIONS   R.A., 1964–65 (36).

It shows, not Matlock High Tor, but what is known locally as Matlock Tor, on the right. The spectator is looking northwards.

A replica is:

309 MATLOCK TOR, MOONLIGHT

Detroit Institute of Arts

SIZE   25 × 30 in / 63.5 × 76.2 cm   pp 88, 90   **218**

Signed 'IWP'.

EXHIBITIONS   Smith College, 1955 (10); New York, 1960 (18).

See Buckley, 1955, p. 271; Rosenblum, 1960, Fig. 7.

310 MATLOCK TOR, DAYLIGHT

Fitzwilliam Museum, Cambridge reproduced by permission of the Syndics

SIZE   28½ × 38½ in / 72.4 × 97.8 cm   pp 88, 90   **248**

PROVENANCE   Acquired 1948 from London Art Market. Formerly believed to be a view of Dovedale, but clearly the same scene as shown in the Mellon and Detroit pictures, with the sun breaking through a cloud as in the *View of Florence*. For this and related pictures, see Buckley, *loc. cit.*

A View of Cromford Bridge Its Companion of Arkwright's Mills Sold to D. P. Coke, £52.10; among pictures of c 1780. The view of *Cromford Bridge* has disappeared. The other is:

311 ARKWRIGHT'S COTTON MILLS, BY NIGHT

I. M. Booth Esq,

SIZE   34 × 45 in / 86.3 × 114.3 cm   pp 55, 90–1, 125, 165–7   **244**

PROVENANCE   Has been in the Coke family since acquired by Daniel Parker Coke, until quite recently.

EXHIBITIONS   Graves' Galleries, 1910 (88).

A View of Cromford; among pictures of the late 1780's. The date would fit: R.A., 1789 (137). *Derby Mercury*, 30th April—7th May 1789 describes as features of the exhibited picture: a 'thin transparent cloud, gliding over the distant objects', and 'the front rocks'.

A small picture of the View of Cromford Bridge moon light for M^{rs} (name illegible).

312 ARKWRIGHT'S COTTON MILLS, BY DAY

Formerly Colonel M. H. Grant

SIZE   23 × 30 in / 58.4 × 76.2 cm   pp 90, 124³, 166–7   **331**

It passed to the London Art Market in the 1950's from Col. Grant's Collection, but has now disappeared.

(This is also the case with its companion, listed below).

313 WILLERSLEY CASTLE, CROMFORD

Formerly Colonel M. H. Grant

SIZE   23 × 30 in / 58.4 × 76.2 cm   pp 90, 167   **330**

Country Life, 14th March 1952, illus. to accompany article by Colonel Grant. Companion to above.

These two cannot be before 1790 since Willersley was not ready until then.

314 CUT THROUGH THE ROCK, CROMFORD

Dr. and Mrs. William S. Dale

SIZE   18⅛ × 22⅛ in / 46 × 56.2 cm   pp 90, 138, 167   **333**

PROVENANCE   Holland Collection.

XI DOVEDALE

A View in Dove Dale & its Comp. of Cosmato for Mr Gisborne at 50 Gs, £52.10
The first is:

315 VIEW IN DOVEDALE

Viscount Scarsdale

SIZE   18 × 25 in / 45.7 × 63.5 cm   pp 89–90, 134   **255**

Signed and dated bottom left: 'I.W.P. 1786'.

PROVENANCE   Passed from Gisborne Collection through Mrs. Griffiths, to Curzon (before 1922).

EXHIBITIONS   Derby, 1883 (63), lent by Mrs. Griffiths.

Smith and Bemrose, 1922, illus. opp. p. 58. Companion to *Cosimato* also at Kedleston (Cat 262).

A View in Dove Dale Morn. Companion in D^o Moonlight 3 q^{rs} sold to E^d Mundy Esqr, £31.10. each; among pictures of the mid 1780's. The first is:

316 DOVEDALE IN SUNLIGHT

Col. Sir John Crompton-Inglefield

SIZE   25 × 31 in / 63.5 × 78.7 cm   pp 90–1, 97   **258**

Signed with initials bottom right on stone: 'I.W.'.

PROVENANCE   Miller Mundy Collection.

EXHIBITIONS   Could well be Robins's Rooms, 1785 (18), and its companion by moonlight (see next entry) No. 19; Derby, 1934 (112); Tate, 1958 (24) for further details.

317 DOVEDALE BY MOONLIGHT

SIZE   25 × 31 in / 63.5 × 78.7 cm   pp 90–1, 97   **261**

Signed with initials bottom centre: 'I.W.'.

PROVENANCE   William Martin; Capt. and Mrs. R. Langton Douglas.

EXHIBITIONS   New York, 1960 (22).

Everything points to the Oberlin picture being the companion to Mundy's daylight: no other moonlight *Dovedale* is recorded of the correct size (3 qrs.); a version of the Oberlin picture is in fact in the same collection as the daylight scene, suggesting there is a connection; and the style indeed suggests *c* 1784–88. See Hamilton, 1954, *passim*.

Allen Memorial Museum, Oberlin College

318 DOVEDALE—MORNING

SIZE   20 × 29 in / 50.8 × 73.6 cm   p 90[2]   **264**

PROVENANCE   ? William Bemrose (see below).

EXHIBITIONS   Derby-Leicester, 1947 (45).

Bemrose lent a 'Dovedale (morning)' described as $29\frac{1}{2}$ × 21 inches, to Derby in 1883 (84). The very unusual dimensions suggest that this is the picture, and the provenance is confirmed by a recent label on the reverse. The picture is late.

H. R. Edwards Esq

319 'DOVEDALE'

SIZE   25 × 33 in / 63.5 × 83.8 cm   pp 83[4], 90, 92, 125   **252**

Signed and dated on further bank right of tree roots: 'I.W.Pinx.!/1786'.

EXHIBITIONS   Derby, 1883 (90); 1934 (114).

A sepia drawing on paper, $14\frac{1}{4}$ x 21 in (36 × 53 cm) in Derby Art Gallery, illus. 1934 catalogue, plate XV, said to be from the Gisborne Collection, is a study for this painting. The 1934 catalogue states categorically that the scene is not of this district.

Presumably from Sir Robert Wilmot's collection but nothing in Wright's Account Book gives us a clue to the subject or its destination.

Mrs. George Anson

Two ovals of Dove Dale wth frames 40 G[s] for Boothby, £42. *c* 1785.

A small oval of Dovedale for M[r] Parsons, £14.14; among pictures of the same period.

XII LAKE DISTRICT

A View of Borrow Dale sunset, £31.10; among pictures of *c* 1786–88.

A small picture of Borrow dale, T. Tate, £12.12; among late pictures.

The presence in the Account Book of the first picture among others of 1786–88 makes one think that Wright's intention to visit the Lakes in the autumn of 1786 (see his letter to Daulby, 7th February 1786, quoted Bemrose, 1885, pp. 86–87) was carried out.

Keswick Lake wth Skiddaw in the distance, immediately preceding a date in January 1796. This might be the picture catalogued in the Sale, Christie's, 6th May 1801 (42) as 'A View of Ullswater Lake and Skiddaw' sold for £21 to 'Sters'.

A view upon Ullswater morn., £36.15, of about the same date as the above. This is followed by **D[o] upon Keswick Lake sunset Norris,** for the same price, suggesting they were pairs. Three entries on, what is likely to be a repetition of the first of these: **A View upon Ullswater morning Norris,** again at the same price. So Norris bought views of both lakes.

A pencil drawing in the Derby Art Gallery ($12\frac{7}{8}$ × 19 in / 32.7 × 48.2 cm), not by Wright, is a schematic study for a *Keswick Lake* by him. 'Keswick Lake' is inscribed in another hand in the top left hand corner, and there are other annotations ('grass', 'sand', etc.).

320 DERWENT WATER, WITH SKIDDAW IN THE DISTANCE

Mr. and Mrs. Paul Mellon

SIZE   22 × $31\frac{1}{2}$ in / 55.8 × 80 cm   P 93   **354**

PROVENANCE   New York Market 1967.

321 VIEW OF THE HEAD OF ULLSWATER LAKE

Formerly Arkwright Collection

A large picture of Ullswater; among pictures of 1795. This is presumably:

SIZE   c 63 × 70 in / 160 × 177.8 cm   pp 20, 22, 94[5], 168–9   **345**

PROVENANCE   Remained on the artist's hands; sale, Christie's, 6th May 1801 (57); 'A large and romantic View of the Head of Ullswater Lake from Lyson's Tower in Graystone Park, the seat of the Duke of Norfolk', bt. for £315 by Carr for Arkwright; Willersley Castle Sale (Knight, Frank & Rutley) 7th–11th June 1927 (627), illus. catalogue.

EXHIBITIONS   International Exhibition, 1862 (56); Derby, 1883 (70).

Philips describes it as his last work, not entirely finished, and regards it as 'the finest of all his landscapes'. Farington (Diary, entry for 20th October 1796, pp. 805–807) says that Philips reports that everything is finished except the foreground. Letter from Holland to Philips, 16th January 1798 (MS. Derby Public Library) says the foreground remained unfinished at Wright's death.

322 ULLSWATER, SUNSET

Formerly Hardman Collection

A smallish picture of Ullswater Sun set to Mr Hardman, £42, among pictures of 1795.   p 93

PROVENANCE   'A scene on Ullswater Lake… a sunny evening effect…' was sold at Manchester (Emporium), 21st February 1817 (132) for 60 guineas. It is presumably the Hardman picture since nothing of this description was in the later Hardman sale.

A pencil drawing (13½ × 19 in / 34.3 × 48.2 cm) in the Derby Art Gallery, probably not by Wright, has in the artist's hand in the top left hand corner: 'Ullswater J.W', and in another hand: 'Outline of the picture which Mr Wright painted for Mr W. Hardman, Manchester'. The composition is the same as that for a sketch of the picture in Farington Diary, entry for 27th October 1796, p. 809. A painting by Wright of this view of Ullswater (not the Hardman picture since it differs from the sketch in Farington) is:

323 ULLSWATER
R. D. Plant Esq.

SIZE   20½ × 17½ in / 52.2 × 44.4 cm   p 93   **355**

PROVENANCE   Cyril Plant.

A third drawing (though again not by him) in the Derby Art Gallery is inscribed 'Coniston Lake', but no painting of this subject is recorded in the Account Book.

324 RYDAL WATERFALL

Derby Museum & Art Gallery

A smallish one (picture) **of the little Cascade at Sr Mic la Flemings, sold to Mr. L. Philips & paid for, £31.10**

SIZE   22½ × 30 in / 57.1 × 76.2 cm   pp 93, 138, 140   **352**

Signed and dated on a stone right: 'I.W.Pinx.^t/1795'.

PROVENANCE   Bought by Philips, 1795; Philips Sale, Manchester, 1814 (31), bt. H. W[right]; Cade Collection; Frederick Barnes Lott by 1922; from whence passed to Derby after 1934.

EXHIBITIONS   Derby, 1866 (199); Tate, 1958 (33) for further details.

Waterfall in the garden of Sir Michael le Fleming's house, Rydal Hall. The last touches were put to the picture in December 1795 (see letter to Philips of 18th December, quoted Bemrose, 1885, p. 96).

D.^o (a smallish picture) **of Windermere with Langdale pikes sold to Mr T. M. Tate, £42.** The original is lost, but a copy showing Windermere with Langdale Pikes and a man 'pushing off a boat' (see below), belongs to Sir Gilbert Inglefield (22 × 30½ in / 55.9 × 77.5 cm). Exhibited Derby, 1934 (128) as 'Grasmere'. Postscript to a letter from Wright to Philips, 29th May 1795 (MS. Derby Public Library; passage not transcribed by Bemrose, 1885, p. 95): 'My friend T. Tate has bought a picture I painted soon after my return from ye Lakes of Langdale Pikes seen from Low wood. When I have put a figure in, pushing off a boat, it is to be sent to Manchester for your inspection'.

A view of the outlet of Whyburn Lake for my friend T. Tate, £42; among the very last pictures.

325 **OUTLET OF WYBURNE LAKE**

Formerly London Art Market

SIZE $22\frac{1}{4} \times 30\frac{1}{2}$ in / 56.5 × 77.5 cm   PP 93, 139   **353**
Inscribed on the stretcher (possibly an incorrect copy of an inscription on the original canvas before the relining) is 'Outlet of Wyburne Lake or Leathers Water J. Wright of Derby 1796 Pinx!' (He never signed like this).
This is the last date recorded on a picture by the artist.

326 **LAKE DISTRICT LANDSCAPE**
Private Collection, U.K.

SIZE   25 × 48 in / 63.5 × 121.9 cm
Signed and dated bottom right: 'IWP/1794'.   P 93   **346**
PROVENANCE   Julius Weitzner, New York, 1953; with Messrs. Agnew in the late 1950's.

XIII ELSEWHERE IN GREAT BRITAIN

A View in Wales, Storm sold to my friend M.ͬ Tom.ˢ Tate, £31.10; among pictures of c 1790.

A small picture of Canarvon Castle. Night, £10.10; among pictures of the early 1780's. This might be the 'View of Carnarvon Castle by Fire and Moonlight, unfinished', sold Christie's, 6th May 1801 (17), bt. Goulding for £5.15.6.
Since Wright is not known to have travelled to Wales, he may have been basing his compositions on Wilson.

A View of Warwick Castle Moon L. for M.ͬ Cutler, £36.15.

A View in Scotland half length Moon light for my friend Tate, £63; among pictures of 1791–92. A few entries away from this is: **A View of Dunkield evening comp**(anion) **to the moon light w.ᶜʰ Tate has** (then the words added) **sold to M.ͬ Wakefield, £75.10.**
These two pictures are discussed by Wright in letters to Philips, 1792–93. On 24th September 1792 he notes he has finished the *Moonlight* (Bemrose, 1885, p. 90). On 31st December that year he announces he has prepared a canvas of the same size, 'for an evening effect on another view of the River Tay at Dunkeld' (*op. cit.* p. 92). On 26th February 1793 (*op. cit.*, pp. 92–93) he contemplates exhibiting that year the evening view of Dunkeld which is now 'near finished'.

A Ferry over the river Tay at Dunkield in Scotland. Moon light rec.ᵈ 29–1 (meaning he had received £29.1), **£36.15;** among late pictures. This was evidently smaller than the other two. A letter from Wright to Philips, 29th June 1794 (Bemrose, 1885, p. 93) proves it was sold to Philips and is about to be dispatched. It, along with a *Vesuvius* also for Philips (see Appendix B, No. 18), was: R.A., 1794 (232).

XIV UNIDENTIFIED LANDSCAPES (see also VI and VIII)

i Gorges, Waterfalls (See also these subjects under Terni and Rydal)

327 **RIVER IN A ROCKY GORGE**

Private Collection, U.K.

SIZE $11\frac{1}{2} \times 17$ in / 29.2 × 43.2 cm   p 84[6]   **263**
On reverse of the original canvas is the inscription: 'J. Wright/1787', perhaps not a signature.
EXHIBITIONS   Derby, 1934 (118).

328 **ROCKS WITH WATERFALL**
Major J. W. Chandos-Pole

SIZE   Unknown.   pp 11, 36, 55, 75   **112**
Pre-Italian journey (? early 1770's).
Possibly S. of A. 1772 (371).

An upright of a rocky Scene wth a waterfall, £10.10; among very late pictures. The only known picture (not otherwise identified) which corresponds to this description and has the advantage of being small enough to be priced so low is:

329 **ROCKY LANDSCAPE WITH A WATERFALL**

Private Collection, U.S.A.

SIZE   19$\frac{1}{4}$ × 13$\frac{1}{2}$ in / 48.9 × 34.3 cm   p 94^5 **351**
PROVENANCE   Cade Collection; Mrs. Wheler; sale, Sotheby's, 10th December 1958 (115); London art market, 1962.
EXHIBITIONS   Derby, 1870 (206); New York, 1960 (16).
A label glued to the reverse of the frame, similar to the label on the reverse of the *View of Florence* (q.v.) and comparatively modern, says it was sold to John Leigh Philips; was bought by the artist's family at the Philips Sale, Manchester, 1814; passed to various members of the Cade family and was bequeathed by a Cade to Bemrose's daughter Mrs. Wheler. There was a 'Landscape with a waterfall' in the Philips sale (No. 13) but it was not this one since the Philips picture was a 'stormy effect'.

ii Landscapes with Gothic Ruins and Castles

A Circular picture Moon light for Mr Birch, £21 among pictures of the late 1780's. This might well be:

330 **LAKE WITH CASTLE ON A HILL**

Gooden & Fox Ltd

SIZE   Circular, diam. 24 in / 60.9 cm   pp 90, 92   **262**
Signed and dated 1787 on reverse
PROVENANCE   Colonel Grant.
EXHIBITIONS   A 'Landscape, moonlight' was lent by Joseph Birch to Liverpool R.I., 1823 (107).
Based on Wilson, illus. Constable, 1953, plate 125b.

331 **LANDSCAPE WITH DALE ABBEY**
Sheffield City Art Galleries

SIZE   28$\frac{1}{2}$ × 39 in / 72.4 × 99 cm   pp 89^3, 90, 92   **249**
Constable, 1953, plate 159c as attributed to Wright; see also Constable, p. 149. A moonlight landscape in the Cade Collection (see No 305) has elements of the same scenery.

332 **LANDSCAPE WITH RUINED CASTLE**
Dr. and Mrs. William S. Dale

SIZE   12 × 18 in / 30.5 × 45.2 cm   pp 93, 138   **349**
PROVENANCE   Holland Collection.

333 **LAKE BY MOONLIGHT WITH CASTLE ON HILL**

Palmer-Morewood Collection; on loan to Brighton Art Gallery

SIZE   22$\frac{7}{8}$ × 30 in / 58 × 76.2 cm   p 92   **292**
Signed and dated: 'I.W.Pinx^t 178[8?]'.
EXHIBITIONS   Derby, 1934 (94).
A pair to the Palmer-Morewood *Cottage on Fire* (see below).
Waterhouse, 1953, plate 171A. Waterhouse was unable to read the last digit of the date but an '8' is the most probable.

iii Houses on Fire

334 **COTTAGE ON FIRE**

SIZE   22$\frac{7}{8}$ × 30 in / 58 × 76.2 cm   p 92   **293**
EXHIBITIONS   Derby, 1934 (96).
Pair to *Lake by Moonlight with Castle on Hill* of 1788 (?), see above.
It is tempting to deduce that these two were the *Moonlight* painted for Bird, and the *Cottage on Fire* also planned to be painted for him (see below), but the date 1788 would be too late for them. The relevant pictures are cited in the Account Book as follows:

A Cottage on fire sold to M.ʳ Cutler, £36.15; among pictures of *c* 1788. This is followed by: **A Companion Moon Light sold to M.ʳ Bird Liverpool, £31.10.**
Letter from Wright to Long, 28th March 1787 (Inglefield MSS): 'I have… taken the liberty of addressing a case of pictures to you, the one Moon light, the other the effect of Fire, the latter I have painted for a M.ʳ Cutler who lives at No. 5 Suffolk Lane Cannon Street, if he approves of the moon light he will take both & pay you immediately for them: but if he rejects it, pray give it house room till you hear further from me… He is quite a Stranger to me…' Letter to Long, 22nd April 1789 (MS. National Portrait Gallery, extra-illustrated Bemrose): 'I am happy to hear M.ʳ Cutler is well pleased wᵗʰ his picture [the *Cottage on Fire*] & that you approve of it, & think the effect true…' Wright asks Long to pack up the Moonlight and return it 'as I have the like Companion of a cot on fire to paint to it for a Gentᵐ in this neighbourhood…' The moonlight, and perhaps also the second fire picture, were then sold to Bird.

Palmer-Morewood Collection;
on loan to Brighton Art Gallery

335 FIRE SEEN THROUGH TREES

SIZE   16 × 21½ in / 40.6 × 54.6 cm   pp 92, 138   **332**
Signed and dated bottom right: 'I.W.P.ʳ 1793'.
PROVENANCE   Holland Collection.
EXHIBITIONS   New York, 1960 (26).
This is presumably the picture referred to in a letter from Wright to Philips, 26th February 1793 (quoted Bemrose, 1885, p. 92): '…a small one of an effect of fire, seen through a dark group of trees, with a large piece of water, reflecting the objects about it…' It cannot be the picture listed in the Account Book as: **A small picture of a Cottage on fire seen thro' a group of trees for my friend Holland sketch, £10.10**; there is no sign of a cottage in this predicament.

Dr. and Mrs. William S. Dale

336 COTTAGE ON FIRE

SIZE   25 × 30 in / 63.5 × 76.2 cm   p 92   **303**
Signed bottom right: 'I.W.Pinx!'.
EXHIBITIONS   Sheffield, 1950 (24).
Given by F. W. Hampshire, 1936.

Derby Museum & Art Gallery

337 COTTAGE ON FIRE
Mr. and Mrs. David Giles Carter

SIZE   22¾ × 29¼ in / 57.8 × 74.3 cm   p 92   **307**
PROVENANCE   London Art Market 1966.

338 COTTAGE ON FIRE

SIZE   22¼ × 31½ in / 56.5 × 80 cm   p 92   **306**
Signed bottom right: 'I Wright'. It may originally have been signed with initials, and the full name added.
EXHIBITIONS   R.A., 1964–65 (174).

Mr. and Mrs. Paul Mellon

The last three are presumably listed in the Account Book but cannot be identified. The remaining pictures listed in the Account Book are as follows (alphabetically under purchasers):

A Cottage on fire for M.ʳ Court, Bristol, £42; among pictures of 1790–92. Letter from Wright to Philips, 24th September 1792 (quoted Bemrose, 1885, p. 90): 'I am going to begin a Cottage on fire for a Gentleman at Bristol. He has offered me 50 Gs. to finish it highly'.

Cottage on fire for M.ʳ Cunningham, £21; among very late pictures.

A Cottage on Fire sold to M.ʳ Hardman, £36.15; among pictures of *c* 1790. Letter from Wright to Philips, 26th February 1793 (Bemrose, *loc. cit.*, p. 92) proves that by this date the picture was already in Hardman's possession. It was a three-quarters, according to Farington (Diary, entry for 27th October 1796, p. 809). Manchester Institution, 1831 (124).

A Cottage on fire for Miss Linwood, £42; among pictures of 1790–92. Miss Linwood sale, Christie's, 23rd April 1846 (42).

A Village on fire for M.ʳ Lowe, £36.15; (changed to 35 guineas), among late pictures. A *Village on Fire* was lent to Derby 1870 (56) by Drury Lowe. Wright also lists a **Village on Fire** at £63. One of these two could have been: R.A., 1794 (233).

A Cottage on fire Norris, £42. One of the last pictures.

D.ᵒ of D.ᵒ (Cottage on fire) **50 Gs. to M.ʳ N. Philips, £52;** among very late pictures. Letter from Wright to J. L. Philips 27th December 1794 (Bemrose, *loc. cit.*, p. 94) makes clear that N. Philips had ordered the picture by that date and intended sending it to America. By 18th December of the following year (*loc. cit.*, p. 96) this was sent off to Nottingham with other pictures.

A small picture of a fire seen thro' a wood. Sold to Rev.ᵈ Holden Shuttleworth, £26.5. Among very late pictures.

iv After Cozens

A Close scene morning from Cozens sold to B. Boothby Esq.ʳ, £31.10.
A Sun Set a bold sea shore from Cozens sold to M.ʳ Boothby, £31.10.
What may be a repetition of the Boothby picture is: **A Sun Set from Cozens frame for d.ᵒ, £31.10.**

The Close scene from Cozens Blot for S.ʳ R.ᵈ Wilmot, £31.10.

These are all (3 or 4) *c* 1786–88.

v Storms

A small Storm. both (this and a *Lighthouse* sold to John Leigh Philips) **sketches to M.ʳ N. Philips, £10.10;** among the latest pictures. Letter from Wright to J. L. Philips, 27th December 1794 (quoted Bemrose, 1885, p. 94) mentions this as a 'Sea Storm' which N. Philips intends sending to America. For further details, see Tate 1958, under No. 32.

Its Companion (of a small *Italian Lake by Moonlight* sold to Holland) **A Land Storm.**

vi Seashores. Lakes

339 **LAKE LANDSCAPE** Dr. and Mrs. William S. Dale	SIZE 12¼ × 18¼ in / 31.1 × 46.3 cm PROVENANCE Holland Collection.	p 93	**350**

A Sea Shore seen thro' an arch in the Rock given to L. Philips. About 1789.
A sea Shore seen thro' an arch in y.ᵉ Rock sun set Holland. After 1790. This might refer to:

340 **SEASHORE THROUGH ARCH**	SIZE 19⅝ × 15¾ in / 49.8 × 40 cm PROVENANCE Holland Collection EXHIBITIONS New York, 1960 (14).	p 138

Two landscapes are superimposed one on the other. The picture is as a result difficult to read.

Dr. and Mrs. William S. Dale

A small picture of a view by the sea side sun rising. Sold to my friend Tate, £12.12. Among very late works.

The Sea Shore moon light for M.ʳ Harvey, £31.10; among pictures of the mid 1780's.

vii Miscellaneous

A small Moon light without y.ᵉ Moon appearing for M.ʳ Boothby, £26.5; among pictures of the mid-'80's.

A Wood Scene by Moonlight w.ᵗʰ frame sold to M.ʳ Thompson, £31.10; among pictures of the mid-'80's.

Jan.ʸ 2.ᵈ (1783) Two small Landskyp, £21.

341 **LANDSCAPE**

Mrs. Mackeig Jones

SIZE   Unknown   p 149
PROVENANCE   Wedgwood family. The present owner was born a Wedgwood. On the reverse is an inscription: 'The gift of Joseph Wright to his friend Jos. Wedgwood, Esq., the patron and encourager of living artists, 1787'.
The subject and dimensions are not known to the author.

342 **MOONLIGHT**

The University of Liverpool
on loan to Walker Art Gallery

SIZE $36\frac{1}{8} \times 50$ in / 91.7×127 cm   pp 92–3   **344**
Signed and dated on rock left: 'I.W.P/1792'.
PROVENANCE   Hugh Rathbone, Greenbank, Liverpool.

Appendix A
Wright's Exhibited Pictures[1]

1 The shorthand used throughout will be comprehensible if the first entry below is explained. Wright showed at the Society of Artists in 1765 (Cat. No. 163) the *Gladiator* which he sold to Dr. Bates and which is now in a private collection, U.K.

I PICTURES EXHIBITED BY WRIGHT AT THE INCORPORATED SOCIETY OF ARTISTS OF GREAT BRITAIN

1765   (163)   *Three Persons Viewing the Gladiator by Candle-light*. Dr. Bates. (Private Collection, U.K.)

1765   (164)   *A Conversation Piece*. ? James Shuttleworth. (? Lord Shuttleworth.)

1766   (195)   *A Philosopher giving that lecture on the Orrery, in which a lamp is put in place of the Sun*. 5th Earl Ferrers. (Derby Museum & Art Gallery.)

1766   (196)   *A Portrait of a Lady, whole length.*? (?)

1766   (197)   *Head of a Gentleman.*? (?)

1767   (188)   *Portrait of a Gentleman, whole length.*? (?)

1767   (189)   *A small Candle-light.*? (?)[2]

1767   (190)   *Ditto, its Companion.*? (?)[2]

1768   (193)   *An Experiment on a Bird in the Air Pump*. Dr. Bates. (Tate Gallery.)

1768   (194)   *Two Candle-lights.*? (?)[2]

1769   (196)   *A Philosopher by Lamp light*. ? (?)[3]

1769   (197)   *An Academy by ditto*. 1st Lord Melbourne. (Mr. and Mrs. Paul Mellon.)

1769   (198)   *A Lady*. ? (?)

1769   (199)   *A Conversation*. ? (?)

1770   (154)   *Portrait of a Gentleman, Painted by an Artificial Light*. ? (?)

2 One of the two pairs of candlelights shown in 1767 and 1768, might be the two Wright sold to his friend Thomas Coltman (now Rogers-Coltman Collection); the other pair, the candlelights sold to Lord Exeter. The latter are large and so cannot have been the ones shown in 1767.

3 Bemrose transcribes 'candlelight' instead of 'lamplight'.

4 This picture, painted in Liverpool *c* 1769, may have represented Master John Ashton with his dog. It was destroyed during the second world war but a good copy exists by one Williamson in the Bostock Collection. This No. 303 is not in the published catalogue of the Society of Artists, but appears in Bemrose's transcription, 1885, p. 13. He may have had access to a manuscript addition.

5 Conceivably the *Coltman Group* (Rogers-Coltman Collection).

6 The picture in Derby is dated 1795 but see the discussion in the *catalogue raisonné*.

7 The companion (untraced) is known from an old photograph in N.P.G. extra-illustrated Bemrose.

1770 (155) *A Conversation of Girls*. E. Parker. (Heirs of Oliver Vernon Watney.)

1770 (303) *Child with a Dog*. ? Ashton family of Woolton Hall, near Liverpool. (? destroyed)[4]

1771 (200) *A Lady and Child, whole length*. ? Col. Edward Pole. (? Major J. W. Chandos-Pole.)

1771 (201) *A Blacksmith's Shop*. 1st Lord Melbourne. (Mr. and Mrs. Paul Mellon.)

1771 (202) *A small Ditto, viewed from without*. E. Parker. (?)

1771 (203) *A small Conversation*. ? (?)[5]

1771 (204) *Portrait of an Officer*. ? (?)

1771 (205) *A Young Lady Undressing at her toilet by Candle-light*. E. Parker. (?)

1771 (206) *An old woman Knitting by Candle-light*. E. Parker. (?)

1771 (209) *The Alchymist, in Search of the Philosopher's Stone, discovers Phosphorus, and prays for the successful Conclusion of his operation, as was the custom of the Ancient Chymical Astrologers*. Unsold. (Derby Museum & Art Gallery.)[6]

1772 (369) *A Portrait of an Officer, a small whole length.* ⎫ Colonel Heathcote. Captain Milnes. (The latter belongs to Mrs. Lawrence Copley Shaw.)

1772 (370) *A Portrait of an Officer, ditto, ditto.* ⎭

1772 (371) *A Landscape*. ? (? Major J. W. Chandos-Pole.)

1772 (372) *A Blacksmith's Shop*. Robert Alexander of Edinburgh. (Private Collection, U.K.)

1772 (373) *An Iron Forge*. 2nd Lord Palmerston. (Admiral of the Fleet Earl Mountbatten of Burma.)

1772 (417) *An history, Miravan, a young nobleman of Ingria . . .* Milnes. (Derby Museum & Art Gallery.)

1773 (370) *A Captive King*. Unsold. (?)

1773 (371) *An Iron Forge, viewed from without*. Empress of Russia. (Hermitage Museum, Leningrad.)

1773 (372) *An Earth Stopper on the Banks of the Derwent*. Earl of Hardwicke. (Derby Museum & Art Gallery.)

1774 (321) *The Old Man and Death*. Unsold. (Wadsworth Atheneum, Hartford, Conn.)

1775 (223) *A Smith's Forge, altered from his first design*. ? Robert Alexander of Edinburgh. (? Private Collection, U.K.)

1776 (147) *An Eruption of Mount Vesuvius*. John Milnes of Wakefield. (?)

1776   (148)   *The Annual Girandola, at the Castle of St. Angelo, at Rome.* John Milnes of Wakefield. (?)

1791   (219)   *Antigonus in the Storm. (From the 'Winter's Tale').* Henry Philips. (Viscount Scarsdale.)

1791   (220)   *Romeo and Juliet. The Tomb Scene. 'Noise again! then I'll be brief'. N.B. The Above Pictures* [Nos. 219 and 220] *were exhibited last year in the Academy; but having been placed in an unfortunate position, owing (as Mr. Wright supposes) to their having arrived too late in London, and have since received alterations, he is desirous they should again meet the public eye.* Unsold. (J. M. Oakes.)

1791   (221)   *Inside an Italian Stable.* ? J. Henderson. (?)

1791   (222)   *Part of the Colosseum.* ? (?)

1791   (223)   *Moonlight, View on the Lake Albano, Italy, Monte Jove in the distance.* ? Philips. (?)[8]

8 Wright's Account Book has the entry: 'A 3 q^{rs} of the Lake of Albano with the Monte Jove seen thro' the Arch of a Aquaduct...', no purchaser, no price, which might be this.

2 PICTURES EXHIBITED BY WRIGHT AT THE FREE SOCIETY OF ARTISTS

1778   (224)   *A portrait.* ? (?)

1783   (4)   *Moonlight.* ? (?)

1783   (89)   *Boy blowing a Bladder.* ? Unsold. (?)

3 PICTURES EXHIBITED BY WRIGHT AT THE ROYAL ACADEMY

1778   (357)   *An Eruption of Mount Vesuvius, with the Procession of St. Januarius' Head.* Empress of Russia. (Pushkin Museum, Moscow.)

1778   (358)   *A Grotto by the Sea-side, in the Kingdom of Naples, with Banditti; a Sunset.* Josiah or Joshua Cockshutt. (G. Meynell Esq, M.B.E.)

1778   (359)   *Edwin, from Dr. Beattie's Minstrel.* Milnes. (Lady Cynthia Colville.)

1778   (360)   *Stern's Captive.* ? (? Derby Museum & Art Gallery.)

1778   (361)   *The Girandola, a grand firework exhibited at the Castle of St. Angelo, in Rome.* Daulby. (?)

9 Listed in R.A. catalogue under 'omitted',

1778   (411)   *Neptune's Grotto at Tivoli.* Daulby (?)[9]

10 Wrongly transcribed by Bemrose as 'candlelight'.

1779 (358) *The Girandola, or Grand Fire work at the Castle of St. Angelo, in Rome; Companion to the Vesuvius he painted last year* [e.g. 1778 (357)]. Empress of Russia. (Hermitage Museum, Leningrad.)

1779 (359) *Virgil's Tomb, with the Figure of Scilius Italicus, who bought an estate enriched with this very tomb. He was frequent in his Visitation to this monument of his master.* Unsold. (? Col. Sir John Crompton-Inglefield.)

1779 (360) *Neptune's Grotto at Tivoli.* Milnes. (?)

1779 (361) *Two Boys, whole Length.* ? Pickford. (? Cat No 119.)

1780 (158) *Eruption of Mount Vesuvius.* ? (?)

1780 (203) *A Cavern, with the Figure of Julia, banished thither by his grandfather, Augustus.* Cockshutt. (G. Meynell Esq, M.B.E.)

1781 (23) *A Philosopher by Lamp-light.* Unsold. (Cat No 194.)[10]

1781 (61) *Cavern in the Gulf of Salernum, Sunset.* Hardman. (?)

1781 (100) *Maria, from Sterne, a companion to the Picture of Edwin, exhibited three years ago.* Unsold. (Derby Museum & Art Gallery.)

1781 (112) *Cavern in the Gulf of Salernum, Moonlight.* Hardman. (?)

1781 (181) *Portraits of Three Children.* Walter Synnot. (Mrs Michael Hawker)

1781 (224) *Virgil's Tomb by Moonlight.* ? (?)

1781 (245) *Portrait of a Gentleman.* Brooke Boothby. (Tate Gallery.)

1782 (165) *Two Young Gentlemen in the Character of Archers.* Mundy. (Oscar and Peter Johnson Ltd, Loundes Lodge Gallery, London)

1782 (231) *Old Man's Head, in the character of an Apostle.* ? John Holland of Ford. (? Mrs Edward Maclean Stewart.)

1788 (81) *Mæcena's Villa at Tivoli.* Unsold. (?)

1788 (83) *Cicero's Villa, near Salerno.* ? Unsold. (?)

1788 (96) *View near Mare Chiare, on the shore of Paussillipo.* ? (?)

1788 (98) *The Convent of St. Cosimato, near Vicobaro, and remains of the Claudian Aquaduct, on the River Arno.* ? Gisborne. (? Viscount Scarsdale.)

11 This showed a lighthouse by moonlight, and may be 'Moonlight on the coast of Tuscany in the Mediterranean' for John Milnes and/or *Lighthouse on the coast of Tuscany* in the Tate.

12 Wright's Account Book lists: A large one of Dº [*Cicero's Villa*]—sun setting after a shower... Edward Mundy', £84, and 'Moonlight on the Coast of Tuscany in the Mediterranean, companion to the large picture of Cicero's Villa... Mr. Jno. Milnes', £63.10. No. 26 in the 1789 exhibition might well be the Mundy picture.

1788 (234) *View in the Alps, on the side next Italy, in the Duchy of Milan.* ? Poploe Birch. (?)

1789 (9) *A Moonlight.* ? John Milnes. (? Tate Gallery.)[11]

1789 (26) *Cicero's Villa, an Evening.* ? Edward Mundy. (?)[12]

1789 (67) *The Prison of the Capitol.* ? (?)

1789 (74) *Ruins of the Colloseo, in Rome.* Either this or No. 107 to Machlin. (?)

1789 (87) *A Boy and Girl engaged with a Bladder.* Hardman. (?)

1789 (107) *Ruins of the Colloseo, in Rome, with Banditti.* Either this or No. 74 to Machlin. (?)

1789 (137) *View of Cromford, near Matlock.* ? Unsold. (?)

1789 (153) *A Girl blowing a Charcoal Stick.* Daulby. (?)

1789 (236) *A Dead Soldier, his Wife and Child, vide Langhorne's Poems.* Philips. (?)

1790 (1) *Romeo and Juliet, Act V, Scene last.* Unsold. (J. M. Oakes Esq.)

1790 (221) *Scene from the 'Winter's Tale, Act iii, latter end of the sixth scene.* Henry Philips. (Viscount Scarsdale.)

1794 (107) *An Eruption of Vesuvius.* John Leigh Philips. (?)

1794 (232) *A Lake in Dunkeld, in Scotland, Evening.* John Leigh Philips. (?)

1794 (233) *A Village on Fire.* ? (?)

4 PICTURES EXHIBITED BY WRIGHT AT THE SOCIETY FOR PROMOTING THE ARTS IN LIVERPOOL

1784 (115) *Virgil's Tomb with Silvius Italicus.* ? (?)

1784 (116) *Eruption of Vesuvius.* ? Daulby. (?)

1784 (117) *Girandola.* Daulby. (?)

1784 (118) *Cascade at Terni.* ? (?)

1784 (119) *Cascade at Neptune's Grotto, with the Sibyl's Temple at Tivoli.* ? Daulby. (?)

1784 (120) *View of a Lake between Rome and Florence by moonlight.* Daulby. (?)

1784 (121) *View of the Inside of a Cavern.* ? (?)

1787 (117) *Julia in cavern.* Daulby. (?)

1787 (118) *Girandola 'on a rejoicing night'.* ? Daulby. (?)

1787 (119) *A Distant View of Vesuvius; from the Shore of Pausilippo.* ? Daulby. (?)

1787 (120) *A Landscape, moonlight.* ? (?)

1787 (121) *An Internal View of a Prison.* ? (?)

5 PICTURES EXHIBITED BY WRIGHT AT MR ROBINS'S ROOMS, 1785[13])

13 We follow for Robins's Rooms the same annotations as in lists of previous catalogues but give shortened versions of catalogue entries. Since Bemrose publishes the entire catalogue (1885, pp. 18–23), further details are not necessary.

(1) *The Lady in Milton's Comus.* Josiah Wedgwood. (Walker Art Gallery, Liverpool.)

(2) *Indian Widow.* Companion to No. 1. Unsold (Derby Museum & Art Gallery.)

(3) *William and Margaret.* Unsold. (? Col. Sir John Crompton-Inglefield.)

(4) *View of the Cascade of Turni in Italy.* ? Unsold. (?)

14 This *Virgil's Tomb* is not marked for sale, and since none of the pictures of this subject are listed in Wright's Account Book with names of purchasers except one which had gone at least five years earlier to Cockshutt, it is possible that the picture exhibited is a *Virgil's Tomb* Wright had recently presented to Hayley. It is more than likely that Hayley would agree to contribute a work to the show.

(5) *Virgil's Tomb by moonlight.* ? Hayley. (?)[14]

(6) *The Lake of Nemi, sunset.* ? (?)

(7) *Julia in a cavern by moonlight.* Daulby. (?)

(8) *Hero and Leander.* Hon. Thomas Fitzmaurice. (?)

(9) *Drowning of Leander.* Companion to No. 8. Hon. Thomas Fitzmaurice. (?)

(10) *A landscape, Morning.* ? (?)

(11) *A Sea Shore, Evening.* ? (?)

(12) *Matlock High Tor—Moonlight.* ? (?)

(13) *Maid of Corinth.* Josiah Wedgwood. (Mr. and Mrs. Paul Mellon.)

(14) *Penelope unravelling her Web.* Companion to No. 13. Josiah Wedgwood. (Mr. and Mrs. Hensleigh Wedgwood, New York.)

(15) *A distant View of Vesuvius from the shore of Posilipo.* Daulby. (?)

(16) *The Companion, in the gulf of Salerno.* ? Daulby. (?)

(17) *A Landscape, moonlight.* ? (?)

(18) *A View of Dovedale, morning.* ? Edward Mundy. (? Col. Sir John Crompton-Inglefield.)

(19) *A View of Dovedale, evening.* Companion to No. 18. ? Edward Mundy. (? Oberlin.)

(20) *Portrait of an Artist.* [*Self Portrait*]. Josiah Wedgwood. (?)

(21) *Guy de Lusignan in Prison.* ? Unsold. (?)

(22) *Portrait of three (of Mr. Leaper's) Children.* John Leaper Newton. (Cat No 100.)

15 'A wood scene by moonlight, wth frame' is listed in Account Book as sold to a Mr. Thompson. The entry appears among pictures shown at Robins's Rooms, so it must be the one here.

(23) *A Wood Scene, moonlight.* Thompson. (?)[15]

(24) *View of Gibraltar during the destruction of the Spanish Floating Batteries, 13th September 1782.* John Milnes of Wakefield. (?)

(25) *Portrait of a Gentleman.* [*John Whitehurst*]. Whitehurst. (John Smith & Sons., Derby).

Appendix B
Paintings of 'Vesuvius' and the 'Girandola'

Since negotiations between Wright and his patrons over purchases of pictures of these subjects are somewhat involved, it is preferable to set out the facts here, rather than to overload catalogue entries.

A *Pairs of 'Vesuvius' and 'Girandola'.*

Wright exhibited only two pairs of these subjects: one at the Society of Artists, 1776 (147 and 148); the other at the Royal Academy, 1778 (357) and 1779 (358), No. 357 at the Academy in the earlier year being a *Vesuvius* 'with the Procession of St. Januarius' Head'. Since the picture in Moscow introduces this Procession it may be assumed that the R.A. pictures were the ones bought by the Empress of Russia. The description of the *Vesuvius* in *The General Advertiser*, May 1778 does not conflict with this identification: 'In the foreground we see the procession, illuminated by the glow behind it, serving as a secondary object to the principal effect... the tinge upon the foliage of the tree, in the foreground is beautiful indeed...' The other at the Society of Artists is therefore the pair that Milnes purchased 'in the Exhibition' (see below).

1, 2 *Milnes pair. Vesuvius: c.* spring 1775. 100 guineas, therefore quite large. *Girandola:* Winter 1775–6. Same size, same price.
   The *Vesuvius* was presumably the one painted in Italy, referred to as having been offered to the Empress of Russia for 100 guineas in the spring of 1775, but rejected (see Wright's letter to his sister, 4th May 1775, Bemrose, 1885, p. 35—cited hereafter as 'B'). The companion of the Girandola was painted at Bath in the following winter, as transpires from a letter from Wright of 15th January 1776 (MS. Derby Public Library; only short passage transcribed by B, p. 44): 'As to the picture of Vesuvius the Town [Bath] rings with commendation of it'. One man wishes to buy it, and: 'Another Gent^{mn} from Salisbury, Mr Pen Wyndham is also very desirous of having it, & will wait the event of the Exhibition [S. of A., 1776] & if not sold then will give me an 100 guineas for it. I have just now finished a companion to it. The Exhibition of a great Fire work from the Castle of St. Angelo in Rome, the one is the greatest effect of Nature the other of Art that I suppose can be. This last picture I have painted to keep me from Idleness'. It still stands, then, at 100 guineas. Next we hear the pictures have gone to the exhibition (letter of 15th April 1776, B, p. 45), and this time there is an offer of 100 guineas for the *Girandola* (see B, p. 46, 8th May). We do not hear of them again until nearly four years later when Wright reports that Milnes bought both at the exhibition (see his letter of 11th January 1780 quoted under No. 16 below). Milnes still had the two companion pieces in 1787, as transpires from a memo. dated 15th September of that year in the Account Book (quoted by B, p. 117).

3, 4 *Russian pair. Vesuvius:* 1778. £300. 63¾ by 84 in. Pushkin Museum, Moscow. *Girandola:* 1778–9. £200. Same size Hermitage Museum, Leningrad. MS. Account Book as 'A large Mount Vesuvius sold to the Empress', £300; 'A Large picture of the Girandolo—companion to the Vesuvius wch was sold to the Empress of Russia', £200. The R.A.

exhibition catalogue specifically states that the *Vesuvius* was 'painted' in 1778. According to the Account Book the *Vesuvius* was sold first. Both pictures belonged to the Empress by the end of 1779 (see letter of 31st December that year, B, p. 85). This letter tells us she gave 500 guineas for them—confirming the prices in the Account Book. The *Girandola* was transferred to Peterhof, 1920.

5, 6   A pair of sketches of the *Girandola* (City Art Gallery, Birmingham) and *Vesuvius* (L. B. Sanderson Esq), each 16¾ by 28 in. They have the spontaneity (though not naturalistic fidelity) which leads one to suspect they were done in Italy after the autumn of 1774 when Wright went to Naples. This theory is supported by the close connection of the picture in Birmingham with some *Girandola* drawings clearly made at the time. Since we do not know the design of Milnes's pictures, it is impossible to say whether they are studies for these; but if they are, then the Liverpool *Girandola* cannot be Milnes's, since the composition of this is quite different from the Birmingham sketch.

B   *Other 'Girandola' pictures known from sources but untraced.*

7   *To Daulby.* £84 (or 40 guineas). 38 by 48 in. MS. Account Book as 'A small picture of the Girandolo sold to M.ʳ Daulby', £84, among pictures of *c.* 1777–8. According to Daulby MS. *c.* 1790 this was the one exhibited at R.A., 1778 (361). It was re-exhibited by Daulby in Liverpool in 1784 (117) and possibly again in 1787 (118). Further passages from Wright's letter of 31st December 1779 (MS. Derby Public Library; not transcribed by B, p. 85) read: 'He [Mr. Sale] mentions also that you wish to know the price of the Girandolo or grand Firework exhibited at the Castle of St. Angelo. I suppose you mean the one you saw at my Room when last in Derby (I am sorry I was from here). I put it into the exhibition [1778] at 100 g.ⁿˢ & I never intended selling it for less as it cost me upward of 6 weeks study, but the scarsity of money has of late lowerd the value of art, & we must do as we can, when we cant do as we wish: tho' I have no reason to complain...' (continues as in B. where Wright offers it for 40 guineas). In the summer of 1780 he announces his intention of sending it to Daulby (see B, p. 85, letter of 4th June). Daulby sale, Liverpool, 27th August 1798 (81), bt. Norris. Exh. Liverpool R.I., 1823 (93), lent by John Moss.

C   *Other 'Girandola' pictures known but unidentified in sources.*

8   Walker Art Gallery, Liverpool, 55¼ by 68⅛ in. See notes under 5, 6 above. Smith and Bemrose, 1922, pp. 28–9 wrongly assumed this was the Daulby picture, but the sizes are quite different. For further details, see Tate, 1958 (15). Since then it has been exhibited 'Settecento a Roma', Rome, 1959 (690). Nothing is known of its history before 1880 when it was presented to Liverpool by Robert Neilson. Exh. Derby, 1883 (49). A pen and wash drawing in the Derby Art Gallery, 13¼ by 20 in. inscribed top left: 'JW Rome June 4.ᵗʰ 1774' is used as a basis for the composition, which is then considerably altered.

D   *Other 'Vesuvius' pictures known from sources but unidentified.*

The following are listed alphabetically under purchasers.
9   *Arnold.* MS. Account Book as 'A distant view of Vesuvius from the shore of posilipo the Eruption principal, sold to M.ʳ Arnold', £31.10. Late '80's.

10   *Bacon.* MS. Account Book as 'A moon light w.ᵗʰ an Eruption of Vesuvius from the Shore of Posilipo w.ᵗʰ. frame sold to Mr. Bacon', £26.5. Ready by 1788, but probably painted *c.* 1783 in view of its position in the Account Book. Small. According to Edwards, 1808, p. 254 this was the picture engraved by William Byrne (1788). B, p. 53 adds that it was exhibited at Robins's Rooms, 1785. This would be No. 15, which had a companion of the *Gulf of Salerno* (No. 16)—and indeed in Wright's Account Book a companion of this description, sold to Holland, follows on the entry for Bacon's *Vesuvius*. However, in October 1786 Wright copied out for Daulby's benefit three entries from the catalogue of

this exhibition (Nos. 7, 15, 16), and it is hard to see why he should have done so unless the pictures belonged to Daulby. No. 7, a *Julia*, certainly did. It is likely therefore that No. 15 was Daulby's *Vesuvius*, and No. 16 a *Salerno* also in his possession. See No. 12 below.

11 *Brown*. Sold to a Mr. Brown for £16.16. Very small. 1779.

Letter to Daulby, 31st December 1779 (MS. Derby Public Library; not in B, p. 85): '...one M.ʳ Brown a Gent.ᵐ from London saw it [Sale's *Vesuvius*] at my Room & was so pleased w.ᵗʰ it he gave me a commission to paint one for him rather shorter than M.ʳ Tate's to make the proportion better, I have finished & sent it Home, he gave me 16 guineas for it...'

12 *Daulby*. MS. Account Book as 'A small picture of a distant view of Vesuvius from y.ᵉ shore of Posillipo sold to Mr. Daulby', £31.10. Smallish, from shore of Posillipo with village of Marechiaro. Ready by Spring 1785.

Presumed to be Robins's Rooms, 1785 (15)—see No. 10 above. Letter from Wright to Daulby, 5th October 1786 (MS. Derby Public Library) reads: 'I shall take care to forward by the first waggon to my friend M.ʳ W.ᵐ Tate at Manchester your picture of the distant view of Vesuvius from the shore of Posilipo, and give him advice of it, I will also endeavour to get the name of the promontory w.ᵗʰ its Buildings. That picture I charge w.ᵗʰ the frame —gs. for the pair,—, that is estimating its companion [the *Gulf of Salerno*, see No. 10 above] at—, because it is not so full of work...' (prices heavily deleted and illegible). The letter quoted in part in B, pp. 87–8 is in fact not dated the same day, though it is bound up with the dated letter and belongs to the same month. It tells us the picture introduces 'the village of Mare Chiare, a place much frequented by the lower class of people in Naples...', and that 'The other house or palazzo on the Hill in the distance is called the pallace of 9 windows, but is inhabited only by servants...' Marechiaro is beyond the Capo di Posillipo, from where Naples itself is invisible, but the sea with its islands must have played a prominent part in the composition.

The *Gulf of Salerno* is not identifiable among Daulby's pictures and he may never have taken it. In fact in the dated letter above, Wright tells us: 'however if you shou'd hereafter approve of another picture as a comp: rather than the one already painted [i.e. the *Salerno*] I shall not insist upon more than—gs. [heavily deleted] unless you should make choice of one very full of work indeed...'

13 *Daulby*. Offered to Daulby for 14–20 guineas. Moonlight with foreground trees. 12 by 17 in. 1779–80.

Letter from Wright to Daulby, 31st December 1779 (MS. Derby Public Library; passages not transcribed by B, p. 85): 'I have now on the stocks a small picture of Vesuvius, it is dead colour'd, & I think if well finish'd will make a clever little picture, it is nearly the same view as Mr. Tate's, but shows more of the semicircular part of the Bay formed by the City of Naples. The Circumstances of the picture are nearly the same, the Lava is running into the Sea & the moon is rising over the Appenines w.ᶜʰ is seen thro' the trees w.ᶜʰ grow on the high Foreground & w.ᶜʰ by extending their dark arms over the fire, give fine contrast & enhance the value of the light. The size is 1 foot 5 i.ⁿ by 1 foot. it may be finish'd from 14 to 20 guineas value...' It must have shown a view rather closer to the mountain than Nos. 29 and 6. Letter to Daulby, 11th January 1780 (MS. Derby Public Library): 'Sir, I am favour'd w.ᵗʰ yours, & agreeable to your request have forwarded the little picture of Vesuvius I mention'd [note in margin: 'it was sent yesterday by Shawcross'] to you in my last, tho' in a situation unfit to be seen, for it is [no] further advanced than a dead colour in some parts, & no where finished, therefore the effect is unequal for w.ᶜʰ you must allow. If you like the general design of it, it will be sufficient incouragement to go on w.ᵗʰ it...' It is not known whether Daulby took the picture.

For another picture of *Vesuvius* offered to Daulby, see below, No. 16.

14 *Gisborne*. MS. Account Book as 'A view of Vesuvius from the shore of posilipo for Mr. Gisborne', £42. *c*. 23 by 33 in. *c*. 1788. Listed in Wright's Account Book on the reverse

of a letter of August 1788 at £44.2. Exh. Derby, 1883 (65) as 23 by 33 in.
Greville, see No. 27 below.

15   *Machlin*. MS. Account Book as 'A view of Vesuvius from the shore of Paussillipo, for Mr. Maclin,' £42. Late '80's.

16   *Milnes*. Sold to Milnes before spring 1776 for £42, withdrawn, and offered to Daulby, 1780. Moonlight, showing islands off the coast. *c.* 29 by 34 in.

Letter of Wright to Daulby, 11th January 1780 (MS. Derby Public Library): '...It has just occurr'd to me that I shall soon have in my possession a picture of Mount Vesuvius, very different from that of Mr. Tates, it is a near View of ye Mountain wch shews the Lava to great advantage, & the distance is made up of the Bay of Naples, the Islands of Procida Ischia Caprea etc. etc. the necks of land breaking into the sea wth the reflection of ye moon, playing between them has a pleasing effect, you shall have it for 30 g^{ns} wch is 10 less than I would paint one for of that size, it being I believe somewhere about 2 feet 10 by 2 ft. 5 In. It is highly finish'd. The reason of it being returned to me is. After Mr. Milnes had purchased the picture above mention'd & a companion of Mount Etna, he saw in the Exhibition [i.e. 1776] a pair of large ones of Vesuvius & the Girandolo, wch he purchased therefore thinks it unnecessary to have two pictures of the same subject, & now [note in margin: 'Mr Milnes has been a great friend to me, having laid out wth me 7 or £800'] wishes to exchange this picture of Vesuvius for a picture of Neptune's Grotto wch I exhibited last year [i.e. R.A. 1779 (360)], & allow me the difference, also make an abatement of 10 Gns [note in margin: 'he gave 40 gns'] wch will make the picture come cheap indeed to you. The picture, if you wish it, shall be sent for your inspection'.

This is the only mention anywhere in Wright's papers of a view of Etna. It is therefore possible that this picture and its companion of *Vesuvius* were the ones that appeared at Christie's in 1783 and were bought by Lord Palmerston for £32.11. and £43.1. respectively. A small notebook kept by 2nd Lord Palmerston at Broadlands has: 'A view of Qtna [Etna] Wright Christie's 1783. 32. 11. 0', and 'A View of Vesuvius during an Eruption by night do [ditto] Wright 43. 1. 0.' Milnes might have wished to get rid of the Sicilian as well as the Neapolitan view.

17   *Palmerston*. See No. 16.

18   *Philips*. Sold to John Leigh Philips. Volcano from close to. 1794.

Letters from Wright to Philips, 19th February and 29th June 1794 (B, p. 93) make clear that he was still working on it in the late winter of that year. A passage not transcribed by B. reads: 'The Gent^m who was to have had the Vesuvius, agreed to give me 60 gs. for it unframed, it is yours wth ye frame at ye same price...' Niece's memoir (Derby Public Library) describes it as the last *Vesuvius* he painted: 'a near view, with figures as high up the mountain as was safe during an eruption, which he considered the finest he had painted...' R.A. 1794 (107). See Nos 25, 26 below.

19   *Poploe Birch*. MS. Account Book as 'D^o [following on Walker picture, see below No. 22] for Mr. Poploe [? Peploe] Birch. Curzon Street May Fair', £42. Late '80's.

20   *Sale*. Ready by 1779.

Extract from letter to Daulby, 31st December 1779 (quoted in part by B, p. 85): 'I have lately rec'd a Letter from my good friend Mr. Sale, who informs me you have seen his Picture of Vesuvius, and are much pleased wth it. I am very happy it meets with his & his friends approbation...'

21   *Tate*. Distant view of Vesuvius. Ready by 1779. An idea of what this picture was like can be guessed from quotations from Wright's letters of 1779–80 quoted under Nos. 11, 13, 16 above. A pencil drawing in the Derby Art Gallery, 7$\frac{5}{8}$ by 9 in. inscribed 'For the picture/ For my friend Tate' shows the lighthouse on the Mole in the foreground, but this

drawing must have been intended for another composition since here the mountain is too close.

22   *Walker*. MS. Account Book as 'A distant View of Vesuvius from the shore of posillipo for Mr. Walker', £32 (? £42). Late '80's.

23   *Wilmot*. MS. Account Book as 'A View of Vesuvius from the shore of posillipo for Edw. Wilmot Esq!', £42. Late '80's.

24, 25, 26, 27   MS. Account Book has 'A sketch of Mount Vesuvius Evening to L. Philips', £10.10. Changed from 'two sketches' by 'daylight'. Two sketches of *Vesuvius*, morning and evening, the latter sold to L. Philips, are priced at £10.10. each. They are among very late pictures. A near view of the volcano is in the Account Book at £63 with no purchaser's name: this might be for Philips also (see No. 18). It also is among the late works. A small *Vesuvius*, a companion to a *Lake of Geneva*, is priced at £21. The latter was bought by a Col. Greville. The Philips picture was in Philips sale, Manchester, 1814 (28).
  Among pictures of the late '70's is listed in the Account Book a *Vesuvius* for £200. This could be a repetition of the entry for the Moscow picture, though in fact £100 more was charged for it. Among pictures of the mid-'80's is listed a *Vesuvius* from Posillipo on panel at £42. This may be the repetition of the entry for Sir Robert Wilmot's picture (see No. 31 below). A picture of *Vesuvius* with a view of the Bay of Naples, 25 by 31 in. was bought in at Christie's, 6th May 1801 (27) and resold Derby, 11th October 1810 (2), bt. Snowdon, Spondon.

E   *Other 'Vesuvius' pictures known and identified in early sources.*

28   *Beridge*. MS. Account Book as 'one of the above size [i.e. small oval] of Vesuvius, sold to Dr. Beridge', £10.10. Exh. Derby, 1870 (577); 1934 (69). Private Collection, U.K. Probaby early '80's.

29   *Derry, Bishop of*. MS. Account Book as 'Vesuvius for the B? Derry, £105, entry deleted. Offered to the Bishop of Derry but Wright refuses to part with it. Late '70's. 49 by 71 in. Niece's memoir, followed by B, p. 43 describes the Bishop's rudeness and Wright's refusal to part with the picture to him. Hayley writes a poem describing the episode (B, pp. 43–4). It remained in the artist's possession; was in the 1801 (65) and 1810 (9) sales but both times bought in, and now belongs to Miss Cade in Porthcurno, Penzance. Exh. B. I. 1817 (130); Derby, 1866 (168).

30   *Mundy*. MS. Account Book as 'A distant view of Vesuvius from the shore of Posillipo bigger than ½ length. to M! Edward Mundy', £84 (changed from £103), among pictures of the late '80's. The picture is inscribed bottom left in a later hand 'J. Wright fec!/Derby 1780' but this is a wrong interpretation of the artist's own signature bottom right: 'IW. P! 178[9?]'. The last digit of the date is most likely to be a '9' since the picture belongs in style with Mrs. Anson's of *c.* 1788. For further details, see Tate 1958 (20). A skilful copy in the Derby Art Gallery. Still in the same family (Peter Miller Mundy Collection).

31   *Wilmot*. MS. Account Book as 'A picture of a distance View of Vesuvius from the Shore of Posilipo painted on pannel / S! R! Wilmot', £42. Has remained in the same family since it was painted. (Mrs. George Anson, Catton Hall). Exh. Derby, 1833 (92). In the Account Book is the entry: 'A distant View of Vesuvius on pannel', in a bill with other pictures, made out to Sir Robert Wilmot. It is on the reverse of a fragment of a letter dated 27th August 1788.

F   *Other 'Vesuvius' pictures known but not identified in early sources.*

32   *Eruption of Vesuvius*. Canvas, 40 by 50 in. University College of Wales, Aberystwyth.

Label on reverse (? mid- or late nineteenth century): '"Vesuvius in Action at Night" by Joseph Wright of Derby'.

33, 34 *Two views of Vesuvius.* Copper (oval), each 7½ by 9 in. Christopher Norris.

35 *Vesuvius in eruption.* Canvas, 47½ by 67 in. Derby Museum & Art Gallery.
Purchased from the Bemrose Collection, 1927.
Very likely the picture painted in the winter of 1774–5 (see p. 77).
This means that Wright painted at least 27 views of *Vesuvius*, and at least 4 of the *Girandola*, without counting the copper panels (33, 34 above), and several drawings and a gouache in the Derby Art Gallery. Only 8 of *Vesuvius*, and 3 of the *Girandola*, are now known.

Bibliography

These publications are cited in the text under shortened titles as shown in the margins of the following pages. Publications not included in this bibliography are cited in full in the text. Manuscripts, books and articles essential for Wright studies are shown with an asterisk.

1 MANUSCRIPT MATERIAL

*Bound up volume of 'Original and other Documents relating to Joseph Wright of Derby. Collected by Wm. Bemrose, Jun. 1877'. Derby Public Library. Contains (a) Wright's Journal during his travels in Italy (1774–5), in his own hand in pencil. Extracts from these are published by Bemrose, 1885, pp. 37–41 (see below 'Publications on Wright'). (b) Rough draft of MS. biography of Wright by his niece Hannah (see below, MS. 2, Derby Public Library). (c) Accounts and letters relating to Wright.

MS. 1, Derby Public Library

Bound up volume containing fair copy of MS. biography of Wright by his niece Hannah. This is dated 1850 on the flyleaf. Derby Public Library. It does not differ in essential features from the rough draft. It contains many more quotations from letters, exhibition catalogues etc., but no material which is not available from the original sources. This biography is used extensively by Bemrose, 1885, *passim*.

MS. 2, Derby Public Library

*Bound up volume of letters from Wright to J. L. Philips and Daniel Daulby. It contains a letter to O. Humphry of 24th July 1775, and also some correspondence with Boydell. Derby Public Library. Most, but by no means all of these letters are published by Bemrose, 1885.

MS. Derby Public Library

Bound up volume containing miscellaneous material relating to the artist, including early catalogues. Some printed material. Derby Public Library.

MS. Derby Public Library

*Wright's MS. Account Book. It contains lists in his own hand of most of his pictures, with prices and in some cases names of purchasers. There are also a few miscellaneous notes, accounts etc., and drawings. National Portrait Gallery. The book was kept up for most of his working life. The lists of pictures are transcribed by Bemrose, 1885, pp. 118–24. A few errors and omissions in Bemrose's transcription are noted by Nicolson, 1954, p. 80; see below 'Publications on Wright'.

MS. Account Book

*Extra-illustrated copy of Bemrose, 1885. On loan to National Portrait Gallery. From Bemrose Collection. Specially bound up copy of his book with the addition of some autograph letters to Hayley 1783–89 (unpublished), press cuttings, photographs of paintings by Wright, and other material, some printed.

N.P.G. extra-illustrated Bemrose

Extra-illustrated copy of Bemrose, 1885, compiled by Llewellyn Lloyd Simpson. Collection heirs of J. M. Eardley Simpson. Additional material includes autograph letters by Wright, extracts from which are published by Bemrose, 1885; drawings by Wright; printed catalogues and press cuttings.

Eardley Simpson extra-illustrated Bemrose

*Autograph letters to Hayley (c 1782–89). Collection Sir Gilbert Inglefield. Unpublished.

Inglefield MSS.

MS Diary of Thomas Buxton of Bradbourne. Derby Public Library. Entries from April 1776 onwards.

MS. Buxton

*Diary of Joseph Farington, R.A. All extracts quoted are taken from the typescript copy in the Print Room of the British Museum, by gracious permission of H.M. The Queen.

Farington Diary followed by page reference to typescript	The published volumes (*The Farington Diary*, ed. James Greig, 8 vols., London, 1922 ff.) contain very few of the quotations used.
Humphry MSS. R.A.	Ozias Humphry Correspondence, 1773 onwards. Royal Academy. Letters to and from Humphry.
Daulby, MS. *c* 1790	Manuscript list of *c* 1790 of Collection of Daniel Daulby, Jn., Liverpool Public Library, Local History D. 5822.
Whitley Papers	W. T. Whitley Papers. British Museum Print Room. These scraps contain little original material but some references to contemporary newspaper reports which have proved useful.
Thorpe/Arundell MSS.	Father Thorpe's Letters to 8th Lord Arundell of Wardour, in possession of Mr. R. J. R. Arundell.
Barlaston MSS.	★Autograph letters from Wedgwood to Bentley (1773–79), Wedgwood to Wright (1784) and Wright to Wedgwood (1782–89). Wedgwood Museum, Barlaston, Stoke-on-Trent. A few published in edition of Wedgwood's letters of 1903, and in Finer & Savage (see below 'Other Publications'), but most are unpublished.
Keele MSS.	Autograph letters from Wright to Wedgwood (1779–89). Library. Keele University, Nos. Etruria 1–669 to 1–677. Unpublished.
Browne MS.	Michael Browne, *Arkwright, Industry & Architecture*. Diploma Thesis in Architecture, Imperial College of Science, 1963.
Arkwright MSS.	8 Letters from Wright to Richard Arkwright junior, between 21st January 1790 and 27th June 1791. Collection Col. Peter Arkwright.

2 PUBLICATIONS ON WRIGHT

Catalogues in which works by Wright are cited are listed separately.

Hayley, 1783	1783 William Hayley, *Ode to Joseph Wright, Esq., of Derby*, Chichester, 1783. Republished in:
Hayley, 1785	1785 William Hayley, 'to Mr. Wright of Derby, on his Picture of the attack of Gibraltar', *European Magazine*, March 1785, p. 226. (see also Hayley's *Poems and Plays* under section 4, below, 1788).
	1795 *Gentleman's Magazine*, June 1795.
Obituary, 1797	1797 *Gentleman's Magazine*, September 1797, p. 804. Anon. Obituary of Wright. (Compiled from material supplied by J. L. Philips.)
Philips, 1797	[J. Leigh Philips], 'Memoirs of the Life and Principal works of the late Joseph Wright Esq., of Derby', *Monthly Magazine*, October 1797, pp. 289–94.
Bemrose, 1863–4	1863–4 W. Bemrose, 'Wright of Derby. A biographical sketch', *Reliquary*, XV and XVI, 1863–4, pp. 176 ff.; pp. 209 ff. Reprinted with additions, London, no date.
Bemrose, 1872–3	1872–3 W. Bemrose, *Reliquary*, LI, 1872–3, p. 176.
Thomson, 1883	1883 D. C. Thomson, 'Joseph Wright of Derby', *Art Journal*, 1883, pp. 205–08.
Bemrose, 1885	1885 ★William Bemrose, *The Life and Works of Joseph Wright, A.R.A. commonly called 'Wright of Derby'*, London, 1885.
Smith and Bemrose, 1922	1922 S. C. Kaines Smith and H. Cheney Bemrose, *Wright of Derby*, London, 1922.
Shurlock, 1923	1923 F. W. Shurlock, 'The Scientific Pictures of Joseph Wright', *Science Progress*, 1923, pp. 432–7.

Grundy, 1930–1   1930–1 C. Reginald Grundy, 'Wright of Derby', *Connoisseur*, December 1930; January 1931.

Morris, 1931   1931 Roy Morris, 'Joseph Wright, A.R.A.', *Artwork*, Autumn 1931, p. 196.

Morris, 1932   1932 Roy Morris, 'Joseph Wright, A.R.A.', *Apollo*, January 1932.
Morris, Engravings, 1932   Roy Morris, 'Engravings after Joseph Wright, A.R.A.', *Print Collector's Quarterly*, April 1932.

Buckley, 1952   1952 *Charles E. Buckley, 'Joseph Wright of Derby', *Magazine of Art*, April 1952, pp. 160–67.

Buckley, 1953   1953 Charles E. Buckley, 'An eighteenth century British Painting', *Wadsworth Atheneum Bulletin*, April 1953, p. 2.

Nicolson, 1954   1954 Benedict Nicolson, 'Joseph Wright's early Subject Pictures', *Burlington Magazine*, March 1954, pp. 72–80.
Hamilton, 1954   C. Hamilton, 'A Landscape by Wright of Derby', *Allen Memorial Art Museum Bulletin*, 1954, pp. 16–22.

Buckley, 1955   1955 Charles E. Buckley, 'An English Landscape by Joseph Wright of Derby', *The Art Quarterly*, Autumn 1955, pp. 265–71.

Honour, 1956   1956 Hugh Honour, 'Two Letters from Joseph Wright of Derby', *Connoisseur*, November 1956, p. 188.

Buckley, 1957   1957 Charles E. Buckley, 'Joseph Wright of Derby in mezzotint', *Antiques*, November 1957.

Shipp, 1958   1958 Horace Shipp, 'Wright of Derby', *Far and Wide*, Spring 1958, pp. 17–21.
Shipp, *Apollo*, 1958   Horace Shipp, 'Joseph Wright of Derby', *Apollo*, April 1958, pp. 118–23.
Robinson, 1958   Eric Robinson, 'Joseph Wright of Derby: the Philosophers' Painter', *Burlington Magazine*, June 1958, p. 214.

Crombie, 1959   1959 Theodore Crombie, 'Wright of Derby's "Indian Widow"', *Apollo*, October 1959, p. 107.

Rosenblum, 1960   1960 Robert Rosenblum, 'Wright of Derby: Gothick realist', *Art News*, March 1960, pp. 25–27; 54–55.

Nicolson, 1962   1962 Benedict Nicolson, 'Two Companion Pieces by Wright of Derby,' *Burlington Magazine*, March 1962, pp. 113–17.
Buckley, 1962   Charles E. Buckley, 'Wright of Derby's Portraits of Mr. and Mrs. William Chase', *Yale Art Gallery Bulletin*, April 1962, pp. 43–48.
Rosenblum, 1962   Robert Rosenblum, 'Sources of two paintings by Joseph Wright of Derby', *Journal of the Warburg and Courtauld Institutes*, XXV, Nos. 1–2, 1962, pp. 135–6.

Nicolson, 1965   1965 Benedict Nicolson, 'Thomas Gisborne and Wright of Derby', *Burlington Magazine*, February 1965, pp. 58–62.
St. Louis Bulletin, 1965   *City Art Museum of Saint Louis, Bulletin*, November-December 1965, pp. 2–3.

Nicolson, 1966   1966 Benedict Nicolson, *Wright of Derby*, 'The Masters' series, No. 22, London, 1966.

3 CATALOGUES IN WHICH WORKS BY WRIGHT ARE CITED

When referred to in the text, catalogue numbers follow the shortened titles in brackets. Not all catalogues in which Wright's works appeared are listed below: the following is a selection of the more important. Catalogues of collections as well as of sales and exhibitions are listed here. Paintings by Wright shown during his lifetime at the Incorporated Society of Artists, the Free Society of Artists, the Royal Academy, at Liverpool and at Robins's Rooms (1785) are listed in detail in Appendix A. The sale catalogues of Wright's unsold pictures after his death (1801 and 1810) are reprinted in Bemrose, 1885, pp. 107–14 and are not listed here. The same goes for the Philips sale catalogue. For further details about loans, see A. Graves, *A Century of Loan Exhibitions*, under Wright. 'British Institution' and 'Royal Academy' are shortened to 'B.I.' and 'R.A.' in the text.

Shakespeare Gallery, 1790	1790	*A Catalogue of the Pictures Ec, in the Shakespeare Gallery, Pall-Mall*, London, 1790.
Strutt, 1827, 1835	1827	*A Catalogue of Paintings, Drawings... in the Collection of Joseph Strutt, Derby*, Derby, 1827. Some additional entries in a catalogue of the same title published Derby, 1835.
Hardman, 1838	1838	*A Catalogue of the... Collection of Paintings... the Genuine property of late Thomas Hardman, Esquire... sold by auction... at the Large Room in the Exchange, Manchester... 18th... 19th of October 1838 and subsequent days...'*
Derby, 1866	1866	*Catalogue of the Art and Industrial Exhibition... Corn Exchange*, Derby, 1866.
Derby, 1870	1870	Midland Counties Exhibition, Derby, May 1870.
Derby, 1883	1883	*Catalogue of the Paintings by Joseph Wright, A.R.A....*, Corporation Art Gallery, Derby, 1883.
R.A., 1886	1886	*Catalogue of the Exhibition of works by the Old Masters, including a selection from the works of Joseph Wright (of Derby), A.R.A.*, Royal Academy, 1886 Winter Exhibition.
Graves' Galleries, 1910	1910	*Catalogue of Loan Exhibition of Works by Joseph Wright, A.R.A. of Derby*, Graves' Galleries, London, undated [1910].
Derby, 1934	1934	★*Wright of Derby: Catalogue of the bi-centenary Exhibition of Paintings...*, Corporation Art Gallery, Derby, 1934.
R.A., 1934		*Exhibition of British Art c 1000–1860*, Royal Academy, 1934.
Derby-Leicester, 1947	1947	Exhibition of paintings by Wright in Derby and Leicester.
Sheffield, 1950	1950	*Pictures by Joseph Wright of Derby*, Graves Art Gallery, Sheffield, 1950.
R.A., 1951	1951	*100 years of the Royal Academy*, Royal Academy, 1951.
Smith College, 1955	1955	*Joseph Wright of Derby 1734–1797*, Smith College Museum of Art, Northampton, Mass., January 1955.
Canada, 1957–58	1957–8	*British Painting in the Eighteenth Century*, Canadian Museums, Toledo Museum of Art, 1957–58.
Tate, 1958	1958	★*Joseph Wright of Derby 1734–1797*, Tate Gallery and Walker Art Gallery, Liverpool, Arts Council of Great Britain, 1958.

Norwich, 1959   1959 *Joseph Wright of Derby A.R.A.*, Norwich Castle Museum, January–February 1959.
Tate, 1959   Romantic Exhibition, Tate Gallery.

New York, 1960   1960 *Joseph Wright of Derby 1734–1797*, Durlacher Bros., New York, March 1960.

R.A., 1962   1962 *Primitives to Picasso*, Royal Academy, 1962.

Richmond, 1963   1963 *Painting in England 1700–1850. Collection of Mr. and Mrs. Paul Mellon*, Virginia
                                           Museum of Fine Arts, Richmond, Virginia, 1963.

Matlock, Spring 1964   1964 *Joseph Wright of Derby (1734–1797)*, Tawney House, Matlock, April 1964.
Matlock, Autumn 1964   *Paintings from local collections, 17th–19th century*, Tawney House, Matlock, Septem-
                                           ber–October 1964.

R.A., 1964–65   1964–65 *Painting in England 1700–1850 from the Collection of Mr. and Mrs. Paul Mellon*,
                                           Royal Academy, 1964–65.

Yale, 1965   1965 *Painting in England 1700–1850 from the Collection of Mr. and Mrs. Paul Mellon*,
                                           Yale University Art Gallery, 1965.
Indianapolis, 1965   *The Romantic Era, Birth and Flowering 1750–1850*, Art Association of Indianapolis.

Birmingham, 1966   1966 *Lunar Society of Birmingham*, Museum and Art Gallery, Birmingham, 1966.

4 OTHER PUBLICATIONS

Ferguson, 1760   1760 James Ferguson, *Lectures on Select Subjects in Mechanics, Hydrostatics, Pneumatics, and
                                           Optics...*, London, 1760–

Critical Examination, 1767   1767 *A Critical Examination of the Pictures, Sculpture, Designs in Architecture, Medals,
                                           Drawings, Prints &c exhibited at the Great Room, in Spring Gardens, Charing Cross,
                                           April 22 1767*, London, 1767.
Le Pour et le Contre, 1767   *Le Pour et le Contre being a poetical Display of the Merit and Demerit of the Capital
                                           Paintings exhibited at Spring Gardens...*, London, 1767.

Candid Observations, 1772   1772 *Candid Observations on the Principal Performances now exhibiting at the New Rooms of
                                           the Society of Artists...*, London, 1772.
Hamilton, 1772   Sir William Hamilton, *Observations on Mount Vesuvius...*, London, 1772; 2nd ed.
                                           1773.

Bray, 1778, 1783   1778 William Bray, *Sketch of a Tour into Derbyshire and Yorkshire*, London, 1778; 2nd
                                           (revised) ed. 1783.

Hamilton, 1779   1779 Sir William Hamilton, *Campi Phlegraei, Observations of the Volcanoes of the Two
                                           Sicilies...*, 2 vols., Naples, 1779.

Hayley, 1788   1788 William Hayley, *Poems and Plays*, six volumes. Vol. I contains *An Essay on Painting*
                                           and *Ode to Mr. Wright of Derby 1783*.

Pilkington, 1789   1789 James Pilkington, *A View of the Present State of Derbyshire with an Account of its most
                                           remarkable Antiquities*, 2 vols., Derby, 1789.

Hulton, 1791   1791 W. Hulton, *The History of Derby...to the year* MDCCXCI, London, 1791.

Keir, 1791   [James Keir], *An Account of the Life and Writings of Thomas Day, Esq.*, London, 1791.

Whitehurst, 1792   1792   *The Works of John Whitehurst, F. R. S. with Memoirs of his Life and Writings*, London, 1792.

Seward, 1804   1804   Anna Seward, *Memoirs of the Life of Dr. Darwin...*, London, 1804.

Edwards, 1808   1808   Edward Edwards, *Anecdotes of Painters...*, London, 1808.

Barry, 1809   1809   *The Works of James Barry...*, 2 vols., 1809.
Carey, 1809   William Carey, *Letter to I...A...Esq., A Connoisseur, in London*, Manchester, 1809.
Hayley, 1809   William Hayley, *The life of George Romney*, Esq., Chichester, 1809.

Seward, 1810   1810   *The Poetical Works of Anna Seward with Extracts from her Literary Correspondence. Edited by Walter Scott, Esq.*, 1810.

Davies, 1811   1811   Rev. D. P. Davies, *A new historical and descriptive View of Derbyshire...*, Belper, 1811.

Farey, 1811–17   1811–17   John Farey, *General View of the Agriculture and Minerals of Derbyshire... drawn up for the Consideration of the Board of Agriculture...*, London, I, 1811; II, 1815; III, 1817.

Lysons, 1817   1817   Rev. Daniel Lysons and Samuel Lysons, *Magna Britannia...*, Vol. V on *Derbyshire*, 1817.

Edgeworth, 1820   1820   *Memoirs of Richard Lovell Edgeworth Esq. Begun by himself and concluded by his Daughter Maria Edgeworth*, 2 vols., London, 1820.

Hayley, 1823   1823   ★*Memoirs of the Life and Writings of William Hayley, Esq... written by himself... and memoirs of his son Thomas Alphonso Hayley the young Sculptor*, ed. John Johnson, Ll.D., 2 vols., 1823.

Glover, 1829   1829   Stephen Glover, *The Directory of the County of Derby... Accurately taken during the years 1827, '8 and '9*, Derby, 1829.

Romney, 1830   1830   Rev. John Romney, *Memoirs of the Life and Works of George Romney...*, London, 1830.

Bousfield, 1832   1832   Rev. H. N. Bousfield, *The Chantry House, Newark*. Undated pamphlet, contains poem by Bousfield dated 1832.

Baines, c 1835   c 1835   Edward Baines, *History of the Cotton Manufacture in Great Britain...*, London, c 1835.

Gandon, 1846   1846   *The life of James Gandon Esq... from material collected and arranged by his son James Gandon, Esq.*, assisted by T. J. Mulvany, Dublin, 1846.

Redgrave, ed. 1947   1866   Richard and Samuel Redgrave, *A Century of British Painters*. 1st ed. 1866, new ed., London, 1947.

Henderson, 1867   1867   E. Henderson, *Life of James Ferguson, F. R. S....*, Edinburgh, London and Glasgow, 1867.

Mayer, 1876   1876   Joseph Mayer, *Early Exhibitions of Art in Liverpool*, privately printed, Liverpool, 1876.

Coke, 1880   1880   *Coke of Trusley... A Family History*, compiled by Major John Talbot Coke, privately printed, 1880.

Cox, 1890   1890   Rev. J. Charles Cox, *Three Centuries of Derbyshire Annals...*, 2 vols., London, 1890.

Tilley, 1892–1902   1892–1902   J. T[illey], *The Old Halls, Manors and Families of Derbyshire*, 4 vols., London, Buxton, 1892–1902.

Jeayes, 1896   1896   *Descriptive Catalogue of the Charters and Muniments at Radbourne in the possession of Reginald Walkelyne Chandos-Pole, Esq. at Radbourne Hall.* Compiled with introduction and index by Isaac Herbert Jeayes, London, 1896.

Williamson, 1897   1897   George C. Williamson, *Richard Cosway, R.A. and his life and pupils*, London, 1897.

Cox, 1899   1899   Rev. J. Charles Cox, *Calendar of the Records of the County of Derby*, London, 1899.

Wedgwood, 1903   1903   *Letters of Josiah Wedgwood 1772 to 1780*, London, 1903.

Ward and Roberts, 1904   1904   Humphry Ward and W. Roberts, *Romney*, 1904.

Hodgson and Eaton, 1905   1905   The late J. E. Hodgson, R.A. and Fred. A Eaton. M.A., *The Royal Academy and its Members 1768–1830*, London, 1905.

Copley-Pelham, 1914   1914   *Letters & Papers of John Singleton Copley and Henry Pelham, 1739–1776*, Massachusetts Historical Society, 1914.

Dibdin, 1917–18   1917–18   E. Reinbault Dibdin, 'Liverpool Art and Artists in the eighteenth century', *Walpole Society*, VI, 1917–18, pp. 59 ff.

Unwin, 1924   1924   George Unwin (with chapters by Arthur Hulme and George Taylor), *Samuel Oldknow and the Arkwrights*, Manchester, London and elsewhere, 1924.

Childe-Pemberton, 1925   1925   William S. Childe-Pemberton, *The Earl Bishop...*, 2 vols., London, 1925.

Whitley, 1928   1928   ★William T. Whitley, *Artists and their Friends in England, 1700–1799*, 2 vols., London, 1928.

Gignilliat, 1932   1932   George Warren Gignilliat, Jr., *The Author of Sandford and Merton, A Life of Thomas Day, Esq.*, New York, 1932.

Torrington, 1935   1935   *The Torrington Diaries, containing the Tours through England and Wales of the Hon. John Byng (later fifth Viscount Torrington) between the years 1781 and 1794*, ed. C. Bruyn Andrews, 1935.

Walpole, 1937   1937   Horace Walpole, *Anecdotes of Painting in England 1760–1795*. Edited by F. W. Hilles and Philip Daghlian, Yale U. P., 1937. Containing Walpole's Collection of contemporary extracts, V; pp. 119–22.

Bell, 1938   1938   *Annals of Thomas Banks, Sculptor, Royal Academician...*, ed. C. F. Bell, Cambridge, 1938.

Klingender, 1945   1945   F. D. Klingender, 'The Industrial Revolution and the Birth of Romanticism', *Apropos*, No. 4, pp. 20–24.

Todd, 1946   1946   Ruthven Todd, *Tracks in the Snow*, London, 1946.

Boase, 1947   1947   T. S. R. Boase, 'Illustrations of Shakespeare's Plays in the seventeenth and eighteenth centuries', *Journal of the Warburg and Courtauld Institutes*, X, 1947, pp. 83 ff.
Klingender, 1947   ★F. D. Klingender, *Art and the Industrial Revolution*, London, 1947.

Chaloner, 1950–53	1950–53	W. H. Chaloner, 'Charles Roe of Macclesfield (1715–81): an eighteenth-century Industrialist', *Lancashire and Cheshire Antiquarian Society Transactions*, Vols. 62–3, 1950–53, pp. 133–56; 52–86.
Jones, 1951	1951	'Memoirs of Thomas Jones', *Walpole Society 1946–1948*, London, 1951.
Harris, 1951		Stanley A. Harris, 'Robert Adam (1728–1792), architect, and Woolton Hall, Liverpool', *Hist. Soc. of Lancashire and Cheshire*, 1951, pp. 161 ff.
Waterhouse, 1953	1953	Ellis Waterhouse, *Painting in Britain, 1530 to 1790, Pelican History of Art*, London, 1953.
Pevsner. 1953		Nikolaus Pevsner, *Derbyshire (The Buildings of England* series), London, 1953.
Constable, 1953		W. G. Constable, *Richard Wilson*, London, 1953.
Robinson, 1953		Eric Robinson, M.A., 'The Derby Philosophical Society', *Annals of Science*, 15th December 1953.
Andrews, 1956	1956	C. Reginald Andrews, *The Story of the Wortley Ironworks*, Nottingham, 1956 (revised 2nd ed.).
Voisine, 1956		Jacques Voisine, *J.-J. Rousseau en Angleterre à l'Epoque Romantique*, Paris, 1956.
Connell, 1957	1957	Brian Connell, *Portrait of a Whig Peer…*, London, 1957.
Rosenblum, 1957		Robert Rosenblum, 'The Origins of Painting: A Problem in the Iconography of Romantic Classicism', *The Art Bulletin*, December 1957, pp. 279–90.
Schubert, 1957		H. R. Schubert, *History of the British Iron and Steel Industry*, London, 1957.
Fitton and Wadsworth, 1958	1958	R. S. Fitton and A. P. Wadsworth, *The Strutts and the Arkwrights*, Manchester U. P., 1958. (reprinted 1964).
White, 1958		W. Douglas White, 'The Whitehurst Family', Supplement to *Derbyshire Miscellany*, March 1958.
Merchant, 1959	1959	W. Moelwyn Merchant, *Shakespeare and the Artist*, London, 1959.
Smith, 1960	1960	Bernard Smith, *European Vision and the South Pacific 1768–1850…* Oxford, 1960.
Mantoux, 1961	1961	Paul Mantoux, *The Industrial Revolution in the eighteenth century*, London, 1928; new ed. 1961.
Schofield, 1963	1963	Robert E. Schofield, *The Lunar Society of Birmingham…*, Oxford, 1963.
Barbier, 1963		Carl Paul Barbier, *William Gilpin…*, Oxford, 1963.
Whinney, 1964.	1964	Margaret Whinney, *Sculpture in Britain 1530 to 1830*, London, 1964.
Finer & Savage, 1965	1965	*The Selected Letters of Josiah Wedgwood*, ed. Ann Finer and George Savage, London, 1965.
Waterhouse, 1965		Ellis Kirkham Waterhouse, *Three Decades of art 1740–1770*, Philadelphia, 1965.
Stevens, 1965		*The Journal of the Rev. William Bagshaw Stevens*, ed. Georgina Galbraith, Oxford, 1965.
Swindell, 1965		K. Swindell, 'The Cromford Cotton Mills, Their Life and Location', *East Midlands Geographer*, December 1965.
Chapman, 1965		S. D. Chapman, 'The Transition to the Factory System in the Midlands Cotton Spinning Industry', *Economic History Review, XVIII*, No. 3, 1965.
Chapman. 1967	1967	Stanley D. Chapman, *The Early Factory Masters*, Newton Abbot, 1967.

Separate indices are provided in Vol II of present owners and public collections, and the principal subjects of pictures, with references to catalogue numbers. These are therefore not included in the general index here. Nor are names of sitters who, though not separately indexed, can easily be found since they are listed alphabetically in the text part of the catalogue. However, in innumerable cases, sitters are discussed in the text without special reference to their portraits by Wright, and these references are given here. We also index references to sitters whenever they are mentioned in other connections in the catalogue.

References to pictures wherever mentioned in the text are not indexed, since these references are given in each catalogue entry. Names mentioned incidentally in the catalogue are indexed but a selection only has been made: to have included all names would have made the index unwieldy. Thus, 18th but not 19th and early 20th century collectors are included. So also are engravers, but readers are warned that not all engravings after Wright's work are recorded. The Appendices are also indexed here.

Numbers above the line refer to footnotes. Numbers in Roman type are page numbers; in italics, are catalogue numbers.

Wright of Derby is described as 'W.' throughout this index.

Index